REVOLUTIONARY STRUGGLE

1947–1958

Volume 1 of the Selected Works of Fidel Castro

Edited and with an introduction by
ROLANDO E. BONACHEA *and* NELSON P. VALDÉS

REVOLUTIONARY STRUGGLE

1947–1958

Volume 1 of the Selected Works of Fidel Castro

THE MIT PRESS

Cambridge, Massachusetts, and London, England

This book was set in Linotype Janson by Publishers' Composition Service, Inc., printed on Mohawk Neotext Offset by The Alpine Press Inc., and bound by The Colonial Press Inc. in the United States of America.

Library of Congress Cataloging in Publication Data

Castro, Fidel, 1927–
  Revolutionary struggle.
  Bibliography: p.
  1. Cuba—History—1933–1959—Addresses, essays, lectures. 2. Cuba—History—1959- —Addresses, essays, lectures. 3. Communism—Cuba—Addresses, essays, lectures. I. Bonachea, Rolando E., ed. II. Valdés, Nelson P., ed. III. Title.
F1788.C2713 1972   972.91'064'0924 [B]   74-103892

ISBN 0-262-02065-3 (hbd)
ISBN 0-262-52027-3 (pbk)

To Maxine and Katheryn

No es que los hombres hagan pueblos, sino que los pueblos en su hora de génesis suelen ponerse vibrantes y triunfantes, en un hombre.

A man does not make a nation, but a nation at its birth may find its vibrant and triumphant voice in a man.

JOSÉ MARTÍ

Contents

Preface

One can begin to understand the impact of the most fundamental revolution in modern Latin American history by objectively analyzing the words of the man who guided it. This volume encompasses Fidel Castro's chief statements from the late 1940s to the time when Fulgencio Batista finally ended his control over Cuba's destiny in the early hours of January 1, 1959. Included are letters, articles, manifestos, speeches, military and political field orders, interviews, press releases, proclamations, appointments, and decrees.

Through these selections every facet of Castro's central role as the leader of a revolutionary process can be ascertained to form a clear picture of one of the most dynamic revolutions of all time. Nonetheless, it would have been a mistake for us as editors to have been concerned solely with Castro's statements without placing them in the correct historicopolitical context. Therefore, we have written an unusually long introduction. Fidel Castro's political career and the subsequent revolutionary upheaval in Cuba have been marked by such differences of views that we felt only a thorough discussion could provide the right context for understanding the readings.

Basically, the introduction seeks to show that in Cuba there has always existed a revolutionary tradition that is anti-imperialist, nationalist, usually devoid of a systematic ideology, and above all action oriented. Moreover, almost all Cubans in the twentieth century have sought ideological guidance from José Martí, who dealt with problems in the nineteenth century similar to those of the twentieth century.

The 1933 revolutionary movement, as we shall show, degenerated into gangsterlike action groups by the 1940s. It was in one of these groups that Fidel Castro initiated his career and received practical political training. It can be said that he did not depart from Cuba's revolutionary tradition. He relied on Martí's interpretations, he was anti-imperialist and nationalist, and above all he was a man of action.

The insurrectionary process (1952–1958) was not only a struggle against the dictatorship of Fulgencio Batista but also a struggle among revolutionary leaders and their organizations for control of the whole movement. In most cases the participants in the revolutionary process were men propelled by altruism, patriotism, and a thirst for political power.

It is in the 1950s that Fidel emerges as a brilliant political strategist, military tactician, and psychologist who captures the moods of his people. He displays that resourcefulness and imagination without which a revolutionary is doomed. Perhaps for that reason the selections in this volume, which are full texts of the Spanish originals, are mainly political and military statements that present the man as an astute politician rather than an ideologue. Fidel was concerned more with strategy and tactics than with theory.

We hope that this volume will contribute toward a more rational understanding of Fidel Castro and the Cuban Revolution. A comprehensive bibliography of Castro's works through 1958 has been included as a tool for research.

Prior to 1952, writings by Fidel Castro are sketchy and hard to find. In the early 1940s, Fidel was a university leader and participated in a political group called Unión Insurreccional Revolucionaria, but most of his speeches were neither transcribed nor recorded. In 1950–1951, he traveled throughout Cuba speaking on behalf of the Partido del Pueblo Cubano. Copies of the speeches were kept, but we have been unable to consult them because many were published in the Havana newspapers *Alerta* and *La Calle*, neither of which can be obtained in the United States.

The selections of 1952–1958 are comprehensive, although we cannot claim definitiveness for them. There are many documents written by Fidel Castro that the Cuban government has failed to publish. Furthermore, there are Cuban exiles who possess important letters from Castro but refuse to make them available to scholars.

Finally, we are aware that the work of those who write on contemporary historical events is always inconclusive. This is so because later previously classified official documents are opened, memoirs are written by participants to shed new insights into specific events, and new material becomes available. Furthermore, it is difficult to obtain necessary sources in the United States or to travel to Cuba. The difficulties are compounded by those who, wanting to keep their "heroes" shrouded in myth and legend, sometimes do not hesitate to threaten those who seek out the facts. Therefore we cannot claim this to be a definitive work, and the reader will observe in the text certain gaps that, in our opinion, still exist. The views expressed are our own, and the research and writing were not financed by any institution but rather through our own meager resources.

We should like to thank the following friends who helped in many different ways toward the completion of this volume: Edwin Lieuwen, chairman of the History Department at the University of New

Mexico, and Martin C. Needler, chairman of the Inter-American Studies Division, who read the manuscript; Professor Luis E. Aguilar of Georgetown University and Professor Gilbert Merkx of the University of New Mexico, with whom we have been fortunate enough to share many stimulating discussions on revolution; Professor Janice Hopper of Georgetown University, who has been a constant source of encouragement; Professor Andrés Suárez of the University of Florida in Gainesville; Fred Padula, who read portions of the manuscript; Marcelo Fernández Zayas, who advised us; Maxine Valdés, who worked patiently on different portions of this volume; Arhán Pérez, Allen Cooper, Bill Orsen, Manuel Wright, and Jim Kennedy, who helped us in different ways; Jay Mallin of the University of Miami, who lent us some material; and Luis Conte Agüero, whose collection of personal letters was extremely useful.

The help of the following institutions and their staffs where the research was conducted is gratefully acknowledged: the University of New Mexico's Zimmerman Library, the Georgetown University Library, Harvard's Widener Library, the Hispanic Foundation at the Library of Congress in Washington, D.C., and Stanford University Library. Finally, our special thanks to the Instituto Cubano de Amistad con los Pueblos.

R.E.B. and N.P.V.
Albuquerque, New Mexico
August 15, 1970

Chronology of Major Events in Cuban History

1868	War of Independence begins.
1898	Battleship *Maine* explodes in Havana harbor, and the U.S. declares war on Spain. After several months a peace treaty is signed, and Cuba becomes protectorate of the United States.
1901	Platt Amendment attached to Cuban Constitution gives the United States the right to intervene.
1906–1909	Second U.S. intervention occurs.
1917–1922	Third U.S. intervention occurs.
1925–1933	Gerardo Machado rules Cuba.
August 13, 1927	Fidel Castro is born.
1933	Nationalist revolution ousts Machado, and Ramón Grau becomes provisional president.
1934	Fulgencio Batista removes revolutionary government.
1934–1940	Batista controls Cuba through puppet governments.
1940–1944	Batista is president of Cuba.
1944–1948	Ramón Grau serves as president.
1948–1952	Carlos Prío serves as president.
March 10, 1952	Fulgencio Batista takes over power through military coup.
July 26, 1953	Castro attacks Moncada Barracks and is captured.
May 15, 1955	Castro and his followers are released from prison.
July 7, 1955	Castro goes into exile, visits U.S. and Central America, prepares expedition in Mexico.
November 30, 1956	Santiago revolt is led by Frank País.
December 2, 1956	*Granma* landing takes place.
March 13, 1957	Assault on Presidential Palace is made by Directorio Revolucionario.
May 27, 1957	*Corintia* landing takes place.
July 30, 1957	Frank País is killed.
April 9, 1958	General strike fiasco occurs.

June 1958   Batista military offensive against rebels begins.

August 1958   Regime's offensive ends, and revolutionary counterattack starts.

January 1, 1959   Batista leaves power, provisional junta is set up, and Castro calls general revolutionary strike against junta.

Cuban Political Parties and Organizations before 1959

ABC   A secret terrorist organization of the 1930s taking its name from the first three letters of the alphabet.

AIE   Ala Izquierda Estudiantil. A left-wing and Marxist-oriented student group in the 1930s. Its leaders included Raúl Roa, among others.

ARO   Acción Radical Ortodoxa. The political group of the late 1940s advocating armed insurrection. Fidel Castro was one of its leaders.

CSU   Comité de Superación Universitaria. A university student group in the 1940s.

DEU   Directorio Estudiantil Universitario. A revolutionary organization of university students in the 1930s. Founded by Carlos Prío Socarrás and Ramiro Valdés Daussá.

DR   Directorio Revolucionario. A revolutionary organization formed to overthrow the Batista regime in late 1955 and led by José Antonio Echevarría.

FEU   Federación Estudiantil Universitaria. A federation of university students greatly concerned with Cuban politics. It was led in the 1950s by José Antonio Echevarría.

JL   Junta de Liberación. A Cuban exile group of Batista opponents formed in the United States in 1957.

LC   Legión del Caribe. The Caribbean Legion was formed in the 1940s primarily by Dominican exiles and adventurers. It attempted to overthrow various dictatorships in the Caribbean.

M–26–7 Movimiento 26 de Julio. The 26th of July Movement was the anti-Batista organization led by Fidel Castro and Frank País. July 26 was the date of Castro's attack on the Moncada army barracks in 1953.

MNR   Movimiento Nacionalista Revolucionario. A political group formed in 1953 and composed mostly of upper-middle-class university students. Its leaders were Rafael García Bárcena and Armando Hart.

MSR   Movimiento Socialista Revolucionario. A left-wing and anti-communist terrorist organization of the 1940s. Among its leaders was Mario Salabarría.

OA   Organización Auténtica. An action-oriented splinter group that broke away from the Auténtico Party. Its leader was Carlos Prío Socarrás.

PAU   Partido Acción Unitaria. Fulgencio Batista's political machine.

PPC   Partido del Pueblo Cubano or Ortodoxo Party. The Cuban People's Party, formed in 1947 under the leadership of Eduardo Chibás on a broad reformist and anti-Auténtico program.

PRC   Partido Revolucionario Cubano or Auténtico Party. The Cuban Revolutionary Party was the party of Ramón Grau San Martín and Carlos Prío Socarrás, founded by Grau after his expulsion from the presidency in 1934.

PSP   Partido Socialista Popular or Communist Party. The People's Socialist Party was the Cuban Communist Party and was led by Blas Roca, among others.

SAR   Sociedad de Amigos de la República. An association of influential Cubans who attempted to find a peaceful solution to Cuba's problems. The group's leaders included Cosme de la Torriente and José Miro Cardona.

UIR   Unión Insurreccional Revolucionaria. A left-wing terrorist group and the MSR's main enemy. Jesús Diegues was one of the main figures, as was Fidel Castro.

REVOLUTIONARY STRUGGLE

1947–1958

Volume 1 of the Selected Works of Fidel Castro

Introduction

During the night of April 9, 1895, a small boat sailed across rough Caribbean waters from the Dominican Republic, moving a handful of men toward Cuba. In a few hours they landed on the island to continue the war of independence initiated against Spanish colonialism almost thirty years earlier. The war of liberation had been brutal, claiming thousands of lives over the years, including those of many of its leaders. Yet just when victory was in sight, in 1898, the United States declared war on Spain, intervened in Cuba, and put an end to the struggle. It was inglorious indeed for the many Cubans who had fought so long only to witness victory snatched from their hands by North Americans, who claimed all the credit for Spain's defeat.

Independence had been thwarted. Spanish colonial power was replaced by U.S. domination, and the island remained under the control of foreigners. In 1901, North American control was assured legally by passage of the Platt Amendment, which was attached to the Constitution and gave the United States the right to intervene in Cuba at will. It was passed by the Cubans (by one vote) because otherwise U.S. troops would have remained in Cuba. The republic was born, but not before institutionalizing its dependence on the United States.

Furthermore, although the United States had defeated Spain militarily, in reality it had saved the reactionary Spanish classes. The Cubans had almost driven out the Spanish, but with North American intervention they were allowed to stay and soon became close collaborators with the United States. The result was, as a radical Cuban historian noted in the 1940s, that "before independence the Spaniards feared the Cuban; today the Cuban fears the Spaniards."[1] The Spanish supported intervention and annexation. Their power increased after the war, and by the 1950s they constituted one of the most reactionary sectors of the society.

Thus Cuba tragically entered the twentieth century, still convinced that some day complete independence would be attained.

Out of this frustrated attempt at independence grew the strong revolutionary tradition to which Fidel Castro became heir. The ideal of independence took root in the hearts of Cuban youth. Every new generation felt compelled to sever the island's dependence on the

[1] Emilio Roig de Leuchsenring, *Los grandes momentos políticos cubanos en la república: Ingerencia, reacción, nacionalismo* (Havana, 1943), p. 24.

United States.[2] And all radical nationalists, including Castro, turned for inspiration to the works of José Martí (1853–1895), Cuba's foremost intellectual and an outstanding leader of the war of independence against Spain.

Martí outlined Cuba's problems and offered systematic solutions. He developed the ideals of cultural, economic, and political independence which set the foundations for a national identity. Cuba's true destiny, Martí suggested, could be attained only when all foreign control had disappeared. Thus, Cuban nationalism expressed itself in an anti-imperialist stand.

As independence was an immediate necessity, the class struggle had to be set aside, according to Martí. To fight the foreigners, a united national front was essential, and class differentiations had to be disregarded. Revolutionary activity needed the support of all Cubans, a belief shared by radical youth over the years. Once independence was obtained, a social revolution would follow.

The war of independence, as envisioned by Martí, had two functions. First, it would free the island from Spanish domination. Second, it would make the completely independent nation of Cuba a barrier against U.S. imperialism throughout the rest of the hemisphere. His last letter declared:

> At last I am daily risking my life for my country and . . . for my duty of preventing in time, by securing the independence of Cuba, the spread of the United States across the Antilles and of stopping it from pouncing with this added impetus upon our American lands.[3]

Thus, Cuba was to be the last front against Spanish colonialism and the first against U.S. expansion. But North American intervention had frustrated national liberation, and instead of the bulwark Martí foresaw, Cuba became one of the first Latin American nations to be thoroughly penetrated by U.S. capitalism. The experience was traumatic.

Lacking national leadership and with its goals thwarted, the society

[2] Cuban scholarship dealing with the island is filled with references to generational conflicts, but this tendency has been disregarded by most foreign scholars, who have persisted in their utilization of a class-oriented methodology. A structural analysis of Cuba ought to be complemented by a generational approach to its social and political history. This task, however, cannot be undertaken here. See Nelson P. Valdés and Rolando E. Bonachea, "Social Structure, Generations, and Class Consciousness" (manuscript, 1969), and Dennis B. Woods, "The Long Revolution: Class Relations and Political Conflict in Cuba, 1868–1968," *Science and Society*, vol. 34, no. 1 (Spring 1970).

[3] Emilio Roig de Leuchsenring, *Martí Anti-Imperialist* (Havana: Book Institute, 1967), p. 41.

could neither comprehend nor control the rapid transformations taking place. The introduction of capital and technology from the United States had caused enormous socioeconomic changes, and apprehension seized those who perceived the growing North Americanization. Cuba had radically broken with the past, but without really changing. Now Washington, instead of Madrid, dictated its future. Cuba remained with a colonial status.

The extensive investment of U.S. capital in the island brought about the progressive proletarianization of the countryside.[4] From 1903 to 1927, production increased rapidly, primarily in the sugar sector. Consequently, rapid economic growth caused an increased demand for manpower. Laws were instituted to promote immigration, and from 1902 to 1919 Spaniards accounted for 97 percent of all immigrants to Cuba.[5] One such immigrant was Angel Castro, who went to the island just a few years earlier.

Fidel Castro's Childhood

Angel Castro Argiz was born in the city of Lugo, in the conservative region of Galicia, Spain. In the 1890s, while still a youngster, he emigrated to Cuba to make his fortune. Like thousands of Spaniards, he went into the production of sugar, settling in Mayarí, Oriente Province.

Mayarí was a small, dusty town of wooden shacks. Most of the people were sustained by the United Fruit Company, whose lands encircled the town.[6] According to Fidel Castro, this was also the area where, in 1901,

> A certain Preston bought 75,000 hectares of land in the Nipe Bay area for $400,000, that is, less than $6 a hectare. The valuable hardwood forests alone that covered that land and that went into the

[4] From 1902 to 1921, U.S. investment skyrocketed from $80 million to $1.2 billion. It is reported that from 1913 to 1928 it increased 536 percent. See Robert F. Smith, *The United States and Cuba: Business and Diplomacy, 1917–1960* (New York: Bookman Associates, 1960); Francisco Pardeiro, "Penetración de la oligarquía financiera yanqui en la economía de la Cuba capitalista," *Universidad de la Habana*, nos. 186–188 (July–December 1967), pp. 193–259; "History of the Penetration and Control of Cuba's Economy by Yankee Imperialism," *Granma* (Havana), October 20, October 27, November 10, November 17, December 1, 1968.

[5] Grupo Cubano de Investigaciones Económicas, *Estudio Sobre Cuba* (Coral Gables: University of Miami Press, 1963), p. 378. For a description of this immigration process, see D. C. Corbitt, "Immigration in Cuba," *Hispanic American Historical Review*, vol. 22 (May 1942), pp. 304–308.

[6] In the 1940s some of the residents of Mayarí constituted a large portion of the labor force used by the American government-owned Nicaro Nickel Company.

furnaces of the sugar mills were worth many times that sum. With bulging pockets, they came to a country impoverished by thirty years of struggle, to buy up the nation's best land at less than $6 a hectare.[7]

Angel Castro was not deterred by the backward conditions of the area. Like many Spanish immigrants, he sought and attained rapid enrichment, though he began with no capital. Over the years Angel became wealthy, possessing by the 1950s more than half a million dollars and 23,300 acres of sugar land—acquired, according to his son, by exploiting peasants.[8] This left a lasting impression on Fidel.

Angel Castro married a Cuban who bore him his first two children, Lidia and Pedro Emilio. By then he owned a prosperous lumberyard, which enabled him to purchase "Las Manacas" farm, in the residential district of Birán in Mayarí, where he cultivated sugar cane. At "Las Manacas" he had a love affair with a peasant girl, a household servant. After the death of his first wife, Angel Castro married the girl, Lina Ruz González, who already had borne him three children, Angela, Ramón, and Fidel.[9] The couple had four other children, Juana, Raúl, Emma, and Agustina, after their marriage. Fidel was born August 13, 1927.[10] Like many other Cuban revolutionaries, he was a *first*-generation Cuban.[11]

[7] Fidel Castro, "Our History Is Now One Hundred Years Old," *Granma* (Havana), October 13, 1968.

[8] Lee Lockwood, *Castro's Cuba, Cuba's Fidel* (New York: Macmillan, 1967), p. 25. Some observers have alleged that Fidel's father obtained his wealth by moving fences, thus expanding his land, and coercing neighbors into selling their lands. The allegations, however, have not been documented.

[9] Juan Bosch, who had known Fidel since the 1940s, maintains that Fidel's illegitimacy later had traumatic effects. See "República Dominicana: Entre la terquedad y la ambición," *Bohemia Libre* (New York), October 13, 1963, p. 7.

[10] There is no agreement as to the year Castro was born. Some say it was on August 13, 1926 (for example, Herbert Matthews and Luis Conte Agüero), whereas Cuban government versions give the date as August 13, 1927. See Herbert Matthews, *Fidel Castro* (New York: Simon and Schuster, 1969), p. 17; Luis Conte Agüero, *Fidel Castro, vida y obra* (Havana: Editorial Lex, 1959), p. 7; "Síntesis cronológica de la vida de Fidel," *Revolución* (Havana), May 3, 1963, p. 3; *Political, Economic, and Social Thought of Fidel Castro* (Havana: Editorial Lex, 1959), pp. 5–19.

[11] It is significant that so many Cuban revolutionaries are first-generation Cubans. Such are the cases of José Martí, Julio Antonio Mella (founder of the Cuban Communist Party and leader of the student movement in the 1920s), Antonio Guiteras (leader of the revolutionary movement in the 1930s), Abel and Haydée Santamaría (participants in the Moncada attack), Faure Chomón (leader of the Directorio Revolucionario), Calixto Sánchez (leader of the Organización Auténtica or OA), Joe Westbrook (Directorio), Faustino Pérez (leader of the 26th of July Movement), Manolo Fernández (26th of July), Enrique Oltuski (26th of July), the Ameijeiras brothers (26th of July), the Menoyo brothers (OA), García Lavandero (OA), and many others.

For his first few years, Fidel seems to have led a carefree, bucolic existence. There was a certain simplicity in his home, which Lina managed to run in an orderly way. A healthy, tall, thin, and agile youngster, he ran around the farm barefoot, played with his dogs, and rode his horse. He enjoyed swimming with friends in the Birán River, but his great love was the sea, a few miles to the north. Fidel made frequent visits to the fishermen to hear their tales of adventure and of their struggles with sharks.[12]

A spoiled child, he often had unexpected reactions and tantrums. When he wanted to do something, his parents would usually let him. Herbert Matthews claims that at the age of six Fidel wanted to go to school, but his old, conservative father did not see any point in getting an education. Thereupon, Fidel threatened to burn down the house if he was not sent to school.[13]

He had his way. He received his primary education in Mayarí and at La Salle School in Santiago de Cuba. Later he changed to a boarding school run by the Jesuits in Santiago. In 1942 Fidel arrived in Havana to continue his studies under the Jesuits at Belén High School. He was a good student and graduated in 1945. His major interests were history, sociology, geography, and agriculture. He was also good in sports, being proclaimed the best high school athlete in Cuba in 1943–1944. His main interest, however, was in social problems; he had a great concern for the poor. A close friend of his at that time writes:

> When his teachers could not find him and wanted to talk to him, they knew that the best thing to do was to go to the kitchen where he would probably be found talking to the cook or some other humble employee about their problems and agonies.[14]

It was in high school that Fidel became acquainted with the works of José Martí. He read Martí voraciously and was deeply moved by the man's honesty, intellectual commitment, and revolutionary actions. José Martí became his model and primary moral influence. From then on he would try to act, speak, and write in the same manner as the leader of the war of independence.

Fidel also learned of Cuba's tragic history. He discovered that the republic created in 1902 was essentially a colony guided by the principles of the Platt Amendment, and that Cuba's true identity and place in the world were something to fight for, something yet to be accomplished.

---

[12] "Hechos y fechas en la vida de Fidel, publicados en la prensa de la Unión Soviética," *Revolución* (Havana) May 4, 1963, p. 3.
[13] Matthews, *Fidel Castro*, p. 21.
[14] Conte Agüero, *Fidel Castro*, p. 23.

These were not new thoughts, nor did they originate with Fidel Castro. To understand his political behavior and thinking, it is extremely important to consider, at least briefly, Cuba's recent sociopolitical history and its revolutionary tradition. Fidel is a product of his country's history, and to that history he is inextricably tied.

Developing a National Consciousness

At the time that Angel Castro settled in Oriente Province, Cuba was undergoing deep social transformations. These changes left the country with an economy owned and operated by the United States and with a monoculture in which only sugar was produced. Sugar production always entailed seasonal unemployment for the rural proletariat that had evolved; at the same time, however, there was great prosperity. When World War I devastated Europe, Cuba was enriched. The island supplied sugar to the Allies, producing a fantastic but short-lived boom. Sugar prices collapsed in September 1920. Banks refused to give credit; the small private sugar mills went bankrupt and were absorbed by the large U.S. corporations.[15] Close to 75 percent of the sugar industry passed into North American hands by this process.

With the traditional bourgeoisie destroyed and foreign capital rigidly controlling the conventional economic power bases, new social groups could acquire wealth and power only by entering the political arena.[16] But recurrent political instability allowed little time for this new social class to develop a coherent political and social consciousness. Thus, no one class effectively represented the interests of the nation.

Economic growth was paralleled by a cultural crisis, in which many lost their identity and purpose.[17] People felt powerless to change their destiny or that of their own country. Everything seemed to be dominated and defined by foreigners. Yet under those foreigners, conditions had visibly improved in some ways. Roads and schools were built, jobs opened up, and health-care facilities grew. Conformism, the "Plattista" mentality (after the Platt Amendment) was the order of the day. To object to these changes was considered unpatriotic.

[15] Hugh Thomas, "Middle Class Politics and the Cuban Revolution," in Claudio Véliz (ed.), *The Politics of Conformity in Latin America* (London: Oxford University Press, 1967), p. 251.

[16] This thesis originated with Merle Kling, "Towards a Theory of Power and Political Instability in Latin America," *The Western Political Quarterly*, vol. 9 (March 1956), pp. 21–35.

[17] The 1920s witnessed an increase in illiteracy, violence, and corruption, while "Cuba lost its own characteristics." See Fernando Ortiz, *La decadencia cubana* (Havana: Imprenta La Universal, 1924).

Nevertheless, the sense of frustration was overwhelming. The generation that had been born under Spanish colonialism and had attained adolescence in the early years of the republic, though too young to fight the war of independence, declared itself defender of Cuban national identity. Unable to liberate the island, these people found refuge in seeking its essence, trying to create a self-consciousness, an awareness that would bind Cubans together and transcend their fatalism. This transitional generation was concerned essentially with "culture," because cultural criticism was considered a necessary condition for engaging in future political activity.

Castro has attested that the revolutionaries owed a great debt to those intellectuals who began to implant a national consciousness, a national spirit, in the Cuban people, because it was a necessary foundation from which the struggle for national liberation would continue.[18] The furthering of nationalism, he suggested, was a continuation of the war of independence.

Cultural criticism soon evolved into a more politically committed stand. Many intellectuals concluded that it was worthless simply to look for what was unique in Cuba's culture; instead they turned to the ideals of José Martí. Martí was discovered by this generation because of their common desire for the termination of Cuba's colonial status. The Martí cult that grew from then on represented a return to revolutionary ideals, a reestablishment of a nationalist and anti-imperialist continuity that had been broken years earlier.[19]

In the 1920s Cubans were also influenced by other Latin American intellectuals such as José Enrique Rodó (Uruguay), José Ingenieros (Argentina), Joaquín González (Chile), José Vasconcelos (Mexico), and José Carlos Mariátegui (Peru). Moreover, the Mexican Revolution of 1910 and the Russian Revolution of 1917 emphasized to this radical generation what Martí had maintained years before: Only violent revolution could terminate the island's dependence on the United States and bring about a more just social order. Romanticism and idealism were growing hand in hand with revolutionary fervor.

The first action of the new postwar generation (often called the 1923 generation) took place on May 13, 1923, when thirteen young radical intellectuals[20] boldly and publicly repudiated the government's

[18] Fidel Castro, "Ante la agresión económica no nos quedamos impasibles," *Revolución* (Havana), June 24, 1960, pp. 1, 14.

[19] Francisco Ichaso, "Ideas y aspiraciones de la primera generación republicana," in Ramiro Guerra et al., *Historia de la Nación Cubana* (Havana: Editorial Historia de la Nación Cubana, 1952), pp. 335–337.

[20] Several were members of the newly founded Communist Party, which was then romantic and nationalistic in outlook.

corruption and lack of representativeness. They formed an organization called the Falange de Acción Cubana, which persuaded Cuban youth to take a more active role in politics. At the same time, other new social forces began to appear, including newly founded labor unions that launched a series of strikes because of the deterioration of the rural economy after the crisis of the 1920s. The students were organizing also, and there was the influence of revolutionaries who had sought refuge in Cuba after fighting the dictatorships of other Latin American nations.[21]

Amid the growing social unrest and economic problems, a political crisis brewed. Gerardo Machado, who had been elected to the presidency, became ever more determined to remain in power. In March 1927 he presented a bill to the Cuban Congress to legalize his continuation in power. While Congress debated the bill, Machado created what became known as *cooperativismo*. His idea was that there was enough wealth for all politicians, so there was no need to fight and kill one another; instead they should cooperate to monopolize the political structure of the nation.[22]

The young men and women who demanded political honesty and a radical transformation of society denounced the system, which forbade the creation of new political parties, thereby closing all peaceful channels for the opposition. The youth demanded power, but were faced with a ruling elite blinded by its own hunger for power. To struggle against Machado, students and young workers formed the Directorio Estudiantil Universitario (DEU).[23]

Resistance grew with the amendment to the constitution, extending Machado's term of office. In May 1929 Machado began his second term, after winning an election in which no opposition candidates were permitted to participate.

The worldwide economic depression of 1930 caused serious hardships in Cuba and gave Machado an excuse for ruthless supression. Nonetheless, opposition continued to increase, and by 1931 the general

[21] Maria Villar Buceta, "Minorismo y minoristas," *Universidad de La Habana* (Havana), March–June 1964, pp. 59–66; Carlos Ripoll, *La generación del 23 en Cuba* (New York: Las Americas Publishing Co., 1968). On the role of the labor unions, see Charles Page, "The Development of Organized Labor in Cuba" (Ph.D. dissertation, University of California, Berkeley, 1950).

[22] Ernest Gruening, "Cuba Under the Machado Regime," *Current History*, vol. 34 (May 1931), pp. 214–219; and Russell Porter, "Cuba Under President Machado," *Current History*, vol. 37 (April 1933), pp. 29–34.

[23] The DEU in 1927 and 1930 was similar, although the leadership changed due to imprisonment, exile, and death. By 1930 it was also less leftist-oriented, although more inclined toward action and terrorism, than in 1927.

discent of the population pressured the traditional opposition parties to reconsider their position with regard to Machado.

The parties first attempted to establish a "cordial understanding" with the dictator, but failed.[24] The traditional politicians then tried to start a guerrilla war, but once again were unsuccessful. This fiasco finally discredited them. From that time on, revolt was led by young people and would take place in the cities rather than the countryside.

Division, however, soon displaced generational unity. When the DEU ranks split, its left wing became the Ala Izquierda Estudiantil (AIE) and its right wing formed the ABC. The AIE, which followed a Marxist though not necessarily communist line, emphasized the class struggle,[25] whereas DEU had a generational outlook.

The ABC was organized by exasperated youth who considered action and terrorism the only solution to the problems of the country. It represented a new form and style of struggle—a clandestine action group modeled on the French terrorist society described by Victor Hugo in *Les Misérables*. Unlike the organization in Hugo's novel, however, the Cuban ABC was composed of men who had no close relations with the working class.[26]

These trends are extremely important in comprehending Fidel Castro's political career. As will be seen, Fidel identified with a generational outlook, favoring revolutionary violence over theory and disparaging those who preferred to become theoreticians rather than foment a revolution.

In 1933, the terrorism of action groups and popular opposition to the Machado administration increased. The political forces in Cuba were divided between Plattistas, who wanted the United States to intervene to remove Machado without structural changes, and those

[24] Cosme de la Torriente was actively engaged in the "cordial understanding" formula. In the 1950s he participated in a "civic dialogue" with dictator Batista in order to find a peaceful solution to the conflict between the government and the opposition.

[25] Almost all the AIE leaders had a bourgeois background, and a large percentage held law degrees from the University of Havana, at the time the only university in Cuba. The AIE was led by Raúl Roa, Aureliano Sánchez Arango, Alberto Saumell, Gabriel Barceló, Pablo de la Torriente Brau, Marcos García Villaroel, Charles Simeón, José E. Borges, Teté Casuso, Salvador Vilaseca, José Utrera, and others.

[26] The ABC leaders were Jorge Mañach, Francisco Ichaso, José Martínez Sáenz, Juan Andrés Lliteras, Carlos Saladrigas, Emeterio Santovenia, Francisco López, Aurelio Espinosa, Ramón Hermida, Fulgencio Batista, and others. See Mario Riera Hernández, *Cuba Libre, 1895–1958* (Miami: Colonial Press, 1968), p. 126; and Eddy Chibás, "Hacia donde va Cuba," *Bohemia* (Havana), August 26, 1934, pp. 63–64.

who demanded nonintervention while advocating thorough social changes. In 1933, Franklin Delano Roosevelt made his position explicit by sending a special emissary to Cuba: Ambassador Sumner Welles. His mission was to "mediate" between the different political groups in Cuba, and to this effect a mediation committee was formed. This action provoked even more dissension among the badly divided youth.[27]

1933: Revolution and Reaction

Social and political forces obliged Machado to resign. North American mediation played an important role, but the dictator was overthrown mainly by a general strike that began on August 5, 1933, and terminated in an army revolt. Thereafter the new generation[28] was further split when the ABC joined the government formed by Ambassador Welles and headed by Dr. Carlos Manuel de Céspedes, while the DEU and the AIE stood aside.[29] The new government was established, with the consent of the military, in order to forestall a possible takeover by the revolutionary forces. A whirlwind of confusion ensued.

The Céspedes government did not remain long in power. On September 4, 1933, noncommissioned officers and enlisted men of the army revolted against the older, higher-ranking officers. The revolt began as a protest against nonpayment of wages and because of dissatisfaction with officers who had collaborated with the Machado regime. The DEU enthusiastically joined the military men led by Fulgencio Batista as a junta of five men assumed power.[30]

A new generation at last, with new ideas, new men, and new pro-

[27] The committee was composed of Cosme de la Torriente, Joaquín Martínez Saénz (a member of ABC), Rafael Santos, Wilfredo Albanes, Hortensia Lamar, Nicasio Silveiro, Manuel Dorta Duque, and others. See also Sumner Welles, *The Time for Decision* (New York: Harper and Brothers, 1944), p. 195.

[28] The "new generation" refers to what is generally called the "generation of 1923" and the "generation of 1933," which some authors have called the "generation of the 1930s." We consider these different terms to describe a generation that went through different political stages during a ten-year period. Throughout the text we use the terms interchangeably.

[29] Margaret Naegle, "Sumner Welles' Mediation in Cuba" (Master's thesis, University of New Mexico, 1964), p. 121. The new government was composed of Carlos M. de Céspedes, Cosme de la Torriente, Federico Laredo Brú, Joaquín Martínez Saénz, José A. Presno, Demetrio Castillo, Carlos Saladrigas, Eduardo Chibás, Sr., Guillermo Belt, and Nicasio Silveiro.

[30] In mid-August 1933 the enlisted men had formed a clandestine organization that articulated their grievances; it was led by Fulgencio Batista, Pablo Rodríguez, José Euleterio Pedraza, Manuel Lopez, Juan Estevez, Angel Echevarria, Mario Hernández, and Cruz Vidal. The best account of this group is in Ricardo Adam Silva, *La gran mentira: 4 de septiembre de 1933* (Havana, 1947). The junta installed after the revolt consisted of Ramón Grau San Martín, Sergio Carbó, José Miguel Irrisarri, Porfirio Franca, and Guillermo Portela.

cedures, had taken over the political and military structure of the nation. But the junta lacked the support of many of its contemporaries and, most importantly, of the United States. Internal differences within the junta (known as the *pentarquía*) over the issue of political power necessitated the delegation of decision-making powers to one person. On September 10, 1933, Ramón Grau San Martín was inaugurated as provisional president.[31]

A manifesto issued in Havana in November 1956 by the 26th of July Movement acknowledges the contributions of that brief administration:

> In the "100 days" that the revolutionary forces held power, they did more in defense of the interests of the nation and of the people than all the governments of the preceding thirty years.[32]

Besides the repeal of the Cuban constitution and the Platt Amendment, progressive labor and social measures gave the Cuban people, at long last, a feeling of confidence in themselves. Unfortunately, their taste of self-government was short-lived.

Twenty days after the revolutionary government was established, thirty U.S. warships surrounded Cuba because Welles's successor, Ambassador Caffery, considered the new government communist inspired. Meanwhile in Oriente Province the AIE organized soviets, captured thirty-six sugar mills, formed red guards, and tried to establish an independent communist zone.[33] Grau's government was in the unenviable position of trying to carry out a social revolution while fighting both right and left. Moreover, it had only tenuous control over the armed forces. Caffery claimed that the revolutionary government did not represent the will of the Cuban people and was incapable of maintaining order, but in reality it was not recognized because the United States was afraid it would carry out a thorough social revolution that would put an end to North American hegemony over the island by following the precepts outlined by José Martí almost forty years earlier.

Grau's ambivalence allowed the political leadership of the movement to fall into the hands of the radical twenty-six-year-old minister of

[31] Ramón Grau San Martín was a professor of medicine of the University of Havana. He was chosen to preside over the government because of his moderate views and dispassionate behavior.

[32] The manifesto was probably written by Dr. Mario Llerena. It appears in its entirety as "Manifiesto-programa del Movimiento 26 de Julio," in Enrique González Pedrero, *La revolución cubana* (Mexico: UNAM, 1959), p. 98.

[33] The communists were active in trying to blackmail Franklin D. Roosevelt, by creating chaos in Cuba, into establishing relations with the USSR. The soviets, however, were crushed by the military under the command of Batista.

the interior, Antonio Guiteras. The revolutionary bent of the Grau administration was due mainly to Guiteras, who favored agrarian reform, industrialization, housing reform, and the curtailment of North American influence.[34] Guiteras constantly made his dislike for Batista obvious. He tried unsuccessfully to destroy Batista's power by creating a marine corps independent of the army. In January 1934 he asked the president to consent to Batista's removal from his military post. Grau refused, and on January 15, 1934, Grau himself was forced to resign by Batista. Guiteras tried to take power but could find no consistent support.

Batista, on the other hand, had been shrewdly and skillfully consolidating his position within the military. He had given the civilians a measure of political power as long as they could be useful, while keeping the military his own domain. In Guiteras he found a challenger, and Batista did not hesitate to remove the civilians from power. This tactic was successfully repeated with subsequent civilian governments. This military *caudillo*, a key figure in Cuban political history, and his followers were, after all, as conservative as the officers they had removed from power months earlier. Years later Fidel Castro was to observe:

> The conditions under which the 1933 revolution developed could not allow a revolution to subsist. The army did not change; it was the same army Machado had. . . . It was logical for them to end up doing what they did: to overthrow the revolutionary government.[35]

Nonetheless, he reminded the Cuban people of the influence that the revolutionaries of the 1930s had on later revolutionaries, calling them in the same speech "an inspiration for us." From their experience he concluded that in order to mount a successful revolution, the army had to be destroyed.

The revolution of 1933 failed partially because this new generation was permeated by dissension. Futhermore, the revolutionary government that was created in September 1933 was put in power by a new

---

[34] Guiteras took over the American-owned Cuban Electric Company, cut the service rates, enacted a law for an eight-hour workday and a minimum wage, repudiated Cuba's debt to the Chase Manhattan Bank, dissolved the political parties that supported Machado, distributed land, made unionism compulsory, and insured workers' retirement and security among other things—all during his ninety days in power!

[35] Castro, "Ante la agresión económica no nos quedamos impasibles." It is worth noting that a similar process took place in Guatemala in 1954. The Arbenz regime was overthrown with ease because the government did not control the military. Guatemala in 1954 reinforced the conclusions Fidel had reached about the failure of the 1933 revolution in Cuba.

wave of military leaders and not by the efforts of the revolutionaries. The latter were, in fact, given a government to run; they never attained political power by themselves. Their great handicap was their failure to achieve control over the military, with whom final power rested.

The new government, formed by Batista with Uncle Sam's blessing, put an end to the attempt at social revolution.[36] Cuba would be for many years under the aegis of Fulgencio Batista.

The social revolution was frustrated; nonetheless, important and deep-seated changes had occurred in Cuban society. The traditional political parties and officer's corps were almost entirely obliterated, while those involved in the labor movement and the students actively entered politics. In addition, the Cuban armed forces emerged as a decisive new factor in Cuban politics. Finally, revolutionary violence and terrorism became commonplace political practices.

A new kind of conservative politics was inaugurated on January 18, 1934, when Colonel Carlos Mendieta became president.[37] He restored "law and order" and guaranteed the United States full restoration of confiscated property. The United States immediately extended diplomatic recognition to the new government and abrogated the Platt Amendment once the Cubans agreed to sign a reciprocal trade agreement, giving the United States a "practical control" of the Cuban market.[38]

The consequences of the 1934 treaty and the ensuing sugar quota system were devastating for Cuba. The terms of the system did not permit the Cuban sugar industry to return to predepression levels of production, and the smaller size of the quota increased unemployment. After 1933 the number of sugar mills declined. The quota system stabilized the nation's economy, but at a low level of productivity, and although Cuban sugar producers were rewarded by U.S. subsidies, the people did not fare very well.

The counterrevolutionary government of "national conciliation" became increasingly dictatorial, forcing revolutionaries into exile or underground activity. Opposition grew, and once again Cuba was enveloped by revolutionary struggle.

[36] The new government was formed by Carlos Mendieta, Cosme de la Torriente, Felix Granados, Gabriel Landa, Luis Baralt, Joaquín Martínez Saénz, Juan Antiga, Santiago Verdeja, Miguel Mariano Gómez, Daniel Compte, Roberto Méndez Peñate, Carlos de la Rionda, and Emeterio Santovenia.

[37] Batista ruled through puppets from 1934 to 1940. The nominal heads of state were Carlos Mendieta (1934–1936), Miguel Mariano Gómez (1936), and Federico Laredo Brú (1936–1940).

[38] Smith, *United States and Cuba*, pp. 141–164.

Revolutionary sectors remained split in terms of political strategies and outlook. The "ideologues," led by former president Ramón Grau, believing that it was impossible to fight against Batista's military might, went into exile. This left a leadership vacuum within the "electoralist" sector, which favored peaceful resistance. Meanwhile, Antonio Guiteras continued to lead those "men of action" who still advocated armed insurrection to regain power.

Guiteras created Joven Cuba in order to coordinate a national uprising, establish socialism, and end Cuba's colonial status. Its activities were financed by kidnapping and bank robbery, its main political instruments were terrorism and assassination, and its primary target was the ABC. After the failure of a general strike that he helped labor leaders to organize, Guiteras decided to go to Mexico to form an armed expedition. But as he sailed from the island on May 8, 1935, he was captured by Batista's henchmen and shot to death.[39] With the death of Guiteras, the persistent rebel, the men of action lost the only person capable of channeling their revolutionary violence toward practical political goals.

Leaderless, the action groups retained only the technique of violence. Unable to overthrow the Batista regime, many joined the electoralists and helped create the Partido Revolucionario Cubano (PRC), whose goal was to realize the ideals of José Martí and the principles for which the revolutionary government stood. The Auténticos, as the party was generally known, espoused the principles of "nationalism, socialism, and anti-imperialism" by peaceful means.[40]

In December 1939, electoralist PRC leaders, including former President Grau, returned from exile to participate in a Constitutional Assembly and prepare for the following year's elections. Grau's return acknowledged and legitimized Fulgencio Batista's control of Cuba. It also demoralized the rank and file of the action groups, which still considered Batista and the armed forces the enemy and main cause of the failure of the 1933 revolution. Nonetheless, Auténtico participation in the Constitutional Assembly made possible the adoption, at least theoretically, of many of the 1933 ideals.

[39] Jesús González Cartas, "Los hechos del Morrillo: crimen y coartada," *Bohemia* (Havana), December 26, 1948, pp. 42–43, 80; José D. Cabús, "Grau odiaba a Guiteras," *Bohemia* (Havana), September 26, 1948, pp. 28–29, 80; Paulino Pérez, "Batista es el responsable directo de la muerte de Guiteras," *Bohemia* (Havana), October 3, 1948, pp. 32–33, 82.

[40] Ramón Grau San Martín, "Definición de la doctrina auténtica," in Diego de Pereda, *El nuevo pensamiento político de Cuba* (Havana: Editorial Lex, 1943), p. 232.

In 1940 Batista was elected president with the backing of commu- nists, conservatives, and the armed forces.[41] The PRC was defeated because its structure and financial resources were not well developed and because military terror was used against it during the campaign. Also, it had signed a conciliation pact with Batista agreeing that the provisions for free and direct ballots approved in the 1940 Constitution need not apply in the immediate election.

The Batista regime (1940–1944), aided by World War II and the world demands for sugar, managed to improve conditions in the island and reduce the polarization of Cuban society. Temporarily, at least, Cubans breathed easier under a delicate stability.

In 1944, after eleven years in the opposition, the 1930s generation finally obtained power. Why Batista allowed this to happen is not difficult to perceive. After the war, democracy enjoyed brief interna- tional popularity, so elections looked good. On this subject Fidel has remarked:

> The world was shaken by a wave of popular enthusiasm and democratic optimism, a world which with the last shots in Europe conceived hopes for a happier and more humane future for its peoples. Batista then yielded to world public opinion.[42]

One must also bear in mind that Batista still controlled the military, where the real power lay, and therefore had nothing to lose but a bad reputation. So while Batista was dealing in real estate in Daytona Beach, the Auténticos took over and proved that they could be just as corrupt as they accused him of being.

President Ramón Grau San Martín (1944–1948) improved the condi- tions of *organized* labor, built new roads and housing projects, began a rural school program, and made provisions for the aged, invalids, widows, and homeless children. He also improved health facilities, and his government regulated the economy and tried to implement a more equitable distribution of income. Moreover, World War II brought immense prosperity to the first Auténtico administration. But the early revolutionism gradually cooled, as the government had to ally itself with conservative forces to remain in power. By 1944, it had moved away from socialism and nearer to welfare capitalism and consensus politics.

---

[41] For a discussion of the relations between Batista and the communists, see Robert J. Alexander, *Communism in Latin America* (New Brunswick, N.J.: Rut- gers University Press, 1957), pp. 278–285.

[42] "Manifesto No. 1 to the People of Cuba" in this volume.

At about the same time that the Auténticos attained power, Fidel Castro entered college and began his political career.

The University Years

Background. When Fidel Castro entered the University of Havana in 1945, it was far from an ivy-covered citadel where the roughest activity was football. Gunmen lurked around every corner, and their games were deadly. Students and faculty alike were terrorized by a few groups of power-hungry gangsters, mostly nonstudents. In fact, Fidel remarked in 1959 that his four years at the University of Havana were much more dangerous than all the time he fought against Batista from the Sierra Maestra.[43] To see how and why these conditions came to be, it is necessary to go back as far as 1939.

At that time Batista and the leaders of the PRC had reached an understanding, leaving the underground "action groups" of the anti-Machado struggle without function or leaders. Nonetheless, these experts in sabotage, weapons, and terrorism continued their cold-blooded murdering of opponents, without regret and with the slightest motivation. During the Batista administration (1940–1944), the insurrectionists found refuge at the University of Havana and in some labor unions, where they degenerated into mercenary gangs. Batista's firm control prevented any major violence, but when the Auténticos came to power in 1944 with a weak government, violence once again erupted. The Grau administration took advantage of the insurrectionists' existence by providing government jobs for group members. In return, they assassinated communists to help Grau gain control of the university or the labor unions. The Auténticos also used action groups as bodyguards and shock troops, a force conveniently independent of the Batista-controlled military. The very corruption of the Grau regime thus contributed to the spread of political violence, for it lacked the moral authority to command respect and orderly behavior.

There are other reasons for the incredible violence and terror that swept the nation.[44] First, violence always has been an important tradition in Cuban culture for solving disputes. The action groups also reflected many unresolved tensions, for no one agreed on what was legitimate in order to control power. Many groups and individuals believed that power in itself was the most important goal, regardless of the means employed to obtain it. Social unrest evolved into violence

---

[43] "Fidel Castro visitó la Universidad," *Diario de la Marina* (Havana), January 14, 1959, pp. 1, 9b.

[44] The varieties of motives explain why the action groups could be different things to different people. There were romantics, gangsters, and terrorists side by side.

also because many people could still earn a living only through extortion. The use of armed violence could quickly bring fame and fortune, and the romantic image of the man of action attracted young people. There were terrorists who dispensed "revolutionary justice" to those whom the state had failed to prosecute during the Machado-Batista regimes, and others whose goal was vengeance for fallen comrades.[45] Finally, there was a handful of individuals who either found revolutionism a vocation or sincerely believed that insurrection was still necessary to establish a revolutionary government.

These violence-prone gangs, although functioning in a university environment, had few ideological interests. Their politics were a strange mixture of anti-imperialism, a trigger-happy sort of anarchism, and anticommunism. Their anti-imperialism was passionate, yet they lacked any understanding of the real influence of the United States over the island. Their anticommunism stemmed from their low educational level,[46] aversion to serious thinking, and distrust of those who discussed theoretical issues without acting—which was generally the case of the communists. Although their vision of a new world may have been limited, action delighted them.

Control of the university was important because it was one of the main power centers in national politics, where the groups wanted to gain influence.[47] University leadership assured a future position in national politics. Furthermore, to belong to the leadership elite meant automatic good grades with almost no studying.

In the late thirties the action groups, then called *bonches*,[48] formed a puppet student organization (Asociación Estudiantil Alma Mater) at the University of Havana in order to undermine the control of the student government and university authorities. They utilized their

[45] Letter of Jesús Diegues (leader of Unión Insurreccional Revolucionaria) to one of the authors on December 15, 1969. Also see Rolando Masferrer, "Violencia revolucionaria y degeneración," *Tiempo en Cuba* (Havana), April 24, 1948, p. 12.

[46] Andrés Suárez, *Cuba: Castroism and Communism 1959–1966* (Cambridge, Mass.: The M.I.T. Press, 1967), p. 15.

[47] Of the many action groups in the 1940s, the following, with leaders' names in parentheses, were the most important: Unión Insurreccional Revolucionaria (Emilio Tró, Jesús Diegues); Legión Revolucionaria de Cuba (Julio Salabarría, Antonio Acosta); Joven Cuba (Lauro Blanco, Manuel Fernández); Acción Revolucionaria Guiteras (Jesús González Cartas); Alianza Nacional Revolucionaria (Lazaro Cruz, Mariano del Val); Asociación de Veteranos (Vidal Morales, Rafael del Pino); Movimiento Socialista Revolucionario (Rolando Masferrer); ATOM (Ernesto de la Fé); and Asociación de Ex-Combatientes Anti-Fascistas.

[48] Cuban slang meaning "gang." The term appears to come from the English word "bunch." See "El viejo bonchista," *Tiempo en Cuba* (Havana), October 3, 1948, p. 8.

experience with coercion to take over the university, and students had to carry a book in one hand and a gun in the other to feel some degree of safety.

The university's autonomy offered a safe refuge for the *bonchistas*. Many students who sought unsuccessfully to become university leaders joined the gangs, hoping to gain prominence by bullets where ballots had failed. They used all kinds of criminal tactics to achieve control over several departments of the university. Recognizing the threat posed by the *bonchistas* in university politics, the student, faculty, and administrative leaders rapidly reacted by forming the Comité de Superación Universitaria (CSU), which had the backing of the university police and adopted the methods of the action groups.[49] The CSU's objective was to annihilate the action groups through violence, and before long it had unleashed a wave of repression.

On June 4, 1940, war broke out between the two factions, and Antonio Morín Dopico, a *bonchista* leader, was wounded. Five days later a member of the CSU was machine-gunned while coming out of a class. Many Cubans shared the CSU's outrage at the August 15 murder of Ramiro Valdés Daussá, an engineering professor who had tried to curb *bonchista* violence. The university reacted by expelling those students who were members of the action groups. However, the CSU betrayed the confidence of university sympathizers by assassinating several professors who disagreed with its methods. It was officially dissolved, but continued surreptitiously to control university politics through the student federation.

After recurrent waves of terror and counterterror, the old *bonchista* leaders formed the Unión Insurreccional Revolucionaria (UIR), and their anti-*bonche* counterparts formed the Movimiento Socialista Revolucionario (MSR). These were the two major action groups operating in Havana in 1945.

The UIR was led by Emilio Tró, a veteran of the Spanish Civil War who had also fought with the U.S. Army in Guadalcanal. The UIR membership included former *bonchistas*, anarchists who had fought in Spain, and Tró's comrades from the war in the Pacific.[50] According to

[49] The leaders of the CSU were Ramiro Valdés Daussá, Mario Salabarría, Cándido Mora, Manolo Castro, Eufemio Fernández, Roberto Pérez, Roberto Meoqui, and Oscar Fernández Caral. See "Manolo Castro, 1910–1948," *Tiempo en Cuba* (Havana), February 27, 1949, p. 13.

[50] José A. Duarte, *Historiología Cubana* (Hollywood, California, 1969), vol. 4, p. 689 (mimeographed). The UIR leadership was composed of Emilio Tró, José de Jesús Jinjaume, Armando Correa, Vidal Morales, Luis Padriene, Jesús Diegues, Rafael del Pino, Calixto Sánchez, Orlando García, and others.

one of the founders, UIR was created "above all to sanction the assassins and henchmen who walked freely and with impunity in our streets."[51]

The MSR was formed in October 1945 after Rolando Masferrer and some of his followers broke with the Communist Party. Masferrer, who had fought on the Republican side during the Spanish Civil War, had been a Communist Party thug (1940–1945) at the University of Havana. The MSR had three goals: to create a revolutionary socialism that would oppose communism, U.S. imperialism, and the Auténticos; to destroy the UIR and other action groups for being adventurist and counterrevolutionary; and to liberate the Dominican Republic from the dictatorship of Rafael Trujillo.[52]

From 1940 on, the MSR exerted total control over the University of Havana. To enroll, even to pass examinations, students were required to be in good standing with the organization. With the assistance of the MSR, Manolo Castro, who was a founder of the CSU, established a virtual dictatorship over the students.[53] From 1940 to 1946, he completely controlled the university's politics. To challenge his power was an invitation to mortal combat. Students had only two options: tolerate MSR rule or defy it by joining a different action group.

This was the situation in 1945 when, at the age of nineteen, Fidel Castro enrolled at the University of Havana.

Fidel at the University. Fidel had come to study law and was attracted by student politics from the very outset. He was a good speaker, and many were impressed by his remarkable memory and powerful physique. He was determined to become a university leader, and he accomplished his goal with amazing recklessness and courage. Realizing that

[51] Letter of Jesús Diegues to one of the editors (December 15, 1969).

[52] *Movimiento Socialista Revolucionario, Acuerdos y resoluciones* (Havana), 1949, pp. 5–64. The MSR leaders were: Rolando Masferrer, who later became a senator for the PRC and ended up supporting the Batista dictatorship in 1952, after which the MSR further degenerated into a sort of personal private army known as the *Tigres de Masferrer;* Eufemio Fernández, who became Prío's chief of police and a founder of the Caribbean Legion; and Juan Bosch, the Dominican writer and exile who believed the action groups would liberate his country, although his relationship with the MSR eventually declined. See Boris Goldenberg, *The Cuban Revolution and Latin America* (New York: Praeger Publishers, 1965), p. 149; and Rolando Masferrer, "El Movimiento Socialista Revolucionario," *Tiempo en Cuba* (Havana), May 1, 1949, pp. 14–15.

[53] Manolo Castro was an engineering student and aided Ramiro Valdés Daussá in the curbing of action groups from 1940 to 1944. He was not related to Fidel Castro.

he needed the support of an action group with which he could challenge the MSR's hegemony over the university, Fidel joined the UIR
in 1946.[54]

In 1947, the UIR resolved to remove the MSR from the University
of Havana. Manolo Castro's term as president of the student federation
had ended, and elections were forthcoming. Further evidence of
Fidel Castro's anticommunist background is the fact that the UIR
made an alliance with some Catholic students and presented as their
candidates Humberto Ruiz Leiro, Fidel Castro, and José I. Rasco. On
the other hand, the MSR allied with the young communists and ran
Enrique Ovares, José Luis Massó, and Alfredo Guevara.[55] The latter
won by a very small margin.

Violence continued unabated. On May 26, 1947, an MSR leader,
Orlando León Lemus, was wounded. A day later several "revolutionary" organizations threatened to kill him because he had exploited
the title of revolutionary to enrich himself.[56] The MSR quickly replied
by machine-gunning several UIR members. After many such bloody
incidents, President Grau met with representatives of both groups.
Realizing that both fought for a larger share of wealth, power, and influence, the president agreed, incredibly enough, to divide most government agencies between them. Why Ramón Grau would opt for
such a solution remains a mystery. Perhaps he hoped that by furnishing
both groups with sufficient weapons he would cause them to annihilate
each other. Or, lacking the courage to take a strong stand, he allowed
the action groups to dictate terms to him.[57] In any case. Cuba's govern-

[54] Jesús Diegues, leader of the UIR, has stated, "Fidel Castro used us for his
own political battles within the university without ever really identifying [pub-
licly] with UIR" (Jesús Diegues, letter of December 15, 1969, to one of the
editors). A Cuban reporter has argued that Fidel opposed political gangsterism
during his university years. This is true if one refers only to the activities of the
MSR and not to those of the UIR. See Ernesto Montaner, "Hermanos contra
hermanos," *Bohemia* (Havana), May 2, 1954, pp. 58–90.

[55] Ruiz Leiro and Rasco are today in exile. Alfredo Guevara, who was at the
time a communist, soon became a good friend of Castro, although they had run
for election on opposite sides. Today he heads the Film Institute in Cuba. Both
Ovares and Massó are in exile.

[56] "Historia de una trifulca," *Tiempo* (Mexico), October 3, 1947, pp. 15–16. The
organizations that attacked the MSR were the UIR, Joven Cuba, Alianza Nacional
Revolucionaria, Asociación Libertaria de Cuba, and Asociación de Ex-Combatientes
Anti-Fascistas.

[57] Ramón Grau has been considered a revolutionary by most people who have
studied twentieth-century Cuba. But Grau refused to take a militant stand against
Batista's power in 1933–1934; he favored electoral politics in the 1940s; and when
Batista staged his coup in 1952 he continued to defend the idea of ballots instead of
bullets, even when elections were impossible. Grau also disagreed with the revolutionary government established in 1959; nonetheless, he remained in Havana until
his death in 1969. At least his lack of initiative was a consistent characteristic.

ment began to be ruled by terrorist elites. Ironically, many scholars still consider Grau's administration one of the most "democratic" Cuba ever had![58]

The population watched in stunned disbelief as one action group tried to destroy the other in order to control a particular ministry, the black market, or the "protection" of businessmen. The bloodiest and most spectacular fights took place between some UIR and MSR members who had become national police officers. Emilio Tró, leader of the UIR, was granted the rank of major and placed in charge of the National Police Academy, while Mario Salabarría of the MSR was given the same rank and control of the national police investigation department. In 1947 alone, Havana had five different police chiefs, as they were forced to resign or were murdered by some terrorist turned policeman.[59] Hit-and-run attacks from fast-moving cars reached a peak in the summer of 1947. On September 2, 1947, the police section that was under the MSR attempted to kill Emilio Tró. Ten days later an MSR policeman was killed in retribution for the attempt. Thereafter Mario Salabarría, entrusted to investigate the murder of one of his men, arranged for the arrest of Tró.

On September 15, 1947, Tró was surrounded by MSR gunmen while dining at the home of the chief of police in Marianao (a suburb of Havana) on Orfila Street. A fantastic three-hour gun battle, ending in Tró's death, followed. He had eighteen bullets in his body. Several other persons, including a pregnant woman, were also killed by the police. The entire battle was heard over the radio by an astonished public and a passive government.

Fidel and several UIR members were outraged by the death of their leader. They seethed with anger at their inability to avenge his death, but at the time they were participating in an MSR attempt to train an expeditionary force for an invasion of the Dominican Republic.

[58] Such a generalization should be revised, for it is erroneous to consider a government democratic simply because it has a congress, an elected President, and the military does not rule. For instance, during the entire Grau administration, the Congress was convened only three months, and its budget was never approved by an Auténtico-dominated Senate, making it possible for the president to use extraordinary budgetary decrees accountable to no one. See Carlos M. Lechuga, "En cuatro años el Congreso no trabajó mas de tres meses," Bohemia (Havana), October 10, 1948, pp. 18–19, 186; and "Presupuestos," Tiempo (Mexico), January 3, 1947, pp. 20–22.

[59] During the Grau regime (1944–1948), 64 political assassinations were committed, 33 persons were wounded by the action groups, and over two dozen individuals were kidnapped; there were also 100 assassination attempts. See "Los atentados políticos durante el gobierno del Dr. Grau," Bohemia (Havana), October 10, 1948, pp. 86–88; "Cinco jefes de policia hemos tenido en los últimos doce meses," Diario de la Marina (Havana), January 2, 1948, p. 2.

Had they expressed their own views in such a situation, Fidel and his companions probably would have been murdered on the spot—even though one purpose of cooperating in the invasion, according to some of the more idealistic MSR members, was to ease tensions with the UIR. The MSR also established a revolutionary committee of Rolando Masferrer, Eufemio Fernández, Armentino Feria, José Casas, Daniel Martín, Manolo Castro, and Carlos Gutiérrez Menoyo to coordinate activities with the Dominican leadership of the expedition and their revolutionary junta formed by Angel Morales, Juan Rodríguez, Juan I. Jímenez, Leovigildo Cuello, and Juan Bosch.[60]

For several months more than 1,200 Dominican exiles, Caribbean adventurers, soldiers of fortune, and members of Cuban action groups had been congregating in Oriente Province. They were a sort of international revolutionary brigade, believing in violent action. They had the financial and logistical support of some of the leaders of the democratic left in the Caribbean area and the Grau government. Their anticommunism, it must be noted, always was equal to their anti-imperialist sentiments.

In July 1947, Fidel Castro joined the expedition after working out a truce with the MSR. He sincerely believed that a dedicated revolutionary had to oppose ruthless dictatorships and make his solidarity available when required—and he felt that the time had come for him to do so.

Fidel received military instruction at the Instituto Politécnico at Holguín, in northern Oriente Province. The people of Holguín, like the rest of the Cuban population, knew that men were training to invade another nation. On July 29, 1947, the young men were taken to the port of Antilla, where they boarded three ships. The following day they reached Cayo Confites, a barren and desolate key off the port of Nuevitas in Camagüey Province. For fifty-nine days they lingered on the mosquito-infested key, awaiting orders that never came. In late September the Grau administration canceled the expedition.

The expedition was called off because earlier that month the United States had notified the Cuban government of its concern that an inva-

---

[60] Information on this expedition is scattered among various sources. See Robert D. Craswell, *Trujillo, the Life and Times of a Caribbean Dictator* (New York: Macmillan Co., 1966), pp. 237, 239; "Síntesis cronológica de la vida de Fidel," *Revolución* (Havana), May 3, 1963, p. 3; J. L. Wangüemert, "El diario de Cayo Confites," *Carteles* (Havana), October 12, 1947, pp. 32–33, 36–37; October 19, 1947, pp. 36–37; November 2, 1947, pp. 46–69; Jorge Yáñez, "Cincuenta y nueve días con los expedicionarios de Cayo Confites," *Bohemia* (Havana), November 16, 1947, pp. 28–29; and Conte Agüero, *Eduardo Chibás*, p. 531.

sion of another country violated international law and would increase conflicts in the Caribbean. And as if pressure from Washington were not enough, government authorities had discovered that the expeditionary force was also going to be used to help overthrow the Cuban regime in a plot headed by the minister of education, who hoped to become the head of a new government. Thus the army swiftly aborted the enterprise by arresting the expeditionaries.

The confused men, who did not know of the planned MSR coup, were placed in a Cuban navy frigate, which was to take them from the inhospitable key to Havana. However, fearing that the MSR would kill him now that amnesty was no longer in effect, Fidel jumped overboard and swam ashore across the bay of Nuevitas. A few days later the expeditionaries were freed.[61]

On September 30, 1947, just a few hours after escaping from the navy frigate, Fidel participated in a student rally at the University of Havana. He spoke to honor the memory of a student killed by the Machado dictatorship and attacked the government for betraying the Dominican liberation cause. Other mass meetings denouncing the government followed.

High-school and university students began protesting against the influence of gangsters in the government. On October 9, 1947, a student strike was instigated to call for the removal of Minister of Education José M. Alemán from the cabinet. Fidel, in the days following, denounced political gangsterism and dared to call some of the thugs by name. From then on, he escaped several MSR assassination attempts by sheer luck. On one occasion, Fidel has said, he was challenged in the early hours of the morning by a fellow student to fight out their differences. Not knowing that several men had prepared an ambush, Fidel agreed to meet his contender at the university stadium. "It was a miracle that I came out from that alive," he said years later, without specifying how he managed to escape.[62]

In 1948, Fidel was elected to the presidency of the Association of Law Students. He also published a mimeographed bulletin, *Acción*

[61] Most of the men released left Cuba and went to Costa Rica, where they formed the Caribbean Legion (CL) which helped José Figueres capture power there in early 1948. In 1949 the CL went to Guatemala, where they supported the governments of Arévalo and Arbenz. After 1954 the CL moved to Mexico, establishing contacts with some of Castro's followers. See John P. Bell, "The Costa Rican Revolution of 1948" (Ph.D. dissertation, Tulane University, 1969); "La Legión del Caribe," *Bohemia* (Havana), June 26, 1949, pp. 67–70; and Alberto Bayo, *Tempestad en el Caribe* (Mexico, 1950), pp. 95–201.

[62] "Fidel Castro visitó la Universidad," *Diario de la Marina* (Havana), January 14, 1959, pp. 1, 9b.

Universitaria (*AU*), whose main target was Manolo Castro's group.[63]

On February 22, 1948, Manolo Castro was assassinated. A cousin of the murdered man accused Fidel Castro of having participated in the murder plot.[64] He and three close friends were arrested but soon released for lack of evidence. Once freed, Fidel analyzed the situation this way:

> Rolando Masferrer wants to take over the leadership of the university. . . . We have not allowed him to do so, in spite of the coercion and violence practiced against us for quite some time. . . . He wishes to incite action against our lives, using Manolo Castro as a pretext; in other words, he wishes to profit from the death of a friend.[65]

Such a declaration was, to say the least, dangerous.

Fearing reprisals, Fidel and the other three students decided to leave Cuba. The opportunity to go abroad presented itself from an unexpected direction: Argentina.

At the time, populist dictator Juan Domingo Perón of Argentina was forming Latin American organizations that would be nationalist and anti-imperialist. One of these was to be the Latin American Student Association. Through a representative in Havana (Cesar J. Tronconi), he was able to persuade Havana University leaders to share in laying the groundwork for the organization. The first step was a student congress opposing colonialism and imperialism.

Fidel, as leader of the law students, was directly involved in its planning; in fact, Cubans were in charge of most of the planning and coordination. After several meetings it was agreed that a preparatory meeting for the future congress be held at Bogotá, to coincide with the Ninth Inter-American Conference, which Perón wished to disrupt.[66] On March 15, 1948, Fidel outlined the goals of the congress:

> We hope that this action will initiate a movement of larger proportions which will find support in all of Latin America, es-

[63] *AU* was edited by Fidel, Rafael Díaz Balart (who became his brother-in-law and subsequently joined Batista's cabinet in 1952), and Baudilio Castellanos (a close friend of Fidel's, a member of UIR, and the first client Fidel had as a lawyer). Castellanos was the defense lawyer for the men who attacked the Moncada Barracks in 1953 and today works for the Castro government. Balart is in exile.
[64] "Acusa un sobrino de Castro a los miembros de la UIR," *Diario de la Marina* (Havana), February 22, 1948, p. 1.
[65] "On the Death of Manolo Castro" in this volume.
[66] Jaime Suchlicki, *University Students and Revolution in Cuba* (Coral Gables, Fla.: University of Miami Press, 1969), p. 53. Besides Fidel, the Cuban university leaders organizing the student conference were Enrique Ovares, Alfredo Guevara, Justo Fuentes, Pedro Mirasou, Armando Gali-Menéndez, Aramis Taboada, Rafael del Pino, and Alfredo Esquivel.

pecially among university students, united under the banner of the anti-imperialist struggle. . . . The Cuban and Argentine university students favor the holding of the "First Latin American Congress of University Students." . . . To do so, preparatory sessions will be held after the first week of April in Bogotá, to prepare the agenda of the congress. . . . As you will note, we are trying to hold the preparatory sessions of the congress at the same time as the Inter-American meeting in Bogotá in order to support the demands against colonialism which will be presented by several Latin American countries. Those demands will be easier to carry out if we precipitate a wave of protests.[67]

On March 31, 1948, Fidel reached Bogotá, where for several days he and Enrique Ovares heatedly discussed who should preside over the congress. Ovares, as president of the Cuban University Student Federation, stated it was his duty to do so, whereas Fidel argued that it would help his own political career. Ovares prevailed.[68]

Later, on April 9, Jorge E. Gaitán, leader of the Liberal Party, was assassinated shortly before he was to meet with the Cuban delegation about speaking at the congress. His death sparked a popular riot that ripped through the city of Bogotá. Fidel Castro and Rafael del Pino participated in the revolt, convinced that this was their duty as revolutionaries. Both joined a group that attacked a police station from which rifles were taken and distributed to the population with a call for revolution. Having failed in his attempt to help the Dominican Republic free itself from dictatorship, Fidel now wanted to aid a revolt that he felt could evolve into a national revolution. His actions had nothing to do with communism, although the communists did want to sabotage the Inter-American Conference.

The Colombian authorities soon discovered the Cubans' activities and tried to arrest them, but Fidel and others took refuge in the Cuban embassy. On April 13, 1948, they returned to Havana in a Cuban government-chartered plane and refused to make any statements.[69]

Back in Cuba, Fidel was still concerned about his own safety. Many had sworn to kill him, and he had no choice but to continue resorting to force. Those were days in which few could be trusted; everyone,

[67] "Primeros pasos del movimiento latinoamericano contra el coloniaje europeo en este continente," *Bohemia* (Havana), March 17, 1957, pp. 62–63.

[68] Suchlicki, *University Students*, p. 53. See also Lacides Orozco, "Dos cubanos repartían armas," *Diario de la Marina* (Havana), April 20, 1948.

[69] "Llegó de Bogotá un avión conduciendo siete refugiados," *Diario de la Marina* (Havana), April 14, 1948, p. 1. The students were Fidel Castro (twenty-one years old), Rafael del Pino (twenty-one), Enrique Ovares (twenty-three), and Alfredo Guevara (twenty-two). A picture of Fidel in Bogotá appears in *Bohemia* (Havana), April 25, 1948, p. 7 (supplement); see also "Síntesis cronológica de la vida de Fidel," *Revolución* (Havana), May 3, 1963, p. 3.

it seemed, was involved in some conspiratorial network or intrigue.

At the university the UIR successfully captured the support of several university leaders, but the campus police remained dominated by its rival, which tried to disarm the UIR people a number of times. They usually failed to do so and always brought about more disorder and killings. On June 6, 1948, Oscar Fernández Caral, a campus police sergeant, was slain. Before dying he allegedly declared that Fidel Castro had shot him.[70] A witness verified the accusation. Three days later Fidel stated that he was innocent and that the entire accusation was part of a plot to do away with him.[71] The witness later retracted his statement, affirming that the police coerced him into incriminating Fidel. The real assassins were never discovered, for witnesses were afraid to testify.

Assassinations, actual and attempted, subsided somewhat in late 1948, although demonstrations, mass meetings, and labor strikes continued to haunt the Auténtico administration. For a few hours, on September 9, 1948, a popular rebellion seemed imminent in Havana. Fidel Castro and Justo Fuentes led a gang of students who captured and burned several buses to protest an unpopular increase in bus fares.[72] Some UIR members took advantage of the situation to commemorate the first anniversary of Tró's death by creating chaos throughout the city. The conflict, however, did not last long because the government abrogated its decree to raise bus fares. The insurrectionists had failed in a Cuban version of the "Bogotazo." In the end they settled for a rally on September 15 to honor their murdered leader. Fidel attended that meeting, at which several UIR leaders spoke. Fifteen days later, a similar session was held at the University of Havana. While Fidel spoke about Emilio Tró, a fistfight between rival gangs abruptly ended the meeting.

Shortly thereafter, on October 12, 1948, Fidel married a philosophy student, Mirta Díaz Balart. She came from a wealthy Cuban family that disapproved of the union. On September 15, 1949, a son, Fidel, was born.

Throughout 1949 labor unrest, student unrest, and gang warfare continued, with Fidel in the middle of it all.[73] Established institutions

---

[70] Ernesto Rodríguez Suárez, "Cuatro años de asesinatos impunes," *Tiempo en Cuba* (Havana), October 10, 1948, p. 51.

[71] "The Assassination of Sergeant Fernández Caral" in this volume.

[72] "Tiene serios carácteres la protesta iniciada por los estudiantes," *Diario de la Marina* (Havana), September 10, 1948, pp. 1, 21.

[73] In January 1949 transport workers went on strike, while students refused to pay the increase in bus fares. Fidel played a central role in the student demonstrations. See Fidel's speech in this volume, "Against an Increase in Bus Fares."

remained inert while the nation bordered on social chaos. Although the UIR successfully displaced the MSR from student politics, the latter continued fighting to regain control.[74] A liberal Havana daily commented in an editorial:

> Violence holds sway in the halls of the university. Professors and students are nothing but the prisoners of a few groups of student gangsters who impose their will at gunpoint. . . . The University Council has declared its inability to remove these gangs because of the lack of coercive power.[75]

Political violence and extremism are as Cuban as the palm trees, and Fidel Castro was a product, rather than a cause, of the profound and unresolved tensions in Cuban society. A substantial portion of his political viewpoints can be traced to these university years. When he left in 1950, he had a degree in civil and diplomatic law and a keen understanding of political power and the role that violence played in a very weak and barely legitimate political structure. If Fidel later chose the path of insurrection, it was natural for him, as well as for many others. He developed in an environment of turbulent political conflict with little relation to theoretical or ideological models borrowed from abroad.

It would be a mistake to confuse his radicalism with communism; in fact, the men with whom Fidel identified considered the Cuban Communist Party conservative. According to a close friend of his, Fidel attended courses in Marxist studies offered at the university by the Communist Party throughout 1949.[76] But the implication that he was a Marxist does not seem to be true if one studies his speeches and writings of that period. In fact, during those years Fidel was a member of the Ortodoxos, a political party that, although radical, was thoroughly anticommunist.

Fidel and the Ortodoxo Party

The Partido del Pueblo Cubano (PPC), also known as the Ortodoxos, was formed because the administration of Ramón Grau (1944–1948) and of Carlos Prío Socarrás (1948–1952) completely discredited the

---

[74] It is interesting to note that the MSR, along with the minister of education, formed a student committee to get rid of the UIR. Years later, many of the members of the committee formed the Directorio Revolucionario to fight against Batista and to take away the revolutionary leadership from Fidel Castro. The group included Enrique Rodríguez Loeches and Humberto Castelló. See "CESU," *Tiempo en Cuba* (Havana), June 5, 1949, p. 5.

[75] Editorial, *El Mundo* (Havana), September 5, 1949, p. 11.

[76] Baudilio Castellanos, "La historia me absolverá, documento esencialmente marxista," *Revolución* (Havana), July 18, 1962, p. 6.

Auténticos (PRC).[77] They permitted all types of excesses, from political assassination to corruption. Also, Auténtico conservatism and neglect of its original program, along with a return to traditional practices, disillusioned many Cubans. Cynicism abounded.

Many were convinced that, although forty-odd years had passed since the establishment of the republic, the national leaders were unable to solve Cuba's problems. This was the dismal political milieu when Eduardo Chibás arose from the ranks of the Auténtico Party to interpret the prevailing problems.[78] Through his oratory he denounced the political gangsterism, graft, and corruption of the Auténticos and moved the masses to his side. The young were especially attracted by this charismatic man who, more than a politician, was an ethical and messianic agitator. Throughout the 1940s Chibás gained the support of committed young Auténticos, causing a split within the ruling party. To some extent the split was sparked by Ramón Grau's announcement that he would run for reelection. The young members of the PRC, including Fidel and several other students, had protested.[79] Thus, on May 15, 1947, the youth section of the PRC met under the leadership of Eduardo Chibás and formed the Partido del Pueblo Cubano (PPC), which considered itself the true heir of Cuban revolutionary ideals.

Fidel Castro was one of the founders of the party and was extremely impressed by Chibás, whom he followed everywhere.[80] He learned from Chibás that charismatic leadership plays a very important role in a social movement and that the Cubans are attracted by symbolism in struggles. The successful use of symbolic acts through propaganda was a very efficient weapon for waging political warfare. In one instance, Chibás used as the emblem of the Ortodoxo movement a broom, to symbolize sweeping away past practices and corruption. He strongly influenced the social and political processes of Cuba with his emphasis on ethics. This produced widespread unrest; people began to judge their political rulers, not in terms of whether they improved the

[77] Carlos Prío Socarrás (1903–   ) was a founder of DEU in 1930 and was a close collaborator with Grau until the 1950s within the Autentico party. In 1960 he went into exile.

[78] Eduardo Chibás (1907–1951) was born of rich parents. From 1927 on he participated in revolutionary activities. In 1930 he formed the DEU, and later the PRC; in 1946 he was elected senator. The best biography of Chibás is that of Luis Conte Agüero, *Eduardo Chibás, adalid de Cuba* (Mexico: Editorial Jus, 1955).

[79] "Against the Reelection of Ramón Grau San Martín" in this volume.

[80] Besides Chibás, the leaders of the PPC were Pelayo Cuervo, Manuel Bisbé, Luis Orlando Rodríguez, Alberto Saumell, Rafael García Bárcena, Hugo Mir, Orlando Castro, Luis Emilio Ochoa, and Luis Conte Agüero. Goldenberg, *The Cuban Revolution*, p. 150, mistakenly states that Fidel joined the PPC after he traveled to Bogotá in April 1948.

standard of living, but by how honest they were. Thus, the Auténticos were faced with internal division and began to lose influence among the masses.

Chibás continued firm in his stand and cleverly used propaganda to gain influence. Radio broadcasts, he maintained, were as deadly in the political sphere as weapons. Consequently, he opposed the idea of insurrection or any other form of armed struggle to obtain power. In this respect, Chibás was a legally oriented, charismatic leader, which separated him from some of his revolutionary young constituents.

Within the Ortodoxo movement, Fidel created a splinter group favoring insurrection. Functioning primarily within the youth section of the party, the Acción Radical Ortodoxa (ARO)[81] was consistently opposed by the leaders of the movement. The ARO was closely tied to those individuals entering the PPC from the action groups. Most of them came from the UIR and on a number of occasions tried to force the Ortodoxo leaders into armed revolt.[82]

Nonetheless, Fidel and other insurrectionists traveled throughout Cuba in 1948 asking the people to vote for Chibás for president. The Ortodoxos however lost that election for several reasons. The party did not have sufficient time to create an efficient electoral machine; it was participating in a presidential election only eleven months after its formation. Moreover, the electoralist party leadership was divided between those who favored an alliance with other political parties and those who, like Chibás, followed a line of political independence, opposed to all types of alliances. This independence caused the PPC to lose many votes. Finally, it lacked the financial resources to wage a fruitful campaign.

The Ortodoxos did not differ from the Auténticos ideologically. Rather, they viewed themselves as true representatives of a revolutionary tradition betrayed by the ruling party. Chibás stressed the fact that the early revolutionism of the Auténticos had gradually cooled off

[81] Not to be confused with the Acción Revolucionaria Oriental whose initials were also ARO.

[82] Within the ranks of the Ortodoxos could be found two factions, one composed of the party leadership and favoring electoral methods for gaining revolutionary goals, the other of young militants who opted for revolutionary means. From 1948 on, a series of internal discussions occurred within the PPC between the two groups. While originally concerned with the meaning of being a revolutionary, by 1952 the debate had come to be focused on the question of revolutionary versus electoral means for achieving power. See Francisco Ichaso, "La coalición liberal-demócrata," *Bohemia* (Havana), April 4, 1948, pp. 28, 54. On the leadership's opposition to ARO militancy, see "Niegan la existencia de un organismo dentro del Partido del Pueblo Cubano," *Diario de la Marina* (Havana), September 1, 1948, p. 12.

because it had had to ally itself with conservative forces in order to remain in power. Fidel, like Chibás, believed that the Auténticos had betrayed their historic mission for a social and political revolution. Moreover, traditional methods of ruling condemned in 1933 had continued.

After graduation from the university, Fidel opened a law office in the old section of Havana. His clients included students who had rioted against the government, an association of coal workers, and vegetable vendors of Havana's biggest marketplace. In 1951 he was the lawyer for the prosecution against Major Rafael Casals Fernández and Lieutenant Rafael Salas Cañizares, both policemen who murdered a worker demonstrating against the government. However, the trial never took place because of the Batista coup.

Fidel also continued to take part in student politics at the university. During this period he spoke daily on an Ortodoxo-sponsored radio program denouncing the government. One of the more spectacular episodes was his exposure of unfair labor practices by President Prío toward his farm workers in 1952. His political activities and his law practice took up most of Fidel's time.

As the presidential campaign for the elections of June 1952 began to gather momentum, everyone expected Ortodoxo leader Eduardo Chibás to win. He had become the most influential political personality on the island because he was honest and truthful—unique qualities at the time. The discreditation of all other adversaries gained him support, but in 1951 he made an unfortunate mistake. He charged Aureliano Sánchez Arango, the minister of education, with using funds from the education budget to purchase real estate in Guatemala and other Central American nations. Sánchez Arango challenged Chibás to prove his charges. Four days later, over national radio, Chibás presented concrete proof of the minister's misappropriation of funds but had no evidence relating to the purchase of land in Guatemala. Soon afterward, the Auténtico administration began a campaign to discredit Chibás, stating that he had lied to the Cuban people and that he was purely and simply a demagogue.

On August 5, 1951, Chibás declared over the radio that, although he did not have proof to present, his accusation was true. He then reviewed his political life and said he felt that the people doubted him because there was too much cynicism in the hearts of Cubans. He ended by making this affirmation:

> Comrades of the Ortodoxo movement, keep moving forward! Let us fight for economic independence, political freedom, and social justice! Let us sweep away the government thieves! People of

> Cuba, stand up and move forward! People of Cuba, wake up!
> This is my last knock at your conscience.

Seconds afterward, in a last desperate, symbolic act, Eduardo Chibás shot himself.[83]

Fidel, though stunned as Chibás shot himself before his eyes, immediately took him to the hospital, where he died a few days later.

The leader was dead, but his message remained: Cuba was a colonial republic, which fought to become an independent nation, free to determine its own destiny, as all revolutionary leaders since José Martí had dreamed.

Factional quarrels within the PPC followed Chibás's death. The insurrectionists battled the electoralists, who eventually gained the leadership. Capitalizing on the immense popular emotion unleashed by Chibás's death, the electoralists believed they could win the forthcoming elections.

Although Fidel belonged to the insurrectionist ARO, he ran for the post of representative. He hoped to revolutionize the society from within. Years later Fidel stated that he had hoped to present a revolutionary program once he was in congress. Although he did not expect the program to be approved, he would then have had a platform from which the people could be mobilized.[84]

These elections, however, were never to take place. On March 10, 1952, Fulgencio Batista once again staged a coup d'état, and electoral politics and constitutional order came to an end.

Batista's Coup

Contrary to popular belief, Fulgencio Batista did not engineer the coup. Several junior officers believed that the regime could be overthrown because of the lack of discipline prevalent in the ranks. It was well known that promotion within the armed forces was dependent on President Prío's favoritism. The lack of promotions plus a thirst for power and wealth motivated these officers. Their plan was simple: take over the command posts and neutralize the high command. Once the plan was developed completely, it was presented to Batista. He agreed to lead the coup as a civilian.[85] He insisted on only

---

[83] There are differing interpretations as to whether Chibás was just trying to impress the Cuban people, hoping to win their total allegiance with such an act in order to win the presidency. There was a precedent: In 1946, he shot himself and was later elected senator. Chibás quotation from Luis Conte Agüero, *Eduardo Chibás, adalid de Cuba* (Mexico: Editorial Jus, 1955), p. 784.

[84] Lockwood, *Castro's Cuba, Cuba's Fidel*, p. 140.

[85] The coup followed the pattern of the "swing man" posited by Martin C. Needler, *Political Development in Latin America* (New York: Random House, 1968) pp. 68–69. For a brief but thorough description of the plans, see "Reseñó

one condition: He would set the date. Shielded by a façade of electoral politics, Batista joined the conspiracy. Two of the most important men behind the coup were at the time facing twenty years' imprisonment for the murder of a worker a few months earlier.[86]

In January 1952, President Carlos Prío (1948–1952) received a letter from a woman in Oriente Province reporting a military conspiracy against his government. The chief of the army, however, insisted that there was no conspiracy, only rumors.[87]

On March 10, 1952, Fulgencio Batista swiftly carried out the coup. President Prío was taken by surprise by a method very similar to that used in Batista's famous September 4, 1933, "sergeants' revolt." The difference was that Prío, unlike Machado, was not a dictator. And this time the conspirators were lieutenants and captains instead of sergeants. From a corrupt democracy Cuba shifted to a corrupt dictatorship.

Batista moved into Camp Columbia at 2:40 A.M., and one hour later he controlled most of Cuba's military posts. Prío tried to resist at the Presidential Palace, but he refused to arm university students and the people as the Federación Estudiantil Universitaria (FEU) demanded.[88] Instead, not knowing what to do but aware of the loyalty of some military command posts in the provinces of Matanzas, Las Villas, Camagüey, and Oriente, Prío left by car for the city of Matanzas but was not permitted to get there. Unable to rally troops to his side, he eventually sought refuge at the Mexican embassy. It must be noted that the navy and police remained loyal to Prío on the morning of the coup, but Batista later won their support by raising their salaries.

The usurper later announced that his coup was designed to end rampant gangsterism, eliminate governmental dishonesty, and preempt a coup that Prío supposedly had planned for April 15, 1952, because he knew that the Auténticos would be defeated in general elections that June. According to Batista, the military would retain power until

---

Batista como ocurrió el 10 de marzo," *El Mundo* (Havana), July 10, 1952, pp. 1, A8.

[86] The two men were Major Rafael Casals Fernández and Lieutenant Rafael Salas Cañizares of the Havana police. Batista referred to Salas as "fat Salas"; he was killed in 1956.

[87] The chief of the army asked Captain Leopoldo Pérez Coujil, who at the time was in charge of the Bureau of Investigations, to keep surveillance over Batista's activities, but Pérez Coujil turned out to be an agent of Batista.

[88] "Recorrido del Dr. Prío desde Palacio al exilio," *El Mundo* (Havana), March 12, 1952, pp. 1, 10. The university students had sent a delegation composed of Alvaro Barba, José Hidalgo, Agustín Valero, Danilo Baeza, and Orestes Robledo to request Prío to supply them with arms. See "10 de marzo de 1952: una fecha negra en la historia," *Bohemia* (Havana), March 8, 1959, p. 70.

"law, order, and justice" had been established by what he called the "revolutionary government."[89]

On March 11, Batista assumed the post of prime minister and formed a cabinet. The political sectors of the nation reacted in different ways. The Ortodoxos vowed to fight the coup, and the Auténticos denounced it but failed to take a militant stand. A large number of political, commercial, industrial, and land interests, in contrast, emphatically supported the new government. Batista received pledges of support from the major banks, associations of landowners and cattlemen, the Chamber of Commerce, and the Veterans of the War for Cuban Independence; the communications media promised to bar "demagogues" from using their facilities.[90]

The true reasons behind Batista's coup were two. First, he knew he could not win the elections for the presidency. His Partido Acción Unitaria (PAU) did not even have enough popular leaders to run for senatorial offices in several provinces. Second, Batista's military and civilian cronies were being displaced by the new parasitical social class spawned under Auténtico rule. In other words, the Batistianos wanted to keep a monopoly over the state budget. The appropriation of the national treasury always has been a major factor in Cuban politics.

Of all Cuba's power groups the students were the most outraged by the coup. At the University of Havana, the banner of antimilitarism was raised along with a cry for the defense of the constitution. Some students wanted to fight. Many of the young awaited weapons, which they never received. The young Ortodoxos who espoused an insurrectionary thesis also gathered at the university. Among them was Fidel Castro. After three tense days of waiting, the students concluded that they lacked the resources to wage an efficient struggle. The students' attitude toward Batista's coup was outlined in an FEU manifesto on March 14, 1952, calling for a united opposition and the

[89] "Promete Batista un régimen de paz," *El Mundo* (Havana), March 11, 1952, pp. 1, 9. It is questionable whether Batista really wished to put an end to the trigger-happy groups roaming every major city. Batista kept himself in power by using such groups as ATOM and its leader Ernesto de la Fé (who was put in charge of government propaganda) and Masferrer's MSR. Shortly after the coup, Masferrer returned from a talk with Batista and canceled plans he had originally made with Charles Simeón, a traditional anti-Batista fighter, to issue a special edition of *Tiempo en Cuba* (the MSR organ) denouncing Batista's action. Instead, armed MSR men (including Valentín González, known as "El Campesino" in the Spanish Civil War) went to the University of Havana to prevent any resistance against Batista. See "Rebeldía en el recinto universitario," *El Mundo* (Havana), March 11, 1952, p. 9.

[90] See *El Mundo* (Havana), March 13, 1952, pp. 1, 8, 9; and March 14, 1952, pp. 1, 8.

creation of a plan to fight for the reestablishment of democracy.[91] Two days later, at a meeting called by the Ortodoxo leaders, the insurrectionalist faction demanded a more militant stand and street fighting. The impatient youth insisted on a clear definition of what the leadership considered "adequate resistance."

From the outset those in the opposition attempted to remove Batista legally, but they soon learned that a military regime could be displaced only by armed struggle. Meanwhile, from his exile, the former president petitioned the judiciary to declare the new government unconstitutional. The Ortodoxo leaders did likewise. On March 15 they sent a representative to the Organization of American States in Washington to demand inter-American intervention to restore democracy in Cuba.

Playing on Cuban nationalism, Batista shrewdly repudiated the PPC leaders by reminding them that Cuba's sovereignty had to be respected. Political parties, he argued, should not resort, as in the old days, to reliance on foreign intervention.[92] In any case, the protest of the PPC was not even considered by the inter-American organization. The PPC next presented a brief to the Court of Appeals, demanding that Batista's government be declared illegal.

Three days after the coup, on March 13, Fidel Castro wrote "Revolución no: Zarpazo!" entreating "courageous Cubans to sacrifice and fight back!" but failing to outline a plan of how to do so.[93] He simply denounced the past Auténtico administrations and Batista's rule. Thereafter he presented a brief to the Court of Appeals in Havana to request punishment of those who had disrupted the public order by a military coup.[94] He demanded one hundred years in prison for Batista, but the court dismissed the brief. Peaceful and legal solutions had resulted in failure. For Cuban radicals it was increasingly evident that only one path remained open: conspiracy and insurrection.

In the meantime, the two largest political parties (Auténtico and Ortodoxo) were disintegrating, mainly because of a lack of effective leadership and unity of action. The government completed the debacle

[91] Among the signers of the manifesto were Alvaro Barba, Eduardo Hart, and José Antonio Echevarría, all of whom would later play important roles in the anti-Batista struggle.

[92] "Repudia la apelación a la OEA," *El Mundo* (Havana), April 1, 1952, pp. 1, 10. See also "Elevan los ortodoxos apelación a la OEA," *El Mundo* (Havana), March 28, 1952, p. 1.

[93] "Proclamation on Batista's Seizure of Power" in this volume.

[94] "Brief to the Court of Appeals" in this volume. It must be noted that the brief was presented on March 24, 1952, and not on March 10, 1952, as it appears in a Cuban publication. See "Cronología de los cien años de lucha (1868–1968)," *Revista de la Universidad de La Habana* (Havana), October–December 1968, p. 230.

by ordering the dissolution of all parties and the suspension of all constitutional guarantees. Meanwhile the Council of Ministers released a declaration designating the March 10 coup as the "continuation of the revolutionary aspirations that began in 1927 and culminated in the 1940 Constitution."[95] Batista, like the leaders of the Auténticos and Ortodoxos, was exploiting the rhetoric of revolutionary tradition. In doing so Batista placed the opposition leaders in a dilemma by challenging their oft-stated commitment to revolution. Older political leaders, however, refused to accept the insurrectionary thesis. These men were either too old or too conservative to lead a revolt. They were too far removed from reality to consider the final consequences of the changes that had occurred. The old leaders lost their remaining hold on the young when their revolutionary rhetoric proved to be bankrupt.

Among the Ortodoxo group's greatest weaknesses was its lack of an insurrectionary tradition. Whereas the Auténticos formed a political party after they had participated in armed revolt and conspiracies, the Ortodoxos sprang from public dismay over the dishonesty of the Auténticos. The Ortodoxo revolt was one of principle, not of weapons. It lacked cadres who had previously engaged in revolution; its members were part of a liberal Cuban bourgeoisie that had envisioned social justice through evolution. They wanted to acquire power in electoral competition and abhorred violence. Once faced with the necessity for armed struggle, they were caught in a whirlwind of confusion. Moreover, Batista's move took place at a moment of intense competition for the leadership of the party. The coup d'état divided the PPC still further.

Once again, action-oriented groups surfaced throughout the island. They were composed of young people from the University of Havana and the surrounding area, many of humble origins, who also were militants of the Juventud Ortodoxa. In addition, there were veterans of the Spanish Civil War, the Confites expedition of 1947, veterans of World War II, and men from the Caribbean Legion, not to mention those who had belonged to the ABC, Joven Cuba, and the DEU of the 1930s. Two factions favored armed violence. One, made up of old revolutionaries who had fought against the Machado dictatorship, was composed almost totally of Auténticos. The other was young, inex-

[95] The fact that a reactionary military regime should come out with such a declaration is evidence of the revolutionary tradition that had been impregnated in the minds of many Cubans since the 1920s. It must be noted that the revolutionaries fighting against Batista also returned to those same traditions. See "Ley Constitucional de la República de Cuba," *El Mundo* (Havana), April 5, 1952, pp. 7–10.

perienced in armed revolt, and Ortodoxo in political commitment. Inexperienced youths and seasoned veterans went underground, and the experienced men took the lead. Invasions were planned from abroad and financed by Carlos Prío. In the second week of June 1952, rumors spread that Eufemio Fernández, leader of the Caribbean Legion and a Prío follower, was training with 2,000 men in Guatemala to invade Cuba.[96] In the end, most of the veterans died in the struggle or retired, and the young generation acquired hegemony over revolutionary violence.

The Auténticos who followed Prío planned a military coup, but this was prematurely uncovered. The idea was essentially to bomb the Presidential Palace and important military garrisons from planes stolen from the Cuban air force. Mexico and Guatemala were to be used as bases of operation.[97] There were also other conspiracies that need not be considered here.

Conspiracy Begins

Advocates of violence were everywhere. Their headquarters was the University of Havana, where university autonomy provided good cover. Fidel Castro was a major participant in these groups. Having established the first contacts, he began to work with a unit of Ortodoxos. At one of their meetings, held at the home of José Duarte in a residential section of Havana, agreement was reached on the necessity of creating an efficient revolutionary organization, but nothing definitive came of it. Fidel therefore began to act independently.[98]

At the university Fidel defended armed confrontation; young men who listened agreed. Fidel's organizational skills became evident during this period. He coordinated revolutionary groups that appeared

---

[96] "Arrestan al ex-concejal Cándido de la Torre al llegar de Estados Unidos," *El Mundo* (Havana), June 12, 1952, p. 9. Fernández, a former member of the MSR, was leader of Acción Revolucionaria Guiteras for a time and became chief of the national police during the Grau administration. On several occasions he proposed to former President Prío that Batista be assassinated.

[97] Among the conspirators were Carlos Prío Socarras, José Figueres of Costa Rica, Senator Arturo Hernández Tellaheche, Manuel A. de Varona, Juan Bosch of the Dominican Republic, and Jesús González Cartas. "Detenidos 10 civiles y policias," *El Mundo* (Havana), August 2, 1952, pp. 1, 10; "Planean invadir La Habana y bombardear campamentos militares," *Ataja!* (Havana), July 27, 1952, p. 1.

[98] The following persons participated in the meeting: Rubén Acosta Carrasco (PPC); Roberto Agramonte (PPC); José Lauro Blanco (UIR); Guido Bustamente Luque; Fidel Castro (PPC); Orlando Cuervo Galano; Lazaro Cruz; José Diago Valdés; Carlos García Garbalena; Ovidio Juncosa; Feliciano Maderne; Juan Manuel Márquez (ARO); Carlos Morales; Francisco Ortega; José Duarte (PPC). Interview with José Duarte on November 4, 1969. According to Duarte, Castro made a vehement denunciation of gangsterism and the UIR at that meeting.

throughout the island, attracted primarily by the charismatic power of his personality.[99] In an interview Castro later said:

> Once the coup d'état of the tenth of March took place, everything changed radically. *My idea then became, not to organize a movement, but to try to unite all the different forces against Batista.* I intended to participate in that struggle simply as one more soldier. I began to organize the first action cells, hoping to work alongside those leaders of the party who might be ready to fulfill the elemental duty of fighting against Batista. . . . But when none of these leaders showed that they had either the ability or the realization of the seriousness of purpose or the way to overthrow Batista, it was then that I finally worked out a strategy of my own.[100]

Several groups were discovered by Fidel at the University of Havana. One of these centered on Abel Santamaría, a young man of twenty-four who in 1952 worked as an accountant for a Pontiac subsidiary in Havana. In 1947, he had moved from a sugar mill in the countryside to the capital in search of better working opportunities and an education. In Havana he had joined the Ortodoxo movement and later met Castro at party headquarters on Prado 109, Havana.[101] Abel was deeply affected by the death of the Ortodoxo leader Eduardo Chibás. That same year, 1951, his sister Haydée moved into his apartment in Havana. After Batista's coup, young people met at their apartment to have a good time and to discuss politics, and a coherent group began to emerge. Two other accountants also attended these meetings: Jesús Montané, who worked for the Havana subsidiary of General Motors, and Boris Luis Santa Coloma, who worked for a subsidiary of Frigidaire. Montané and Abel were both members of the peasant section of the PPC.

The Santamaría group published a mimeographed underground paper, *Son Los Mismos*, which periodically condemned the Batista

[99] Hugh Thomas, in his article "Middle Class Politics," p. 258, and *Cuba: The Pursuit of Freedom* (New York: Harper & Row, 1971), p. 824, contends that Fidel formed the nucleus of a personal political following based on accidental acquaintance with the branch of the Ortodoxo youth established in the small town of Artemisa. The facts show, however, that Fidel consciously organized his followers by coordinating a number of different groups, of which Artemisa's was just one.

[100] Lockwood, *Castro's Cuba, Cuba's Fidel*, pp. 140–141. Italics added.

[101] There are two other versions as to when Fidel Castro and Abel Santamaría met. Marta Rojas maintains they knew each other prior to the Batista coup of March 1952, whereas an interview with two close friends of Abel's reveals that the men met after Batista's coup. See Marta Rojas, *La Generación del Centenario en el Moncada* (Havana: Ediciones R, 1964), p. 48; Lisandro Otero, "Entrevista a Haydée Santamaría y Melba Hernández," *Juventud Rebelde*, July 25, 1966, p. 5. It is possible that they knew each other before the coup but did not begin to work together until after March 1952.

regime. This paper was hardly influential in Havana, but it united those men and women who found meaning in their activities and considered their work important.[102]

On May 1, 1952, the group went to Colón Cemetery to honor the memory of an assassinated labor leader. There they met Fidel Castro and discussed the necessity of cooperating in their denunciation of the regime. A few days later Montané, Santamaría, and Castro went to the central town of Colón in Matanzas Province to see Dr. Mario Muñoz, a physician who knew how to set up clandestine radio stations. They all wanted a radio station to broadcast a meeting that was to be held on May 8, 1952, at the University of Havana to commemorate the death of Antonio Guiteras, the anti-imperialist revolutionary leader who had been murdered by Batista's repressive forces in 1935. The meeting was broadcast, though with technical difficulties that prevented most of Havana from hearing the speeches made from inside the university.

From May 1952 on, Fidel Castro frequently visited the Santamaría apartment to discuss plans. On May 20 an issue of *Son Los Mismos* was distributed at the University of Havana. It was Fidel who proposed, shortly thereafter, to change the name of the paper to the more militant *El Acusador*. Then Fidel became the political editor of the paper, with Raúl Gómez García and Abel Santamaría assistant editors.

On August 16, 1952, a mass rally was called by the Juventud Ortodoxa at Colón Cemetery to commemorate the first anniversary of the death of Eduardo Chibás.[103] At the demonstration thousands of young men and women marched from the University of Havana to the cemetery. Leaders of the Ortodoxos spoke at the rally, and a recording of Chibás's last speech was played to a crowd overcome with emotion. Fidel and the Santamaría group distributed the first issue of *El Acusador* among the people. The military intelligence and the police rapidly reacted by arresting them. Only Fidel and Haydée Santamaría escaped. In that issue of *El Acusador* Castro had two articles written under the pseudonym "Alejandro." One of these stated:

> The movement is revolutionary and not political. Politics is the consecration of the opportunism of those who have the means and the resources. The Revolution opens the way to true merit to those who have sincere courage and ideals, to those who risk their

[102] The group was composed of Abel Santamaría, Haydée Santamaría, Melba Hernández, Elda Pérez, Jesús Montané, Raúl Gómez García, Pedro Miret, and Boris Luis Santa Coloma, who was Haydée's fiancé. Their paper was printed on an old mimeograph machine worth seventy-five dollars and donated by Adolfo Vázquez Cuadrado.

[103] It seems that Fidel was not allowed to participate in the planning of the rally. See "Organizan acto jóvenes del PPC," *El Mundo* (Havana), July 26, 1952.

lives and take the battle standard in their hands. A revolutionary party requires a revolutionary leadership, a young leadership originating from the people, that will save Cuba.[104]

Fidel maintained in his article that it was necessary to attract young Ortodoxos to the revolutionary cause.[105] Thus began the infiltration of the youth section of the PPC. The attraction and co-optation of young Ortodoxos was a natural outcome, for the national leaders remained incapable of action while they were imprisoned for allegedly inciting the people to overthrow the regime. It should be noted that as late as August 1952 Fidel Castro still appeared to believe that the Ortodoxo leaders could lead the battle against Batista, and on several occasions he expressed his solidarity with the national leadership. Such expressions, however, may have been a cover required by his underground activities.

At first most of the proselyting was done by the close associates of Castro who in 1948 had formed the radical ARO caucus within the party.[106] This group also had edited an underground newspaper and for more than four years had proclaimed that a revolutionary party could attain power only by armed struggle.

From ARO and the Abel group Fidel selected young men who thought as he did. They formed the nucleus of the future 26th of July Movement. Their primary function was to discover young people with similar ideas and integrate them into the newly emerging organization. Their first organizational meeting took place during the first week of September 1952 in an accountant's office in the old section of Havana. Most of the participants were accountants from the PPC who also believed that armed struggle was the only solution to the national crisis.[107] At that meeting Fidel stated:

> All those who join the movement will do so as simple soldiers; any merit or post which one might have had in the Ortodoxo

104 See "Critical Assessment of the Ortodoxo Party" in this volume.

105 The leaders of the Juventud Ortodoxa at the national level were: Max Lesnick, secretary general; Omar Borges, national secretary; Luis López Pérez, propaganda secretary; José Iglesias Lastra, municipal secretary; Francisco Cardona Orta, finance secretary; Mario Rivadulla, national leader; Pedro Guzmán, national secretary of meetings; and Salvador Lew, organization secretary.

106 ARO was composed of Fidel Castro, Juan Manuel Márquez, Antonio López, Sergio González, Roberto Mederos, Gerardo Sánchez, Elpidio Sosa, Pablo Cartas, Blas Castillo, Hugo Mir, and others, many of whom participated in the Moncada attack in 1953. The ARO militants consisted of members of the PPC from the Havana districts of Marte, Tacón, Vives, Arsenal, and Jesús María, all of which were of a working-class nature. See Agustín Alarcón, "Papel revolucionario del grupo del Parque de la Fraternidad," Revolución (Havana), January 29, 1959, p. 2.

107 Carmen Villar, "El asalto al Moncada (Entrevista con Oscar Alcalde)," Juventud Rebelde (Havana), July 20, 1966, p. 10. The reasons why accountants would enter revolutionary politics remain to be analyzed.

Party will not matter here. The fight will not be easy, and the road to be traveled will be long and arduous. We are going to take up arms against the regime.[108]

Ernesto Tizol, one of the participants at the meeting, stated in an interview years later:

We were militants of the Ortodoxo Party when the military coup took place. In a conspiratorial meeting held in Havana, I met Fidel as he outlined his insurrectional line which was followed by the group. That group, from then on, engaged in extracting those *compañeros* from the Juventud Ortodoxa who favored armed struggle and moved away from the bosom of the party.[109]

The infiltration of the Juventud Ortodoxa was a logical step, for it was the most radical political group with any substantial influence in Cuban politics at the time.[110]

On June 25, 1952, the Juventud Ortodoxa issued a manifesto opposing electoral politics and the static isolationism maintained by the party's national leadership. The declaration also stated:

We support the line of revolutionary action, of fighting in the streets, and open warfare against the de facto government in order to create the necessary conditions for the Cuban people in a given moment to do away with the heavy burden that the government imposed on us on March 10. Batista today, like Machado yesterday, cannot be overthrown with little pieces of paper.[111]

The national leadership responded by rejecting the demands of its youth section and reaffirming its opposition to violent revolt. Thereafter, young men and women began to look for a new direction: Many joined Fidel Castro, while others sought to create their own factions and sects.

Individuals recruited by Fidel Castro were organized into cells. Antonio López and Juan Manuel Márquez, both members of ARO and close associates of Fidel, were given command of a group of twenty-

[108] Marta Rojas, *El Juicio del Moncada* (Buenos Aires: Ediciones Ambos Mundos, 1966), p. 27.

[109] Carlos Nicot, "No hay problema, es el pollero (Entrevista con Ernesto Tizol)," *Revolución* (Havana), July 25, 1963, p. 1.

[110] The influence of communists, Trotskyists, and anarchists among the people was not large, although some authors argue otherwise. For an overestimated account of the communist influence, see Maurice Zeitlin, *Revolutionary Politics and the Cuban Working Class* (Princeton, N.J.: Princeton University Press, 1967).

[111] The expression "little pieces of paper" refers to a comment made by dictator Machado in 1933, when he sarcastically said that he could not be removed from power with *papelitos*, that is, manifestos. See "Considera la juventud del Partido del Pueblo Cubano que la línea política actual no es correcta," *El Mundo* (Havana), June 26, 1952, p. A7.

five men from the Havana suburb of Marianao. This group partic-
ipated in the attack on the Bayamo Barracks in Oriente Province on
July 26, 1953, while Fidel simultaneously led an attack on the Moncada
Barracks, also in Oriente. Of the twenty-five men who attacked the
Bayamo garrison, fourteen were killed.

A man from the Marianao group has stated that they usually met at
the Liceo Ortodoxo, where they were joined by Castro. They went
there to discuss politics. He says:

> One day a friend told me that Fidel Castro was organizing a
> group of men for an attack. I went to the liceo, looking for Fidel,
> and found him in a small room at the back of the building. I
> told him I wanted to join his group. He asked me what my name
> and address were and promised to come and see me soon. I saw
> him a week later, and even though he had only seen me once be-
> fore, he remembered my name and address. It was then that I was
> made a member of this group.[112]

Finally, a large contingent of men from Artemisa and Guanajay in
Pinar del Rio Province joined the movement. This Artemisa group
emerged after the Batista coup, when young workers and students led
by José ("Pepe") Suárez published a manifesto and afterward formed
a revolutionary cell. Suárez had been a friend of Fidel's for some time
and a leader of the Juventud Ortodoxa. His followers were young
Ortodoxos, most of them workers, many of them from the countryside.[113]

The Artemisa group, like the others, was very young. A member
of the group stated in an interview:

> By December 1952, we formed a contingent of 250 young men.
> Flores Bentancourt, the oldest, was thirty years old. At the time I
> was twenty-four. There were numerous young men who were
> seventeen and eighteen years old.[114]

By the end of 1952, Fidel Castro had visited Artemisa, making
preparations for future activities. The revolutionary leaders met at the

---

[112] Marta Matamoros, "Storming Bayamo's Army Garrison," *Gramma* (Havana), July 16, 1967, p. 2.
[113] Rojas, *El Juicio del Moncada*, p. 28; Jacinto Granda, "Artemisa y la Revolución," *Juventud Rebelde* (Havana), July 25, 1966, p. 2. The exact date of the Artemisa group's formation is unknown, but it was probably in April or May 1952.
See Comandante José Ponce Díaz, "Recuerdos del ataque," *Verde Olivo* (Havana),
July 26, 1963, p. 17. The members of the first nucleus were José Suárez, Ramiro
Valdés, Ciro Redondo, and Julio Díaz.
[114] Vicente Cubillas, "Los artemiseños en el Moncada," *Revolución* (Havana),
July 22, 1963 (supplement), p. 7. Statement made by Severino Rossell Gon-
zález.

Masonic Lodge of Artemisa, where one of their members was the treasurer.[115] They agreed that revolutionary cells must be created, and Ramiro Valdés was assigned that task. Thereupon, seven cells in Artemisa and four in Guanajay were organized with ten men in each. The traditionally rebellious Artemisa region was an excellent training ground. It was sufficiently rural to permit military maneuvers. Moreover, it was removed from the prying eyes of Batista's urban secret service, yet close enough to the capital to allow rapid mobilization if necessary. Castro considered the Artemisa group one of his best because most of the men were expert marksmen. In the early days of June 1953, thirty men from Artemisa were chosen to participate in the Moncada attack. Two others refused to participate. All were hand-picked by Castro.[116]

Months were spent training the inexperienced youths in the use of weapons, personal defense, and military tactics. Political education was imparted by reading the works of José Martí. A complex structure was organized to supply arms and financial support.

One afternoon during the training on a farm near Los Palos, in Pinar del Rio Province, a rifle was damaged. The young men began to look in the high grass for a small spring that had fallen from it. Time passed, night fell, and it began to rain. Most of the men stopped looking; only one man continued the search despite the dark and rain. Eventually he found the lost part. It was Fidel who had demonstrated such strong will and perseverance. He turned to his followers and said, "See, this shows that perseverance will bring about our victory."[117]

The fervor of the new generation became evident in their military training and political commitment. There was not a single demonstration, meeting, or rally in which they failed to participate in order to repudiate the government. They were self-confident and defiant. On January 27, 1953, thousands of youths marched from the University of Havana to downtown Havana to commemorate the centennial of José Martí's birth. The Fidelistas mobilized and participated in a

[115] Luis Rolando Cabrera, "El Comandante García Collazo, una gran lección de coraje," *Bohemia* (Havana), July 12, 1959, p. 9; and Cubillas, "Los artemiseños en el Moncada." The participants in the meeting were Fidel Castro, Pastorita Núñez, Ismael Ricondo, Julio Díaz, Ciro Redondo, Abel Santamaría, Ramiro Valdés, José Suárez, Jaime Acosta, and René García Collazo.

[116] One author states that thirty-five youths were chosen from Artemisa and five from Guanajay, but most sources give the number as thirty. See Cubillas, "Los artemiseños en el Moncada" (also for Castro's esteem for their marksmanship), and Miguel Enrique, "Pinareños en el Moncada," *Bohemia* (Havana), July 22, 1966, p. 13.

[117] Marta Rojas, "Enseñanzas del Moncada," *Juventud Rebelde* (Havana), July 25, 1966, p. 9.

breathtaking torchlight parade through the streets. Melba Hernández relates the event:

> From the university came thousands of young people with their torches. We were among them, as an organized group. Our torches had large nails with which to reply to the police if they attacked us. We marched shoulder to shoulder in a disciplined manner. The people were very impressed when they saw us go by. I heard some of them say, "Those who go there are the communists!"[118]

The MNR Revolt. An atmosphere of rebellion now prevailed on the island. On January 15, 1953, the police shot a student, who succumbed to his wounds the following month. On February 14, he was buried with a Cuban flag over his coffin and the following thought of Martí inscribed on a black cloth: "The blood of the good is not spilled in vain." From then on, more students considered themselves the representatives of the Cuban people, the conscience of the nation. Soon students were flocking to the Movimiento Nacionalista Revolucionario (MNR), led by Rafael García Bárcena, a philosophy professor at the University of Havana. Bárcena was a member of the Directorio Estudiantil of 1930, a founder of the Auténticos, and later a leading exponent of the faction that, along with Eduardo Chibás, formed the PPC. He had been on the faculty of the Escuela Superior de Guerra, a school for military officers, for six years. Although he resigned in March 1952, he continued his contacts with some of the officers after the Batista coup.[119]

The MNR, founded on May 20, 1952, at the University of Havana, proclaimed that it fought not merely for a change of ruler but for an end to "national evils." Using his influence within the officers' corps, Bárcena planned a bloodless coup against Batista. His military and civilian followers would take over Camp Columbia by surprise and dismiss the military strongman. But although the philosophy professor knew his theoretical models, he underestimated the military intelligence service. On April 5, 1953, the MNR members were caught by surprise,

118 Melba Hernández, "Siempre supimos que el asalto al Moncada culminaría en la victoria," *Verde Olivo* (Havana), July 28, 1963, p. 30.
119 "Datos biográficos de García Bárcena," *El Mundo* (Havana), July 8, 1952, p. A8. The members of the MNR who later would become important revolutionary figures included Rafael García Bárcena, Eva Jímenez, Mario Llerena, Fernando Sánchez Amaya, Manuel Fernández, Faustino Pérez, Armando Hart, Enrique Hart, Manuel Carbonnell, Danilo Mendez, Orlando Ventura Reyes, Joe Westbrook, José Luis Varona, and Angel Boan. See Clara Hernández, "Combatientes clandestinas," *El Mundo* (Havana), August 21, 1968, p. 2.

rounded up, and imprisoned.[120] Many suffered terrible tortures. Thirteen persons were given prison sentences, whereas fifty-four others were freed. Bárcena himself received a two-year sentence, although he denied planning to take over the Camp Columbia army headquarters. The MNR conspiracy was important, even though it failed. Many of the young people who participated in the plan were the sons of wealthy families in Havana. Furthermore, Bárcena was a widely known and respected intellectual, journalist, and politician. He was one of the last representatives of the 1930s generation still moved by the ideals of José Martí.

With Bárcena's imprisonment the MNR crumbled, and most of its members joined other groups.[121] Nonetheless, it had a lasting strategic and ideological influence. Its failure demonstrated that a revolutionary movement could not function nonviolently nor could it work within the military structure to bring about change.[122] Furthermore, the MNR program suggested a fundamental principle: that the new younger generation had to organize independently to attain power.

The Montreal Pact. The MNR fiasco conclusively demonstrated the disarray within the Ortodoxo movement.[123] The ever-growing struggle within the leadership was defined by mid-January 1953, when a faction led by José Pardo Llada and Emilio Ochoa opted for an alliance with their political enemies, the Auténtico Party. The followers of Roberto Agramonte, a sociology professor at Havana University, on the other hand, considered such a movement a betrayal of Ortodoxo principles.

After the first Ortodoxo split early in 1953, there was a second schism on March 18, 1953, when the powerful Ortodoxo leader and sugar potentate from Oriente Province Fernández Casas decided to participate in the elections promised by Batista for November of that year. A few days later, however, the government announced the post-

---

[120] "A la Cabaña 60 detenidos," *El Crisol* (Havana), April 6, 1953, p. 1; and "Sesenta muchachos al mando del Dr. García Bárcena intentaban tomar por asalto el campamento de Columbia," *Alerta!* (Havana), April 6, 1953, p. 1.

[121] Faustino Pérez, Frank País, Armando Hart, Vilma Espín, José Tey, Manuel Fernández, Angel Boan, Mario Llerena, and Fernando Sánchez Amaya eventually joined the 26th of July Movement; Eva Jímenez, Joe Westbrook, Faure Chomón, Domingo Portela, and others joined the Directorio Revolucionario.

[122] According to Jaime Suchlicki, García Bárcena had invited Castro to participate in the revolt, but he refused, considering it "suicide." See Suchlicki, *University Students*, pp. 61–63.

[123] García Bárcena was not a member of the PPC at the time of his plot because the party did not allow a member to form another political organization. See "Causaron bajas en el PPC por indisciplina," *El Mundo* (Havana), December 31, 1952, p. A7.

ponement of elections until June 1, 1954, on the grounds that conspiratorial activities by the opposition had destroyed the peaceful climate required for holding them.[124]

Once the possibility of immediate elections was denied, politicians conceived of still more legal expedients to remove Batista. Steps were taken to establish a united opposition front, but the two major opposition parties split over the issue of a strategic alliance. Nonetheless, an Auténtico faction led by Carlos Prío Socarrás and the Ortodoxo splinter group following Emilio Ochoa and José Pardo Llada favored cooperation.[125] They met in Montreal, Canada, to discuss a program. The Montreal meeting further divided the Auténtico and the Ortodoxo parties. Interparty conflict became vehement, virulent, and militant. The Auténtico faction led by former president Ramón Grau San Martín opposed the pact simply because he wanted to seize party leadership from Carlos Prío, and this was as good an excuse as any to make an issue. This same desire for power motivated Grau to run for reelection in 1953 and 1954. Aureliano Sánchez, also an Auténtico, disagreed with both Prío and Grau. He did not want an alliance with the Ortodoxos because he hated the party, nor did he favor the reformist and nonviolent methods of Grau. On the Ortodoxo side, Roberto Agramonte wanted civic resistance without the use of armed violence or alliances. Then there were the counterparts of Grau in the PPC, those who wanted an electoral solution, led by Fernández Casas and Carlos Márquez Sterling. Thus, within the Auténtico and Ortodoxo ranks could be found those who favored coalition politics (Prío and Ochoa), electoralism (Grau and Casas), civic resistance (Agramonte), and revolutionary action (Arango and Castro).[126]

[124] *Hispanic American Report*, vol. 6, no. 2 (April 1953), p. 14.

[125] The Ortodoxo faction was represented by Emilio Ochoa, José M. Gutíerrez, José Pardo Ilada, Isidro Figueroa, Raúl de Jan, and Javier Lescarro. The Prío faction was composed of Carlos Prío, Guillermo A. Pujol, Manuel A. de Varona, Eduardo Suárez Rivas, Juan A. Rubio Padilla, Carlos Hevia, Antonio Santiago, Aracelio Azcuy, Luis Gustavo Fernández, and Rafael Izquierdo. See "Discuten la unidad ortodoxos y auténticos," *El Mundo* (Havana), June 2, 1953, pp. 1, A8; "Acuerdo entre el PRC y el PPC," *El Mundo* (Havana), June 3, 1953, pp. 1, A11.

[126] The Agramonte stand within the Ortodoxo movement was supported by the national directorate of the party, the peasant section led by Rolando Espinosa, the professional section led by Salvador Massip, the labor section of Emilio Ilenín, the youth section led by Mario Rivadulla, and the women's section of María Teresa Freyre. Within these sections, however, there were the cases of the Havana provincial committee of the party, a section of the professionals and the Juventud Ortodoxa of Havana, the municipal committees of the party, and various national leaders who wanted an alliance with the PRC. The electoral stand had the support of the national organizational committee of the party. See "Respaldan acuerdos de Montreal," *El Mundo* (Havana), June 5, 1953, p. A7; "El acuerdo de Montreal considera la enorme zona de opinión no partidarista," *El Mundo* (Havana), June

The declaration of Montreal issued on June 2, 1953, stated in part that: (1) the Cuban crisis could be solved only by restoring the 1940 Constitution; (2) the Batista regime was unable to restore political institutions to the people and bring about elections; (3) after the removal of Batista, a provisional government would restore the Electoral Code of 1943 and guarantee official neutrality in elections;[127] (4) the signing political factions categorically rejected and condemned attacks on individuals, gangsterism, and terrorism as forms of struggle; (5) the two factions would appoint commissions to structure efficiently the efforts to carry out their objectives, reiterating that they did not form an electoral coalition.[128]

No reference was made to armed revolt, either to favor or condemn it, although it seemed to be implied that the Montrealistas wanted to find a peaceful resolution to their conflict with the government. The Partido Socialista Popular, that is, the communists, were not invited to participate.[129] Several authors maintain that Fidel Castro had no relation whatsoever with the Montrealistas; there are others, however, who claim that he had close contacts with them.

Andrés Nasario Sargen, at the time an Ortodoxo leader from Las Villas Province, has stated that the Montrealistas agreed on a national uprising whose military coordinator was to be Juan Manuel Márquez (a man closely tied to Fidel).[130] Fidel supposedly became the coordinator for three municipalities in Pinar del Rio, one of which was that of

---

7, 1953, p. A9; "Traidores al testamento de Eduardo Chibás," *El Mundo* (Havana), June 3, 1953, p. A7; "Consideran politiquero el pacto Auténtico-Ortodoxo," *El Mundo* (Havana), June 5, 1953, p. A7.

[127] A month later the United States Government issued a "13-point Declaration" with regard to U.S.-Cuban relations, in which it was clearly stated that Washington favored the alteration made by Batista of the Electoral Code, and condemned the 1943 Electoral Code because it allowed political parties with 2 percent of registered electors to run for elections, that is, the Communist Party, which in 1948 had 2.54 percent. This declaration, disregarding other major changes in the code, torpedoed point 3 of the Montreal declaration.

[128] "Carta de Montreal," *Bohemia* (Havana), June 7, 1953, p. 77.

[129] It should be noted that the professional section (*sección de profesionales*) of the Ortodoxos led by Dr. Raúl de Jan wanted the communists to be included in the conversations at Montreal. See "La sección de profesionales," *El Mundo* (Havana), June 11, 1953, p. A7; "Responden a Ortodoxos los Apristas," *El Mundo* (Havana), June 10, 1953, p. A7; "Disienten sobre el nuevo pacto," *El Mundo* (Havana), June 19, 1953, p. A7.

[130] Interview with Andrés Nasario Sargen, Miami, Florida, September 2, 1969. Baeza Flores also states that the Prío and Ochoa factions were preparing for "armed struggle." See Alberto Baeza Flores, *Las cadenas vienen de lejos* (Mexico: Editorial Letras, 1960), p. 312; and José Suárez Nuñez, "Batista ha cogido un león por el rabo, veremos como lo suelta," *Baraguá* (Honduras), November 15, 1966, pp. 1, 8.

Artemisa. According to this version, Castro broke party discipline a month later by attacking the military barracks in Santiago de Cuba. This version appears doubtful primarily because the time interval of a month and a half was too short to prepare the type of action carried out by Fidel at Moncada.

The evidence available suggests that if secret agreements were reached, they probably did not deal with armed struggle.[131] The Montrealistas were concerned primarily with setting up an alliance. They could not outline a program of action because their own ranks were divided. It was a matter of priorities, in which coalition politics had precedence over revolutionary tactics. Moreover, the overriding issue was the claim of Carlos Prío that he was the legitimate heir to power.[132] The internal splits and mutual recriminations showed the inability of the two parties to attain any kind of working unity.

Moncada: The Plan Unfolds

Meanwhile, in February 1953, Fidel Castro and Abel Santamaría began to make preparations for the attack on the barracks, a project that was to remain secret from all other members of the group. The training in personal defense and commando tactics proceeded at the Rancho Los Palos near Madruga, in the towns of Pijirigua, Capellanía, Cotorro, and El Cerro, and on the roof of the Department of Science of the University of Havana.

Ernesto Tizol Aguilera, who owned a business in Miami, was contacted and persuaded to join the group. His mission was to move to Santiago de Cuba and start a chicken farm. Shortly thereafter, in April 1953, the small two-acre farm "El Siboney" was leased from José Vázquez. The farmhouse was old and spacious, located on the road that led to the famous Siboney Beach, where the commander of the Moncada Army Barracks, Colonel Alberto del Río Chaviano, owned a house. It was also fifteen minutes away from downtown Santiago de Cuba and only a few kilometers from the foothills of the Sierra Maestra.

Soon after the acquisition of "El Siboney," Fidel began to ship ammunition and weapons to the farm. The owner of Thion Laboratory

---

[131] The proceedings of the Montreal meeting have not been published, and many of the participants, the majority of whom are in exile today, refuse to make them available.

[132] Some people argue that in Montreal it was agreed to place Prío in power once Batista was deposed. See Roberto Agramonte, "Ochoa se propuso destruir la Ortodoxia y entregarla a Prío," El Mundo (Havana), June 13, 1953, p. A7; Tony Dehaloza, "Ni Batista ni Prío constituyen una solución nacional (entrevista con Roberto Agramonte)," Bohemia (Havana), June 14, 1953, pp. 82, 94.

lent his business sample bags in order to transport some of the equipment without arousing suspicion. Other equipment was shipped to the
farm in boxes and the remainder taken personally by the conspirators.

Melba Hernández was given the delicate mission of persuading an
army sargeant, Florentino Fernández, who was a sympathizer and
eventually a member of the group, to supply a large number of the
army uniforms that the revolutionaries used in their surprise attack on
the army barracks. The uniforms were sewn by Melba and her mother
Elena Rodríguez, Elita Dubois (wife of conspirator José Luis Tasende),
Nati Revuelta, and Delia Terry at Melba's home at 107 Jovellar Street
in Havana. The weapons and uniforms were taken to Siboney by
Fidel, who sometimes dropped in with Alcalde or with "Ñico" López
and Chenard.

As the hour to strike drew near, Abel moved to Santiago, followed
by his sister Haydée, who posed as his wife. Shortly thereafter, Fidel
asked Melba to prepare to leave for Santiago, where she would join
Abel and Haydée. Melba recalls:

> I remember that I went to a florist shop on Neptuno Street to ob-
> tain a flower box where we could place the shotguns which I
> would take as part of the valuable luggage. I took the train in the
> evening toward Santiago, even though I did not know where I
> was really going. Ernesto Tizol accompanied me to the train. In
> Santiago, Abel, Renato Guitart, and Elpidio Sosa awaited me.[133]

Throughout this time rumors of forthcoming revolts were everywhere. The New York magazine *Visión* stated on June 17, 1953, that
a revolt would occur in Cuba within a few weeks. A few days later
rumors spread that the dreaded Caribbean Legion had 1,500 men training to invade the island.[134] Batista remarked:

> There will be no revolution. A revolution needs the support of
> the people. I know very well that the armed forces and the people
> support me.[135]

The 26th of July. On July 24, 1953, Castro ordered his men to leave
for Santiago de Cuba. There some lodged at a home on Celda Street,
others at a house in the Sueño residential district, and the rest in two
hotels. For security reasons, no one knew his final destination: "El
Siboney."[136]

[133] Hernández, "Siempre supimos que el asalto al Moncada culminaría en la
victoria," p. 31.
[134] "Denuncia una conspiración en el Caribe," *El Mundo* (Havana), July 7,
1953, p. 1.
[135] "Afirma Batista que Prío hace daño a Cuba hablando de inminente revolución," *El Mundo* (Havana), July 4, 1953, p. 1.
[136] Marta Rojas, "Moncada, secreto militar," *Verde Olivo* (Havana), July 26,

The revolutionaries had departed from Artemisa in Pinar del Rio, where most of the attackers lived; from 164 25th Street, 107 Jovellar Street, and Marianao in Havana, and from the towns of Colón and Calabazar. They traveled by bus, train, and car. Some of the men from Artemisa stopped in Havana, where they stayed at a house on Basarrate Street, a few blocks from the University of Havana. There they were given train tickets to Santiago, arriving at dawn on July 25 and checking into the Hotel Rex. At midnight on July 25, the different groups began to converge on "El Siboney," still unaware of their target.

Soon Fidel arrived to explain the mission and distribute the weapons. He explained that the main thrust of the attack would be against the Moncada Army Barracks of Santiago de Cuba, with a simultaneous assault on the army barracks at the town of Bayamo to prevent military supplies and reinforcements from being sent from Holguín to Santiago. They would wear army uniforms in order to facilitate entrance.

Just before the attack Fidel tried on the largest uniform, and a problem arose: It did not fit! Tomás Toledo writes:

> I remember that when Fidel tried on the biggest uniform it still would not fit him. Looking at himself in the mirror, he worried that he would not look—for the glorious assault on the Moncada—like a soldier of the regime, the role we were to play in attacking the garrison. He had the same worry when Abel tried on his uniform. "Look, Abel," he said, "you have to act like a military man."[137]

As the hour drew near, Fidel asked for volunteers to take Post 3 of the barracks. Jesús Montané, one of the participants, recalls:

> Post 3 was the most dangerous mission of the assault because it would open the doors of the barracks. . . . It was decided that Raúl Castro would take over the Palace of Justice, and then when Fidel saw *compañero* Abel step forward, along with those who had volunteered to take over Post 3, which in reality was the most important mission of that heroic action, he said, "Abel, you cannot go in that action, you are the second in command of the organization and what would happen if we both got killed? No one would know what has happened here and we would be left without direction."[138]

1963, p. 17. Renato Guitart, thanks to his connections in Santiago, was able to supply Castro with the plans of the inside of the Moncada Barracks. He died during the attack. Also see Marta Rojas, *La Generación del Centenario en el Moncada* (Havana: Ediciones R, 1964), pp. 95–96.

137 Tomás Toledo, "Background on the Assault on Moncada and Bayamo Garrisons," *Granma* (Havana), June 18, 1967, p. 11.

138 Jesús Montané, "El asalto al Moncada," *Verde Olivo* (Havana), July 19, 1964, p. 22.

When the time for departure finally arrived, Fidel ordered Haydée and Melba to remain in the farmhouse, an order that both women obviously resented. Dr. Muñoz, the group physician, proposed that they go along with Fidel to the Civil Hospital, where they could be useful in caring for the wounded. Fidel agreed. At 4:30 A.M. on July 26, Fidel spoke to the men and women briefly.[139] At the last minute some of the men refused to participate in what they considered to be an insane adventure.

One hundred and thirty-five men, at 5:15 A.M., began to move toward the city of Santiago de Cuba.[140] Twenty-six cars were used. Meanwhile, the city continued to celebrate the traditional carnival festivities. Military officers from the Moncada, who had not taken any precautionary measures against a surprise attack, got drunk while celebrating their holidays in private parties.

The cars moved without difficulty. The first one, leading the column, carried those who had volunteered to take Post 3. They had .22-caliber rifles, shotguns, and knives. On entering the city, the cars divided into two groups. The first, led by Fidel and Abel, would attack the garrison and vicinity, while the second group, made up of fifty men, would serve as a reserve force. Tragically for the revolutionaries, the second force got lost when it made a wrong turn. (They had never traveled the route before the attack!)

Meanwhile, Fidel and fifty-three men continued to move toward the Moncada. Raúl Castro with ten men separated from the first group and took several buildings in the area. Julio Reyes, Raúl Gómez García, and several others tried to reach a nearby radio station to call the people to revolt. They failed to do so. Abel Santamaría, his sister, and twenty-one men occupied the Civil Hospital across from the barracks.

The men who were to capture Post 3 were foiled in their plan, according to the revolutionaries' version, when they met an army sentry jeep. The ensuing fire alerted the garrison immediately.[141] Hours later, Fidel ordered a retreat because he did not have sufficient men or am-

---

[139] "This Movement Will Triumph" in this volume.

[140] It is debatable how many men really participated in the insurrection or in the attack proper. Some sources state that 126 men participated, others offer the figure of 165. See Robert Merle, "Moncada, primer combate de Fidel Castro," *Bohemia* (Havana), July 22, 1966, pp. 50–51; Matthews, *Fidel Castro*, p. 65.

[141] An army officer has provided a different version. According to him, the revolutionaries entered the barracks after surprising the sentries and killing them with knives. Inside the barracks a fierce battle was fought, and finally the revolutionaries were forced to retreat. (One must note that it is possible that the revolutionaries were aided by several soldiers from inside the barracks, although this point has not been thoroughly cleared.) See Colonel Pedro A. Barrera Pérez, "Por qué el Ejército no derrotó a Castro," *Bohemia* (Havana), August 6, 1961, pp. 28–29.

munition. Discipline soon broke down as many men panicked. Some
went their own way; others found refuge in the Civil Hospital nearby.

The rest of the men retreated with Fidel. Completely exhausted and
filled with fear, about sixty men reached "El Siboney."[142] There Castro
spoke to what was left of his revolutionary force. Whoever wanted to
follow him could do so, he said; he was going to the mountains to
fight. At that point arguments in favor of and against the idea burst
out. Most of the men agreed that they could not succeed and decided
to disperse. Many gave themselves up and later were murdered.
Eighteen men decided to follow their leader. They formed a small
troop, most of whom were from the city of Artemisa.

One member of the group got lost and later was found dead. Once
again they discussed what to do and agreed to continue their march
toward the mountains. Finally they reached a house where an old
woman instructed her grandson to guide them quickly to the Gran
Piedra Mountains. From there they could gain easy access to the
Sierra Maestra. With a young black man for a guide, they reached
Sevilla Arriba. As one participant recalls:

> We found a black man who refused to sell us some chickens.
> Fidel, usually so persuasive, was not able to convince him. The
> black man told us that his brother lived farther ahead, and he
> would sell us the chickens. Fidel told him to accompany us to his
> brother's house; he went and found the brother, who killed a
> pig. He knew about the Moncada. All of that zone was inhabited
> by blacks and mulattoes. Fidel gave the man a nickel-plated .45
> pistol, and the man told us about his fight with the land owners,
> to which Fidel replied, "When they come to bother you, open
> fire with this pistol. Don't believe in anyone. Defend what is
> yours."[143]

The men proceeded to the house of some relatives of the black
peasant, where they changed their clothes, rested, and listened to Batista's speech to the nation recounting the events of the Moncada. It
was now July 27. Afterward they continued the march, hiding from
reconnaissance aircraft, and aware that the army already was tracking
them closely.

On July 29 and 30 the men camped. They were weary, and the
wounded were suffering badly. Among the wounded,

> Reinaldo Benítez was very bad due to a bullet wound in his leg.
> Jesús Montané, who has flat feet, could barely walk. We had to

---

[142] There are two different estimates as to how many men gathered at the
farm. Some state the number was thirty-eight, of whom twenty decided to give
themselves up. Others provide a figure of between sixty and seventy. See Vicente
Cubillas, "Los artimiseños en el Moncada," *Revolución* (Havana), July 22, 1963
(supplement), p. 9.
[143] *Ibid.*

drag them both. The evening of Thursday found us in a canyon, and we decided to spend the night there. A little while after having halted, we heard a shot. It was Mario Lazo, whose gun had misfired, piercing his shoulder. Already three casualties in the ragged troop![144]

After this incident the men spoke to Fidel about their condition. The main problem was presented by the wounded men, who could no longer climb mountains. Although the men did not want to split up, Fidel thought otherwise and ordered two men to carry the wounded to Santiago. Rosendo Menéndez and Antonio Rosell accepted the mission. They hid in a cave and stopped Lazo's bleeding with a plug of tobacco. In spite of the rain, Menéndez, Benítez, and Montané decided to continue looking for the road to Santiago. Lazo and Rosell took another road and eventually found the home of Benjamín Arza, an Auténtico sympathizer who hid them on a hill behind his farm for a month.[145] On August 29, they left for Santiago, where they were taken to the residence of Alfredo Guerra in the Vista Alegre residential district and where they remained for three days. There they separated, and Rosell was sent to the home of José Espín, where he hid for two months before asking for political asylum at the Guatemalan embassy in Havana.[146] Meanwhile, Menéndez, Montané, and Benítez were captured before reaching Santiago.

Several men surrendered to the authorities, fearing death if they continued fighting because of the merciless terror unleashed by the government.[147] Sixty-seven revolutionaries were executed after being captured; the armed forces felt they had to set an example to discourage further uprisings. Fidel Castro and his now-reduced band of followers continued their desperate attempt to reach the Sierra Maestra.

Monsignor Enrique Pérez Serantes of Santiago de Cuba appealed to the authorities on behalf of the revolutionaries. Colonel Chaviano thereupon accepted the archbishop's offer of mediation to obtain the surrender of Castro and his men. On Friday, July 31, Pérez Serantes, accompanied by Justice Subirat Quesada, Antonio Guerra, and Fernando Canto, unsuccessfully attempted to establish contact with the rebels.

On August 1, 1953, a sixteen-man rural guard patrol under the command of Lieutenant Pedro Manuel Sarría surprised Castro and his

[144] *Ibid.*, pp. 9–10.
[145] Arza's wife was the aunt of Fidel's wife, Mirta Diaz Balart.
[146] Espín was the father of Vilma Espín, who later married Raúl Castro.
[147] The romanticized versions of the Moncada attack always fail to mention these surrenders. See "Acogiéndose al bando militar se están presentando algunos de los atacantes del Moncada," *El Mundo* (Havana), July 31, 1953, pp. 1, A8.

friends and opened fire on them. The rebels surrendered. According to Sarría, Castro was captured with Francisco González Calderín, Oscar Alcalde, José Suárez, Juan Almeida, Jesús Montané, Armando Mestre, and others whose names he could not recall.[148]

An army communiqué stated:

> In the early morning hours of August 1, 1953, on the farm "Cilindro," property of Francisco Sotelo Piña, in the district of Sevilla, in the municipality of Caney, after a fight between members of squadron 11 of the rural police and rebels . . . the leader of the movement, Fidel Castro Ruiz [sic], 26 years old, resident of Street 18, Number 365, Vedado, Havana, was captured.[149]

On receiving the news of the rebels' capture, the Oriente command dispatched twenty men to take the prisoners. The rebels were to be executed. But Lieutenant Sarría, who had known Castro at the University of Havana, refused to turn the prisoners over to the detachment. Instead, he personally escorted them to army headquarters, where Colonel Chaviano awaited news of their death. Chaviano reprimanded Sarría for not having carried out his orders, to which Lieutenant Sarría replied, "If you want, you kill them, Colonel."[150]

It was too late, however, to do so. Public opinion was outraged by the bloodbath. Few revolutionaries had escaped the military roundup. The majority had peacefully given themselves up, and yet they were murdered afterward. Eighty men were murdered by the military; just five were reported wounded. Only luck and public opinion spared the lives of Fidel, Raúl and some of his closest associates—most of whom were captured beside him.[151]

The revolutionary plan had failed. The group had hoped to spark the masses by a heroic and exemplary action; it did not work. Nonetheless, the conception was entirely Cuban. The idea of a small and well-organized minority attempting a political stroke by force began with Antonio Guiteras; thus the Cubans did not need a foreign model.

---

[148] Alfredo Echarry, "Yo capturé a Fidel Castro (entrevista con Pedro M. Sarría)," *Juventud Rebelde* (Havana), July 25, 1966, p. 4. A different version states that at the time of his capture Castro had only two other men with him. See "Cuando Sarría detuvo a Fidel Castro y a sus 2 compañeros el sábado 1 de Agosto de 1953," *Revolución* (Havana), July 26, 1962, p. 15. It should be noted that Jesús Montané was captured elsewhere.

[149] "En la cárcel de Santiago de Cuba ocho fugitivos capturados," *Diario de la Marina* (Havana), August 2, 1953, pp. 1, 39.

[150] Rodolfo Rodríguez, "Por qué Fidel Castro no fue asesinado al capturarlo el Ejército en Oriente," *Bohemia* (Havana), March 8, 1959, pp. 63, 112. On August 20, 1957, Sarría was sentenced to one year in prison for conspiracy.

[151] Perhaps some influence was exerted by Fidel's family too. His brother-in-law was still a member of the cabinet, and the Castro Ruz family was influential in Oriente Province.

It was Guiteras who organized a handful of "audacious young men"[152] to assault and take the Moncada Barracks in 1931. Its capture, Guiteras (and Castro) believed, would precipitate a revolt throughout the province, which in turn would cause a national uprising.[153] The 1931 plan, however, was never carried out.

Did the conditions exist for a rebellion in Oriente province? Fidel believed so. He did not think that political agitation among the masses was necessary, because the masses were already impregnated with the revolutionary ideals of Eduardo Chibás. In fact, during the attack the revolutionaries planned to broadcast Chibás's last speech (August 1951), which called on the people for a more committed stand. A manifesto[154] and some poems also were to be read on the air, but owing to several errors no broadcast was ever made.

Years later, Castro summarized his strategy as follows:

> We had no economic resources, no arms, but we started out with the thesis that the revolutionary arms were in Cuba, perfectly stored, and kept in the army posts. And it was from there that we had to seize the arms they had in the forts to begin the revolutionary struggle. We planned an attack on the main fort in Santiago de Cuba and another in Bayamo. . . . We would capture the arms and later force a surrender of other units in the province, and produce an uprising in Oriente Province, which has had a fighting tradition since the times of the struggle for independence. The idea was to produce a provincial uprising, capture the arms from the enemy, and then use the radio stations to win the support of the masses in the whole country.[155]

The people, however, did not support the uprising. Nonetheless, the plan was well prepared, for it took into consideration the unique attitudes of the region.

Oriente Province has had a tradition of rebelliousness since the nineteenth century. It was in Bayamo that the war of independence against Spain had found its greatest support and that the independence ideals had burned most strongly. It was there also that in the 1930s the peasants had taken over land from their owners. Furthermore, Oriente offered certain military benefits.

The province was the farthest from the capital. While the regime kept tight security measures in Havana because Batista feared a mili-

---

[152] The phrase is taken from Rogelio L. Bravet, "Antonio Guiteras, el precursor," *Bohemia* (Havana), May 6, 1966, p. 6.

[153] Calixta Guiteras Holmes, *Biografía de Antonio Guiteras* (Havana: Municipio de La Habana, 1960); "Guiteras: líder anti-imperialista," *Revolución* (Havana), May 8, 1961, pp. 1, 10.

[154] "The Cuban Revolution" in this volume.

[155] Saul Landau, "Interview with Fidel Castro," *Eyewitness* (San Francisco), vol. 2, no. 1 (1970), pp. 1–2.

tary coup, provincial barracks were more lax. Also, in the 1950s it was considered unthinkable to unleash a frontal attack on the military. Castro has stated:

> There was a saying, which had been repeated for no one knows how long, to the effect that a revolution could be made with the army or without the army, but never against the army. . . . The idea of a revolution against the army, against the armed forces, against the system, seemed an absurd idea to many.[156]

The simultaneous attack on the Santiago and Bayamo barracks initiated a new version of armed struggle. Though urban oriented, revolutionary action moved away from the capital and centered on the constituted armed forces. This was unique in Cuban political history, and the Moncadistas set an example for a generation to follow.

The military defeat, in the long run, turned into a political victory, for Fidel Castro and his followers became the vanguard of a generation that desperately wished to act and found itself with almost all avenues of social mobility closed.[157] A participant in the revolutionary struggle stated succinctly:

> With the Moncada our generation broke its ties with the past and won for itself the right to orient and lead this stage of the Cuban revolutionary process, fulfilling in this way its historic mission.[158]

Breaking with the past, however, did not mean escaping from it. The insurrectionist plans failed, and the revolutionaries were killed or imprisoned. Few escaped the heavy hand of the regime.

Fidel in Prison. The revolutionaries spent several weeks in Boniato Prison, just a few miles from the city of Santiago. While awaiting trial, they were reasonably well treated, although their diet was poor. They could exercise and have books in their cells. Fidel, in solitary confinement, avidly read works from the prison library and prepared the defense for the forthcoming trial. He also managed to communicate regularly with his fellow inmates through written messages, for the guards pretended not to see.

---

[156] Fidel Castro, "History Creates Objective Conditions, but Men Create the Subjective Ones," *Gramma* (Havana), July 31, 1966, pp. 9–12.

[157] Suárez, *Cuba: Castroism and Communism*, p. 20. For blocked social mobility as one of the preconditions of the Cuban Revolution, see Ramón Eduardo Ruíz, *Cuba, The Making of a Revolution* (New York: W. W. Norton and Co., 1968), pp. 141–163; James O'Connor, "The Foundations of Cuban Socialism," *Studies on the Left*, Fall 1964, pp. 97–117; and Cuba, Consejo Nacional de Economía, *El empleo, el sub-empleo y el desempleo en Cuba* (Havana, 1958).

[158] Francisco A. Pardeiro, "La valerosa acción de Santiago," in René Ray (ed.), *Libertad y revolución* (Havana: n.p., 1959), p. 17.

On September 21, 1953, the trial began. Fidel, acting as his own lawyer, questioned witnesses and consistently denounced the regime's crimes. In the audience were reporters, lawyers, and opposition leaders who heard Castro present his version of the attack. The government, frightened and embarrassed, did not want the proceedings known to the public because unrest could result. In order to maintain the necessary secrecy, Colonel Chaviano ordered that Fidel be held incomunicado. The court was to be told he was ill. However, the prison physicians who signed the document testifying to Fidel's illness were sympathizers of the revolutionary cause. Castro was warned of the government's plan and promptly took steps to foil it.

On September 26, when Fidel was to be called into the court, a military officer handed the judge a letter that stated:

> The main defendant has not been brought to court according to the report from the assistant chief to Colonel Chaviano because he is presently ill in jail as shown in the enclosed medical certificate.[159]

Then Melba Hernández, who had been in a cell adjacent to that of the revolutionary leader, burst out, "Fidel is not sick!" and produced a folded letter written by Fidel and concealed in her hair. The message stated that in order to prevent the disclosures of the horrible crimes committed against the revolutionaries, he was not permitted to be present in court. "This is why I have been informed that I shall not appear before the Court. I am supposed to be sick. The fact is that I am in a perfect state of health and suffer no disease."[160] Nonetheless, the prison authorities did not permit Castro to appear at the trial. Furthermore, he was transferred to the most isolated corner of the prison and kept in solitary confinement.

The other revolutionaries did not ask for mercy; they maintained their stand courageously. Fidel later stated, "Although absent from the trial, I was able to follow it in all its detail from my cell,"[161] as his comrades continued to furnish him with information.

On October 13, 1953, the Moncada survivors were sent to the prison on the Isle of Pines, while Fidel remained in Santiago de Cuba for his special trial three days later. The authorities, hoping for the greatest secrecy, held it in a nurses' lounge at the Santiago Civil Hospital. The proceedings were not published, nor was Castro's own defense ever recorded.[162] In the end, Fidel was sentenced to fifteen years in prison.

---

[159] Rojas, *La Generación del Centenario*, p. 151.
[160] "Letter to the Court of Appeals" in this volume.
[161] "History Will Absolve Me" in this volume.
[162] Castro's address was later expanded and issued in 1954 as "History Will Absolve Me."

On arrival at the Isle of Pines, he was placed with some of his comrades. Jesús Montané, one of the prisoners, recalls:

> From the outset Fidel told us that our imprisonment should be combative, and we should acquire rich experience from it, experience that would help in the continuation of the struggle once we are freed.[163]

A school was formed to improve the education of the men and to prepare them ideologically for the struggle ahead. Fellow inmates gave classes in mathematics, Spanish, geography, Cuban history, English, and philosophy.[164] The poorly educated men were amazed that there was so much to be learned and were grateful to those who taught them. However, the school, which never functioned well, was closed in late 1953. Fidel was again placed in solitary confinement. His cell had no electric light or water, but he managed to build an oil lamp in order to read works by Max Weber, Karl Mannheim, Anatole France, José Carlos Mariátegui, José Martí, and Balzac, among others. "The weeks are long," he said, "but a good book makes them shorter."[165]

In the solitude of prison Fidel worked out the revolutionary program for the movement. The July 1953 manifesto had dealt with generalities such as becoming identified with the programs of Joven Cuba, ABC Radical, and the Ortodoxo Party, as well as with the ideals of José Martí and other revolutionary leaders. But it was necessary to be more precise than simply to be in favor of diversification of agriculture, industrialization, and social justice.

On December 12, 1953, Castro wrote a letter to Luis Conte Agüero, a close friend and a major Ortodoxo spokesman.[166] In it he presented detailed information on the crimes committed against the men who had attacked the Moncada. He then stated, "If our revolutionary effort had succeeded, it was our objective to place power in the hands of the most devoted Ortodoxos." Clearly, Fidel was aware that he needed the aid of some of the PPC leaders to maintain any power within the party structure. He added, "Speak with Dr. Agramonte [Ortodoxo leader], and show him this letter. Tell him that we feel completely loyal to the purest ideals of Eduardo Chibás; that those who fell in Santiago de Cuba were militants of the party he founded." Fidel identified his followers with the party, hoping the party would reciprocate.

Once in control of Oriente's capital, the letter continued, the revolutionaries immediately would have decreed the six revolutionary laws

---

[163] Jesús Montané, "Del 26 de Julio de 1953 al 15 de Mayo de 1955," *Verde Olivo* (Havana), July 28, 1963, p. 22.

[164] Hilario Chaurrondo, "Con los muchachos del Moncada," *Diario de la Marina* (Havana), January 16, 1959, p. 8A.

[165] Conte Agüero, *Fidel Castro*, p. 196.

[166] "A Letter from Prison" in this volume.

cited in the letter. The letter was later condensed and issued as a manifesto to the Cuban people, but this document did not satisfy Fidel. He wanted a more dramatic and ideologically coherent statement around which to create a new revolutionary organization.

On February 20, 1954, Melba Hernández and Haydée Santamaría were released from prison, having served a six-month sentence. Both immediately established contact with Fidel in order to build a new organization and soon became Fidel's most efficient aides.

Despite his isolation, Fidel's morale was high. He eagerly outlined the steps to be taken and, thanks to his indifferent guards, issued orders to the two women. They soon asked Castro for a document that would explain the goals of the new revolutionary movement.[167]

In a letter on April 17, 1954, to Melba Hernández, Fidel confessed he was working on a pamphlet of great ideological importance.[168] He also emphasized the role of propaganda in a revolutionary struggle, saying that he considered it the "soul of every struggle" and stressing the need for an unceasing campaign to denounce the crimes of the regime. He also pointed out the need to coordinate all his followers and concluded:

> Deal with the people artfully and with a smile. Follow the same tactic used in the trial: Defend our viewpoints without making unnecessary enemies. There will be enough time later to crush all the cockroaches together.

Little by little, the manuscript was smuggled out of prison, to be printed in the underground. Melba and Haydée received instructions that outlined the format. Fidel even went so far as to tell them what kind of type face to use and how much space to leave between paragraphs. Then one day he ordered his aides to print 100,000 copies of the pamphlet. Haydée Santamaría recalls:

> When we were told by Fidel that we should print 100,000 copies of "History Will Absolve Me" we thought he had gone out of his mind in prison. How could we print 100,000 if 500 were almost impossible?[169]

To this objection Fidel replied that there was no difference between printing 25 copies and 100,000. It was just a matter of time and paper. Eventually, 10,000 copies were printed and distributed throughout the island by two men.

---

[167] Francisco de Armas, "Como se editó en la clandestinidad la primera edición de 'La historia me absolverá,' " *Hoy* (Havana), July 21, 1963, p. 4.

[168] The letter and the pamphlet are in this volume. The pamphlet, the famous "History Will Absolve Me," is a reconstruction of the speech allegedly made by Castro in his own behalf before the court months earlier.

[169] Haydée Santamaría, *Haydée habla del Moncada* (Havana: Instituto del Libro, 1967), p. 83.

The "History Will Absolve Me" pamphlet repeated charges made by Castro at his trial and elaborated on the crimes committed by the military. It also incorporated ideas that had appeared in Castro's letter of December 12, 1953, to Conte Agüero. The pamphlet, however, referred to only five, not six, revolutionary laws.[170]

The solutions to Cuba's social and political ills proposed in "History Will Absolve Me" were not original and hardly as radical as they may seem. Almost all the Cuban people had the same ideas, although it is questionable how much they really desired their implementation. Rather than doing away with private ownership, the document expressed a wish to extend it by expanding a rural and urban middle class.

The document, however, was not read by the population at large. A new revolutionary movement, Fidel rapidly realized, could not be formed from prison. He was also aware that his military fiasco had discredited the insurrectionist thesis. The majority of the Cubans wanted a solution to the nation's political crisis, and electoral politics seemed once again to be the only possibility.

As his influence declined, disillusionment took possession of him. Feeling powerless in his lonely cell, he burned with anger and frustration. At times he thought he could not endure it any longer. In a letter written on June 19, 1954, he stated:

> My situation cannot be any harder. I do not know whether it is the mental torture of being alone, or seeing the incredible things that are happening. How could these things [his solitary confinement] be done in Cuba with absolute impunity, and amidst the great indifference of almost everyone?[171]

His political concerns, however, were temporarily overshadowed by a personal crisis. On July 17, 1954, the minister of interior announced the dismissal of Mirta Díaz Balart, who had been receiving a sinecure through her brother, the undersecretary of interior. At first Fidel refused to believe that his wife had been on the Batista payroll. That very day he wrote to her, saying that he did not believe it, that it was slander and should be fought in court. "I understand your sadness, but count on my unconditional trust and love," he told her.[172] He thought someone else must have been taking checks in her name.

In a letter to Luis Conte Agüero, he called the charge "a damned,

[170] Castro referred to six revolutionary laws in his letter to Luis Conte Agüero (December 12, 1953); see this volume. The fifth law in the letter to Conte Agüero stated that all civil servants employed by the Batista regime were to be dismissed. This law was deleted in "History Will Absolve Me" (see text).
[171] Conte Agüero, *Fidel Castro*, p. 174.
[172] *Ibid.*, p. 183.

cowardly, indecent, intolerable, and base machination against me."[173] He reiterated that he trusted his wife and considered the whole thing an attempt to discredit him in the eyes of the Cuban people. He accused the minister of the interior of being effeminate and sexually degenerate, and he added:

> I am blinded by rage, I can hardly think anymore. I am ready to challenge my brother-in-law to a duel. The prestige of my wife and my revolutionary honor are at stake.[174]

The real blow fell on July 21 when Fidel learned through his sister, Lidia Castro, not only that the accusation against Mirta was true, but that she also had decided to terminate their marriage. His reaction was sorrowful but restrained. They were divorced in late December of that year.

This was a period of great tribulation for Fidel. Not only had his faith in his wife been crushed, but with the prospect of elections the influence of the insurrectionists was dwindling. He began to feel that perhaps all his work and sacrifice had been for nothing. Writing to Conte Agüero on July 31, 1954, he stated:

> I consider the movement above me, and the very moment I realize that I am not useful to the cause for which I have suffered so much, I will kill myself.[175]

For a time it seemed that Cuba might solve its crisis peacefully. In May 1954, Batista repealed the drastic measures giving him martial-law powers and declared an amnesty for political exiles and some political prisoners (the Moncadistas were excluded). He also promised to hold free and honest elections on November 1, 1954. But the opposition was ambivalent and divided, although a strong electoralist undercurrent predominated.

The Auténticos and Ortodoxos remained divided. The weak rapprochement reached at Montreal in June of 1953 ended a year later when Aureliano Sánchez Arango (an Auténtico leader) declared that Chibás had shot himself in 1951 as a publicity stunt. The Ortodoxo leaders immediately demanded that Carlos Prío deny Sánchez Arango's declaration. When he did not do so, the PPC in July 1954 broke entirely with the Auténticos, ending any possibility for a united front.[176]

The Auténticos also continued to be split between those who followed the electoralist position of Ramón Grau and those who stood

---

[173] *Ibid.*, p. 184.
[174] *Ibid.*, p. 185.
[175] *Ibid.*, p. 190.
[176] "La ruptura del Pacto de Montreal," *Bohemia* (Havana), July 4, 1954, p. 53; and *Hispanic American Report*, vol. 7, no. 7 (August 1954), p. 19.

for the insurrectionist ideas of the exiled Carlos Prío.[177] The Ortodoxos, on the other hand, attained an uneasy unity under the leadership of Raúl Chibás (brother of Eduardo). They favored what was termed *conditional electoralism.* They agreed to participate in the forthcoming elections only if Batista concurred with certain conditions: the restoration of the 1940 Constitution and the right to vote for individuals instead of entire tickets; the release of all political prisoners; the abrogation of all repressive laws; permission for all political exiles to return to the country; and the establishment of a neutral government six months prior to the election. Batista refused some of the conditions, and as a result the Ortodoxos decided not to participate.

On October 30, 1954, Ramón Grau withdrew from the presidential race because the elections would have been rigged, leaving Fulgencio Batista the only contender. Thus, on November 1, Batista won the presidency by default. He hoped that at last his regime would have legitimacy. An existing undercurrent, however, was to present him with a different situation.

Throughout the electoral campaign Fidel Castro opposed those who participated in it. He argued that if Batista, unable to win the elections of 1952, required a coup to achieve power, it would be childish to believe he would cede power if defeated in honest elections. But such a thing could not happen, since honest elections would not be permitted. That was why to participate in the elections was to play into the hands of a dictatorial and illegal regime. Fidel's followers also denounced the electoral farce. In every political meeting held by their adversaries they cried for violent revolution.

After Batista's uncontested "victory" at the polls, disillusionment was widespread. Electoral politics, after all, had not provided a real solution. Batista concluded that such a situation could lead to insurrection unless the people changed their minds about his government; he therefore began a policy of reshaping the regime's image.

The regime was torn by internal conflicts. Fulgencio Batista loved power and wanted to remain in office as long as possible. At the same time, he longed for the support of the Cuban people. It was the irreconcilable paradox of an illegitimate ruler dreaming of legitimacy. Thus, on some occasions he used repression against militant adversaries and then suddenly relaxed it, hoping to create a liberal environment in which his flexibility would win him support. Batista was caught in

---

[177] It is possible that Sánchez Arango made his declarations on purpose, for it would have made the Auténticos the only faction that espoused rebellion without being in prison. See Francisco Ichaso, "Polémica y tercer frente," *Bohemia* (Havana), June 27, 1954, p. 57.

a vicious cycle. Repression was followed by a liberal policy that allowed opponents to challenge his rule, making repression a necessity once again.

Both tendencies had advocates within the regime. The *tanquistas* (tank section of the army) favored repression and disregarded even the mere façade of constitutional government; the "civilians" (led by Prime Minister Jorge García Montes) hoped to find a peaceful solution to Cuba's political conflicts. The "civilians" believed that the trust of the Cubans would be won through maximum restraint.

Batista was caught in the middle. He used his power and influence to play one group against the other, aware that he could not be totally dependent on either. Thus, whenever the militarists seemed to increase in power, Batista would move in the opposite direction until he had no choice but to join those who favored a harder line.

The regime's contradictions were successfully exploited by Fidel. In the late summer of 1954, knowing that Batista wanted to move toward a constitutional democracy, Castro from his cell began to inspire a campaign for the release of all political prisoners. The campaign, led by Luis Conte Agüero, centered on Fidel, who was presented as a "rebel," and made him better known in the eyes of the public.

Fidel's followers argued that it was politically imperative to release all political opponents if the government hoped to acquire legitimacy.[178] The campaign for amnesty continued for almost a year. Many prominent and influential individuals raised their voices on behalf of the prisoners, and finally the government relented. On May 7, 1955, Batista signed the law granting amnesty. Eight days later, Castro and the other twenty–nine Moncadistas were released. He had served twenty-two months of a fifteen-year sentence.

Political Struggle in Cuba

On his release on May 15, 1955, Fidel embraced an army officer at the prison door. He tried to express his friendship toward the military. The revolutionaries, he argued, did not go to the Moncada Barracks to fight against the soldiers. Rather, they had wished to struggle against just one man. Then he added, "Against the Cuban army we have no ill feelings, and we feel admiration and respect for the courageous soldiers who died there."[179]

[178] Luis Conte Agüero, "Traslado a la Cabaña," *Diario Nacional* (Santiago), April 5, 1955.
[179] Conte Agüero, *Fidel Castro*, p. 230. It should be pointed out that some soldiers appear to have supported the Moncada attack.

Fidel was trying to sow dissent. There were sectors of the armed forces that vehemently opposed his release, while some government officials and officers favored it, hoping to create a peaceful and orderly climate. At the same time, Fidel expressly urged the holding of immediate general elections to resolve the political difficulties of the nation.[180] New elections were imperative, but unacceptable to a regime that persisted in its selfish power hunger. Batista instead promised to hold elections in 1958 when his term supposedly ended.

Fidel devoted most of his energies to excoriating the regime and organizing the future 26th of July Movement cadres. The November 1954 elections, he pointed out, had been a mockery. In several articles the regime's conciliatory measures were presented for what they truly were: a sham that hid the reality of oppression. Behind the façade of flexibility, he said, remained the fact that the regime lacked legitimacy and was unwilling to give up any of its power. It was clear to him that the government did not have the slightest desire to find peace. And whenever he could, he continued to denounce the murders of his comrades. Batista was mercilessly damned. The government's spokesmen were quick to reply. Using all sorts of epithets, they threatened the lives of the Moncadistas and that of Fidel in particular.[181] The uneasy truce between government and opposition was collapsing.

On May 21, 1955, the PPC released a manifesto that Fidel had helped to draw up. It stated that Cuba was now in an economic crisis owing to the lack of funds and credits, a public debt amounting to $652 million, and the government's restriction on sugar production. The "economic crisis," continued the manifesto, "has given rise to a social crisis in which salaries have declined and unemployment [has been] augmented." There also existed "political persecution of the opposition, the enrichment of the government officials by privilege, fraud, illegal gambling, smuggling, and administrative corruption." Like Fidel's earlier statement, the Ortodoxos affirmed:

> We do not fight against military institutions. This is a struggle against a regime that began with the complicity of some members of the armed forces.[182]

Rather than calling for immediate general elections, the PPC presented the following conditions in order to begin any type of meaningful discussions with the government: (1) restoration of the 1940

[180] "Retornan al seno de la familia cubana los presos sancionados por causas de origen político, *Diario de la Marina* (Havana), May 17, 1955, pp. 1, 16A.
[181] See "Murderers' Hands" in this volume.
[182] "En un manifiesto ratifica su ideología la Ortodoxia unida," *Diario de la Marina* (Havana), May 22, 1955, pp. 1, 2A.

Constitution; (2) complete constitutional guarantees to the opposition, including political exiles; (3) cessation of attacks on citizens; and (4) an end to censorship.

Three days later Batista responded. On May 24, 1955, Ortodoxo radio and television programs were suspended by decree. After the publication of an article in the leading Cuban magazine *Bohemia* on May 29[183] in which Fidel persisted in his condemnation of Batista, Castro was prevented from making any public speeches. He was permitted, nonetheless, to continue writing. The regime was showing its reluctance or ambivalence toward going to extremes as well as recognizing Fidel's magnificent and dramatic oratorical skills.

Freedom of the press became a dangerous weapon. The assassinations committed in July 1953 by the military were finally disclosed. The people were shocked, becoming further alienated from a regime already lacking in legitimacy. In his daily columns, Fidel hurled fulminating accusations, contributing to the further erosion of the regime's credibility.

Feelings and emotions ran high. The military, in an ugly mood, demanded a stern hand from the government. In the meantime, the moderates in the Batista administration watched in dismay as their hopes for normalcy withered. The police began a wave of beatings and assassinations that was paralleled only by the terrorist activities of some opposition groups.

Bombs exploded daily throughout the island, destroying buildings with little strategic value or relation to the regime. The implacable logic of these clandestine groups was simply centered on fomenting chaos. Having no concern with political realities, they had no use for propaganda or proselytism. Fidel disagreed with their tactics. Terrorism, he argued, only benefited the regime. He expressly alleged that the bombings were probably the work of provocateurs trying to discredit the revolutionary cause, and they also offered real justification for a more dictatorial and repressive stand by the government.[184] He wanted no part of it.

Publicly assuming the role of favoring peace, Fidel even stated that armed struggle was not necessary to bring about a revolution. "Sometimes, a mass movement," he emphasized, "can accomplish what an insurrection cannot."[185] Privately, however, he thought otherwise. He clearly perceived the political situation in its true dimensions. Batista wanted to continue in power, and only armed insurrection could remove him. But before engaging in revolutionary violence, Fidel

---

[183] "Chaviano, You Lie!" in this volume.
[184] "Against Terror and Crime" in this volume.
[185] *El País* (Havana), May 21, 1955, p. 1.

perceptively maintained, it was necessary to demonstrate to the Cuban people that there was no other path left because of the regime's inflexibility. Revolution was a last resort encouraged by the enemy.

Jesús Montané, one of the Moncada survivors, has stated that on the very day they were released, the twenty-nine men ratified their decision to continue armed struggle.[186] Their function, however, would be to agitate in such a manner as to demonstrate the oppressive character of the government. While appearing to favor peaceful struggle, they were to create an insurrectionary consciousness in the people. Political ferment had to be utilized to the utmost, as well as the regime's promises of respect for freedom of expression.

A small cadre composed of Fidel's closest associates dedicated itself to carrying out those goals. In doing so, they were following the organizational lines developed by their leader in prison. The revolutionary movement, Fidel had written in prison, would have to be formed at first around the core of men who had attacked the Moncada: "I have to organize the men of the 26th of July and unite in an unbreakable body all of these fighters who are in exile, prison, or in the streets."[187] This detachment, united by ties of friendship, common experience, and sacrifice, numbered close to eighty men. Fidel affirmed that this revolutionary vanguard would be characterized by perfect discipline, constituting "a valuable resource in order to form fighting cadres for peaceful or insurrectionary goals." Afterward, they would form a "large civic and political movement that will command the necessary force to conquer power by peaceful or revolutionary means." Declaring that the primary task was that of uniting his closest followers and associates, Fidel argued, "our task should be, first of all, that of uniting our fighters. It would be lamentable if widespread desertions occurred in our ranks because of a lack of persuasion." Elaborating on his ideas, he maintained that, beginning with what he had at the moment, he expected an extraordinary multiplication of forces to follow which would "defeat the reigning political system." He then added:

> The indispensable conditions for the formation of a true civic movement are ideology, discipline, and leadership. The three are essential, but leadership is basic. . . . A movement cannot be organized in which everyone believes himself to have the right to issue public statements without consulting anyone; nor can anything be expected of a movement integrated by anarchic men who at the first disagreement take the post they consider most convenient, breaking and destroying the structure. The propaganda and organizational apparatus should be such and so powerful that

---

[186] Montané, "Del 26 de Julio de 1953 al 15 de Mayo de 1955," p. 23.
[187] Conte Agüero, *Fidel Castro*, p. 192.

it would implacably destroy anyone who tries to create tendencies, cliques, schisms, or rebels against the movement.[188]

These ideas were not publicized. Rather, Fidel continued to speak of peaceful struggle. Some young Ortodoxos at first were surprised with this position; after all, he was now their leader, and the party recognized him as its hero. Their fears were somewhat assuaged, however, after Fidel, on being offered a post in the party leadership council, declined the offer.[189] He argued that he had not fought for a post, nor did he want to be co-opted into such a position. Fidel preferred to function at the grass-roots level, close to the people, and with a greater degree of freedom of action to form a revolutionary organization.

Fidel enthusiastically gathered his closest associates to form the first revolutionary cells. No exact date can be pinpointed as to when the first organizational session took place. The difficult task of ascertaining the date is complicated by contradictory accounts by participants. The plan was undoubtedly conceived in its primitive stages while Fidel was in prison. According to Haydée Santamaría, the first meeting at which it was agreed to establish a revolutionary structure that would function within the Ortodoxo movement took place on May 15, 1955. Faustino Pérez provides a different account. He claims that the 26th of July Movement was formed in Havana "around mid-1955" when Castro was still in Cuba.[190] A still different version offers July 19, 1955, as the date of the creation of the revolutionary movement in Mexico.[191]

Fidel in Exile

Underground activities became ever more difficult. Fidel met government resistance and threats wherever he turned. He soon concluded that it was impossible for him to set up the conspirational structure he needed. Thus, on July 7, 1955, he left Cuba. Before departing, he composed a letter to prominent political leaders which stated:

[188] Conte Agüero, *Fidel Castro*, pp. 192–193.

[189] "Constítuido el Consejo Director del P.P.C.," *Diario de la Marina* (Havana), May 15, 1955, p. 2A.

[190] Faustino Pérez, "La lucha contra Batista," *El Mundo* (Havana), December 2, 1964, pp. 1, 7.

[191] Theodore Draper states that the M-26-7 (26th of July Movement) was "formally launched" on July 19, 1955. René Ray (the source used by Draper) does not provide such an explicit statement. Rather, he declares in a very confusing sentence (the sentence begins with one date and ends with another) that the "idea of organizing the 26th of July Movement was conceived" in a meeting held either on May or July 19, 1955. Ray states that Faustino Pérez was at the meeting. If that is the case, then the meeting was held in Cuba because Pérez was *not* in Mexico at the time. See Theodore Draper, *Castroism: Theory and Practice* (New York: Praeger, 1965), and Ray (ed.), *Libertad y revolución*, p. 11.

> I am leaving Cuba because all doors of peaceful struggle have
> been closed to me. . . . I will reside somewhere in the Caribbean.
> From trips such as this, one does not return, or else one returns
> with the tyranny beheaded at one's feet.[192]

A month later from Mexico City, Fidel presented the reasons for his
departure in greater detail. Every instrument of power, he said, had
been successfully used to silence him. This demonstrated the extent
to which any type of "moral protest" was doomed because of the
"shameful coalition of oppression, vested interests, and general hypocrisy." He added that "only the unconditional supporters of the regime
or those who play the game of a docile and inoffensive opposition have
the right to meet freely."[193] Immediate general elections without
Batista were the only decent and honorable conditions for a compromise. If the regime did not accept it, revolution was the only possible
course.

Origins of the 26th of July Movement. Many in the opposition thought
otherwise. Traditional politicians and civic leaders, hoping a compromise could be reached, fostered a "civic dialogue" between the government and the opposition through the auspices of the Sociedad de
Amigos de la República (SAR), headed by Cosme de la Torriente.[194]

Members of the SAR were convinced that their fear of revolution
would be shared by the regime, and that that fear would force the regime to call for a new presidential election. Time would prove their
premise ill founded, but 1955 momentarily, at least, seemed to offer
a future to the moderate forces in Cuban politics. This hope was
strengthened when Carlos Prío, who had been one of the oppositionists
favoring violence, had a change of heart after a plan to assassinate
Batista was uncovered.[195] In mid-August, Prío stated that the opposition had to engage in political rather than military struggle. On Au-

---

[192] "Letter to Prominent Political Leaders" in this volume.

[193] "Manifesto No. 1 to the People of Cuba" in this volume. It should be noted
that Theodore Draper confuses this manifesto issued on August 8, 1955, with the
"Message to the Congress of Ortodoxo Militants" (August 15, 1955) and an article written in *Bohemia* (December 25, 1955), all of which appear in this volume.
See Draper, *Castroism: Theory and Practice,* footnote 11.

[194] A veteran of the war of independence, de la Torriente formed a mediation
committee in 1933 to find a peaceful solution between the opposition and Machado's dictatorship. See Francisco Ichaso, "Hacia el diálogo cívico," *Bohemia*
(Havana), August 28, 1955, pp. 39, 112.

[195] "José Antonio Echeverría en el tiempo y en la acción," *Revolución* (Havana), March 13, 1963, pp. 8-9; *Hispano* (Mexico), August 15, 1955, p. 28. The
plot was to be carried out by the Organización Auténtica of Prío and the university students around José A. Echeverría (at the time leader of the University
Federation).

gust 11, 1955, after three years in exile, he returned to Havana with the government's permission to participate in the civic dialogue.

Fidel, observing from Mexico, was appalled by the state of national confusion and uncertainty. For political leaders to choose compromise, he said, simply disoriented the masses at a moment when it was necessary to show the true colors of the regime. The choices were obvious to Fidel: revolution or submission. On several occasions he warned against "those who advise you to submit."[196] Three days before the return of the deposed president, Fidel issued a manifesto announcing the formation of a revolutionary movement that would use violence to oust the government.

> The 26th of July Movement is formed without hatred for anyone. It is not a political party but a revolutionary movement. Its ranks are open to all Cubans who sincerely desire to see political democracy reestablished and social justice introduced in Cuba. Its leadership is collective and secret, formed by new men of strong will who are not accomplices of the past.

The program, which was defined as "broad and courageous," consisted of fifteen points (see text).[197]

Young Cubans who could not accept conciliatory moves were attracted by Fidel's militancy. Many joined his cadres to fight against the civic dialogue in order to intensify the nascent revolutionary mood. At every rally the Fidelistas cried out for revolution, and they painted revolutionary slogans throughout the country. The number "26" was found on walls, bathrooms, schoolrooms, restaurants–everywhere. It symbolized the growing rebellious spirit of a generation. Fidel Castro and his followers were carrying on a twofold political struggle. On the one hand, they fought the regime; on the other, the moderate opposition. From Mexico, Fidel issued orders to his men in Cuba: Organizing the revolutionaries, denouncing the electoralists, and infiltrating the Ortodoxo movement were the most important aims.[198]

On August 15, 1955, the Ortodoxo Party held a national congress to discuss whether to participate in SAR's civic dialogue. The national leadership favored such a move, whereas the Fidelistas did not miss the

[196] For example, "Manifesto No. 1 to the People of Cuba" in this volume.

[197] *Ibid.* Point 12 of this program, which calls for legislation against discrimination based on race or sex, contradicts Hugh Thomas's assertion that racial discrimination was a matter that "Castro never mentioned . . . in any of his speeches or programmes before the revolution." Thomas, *Cuba*, p. 1121.

[198] In 1955 the underground leaders of the M–26–7 in Cuba were Armando Hart, Faustino Pérez, Haydée Santamaría, Melba Hernández, Pedro Miret, Antonio López, José Suárez, Pedro Aguilera, and Luis Bonito.

opportunity to present their position and demand a revolutionary line. Throughout the meeting the latter sought converts among the young delegates and at the end read a message sent to the delegates by Fidel Castro. This message, distributed in mimeographed form, stated that if the members of the Ortodoxo movement believed in the possibility of immediate general elections, they were either naïve or fools, for Batista would never consent to presidential elections. Furthermore, to recognize an illegitimate, dictatorial, and discredited regime, he argued, would be a betrayal of the party's principles. The time had come, the message continued, for the Ortodoxos to decide on a clear and positive position. The party had to demonstrate its readiness to fight for the people's rights, and it was difficult to believe that the smallest concession from the dictatorship could be gained if demands were introduced "with a beatific confession of pacifism."[199]

The delegates applauded the document with great enthusiasm. At that moment Faustino Pérez, a Fidelista leader, took over the microphone and urged a more concrete demonstration of support for the revolutionary line. Faustino recalls that "for the first time in my life I spoke in public and proposed to that huge assembly that the strategy of armed insurrection and the general strike be adopted."[200] The 500 delegates from all parts of Cuba unanimously approved the proposal, rejecting all negotiation and compromise. Immediately afterward the delegates adjourned, escaping a police raid by mere seconds.

The revolutionary thesis of the Fidelistas had at last been adopted by a political party. For the first time a national political organization clearly stood for armed struggle, but the Fidelista victory was primarily symbolic, for in subsequent months the party leadership continued to seek accommodation with the government. Nonetheless, the victory of the revolutionary line at the congress was the direct consequence of a daring and committed group of young men who carried out Fidel's orders to the best of their abilities.

Too often these young people, totally dedicated to revolution, have been forgotten, while Fidel Castro has been given disproportionate recognition. Clearly, Fidel inspired many who were drawn by his charisma and far-reaching perception or were impressed by his ideas. But these youths also felt a missionary zeal; they saw themselves as a group with a destiny to fulfill. They were men and women with a boundless faith in the regeneration of the nation.

Youthful revolt was a response to brutal police violence. It was the

---

199 "Message to the Congress of the Ortodoxo Militants" in this volume.
200 Faustino Pérez, "La lucha contra Batista," *El Mundo* (Havana), December 2, 1964, pp. 1, 7.

product of concrete, arbitrary torture rather than the consequence of intellectual protest. Politicians could justify an understanding with the government; after all, it was youth who suffered most under Batista. To be young was sufficient cause to incur the capricious wrath of the police. Hence, youth would opt for revolution, old professional politicians for compromise. The year 1955 marked the parting of the ways, because the older generation was merely aware of the prevailing climate of terror and brutality, whereas the youth of Cuba experienced it firsthand.

The Call for Revolution. Meanwhile, the nonpartisan solution sought by SAR faced numerous obstacles. Cosme de la Torriente, on several occasions, sought to have personal discussions with Batista, hoping he could persuade the president to hold new elections. But prior to December 1955 Batista refused to have any sort of conversation. This rejection by the government provided Fidel with more arguments to denounce mediation. In a speech to Cuban émigrés in New York on November 1, 1955, he predicted that "in 1956 we will be free or we will be martyrs." He then proceeded to analyze the civic dialogue movement, pointing out that the regime had clearly refused to listen to the proposals of the opposition groups presented through the SAR. If the government did not want compromise, Fidel continued, it would be faced with revolution. If the opposition refused to take the road of armed struggle, the men of the 26th of July Movement would discredit and intimidate them:

> The militants of the 26th of July Movement will attend all the meetings to be organized in Cuba, regardless what opposition party organizes them, to shout a speech for the masses: Revolution! Revolution! Anyone who gets permission for a public meeting can count on an assured public.[201]

The Fidelistas had the opportunity to implement their tactics at a mass meeting held on November 19, 1955, in Havana by SAR. The gathering, one of the largest in Cuba's history prior to 1959, was called to show popular support for Cosme de la Torriente's electoral formula. The views of SAR were backed by major opposition leaders, including the national leadership of the Auténticos and Ortodoxos. One speaker after the other, expressing the naïve hopes of most of the people, denounced violence while pleading for general elections. Revolutionists in the crowd at the same time fervently called for revolution while constantly cheering Fidel Castro.[202]

[201] "Speech in New York" in this volume.
[202] Mario Riera Hernández, *Cuba Libre, 1895–1958* (Miami: Colonial Press, 1968), p. 197.

Lacking a consensus, the people became progressively enraged at the rally, which ended in violence and chaos. Fistfights and the throwing of bricks and chairs terminated the rally that had been called in support of peaceful political struggle. The dissatisfaction of young oppositionists toward their elders had taken a significant turn. Hectic times were to follow, in which the moderates would be increasingly intimidated by revolutionists and government authorities alike.

Several days later, still in exile, Castro spoke to his sympathizers in Miami. There he denounced the "embezzlers" who had joined SAR. "It was a depressing spectacle," he said, "to listen at the SAR meeting to the voices of men who have enriched themselves in power, who represent no moral ideals, and who are as guilty of Cuba's ills as Batista himself." The embezzlers, he argued, had joined the opposition to exonerate themselves, but in fact they were the friends of the dictatorship.[203]

The political atmosphere of Cuba was propitious for violence. Confronted with an inflexible and often confused regime, plus a large segment of the opposition seeking pacification, revolutionaries, independent of Castro's movement, sprang up to pursue a deliberate policy of intrigue.

In late November of 1955, several leaders of the University Student Federation (FEU) met secretly to analyze the existing political situation. Led by José A. Echevarría, FEU president, the group concluded that armed struggle had become imperative. Faure Chomón, who participated in the meeting, recollects that an agreement was reached as to how indispensable it was to "accentuate the insurrectionary consciousness of the people by the radicalization of massive demonstrations." Violence was to be incorporated into all types of political demonstrations, Chomón stated, because "that would emphasize much more the oppressive and criminal characteristics of the tyranny and would augment popular discontent, thus strengthening the insurrectionist line." Furthermore, the conspirators calculated that violent demonstrations would liquidate conciliation, "the electoral promises of the tyranny, and provoke the closing of the university, which would stigmatize the pseudo-opposition cooperating with the dictatorship."[204]

Soon a wave of student riots and demonstrations swept the island. On November 27, FEU organized meetings in more than a dozen cities to commemorate eight students murdered by Spanish colonialism in 1871. In Santiago de Cuba and Havana many students were brutally beaten by the police, more than ten were wounded, and about fifty

---

[203] "Speech at Flagler Theater" in this volume.
[204] Javier Rodríguez, "José Antonio Echevarría y la clase obrera," *Bohemia* (Havana), March 10, 1967, p. 53.

were arrested. But the students, anticipating the police reaction, had organized armed cadres to retaliate.[205] On November 29, FEU protested the numerous arrests and insisted on carrying out a three-day national student strike to express solidarity with the arrested men. In the succeeding days only primary schools remained open, while a series of clashes between the police and students developed at the university and several high schools in the capital.

On December 1, 1955, all meetings were banned by the minister of the interior because they were used to incite revolution, but the next day university students, led by Echevarría of the FEU, marched from the steps of Havana University to the home of the SAR leader. They were to deliver a statement proclaiming that revolution remained the only path open to those who truly opposed dictatorship. The organizers, once again, counted on the brutality of the police to enhance their revolutionary cause. The students had formed an armed commando unit that shot at the police as they tried to break up the demonstration. Several persons, students as well as policemen, were wounded in the encounter. Faure Chomón, a member of the commandos, affirms that throughout those hectic days the students continued to attack the police. On a number of occasions policemen were wounded in order to encourage violent repression, to destroy any possibility of compromise, and to "augment the people's hatred toward the dictatorship."[206]

Another incident occurred on December 4, when the Cuban national baseball championship game in Havana was interrupted by fifteen students who rushed onto the field carrying banners reading "Abajo Batista!" (Down with Batista!). The police savagely beat the helpless youths in the middle of the baseball field. This event had deep national repercussions because thousands of persons witnessed the whole affair on television.

Clashes persisted. On the anniversary of the death of Antonio Maceo (December 7, 1955), a black leader of the independence struggle, more rallies were held in spite of government threats. Throughout the island dozens were arrested or injured; in Ciego de Avila, Camagüey Province, Raúl Cervantes was mortally wounded. The popular Ortodoxo youth leader died three days later. "Instantly he became a new martyr whose funeral was made into a gigantic symbol of political protest."[207]

In a public declaration on December 12, 1955, FEU stated:

> Because of the series of outrages that the students and people of Cuba have recently suffered from the repressive forces of the dic-

205 *Ibid.* This fact was not disclosed by the revolutionists until after 1959.
206 *Ibid.*
207 Suchlicki, *University Students*, p. 68.

tatorship, the FEU has chosen December 14 as the Day of Popular Protest. The protest will consist in all workers and people stopping their labor for five minutes at 10:00 A.M.[208]

The temporary national strike was a success despite the moves and precautions taken by the regime and the Batista-dominated labor unions. The collective protest, improvised in less than two days, represented the first national mobilization of the people since 1952. Meanwhile, the dissatisfaction of sugar workers spread because of a decline in wages and the arbitrary price of sugar, set by the sugar producers in order not to have to give a bonus to the workers. The revolutionists of FEU, who in early December 1955 had formed the Directorio Revolucionario (DR) as the armed instrument of FEU, established contacts with labor leaders and organized a sugar workers' strike.[209] They argued that it was now time for the students to show their solidarity with the labor movement.

On December 20, half a million workers unleashed the strike. Militants of DR were to be found throughout the countryside. The government reacted violently, imprisoning, beating, and shooting the proletariat. The workers fought the police, the rural guard, and the military while taking control of twelve sugar towns, blocking all traffic through the central provinces, and closing down thirteen sugar mills.

The demands of the sugar workers for extra wages were granted by Batista on December 30, 1955, over the persistent opposition of wealthy sugar producers. This was done because the government was threatened by an economic strike that began to develop into a political instrument to remove Batista. Thus the regime's survival took precedence over the interests of the sugar producers. The move alienated the latter but successfully dampened the fiery revolutionary momentum and ended the newly created student-worker alliance. Economics took precedence over politics in the eyes of the proletariat, and the regime considered political power more important than the assurance of profitable returns for a small circle of supporters.

Concurrent with the disorders in the island, Castro had traveled to the United States to organize the exiles and émigrés behind his leadership and build the financial backbone of the M–26–7 (26th of July Movement). In a letter on October 8, 1955, Fidel outlined his planned

[208] Rodríguez, "José Antonio Echevarría," p. 53.
[209] The best published account of the DR can be found in Suchlicki, *University Students*, pp. 70–86. The DR was formed by José A. Echevarría, Fructuoso Rodríguez, Joe Westbrook, Tirso Urdanivia, René Anillo, Faure Chomón, Jorge Valls, Felix Armando Murias, Julio García, Wilfredo Ventura, Orlando Blanco, Rodríguez Loeches, and others.

campaign to unite Cubans in an "orderly, serious, and large-scale movement" that would bring about the liberation of Cuba as well as a
"radical and profound change in the national life."[210] With the assistance of various exile associations, he soon formed "Patriotic Clubs of
the 26th of July" in New York City, Washington, Bridgeport, Chicago,
Philadelphia, Union City, Miami, Tampa, and Key West. Fidel was
consciously repeating the organizational methods used by José Martí
in the 1890s when he structured the exile community in such a way as
to make the waging of a liberation war successful. He consistently
emphasized a major theme: The émigrés have been forgotten by
everyone, but they will be the ones to help Cuba liberate itself from a
dictatorship and change the socioeconomic circumstances that forced
them to seek jobs in the United States.

In a manifesto issued on December 10, 1955, he asserted that seven
weeks of tireless effort devoted to organizing the Cubans from the
Canadian border to Key West had produced "the best of results."
Urging each unemployed émigré to donate a dollar a week and those
working the earnings of one day's labor a month, Fidel noted that he
had dedicated himself to an austere life. He felt that he had the "moral
authority and courage" to ask for financial assistance because he was
giving the country his youth and his life "without asking anything of
anyone" for himself. He concluded with the warning that no form of
collection through coercion or violence was supported by the movement.[211]

Three days later, in a letter to the committee heading the New York
Patriotic Club, Fidel commented in despair that, although he had believed the émigrés of that city would give him aid, they had not done
so. "In New York, where the Patriotic Club enjoys the greatest enthusiasm of the émigrés, everything is in sad shape." Charging that the
reason for this lay in personality clashes, Fidel hinted that the leadership of the club should be unified. On December 24, 1955, he again
wrote to the New York club:

> Although at first I agreed with the idea of different clubs in the
> city of New York, I am now convinced that the ideal thing would
> be to unite all efforts in one single large club.[212]

He went on to add that a drive to gain 1,000 members, each paying
two dollars per week, had to begin immediately if the movement was
to survive. After two weeks without an answer, Fidel again wrote to
his followers in New York. Why had he received no letters in reply?

[210] Conte Agüero, *Fidel Castro*, p. 322.
[211] "Manifesto No. 2 to the People of Cuba" in this volume.
[212] Conte Agüero, *Fidel Castro*, p. 349. Text quotation preceding p. 345.

Had they been lost? No, he concluded that the leaders of the Patriotic Club in New York were irresponsible, lacked loyalty, and had forgotten their friendship toward him. He then asked for a weekly report.

Fidel's discouragement can be discerned from a letter written to Celestino Rodríguez, leader of a Patriotic Club in Bridgeport, Connecticut, on February 12, 1956:

> At times I have the feeling that in the comfortable refuge of a country where work is abundant and high salaries are earned, where the people are not forced from their homes in the middle of the night, or tortured or persecuted, the émigrés forget the desperate situation of our brothers in Cuba.[213]

Moreover, grave differences had arisen between Fidel and the leaders of the Ortodoxo Party. The conflict revolved around what type of stand the party should take, and the issue was to a large degree determined by Batista's co-optation tactics at the end of December 1955. At that moment it was necessary for Fulgencio Batista to avert an uprising. He desperately needed time to "pacify" (repress) the students while keeping the major political parties passive. Thus, in the first week of 1956 Batista invited the leader of SAR to a meeting at which it was agreed that a peaceful solution had to be found. The president-dictator gave the impression that he would grant the opposition's demands for presidential elections and agreed to another meeting at the end of the month. At that point, many thought it was unnecessary to continue the violent struggle if the regime really meant what it promised. The calm that Batista needed returned, and moderate politics once again seemed a possibility.

Fidel's Rift with the Ortodoxos. The Ortodoxo Party, which throughout the disorders of late 1955 between the students, workers, and the police denounced conciliatory moves, remained the major obstacle. To be successful, any dialogue needed to have their participation. Thus, in early February 1956, SAR publicly exhorted the PPC to join discussions with the government in order to achieve peace.

On February 20, the Ortodoxo leaders responded by agreeing to consider the matter at a future meeting. This was a complete reversal of the resolution passed by the party congress seven months earlier when revolutionary methods had been proclaimed.

Nonetheless, the party leadership, which in private disagreed with the rank and file, met on February 23, 1956, in order to take a definitive

---

[213] "Letter to Celestino Rodríguez" in this volume.

stand.[214] As the leaders met at the home of Dr. Manuel Dorta Duque in a Havana suburb, a crowd gathered in the street and shouted "Down with the traitors!" "Down with mediation!" Despite the harassment, deliberations began. In the middle of the discussion the group made up of Castro's followers had assembled outside the house, although guards had been set up by the national leadership. What ensued has been described by a participant:

> We painted signs and posters rejecting any mediation attempts by the Ortodoxos. Then we proceeded to Dorta Duque's home and assembled in front of his house, though they did not bother about our demonstration. Later we decided to enter the house according to the instructions given to us by Antonio López [one of the underground coordinators of the M-26-7 in Cuba]. As we attempted to force our way in, we realized that some people inside were armed with steel pipes and bats. A fight followed in which we used our posters. One of our friends was hit on the head and bled profusely. It had not been our intention to use violence, but at any rate we broke up the meeting.[215]

Soon afterward the police arrived and dispersed the demonstrators. The meeting continued, and Antonio López, who had arrived, then stated to the leaders of the PPC: "Gentlemen, we oppose conversations with the government, but we repudiate what has occurred here. The 26th of July Movement has nothing to do with it."[216] The Ortodoxo leaders were not satisfied and demanded a condemnation of the event from Fidel Castro himself. They also agreed to enter negotiations with the regime, as all other opposition parties already had done. This initiated a wave of recriminations from the Ortodoxo Party and the 26th of July Movement which culminated in their definitive break.

In an article written from Mexico on March 5, 1956, Fidel replied to the PPC leadership.[217] He began by asserting that he did not owe an explanation to anyone, because he was not responsible for the events that had taken place. The national leadership, he continued, had no right to suppose that the 26th of July Movement had anything to do with the disruption. It was a cynical accusation, just as the regime had viciously spread the myth that the Fidelistas were violent crim-

[214] The meeting was attended by Raúl Chibás, Luis Conte Agüero, José Iglesias, Armando Muza, Ernesto Stock, Raúl Primelles, Mario Rivadulla, Marta Freyre, Pastora Núñez, Nasario Sargen, Rubén Acosta, Omar Borges, Erasmo Gómez, Max Lesnick, Enrique Barroso, José Manuel Gutiérrez, Roberto Agramonte, Pelayo Cuervo, and Manuel Bisbé.
[215] Interview with Miguel Roché, Washington, D.C., March 17, 1970.
[216] "Ortodoxos," *Bohemia* (Havana), March 4, 1956, p. 71.
[217] "The Condemnation They Demand of Us" in this volume.

inals. If the M–26–7 had promoted "the unfortunate incident," he pointed out, "we would not hesitate to say so publicly." He also added, "I cannot justify by any means" those who interrupted the meeting, "but I can understand it perfectly: It was a spontaneous and lawless action by unorganized elements of the masses." Who was to be blamed? The Ortodoxo leadership, Fidel replied, because it had changed from a radical to a conservative position, thereby deceiving their own rank and file. The incident was the consequence of the change. Fidel ended by insinuating that a break between the 26th of July Movement and the Ortodoxo Party seemed imminent, although "it would be profoundly painful," since the national leaders persisted in their erroneous position.

The Fidelista outlook was strengthened on the third anniversary of the coup d'état. On March 10, 1955, Fulgencio Batista spoke to the Cuban people announcing presidential elections for the *end* of his term in 1958. The civic dialogue, and all moderate or peaceful solutions, had been rejected by the regime. Nine days later Fidel Castro, after several disputes with Ortodoxo representatives, formally broke with the party.[218]

After repeating that the M–26–7 did not constitute a tendency within the party but was simply the revolutionary apparatus of the followers of Eduardo Chibás, Fidel stated:

> The 26th of July Movement is not different from the Ortodoxo Party for the followers of Chibás. It is the Ortodoxo movement without a leadership of landlords . . . without sugar-plantation owners . . . without stock-market speculators, without commercial and industrial magnates, without lawyers for the big interests or provincial chieftains, without incompetent politicians of any kind.[219]

It soon became evident that the military on whom Batista depended to maintain his power was not the monolithic force it was purported to be. Within the military there were the advocates of repressive measures and complete military control. Known as the *tanquistas* because their leadership originated in the tank corps, they had participated in the coup of 1952. There were also the *puros* ("pure ones"), who had not supported the coup. On April 3, 1956, a planned coup by the *puros*, who also favored civilian control and a return to democratic government, was aborted, and the conspirators were arrested. They had

---

[218] For the Ortodoxo viewpoint as expressed by the national leadership, see Enrique Barroso Dorta, "Palos si bogas, y palos si no bogas," *Bohemia* (Havana), March 18, 1956, pp. 53, 81.
[219] "The 26th of July Movement" in ths volume.

planned to arrest Batista and hold immediate general elections.[220] Referring to the *puros*, Fidel said, "One of the first measures of the victorious revolution will be the reinstatement of those honest military men to their posts."[221] But the division within the military had moved the regime toward a more recalcitrant position in which issues were solved by ruthless repression and a strong hand.

As unrest continued, the revolutionaries became further convinced that the military was crumbling from within. The opportune time for action, they felt, had arrived. During the month of April several confrontations between police and students took place. On the twenty-ninth of that month the Goicuría Barracks in the city of Matanzas was attacked by an action group belonging to Carlos Prío's Organización Auténtica (OA). The OA militants were displeased with Prío's conciliatory maneuvers and intended with their attack to put an end to them by directly implicating the Auténtico leader. The military assault ended in a fiasco, as the men, crying "Viva Prío!" entered the barracks and were cut down by machine-gun fire. Nonetheless, the attack was politically successful. The death of thirteen revolutionists forced Carlos Prío to go into exile. Fidel compared the murder of the attackers to the Moncada:

> It is clear that the government was well informed about the planned attack on the barracks. The government could have prevented it; nevertheless, it preferred the massacre.[222]

Forming the Expeditionary Force

With unrest spreading in Cuba, Fidel in Mexico organized incessantly. At first, in mid-1955, with little money and few weapons or men, he asked Colonel Alberto Bayo, an instructor at the School of Military Aviation in Mexico, to aid him in the training of the men who would invade Cuba.[223] When Bayo, a Cuban who had fought as a guerrilla in the Spanish Civil War, asked him whether he had the men or the money required for such an enterprise, Fidel said no, but he felt certain that in a few months he would have both. Bayo, believing Fidel's dream to be unrealizable, agreed to train the men once they were recruited.

[220] Although Batista denied it, the *puros* had connections with some prominent political opponents, such as Justo Carrillo, Valeri Busto, Luis Conte Agüero, and Felipe Pazos. See "Consejo de guerra," *Hispano* (Mexico), April 16, 1956, p. 27.
[221] "Interview in Mexico" in this volume.
[222] *Ibid.* A different version has been presented in "La acción del Goicuría fue para atajar el electoralismo," *Revolución* (Havana), April 28, 1960, p. 3.
[223] Bayo was born in Cuba in 1892 and left the island six years later. He fought for eleven years under the flag of the Spanish monarchy against Rif tribesmen in Morocco. He attended West Point and was a participant in several conspiracies planned by the Caribbean Legion in the 1940s.

Months later, in February 1956, an underground representative of the M–26–7 arrived in Mexico City with $8,000 from Cuba. Fidel was joyous at the realization that thousands of Cubans had contributed to the revolutionary cause and enthusiastically affirmed to his close friends that at last "the expedition was assured."[224]

Immediately Fidel informed Bayo that money had been collected and that Moncada veterans, several Cubans from the United States, Central America, and the island, as well as several Latin American volunteers, awaited training. Bayo replied in amazement that he would teach the men for three hours daily, to which Castro replied, "No, General Bayo, we want your entire day. You have to dedicate all your time to our training."[225] The sixty-five-year-old veteran eagerly complied, believing he would become the military leader of the expedition while the young revolutionary would concern himself with politics and with organization.

The $8,000 undoubtedly covered only essentials. Fund raising outside and inside the island continued, but the foundations for the creation of a revolutionary force had been laid. In March 1956, weapons were purchased and six houses rented in Mexico City. Each house lodged from five to ten men, followed strict military discipline, and was headed by a group leader who set the example of revolutionary responsibility for all the others. All had to clean house, wash clothes, and cook. They did not receive any salary, and no one was permitted to leave the house alone or return after midnight. The reading of Cuban periodicals and discussions of events taking place in the country were compulsory. Moreover, the men could not drink or have girl friends.[226] The latter rule, however, was overlooked. Nonetheless, it was a Spartan existence.

At first the revolutionists learned guerrilla warfare in Bayo's classes. The constantly emphasized need for discipline was merged with techniques for making bombs and carrying out sabotage. Drill practices were held in very small rooms, but the men did not mind, because a spirit of fellowship and high morale were developing. Clandestine instructions created a sense of heroism and adventure. After five or six weeks, these future *guerrilleros* were transferred to the "Rancho Las Rosas" in the Chalco district, a few miles from the Mexican capital and in the foothills of the volcano Popocatepetl. The ranch had been

224 Faustino Pérez, "A diez años del Granma," *Verde Olivo* (Havana), December 11, 1966, p. 21.

225 Alberto Bayo, *Mi aporte a la revolución cubana* (Havana: Imprenta Ejército Rebelde, 1960), p. 21.

226 *Ibid.*, p. 27; Fernando Sánchez Amaya, *Diario del Granma* (Havana: Editorial Tierra Nueva, 1959), p. 11.

acquired by Bayo in a dubious manner. Posing as the representative of a Salvadorian colonel, Bayo told the owner of the ranch, a man named Rivera who had fought side by side with Pancho Villa, that he was willing to buy the ranch for $24,000 if his men were allowed to improve the property for several months. During six months, Bayo argued, he would pay a token rental of $8 a month, at the end of which time he would buy the ranch.[227] Thus, the revolutionaries acquired a ranch ten miles long and six miles wide, with mountains nearby, for the incredible price of $48 for half a year!

The men found the conditions hard and the tasks demanding. They were taught guerrilla exercises, ambushes, hit-and-run tactics, shooting, mountain climbing, the making of Molotov cocktails, grenades, and booby traps. They were also instructed to make long marches at night.

On one occasion one of the trainees, a Cuban rural teacher, refused to walk for thirteen to fifteen hours every day with his comrades, precipitating an internal crisis that demanded Fidel's intervention. Fidel, who did not himself participate in the training sessions because of a busy schedule of organizing, accused the man of breaking discipline, of sabotaging the movement, and of being a traitor. Others even demanded his death, but in the end Fidel resolved that the man had to be imprisoned until "we had left Mexican territory." Days later, however, moved by the sympathy awakened by the accused comrade, his public regret, and his hard work, Fidel dismissed the charges.[228]

On June 10, 1956, while his men continued training, Fidel arrived in San José, Costa Rica.[229] He spoke with members of the social democratic party, Liberación Nacional, and sought financial support from Cubans there. His followers were informed that an expeditionary force would soon land on the island. Five days later he arrived in Mexico City, where his well-trained guerrilla unit awaited him. The Fidelistas were now a clear and present danger to the Batista regime. For this reason Cuban agents repeatedly inspired or paid Mexican authorities to raid the revolutionary camp and arrest its leaders.

Plans also were made to assassinate Fidel. A Batista agent made two trips to Mexico to carry out the plans but concluded that it was very difficult because of Fidel's precautions.[230] Once the assassins realized that it was impossible to commit the crime, they urged the Dirección Federal de Seguridad, Mexico's federal police, to arrest the revolu-

---

[227] Bayo, *Mi aporte*, pp. 65–67. One author mistakenly states that Bayo paid close to $26,000 for the farm. See Daniel James, *Che Guevara, a Biography* (New York: Stein and Day, 1969), p. 85.

[228] Bayo, *Mi aporte*, pp. 91–98.

[229] *Revolución* (Havana), July 26, 1959, p. 1.

[230] See "Enough Lies!" in this volume.

tionaries. On June 21, 1956, Fidel was arrested at night while walking with Ramiro Valdés, a veteran of the Moncada. Fidel recalled:

> On that occasion I could have died accidentally. I remember that Ramirito and I walked through this street when we became aware that a number of cars were following us, inside of which were several suspicious individuals. We thought they were assassins hired by Batista. I told Ramiro to follow me and did not realize when I reached the corner, where there was a building under construction, that he had been arrested. I thought my back was secured and saw a group of armed men rapidly get out of a car and try to intercept me. I hid behind a column and when I tried to take out my automatic pistol, a policeman who had taken Ramirito's place put his .45 pistol in back of my head.[231]

The following day, from the Miguel Schultz Prison, Castro issued a statement expressing his hope that Mexico would remain friendly toward the politically persecuted. He again stated that he would continue to fight for Cuba's freedom and denounced the charge that his movement was tied to communism or to former President Carlos Prío.[232] Forty other revolutionaries were arrested on June 26 at the training ranch and held incommunicado for twenty-seven days, accused of illegal possession of weapons and violation of an immigration law prohibiting conspiracy against other governments. The men were severely beaten, badly mistreated, and threatened with extradition.[233]

Days later, a lawyer interceded on Castro's behalf, but the latter refused to be freed as long as his followers continued to be incarcerated. Thanks to the good offices of Lázaro Cárdenas, former Mexican president, most of the men were released on July 25, 1956.

Ceaseless police harassment placed members of the revolutionary group in a difficult position. With their equipment seized and the old *campamentos* closely watched it was imperative to change plans, prepare new training centers, and purchase additional weapons. This required more money.

After seriously considering the problem, Fidel concluded that, because of the meager resources available to the movement, only Carlos Prío could provide the necessary capital. Otherwise, it would take many months to collect small individual sums from sympathizers,

[231] Mario Menéndez Rodríguez, "Fidel Castro habla para Sucesos," *Bohemia* (Havana), October 28, 1966, p. 14. There is no definite agreement as to whether Castro and his men were arrested on June 20 or 21.

[232] See "On the Arrest of Cuban Revolutionaries in Mexico" in this volume.

[233] See "Enough Lies!" in this volume. Ernesto Guevara, who was among those arrested, was kept in prison for fifty-seven days. For more on the relationship between Castro and Guevara, see Rolando E. Bonachea and Nelson P. Valdés (eds.), *Che: Selected Works of Ernesto Guevara* (Cambridge, Mass.: The M.I.T. Press, 1969), pp. 6–38.

a method that would delay the revolutionary timetable of landing in Cuba before the end of the year. Thus, in September 1956, Fidel Castro met the Auténtico leader for the first time, after swimming across the Rio Grande from Mexico to the United States. What agreements were reached during their rendezvous at the Casa de Palmas Hotel in McAllen, Texas, has never been made public, but Fidel received at least forty or fifty thousand dollars to continue his plans.[234]

With little time left, an intensive program of training was prepared. Camps were opened in Tamaulipas, Jalapa, Boca del Río, and Ciudad Victoria, all away from the Mexican capital. Instruction was given by Bayo's best students, for the old man had been retained in prison. One of the instructors was a Cuban veteran of the Korean War.

Study groups were also set up at the camps to consider Cuban problems and how they could be solved once the revolutionaries had attained power. The 26th of July manifestos and the works of José Martí were read avidly. The men who had led an active political life lectured about their experiences, and discussions were held on the reasons why the revolution of 1933 had failed. They also took stock of the lessons that could be learned from the recent Guatemalan debacle.[235] Fidel, at the time occupied with other endeavors, did not participate in these sessions, but Ernesto Guevara, among others, played a central role.

In early October 1956, Castro purchased the yacht *Granma* for $15,000 from a North American family living on the Gulf coast of Mexico. The *Granma* was seventy-five feet long, designed to carry only ten passengers, and in desperate need of repair. For an entire month repairs were made in the dark of the night, although one of the engines and a clutch continued to malfunction despite all the effort put into it.

Fidel was a hard taskmaster, and relations between him and the underground leaders were not without conflict. The men and women working inside the island often felt that the *líder máximo* had lost touch with reality and demanded more from them than was humanly possible to accomplish. In order to ascertain the strength of the 26th of July Movement underground and to coordinate its activities with those of the expeditionaries, Fidel conducted several meetings with his men in Mexico.

[234] Luis Dam, "El grupo 26 de Julio en la cárcel," *Bohemia* (Havana), October 28, 1966, p. 14. The Cuban chief of intelligence reported that Prío gave $200,000 to Castro. See "Denuncian próxima insurrección," *El Mundo* (Havana), November 13, 1956, pp. 1, A8.

[235] In June 1954, the Arbenz government of Guatemala was overthrown by counterrevolutionary forces with the aid of the United States Government.

Throughout September 1956, the underground leaders from all of Cuba's provinces except Oriente met with Castro in Mexico City. It was agreed that rather than training in Mexico as originally planned, they would prepare clandestinely for the time when Fidel would land on the island. This new plan called for instigation of a national rebellion, culminating in a general strike, simultaneously with the planned landing.[236]

The only dissident was the popular and independent young leader of the Oriente underground, Frank País, second only to Fidel in his influence over the 26th of July Movement.[237] The twenty-one-year-old son of a Baptist minister, Frank had been president of the Student Association of the National Teachers' College in Santiago de Cuba and taught at a Baptist school. A poet and a musician, he was also a great admirer of José Martí. In 1953 he had formed an underground group, Acción Revolucionaria Oriental (ARO), to recruit, collect weapons, mimeograph a newsletter, and engage in small-scale sabotage.[238] He gained support for the revolutionary cause throughout Oriente among high-school and university students and workers. However, most of the militants came from the youth section of the Ortodoxo Party, which by that time almost totally sided with Castro. It is possible that in mid-1955 País agreed to merge ARO with the 26th of July Movement and become its national underground coordinator for sabotage and other revolutionary actions.[239] Nonetheless, the Fidelista underground developed slowly.

While all the other underground leaders agreed to the plan of a coordinated invasion and uprising, Frank País alone held out. From October 23 to 28, he discussed it with Fidel. He felt that Oriente was not yet prepared for such an undertaking. As the landing was to take place in the province, his cooperation was essential, and for five days

[236] Armando Jiménez, *Sierra Maestra: la revolución de Fidel Castro* (Buenos Aires: Editorial Lautaro, 1959), p. 47.

[237] The 26th of July Movement was organizationally divided into two leaderships. The national leadership (*dirección nacional*), residing in Cuba, was composed of twenty-five members, all of whom nominally had the same power. The general leadership (*dirección general*), based in Mexico, was led primarily by Castro.

[238] There is no consensus as to the real name of País's organization. Three other names can be found among Cuban sources: Acción Liberadora, Movimiento de Acción Liberadora de Oriente, and Acción Nacional Revolucionaria. See "Trayectoria revolucionaria de Pepito Tey," *Revolución* (Havana), November 30, 1959, p. 19; "Biografía de Frank País," *Revolución* (Havana), July 30, 1962, p. 9; and Gregorio Ortega, "Frank País," *Lunes de Revolución* (Havana), July 26, 1959, pp. 16–17.

[239] Guillermo Cabrera, "Frank y la lucha clandestina en Santiago," *Juventud Rebelde* (Havana), July 30, 1966, p. 8.

the two men argued bitterly. País said he was "doubtful of the action groups' efficiency because they were unprotected, unprepared, and uncoordinated."[240] Fidel suggested that Frank work harder to pave the way for rebellion. He had promised to land in 1956, and he would do it.

Under the spell of Fidel's eloquence but still against his better judgment, Frank finally agreed to the plan. He was put in charge of taking over the city of Santiago de Cuba and coordinating the revolt in all of Oriente Province while Fidel would be landing at Niquero, in western Oriente, where one hundred waiting revolutionaries would join his invading force.

Fidel also realized that it was essential to establish some sort of coalition with other revolutionary groups. Only their active participation in a nationwide revolt could ensure Batista's ouster.[241] To this end he met during September and October 1956 in Mexico City with José Antonio Echevarría, twenty-four-year-old leader of the student-based Directorio Revolucionario and president of the Federation of University Students (FEU).

In Echevarría, Fidel had met his match. Powerfully built and charismatic, José Antonio was every bit as skilled and persuasive an orator as Fidel himself. The two revolutionaries had been avowed adversaries since the 1940s when they had belonged to rival cliques.[242] Nonetheless, a precarious alliance was reached in the form of the "Mexico Pact," which recognized the "ideological unity" of a revolutionary generation as represented by the 26th of July Movement and the FEU.[243] Its authors denied an accusation by Batista that they had dealings with Rafael Leónidas Trujillo, the dictator of the Dominican Republic (Batista had made the charges in the hope of uniting the Cubans behind the government against a "foreign threat").[244] Even though the Mexico Pact publicly stated that the two organizations had decided to

[240] "Carta de Frank a Fidel," *Verde Olivo* (Havana), August 1, 1965, p. 6.

[241] In late 1956, Fidel met with members of the Organización Auténtica and signed a coalition pact. The terms have never been made public, but it is interesting that all the participants had formerly belonged to the UIR. Source: letter of Jesús Dieguez to the authors dated December 15, 1969.

[242] To some degree it could be argued that the Directorio could trace its roots, in terms of many of its members, to the Movimiento Socialista Revolucionario of Rolando Masferrer, whereas the 26th of July Movement was to a large extent formed by individuals who had been very closely tied to the Unión Insurreccional Revolucionaria of Emilio Tró. As previously noted, each group hated the other in the 1940s, and that hatred was passed on to the ranks of the DR and the M-26-7.

[243] Echevarría signed the pact as an official of the FEU rather than as head of the DR. It must be noted that this was a mere symbolic act, for he had not consulted with other FEU officials. His unilateral action bound the DR in practice but the FEU only in name. For text of the pact, see this volume.

[244] Trujillo wanted to foster civil war in Cuba in order to take advantage of

unite their efforts "in order to overthrow the tyranny and carry out the Cuban Revolution," they could not agree on a common strategy. They called for a united front, yet neither would concede to the other's strategic thinking.

The Directorio had its power base mainly in the city of Havana. Whereas it wanted revolutionary action centered in the capital, Fidel hoped for an islandwide revolt with Oriente, the region most remote from Havana, bearing the brunt of the fighting. The Directorio called for *golpear arriba* ("strike at the top") because of its belief in terrorism and sabotage accompanied by the systematic assassination of major political figures. This group felt that a series of political murders, culminating with Batista's, would put the revolutionaries in power. Fidel, in contrast, thought that this approach would only do away with men, not destroy the system itself; it allowed for political change but hardly touched the main bastion of the established institutions—the armed forces. Strike at the military in order to carry out a thorough social revolution—this was his thesis.

Strategy was not the only area of conflict. It was a case of an irresistible force meeting an immovable object: Both leaders were extremely popular and powerful in their groups, and neither was willing to give up his position. During their discussions Fidel proposed that the Directorio dissolve as a separate organization and became part of his movement. Echevarría replied sardonically that he liked the idea as long as it was the M–26–7 that did all the dissolving (an idea that the DR leader had proposed several months earlier).

In the end, they simply agreed to support each other while working independently. Such had been the outcome of the meeting between the two leaders when Echevarría returned to Cuba on October 24, 1956. It was not long before DR's thesis of striking at the top was put into practice. On October 28, several Directorio men murdered the chief of military intelligence and seriously wounded some others.[245] The

---

the sugar deficit that such a climate would create in the island. Although on several occasions Fidel denounced the charges (see "Cuba and the Dominican Republic" in this volume), the available evidence suggests that after all there were ties between the revolutionists and Trujillo. For example, on one occasion David Figueredo, a member of the M–26–7, worked with a Trujillista action group in Cuba and through them obtained weapons for the Fidelista cause. See Lester Rodríguez, "30 de Noviembre de 1956," *Hoy* (Havana), December 2, 1963 (supplement), and Eduardo Yasells, "Recuerdos sobre Frank y Daniel," *Verde Olivo* (Havana), August 4, 1963, p. 8.

[245] The attack was made by Pedro Carbó Servía and Rolando Cubela. The former died months later and the latter became a revolutionary leader who in 1965 was arrested by the revolutionary government for planning Fidel Castro's assassination—that is, for wanting to use an old Directorio tactic. See "Como se produjo el atentado," *El Mundo* (Havana), October 30, 1956, pp. 1, A4.

police retaliated the next day by entering the Haitian embassy, where ten revolutionaries had sought refuge, and killing the men. Also, the chief of the Cuban police was shot down while leading the attack.

Such a display of violence and terror was immediately condemned by major sectors of society. In a November 19, 1956, interview with the progovernment paper *Alerta*, Castro also raised his voice against the action:

> I do not condemn [assassination] attempts as a revolutionary weapon if the circumstances require it. But such attempts cannot be indiscriminately perpetrated. I do not know who carried out the assault on Blanco Rico, but I do believe that, from a political and revolutionary standpoint, assassination was not justified because Blanco Rico was not a henchman.[246]

Castro's remarks were resented by the Directorio, and the political ambitions for leadership of the revolutionary movement no doubt accentuated the rivalry. Members of the Directorio viewed Fidel's statement as a maneuver to discredit them before the Cuban people. In their eyes, Fidel could not be trusted, and furthermore they felt it was time to redefine relations between the groups.

In that same interview, Fidel gave the impression of favoring a united front, while attacking violent methods. He said that he would gladly give up insurrectionary plans if his program for "national unity" were carried out. The main points of the program were: (1) immediate appointment by government and opposition of a president who would inspire trust in all Cubans; (2) general elections within ninety days; (3) breaking diplomatic relations with the Dominican Republic; (4) presenting a formal denunciation of Dominican plans to invade Cuba before the Organization of American States; (5) freeing all military personnel arrested on April 4, 1956; (6) amnesty for all social and political prisoners and national mobilization to defend the country.

If this program were not carried out within two months, Fidel concluded:

> The 26th of July Movement will be free to initiate at any moment the revolutionary struggle as the only possible solution. We ratify entirely our 1956 promise: We will be free or we will be martyrs.

Meanwhile, in Mexico serious difficulties were being encountered by the Fidelistas. On November 22, 1956, the federal police in Mexico City, thanks to a Cuban spy among the revolutionaries, captured weapons valued at $56,000.[247] A few minutes later a police officer

---

[246] "Entrevista con Fidel Castro," *El Mundo* (Havana), November 20, 1956, p. A9.

[247] The agent was Rafael del Pino, a long-time friend of Fidel's, who was in charge of purchasing weapons in the United States for the M-26-7. He accom-

friendly to the cause warned Fidel and his men to move immediately to avoid arrest. Thus, Fidel ordered his men to mobilize and meet at the small port of Tuxpán on the Gulf of Mexico.

The Crossing of the Granma

On November 25, 1956, the yacht *Granma* prepared to sail from the small port of Tuxpán, about 150 miles north of Veracruz. It was 2:00 A.M., and there was a storm so severe that navigation had been prohibited. In the strong north wind, sheets of freezing rain assailed the shivering band of expeditionaries. The silence was broken only by the storm and the distant barking of dogs.

After weapons, ammunition, equipment, and food had been placed in the boat, hushed voices gave the order, and eighty-two men clambered aboard. Faustino Pérez recalls, "'We all tried to board the yacht at the same time, fearing that there would not be room for everyone."[248] Nearly fifty other men were left behind because there was not enough space.

With lights out and men lying breathless in piles on the floor, the *Granma* quietly moved out of Tuxpán harbor. One hour later they were in the Gulf of Mexico, singing the Cuban national anthem. Fidel had told them, "If we leave, we shall get there. If we get there and last seventy-two hours, we shall win."[249]

Before them lay the tip of the Yucatán Peninsula. After passing north of that, they would enter the Caribbean and head down toward Niquero, Oriente Province, at the southwestern end of Cuba. The engines were malfunctioning, and for a time Fidel feared he would have to change his plans and land in the western province of Pinar del Río, less than 100 miles northeast of Yucatán.

This particular group of island dwellers made poor sailors. The *Granma* was tossed by enormous waves and lashed with heavy rain. Water filled the boat, and the pumps failed to work. Wracked by seasickness, the men began bailing with the two available buckets. The only lifeboat, designed, like the *Granma*, to hold just ten persons, had holes in the bottom. And Yucatán was still over eighty miles away. Everything looked hopeless, when at last the water pumps began to function.

Making only 7.2 knots an hour, the *Granma* slowly made her way

panied Fidel to Bogotá in 1948. See "$56,000 en armas ocupadas," *El Mundo* (Havana), November 23, 1956, pp. 1, A8.

[248] Faustino Pérez, "De Tuxpán a las Coloradas," in Ray (ed.), *Libertad y revolución*, p. 22.

[249] Pedro García, "Recuerdos de 'la casa bonita,'" *Bohemia* (Havana), May 28, 1959, p. 130.

toward Cuba. The next day was also rainy; then the weather cleared for three days. On November 30 the sea became rough again, but visibility was good. They had reached Grand Cayman, 180 miles south of Cuba. It was the day they had planned to land, and from a Cuban radio broadcast they learned that the revolt, led by Frank País, had broken out in Oriente Province on schedule. (However, the cadres of the M–26–7 in other parts of the island, despite their early assurances, did not revolt because of lack of organization, leadership, or weapons. In Havana it seems that the Fidelista structure was not even informed as to the date of the landing. Moreover, the Directorio did not carry out its plan either.) Now, not only had the people of Santiago been massacred by the regime, but the government had been alerted to the impending landing.[250]

On December 1, Fidel proclaimed the military organization of the expeditionaries, and for the first time the men wore the olive-green uniform of the 26th of July Movement. The next day they reached Cuba, running aground at 6:00 A.M. near Las Coloradas beach in Belic district, somewhat south of their goal of Niquero. Thus, they were unable to link up with a force of about fifty men awaiting them nearby with jeeps, trucks, food, and weapons.[251]

The *Granma* could go no farther. Between the men and solid ground lay two miles of dangerous swamp. They were forced to wade ashore, losing weapons, food, and medicine in the process. A heavy radio transmitter had to be left behind. Fidel was the first off the boat, followed by some members of his general staff. Grouped in three columns, up to their necks in water, with rifles held high, the weary *Granma* expeditionaries began the arduous march toward the mangrove-covered shore.

Hours later they reached firm ground, hungry, exhausted, wet, and

---

[250] On the Havana cadres, see Enrique Rodríguez Loeches, "Menelao Mora: el insurrecto," *Bohemia* (Havana), March 15, 1959, p. 79, and Jorge Valdés Miranda, *Cuba revolucionaria* (Havana: Editorial Ugo, 1959), pp. 157–158. The reason for Directorio inaction remains unclear, although different versions are available from members. Juan Nuiry has simply stated that "the necessary conditions to carry out the Directorio's plans did not exist." Felix Murias, on the other hand, has said that the Directorio lacked time to do anything because it was not notified of the landing until December 2, 1956. Faure Chomón, however, has stated that on November 28, 1956, the Directorio had been informed of Castro's imminent landing but that persecution and lack of weapons made armed insurrection impossible; Chomón says that "in a meeting with the Havana M–26–7 we found that they lacked organization and could not provide us with weapons." See Juan Nuiry, "José Antonio Echevarría, Pensamiento y acción!" *Bohemia* (Havana), March 10, 1967, p. 78; Suchlicki, *University Students*, p. 74; and Faure Chomón, "El ataque al Palacio Presidencial," *Bohemia* (Havana), March 15, 1959.

[251] "El desembarco," *Cuba Internacional* (Havana), May–June 1970, pp. 11–12.

completely covered with mud. But they could not stop. A government warship was visible offshore, and it was obvious they had been spotted. The columns regrouped, and a head count revealed that eight persons were missing, including Juan Manuel Márquez, second in command. Just as a search was about to begin, an airplane was sighted, and everyone ran for cover in the nearby woods.

They had survived seven miserable days of hunger, seasickness, fear, and misfortune. And this desperate group of lost and muddy men, looking more like their own ghosts, was the liberation army promised the Cuban people.

The air force and 1,000 soldiers were diligently searching for the expeditionaries, who had lost all equipment except their weapons and some wet ammunition. Trying to avoid encirclement, they marched without food or water for three consecutive days. Finally, in the early morning of December 5, 1956, the inexperienced and exhausted rebels set up camp near a surgarcane field at Alegría de Pío. They spent most of the day eating sugarcane and nursing the blisters on their feet. Meanwhile, government troops, alerted by a peasant, had surrounded them.

About 4:00 P.M. the rebels—who had not even set up sentry posts—were surprised by a barrage of bullets. Many were wounded or killed there; others found refuge in a nearby forest or cane field. At least twenty Fidelistas met their death as government troops set fire to the cane fields. This first encounter with the forces of the regime had ended in a tremendous defeat for the rebels.

Frightened and lost, the rebels divided into several groups and moved toward the mountains. Many more were captured, tortured, and killed in the process. Fidel, Universo Sánchez, and Faustino Pérez began the long march toward the home of Ramón Pérez (Ramón's brother was an influential leader in the area who had awaited the expeditionaries with help at Niquero days earlier). They hid in a cane field for five days while troops searched for them. Faustino Pérez recalls:

> During the daytime we hid under the fallen sugarcane leaves because airplanes flew over us incessantly. We ate sugarcane and used the morning dew on the leaves to quench our thirst. Then we decided to get out of there. At night we cautiously moved out, using the stars to guide us.[252]

252 Faustino Pérez, "Hablando del Granma," *Revolución* (Havana), December 4, 1959, p. 2. Joaquín Oramas, "The Landing and the First Encounter," *Granma* (Havana), December 11, 1966, p. 9, says that Castro's group hid in the canefields for fifteen days, not five.

The three men finally found rest in a village, where they were fed and informed of military activities in the area. The peasants urged them to surrender. On December 10, the government had offered a two-day truce and had dropped leaflets urging the rebels to surrender and promising not to kill them. As encouragement, the army ceased to advance. Some Fidelistas, who still did not know whether their comrades were alive and free, took advantage of the truce to continue moving to the high mountains. Although many gave themselves up, Fidel refused to do so.

On December 13, 1956, the armed forces officially announced the end of the insurrection and withdrew troops from the area. Four days later Fidel and his two companions reached the regrouping point at the farm of Ramón Pérez. During the succeeding days, other members of the group straggled in and were met with warm embraces and cries of "Viva la Revolución!" The desperation of the last few days gave way to renewed conviction in the triumph of the rebellion. Of the original invading force, twenty-one had been killed and thirty captured. Thirty men, with seven weapons among them, remained to form the core of the future Rebel Army.[253]

In the early morning hours of December 24, Fidel told his men:

> The regrouping of the *Granma* expeditionaries is a definitive sign that the days of Batista are numbered. From now on the army of the 26th of July Movement will not be defeated.[254]

The revolutionists later wrote a letter expressing their gratitude to Ramón Pérez for having helped them regroup, feeding them for eight days, and aiding in establishing contact with the movement throughout the island.[255]

The rebels were successful in making contact because of help from Ramón's brother, Crescencio Pérez, an influential *cacique*, or unofficial leader of the peasants (*guajiros*), in the traditionally rebellious Sierra Maestra area. He established a network to find lost men and to contact the rest of the island. And because the people trusted him, he was instrumental in gaining their loyalty for Fidel and his men. The rebels showed respect for the people, paying for food and being careful not

---

[253] It is alleged that only twelve men had survived and managed to create a guerrilla movement. On several occasions, Fidel has referred to that number or spoken of a "handful of men." Guevara, on the other hand, asserted that there were seventeen men. See Fidel Castro, "History Creates Objective Conditions, but Men Create the Subjective Ones," pp. 9–12; Bonachea and Valdés (eds.), *Che: Selected Works of Ernesto Guevara*, p. 10. We have arrived at our figures by making a list of those who were killed, captured, or managed to escape.

[254] Manuel de J. Zamora, "Pasión y gloria de la alborada revolucionaria," *El Mundo* (Havana), January 18, 1959 (supplement), p. 14.

[255] See "An Expression of Gratitude" in this volume.

to bring reprisals from the soldiers on them. Fidel also found favor with the people through his policy of executing landlords who betrayed *guajiros* suspected of aiding the rebel cause. These policies and aid from Crescencio Pérez (who had known Fidel since their Ortodoxo days in the late 1940s), plus the regime's brutality, eventually brought most of the *guarjiros* of the area to the side of the rebels.

On December 25, 1956, the small group left the farm of Ramón Pérez, marching toward Turquino Peak, the highest in Cuba, whereupon Fidel shouted, "We have won this war!"[256] Fidel's first act, on reaching the top of the mountain on Christmas Day, was to check his altimeter to prove that the height given in Cuban geography books was more than fifty meters off.

In the following weeks the guerrillas kept busy simply surviving. They had to acquaint themselves with the territory, set up a rudimentary guerrilla structure, and establish the necessary contacts with the outside world. One main concern also was evading the enemy, for although the Cuban armed forces made no real effort to eliminate them, a private army under Rolando Masferrer—a long-time foe of Castro's—persistently searched out the revolutionists.[257]

Meanwhile, Batista was announcing everywhere that the rebel leader and all his men had been exterminated. Although the people had little faith in what he said, his words still planted doubt in their minds. When the news came that Fidel and Raúl Castro had been killed, the first thing their mother did was to go to Santiago de Cuba to see about the settlement of their father's inheritance![258]

On January 15, 1957, Batista suspended civil rights. Two days later, having mustered some strength, a Fidelista band of twenty-two men made their first attack on an isolated army outpost. After an hour of intensive fighting, the soldiers, who counted two men dead and five wounded, surrendered. Twelve rifles, one submachine gun, 1,000 rounds of ammunition, plus food and medicine, were seized. The battle of La Plata, as it became known, marked the first military victory of the 26th of July Movement.

[256] "Los sueños del futuro se aproximan," *Revolución* (Havana), December 2, 1959, pp. 1, 15. Interview with Ramiro Valdés.

[257] Masferrer, still leader of the dreaded MSR, commanded 2,000 men who for all practical purposes controlled Oriente Province. See Robert Taber, *M–26: Biography of a Revolution* (New York: Lyle Stuart, 1961), p. 82. Yet the Batista regime also contained such amazing contradictions as the attitude of the Cuban vice-president, who remarked publicly that he admired Castro's rebelliousness although it was politically mistaken. "Sierra Maestra," *Bohemia* (Havana), January 6, 1957, p. 79.

[258] "Problema por la herencia de Castro," *El Mundo* (Havana), December 18, 1956, p. 1.

Not only had morale and resources improved but, more important, the surprise attack was disclosed by the chief of the Army Press and Radio Office of the Batista regime, thereby demonstrating to the Cuban people the continued existence of an insurrectionary band in the Sierra Maestra and its willingness to fight. Consequently, the regime was forced to admit that the revolutionists still posed a threat, something that they had tended to disregard since Alegría de Pío.

In the days following, the army was successfully ambushed, suffering close to a dozen casualties. According to one of the rebels, on January 22, "we were able to defeat the advance guard of a detachment searching for us, commanded by Sánchez Mosquera, a figure of sinister reputation. This was followed by an impasse due to a traitor within our ranks; he betrayed our position to the enemy and we were almost liquidated on three different occasions."[259]

A political offensive, Fidel realized, had to be waged too, for although finances were good, a public image was lacking.[260] Thus, on December 23, 1956, Faustino Pérez, one of the expeditionaries, was sent to Havana to approach the mass media and set up an interview with the rebel leader. The Cubans did not accept the idea, but Herbert L. Matthews, correspondent for the New York Times, welcomed it.[261]

On February 17, 1957, behind military lines high in the Sierra Maestra, the interview took place. A week later, Castro, who had been in desperate need of publicity, was known throughout the world. The New York Times report crushed Batista's censorship and showed definite proof that the guerrillas were active and Fidel Castro was leading them.[262] President Batista and the secretary of defense denied that the interview had taken place, to which the Times replied by publishing a photograph of Castro and Matthews. The regime's credibility was destroyed and its principal officials humiliated. Perhaps more important yet, Fidel gained notoriety, and this embryonic guerrilla be-

[259] Ernesto "Che" Guevara, "El desembarco del Granma," in Antonio Núñez Jímenez, Geografía de Cuba (Havana: Editorial Lex, 1959), p. 576.

[260] The means by which capital was acquired remains questionable. The Moncada attack, for example, was financed by individual contributions, phony checks, and by buying television sets on credit under assumed names and selling them at half their value for cash. It is possible that similar methods were used in the early stages of the guerrilla movement. See Marta Rojas, "Como se sufragaron los gastos para el ataque al cuartel Moncada," Verde Olivo (Havana), July 29, 1962, pp. 36–39; "Documentos gráficos para la historia; contienda civil en la Sierra Maestra," Bohemia (Havana), March 17, 1957, p. 69.

[261] Faustino Pérez, "La sierra, el llano: una misma lucha," Pensamiento Crítico (Havana), August 1969, pp. 67–93.

[262] Censorship was lifted in Cuba the day after the interview was published, thus allowing Cubans to read it.

came, in name more than in fact, the center and symbol of the opposition.

From the reports available, the guerrillas appeared quite strong to the Cubans. Herbert L. Matthews estimated their number at ninety; Castro himself stated: "We have been fighting for seventy-nine days now and are stronger than ever. The soldiers are fighting badly; their morale is low and ours could not be higher."[263] In reality the situation was not that rosy. In February the guerrillas' morale was low, ideological convictions had practically disappeared, and many *guerrilleros* requested more dangerous duties in the cities just to "escape from the hard life in the mountains."[264] After a government ambush on February 9, several men deserted, and others were told to get out because of their demoralizing effect on the troops.[265]

They marched slowly, hungry and lost, under torrential rains. Every minor incident caused irritation, and the men cursed one another, disrupting what little discipline was left. Possibly only at night, when they rested and spoke of their dreams and loves, did they find some comfort or peace. But still, in the back of their minds must have clung the fear of more ambushes. These men, with little education, spoke of becoming agronomists, physicians, politicians, or military men once the rebellion had succeeded. On the night of March 11, 1957, Fidel said to his men:

> *Compañeros*, it is true that on three occasions we have almost perished. It is also true that the enemy threatens us everywhere, while denying our presence here; it is true that we have only twelve rifles and forty rounds of ammunition for each of us, but we have fulfilled our promise to the Cuban people. We are here![266]

The Presidential Palace Assault

Meanwhile in Havana the Directorio felt compelled to demonstrate its determination and willingness to fight. Because they had failed to back up the *Granma* landing, there were many who questioned their convictions and courage. To overthrow Batista thus became not a simple

[263] Herbert L. Matthews, "Cuban Rebel Is Visited in Hideout," *New York Times*, February 24, 1957, pp. 1, 34. Castro had then about twenty men, who continually marched around the camp where the interview was taking place, giving the impression to the *Times* reporter that they had more men.

[264] Ernesto "Che" Guevara, *Obra Revolucionaria* (Mexico: Ediciones Era, 1967), p. 130.

[265] It is possible that at this time, during February 1957, due to desertions the *guerrilleros* numbered only twelve. Hugo Gambini, *El Che Guevara* (Buenos Aires: Editorial Paidós, 1968), pp. 128–129.

[266] Efigenio Ameijeiras, "Esperando el refuerzo," *Revolución* (Havana), April 1, 1963, pp. 2, 3.

political necessity but a matter of honor as well.[267] Also, the competition that had grown between the DR and the M–26–7 over the months forced the followers of José Antonio Echevarría to make a desperate move to take the headlines away from the Fidelistas and move the center of revolutionary activities from the mountains to the capital. Therefore, in early January 1957, the Directorio leadership and former members of an Auténtico action group drew up plans to overthrow the regime.

The plan, an outgrowth of the idea of "striking at the top" (*golpear arriba*), consisted of storming the Presidential Palace with a suicide squad, assassinating Batista, securing the executive mansion, attacking police stations throughout Havana, and aiding some military personnel in staging a coup.[268] The putsch, according to the scheme, would cause the government's collapse, while a radio broadcast would urge the Cubans to take up arms and form popular militias. A provisional civilian-military junta was also to be set up.

On March 13, 1957, the plan was put into action by a heterogeneous group of revolutionists. Side by side were students in their early twenties, veterans of the Spanish Civil War and World War II, and long-time members of action groups that had participated in the Cayo Confites affair or in the many adventures of the Caribbean Legion. The leader of the attack, for example, was Carlos Gutiérrez Menoyo, a first-generation Cuban who had fought in the Spanish Civil War and World War II under General Patton, had participated in the Cayo Confites expedition, and was closely associated with the Caribbean Legion. Also in command was Menelao Mora, a former ABC terrorist. The other participants included former members of the UIR, MSR, and Jóven Cuba.[269]

---

[267] The claim exists that Castro himself sent a letter to Echevarría excoriating his inactivity during the landing. Source: authors' interview with Marcelo Fernández Zayas, Washington, D.C., August 19, 1969.

[268] The role to be played by the military has since been denied by revolutionary authorities on the island. See Faure Chomón, "Fundamentos tácticos del asalto a Palacio," *Bohemia* (Havana), March 13, 1970, pp. 66–71. For a thorough description of the plan and its execution, see Faure Chomón, "El ataque al Palacio Presidencial," *Bohemia* (Havana), March 15, 1959, pp. 80–82, 106; March 22, 1959, pp. 72–74, 96; and April 5, 1959, pp. 68–71, 95.

[269] Mora was a close friend of Antonio Guiteras and, like Menoyo, a former Confites expeditionary. The former UIR, MSR, and Jóven Cuba members such as Eduardo García Lavandero, Enrique Rodríguez Loeches, Humberto Castelló, José L. Wangüerment, Jimmy Morales, and Ignacio González all had a long experience with terrorism. See Faure Chomón, "El ataque al Palacio Presidencial," *Revolución* (Havana), September 11, 1962, p. 12; September 12, 1962, p. 10; September 21, 1962, p. 10; September 22, 1962, p. 10; and Chomón, "The Assault on the Presidential Palace," *Granma* (Havana), March 19, 1967, p. 2.

Altogether, fifty men attacked the Presidential Palace at 3:24 P.M. The guards were momentarily taken by surprise, but the battle was fierce. Minutes later the revolutionists gained ground, as the defenders fled to the upper floors. The men divided into three groups. One group remained in the street, securing a retreat, while another controlled the main floor, and fifteen men reached the second floor, desperately searching for Batista's office. By the time they found it, the dictator was gone. Meanwhile, army tanks and troops, rushed from Camp Columbia, surrounded the president's residence. The 150 men who were supposed to back up the revolutionaries failed to appear, leaving the retreating men without cover. As they attempted to leave the building, they were met with a shower of bullets, and few survived.[270]

While the attack on the president's home was under way, a group of men took over the popular Radio Reloj as planned. José A. Echevarría announced the death of Batista and urged the people to take up arms. Immediately afterward, Echevarría and other men headed toward the University of Havana; but as they approached the campus, they encountered a police patrol. They opened fire, and by a whim of destiny Echevarría was shot dead. The remainder of his group disbanded and sought refuge throughout Havana.

Succeeding days were filled with horror and brutal repression. Bodies of tortured individuals appeared throughout the island, and panic touched almost every member of the Directorio. There was no safe refuge in the capital, but Fidel Castro, from his mountain haven, had time to criticize the tragic assault. In a taped interview with a CBS reporter, he stated that it

> . . . was a useless spilling of blood. The life of the dictator does not matter. . . . I am against terrorism. I condemn these procedures. Nothing is solved by them. Here in the Sierra Maestra is where they should come to fight.[271]

Fidel was simply expressing, for tactical reasons, his opposition to the action of any group not controlled by the 26th of July Movement and his animosity toward a group also seeking revolutionary power. In the struggle over the hegemony of the revolutionary movement, he refused to recognize the Directorio's merits.

On March 24, 1957, the remaining DR leaders met somewhere in the

[270] It is open to speculation why the groups that were to aid the assault did not do so. Those who participated in the attack argue that the others were afraid, lacked leadership, did not believe the plan could succeed, or were too old to act, thus sacrificing their comrades. Those who did not back the action say they were not informed when to go into action, their contact failed, or they were caught in a traffic jam.

[271] "En Cuba," *Bohemia* (Havana), May 26, 1957, p. 97.

capital to discuss the recent tragic events.[272] Agreeing to continue the struggle, they chose to stay in Havana and appointed Fructuoso Rodríguez as the new head of the organization. Several days later, on April 2, they met again and approved a document that was then sent to the mass media. The mimeographed leaflet explained the attack on the palace, paid tribute to the dead men, and made harsh and concrete accusations against those who did not participate in the support action. The names and addresses of men who had failed to show up at the assassination attempt were listed for the benefit of the Batista police, with the argument that they were traitors and deserters. In a complementary circular, various members of the Directorio were also expelled.[273]

Two weeks later, on April 20, 1957, the Directorio's disaster became complete when the remaining top leaders were surrounded in their hideout and murdered. Someone had informed the police.[274] The Directorio now had no leaders, weapons, or resources left; those who managed to survive went into exile. The Directorio, as a significant organization, had come to an end.

The Sierra and Llano Conflict in Oriente Province

The Directorio's demise left the 26th of July Movement the unchallenged exponent of armed struggle. Hence, as the guerrillas' prestige and strength began to grow, the M–26–7 gained adherents and material aid from various sectors of society. On March 16, 1957, new recruits from Santiago de Cuba and Manzanillo, sent by Frank País, joined the insurgents, forming a guerrilla foco that attracted youth, the rural proletariat, and the peasants.[275]

The new recruits went through intensive military training for two months, learning to march for many hours, to sleep without covers,

[272] The leadership in Cuba consisted of Julio García Olivares, Fructuoso Rodríguez, Enrique Rodríguez Loeches, Faure Chomón, Joe Westbrook, Juan Pedro Carbó, José Machado; Rolando Cubela and Eduardo García Lavandero were in exile.

[273] The expelled members included Tirso Urdanivia and Jorge Valls. See Enrique Rodríguez Loeches, "El crimen de Humbolt 7," Revolución (Havana), September 26, 1962, p. 12. A summary version of the first leaflet appears in "La capital el sábado de dolor," Bohemia (Havana), April 28, 1957, pp. 81–84.

[274] According to the Cuban government, the informer was Marcos Rodríguez, who in 1964 was tried and shot. However, at least one author argues that the man who informed the police was Faure Chomón, who then became head of the Directorio. See Carlos Manuel Pellecer, Utiles después de muertos (Mexico: Costa-Amic, 1967).

[275] The rebels numbered approximately eighty men. See Efigenio Ameijeiras, "Esperando el refuerzo," Revolución (Havana), April 1, 1963, pp. 1–9 (supplement).

to eat once a day, to accept discipline, and acquainting themselves with the terrain. Weapons for their training were still scarce, but the first guerrilla base and several intelligence networks were formed, making use of the friendly *guajiros* of the area.

On May 19, 1957, twenty-seven expeditionaries led by Calixto Sánchez, a World War II veteran and first-generation Cuban, left Miami aboard the yacht *Corintia* and landed five days later on the northern coast of Oriente, near the then U.S. government–owned Nicaro Nickel Company. The men, mostly members of the Organización Auténtica, were financed by Carlos Prío and hoped to establish a guerrilla front in the Sierra Cristal Mountains which would compete with Castro's guerrilla band to the south.[276]

Exhausted and hungry from a terrible voyage, the men got lost in torrential rains. On May 28, betrayed by a peasant, twenty-four of them were captured and murdered by the armed forces. Many of these men were the same ones who weeks before had been charged with treason by the Directorio because they had not shown up at the Presidential Palace. Their participation in an ill-conceived expedition, without guides or the necessary resources, and their tragic deaths proved that, despite all recriminations, they were not afraid to fight.

Also on May 28, at Uvero, Oriente Province, eighty Fidelista guerrillas attacked and defeated a small garrison of fifty-three soldiers. Although the insurgents suffered fifteen casualties, it was their first significant victory, because the battle was reported by the mass media, and rebel morale improved. Once again it seemed that Fidel Castro and his men were the indisputable leaders of the armed struggle.

The Uvero incident forced the regime to take drastic measures. On June 1, 2,000 families of the region were evacuated and placed in concentration camps, while the best infantry units were sent to pursue the guerrillas. The troops' ruthlessness, however, alienated Cubans all over the nation, and a barrage of demands forced the government to put an end to its action. Batista, still seeking the support of the population, did stop the offensive, establishing a policy of containment which permitted the growing ranks of the Rebel Army to control most of Oriente's mountains. From then on, Che Guevara wrote later, "the fate of every garrison located far from major troop concentrations" was sealed. Subsequently, every small army post in the Sierra Maestra was dismantled.[277]

Although the rebels were no longer threatened by the army, two

[276] Jorge G. Montes and Antonio Avila, *Historia del Partido Comunista de Cuba* (Miami: Ediciones Universal, 1970), p. 506.
[277] Guevara, *Obra Revolucionaria*, p. 169.

different viewpoints emerged within the 26th of July Movement itself at the very moment that the guerrillas were almost totally dependent on the urban areas for weapons, food, medicine, clothes, intelligence reports, men and money. Frank País's urban underground was at this time a shambles, thoroughly disoriented and almost out of the fight as a result of the November 30, 1956, fiasco. The conflict was over the strategy or method for overthrowing the regime and whether priority should be placed on strengthening the *sierra* (the guerrillas) or the *llano* (the urban underground) and which of the two would shape the movement's policies and programs.

The *sierra*, led by Fidel Castro, believed it was the urban cadres' duty and responsibility to serve the guerrillas, playing a complementary, not primary, role in the struggle against the regime. Guerrilla war, they argued, would in the end oust Batista. Futhermore, the political and military leadership of the organization had to be centered in the mountains because the guerrillas constituted the vanguard of the M–26–7, and security was better kept in the mountains than in the cities. Almost the entire repressive apparatus of the regime was concentrated in the cities, which made it quite difficult for a clandestine structure to defeat the regime successfully. The enemy had to be fought, not at the center of its power, but at the periphery—in the mountains. Thus, the urban structure should follow orders issued from the mountains.[278]

The *llano* position, in mid-1957, was best expressed by Frank País. In a letter dated July 7, 1957, País told Castro that the time had come to develop a "new tactic, a new line." País outlined the need for doing away with so many leaders, centralizing coordination, decision making, and defining everyone's function in the M–26–7 well. Referring to the period after November 1956, he wrote,

> It was necessary in this brief period of time to act a little in a dictatorial fashion, dictating orders and being quite strict; but now we can channel our actions according to a thoroughly studied plan.

He asserted his support for generalized armed struggle (in the mountains and cities), culminating in a revolutionary general strike that would drive Batista from power.

> There has always been talk of a general strike, but in preparing for war this aspect was often disregarded; people have worked at it ineffectively and without faith. It was necessary to work on that and start moving, and Oriente has begun to do so. Now the situation has changed, and it is clear that a general strike is possible and necessary.

[278] This view has been systematically developed by Régis Debray in his *Revolution in the Revolution?* (New York: Monthly Review Press, 1967).

Furthermore, he disclosed the organizational steps to be taken to coordinate such a strike and the formation of labor committees throughout the provinces. According to his plans, all the labor committees were to be organized within a month. Moreover, he emphasized that the policies, strategy, and program of the 26th of July Movement were to be made by a national directorate (*dirección nacional*). Frank told Castro that the *dirección nacional* would have thirteen members. Castro's guerrillas were to be represented by only one delegate (which País even specified should be Celia Sánchez!). Then he added:

> Our war plans foresee the creation of militias, the purchase and introduction of weapons in the regions showing the greater degree of discipline and organization, the widening and reinforcement of the guerrillas, and the opening of new fronts.

Ending with the statement that the M–26–7 programs had been too vague, País announced his decision to provide the organization with a systematic program. Work on this aspect had gone on for several weeks. "If you have some suggestions," Frank told Fidel, "send them to us."[279]

How Castro reacted to País's letter never has been disclosed, but it is doubtful that he took the underground leader's intentions calmly. Furthermore, it is questionable that he would have agreed to have no say regarding the composition of the national directorate or its program. Nevertheless, realizing that the leadership of the "new generation" might be escaping from him, Fidel quickly allied himself with members of the old generation. He did so by calling on two well-known and respected Cubans—Raúl Chibás and Felipe Pazos. The former was the brother of the founder of the Ortodoxo Party, principal of a military preparatory school in Havana, and leader of the Ortodoxos. Dr. Pazos had been the first president of the National Bank of Cuba and was widely known in international business circles.   *168881*

On arriving in the *sierra*, both men met with the Castro brothers. Fidel proposed that a manifesto be drawn up to outline the objectives of the guerrillas and their desire to form a popular front with other opposition forces. The document, as discussed by the men, would be moderate in character but nationalist in content with special emphasis on a broad civic front. Pazos was entrusted with writing the manifesto. According to Dr. Pazos,

> I started drawing up the document; but since I was having a difficult time, I asked Fidel to try. Soon afterward, he returned to me

279 "Carta de Frank a Fidel," *Verde Olivo* (Havana), August 1, 1965, pp. 6–7. Dr. Regino Boti was appointed by País to write on economic problems and solutions, while Dr. Baudilio Castellanos and Carlos Olivares were to discuss the race issue. Carlos Nicot and Vicente Cubillas, "Relatos inéditos sobre la acción revolucionaria del líder Frank País," *Revolución* (Havana), July 30, 1963, p. 2.

with the manifesto. I read it and began, not to edit, but to do some
trimming of what Fidel had written. He looked at me in con-
sternation and surprise. I said, "Look, if we are going to sign this
document together, the style must have something of myself and
of Chibás." Fidel agreed, and the document, which he had written
except for some minor changes I made myself, was drafted.[280]

The historic "Sierra Maestra Manifesto" (see text in this volume) was
issued on July 12, 1957, five days after Frank País's letter.

At the meeting, Pazos had suggested to Fidel that

> the Constitution of 1940 could [be] amended in order that he
> [Fidel] could become president of the provisional government by
> lowering the required age, which otherwise would disqualify him
> by the constitution. [Fidel] said that he had no political ambitions
> whatsoever, that his only intention was to overthrow Batista and
> then return to normal life. As for amending the constitution, he
> was flatly opposed and persuasively argued that such a move
> would alienate many segments of the society, as they would fear
> that once they had assumed the right of amending the constitution,
> what would prevent them from doing so again and again? His
> objective, he said, was to reestablish the Constitution of 1940, not
> to amend it.[281]

Alliance with Chibás and Pazos gave Castro and his cause respectabil-
ity, stature, and importance and opened the door to an accommodation
with old political leaders and professional groups which eventually
would be converted to the idea of insurrection.[282]

Although País's signature was conspicuously absent from the manifesto, as the *llano* leader had in mind a more radical program, no
definite break occurred between the two leaders of the 26th of July
Movement. Perhaps a rupture would have been inevitable, but Frank
País was captured and killed in the streets of Santiago de Cuba on

---

[280] Authors' interview with Felipe Pazos, Washington, D.C. Ernesto Guevara,
however, maintains that the document was written by Pazos and Chibás, and not
by Castro. See *Obra Revolucionaria*, pp. 181–185.

[281] Pazos then suggested that an alternative would be to appoint a weak individual to the presidency, and Castro could assume the post of prime minister
with strong powers. This suggestion also was rejected by Fidel. Authors' interview with Pazos.

[282] As Theodore Draper perceptively pointed out, "As one reads Castro's suc-
cession of statements in 1956–1958, the most striking thing about them is their increasing 'moderation' and constitutionalism." Draper, *Castroism: Theory and
Practice*, p. 15. Che Guevara affirmed that the manifesto was signed by Castro for
purely opportunistic reasons. It was, according to Che, "progressive at that moment" because it tacitly recognized the guerrillas' hegemony within the revolutionary movement. Guevara added, "We knew that it was a minimum program, a
program which limited our effort, but we also knew that it was impossible to establish our will from the Sierra Maestra and that we had to work for a long time
with all sorts of 'friends.'" Guevara, *Obra Revolucionaria*, p. 183.

July 30, 1957. An informer had told the police where he was hiding.[283]
His death brought about an internal crisis within the M–26–7, but
one of Fidel's pressing problems was over. From then on, the Oriente
underground was subordinated to the guerrillas, and the *sierra* thesis
began to dominate the movement.

The death sparked a wave of unrest. Santiago de Cuba was a city in
mourning when, on July 31, País was buried in a 26th of July Movement uniform with the rank of colonel. The following day, the newly
appointed U.S. ambassador, Earl E. T. Smith, visited the city to ascertain the true state of affairs on the island. Two hundred anti-Batista
women, dressed in black, took advantage of the ambassador's tour to
beg him to intervene and put an end to the regime's terror. When the
women began to shout "Libertad, libertad!" the police charged,
beating them brutally. Afterward in a press conference, Smith said he
deplored the "excessive use of force" by the police.[284]

A little later Batista established censorship, while tensions augmented
and a sort of spontaneous general strike paralyzed Oriente, Camagüey,
and part of Las Villas Provinces. The strike effort later collapsed,
because it lacked the necessary organization and was opposed by
major sectors of the economy. After all, Cuba was going through one
of its most prosperous years. Nonetheless, Frank País's assertion seemed
to be true: The conditions existed among the people and the workers
for a strike, but more organizing had to take place. Thus, most members of the newly formed M–26–7 national directorate began to work
toward a revolutionary general strike, while the guerrillas carried out
different plans.[285] The *sierra-llano* conflict persisted, but now the center
of the proponents of a general strike moved from Santiago de Cuba
to the capital.

Intermittent skirmishes with the guerrillas, urban terrorism, and
the people's growing discontent with the government's immorality
further discredited Batista, placing him in an unenviable situation. To

---

283 "Encuentro armado," *El Mundo* (Havana), July 31, 1957, p. 1, and "On the
Death of Frank País" in this volume. The name of the informer never has been
disclosed, but soon afterward he was killed by members of the 26th of July
Movement.

284 "Declaró en Santiago Mr. Smith," *El Mundo* (Havana), August 1, 1957,
pp. 1, A8.

285 It is an open queston as to precisely when the national directorate was
formed. Was it created before or after País died? How were its members appointed? What were its functions and relationships to the guerrillas? Perhaps we
can only say what Andrés Suárez said about it, that it was an "elusive and mysterious body." See Suárez, *Cuba: Castroism and Communism*, p. 33. A list of its members can be found in *Revolución* (Havana), January 24, 1959, p. 8, and July 26,
1959, p. 7.

aggravate matters, he was unable to establish a unified command, for government officials and even entire units conspired against him.

Noncommissioned officers within the armed forces had for several months plotted with the *llano* leadership of the M–26–7 to overthrow the government. A full-scale plan for a national uprising was agreed upon sometime in mid-1957. The barracks at Havana, Cienfuegos, Mariel, and Santiago de Cuba were to be taken, while civilians were to attack police stations and urge the citizenry over a major radio station to go on a general strike. In Havana, a participant recalls the details:

> The plan consisted of the bombing of Navy General Head-
> quarters. The Presidential Palace was to be shelled by a navy
> frigate . . . some of the air force men had been pledged and there
> was talk about the motorized police joining in, but mainly it was
> the navy's show in Havana.[286]

At the last minute the plan was called off. However, the Southern Naval District at Cienfuegos, on the southern coast of Las Villas Province, was not notified. Thus, on September 5, 1957, on schedule, the garrison revolted, and the city was taken. Hours later, after a fierce battle in which the city of Cienfuegos was bombed and strafed by the air force, loyal troops, aided by tanks, surrounded the men. The isolated rebellion was crushed rapidly.[287]

The police and the military intelligence service, which were the two main pillars of Batista's power, tortured and murdered many people suspected of revolutionary activities. However, this brutality offended many career officers, who then became close collaborators with the revolutionary cause. Once again, an apparent fiasco by the opposition weakened the very core of the regime because of Batista's blind and foolish reactions.

Revolutionary Leadership: Exiles versus Guerrillas

Realizing that the military was slowly disintegrating from within, that the regime was incapable of fostering loyalty, and that a united

---

[286] Roberto Pavon Tamayo, "Cienfuegos, September 5, 1957," *Granma* (Havana), September 11, 1966, p. 10. The navy had been anti-Batista since 1933.

[287] Some sources maintain that the plan had *not* been called off, but rather that Santiago was not informed of the correct date and Havana "betrayed" the plans. See Aldo Isidrón del Valle, "Movimiento armado del pueblo contra la tiranía," *Revolución* (Havana), September 5, 1963, pp. 2–3; for a different version, see Faustino Pérez, "Antecedentes del alzamiento de Cienfuegos," *Revolución* (Havana), September 4, 1962, p. 10. Cienfuegos was where those commissioned and noncommissioned officers considered unreliable by Batista were stationed. The most complete account of the revolt there is Julio Camacho, "El alzamiento de Cienfuegos," *Revolución* (Havana), on page 10 of each issue for September 5, 6, 7, 8, and 10, 1962.

front was needed, seven opposition groups met on October 15, 1957, in Miami, Florida.[288] Supposedly the men converging on that tourist resort were responding to the call by the Sierra Maestra Manifesto in mid-July for a united effort, but the Junta de Liberación (JL) formed by them actually reflected the desire of many to neutralize or control the increasing influence of the guerrillas. For instance, they had agreed that the JL would lead the insurrection both politically and strategically.

Felipe Pazos, who had signed the Sierra Maestra Manifesto and was then living in the United States, was invited to attend the meetings. He lacked the proper credentials, so with Lester Rodríguez (then Castro's representative in exile) he wrote to the national directorate of the M–26–7 requesting that this approval be part of the negotiations. Without informing Fidel, the national directorate replied, according to Pazos, in "such ambiguous terms that it was difficult to understand whether they were granting authorization or not. It could be interpreted either way, but we decided to interpret it as if the national directorate granted us the credentials to represent the 26th of July Movement at the negotiations.[289]

In November, the JL issued a manifesto closely resembling the Sierra Maestra Manifesto. It favored establishment of a provisional government which would call for elections "as soon as possible"; restoration of the 1940 Constitution; release of all political prisoners; creation of a career civil service; separation of the military from politics; rejection of Batista's proposed June 1958 elections; free labor union elections; and the promulgation of new economic and social reforms. It also called on the United States to withhold its arms shipments to Cuba as long as a civil war continued.[290] News of this "Unity Pact" did not reach Castro until November 20, when he received the public and secret guidelines of the document. The arrival of those papers, according to Fidel in a letter to the JL dated December 14, coincided with the most intense offensive launched by the tyranny against the guerrillas.

Castro refused to accept the Miami document. Pointing an accusing

288 See "Exilio: batalla de papeles," *Bohemia* (Havana), February 16, 1958, pp. 1–2 (supplement). The representatives were Carlos Prío, Tony Varona, Carlos Hevia (Auténticos); Roberto Agramonte, Manuel Bisbé, Salvador Massip (Ortodoxos); Lucas Moran, Felipe Pazos, Lester Rodríguez (M-26-7); Ramón Prendes, Juan Nuiry (FEU); Faure Chomón, Julio García, Alberto Mora (Directorio); Carlos Monstany, Antonio Silío, Alfredo González (OA); Ángel Cofiño, Pascasio Linares (Directorio Obrero).

289 Authors' interview with Dr. Felipe Pazos, Washington, D.C.

290 Gregorio Selser (ed.), *La revolución cubana* (Buenos Aires: Editorial Palestra, 1960), pp. 125–126.

finger, Fidel stated, "The 26th of July Movement did not designate or authorize any delegation to discuss such negotiations."[291] Thus, the agreement did not bind the M–26–7 because it was never approved by the *dirección nacional*. Furthermore, fundamental principles had been suppressed. Fidel wrote:

> To delete from the unity document the express declaration of refusing any kind of foreign intervention in the internal affairs of Cuba is evidence of lukewarm patriotism and a self-evident act of cowardice. . . . In the unity document, our express declaration of refusing any kind of provisional military junta rule of the Republic has been eliminated.[292]

What truly disturbed the guerrilla leader was the idea that "the revolutionary forces [would] be incorporated into the regular army" once Batista had been ousted. Deploring such a proposal, he added that "the 26th of July Movement claims for itself the function of maintaining public order and reorganizing the armed forces of the Republic."

In addition, Fidel believed that the pact threatened the very existence of the M–26–7 when it promoted the idea that all significant decisions were to be made by the exile body. Without qualms, he claimed the political and military leadership of the revolutionary movement for his Rebel Army. It was a fantasy to pretend to direct "from Miami a revolution that is being waged in all the cities and fields of the island." Abroad, he argued, they were merely carrying out "an imaginary revolution," while in Cuba the guerrillas were "making a real revolution." In other words, unity had to be attained on Fidel Castro's terms.[293]

Soon thereafter the JL was dissolved because of the fear that a united effort would be meaningless without the participation of the Fidelistas. But before this was done, all of the organizations secretly replied to Fidel's letter. The Auténticos reminded him that, contrary to his charge that other groups had not aided his movement, the *Granma* expedition was financed by Carlos Prío. It was the Directorio

[291] This statement contradicts Pazos's assertion that the national direcorate had sent an "ambiguous letter." Either Castro or Pazos is mistaken. If Pazos is right, then the national directorate of the M-26-7 had taken a concrete step to challenge Castro. And Fidel's repudiation of the Junta was aimed at the national directorate. If Castro is right, then it is clear that the exiles were trying to displace the center of the revolutionary movement from the Sierra Maestra to Miami. Either way, these two possibilities explain the abrupt change in Castro's attitude from wanting a broad united front in July 1957 to opposing it five months later.

[292] "Letter to the Cuban Liberation Junta" in this volume.

[293] Castro also proposed Manuel Urrutia Lleó as the future provisional president.

Revolucionario, however, that made the most cutting remarks. Faure Chomón, suggesting autocratic motives in Fidel, wrote:

> No organization can or should, as Dr. Castro has done in a sectarian fashion, claim for itself the representation of a revolution being made by all of Cuba. . . . Dr. Castro should remember the men of the Directorio Revolucionario cannot be given lessons in civics, sacrifice, patriotism, courage, or selflessness. Dr. Castro should remember that while he was in Mexico and the United States, we carried on our struggle. . . . He should remember that before he had arrived in Oriente the Directorio Revolucionario was dealing with colonels Blanco Rico and Tabernilla, while he, in Mexico, lamented the death of the former. Dr. Castro should remember that while he was in the lofty Oriente mountains, we were in Havana assaulting the Príncipe Prison, freeing *compañeros*, shooting Colonel Orlando Piedra [chief of military intelligence], burning fifteen patrol cars . . . and attacking the despot in his own den.[294]

And that, Chomón said, was no imaginary revolution. Nonetheless, with his simple letter Fidel had destroyed the exile's plans. At that moment the fact that he had 120 armed men under his command in the *sierra* demonstrated how Fidel, from a relatively weak position, was still capable of dismantling the designs of other oppositionists.

By the end of the year several battles were fought; and at Hombrito, in an isolated mountain region, the Fidelistas established basic training for recruits, small-scale manufacturing of explosives, boots, and uniforms. There was also a field hospital, and outposts were connected with Fidel's headquarters by telephone. The nomadic life had been transformed; territory was now secured. In February 1958, urban terror and counterterror kept up its relentless pace; the guerrillas began broadcasting over rebel radio, and four guerrilla columns already functioned in the Sierra Maestra.

On March 10, Raúl Castro and Juan Almeida, commanding two columns, were dispatched to open new fronts in Oriente. Raúl, with eighty-two men (twenty-six of whom were unarmed), was placed in charge of an area covering seven municipalities to the northeast of Fidel's group in the Sierra Cristal range. This area had been traditionally rebellious since the nineteenth century. Finally Juan Almeida completed the strategy of forming a triangle of guerrilla operations when he formed a base at El Cobre, west of Santiago de Cuba. The rebels had consolidated and begun expanding.

[294] No specific date appears on the original (authors' copy). A summary of the document appears in "Exilio: batalla de papeles," *Bohemia* (Havana), February 16, 1958 (supplement), pp. 1–2.

Arms Embargo. On January 25, 1958, Batista had returned constitutional guarantees and promised elections—to no avail. But on March 12 he once again abolished civil rights, announced an increase in the military budget, and asked the United States government to deliver weapons that had been on order for months. An opposition lobby, however, had been formed in Washington and pressured U.S. government officials to cancel the military assistance to the Cuban government.[295] On March 14, 1958, the U.S. Department of State informed Batista that it would suspend the shipment of arms to Cuba because the grant-in-aid equipment supplied under the Mutual Defense Assistance Program (which asserted that arms were to be used only for hemispheric defense) had been violated when Batista used those weapons for internal security.

Undoubtedly this action had a significant impact, especially for a country that traditionally tended to seek North American sanction for its policies. United States disapproval simply meant in influential circles on the island that Fulgencio Batista had to go. The following day the professional associations issued a manifesto demanding the resignation of the *caudillo.* Batista, the long-time strong man, was almost totally isolated, relying mainly on very close associates and the dreaded police and paramilitary groups that still depended on him.

The April 1958 Strike: The End Of The Llano. The visible deterioration of the dictatorship led the *llano* (primarily in Havana) to believe that the right moment had arrived for a general revolutionary strike. After many months of hard work, its thesis was to be put into effect based on the optimistic hope that if the capital were brought to a complete standstill, Batista would be ousted. Hence, in the first week of March, Faustino Pérez, the leader of the *llano*, went to the Sierra Maestra to discuss the matter. According to him, the guerrillas "did not have firsthand information on the existing conditions [in Havana]. It was we who provided them with that information, according to what we believed the situation to be."[296] For several days plans were discussed with Fidel.

[295] "Como se logró que E.U. no enviara armas a Batista," *Diario de la Marina* (Havana), March 1, 1959, p. 1C. During the years 1956-57, the United States had delivered 3,000 rifles, 40 machine guns, 4,000 rockets, 7 Sherman tanks, and considerable ammunition to the Cuban government. Requests also had been made for rocket launchers, additional rifles, and hand grenades. In October the shipment of a number of bombs and rockets was revealed by the opposition, causing considerable publicity. See *New York Times*, October 31, 1957.
[296] Faustino Pérez, "A Link in the Chain of Events that Led to Victory," *Granma* (Havana), April 13, 1969, p. 5.

On March 12, 1958, Fidel Castro, as commander in chief of the rebel forces, and Faustino Pérez, delegate of the national directorate, issued a twenty-two-point statement announcing "total war against the tyranny."[297] A general revolutionary strike, they stated, seconded by rebel military action, would put an end to the dictator. The new provisional government, the declaration affirmed, was to be headed by Manuel Urrutia Lleó (a judge who had stated during the trial of some of the *Granma* expeditionaries that oppositionists had the right to revolt against a dictatorship).

The restless and desperate desire of the *llano* to capture the initiative of revolutionary change met a traumatic defeat. On April 9, few workers heard the call for the general strike.[298] The surprise announcement was made, without previous notice, when most of them were working rather than listening to the radio. It was a tactical mistake, intended to surprise the regime which would be unable to take precautionary measures while action groups were to attack important production centers, block main highways, and capture police stations. In the end, the action groups did not carry out their plan because of lack of weapons. Furthermore, the urban cadres of the M–26–7 had made no effort to acquire the support of other groups. One of the strike leaders states, "No one had strong feelings or was enthusiastic about including other organizations, because we felt that they would not constitute an important factor in carrying out our plan."[299] Either the *llano* leadership was naïve and irresponsible or it believed itself self-sufficient, not wanting to share the glory of deposing Batista.

The strike's failure had significant repercussions. First, revolutionary groups finally came to the realization that Batista's power resided chiefly in the police, not the armed forces. His well-disciplined police force was efficient and merciless, exercising absolute control over the urban areas, while the army was lacking in morale and discipline, and was split by internal conflicts. Henceforth, revolutionary action had to be centered in the areas representing the weakest part of the regime, the rural areas. Also, the conflict between the urban underground and the guerrilla fronts ended after the urban resources, leadership, and cadres were obliterated and discredited.

At Altos de Mompié in the Sierra Maestra (May 3, 1958), the leaders of the *sierra* and the *llano* met to discuss the consequences of

[297] See "Total War against Tyranny" in this volume. Eight months earlier Fidel had had only one delegate in the *dirección nacional*, but now he occupied a position challenged only by Pérez.
[298] See "A Call to Strike" in this volume.
[299] Pérez, "Link in the Chain," p. 5.

the April strike fiasco.[300] From early morning until 2:00 A.M. the next day each side heatedly argued against the other. The *llano*, inclined to back up a civilian leadership, denounced the guerrillas' militarist mentality and the threat posed by Fidel's *caudillismo*. The *sierra*, on the other hand, pointed out the inability of the urban resistance to weaken the regime. In the end the *sierra* imposed its view, forcing the *llano* to agree that Fidel should become the commander in chief of all the revolutionary forces of the M–26–7. He also was appointed secretary-general of the national directorate, with the power to appoint five other members, and the urban militias were placed under the Rebel Army's command. Furthermore, the fact that the national leadership remained in the mountains, according to Che, "objectively eliminated some practical problems related to decision making which in the past had impeded Fidel from exerting real authority."[301] All the *llano* leaders, moreover, were replaced, and the entire 26th of July Movement was controlled at last from the Sierra Maestra. Fidel Castro finally had consolidated his control of the political and military leadership of the revolutionary movement.[302]

The 1958 Offensive

The April 9 setback of the urban underground encouraged Batista to move against the rebels in the mountains. It was now possible to move troops from the cities to the countryside, so during May 10,000 soldiers—fourteen battalions and seven companies—were deployed to Oriente Province under the command of General Eulogio Cantillo. On May 24, 1958, in the midst of torrential rains, the military offensive began.

The army moved down from the north and the northeast, through land mines and constant harassment. Fidel moved his eight columns to the west of Turquino Peak to form a front of fifteen miles. He positioned his troops at all natural entrances to the Sierra Maestra. Then, on June 15, the army began closing in from the south. For thirty-five

---

[300] The most thorough discussion of this meeting can be found in Guevara, *Obra Revolucionaria*, pp. 237–241, 250–252; and Interview with Marcelo Fernández Font, Radio Rebelde (Havana), April 9, 1964.

[301] Guevara, *Obra Revolucionaria*, p. 240.

[302] Whether Castro knew beforehand what the consequences of the strike would be and agreed, nonetheless, to let it happen in order to take over the movement is an open question. A good case might be made either way. See José Barbeito, *Realidad y Masificación* (Caracas: Ediciones Nuevo Orden, 1964), pp. 90–91; and "Relato de las acciones en Santa Clara por un responsable del M–26–7," *Revolución* (Havana), April 9, 1962, p. 11.

days government troops gained ground. The crucial moment came on June 19, as Fidel described it:

> In the course of those twenty-four hours, the enemy forces simultaneously penetrated Las Vegas de Jibacoa, Santo Domingo, and continued to advance toward Naranjal in La Plata from Palma Mocha, threatening with annihilation the most advanced platoons of our forces. . . . The enemy had penetrated deeply north and south. Between the troops that were attacking from both directions barely a distance of seven kilometers in a straight line remained.[303]

While Fidel was thus surrounded in the Sierra Maestra, Raúl Castro and the "Frank País" Second Front up in the Sierra Cristal were having better luck. Shortly after June 14, Major Pino Aguila, who commanded the nearly 1,000 troops there, signed a nonaggression pact with Raúl, which enabled the guerrilla forces there to go to the aid of Fidel.[304]

The defenders in the Sierra Maestra, meanwhile, were desperate under enemy bombing. Then they came up with a plan. On June 26 they kidnapped close to a dozen United States citizens and two days later the U.S. consul in Santiago paid a visit to Raúl Castro.[305] His mission was to discuss terms for their release. The plan had worked. Batista buckled under Washington's pressure to save the lives of North Americans, and the bombing stopped. The military objective of the operation was to gain time—to acquire men and material and to rest. The detention of the North Americans paralyzed the war for three weeks, allowing the guerrillas to recuperate and strengthen their positions.

However, there was still the land offensive to contend with. The government troops penetrated further into rebel territory, suffering more ambushes and becoming more isolated from their supply centers. They were losing men, food and ammunition were running low, and they had lost their air cover. In addition, they were constantly bombarded by psychological warfare. Through loudspeakers Fidel urged the troops situated throughout the area to join a truly just cause, to go to the side of the people, and to fight for justice and democracy. He told them they did not have to fight for a dictator whose commanders did not go into battle but stayed home and enriched themselves.

---

[303] "Report on the Offensive: Part 1" in this volume.

[304] Marta Rojas, "El Segundo Frente Oriental Frank País: operación antiaérea," *Bohemia* (Havana), July 5, 1955, pp. 50–51.

[305] José L. Cuza, "Combate del centro industrial de Moa," *Verde Olivo* (Havana), July 14, 1963, pp. 18–24.

Of the thirty battles during the seventy-six-day government offensive, six were significant. One, the battle of Jigüe, began on July 11.[306] Major José Quevedo and his men were encircled by the rebels and left without the logistical support he was supposed to have received. Without food or water and with Castro appealing to them to surrender, the morale within Quevedo's ranks began to deteriorate. Nine days after the battle began, Fidel learned that the army commander had been a classmate at the university. On July 15, the guerrilla leader requested a cease-fire so that a letter could be delivered to Quevedo.[307] A truce was agreed on, and that night the men got together.

Rebel and government soldiers met, embraced, and shared the food dropped from government planes. Quevedo reminded his men that their first duty was to the permanent interests of the fatherland, and that to achieve those ends it was necessary to join the rebel forces. The men agreed; 146 surrendered, and the rebels confiscated a considerable number of weapons and ammunition. Quevedo remained captive and was eventually instrumental in establishing contacts with other army officers which lead to conspiracies within the army by the end of 1958.

Then on July 29, government forces under the command of Lieutenant Colonel Sánchez Mosquera in Santo Domingo suffered about 1,000 casualties and had 400 prisoners taken by the rebels. To compound their problems, torrential rains due to the hurricane season forced the government offensive to a close. The army, demoralized, frustrated, and confused, retreated to the garrisons on the perimeter on August 7. The withdrawal command and all explicit orders were monitored by the rebels, who subsequently turned the retreat into a disorderly rout in which tanks, arms, ammunition, food, and medicine were left behind. The defeat was broadcast to all of Cuba by rebel radio. Soon thereafter the rebel counteroffensive was launched.

Rebel Political and Military Offensive. The rebel leader spoke almost daily to the Cuban people in general and the armed forces in particular. Attempts by the government to deceive the troops were disclosed. Castro also expressed his sympathy with the soldiers who had been sacrificed by the military command.[308]

While the seeds of discord continued to be planted within the military, Fidel attempted to bring about a reconciliation of all opposition forces. Enjoying the power produced by the recent turn of

[306] "The Battle of Jigüe" in this volume.

[307] "Letter to Major José Quevedo" in this volume.

[308] "Proclamation to Batista's Soldiers" and "Report on the Offensive" in this volume.

events, he was able to dictate terms while appearing sincere in his desire for unification.

On July 20, 1958, the "Caracas Pact" or "Unity Manifesto of the Sierra Maestra," proclaimed by Fidel over a rebel radio station, was signed by eight groups.[309] The issue of a common strategy consisting of armed insurrection became central. The declaration also conceived of a general strike which could be successful by the mobilization of every sector of society. In contrast with previous manifestoes, Castro referred in very general terms to "a brief provisional government," the return to a constitutional program, and a minimal program guided by the principles of punishing the guilty, securing the rights of workers, fulfillment of international obligations, and the securing of peace, order, and the socioeconomic as well as political development of Cuba. He also called on all soldiers to stop supporting the regime and demanded a cessation of United States aid to Batista. Finally, the declaration summoned all revolutionary organizations to endorse the declaration and meet later to discuss the basis for a more thorough unity.[310] Relations, however, were still strained among the groups.[311]

Financial assistance poured into the treasury of the guerrillas from all sides. Many, like the sugar planters who did not want their crops burned, thought they were buying a sort of insurance. This is why Fidel by October was willing to spend one dollar for every bullet purchased.[312]

With over 800 armed men at his command, Fidel outlined his strategy. The countryside would soon be in rebel hands, forcing the enemy to retreat to the cities. Then the urban areas would be surrounded and isolated by cutting off all possible land communications. No traffic would be permitted in or out of the cities. At the same time the regime's forces would be weakened by urban terror, culminating in a concerted attack by the *guerrilleros*.

This strategy, however, could not bring about Batista's downfall unless other provinces in addition to Oriente followed the plan and

[309] Text in this volume.

[310] Andrés Suárez asserts that immediately Castro began negotiations to have the meeting held in the Sierra Maestra so that he could control it. See Suárez, *Castro: Cuba and Communism*, p. 28.

[311] Carlos Prío, for instance, opposed the appointment of Manuel Urrutia as the future provisional president. See "Interview with Enrique Meneses" in this volume.

[312] See "Letter to Major Juan Almeida" (October 8, 1958) in this volume. José Bosch, president of Bacardí Corporation, contributed one million dollars, according to one source. Juan Bosch, "Dictadura con respaldo popular," *Ahora!* (Dominican Republic), June 16, 1969, p. 39.

coordinated their actions. The island had to be invaded from the Sierra Maestra.[313] Column 1, named "José Martí" and under Fidel's personal command, as well as Raúl Castro's columns, would stay in Oriente, while two other columns moved westward. That is why on August 18 Major Camilo Cienfuegos was assigned the mission of "leading a column from the Sierra Maestra to Pinar del Río Province to carry out the strategic plan of the Rebel Army."[314] Three days later Che Guevara was entrusted with the invasion of Las Villas Province to harass the enemy, until they were totally paralyzed, and intercept any troop movement from west to east.[315]

In late August two columns, independent of each other, began their journey westward. They numbered 200 armed men who either had graduated recently from the training camp at Minas del Frio or were seasoned fighters. A veteran of the column led by Guevara recalls the details:

> The weather was very bad. A hurricane was beating down on the island, and heavy rains were falling in the zone we were to pass. The first day we walked seven leagues. At night we reached the highway and found some trucks, but they were not of much use, for not far from where we began they got stuck. We had to abandon them and continue on foot under the unceasing rain, walking in deep mud.[316]

After an excruciating forty-five-day march, Guevara reached the Escambray Mountains in the south of Las Villas Province. Camilo Cienfuegos, in the north, had arrived days earlier. Although close to ten men died or were wounded, encounters with the government troops were few in the plains of Camagüey. In his diary Camilo Cienfuegos stated on October 9 that although the enemy had seen them, "they did not try to stop us."[317]

Now they had to carry out an urgent order: to implement the boycott of the November 3 elections called by the government in a hopeless effort to find a political solution. Fidel, on October 10, had decreed that no one could participate in such a farce. Whoever dared to do so

[313] This plan was similar to that of the independence fighters in the nineteenth century. Castro's forces followed the model of Calixto García's troops, while Cienfuegos copied Antonio Maceo; Guevara, interestingly, repeated the actions of Máximo Gómez (a revolutionary born in the Dominican Republic).

[314] "Orders to Camilo Cienfuegos" in this volume.

[315] "Che Guevara Ordered to Invade Las Villas" in this volume.

[316] Oscar Fernández Mell, "De las Mercedes a Gavilanes," *Verde Olivo* (Havana), August 25, 1963, p. 15.

[317] Camilo Cienfuegos, "Diario de campaña," *Revolución* (Havana), November 16, 1959, pp. 28, 31–32. Some maintain that the garrison commanders in the area had been paid to allow the guerrillas to pass by.

could be shot.[318] Thus, in late October intense guerrilla activity aimed at keeping the regime in an unstable position began in Oriente, Camagüey, and Las Villas, while nightly disorders, bombings, and terrorism erupted in Havana and other cities.

The electoral turnout was low and as expected the government's candidate "won." This was another big mistake on Batista's part because he wasted an opportunity to end violence by means of honest elections. Instead he managed to turn the remaining neutral Cubans toward the proponents of armed insurrection. There was no other alternative.

The government's mistakes did not, however, create a more cooperative mood among revolutionary groups. Still lurking in the background was the question of power and who was to rule Cuba ultimately once the rebellion had triumphed. The invasion of Las Villas did not improve the chances of agreement, for the move was viewed by some as a clear example of Castro's desire to establish a foothold in the area and control all the independent guerrilla fronts there.

Fidel was well aware that, if Batista fell, most of the guerrillas operating in the Escambray Mountains would be closer to Havana, center of economic and political power, allowing others to impose their own conditions on future developments. It was therefore imperative to place all the guerrilla groups in Las Villas under the command (or coordination) of the 26th of July Movement.

In mid-1957, several groups had initiated preparations for guerrilla war in the Escambray Mountains. The most influential one was composed of young Auténticos and Ortodoxos from the town of Sancti Spiritus, who felt a regionalistic call to action. They thought the people of Las Villas could not be left behind by the revolutionary actions carried out in Havana or Oriente.[319] There were also veterans of the attack on the Presidential Palace who for one reason or another had not supported the assault. Needless to say, their relations with what was left of the Directorio Revolucionario were far from friendly.

On November 10, 1957, about forty such men formally created a military organization, the Frente del Escambray, in which all other revolutionary groups could function if they did not try to politicize

---

318 See "No-Election Decree" in this volume. On the same date Law Number 3 was issued by Fidel Castro and Dr. Sori Marín (later shot by the revolutionary government for conspiracy). The law established the right to the land, free of charge, for all peasants who had less than 165 acres and who were working on the land when the law was promulgated as tenants, sublessees, or sharecroppers. Landowners were to be compensated by the state.

319 Interview with Andrés Nazario Sargen (a founder of the Escambray guerrillas), Miami, Florida, September 2, 1969.

the insurgents to benefit any specific group. The commanders of the Frente were Eloy Gutiérrez Menoyo and Jesús Carreras.

Complications ensued. On February 7, 1958, seventeen Directorio members sailed from Miami to Nuevitas, most of whom moved toward the Escambray to begin guerrilla activities. With their large number of weapons, the Directorio strengthened the guerrillas, and for a moment collaboration appeared possible. But clashes over leadership soon developed. The Directorio (led by Faure Chomón) wanted the whole guerrilla operation to be under its control, but Menoyo, who had once been a member of the Directorio Revolucionario, disapproved of the proposal because he realized that his authority as commander in chief of the Escambray front would end. Differences also arose over weapons. Chomón argued that the correct strategy was to fight in Havana, to hit at the top, and to reorganize the Directorio's urban underground. Menoyo held to his view that only guerrilla war would be successful. In March the two factions finally split.

Menoyo's group then created the Second Front of the Escambray, a politicomilitary organization jealously guarding its independence.[320] The Directorio, on the other hand, sent some of its men to Havana, while Rolando Cubela, and later Faure Chomón, carried out guerrilla operations in the region.

Such was the situation as Che Guevara marched toward Las Villas to coordinate the efforts of all the guerrilla bands. Several days before entering the province, the Second Front sent a commission to Castro to ascertain why two invading columns were approaching their territory. This commission, headed by the M–26–7 member Víctor Bordón, returned without informing the Second Front of their conference with Fidel. Bordón, however, urged his men to join Che's forces and was immediately arrested for "treason" by Menoyo. On October 9, Jesús Carreras, one of Menoyo's lieutenants, sent Guevara a forceful warning:

> Having news that you are moving toward this zone without having communicated officially with our organization, I want to warn you that this zone is controlled by our guerrillas. We ask you before you enter this zone to make clear your true intentions.[321]

Che ignored the missive. In mid-October he entered the Escambray Mountains by way of the Directorio's zone. Soon one of his patrols was arrested, and then released, by the Second Front. They had trespassed beyond a sign installed by Menoyo and reading "No one can

[320] In mid-July the Second Front allied itself with the forces of Víctor Bordón, a member of the M–26–7.
[321] Letter of Jesús Carreras to Ernesto Guevara, October 9, 1958. Author's photostatic copy (courtesy of Lázaro Asencio).

enter this territory without our authorization." Fidel, when informed of these incidents, ordered Camilo's column, then in the north of Las Villas, to stay there because "the politicorevolutionary situation there is complex, and your presence in the province is indispensable *to help Che establish it solidly*."[322]

On October 21, Che met with Faure Chomón. During the course of the meeting Chomón made it clear, presumably to Guevara's delight, that the forces of the Directorio would not engage in any conversations with the Second Front of Escambray, as he considered them "bandits."[323]

Although Guevara shared Chomón's opinion, particularly with respect to Menoyo, he insisted that it was his mission to bring unity to the Escambray Mountains. However, sixteen days later, on November 7, the 26th of July Movement gave up its efforts at "unity." The leaders told the Directorio that the M–26–7 also shared their feelings with regard to the Second Front of Escambray and that it was best to exclude Menoyo and his men from further conversations. They then suggested that the possibility of an alliance between the M–26–7 and the Directorio should be discussed.

This uneasy alliance between two movements that had fought over the leadership of the insurrection throughout the whole revolutionary process was documented through the Pedrero Pact, which was signed both by Ernesto Guevara for the 26th of July Movement and by Rolando Cubela for the Directorio.

Because the die had been cast and neither the M–26–7 nor the Directorio had any intention of holding conversations with the Second Front, what emerged from this pact, aside from the rhetoric of the document, was the foothold Fidel expected to gain in the Escambray.[324] In essence, the political maneuvering that went on and Guevara's shrewdness as a negotiator playing on the rivalries and emotions of both movements further strengthened the control of the M–26–7 over still another revolutionary group. At the end the Directorio found itself divided, as some of its members were not in accord with what had taken place.

As for Menoyo's Second Front of Escambray, the thesis remained unchanged: that guerrilla warfare and political leadership did not inevitably have to be controlled by the 26th of July. Cooperation was possible, they felt, but not subordination. The ill feelings that arose

[322] "Letter to Major Camilo Cienfuegos (October 14, 1958)" in this volume. Emphasis added.
[323] Faure Chomón, "Cuando el Che llego al Escambray," *Verde Olivo* (Havana), December 1, 1965, pp. 12–18.
[324] "Pedrero Pact" in Bonachea and Valdés (eds.), *Che: Selected Works of Ernesto Guevara*, pp. 41–42.

out of this incident would carry through into the first years of the Revolution.

Guevara scored a brilliant victory. He created the united front and concluded an alliance with one of the two key guerrilla units in the area to the exclusion of the other, which had too weak an organization to react. In the end, the 26th of July would prevail.

In November, a general revolutionary offensive began throughout Oriente Province. A systematic war on transportation was launched simultaneously with attacks against the barracks at Bayamo, Holguín, Manzanillo, and other towns. The sugar harvesting and all military movements had to stop. One after another the barracks passed into rebel hands, and defectors joined the swelling rebel ranks.[325] On November 17, Fidel left his headquarters in the Sierra Maestra and started an offensive on the plains of Oriente with the aid of other rebel columns.[326]

On November 20, at Guisa, the rebels clashed against the most important government forces deployed in Oriente. For almost two weeks both sides fought incessantly; but in the end, on December 6, the *guerrilleros* entered the town. The enemy had suffered 200 casualties; four battalions were forced to retreat; a tank, ninety-four rifles, three mortars, one bazooka, and fourteen trucks were captured. That battle illustrated the increasing control of Oriente by Castro's forces. All roads were closed, telephone and electric services were sabotaged, and the enemy retreated to small pockets of resistance in the major urban areas.

In Las Villas the government faced a similar problem. The forces of Guevara, Cienfuegos, the Second Front, and the Directorio threatened to cut the island in half, completely isolating Havana from two of the larger provinces. Therefore, the government plan made a point of defeating the revolutionists in Las Villas before moving against Castro once again.

On November 29, close to 2,000 reinforcements with tanks and heavy equipment moved toward rebel territory. Nonetheless, isolated barracks continued to fall prey to the *guerrilleros*. By December 18, the outcome could be anticipated: The strategic garrison at Fomento, after several hours of bloody struggle, surrendered and joined Che's forces. Three days later the city of Cabaiguán, which controlled Cuba's major highway, was lost by the army, while Camilo Cienfuegos took Yaguajay, Placetas, Remedios, Caibarién, and Sanctí Spiritus.

[325] See "Communiqué to Paralyze Transportation" and "Orders to the Rebel Army" in this volume.
[326] Carlos Franqui, Rebel Radio broadcast, December 2, 1958, reproduced in *Revolución* (Havana), December 2, 1959, pp. 1, 6.

Under such discouraging defeats the commander of the government forces chose to retreat into Santa Clara (capital of Las Villas Province), where the last battle before opening the way to Havana was to be fought. Naturally, as the guerrillas controlled almost the entire province, Santa Clara was heavily besieged.

In Havana, Batista could not bring himself to fully understand the situation. He had just formed a joint command, which was plagued with rivalries and conflicting opinions as to how to conduct the war. Although he had close to 40,000 armed men theoretically under his authority, he was almost totally powerless. Moreover, the United States had decided to dispose of him, asking through an emissary that he capitulate. Batista was finished.[327]

To complicate the spectacle, during December several conspiracies within the military planned the regime's demise. Castro, who was aware of the plots, contacted General Eulogio Cantillo, then commander of all military forces in Oriente and chief of the Joint General Staff, and asked his cooperation.

On December 28, 1958, General Cantillo arrived for a meeting with Fidel at Oriente Sugar Mill in Palma Soriano.[328] After four hours of talks they finally agreed that Cantillo would lead the army in revolt on December 31. According to Castro himself, Cantillo offered the unconditional support of the armed forces to the revolutionary movement. In Castro's words,

> It was made clear that the support of the armed forces would be unconditional: that the president would be designated by the revolutionaries and what positions would be assigned to the military. The support offered was unconditional, and the plan was examined in all its details. On the thirty-first at 3:00 P.M., the garrison

[327] Ambassador Earl E. T. Smith maintains that by November the United States Government had decided that Batista must be replaced. See his account, *The Fourth Floor* (New York: Random House, 1962), p. 169. On November 2, 1958, Secretary of State John Foster Dulles attended a reception at the Cuban Embassy in Washington, D.C., and spoke with Mr. William Pawley (an American businessman), requesting him to act as an emissary to Batista and persuade the latter to leave the country. In Pawley's words: "I was selected to go to Cuba to talk to Batista and see if I could convince him to capitulate. . . . I spent three hours [with Batista] on the night of December 9. I was unsuccessful in my effort. . . . I offered him an opportunity to live at Daytona Beach with his family . . . to make an effort to stop Fidel Castro from coming to power." See Testimony before the Subcommittee of the U.S. Senate Judiciary Committee to Investigate the Administration of the Internal Security Act, September 2, 1960.

[328] Castro was accompanied by Raúl Chibás, Vilma Espín, Celia Sánchez, Major José Quevedo, and Father Francisco Guzmán. Cantillo came with his helicopter pilot, who did not, however, attend the meeting. See "Juzgan en Ciudad Libertad al ex-general Eulogio Cantillo," *Diario de la Marina* (Havana), May 16, 1959, pp. 1, 9b; and author's interview with Father Francisco Guzmán, Washington, D.C., June 14, 1971.

of Santiago de Cuba would revolt. Immediately thereafter, several rebel columns would enter the city, and the people with the military and rebels would unite, issuing to the country a revolutionary manifesto and inviting all honorable military men to join the movement. It was agreed that the tanks in the city would be placed under our command, and I personally offered to advance toward the capital in an armored column led by tanks. The tanks would be delivered by 3:00 P.M., not because we thought we were going to have to fight, but in case the move should fail in Havana and the need should arise to situate our vanguard as near as possible to the capital, and also to prevent that from occurring.[329]

On the following day (December 29) Cantillo informed Batista of his deliberations with Castro. The two men concluded that a military junta, after Batista had left the country on January 6, 1959, would cut the ground from under the revolutionaries' feet. In the hope of misleading Castro, Cantillo sent him a note recommending that all plans be postponed to January 6, without saying anything about his agreement with Batista.

Fidel, however, was suspicious. Aware that no delay could be allowed for a military junta to take over, he immediately requested and obtained the collaboration of Santiago de Cuba's army chief.[330] Cantillo's agreement, Fidel soon knew, had been an empty gesture aimed at hampering the revolutionary takeover.

On New Year's Eve, Fulgencio Batista was in bad spirits. That day rebels had seized the city of Santa Clara, even after numerous reinforcements had been sent. He was frightened and after some hesitation went to his private office at army headquarters in Havana. There with his close friends and associates, he decided to abandon the country; no other possibility remained. At 2:00 A.M. on January 1, 1959, Batista issued his final declaration while in power. The statement said that the Military High Command had notified Batista of its inability to reestablish order and considered the situation of the country "grave." Then his resignation had been requested. Church and business representatives also had requested him to do so. Batista concluded by appealing to the armed forces and law-enforcement authorities "to obey and cooperate with the new government and the leadership of the armed forces, which will be under the command of Major General Eulogio Cantillo Porras."[331]

The master of the coup d'état, who directly or indirectly had held Cuban politics in his hands since 1934, left that same evening, seeking refuge in the Dominican Republic.

[329] Fidel Castro, Speech of January 2, 1959.
[330] "Letter to Colonel Rego Rubido" in this volume.
[331] "La Renuncia," *Revolución* (Havana), January 5, 1963 (supplement), p. 3.

Cantillo immediately made a ludicrous attempt to set up a civilian-military junta presided over by Dr. Carlos M. Piedra, the oldest magistrate of the Supreme Court.[332] Hearing the news, Fidel acted swiftly, as the future of the rebellion depended on his response. He indignantly issued a proclamation exposing the junta's complicity, the Rebel Army's resolve to continue fighting, and a demand for the unconditional surrender of the armed forces.[333] "Revolution, *yes;* military coup, *no!*" the statement warned, because a military take-over would only prolong the war.

Hours later, Castro read a second declaration over rebel radio.[334] It called for a general strike and made demands similar to the previous ones. Soon thereafter Camilo and Che were ordered to advance on Havana, and Major Hubert Matos took Santiago de Cuba without a shot.

The nationwide strike succeeded in bringing Cuba to a standstill. Yielding to the mounting pressure, the junta disintegrated. Colonel Ramón Barquín, who had been imprisoned for conspiring against Batista, was released. Placed in command of the armed forces, he quickly put Cantillo under house arrest. (The irony here is that Cantillo, hoping to get back in Fidel's good graces, had delegated his authority to Barquín at the last minute!)

In Oriente, Castro appointed Manuel Urrutia provisional president, tactfully granted the military commander of Santiago leadership of the armed forces, and perceptively "moved" the capital from Havana to Santiago de Cuba.

The rush for power was on. In the extreme confusion every organization eagerly ran to Havana, believing that whoever could control Havana would also rule Cuba. Camilo and Che seized the two major military installations there for the M–26–7, while the Directorio set up camp at the University of Havana and the Presidential Palace. The Second Front held small garrisons in the Havana suburbs and some police stations. Meanwhile, in Santiago, Fidel patiently awaited the proper moment to enter Havana and consolidate his power.

An era was over. Yet the issue of who would actually control the government still remained unsolved. Soon a generation of revolutionists would learn that the easiest part of a revolutionary process had ended and the most trying stage, that of radically changing the social, political, economic, and cultural structures of a nation, had just begun.

---

[332] Dr. Ricardo Nuñez Portuondo, Raúl de Cárdenas, Gustavo Cuervo, Alberto Blanco, General Loynaz del Castillo, and General Eulogio Cantillo were members of the junta.

[333] "Instructions to All Commanders of the Rebel Army and the People" in this volume.

[334] "General Strike Proclamation" in this volume.

Supplementary Bibliography

The articles and books listed in this bibliography, which follows the chronology of the Introduction, were also consulted in the writing of the Introduction.

Fidel Castro's Childhood

Angier, Angel I. "La literatura." In *Facetas de la vida de Cuba republicana, 1902–1952,* edited by Emilio Roig de Leuchsenring. Havana: Oficina del Historiados de la Ciudad, 1954.

Castro, Fidel. "Our History is Now One Hundred Years Old." *Granma, Weekly Review* (Havana), October 13, 1968.

González Pedrero, Manuel. *Estudios sobre literaturas hispanoamericanas.* Mexico: Fondo de Cultura Económica, 1951.

"Hechos y fechas de la vida de Fidel publicados en la prensa de la Unión Soviética." *Revolución* (Havana), May 4, 1963, p. 3.

Mañach, Jorge. *La crisis de la alta cultura.* Havana: La Universal, 1925.

Mañach, Jorge. "Revolution in Cuba." *Foreign Affairs,* vol. 12 (October 1933), p. 53.

Marinello, Juan. *Contemporáneos, noticia y memoria.* Santa Clara: Universidad Central de Las Villas, 1964.

Varona, Enrique José. *De la colonia a la república.* Havana, 1919.

1933: Revolution and Reaction

Bonsal, Phillip W. "Cuba, Castro and the United States," *Foreign Affairs,* vol. 40 (January 1962), p. 264.

Cruz, Alberto. "La fórmula insurreccional." *Tiempo en Cuba* (Havana), December 26, 1948, p. 5.

Quintana, Jorge. "Las jornadas revolucionarias de Marzo 1935." *Bohemia* (Havana), May 23, 1948, pp. 30–32, 93; May 30, 1948, pp. 50–52, 84.

Valdés, Nelson P. "Sugar Diplomacy: The United States and Cuba." Unpublished manuscript. Albuquerque, New Mexico: University of New Mexico, 1968.

The University Years: Background

Bárcena, Rafael García. "Constitución y revolución." *Bohemia* (Havana), March 7, 1948, pp. 32–74.

Cueto, Mario G. del. "Como murió Emilio Tró." *Bohemia* (Havana), September 21, 1947, pp. 56–61.

Editorial. *Diario de la Marina* (Havana), June 24, 1948, p. 4.

"La frustración revolucionaria." *Bohemia* (Havana), May 16, 1948, pp. 12, 14.

"Hizo una grave declaración el padre de Morín Dopico." *Diario de la Marina* (Havana), February 10, 1948, pp. 1, 25.

Ichaso, Francisco. "Eso que llaman Revolución." *Diario de la Marina* (Havana), June 26, 1948, p. 4.

Mañach, Jorge. "Hollywood y la niñez cubana." *Diario de la Marina* (Havana), June 26, 1948, p. 4.

Movimiento Socialista Revolucionario, Acuerdos y resoluciones (Havana, 1949), pp. 5–64.

Remos, Juan J. "Yo defiendo a los estudiantes." *Diario de la Marina* (Havana), June 25, 1948, p. 4.

Fidel at the University

"Apoyan los estudiantes la elevación de los salarios." *Diario de la Marina* (Havana), September 15, 1948, pp. 1, 20.

"Efectuada anoche la velada conmemorativa de la muerte de Tró." *Diario de la Marina* (Havana), September 16, 1948, p. 14.

"Fué un complot organizado por los comunistas la revolución en Bogotá." *Diario de la Marina* (Havana), April 13, 1948, pp. 1, 6.

Rodríguez, Gerardo. *Fidel Castro, biografía* (Havana: Fernández y Cia, 1959), pp. 11–12.

"Universidad." *Tiempo en Cuba* (Havana), October 2, 1949, pp. 4–5.

Fidel and the Ortodoxo Party

"Noticiero político: ortodoxos." *Diario de la Marina* (Havana), May 26, 1948, p. 14.

Palacios, Carlos González. "El cinismo político en Cuba." *Bohemia* (Havana), April 18, 1948, p. 27.

Toledo, Tomás. "Background on the Assault on Moncada and Bayamo Garrisons." *Granma Weekly Review* (Havana), June 18, 1967, p. 11.

Torriente, Loló de la. "Eso de Eduardo R. Chibás." *Bohemia* (Havana), August 16, 1963, pp. 1–6.

Torriente, Loló de la. "Una ráfaga en la tormenta." *Bohemia* (Havana), August 15, 1969, p. 7.

"A vueltas con la re-eleccion." *Tiempo* (Mexico), February 7, 1947, p. 18.

Batista's Coup

Castro, Fidel. "Pardo Llada escapó." *Diario de la Marina* (Havana), March 30, 1961, p. 7.

"Critica severamente Prío en Mexico el golpe militar ocurrido en Cuba."
El Mundo (Havana), March 14, 1952, pp. 1, 8.

"Declaró el Dr. Prío en la causa del dia 10 de Marzo." *Diario de la Marina*
(Havana), May 26, 1959, p. 10A.

"Descubren asociación conspirativa." *El Mundo* (Havana), June 3, 1952, pp.
1, 10.

"Explican como se ejecutó la Revolución." *El Mundo* (Havana), March 11,
1952, pp. 1, 5.

"Inadmisible el recurso ortodoxo." *El Mundo* (Havana), April 3, 1952, p. 1.

Lechuga, Carlos M. "Loteria sin billetes." *El Mundo* (Havana), March 14,
1952, p. 7.

Prío, Carlos. "Al Pueblo de Cuba." *El Mundo* (Havana), March 12, 1952,
p. 8.

"Prío se dirige al Tribunal de Garantias." *El Mundo* (Havana), March 27,
1952, p. 1.

"Publicó el fallo sobre el recurso ortodoxo." *El Mundo* (Havana), April 4,
1952, p. 1.

Conspiracy Begins

"Acusado Emilio Ochoa de incitar al pueblo a derrocar el gobierno." *El
Mundo* (Havana), August 26, 1952, pp. 1, A8.

Fernández, Pablo A. "Abel, el amigo de lucha." *Revolución* (Havana), August 7, 1962, p. 7.

Granda, Jacinto. "Artemisa y la Revolución." *Juventud Rebelde* (Havana),
July 25, 1966, p. 2.

Lechuga, Carlos M. "El motor inmóvil." *El Mundo* (Havana), December 17,
1952, p. A9.

Ortiz, Rubén. "El documento ortodoxo." *El Mundo* (Havana), December
18, 1952, p. A7.

Otero, Lisandro. "Entrevista a Haydée Santamaría y Melba Hernández."
Juventud Rebelde (Havana), July 25, 1966, p. 5.

Rodríguez, Leandro. *Historia del pueblo de Artemisa*. Havana: Talleres
Tipográficos La Prueba, 1946.

Villar, Carmen. "El asalto al Moncada (Entrevista con Oscar Alcalde)."
Juventud Rebelde (Havana), July 20, 1966, p. 10.

The MNR Revolt

Alonso, Luis Ricardo. "Es falso que intentara tomar Columbia el Domingo
de Resurrección (Entrevista con García Bárcena)." *Bohemia* (Havana),
April 26, 1953, p. 52.

"La escisión ortodoxa." *Bohemia* (Havana), December 27, 1953, p. 67.

"La inscripición del PPC." *Bohemia* (Havana), December 27, 1953, p. 68.

Lechuga, Carlos M. "Los censores." *El Mundo* (Havana), June 4, 1953, p. A7.

"Niega García Bárcena estar conspirando." *El Mundo* (Havana), July 9, 1962, p. 1.

Moncada: The Plan Unfolds

"Anuncian un golpe de fuerza." *El Mundo* (Havana), June 18, 1953, pp. 1, A12.

Barrera Pérez, Colonel Pedro A. "Por que el ejército no derrotó a Castro." *Bohemia* (Havana), August 6, 1961, pp. 28–29.

Batista, Fulgencio. "Terminó la tolerancia." *El Mundo* (Havana), July 28, 1953, p. 1.

Calle, Enrique O. la. *Cuatro siglos de la historia de Bayamo.* Bayamo, 1947.

Castro, Fidel. "The OLAS Conference: A Great Ideological Victory." *Granma, Weekly Review* (Havana), August 20, 1967, pp. 1–6.

"Continua la labor de Mons. Pérez para una pacificación." *Diario de la Marina* (Havana), July 31, 1953, pp. 1, 23.

García, Andrés. "El asalto al cuartel de Bayamo." *Revolución* (Havana), July 20, 1962, pp. 1, 2.

"Julio: la guerra civil." *Bohemia* (Havana), December 27, 1953, p. 70.

Matamoros, Marta. "El asalto al cuartel de Bayamo." *Granma* (Havana), July 6, 1967, pp. 4–5.

Mila Ortiz, Pablo. "Civiles Muertos." *El Mundo* (Havana), July 28, 1953, p. A8.

"Plan de invasión." *El Mundo* (Havana), July 4, 1953, p. A12.

Ponce Díaz, Comandante José. "Recuerdos del ataque." *Verde Olivo* (Havana), July 26, 1963, p. 17.

Villar, Carmen. "El asalto al Moncada." *Juventud Rebelde* (Havana), June 20, 1966.

Fidel in Prison

Conte Agüero, Luis. "Traslado a la Cabaña." *Diario Nacional* (Santiago), April 5, 1955.

"En la cárcel de Santiago de Cuba ocho fugitivos capturados." *Diario de la Marina* (Havana), August 2, 1952, p. 1.

Hernández, Melba. "Siempre supimos que el asalto al Moncada culminaría en la victoria." *Verde Olivo* (Havana), July 21, 1963, p. 32.

Martorrel, Juan. "Ese hombre no debe hablar!" *Revolución* (Havana), July 22, 1963, p. 4.

Montané, Jesús. "Del 26 de Julio de 1953 al 15 de Mayo de 1955." *Verde Olivo* (Havana), July 28, 1953, pp. 22–23.

"Sancionada la amnistía política." *Diario de la Marina* (Havana), May 7, 1955, pp. 1, 11A.

Political Struggle in Cuba

Pérez, Faustino. "La lucha contra Batista." *El Mundo* (Havana), December 2, 1964, pp. 1, 7.

"Suspenden el programa radical del P.P.C." *Diario de la Marina* (Havana), May 24, 1955, p. 3A.

Origins of the 26th of July Movement

Casuso, Teresa. *Cuba and Castro.* New York: Random House, 1961.

Lesnick, Max. "Prío merece una respuesta." *Bohemia* (Havana), August 14, 1955, pp. 63, 75.

The Call for Revolution

"Cuba Bars Political Meetings." *New York Times*, December 2, 1955.

"Cuban Students Hurt in Riot." *New York Times*, November 29, 1955.

"Diez años de revolución." *Revolución* (Havana), July 25, 1963, pp. 7–8.

"En Cuba." *Bohemia* (Havana), November 20, 1955, pp. 68–69 and November 27, 1955, pp. 68–73.

"Entrevista con Cosme de la Torriente." *Bohemia* (Havana), October 23, 1955, pp. 86–87.

"Se efectuó la concentración oposicionista en la plazoleta de Luz." *Diario de la Marina* (Havana), November 20, 1955, p. 1.

"Ten Havana Students Hurt in Police Fight." *New York Times*, December 3, 1955.

Fidel's Rift with the Ortodoxos

"Five Die in Student Riots." *New York Times*, April 21, 1956.

Ichaso, Francisco. "Y ahora qué?" *Bohemia* (Havana), March 25, 1956, pp. 42–101.

Ramos Lechuga, Arnaldo. "La verdad sobre el ataque al Goicuria." *Bohemia* (Havana), May 30, 1959, pp. 62–64.

Forming the Expeditionary Force

Anillo, René. "Biografía de José A. Echevarría." *Revolución* (Havana), March 13, 1963, p. 7.

Chomón, Faure. "El ataque al Palacio Presidencial el 13 de Marzo de 1957." *Bohemia* (Havana), March 22, 1959, p. 72.

"Como se produjo el atentado." *El Mundo* (Havana), October 30, 1956, pp. 1, A4.

Dam, Luis. "El grupo 26 de Julio en la carcel." *Bohemia* (Havana), July 8, 1956, p. 86.

Galvez, William. "Antes de la partida." *Verde Olivo* (Havana), August 20, 1965, pp. 3–6.

García, Pedro. "Recuerdos de la 'casa bonita,'" *Bohemia* (Havana), May 28, 1961, p. 8.

Infante, Enzo, and Devlofeo, Miguel. "José Tey Blancard." *Verde Olivo* (Havana), December 3, 1967, p. 29.

Resnick, Marvin D. *The Black Beret: The Life and Meaning of Che Guevara.* New York: Ballantine Books, 1969.

Rojas, Marta. "Los días que precedieron a la expedición del Granma." *Bohemia* (Havana), December 27, 1959, p. 12.

Sarabia, Nydia. "Del Tuxpán a las Coloradas." *Bohemia* (Havana), December 2, 1966, pp. 16–22.

The Crossing of the Granma

Barrera, Pedro A. "Por que el Ejército no derrotó a Castro." *Bohemia Libre* (Miami), August 13, 1961, p. 25.

"Dan por terminado el brote insurreccional." *El Mundo* (Havana), December 14, 1956, p. 1.

"Desembarco del Granma: Inicio de la gesta libertaria en Cuba." *Revolución* (Havana), December 2, 1960, pp. 1, 8.

Franqui, Carlos, ed. *The Twelve.* New York: Lyle Stuart, 1968.

"Fue librado encuentro en la Colonia Alegría." *El Mundo* (Havana), December 6, 1956, p. 1.

Guevara, Ernesto. "El desembarco del Granma." In *Geografía de Cuba,* edited by Antonio Nuñez Jiménez. Havana: Editorial Lex, 1959.

Guevara, Ernesto. "La Plata, primera victoria del Ejército Rebelde." *Verde Olivo* (Havana), March 26, 1967, pp. 10–14.

Hidalgo, Mario. "Después de Alegría del Pío." *Verde Olivo* (Havana), December 1964, pp. 8, 10.

"Indican como deben rendirse." *El Mundo* (Havana), December 12, 1956, p. 1.

Oramas, Joaquín. "The Landing and First Encounter." *Granma* (Havana), December 11, 1966, p. 9.

Pérez, Angel. "Yo fuí el primer guia de Fidel al llegar el Granma." *Revolución* (Havana), December 2, 1959, p. 9.

"La Plata, documentos de la tiranía." *Verde Olivo* (Havana), April 2, 1967, pp. 9–13.

"Plazo de 48 horas a los rebeldes para que se presenten." *El Mundo* (Havana), December 11, 1956, p. 1.

"El reencuentro." *Cuba Internacional* (Havana), May–June 1961, p. 21.

The Presidential Palace Assault

"Carta de Fructuoso a Cubela." *Revolución* (Havana), March 13, 1963, p. 2.

"Frustrado el asalto al Palacio Presidencial." *Diario de la Marina* (Havana), March 4, 1957, p. 12A.

García Olivares, Julio. "La operación Radio Reloj." *Bohemia* (Havana), March 15, 1959, pp. 10–12, 152–153.

"La guerra civil." *Bohemia* (Havana), March 24, 1957, p. 79.

Rodríguez Loeches, Enrique. "El crimen de Humboldt 7." *Revolución* (Havana), September 25, 1962, p. 10; September 26, 1962, p. 12.

Rodríguez Loeches, Enrique. "Una charla para la historia." *El Mundo* (Havana), March 13, 1969, pp. 5–6.

Times of Havana, March 14, 1957, pp. 1, 4.

The Sierra *and* Llano *Conflict in Oriente Province*

"Anuncian inicio de ataque final en la Sierra Maestra." *El Mundo* (Havana), June 14, 1957, pp. 1, A8.

Castro, Raúl. "El Combate del Uvero." *Revolución* (Havana), August 11, 1962, p. 10.

Castro, Raúl. "Travesia de la Sierra Maestra al Segundo Frente Oriental Frank País." *Lunes de Revolución* (Havana), July 26, 1959, pp. 35–39.

"Contrarios a la huelga los colonos." *El Mundo* (Havana), August 8, 1953, p. 1.

Cubillas, Vicente. "Martirologio del Corintia." *Revolución* (Havana), May 28, 1960, p. 20.

"Documentos de la tiranía sobre el combate de Uvero." *Verde Olivo* (Havana), May 28, 1967, p. 53.

"La gesta del Corintia." *Bohemia* (Havana), May 24, 1959, pp. 74–75; 96.

"Inician evacuación." *El Mundo* (Havana), June 1, 1957, p. 1.

"Los mártires del Corintia," *Revolución* (Havana), May 27, 1961, p. 6.

"Oponense hacendados a la huelga." *El Mundo* (Havana), August 7, 1957, p. 1.

Saruski, Jaime. "Realengo 18." *Revolución* (Havana), June 3, 1961, pp. 2–3 (supplement).

"Sierra Maestra, un hijo de Crescencio." *Bohemia* (Havana), February 22, 1959, p. 96.

Vázquez Candela, Euclides. "El Segundo Frente Oriental Frank País, pequeña república insurgente." *Revolución* (Havana), March 11, 1963, pp. 1, 8.

Zamora, Cristobal A. "Monte Rus: cuna de la revolución agraria." *Carteles* (Havana), August 9, 1959, pp. 54–55.

Arms Embargo

Bonachea, Rolando E., and Valdés, Nelson P. "United States–Cuban Relations: The Batista Years (1952–1958)." Unpublished manuscript. Albuquerque, New Mexico: University of New Mexico, 1968.

Reyes Trejo, Alfredo. "El Ejército de la tirania." *Verde Olivo* (Havana), November 20, 1966, pp. 19–24; November 27, 1966, pp. 19–29.

The April 1958 Strike: The End of the Llano

Brennan, Ray. *Castro, Cuba, and Justice.* Garden City, N.Y.: Doubleday, 1959, pp. 236–237.

Interview with Marcelo Fernández Font, Radio Rebelde (Havana), April 9, 1964.

"El 9 de Abril de 1958." *Bohemia,* April 19, 1959, pp. 58–61, 111–112.

Rojas, Marta. "El Segundo Frente Oriental Frank País." *Bohemia* (Havana), August 16, 1959, p. 104.

Santos, Juan Carlos. "Operación Antiaérea." *El Mundo* (Havana), September 16, 1966, p. 1.

Rebel Political and Military Offensive

Castro, Fidel. "Malo, pobre y deficiente el Segundo Frente del Escambray." *Revolución* (Havana), January 30, 1961, pp. 16–17.

"Hace diez años." *El Mundo* (Havana), December 18, 1968, p. 1.

Martin, Regino. "II Frente del Escambray." *Bohemia* (Havana), February 1, 1959, pp. 40–42, 142.

Nasario Sargén, Andrés. "Escambray, Crisol de la nueva Cuba." *El Mambí* (Miami), November 1963, pp. 1, 3.

Cuban Newspapers and Periodicals Cited

Bohemia
A liberal weekly magazine until early 1960, when it was taken over by the revolutionary government.

Diario de la Marina
The oldest and most conservative Cuban newspaper. Its influential opinion was pro-Spanish in the nineteenth century and pro-American in the twentieth until its publication was suspended in 1960.

Granma
Since 1965 the official daily newspaper of the Communist Party of Cuba.

Hoy
The official daily newspaper of the Cuban Communist Party from the mid-1930s until 1965, when it was merged with *Revolución* to create *Granma*.

Juventud Rebelde
Since 1965 the official daily newspaper of the youth section of the Communist Party.

El Mundo
A liberal daily newspaper with a strong pro-Auténtico viewpoint. It may have been owned secretly by Carlos Prío Socarrás.

Revolución
The underground newspaper of the 26th of July Movement. It was the Cuban government's official newspaper from 1959 to 1965, when it was merged to form *Granma*.

Tiempo en Cuba
The official newspaper of the Movimiento Socialista Revolucionario in the 1940s.

Verde Olivo
Since 1959 the official weekly magazine of the Ministry of the Armed Forces.

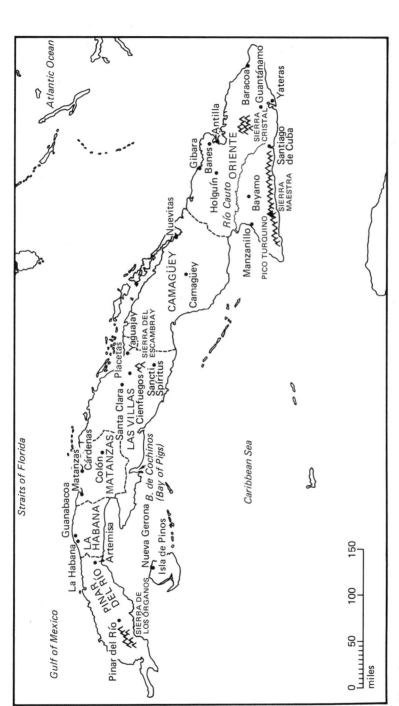

Map of Cuba

Fidel Castro (in circle) participates in a mass demonstration organized by the Federation of University Students of Havana University. The march, held in January 1949, was aimed at stopping an increase in bus fares decreed by the Auténtico administration. (*Prensa Latina*, Havana, Cuba.)

Some of the prominent revolutionaries in the Sierra Maestra in 1957. From left to right: guide known as "Palmero"; the underground leader Marcelo Fernández Font (seated); Ciro Redondo; Fidel Castro (seated); and Camilo Cienfuegos. (Antilles Research Program of Yale University.)

Early recruitment scene in the Sierra Maestra. Facing the *guerrilleros* are *campesinos* who have come to join the rebels. Some of the guerrilla leaders shown here are (from right to left): Efigenio Ameijeiras (only partly visible in profile at extreme right); Ciro Redondo (hat); Juan Almeida; Manuel Fajardo; Ernesto "Che" Guevara; Julito Díaz; "Chao"; Luis Crespo (hat, towel around neck); Ciro Frías; Fidel Castro is in the center. (Antilles Research Program of Yale University.)

Fidel Castro at a brief rest stop from El Hombrito toward La Plata, his headquarters in the Sierra in 1957. (Antilles Research Program of Yale University.)

Major Ernesto "Che" Guevara (center) and Major Rodríguez (left) of the Second Front of the Escambray in Las Villas Province in the fall of 1958, discussing whether Che's guerrillas have a right to be in an area dominated by another revolutionary group. (Courtesy of Andrés Nasario Sargén.)

Major Camilo Cienfuegos, who in the fall of 1958 led a column of *guerrilleros* from the Sierra Maestra Mountains into northern Las Villas Province. He helped Guevara establish the control of Castro's Rebel Army in these areas. (Cuban Ministry of Foreign Relations, Havana.)

Major Juan Almeida's column command post, 1958. The principal function of this base was as a bomb shop and demolition training post—one of several in the Sierra. (Antilles Research Program of Yale University.)

Guerrillero of the Second Front of the Escambray near the city of Santa Clara in late December 1958. (Courtesy of Andrés Nasario Sargén.)

Fidel Castro at La Plata headquarters, Sierra Maestra, in the fall of 1958. (Antilles Research Program of Yale University.)

Part 1
University Years

Against the Reelection of Ramón Grau San Martín
(January 20, 1947)

From the Directorio Estudiantil Universitario to the Cuban People

Cubans:

Before the amazing mockery expressed in the reelection intentions of those who climbed to power mouthing principles which they have betrayed without scruple, the University of Havana once again stands up.

Sad but firm, the dignity and patriotism of Cuba's student youth is acquiring new force. The reasons for this stand are obvious, for all the people know from their own experience the sad results of selfishness and privilege, which are the only true motives behind those who favor the discredited plan to reelect Grau.

All the students raise high the glorious banner for which Mella, Trejo, Floro Pérez, Pío Alvarez, and all our heroes died, and their memory is a call to rebellion.

Our stand is clear and well defined: it is far from partisanship, for it is the product of our soul-searching and our pure ideals.

The Directorio Estudiantil Universitario makes public and solemn profession of its principles and declares:

We consider it a crime against the fatherland to drown it in blood, grief, and shame by encouraging goals that will surely result in civil war.

We believe that the ideas of reelection, extension of the period in power, or even the imposition of candidates can be found only in the sick minds of traitors, opportunists, and the constantly insincere.

We respect the history of the University; we also respect ourselves,

Declaration made by the Central Committee of the Directorio Estudiantil Universitario on January 20, 1947. The Directorio was at the time the name of the university federation. This declaration was signed by Fidel Castro, Rafael Díaz Balart (who later became Fidel's brother-in-law), Baudilio Castellanos (who in 1953 defended in court those who had participated in the Moncada attack), José A. Montes de Oca, Rafael González, Octavio Ortiz, Humberto Ruiz Leiro, Ricardo Valdés, Carlos Miyares, Raúl Granado, Arturo Zaldívar, Isidro Sosa, Andrés Muiño, Angel Miguel García, Jorge Rodríguez, Carlos Guevara, Juan Gros, Enrique Ovares, Santiago Amador, Reinaldo Arza Balart, Eugenio Duarte, G. Rodríguez, Jorge Sidre, Raúl Sotolongo, Eduardo Rizos, Emilio Güira, Hugo Alvarez del Puerto, Manuel Pita, Frank Díaz Balart, Tomás Valdés Booth, Jorge Arredondo, Raúl Rodríguez, Raúl Reyno, and J. Torga. "Declaración del Directorio Universitario," *Diario de la Marina* (Havana), January 21, 1947, p. 2.

and we deeply love our fatherland, for which we desire happiness and progress. Consequently,

WE PLEDGE:

To fight Grau's reelection even if the price we have to pay in the struggle is our own death. "It is better to die on your feet than to live on your knees."[1]

---

[1] This is a general revolutionary and libertarian slogan which Castro sometimes used. Its precise origin is not clear, although it has been attributed to the Mexican revolutionary Emiliano Zapata and was also common among the Republican forces in the Spanish Civil War, according to *Bartlett's Familiar Quotations*. Eds.

The Dignity of Our Freedom Fighters
(November 6, 1947)

The miracle of this moment ought to be emphasized. The men who fought for our independence from Spain still, after fifty years, have the same rebellious spirit. It is a great event when the veterans of our independence struggle ally themselves with the students to lead forward the liberating aims of our past.

The freedom fighters of yesterday trust the young students of today; thus we are continuing their task of achieving independence and justice.

We thank them for the trust they have given us by permitting us to save the political dignity of the University with this symbolic treasure, the Demajagua Bell.[1]

Speech delivered November 6, 1947, at the University of Havana when the students were denouncing government corruption. Luis Conte Agüero, *Fidel Castro, vida y obra* (Havana: Editorial Lex, 1959), p. 25.

[1] The Demajagua Bell is a historic relic, used by the first Cuban independence fighters in 1868 to announce the initiation of the war of independence. The university students used the bell in 1947 to initiate, at least symbolically, a struggle against government graft. The bell was in the custody of Independence War veterans. It must be noted that the bell was later removed from the university grounds by thugs hired by the Ramón Grau administration. Eds.

On the Death of Manolo Castro
(February 25, 1948)

Rolando Masferrer[1] wants to take over the leadership of the university to make it serve his personal interests. We have not allowed him to do so, in spite of the coercion and violence practiced against us for quite some time, as when Mario Salabarría[2] was still free. Now he tries to wash away his guilt and that of his friends of the Movimiento Socialista Revolucionario and attempts to vilify us and, moreover, to justify himself by making that false accusation. He wishes to incite action against us, using Manolo Castro as a pretext; in other words, he wishes to profit from the death of a friend.

Manolo Castro was not fighting in the University any longer, and there was no reason whatsoever for him to be attacked. Far from encouraging the crime, if we had known beforehand what was going to happen, we would have prevented it.

On February 22, 1948, Manolo Castro, director general of sports and well-known student leader, was assassinated. He belonged to the Movimiento Socialista Revolucionario, which at the time was one of the many action groups in Cuba seeking hegemony over Cuban politics. Fidel Castro was denounced by MSR followers as one of the participants in the murder. On February 25, Castro was arrested and later freed. He then released a declaration about the events that had taken place. "Conferencia de prensa de Fidel Castro," *Diario de la Marina* (Havana), February 26, 1948, p. 25.

[1] Former member of the Communist Party, he broke with communism in 1940 and formed the Movimiento Socialista Revolucionario (MSR). Eds.

[2] Member of MSR and in charge of the police in Havana in the 1940s. Eds.

Grau Will Suffer a Shameful Defeat
(May 31, 1948)

A decisive battle is being waged between those who have ideals and those who have vested interests. On the side of the vested interests can be found the government candidates, the cabinet members, and the millions of dollars stolen from the national treasury. Also siding with them are those who have benefited, or hope to benefit, from the present regime. On the idealistic side can be found Eduardo Chibás

"El grausismo está a punto de sufrir la mas vergonzosa derrota," *Prensa Libre* (Havana), May 31, 1948.

and the few who did not give up when victory seemed lost. The people are behind them. Chibás will bring about harmony among Cubans, because many good Auténticos prefer the victory of Chibás to that of Núñez Portuondo. The coalitionists and Popular Socialists prefer Chibás to Prío.[1]

[1] Eduardo Chibás ran for the presidency on the Ortodoxo ticket. Dr. Ricardo Núñez Portuondo was a Liberal Party candidate. Carlos Prío was the presidential candidate of the Auténtico Party. The Popular Socialists were the members of the Partido Socialista Popular (Communist). Eds.

The Assassination of Sergeant Fernández Caral (July 10, 1948)

Last night I read in *Prensa Libre* that at Havana's Fourth District Criminal Court, where charges were made regarding the assassination of Sergeant Caral, it was expected that I would arrive on the scene any moment. But why should I? In order to aid in the unforgivable attempt of implicating myself in something of which I am completely innocent?

There was the testimony of only one witness against me, young Reinaldo Aranda. According to the police record, when shown a photograph of me among other persons, he pointed me out as looking like one of those he had seen firing, which in itself is rather imprecise. Afterward, that statement (which did not even definitely incriminate me) was retracted by the witness in the press and before a judge, Dr. Riera Medina, in a categorical, civic, and courageous manner, in spite of police reprisals and bribes. Thus, the witness received the judge's congratulations.

How can they still try to prosecute me after the only basis of guilt has been destroyed and it has become clear that the witness was bribed and coerced in order to force him to testify against me? Is it not necessary, after this very obvious attempt to hurt me, which has been denounced by the witness himself, that I should have some protection of my rights?

For the same reason that my arrest was ordered after the testimony of witness Aranda, who later declared that he was coerced to make it, the arrest of the authorities accused of coercion and bribery by the same witness ought to be ordered.

Statement made by Castro rejecting accusations of involvement in the assassination of the University of Havana police sergeant Oscar Fernández Caral. See *Introduction* in this volume. *Prensa Libre* (Havana), July 10, 1948.

I believe, honorable Judge Dr. Riera Medina, that my reasons are worthy of consideration. My distrust, Dr. Riera Medina, is based on the fact that Mario Salabarría some time ago came before you with the accusation against Emilio Tró made by a grocer in Vedado, who was almost beaten to death so that he would make the accusation. Afterward, a massacre took place which was supposedly justified by the order of arrest based on a criminal accusation.

On that occasion, before the direct accusation of a witness, you as judge had to limit yourself to ordering the arrest. You fulfilled your duty. But would you have ordered it had you known their intentions and the fatal result?

You are now hearing a similar case, which is even worse because the accusing witness himself has denounced the coercion he suffered.

In the present state of the proceedings, without any evidence against me, there is no reason whatsoever for me to be part of that trial. That is why I will not appear before you. At any rate, who offers me guarantees that the proceedings are going to be honest? I do not distrust you. Your reputation as an honest judge is recognized by all. But what about the others? After the recent distortion of evidence to make us look guilty, what can be expected? Everyone says that the case against Ginjaume[1] is very suspicious, especially after the recently revealed irregularities.

Who would be responsible, Dr. Riera Medina, if my arrest were ordered, obviously without reason, and "some police agents," at the service of treacherous interests that I have fought against, take advantage of the opportunity to assassinate me?

[1] Leader of the Unión Insurreccional Revolucionaria. Eds.

Against an Increase in Bus Fares
(January 30, 1949)

Compañeros:

There are too many rumors circulating that some leaders of the FEU,[1] without its knowledge or consent, have held interviews in the "Vista Alegre" cafeteria with Mr. Saud Juelle, manager of bus lines

"Transporte: Ciudadano, Esconde Tu Kilo!" *Bohemia* (Havana), January 30, 1949, pp. 51, 54–55.
[1] Federación Estudiantil Universitaria. Eds.

21 and 22, and have accepted $2,500 each to prevent the struggle against the raise in bus fares. . . .[2]

[2] On the twenty-fourth of January the Cooperativa de Omnibus Aliados (COA) had raised the bus fair to 1 cent per passenger. The decision of the government to support the increase brought about diverse reaction from the population. At the University of Havana, the members of the Comité de Lucha suggested that the FEU fight the increase. The rumors at the time told of COA financiers having paid some members of the FEU in order to get them not to protest the measure. During the meeting at the University, Castro raised the question, but due to the shouts from the audience he was not able to complete the speech. Castro, in turn, was energetically refuted by Orlando Bosch, president of the School of Medicine. See the same issue of *Bohemia*, p. 54. Eds.

Letter to Amador García Algorri
(December 1951)

Comrade in ideals:

It is Christmas, and with these lines I want to send my sincere greetings to you and your distinguished family.

Recent sad memories dim our happiness during this Christmas season, but new and hopeful signs are emerging from the heat of sacrifice.

For us there is only one possible way of looking for a New Year, and that is by recalling the words spoken by Martí on the last Christmas before he died for freedom: "For a suffering country, there is no New Year other than that of the defeat of its enemies."

With those words I close.

Sincerely,
Fidel Castro

Letter written in December 1951 to a senator of the Partido del Pueblo Cubano. "Fidel siempre fue Fidel," *Bohemia* (Havana), April 26, 1959, p. 149.

I Accuse
(January 28, 1952)

When *Alerta* announced just on time that the President had declared his intention of resigning, Prío called all the news media that very day to deny the news explicitly. However, it was true. Similarly, he had

"Yo acuso," *Alerta* (Havana), January 28, 1952.

denied at the beginning of his administration the news about a government loan while its terms were being discussed.[1] Similarly, he denied his intention to send troops to Korea while a special battalion was being trained, which for other reasons was not sent later.

When Chibás accused him of undertaking great business transactions involving the purchase of apartment complexes in the United States, the President covered his face, blushing like a vestal virgin innocent of sin, and asked for the excommunication of the harsh prosecutor. It was true, and one report of the Economic Commission uncovered the flow of millions out of the country. When Chibás accused him of backing the residential district developments in Guatemala and the lumber empire, this created the most colossal scandal known to political debate. Now we begin to learn the truth of that public denial.

The nature of the facts denied on each of those occasions made the immediate presentation of proof impossible at that time. The corrupt leaders believed they had discovered a new style of hiding their sins, which was to ask for proof of their immorality. They thought in that manner they could escape the public anathema, hiding themselves behind the screen of stock companies.

Very well, I have come today to denounce one of the greatest immoralities of Dr. Carlos Prío Socarrás in all its aspects, which alone could deny him the respect and consideration of our citizenry. It is as grave as to build in New York or to promote residential districts in Guatemala, the only difference being that it is happening here in Cuba; beforehand I challenge him to refute me, because this time I hold the accusation in one hand and the proofs in the other.

Here is the truth that I am attempting to disclose to the people.

At the beginning of his administration, a voracious appetite for land took hold of Carlos Prío. One after another a number of farms were acquired, each of which saw the construction of ostentatious palaces, swimming pools, airports, and a whole series of luxuries. In that manner "La Altura" and "La Chata" and others became famous. However, this was not enough; he then conceived the idea of acquiring a chain of the best farms and most valuable lands in the vicinity of Havana. They extend from Calabazar in the municipality of Santiago de las Vegas and past Managua in the municipality of San Antonio de las Vegas.[2]

Some public voices mentioned some of those farms, and others have never been mentioned. But, above all, the juridical condition of those lands was unknown: the name of the entity in which they appear

[1] Loan made in 1950 benefiting close associates of the President. Eds.
[2] In Havana Province. Eds.

registered, the procedures utilized, the "straw men" who represented the President, and perhaps something still far worse, what channels the President was using to promote those large landholdings.

All of these things I have come to uncover today, as one more stroke in the somber picture of corruption and moral decay which the people contemplate in the present regime.

The story of what I am going to tell dates back several years.

It was about mid-1944. On July 11, before officer René Alarcón of the Judicial Police, a mother announced that her nine-year-old daughter had been brutally abused. I will omit the names of mother and daughter, as well as any other data which could identify those persons. I will also omit other circumstances which, although helpful as demonstrations of the most repugnant and scandalous aspects of this crime, I will pass over out of respect for public sensitivity. The following day the Judge of Instruction of Marianao,[3] Dr. Cabrera Lastre, made the facts known to the pertinent authorities, informing them that he had just opened Case No. 792 in 1944. The following day the same judge issued a warrant for the arrest of Emilio Fernández Mendigutía, considering that the facts related to the accusation had the character of a crime against morals, as foreseen and sanctioned in Article 482a of the Social Code. Bail was set at 3,000 pesos. On August 10, 1944, Emilio Fernández Mendigutía, who was immensely rich, appointed Dr. Amador Bengochea as defense lawyer.

On November 13 of that year at 1:00 P.M., the case began in court. But on April 25, 1945, in the midst of the trial, defense lawyer Dr. Amador Bengochea presented in writing to the court the statement that because of profound differences with the defendant, he was withdrawing from the defense. On that same day, Emilio Fernández Mendigutía presented a written statement to the Fourth Criminal Court which read

> Having been notified yesterday that my lawyer, Dr. Amador Bengochea, has resigned from my defense due to differences with myself, I have come through this letter to appoint as my defense lawyer Dr. Carlos Prío Socarrás, with his law office in this city, "A" Street No. 66 in Vedado; he has accepted my defense and signed this letter as proof of his willingness.

At that date Grau was already governing the country, and Carlos Prío was Senator of the Republic, candidate for president, and one of the most influential persons of the regime.

On appointing him defense lawyer, the defendant was already thinking of taking all possible means to have himself vindicated.

[3] Havana suburb. Eds.

But the Fourth Criminal Court, with a firmness which is a credit to that judicial branch, unflinchingly maintained its decision to administer justice.

On May 24, 1945, the Fourth Criminal Court, composed of justices Manuel E. Romeu, Rogelio Benítez Cárdenas, Jesús Rodríguez Aragón, found Emilio Fernández Mendigutía guilty and imposed the following sentence:

> Considering that the proven facts constitute a crime, he is sanctioned to be deprived of liberty for six years with access to the special interdiction of exercising the right of passive and active suffrage and to fulfill any public position during the sentence. Likewise, we impose a civil obligation to indemnify the person injured, due to moral damages inflicted, with the sum of 10,000 pesos of official currency, being obliged to the payments of quotas and expenses if claimed, and also the sum of 1,000 pesos as payment to defense lawyer Dr. Carlos Prío Socarrás for services rendered.

The "concluding section" of the sentence I will not reproduce because of the sensibilities and scruples mentioned before.

The sentence was appealed on June 18, 1945. After several decisions, it was definitely upheld and ratified in all its parts by the Supreme Court of January 18, 1950, and on June 3 the Supreme Court ordered its fulfillment on July 20 of that year. But by that time Carlos Prío was President of the Republic, and ten days after—without the convicted man having spent one hour in jail—the Chief of State signed Decree No. 182 on August 1, 1950, published in the *Gaceta Oficial* on the fourth of that same month on page 15367, which stated in part the following:

> In exercise of the powers conferred upon me by the Constitution at the request of the Minister of Justice and having heard the Council of Ministers:
> I Resolve: to grant total amnesty to Emilio Fernández Mendigutía, pardoning him from what is left of the sentence of six years imposed on him by the Court of Appeals in its decision of January 18, 1950, dictated in Case No. 792 of 1944 of the Criminal Court of Marianao, as the performer of a crime as well as those accessories as the sentence points out. Given at the Presidential Palace, Havana, August 1, 1950.
> (Signed) Carlos Prío Socarrás, President. Manuel A. de Varona, Prime Minister. Oscar Gans, Minister of Justice.

It was essential to relate the preceding because we shall see immediately its relation to the chain of farms acquired by President Prío between Calabazar and Managua.

The mere enumeration of these farms, their former owners and present ones, as well as the dates of purchase and the manner in which they were given to a certain stock company will disclose the whole matter eloquently.

"Casas Viejas" Farms: Purchased by Emilio Fernández Mendigutía through adjudication in a public auction toward the end of 1943 and given to the Compañía Agropecuaria e Industrial "El Rocío," registered under title 405 before Notary Public Mario E. Pereira on September 10, 1946.

Gordillo Farm: Purchased in a public auction by Emilio Fernández Mendigutía toward the end of 1943 and given to Compañía Agropecuaria e Industrial "El Rocío" and registered under title 405 before Notary Public Mario E. Pereira on September 10, 1946.

San Francisco de Paula o Menocal Ranch: Fourteen *caballerías* of land, with boundaries on the north with the Potrero Lisundia farm, on the south with Potrero Piñales, on the east with Camino Real de Calabazar Barreto, on the west with Dr. Gabriel García's farm.

Formerly they were the property of the heirs of Francisco Otamendi y Durañona, acquired in a public auction by Emilio Fernández Mendigutía and given to Compañía Agropecuaria e Industrial "El Rocío," registered under title 405 before Notary Public Mario E. Pereira on September 10, 1949, and registered in the property registry of Bejucal on page 144, volume 87, dated January 18, 1947.

Galera and Cafetal Avelino Ranch: Thirteen and a half *caballerías*. Boundaries: on the north with the Llanes farm; on the south with Camino Real de Calabazar to Barreto, on the east with the Gavilán farm, and on the west with the San José coffee farm.

Just like the former, it was the property of Otamendi and Durañona's heirs, and it was acquired in public auction by Emilio Fernández Mendigutía and given to the Compañía Agropecuaria e Industrial "El Rocío" and registered in the property registry of Bejucal on page 73, volume 89, on January 18, 1947.

Carlos Prío began to control these farms as soon as he became President of the Republic. A highway that was supposed to go from Calabazar to Managua was constructed immediately, although not all the way to Managua but rather to the heart of those farms under the control of the stock company Compañía Agropecuaria e Industrial "El Rocío." Already by that date Mendigutía had been sentenced by the Court of Appeals of Havana and awaited the adverse judgment of the Supreme Court. It was evident that, taking refuge in the stock company "El Rocío," he had transferred the stock to Carlos Prío Socarrás, in whose hands lay the power to free him of his deserved punishment which was imposed by the courts. Long before receiving amnesty, he was appointed Civil Secretary for the President, a position created just for him, thus becoming an intermediary of the regime for the acquisition of new farms in the surrounding area.

Thus, a year after Prío had been in power and in possession of the previously mentioned farms, Mendigutía, acting as the President's representative, purchased the farm "Pancho Simón," which was the property of Oscar García Montes, in title of sale No. 292 of July 18, 1949, before Notary Public Mario E. Pereira Gallardo, registered in file 52, volume 73, page 8. The tenant farmer who occupied that farm was brutally forced out.

On June 29, 1949, deed 545, before Havana's Notary Public Mario Recio, Prío's straw man Emilio Fernández Mendigutía acquired, from their owners Mmes. María and Guillermina Godínez of León, the farm "Lage" or "Mercedes" adjacent to the just-mentioned farms and with an extension of ten *caballerías* of land, bordering in the north Camino or Calzada of Havana; in the south the farm of Francisco Navarro, in the east the farm of Don Paulino Simón, and in the west the road of Puerto Escondido. It was inscribed in the property registry of Bejucal on page 138, vol. 78, and dated June 6, 1949. All this took place before the amnesty. Besides these farms, Carlos Prío has a mortgage of $50,000, registered in his name in the registry of San José de las Lajas, on the farm "Amelia Maria" of twenty-seven *caballerías* owned by Mr. Gonzalo del Cristo.

Before concluding, I am going to cite some facts about the cultivation and forms of labor established on those farms, in order to unmask the First Executive of our nation.

They are administered by Army Lieutenant Marino Coy, who was a sergeant until the sixth of this month and year, when bypassing the military promotions system as a Christmas gift, President Prío promoted him. The labor in the fields, and this is a very weighty fact, is performed mainly by members of the armed forces. Approximately forty recruits from Managua Camp are sent daily by the Calabazar Highway to the farm, where they enter in a truck with official license plate number 2770. They begin work at 7:00 A.M. and leave at 5:30 P.M.

The stables are cleaned by national police officer Figueredo.

A soldier, Tejeda, takes care of horses.

A brother of the lieutenant-administrator, police officer Neno Coy, also renders his services in various ways.

Besides the soldiers, a dozen peasants from the area also work there. They are picked up before sunrise, at 5:30 A.M., beginning work at 6 A.M., and without rest they labor until 11 A.M. when a twenty-minute break is granted them to eat at the inn, where they must pay

50 cents; then, they return to work from 11:30 A.M. until 6 P.M. For almost twelve hours, they engage in wearisome labor such as shucking corn, piling rocks, and digging coal.

The farms produce essentially small fruits and fruit trees.

Extensive areas are dedicated mainly to the cultivation of sweet potatoes, vegetables, corn, and beans, which have been sold for up to $18 and $20 a *quintal*[4] in the province of Havana.

Thirty-three acres are planted with coffee.

They have planted 7,000 Pestonit avocado tree grafts, whose high price due to their good quality is no less than $30 each, for a grand total of approximately $200,000. At the present time 10,000 holes are being dug to plant an equal number of Pestonit grapefruits.

There are two stables for dairies. In the old stable eighty-seven Hershey cows are milked, and in the new one are others of different breeds. Two hundred breed pigs are presently being raised. The barnyard animals run into the thousands. In machinery they have three bulldozers, around twenty tractors, and a turbine from the Ministry of Health used for irrigation.

Near the main entrance to the Gordillo farm a luxurious chalet is found for recreation, and beside it is a small barracks for the soldiers who guard the several farms.

The working conditions are truly horrible. The soldiers work under the direction of a lieutenant who resides in Rancho Boyeros; when he is not there, work is done under the direction of a corporal. On more than one occasion violent protests because of the hardships of the work have been manifested, and to such a degree that in order to subdue the workers into obedience the authorities have had to utilize persuasive methods and grant some improvements, such as time off Saturday afternoons, which they did not have before.

Worse still is the treatment of the workers who are watched by Lieutenant Coy, wearing a bayonet on his hip, taking advantage of his position as army man with authority that is, of course, arbitrary and tyrannical. The workers are paid only $2.50 a day, from which we must subtract 50 cents for food and 20 cents which Lieutenant Coy's brother charges for giving them a ride to and from work. No peasant family lives on the farms: They all have been removed.

Everything I have stated is rigorously factual, and I invite an honest court to verify it, at whose disposal I will place the evidence that corroborates what I have presented here and demonstrates how Dr. Carlos Prío had no scruples as President of the Republic when he

---

[4] One quintal equals 100 pounds. Eds.

lowered the dignity of his office and his professional decorum by granting amnesty as President to one he could not absolve as a defense lawyer.

I ACCUSE President Prío of prostituting the spirit of presidential pardoning, committing a crime of bribery punished by the Social Defense Code, by granting amnesty through self-evident gifts from the accused and becoming the owner, prior to granting amnesty, of the farms owned by the amnestee Emilio Fernández Mendigutía.

I ACCUSE the President of the Republic of violating labor laws and guarantees of social legislation by submitting the workers on his farm to the most iniquitous exploitation, with shifts of twelve hours of labor and miserable salaries under the direction of military foremen.

I ACCUSE the President of the Republic of mixing and lowering the function of the armed forces of the Republic, turning soldiers into laborers and peons and forcing them into slave labor, taking advantage of his office, putting them to produce for the benefit of his own particular patrimony.

I ACCUSE the President of the Republic of promoting the system of latifundia—proscribed by the Constitution—and contributing therefore to chronic unemployment through the substitution of paid workers by obligatory labor from soldiers.

I ACCUSE President Prío, finally, of betraying the high interests of the nation when intervening in the market as one more competitor in the production of milk, cattle, and agricultural products, produced at a lower price by not paying salaries, and of sacrificing the Cuban peasants for his own convenience.

Part 2
Toward the Moncada

Proclamation on Batista's Seizure of Power (March 13, 1952)

It is not a revolution, but a brutal snatching of power! They are not patriots, but destroyers of freedom, usurpers, adventurers thirsty for gold and power. The coup was not against Prío but against the people. There was confusion, but it was still up to the people to decide things in a democratic and civilized manner and choose their rulers freely and without force. Money will flow in favor of the imposed candidate, no one denies it, but that would not have altered the result, just as it was not altered by the waste of the Public Treasury in favor of the candidate imposed by Batista in 1944.

It is completely false, absurd, ridiculous, and childish to think that Prío planned a coup d'état. Misgovernment was being endured, but then it had been so for years, with the people awaiting the constitutional opportunity to right the wrongs. And you, Batista, who basely escaped for four years and, for three, engaged in useless politicking, appear now with your tardy, unsettling, and poisonous remedy, making shreds of the Constitution, when in only two months we would have reached the goal through appropriate means. Everything you have alleged is a lie, a cynical justification, a dissimulation of what is vanity and not patriotic honor, ambition and not ideals, appetite and not civic greatness.

It was right to remove from office a government of murderers and thieves, and we were trying to do so peacefully with the support of public opinion and the aid of the people. But by what right do the military do so, they who have murdered and stolen without limit in the past? It is not peace but the seed of hatred that has been sown here. It is not happiness but sorrow and sadness that the nation feels looming over this tragic panorama. There is nothing as bitter in the world as the spectacle of a people that goes to bed free and awakens in slavery.

Once again the military boots; once again Columbia[1] dictating decrees, removing and appointing ministers; once again the tanks roaring threateningly in our streets; once again brute force ruling over human reason. We were growing accustomed to living within the Constitu-

"Revolución no, zarpazo!" first appeared in the mimeographed paper *El Acusador* on March 13, 1952. Marta Rojas, "Justa indignación," *Verde Olivo* (Havana), July 25, 1965, p. 19.
[1] Camp Columbia, headquarters of the armed forces. Eds.

tion. For twelve years we had been without enormous blunders, in spite of common errors. Civic peace cannot be achieved except through great effort. You, Batista, have destroyed in a few hours that noble hope of the Cuban people.

Whatever Prío did wrong in three years, you did before him; your coup is, then, unjustifiable. The coup has no basis in morality or in the social or political doctrine of any class; it is simply a product of force, and its justification is falsehood. Your majority is in the army and not in the people. Your votes are rifles and not the will of the people; with those rifles you can make a coup but never win fair elections. Your seizure of power lacks principles that might legitimize it. Laugh if you wish, but principles are in the long run more powerful than guns. The people are formed and strengthened with principles, the people die for principles.

Do not call that outrage, that unfortunate and unsettling coup, that stab in the back of the Republic, a revolution. Trujillo has been the first to recognize your government. He knows who his friends are in the clique of tyrants that afflicts the Americas. It tells us better than anything else the reactionary, militarist, and criminal character of your power snatching. No one believes even remotely in the governmental success of your old and rotten clique; the thirst for power is too great, and the restraints too few when there is no constitution or law other than the will of the tyrant and his accomplices. I know beforehand that your guarantees will be torture and castor oil![2] Your men will murder even if you do not want them to. You will consent because you rely on them. Despots are the masters of the people they oppress and slaves of the forces that sustain their oppression.

Now false, demagogic propaganda will pour out in your name, made by people with good or bad intentions, and contemptible slander will be used against the opposition leaders. This has been done by others before, but it did not change the spirit of the people. Truth lights the destiny of Cuba. The truth that you will not permit to be stated will be known by everyone, carried by word of mouth, though no one will say it in public or write it in the press, and the seed of heroic rebelliousness will grow in all hearts. The truth is a compass that exists in every conscience.

I do not know what pleasure oppressors find in using a whip against human backs, but I know that there is infinite happiness in fighting against oppression, in raising a strong hand and saying, I do not want to be a slave!

[2] Used by the police in Cuba as a form of torture in which a person was forced to drink several bottles of castor oil. Eds.

Cubans: Once again there is a tyrant, but once again we shall have Mellas, Trejos, and Guiterases![3] The fatherland is oppressed, but someday there will be freedom. I invite courageous Cubans to sacrifice and fight back! If our lives are lost, that is nothing. "To live in chains is to live sunk in shame and dishonor. To die for the fatherland is to live!"[4]

[3] Young opposition leaders who fought against the Machado dictatorship in the 1930s. Eds.

[4] The quotation is taken from the last two lines of the Cuban national anthem. Eds.

Brief to the Court of Appeals
(March 24, 1952)

Fidel Castro Ruz, lawyer, with offices in Tejadillo 57, before this court of justice states the following:

The events that motivate this brief are very well known. Nevertheless I come to denounce them formally on my own behalf and to demand the application of existing laws, which (although it may seem absurd in the face of reigning conditions) agree with juridical norms not abolished by anything or anyone, therefore making the duty to comply with them more difficult and overwhelming for the magistrates and more meritorious and worthy for the fatherland.

In the early morning of March 10, a senator of the Republic, betraying his own rights and privileges, entered the military camp of Columbia, following plans made with a group of officers of the army.

Aided by the night, by surprise and treachery, they arrested the legitimate commanders and seized their posts. They took over control, incited all the districts to revolt, and issued a general call to the troops, who assembled tumultuously at the polygon of the camp where they were harangued into turning their weapons against the Constitution and the lawfully constituted government.

The citizenry, completely unaware of the treason, awoke to the first rumors of what was occurring. The violent seizure of all radio stations by the insurrectionists prevented the people from getting news and orders to mobilize and resist.

The nation, unable to act, witnessed a flood of military actions

Brief presented on March 24, 1952, to the Court of Appeals of Havana. "Al Tribunal de Urgencia," *Granma* (Havana), July 26, 1966, p. 5.

which demolished the Constitution, putting lives and property at the whims of bayonets.

The chief of the insurrectionists, assuming absolute power and arrogating to himself omnipotent functions, ordered the immediate suspension of the elections scheduled for the first of June.

The most elemental guarantees were suppressed rapidly.

Like booty, all the state administrative positions were distributed among the leaders of the coup.

When Congress tried to meet in the usual fashion, it was dissolved by gunfire.

At present the total transformation of the republican system is being carried out, and they plan substituting the national constitution, a product of the people's will, with a juridical farce created in the barracks behind the back of popular opinion.

All these events are foreseen and sanctioned decisively in the Social Defense Code in its Article 147, according to which anyone who tries to change directly in full or part, through violent means, the Constitution or the form of government will be imprisoned for six to ten years. In addition, the following precepts could be applied:

Article 148. a. Anyone who promotes an armed uprising against the constitutional power of the state will be imprisoned for three to ten years.

b. The penalty will be from five to twenty years if the insurrection is carried out.

Article 149. a. Anyone who prevents the Senate, the House of Representatives, the President, or the Supreme Court from exercising their constitutional functions will be punished with six to ten years in prison.

b. Anyone who prevents the holding of general elections or plebiscites will be imprisoned for four to eight years.

Article 235. Those who revolt to achieve through violence any of the following objectives are guilty of sedition: (1) To prevent the promulgation or execution of the laws or the free holding of popular elections or plebiscites in a province, region, or electoral district; (2) To prevent a court, authority, officer, or public functionary the free exercise of his functions or the execution of his powers or judicial and administrative powers.

Article 236 a. Anyone who promotes or supports sedition and its main leaders will be imprisoned for three to eight years.

Article 240. Anyone who tries to induce troops or any other member of the armed forces to commit the crime of sedition will be imprisoned for two to five years.

As a result of all these articles and others that would be tedious to enumerate, Fulgencio Batista's crimes have incurred punishment deserving more than *one hundred years' imprisonment.*

It is not enough for the insurrectionists now to argue so easily that the revolution is the source of law.[1] Instead of revolution there has been a "restoration"; instead of progress there has been a "retrogression"; instead of justice and order there has been "barbarity and brute force." There has been no revolutionary program, no revolutionary theory, no revolutionary speeches prior to the coup. They are politicians without followers; they have become stormtroopers of power.

Without a new conception of the state, society, and juridical order based in deeply rooted historical and philosophical principles, there is no revolution generating right. They cannot even be called political delinquents, for, as Jiménez de Asúa, the great criminal lawyer, states, only "those who fight for a socially advanced regime" can be called that. The reactionaries, those who serve the ambitious interests of cliques, will always be simple delinquents for whom the takeover of power will never be justified.

The behavior of this court before the events related will have great significance for the Cuban people. It will show whether judicial power continues functioning or is prevented from acting by the use of force.

It would be well that the judiciary give signs of life when the other two powers have been decapitated, that is, if the judiciary has not been decapitated in the same manner.

A citizen is taken to the Court of Appeals when he is accused of sedition or of any other similar crime. He is tried and, if proved guilty, he is condemned. This has been done many times.

If the citizen refuses to appear, he is declared in contempt of court and the pertinent orders are issued.

The Court of Appeals has the power to put Batista on trial for the crimes committed against Articles 147, 148, 235, 236, and 240; the power to do so has been clearly stated in Article 32 of Decree 292 of 1934 which created this court, as well as in the decree of October 14, 1938, which has been totally accepted in practice.

If, in the face of this series of flagrant crimes and confessions of treachery and sedition, he is not tried and punished, how will this court later try any citizen for sedition or rebelliousness against this illegal regime, the product of unpunished treason? That would be absurd, inadmissible, monstrous in the light of the most elemental principles of justice.

---

[1] "La revolución es fuente de derecho." Eds.

I do not prejudge the thinking of the court. I only expound the reasons on which I base my denunciation.

I resort to logic, I see the terrible reality, and logic tells me that if courts exist in Cuba, then Batista should be punished. And if Batista is not punished and remains master of the state—president, prime minister, senator, major general, civil and military chief, controlling executive and legislative power, owner of lives and properties—then there are no courts, they have been suppressed. A terrible reality?

If that is the case, say so as soon as possible, hang up your robe, resign your post: Let justice be administered by the very ones who legislate and execute; let a corporal sit at last with his bayonet in the august courtroom of the magistrates. I do not commit any offense in stating these things with the greatest respect and sincerity; not to say so is bad, to resign oneself to a reality that is tragic, absurd, without logic, without values, without sense, without glory and honor, without justice.

Dr. Fidel Castro Ruz

Critical Assessment of the Ortodoxo Party (August 16, 1952)

From above the tumult of cowards, the mediocre, and the poor of spirit, it is necessary to pass a brief but courageous and constructive judgment of the Ortodoxo movement after the fall of its great leader, Eduardo Chibás. The formidable *aldabonazo*[1] of the leader of the Ortodoxo movement left the party such an immense wealth of popular emotion that the party was placed at the very doors of power. Everything had been done; the only thing necessary was not to lose that influence on the people.

The first question that an honest Ortodoxo should ask himself is this: Have we enlarged the moral and revolutionary legacy left by Chibás?

This article appeared in the mimeographed paper *El Acusador* on August 16, 1952. It was distributed at the tomb of Eduardo Chibás on the same date. Raúl Castro, "VIII Aniversario del 26 de Julio," *Verde Olivo* (Havana), July 16, 1961, pp. 3–11, and Marta Rojas, *El juicio del Moncada* (Buenos Aires: Ediciones de Ambos Mundos, 1966), pp. 52–54.

[1] *Aldabonazo*, or knock on the door, was the title given to the last radio editorial of Eduardo Chibás before he committed suicide. The editorial stated that only through a hard blow could the apathetic Cuban people be awakened to fulfill their national goals. Eds.

Or have we misused part of that wealth? Whoever believes that up to now everything has been done well, that we have nothing to reproach ourselves for, is a man who demands little of his conscience. Those sterile conflicts that survived the death of Chibás, those colossal scandals that were not motivated by ideology but were purely selfish and personal clashes, still resound like bitter hammerings in our minds. The unfortunate procedure of going to the speaker's platform to discuss Byzantine quarrels was a grave symptom of lack of discipline and responsibility.

March 10 came unexpectedly. But it was to be expected that such a serious event would unearth small controversies and sterile personality conflicts from the party. Did that happen? To the astonishment and indignation of the party's followers the stupid quarrels began again. The guilty fools did not notice that the press was very outspoken when the Ortodoxos attacked one another but not when they attacked the government. The services rendered to Batista by such conduct are not few.

No one will be shocked when such a necessary assessment is made today. The turn of the great masses who suffered that damage in bitter silence has come, and this is the most opportune moment to give an account to Chibás, close to his tomb.

The great mass of the Ortodoxo Party is now arising, more determined that ever. And in these moments of sacrifice it asks: Where are those who were running for office? Where are those who wanted to occupy the places of honor in the assemblies of executives? Where are those who visited political districts influencing people and demanding a place on the platform of large meetings? Why do they not go around today mobilizing the people or demanding places of honor in the front lines of combat?

Those who have a traditional idea of politics will feel pessimistic about such tactics, but for those who have a blind faith in the masses, for those who believe in the indestructible force of great ideas, the indecision of the leaders will not create hopelessness.

The moment is revolutionary and not political. Politics is the consecration of the opportunism of those who have the means and the resources. The Revolution opens the way to true merit, to those who have sincere courage and ideals, to those who risk their lives and take the battle standard in their hands. A revolutionary party requires a revolutionary leadership, a young leadership originating from the people, that will save Cuba.

The Studio of Sculptor Fidalgo
Has Been Destroyed (February 8, 1953)

Five days have gone by. At the time I write this brief note the government has not yet given an explanation of the events of El Calvario,[1] nor has Fidalgo yet appeared.

It happened last Friday, two days after Martí's birthday: At ten in the morning a group of police cars showed up in front of the well-known sculptor's shop in El Calvario, and there the destruction began and later continued in his study located two blocks away. As usual, they completely lacked a judicial mandate; they have never used one.

It was not the police officers who initiated the action; it was Captain Oscár González of the fourteenth police district who supplied the bad example. Taking a sculpture of Eduardo Chibás's face, he furiously threw it on the floor; then grabbing one of Martí's statues, he said he was going to make Fidalgo eat it and afterward he was going to have him build statues of Batista.

It was like an order: Dozens of statues of Martí rolled, destroyed by kicks. The remainder were put in a trash truck and thrown in a corner of the police station. The masks of Chibás were pulverized in a rage; as many busts of patriots as were there were thrown to the floor or taken to the police station. One, the *Virgin of Charity*,[2] had her head taken off; others disappeared. Not a mold was left in one piece, in order to prevent reproduction of the statues.

Thanks to Chenar, *Bohemia*'s courageous and daring contributor, we have obtained irrefutable proof, in spite of the military occupation of the place and the intransigent refusal to allow the press in.

Also, Fidalgo had a beautiful collection of famous hands, fine copies of hands. There were those of Roosevelt, Chibás, Coyula, Miguel A. Quevedo, Guido García Inclán, Judge Justiniani, and other political and scientific personages of the world. They were the products of the artist's whole life and were considered unique in the world. At this time it is not known how many are intact, for the boxes which contained them were also overturned on the ground.

On that same day, María Mantilla presented to Batista the shackles which tortured the ankles of the teacher Martí; in the auditorium a

---

Fidel Castro, "Asaltado y destruído el estudio del escultor Fidalgo," *Bohemia* (Havana), February 8, 1953, pp. 66, 81.
[1] A Havana suburb. Eds.
[2] *Virgen de la Caridad*, Cuba's major religious figure. Eds.

brilliant reception was being prepared for illustrious intellectuals who were visiting Martí's freedomless fatherland.

Fidalgo's crime was to have placed at the base of the statues those words pronounced by the Teacher on an occasion similar to today, "To Cuba, which suffers . . ."

In this manner the entire work of Martí is going to have to be suppressed, removed from bookstores and libraries, because all of it, overflowing with love of the fatherland and human dignity, is a perennial accusation to the men who govern against the sovereign will of the people of Cuba.

Let us hope that they have destroyed only Fidalgo's work, the work of an honest artist, whose hands have sculpted only figures of heroes, and that they have not also destroyed his existence.

Fidalgo is not a man of sensationalism or notoriety. At this time, Wednesday afternoon, the citizenry is alarmed over his unexpected and unjustifiable absence. We have been prudent in this matter until now, as it is too serious to speculate about; but it is also too grave to lose time. We do not want to prejudge, but already the facts accuse. The government now has the word.

The Cuban Revolution
(July 23, 1953)

In the dignity of Cuba's men lies the triumph of the Cuban Revolution —the Revolution of Céspedes, Agramonte, Maceo, and Martí, Mella, Guiteras, Trejo, and Chibás, the true revolution that has not yet ended.[1] The Revolution shall triumph for the dignity and honor of Cuba's men.

This manifesto was written by Raúl Gómez García following instructions from Fidel Castro. The manifesto was released to the Cuban people on July 23, 1953. "Manifesto de los revolucionarios del Moncada a la nación," in *13 documentos de la insurrección* (Havana: Organización Nacional de Bibliotecas Ambulantes y Populares, 1959), pp. 19–21.

[1] Carlos Manuel de Céspedes, Ignacio Agramonte, Antonio Maceo, and José Martí were leaders of the independence war against Spain in the nineteenth century. Julio Antonio Mella was a student leader who organized university students in Havana and later became the first secretary general of the Cuban Communist Party. He was assassinated in Mexico on January 10, 1929. Antonio Guiteras was one of the leaders of the struggle against the Machado dictatorship and was the main leader of the revolutionary government formed in 1933. Guiteras was executed on May 8, 1935, by Fulgencio Batista because of his

The centennial of Martí's birth is the culmination of a historical cycle marked by progression and regression in the political and moral realms of the Republic: the bloody and vigorous struggle for liberty and independence; the civic contest among Cubans to attain political and economic stability; the sorry process of foreign intervention; the dictatorships; the unrelenting struggle of heroes and martyrs to make a better Cuba.

In Cuba the desire to find the true road was awakening. The conscience of the citizenry was ready to produce its best fruit, won through the sacrifice of one of its most visionary patriots and his teachings, when a ridiculous minority led by the most ambitious of all Cubans took over the country, spreading deceitful promises and propaganda. Their objective was to make good people believe that the treacherous coup against our institutions would engender social progress, peace, and work.

Besides the crimes of blood, dishonor, unlimited lust, and theft of the national treasury which were linked to the name of the new ruler there was also a series of assaults against Cuba: institutionalization of the coup d'état to secure military regimes, bribery of Congress and the puppet presidents, violation of executive power, imposition of castes and privileges, dismissal of Congress, illegal appointment of persons to power, removal of mayors and aldermen, physical trampling and abuse of peaceful citizens, and the placing of an inglorious flag at the side of the most glorious of flags.[2]

Shortly after the treacherous coup we witnessed the full reenactment of calamities, anguish, eviction, and hunger which are unequivocal signs of the ambitious government leader and his main cohorts.

The stifling by force of the people's deepest desires brought on the most serious situation ever created by a political event in any era: a decrease in industrial production accompanying the workers' discontent or their dismissal from work; persecution and imprisonment of students for public protest against the regime; isolation and division of the political parties; the flight of frightened capital; imprisonment of those who dared to protest publicly the abuses suffered by the Republic; dissolution of Congress and the death of the Constitution

---

radical and nationalistic ideas. Rafael Trejo was the first student murdered by the Machado dictatorship. Eduardo Chibás was also a leader of the 1933 revolution and a founder of the Partido Revolucionario Cubano and the Partido del Pueblo Cubano. His ideas were anti-imperialist, nationalist, and favored socialism. Chibás committed suicide in 1951. Eds.

[2] The Batista regime had its own flag, which was displayed throughout the island. Eds.

and its rights. On the conscience of the one responsible for all these falls the contempt of free men and the edge of the sword of justice.

Before the pathetic and painful sight of a republic under the capricious whim of one man, the national spirit rises from deep within the souls of honorable men. The Cuban people's unshakable faith rises with their unanimous decision to regain their constitution, their essential freedoms and inalienable rights, trampled ceaselessly by treacherous usurpers.

Before the chaos in which the nation has fallen, the determination of the tyrant, and the godless interests of the men who support him, the youth of Cuba who love freedom and man's dignity stand up in a gesture of immortal rebellion, breaking the insane pact made with past corruption and present deceit.

Before Cuba's tragedy, contemplated calmly by dishonest political leaders, the angry and forceful youth of the centennial stand up in this decisive hour, having no other interest than the desire to honor the unrealized dream of Martí with sacrifice.

In the name of the relentless struggles that have marked the glorious history of Cuba comes the new revolution, rich in men without faults to change once and for all the unbearable situation created by ambitious men. The Revolution identifies with the roots of Cuba's national sentiment, the teachings of its greatest men, and embraces the national flag. We declare before the honor and dignity of the people:

1. Motivated by the most genuine *criollo* values, the *Revolution* comes from the soul of the Cuban people. Its vanguard is a youth that wants a new Cuba, a youth that has freed itself from all the faults, the mean ambitions, and the sins of the past. The Revolution comes from new men with new methods, prepared with the patience, courage, and decision of those who dedicate their lives to an ideal.

2. The *Revolution* declares itself free from the shackles of foreign nations and also free from the influences and appetites of personal ambition. The men who have organized the *Revolution* and represent it have made a pact with the sacred will of the people to conquer the future they deserve. The *Revolution* is the decisive struggle of a people against all those who have deceived them.

3. The *Revolution* declares its respect for the integrity of free citizens and for military men who have not betrayed the nation or surrendered our glorious flag or denied our constitution. In this important hour the *Revolution* salutes all Cubans of dignity, wherever they may be, and publicly welcomes those who identify with it.

4. The *Revolution* declares its firm decision to give Cuba the well-

being and economic prosperity that its rich land, geographic situation, diversified agriculture, and industrialization assure it. These have been exploited by legitimate and illegitimate governments, by unlimited ambition and guilty apathy.

5. The *Revolution* declares its love and trust in the virtue, honor, and dignity of our men and expresses its intention of using all those who are truly worthy in the great task of Cuban reconstruction. These men are found in all places and institutions of Cuba, from the peasant hut to the general headquarters of the armed forces. This is not a revolution of castes.

6. The *Revolution* declares its respect for workers and students, true representatives in the defense of the people's legitimate rights throughout history. The *Revolution* assures them and all the people of the implementation of total and definitive social justice based on economic and industrial progress following a synchronized and perfect plan which will be the result of thorough, thoughtful study.

7. The *Revolution* declares that it recognizes and bases itself on the ideals of José Martí, the program of the Partido Revolucionario Cubano, and the Montecristi Manifesto as well as the revolutionary programs of Jóven Cuba, ABC Radical, and the Partido del Pueblo Cubano (Ortoxodo).

8. The *Revolution* declares its respect for the free nations of America, countries that have achieved with great sacrifice the economic freedom and social justice that are the signs of our times.

9. The *Revolution* declares its absolute and reverent respect for the Constitution of 1940 and would reestablish it as its official code. The Revolution also declares that the only national flag is the Cuban flag, which it will carry, as always, with glory and dedication into battle. There is no other anthem but the national anthem, identified throughout the world by the vibrant stanza, *"To die for the fatherland is to live!"*

In the name of the martyrs, in the name of the sacred rights of the fatherland, for the honor of the centennial.

The Cuban Revolution
July 23, 1953

This Movement Will Triumph
(July 26, 1953)

In a few hours you will be victorious or defeated, but regardless of the outcome—listen well, *compañeros!*—regardless of the outcome, this movement will triumph. If you win tomorrow, the aspirations of Martí will be fulfilled sooner. If the contrary occurs, our action will set an example for the Cuban people, and from the people will arise young men willing to die for Cuba. They will pick up our banner and move forward. The people of Oriente Province will support us; the entire island will do so. Young men of the centennial,[1] as in 1868 and 1895, here in Oriente we make our first cry of "Liberty or Death!"[2]

You know already the objectives of our plan; it is a dangerous plan, and anyone who leaves with me tonight will have to do so willingly. There is still time to decide. Anyway, some of you will have to stay behind because we do not have enough weapons.

Those who are determined to go should move forward. The watchword is not to kill except as the last resort.

This short speech was made by Castro on the farm "Siboney," headquarters of the revolutionaries prior to attacking the Moncada Barracks on July 26, 1953. "Este movimiento triunfará," *Verde Olivo* (Havana), July 26, 1964, p. 5.

[1] Refers to the centennial of Martí's birth (1853–1953). Eds.

[2] This province traditionally led all revolutionary struggles in the island. Eds.

Part 3
Imprisonment

Letter to the Court of Appeals
(September 26, 1953)

Fidel Castro Ruz, lawyer acting in his own defense on Cause 37 of this year, appears before the court and respectfully states the following:

1. There have been attempts to prevent me from participating in this trial because the fantastic lies made up about the heroic events of the twenty-sixth of July would be destroyed by my testimony, and it will not be possible to prevent disclosure of the horrible crimes committed on that day against prisoners, crimes which represent the most horrible slaughter registered in our history. This is why I have been informed that I shall not appear before the court; I am supposed to be sick. The fact is that I am in perfect health and suffer no disease. An attempt is being made to deceive the court in a most shameful manner.

2. In spite of repeated orders by the judiciary demanding that my isolation cease because it is illegal and criminal, I have been totally incommunicado for the fifty-seven days I have been in prison. I have not been allowed to see the sun, to speak to anyone, or to see my family.

3. I have been able to verify with certainty that my elimination is being planned through the pretext of escape, poison, or something similar. To that effect a whole series of plans and plots has been elaborated that would facilitate the fulfillment of that objective. I have repeatedly denounced it. The motives are the same as those I stated in the first part of this letter.

The lives of other prisoners are in similar danger, among them two women who are key witnesses to the massacre that took place on July 26.[1]

4. I request the court to proceed to order my immediate physical examination by a competent and prestigious physician, such as the dean of the School of Medicine at Santiago de Cuba.

I emphatically state the great necessity for a specially designated member of the court to accompany the political prisoners on their

---

Letter written on September 26, 1953, from an Oriente prison. Rosa Hilda Zell, "Seis documentos del Moncada," *Bohemia* (Havana), July 27, 1962, p. 67.

[1] Refers to Melba Hernández and Haydée Santamaría, both close collaborators of Castro during the attack on the Moncada Barracks. Eds.

trips from this prison to the Palace of Justice and back, and to communicate the subject matter of this letter to the local and national bar associations, the Supreme Court, and as many legal institutions as the court deems should know these facts.

The importance of the trial being held demands exceptional obligations. If the trial is carried out under the conditions I have exposed, it will be nothing more than a ridiculous and immoral farce which will be totally repudiated by the nation.

All of Cuba watches this trial. I hope that this court will defend with dignity its rights and honor, which is at the same time the honor of all judicial power before the history of Cuba.

The behavior of the court up to the present and the prestige of the accredited and honorable justices of the Republic allow me to have complete faith in its vigorous action.

As to myself, if I have to give up my rights or my honor to remain alive, I prefer to die a thousand times. "A just principle from the depths of a cave is stronger than an army."[2]

Fidel Castro Ruz
Oriente Province Prison
September 26, 1953

P.S. I designate Dr. Melba Hernández to present this letter in my name. F. C.

[2] José Martí. Eds.

History Will Absolve Me
(October 16, 1953)

Honorable Judges:

Never has a lawyer had to practice his profession under such difficult conditions; never has such an overwhelming accumulation of irregularities been committed against an accused. The counsel and the defendant in this case are one and the same. As the attorney for the defense, I have not been able even to look at the indictment. As the

"History Will Absolve Me" is a pamphlet which allegedly presents the text of the speech delivered on October 16, 1953, by Fidel Castro before the court that sentenced him to nineteen years in prison because of the Moncada attack. There is no original transcript of the speech available. *La Historia Me Absolverá* (Havana: Editora Política, 1964).

accused, I have been kept silent for seventy-six days, shut away, in solitary confinement, completely and absolutely incommunicado, in violation of every human and legal consideration.

He who is speaking abhors with his whole being puerile conceit, and neither his present frame of mind nor his temperament is inclined toward courtroom pose or sensationalism of any sort. If I have had to assume my own defense before this court, it is for two reasons: first, practically I was deprived of a defense; and second, only a man who has been hurt as deeply as I and who has seen the fatherland so forsaken and justice so vilified can speak on an occasion such as this with words that are the blood of the heart and the essence of truth.

There was no lack of generous *compañeros* who wanted to defend me, and the Bar Association of Havana appointed the competent and courageous lawyer Dr. Jorge Pagliery, dean of the bar association of this city. However, he was not permitted to fulfill his mission. The prison gates were closed to him every time he tried to see me. Only after a month and a half, and through the intervention of the court, was he granted ten minutes to speak with me in the presence of a sergeant from the Servicio de Inteligencia Militar.[1] Supposedly, a defendant should speak with his lawyer in private. This right is upheld anywhere in the world, except when it deals with a Cuban prisoner of war in the hands of an implacable despotism which abides by neither legal nor humane rules. Neither Dr. Pagliery nor I would willingly tolerate this clumsy spying on us as we made plans for the trial. Did they want to know beforehand how the incredible lies, which they elaborated around the events of the Moncada, would be reduced to dust and the terrible truths, which they wanted to conceal at all costs, would be exposed? It was then that it was decided that I, being a lawyer, should assume my own defense.

This decision was heard and reported by the SIM sergeant to his superiors, provoking unusual fears; it seems as if some mocking little imp took pleasure in telling them that because of me their plans would go awry. You know only too well, Magistrates, how much pressure has been brought to bear on you to take away from me the right to defend myself, a right which has been consecrated in Cuba by long tradition. The court could not accede to such maneuvers because it would have meant leaving a defendant totally defenseless. The defendant, who is now exercising his right, will not for any reason whatsoever refrain from saying what he has to say. I consider it necessary to explain, first of all, what caused the relentless isolation

[1] Servicio de Inteligencia Militar (SIM) was the military intelligence service of the Batista regime. Eds.

to which I was subjected; what the motive was in keeping me silent; why plans were made, as the court knows, to assassinate me; what grave deeds they want to hide from the people; and what the secret is behind all the strange things that have occurred in this trial. All these I plan to explain with the utmost clarity.

You have stated publicly that this trial is the most significant in the history of the Republic, and if you sincerely believe so, you should not have permitted them to make a mockery of your authority.

The first session of the trial was held the twenty-first of September. More than one hundred persons sat on the bench reserved for the defendants, amid a hundred machine guns and bayonets that noisily invaded the courtroom. A great majority of the accused were not involved in the events; they were under preventive arrest for many days after suffering all sorts of insults and mistreatment in the chambers of the police. But the rest of the accused, a few, were gallantly firm, ready to confess proudly their participation in the battle for freedom, to give an example of cooperation without precedent, and to set free from the claws of jail that group of persons who maliciously had been included in the trial. The two forces which once fought in battle returned to face each other again. Once more the just cause was on our side; the terrible battle of truth against infamy was to be waged. Certainly, the regime did not expect the moral catastrophe which awaited it!

How could they sustain their false charges? How could they prevent from being known what really happened, when these young men were willing to run all the risks—jail, torture, even death should it be necessary—in order to denounce them before the court?

In the first session, I was called on to testify, being subjected to a two-hour questioning by the prosecutor and by the twenty lawyers for the defense. I proved with exact figures and indisputable facts the amount of money invested, how it was invested, and the weapons we managed to get. I had nothing to conceal because, in fact, all had been obtained through sacrifices which had no precedent in the struggles of our Republic. I spoke of the aims which inspired us to carry on this fight and of the humane and generous behavior which we showed in dealing with our adversaries. If I was able to prove that all the falsely accused in this trial did not participate either directly or indirectly in the attack, I owe it to the total support of my heroic *compañeros*, for as I said, they would not be ashamed nor would they repent of being revolutionaries and patriots just because they might suffer the consequences. I was never allowed to speak to them in prison, yet we were in full accord on how to act. When men carry the same ideals within them nothing can isolate them, neither the walls of a jail nor the sod of a cemetery, for the same memory, the spirit, the same idea, the same dignity sustain them all.

From that very moment, the structure of infamous lies which the government had built around the facts began to collapse like a house of cards. As a result the prosecutor understood how absurd it was to keep in prison all those persons who were accused of being promoters[2] of the attack, requesting their immediate provisional release.

When I had finished my testimony at that first session, I asked the Court to grant me leave from the bench of the defendants in order to take my place among the lawyers for the defense; in effect, my petition was granted. Then began for me the task which I considered most important in this trial: to destroy completely the cowardly, malicious, and shameful slanders which have been hurled at our fighters; to reveal with irrefutable evidence the frightful and repugnant crimes which had been committed against the prisoners; and to show the nation, and the world at large, the infinite misfortune of our people who are suffering the cruelest and most inhuman oppression in all their history.

The second session was held on Tuesday, September 22. Scarcely ten people had testified, and already the murders committed in the zone of Manzanillo[3] had been broken wide open. The direct responsibility of the captain in charge of that military post was specifically established and entered into the court's record. There were still 300 persons to testify. What would happen then if, with the overwhelming data and evidence at hand, I had proceeded to question before the court the army men responsible for those deeds? Could the government permit me to do such a thing before the large crowd attending the trial, before journalists, lawyers from all over the island, and before the leaders of the opposition parties, whom it had stupidly seated right in the prisoner's dock, all of whom could hear perfectly well all that was going to be aired here? They would rather dynamite the courtroom with all the judges in it than to let such things happen!

It was decided to remove me from the trial, and this was done militarily. On Friday, September 25, on the eve of the third session, two prison doctors came to my cell. They were obviously embarrassed: "We have come to examine you," they told me. "And who is so worried about my health?" I asked. The truth was I knew the plan the moment I saw them. They could not have treated me with greater

---

[2] The Spanish is *autores intelectuales*. Eds.
[3] Manzanillo: port town in the southwest of Oriente Province where some of the battles between Castro's men and Batista's soldiers took place. Eds.

politeness, and they told me the truth. That same afternoon Colonel Chaviano had appeared at the prison and told them that I "was causing the government terrible damage at the trial" and that they must sign a certificate stating that I was sick and, therefore, could not continue attending the trial.[4] The doctors told me that, as for them, they were ready to resign their jobs, risking persecution, leaving the matter in my hands for me to decide. It was difficult for me to ask those men to sacrifice themselves, but neither could I consent under any circumstances to be a part of the plan. To leave the matter to their own consciences, I limited myself to the answer, "You should know what your duty is; I know mine very well."

After leaving the cell they signed the certificate; I know they did so because they believed, in good faith, that it was the only way out to save my life, which they saw as in great danger. I made no pledge to keep our conversation silent. I have pledged myself only to truth, and if by telling the truth in this case I may injure the material interest of those good professionals, in turn I leave their honor free of any shadow of doubt and this is worth much more. That same night I wrote a letter to the court denouncing the plot and requesting the appointment of two court doctors to testify to my perfect state of health; and I added that if I had to save my life through such trickery as a false certificate I would rather lose it a thousand times.[5] In order to make it very clear to the court that I was resolved to go it alone against so much baseness, I added to my letter the following thought of the Maestro:[6] "A just principle from the depths of a cave is stronger than an army." That was the letter which, as the court knows, Dr. Melba Hernández presented during the third session of the trial on September 26. I managed to get it to her in spite of the unrelenting vigilance to which I was subjected. Of course, immediate reprisals were taken as the result of that letter. Dr. Hernández was placed incommunicado and I, being already in solitary confinement, was sent to the farthest corner of the prison. From then on, all the accused were searched carefully from head to foot before leaving for the court.

The court doctors came on the twenty-seventh and certified that, in effect, I was in perfect health. Nevertheless, and in spite of the reiterated orders from the court, I was never brought up again to any other session of the trial. Add to that the fact that every day unknown persons distributed hundreds of apocryphal leaflets stating that I would

---

[4] Colonel Chaviano: Army commander of Oriente Province. Eds.
[5] See "Letter to the Court of Appeals" in this volume. Eds.
[6] José Martí. Eds.

be rescued from prison. This stupid alibi was invented to explain as an escape the abduction they intended. When this plan failed because of the timely intervention of alert friends, and the falsity of the doctors' certificate was brought up, they had no other alternative for keeping me away from the trial than open and flagrant disrespect of court.

Something surprisingly unusual was taking place, honorable Magistrate. Here was a regime afraid to bring an accused man before the court. A regime of terror and bloodshed was frightened in the face of the moral convictions of a defenseless, unarmed, incommunicado, and slandered man. Thus, after depriving me of everything, they wanted to deprive me also of the trial in which I was the main defendant. You should take into consideration the fact that all this was done at a time when constitutional guarantees had been suspended, the Law of Public Order[7] was being rigorously enforced, and the press and radio were subjected to censorship. What horrible crimes had the regime committed that it so feared the voice of one accused man?

I should emphasize the insolent and disrespectful attitude which the army chiefs have at all times maintained toward you. How many times has this court ordered that the inhuman isolation to which I was subjected cease? How many times did you order that my most elementary rights be unimpaired? How many times have you demanded that I be presented for trial? Yet you were never obeyed. One after the other all your orders were disobeyed. Worse still, in the very presence of this court, during the first and second sessions, a praetorian guard was put at my side to prevent me from speaking to anyone, even during recess, giving you to understand that not only in prison but also in court and in your presence they would not pay the slightest heed to your orders. I was planning to bring up this matter as a question of elementary respect for the court during the session that was to follow but . . . I never returned. And if in exchange for such disrespect I am brought here so you can send me to prison in the name of a legality which they, only and exclusively they, have been violating since March 10, the role which they wish to force you to play is a very sad one indeed. Certainly the Latin maxim *cedant arma togae*[8] has not been observed in this case even once. I beg you to keep that circumstance well in mind.

However, all their measures were completely useless because my brave *compañeros*, with unprecedented patriotism, did their duty to the utmost.

[7] Law doing away with civil rights and establishing censorship. Eds.
[8] *cedant arma togae:* let arms yield to the toga. Eds.

"Yes, we came to fight for the freedom of Cuba and we do not regret having done so!" they said one after the other when called on to testify. And right off, with impressive courage, they addressed the court denouncing the horrible crimes committed against the bodies of their brothers. Although absent from the trial, I was able to follow it in all its details from my cell, thanks to the inmates of Boniato Prison who, in spite of threats of severe punishment, found ways and means to slip into my hands press clippings and information of all kinds. In this way they avenged the abuses and immoralities of Warden Taboada and of Assistant Supervisor Lieutenant Rozábal, who made them work from sunup to sundown building private mansions and on top of that starved them to death, stealing the money destined for their food.

As the trial went on, the roles changed; those who were to accuse became the accused and the accused turned accuser. The revolutionaries were not judged there. He who was judged there forever was a man named Batista—MONSTRUM HORRENDUM! It does not matter that the brave and worthy youths were condemned if tomorrow the people will condemn the dictator and his cruel henchmen. They were sent to the Isle of Pines to live in circular cell blocks where there still lurks the ghost of Castell and where there are still heard the moans of so many murdered men.[9] Kidnapped from society, dragged from their homes, and exiled from their country, they have been sent there to purge in bitter captivity their love for freedom. Do you not believe, as I have said, that under such circumstances it is thankless and difficult for this lawyer to carry out his mission?

As a result of such obscure and illegal tactics by the will of those who rule and the weakness of those who judge, here I am in this little room in the Civil Hospital, where I have been brought to be judged in secret so that I will not be heard, so that my voice will be muffled, and so that no one will learn the things I am going to talk about. Why, then, have an imposing Palace of Justice where the judges, no doubt, would be much more comfortable? It is not wise, I warn you, to impart justice from a room in a hospital surrounded by sentinels with fixed bayonets because the people might believe that our justice is sick . . . and that the prisoner is a captive.

I remind you that our law of procedure establishes that trials shall be held in public. Nevertheless, access to this session has been completely forbidden to the people. Only two lawyers and six reporters, whose newspapers cannot print a single word because of censorship,

[9] Pedro Abraham Castell was prison warden in the Isle of Pines prison during the dictatorship of Gerardo Machado in the late 1920s and early 1930s. Eds.

have been allowed to witness the trial. I can see that my audience
in the room and in the halls is made up of about one hundred soldiers
and officers. I thank you all for the serious and kind attention you
are paying to my words! I only wish that I had the whole army
before me! I know that some day you will burn with the desire to
wash out the terrible stain of shame and blood with which the ambition of a small group of soulless men has smeared the military uniform.
When that day comes, woe betide those who today ride comfortably
on the backs of their noble soldiers—provided the people do not drag
them off long before!

Finally, I should tell you also that I have not been permitted to read
a single treatise on penal law. I am able to use only this small *Code
of Laws* which Baudilio Castellanos, brave defender of my *compañeros*, has just lent me. In the same way, they prevented me from
receiving the books of Martí. Apparently, the prison censor believed
them too subversive; or could it be that I said Martí was the intellectual author of the 26th of July action? They also forbade my bringing any reference work on any other subject. It makes no difference in the least! I bring in my heart the doctrines of Martí and in
my mind the noble ideas of all men who have defended the freedom
of the people.

There is only one thing that I am going to ask from the court, and
I expect it to be granted in compensation for all the abuse and outrage which this defendant has had to suffer, with no protection from
the law: that my right to express myself with complete liberty be
upheld. Otherwise, even the merest semblance of justice would be
totally absent, and the last link of this trial would be, more than any
other, one of disgrace and cowardice.

I confess that I feel somewhat disappointed. I thought the prosecutor would make terrible charges against me and would be ready
to justify, beyond any doubt, the whys and wherefores and the motives for which, in the name of right and justice—what Right and
what Justice?—I should be condemned to twenty-six years in prison.
Two minutes appear to me too short a time in which to ask and
justify that a man should spend more than a quarter of a century behind bars. Is the prosecutor, by any chance, annoyed at the court?
His brevity in this case, as I see it, goes against the solemnity with
which the judges announced, somewhat proudly, that this was a most
important trial; for I have heard prosecutors talk ten times as much,
in a simple case of narcotics, to ask that a citizen be condemned to
six months in prison. The prosecutor has not said one word to support
his petition. I am a just man. I understand how difficult it is for a

prosecutor who swore to be faithful to the Constitution of the Republic to come here in the name of an unconstitutional, de facto, statutory
government with no legal basis (much less any moral) to ask that a
young Cuban, a lawyer like himself, perhaps as decent as he, be sent
to jail for twenty-six years. But the prosecutor is a gifted man, and I
have seen others less talented write lengthy diatribes defending this
situation. How then are we to believe that he lacks the reason with
which to defend it at least for fifteen minutes, regardless of the great
repugnance which such a defense would inspire in any decent person?
Undoubtedly, there must be a grand plot at the bottom of all this.

Honorable magistrates, why so much interest in keeping me silent?
Why does the prosecutor not reason his case? Is it, perhaps, in order
that I may not have a target against which to direct a well-reasoned
counterattack? Has he no juridical, moral, or political ground at all
on which to base, seriously, the question? Is the truth so feared? Or is
it that they wish that I, too, would speak for two minutes and not
touch here the points that have kept some people sleepless since the
twenty-sixth of July? When the prosecutor limited himself to the
reading of five lines of an article of the Code of Social Defense, it
might have been thought that I would circumscribe myself to the same
article and mill around it endlessly, like a slave turning a millstone.
But I shall not accept such a gag by any means, because at this trial
there is more at stake than the mere freedom of an individual: Fundamental questions of principle are being argued here. The right of a
man to be free is on trial; the very basis of our existence as a civilized
and democratic nation is being debated. And when I finish, I do not
wish to have to reproach myself for having left a principle undefended,
a truth unsaid, or a crime undenounced.

The prosecutor's famous little article does not merit a one-minute
reply. I shall limit myself, then, for the moment to a brief juridical
skirmish with him in order to clear the field for the hour when I shall
destroy all the lies, falsehoods, hypocrisy, banalities, and unlimited
moral cowardice on which this crude comedy is based, which since
March 10, 1952, and even before then has been called *justice* in Cuba.

It is an elementary principle of penal law that a charge must cor-
respond exactly to the type of crime defined by the law. If there is no
law exactly applicable to the point under controversy, there is no
offense.

The article in question says textually,

> A penalty of privation of freedom of from three to ten years
> shall be imposed on the perpetrator of an act aiming at promoting
> an uprising of armed men against the *constitutional powers of the*

state. The penalty shall be privation of freedom of from five to twenty years if the insurrection is carried out.

In what country is the prosecutor living? Who told him that we promoted an uprising against the *constitutional powers of the state?* Two things come into view. First of all, the dictatorship oppressing the nation is not constitutional but has corrupted the legitimate constitution of the Republic. A legitimate constitution is that which emanates directly from a sovereign people. Further on I shall fully demonstrate this point, despite all the arguments to the contrary which the cowards and traitors have invested to justify the unjustifiable. Second, the article refers to *powers* in the plural, not singular, because it takes into consideration a republic ruled by a legislative power, an executive power, and a judicial power, which check and balance one another. We have incited a rebellion against a single illegitimate power which has usurped and concentrated in its hands the legislative and executive powers of the nation, thus destroying the whole system which the article of the Code we are analyzing precisely tried to protect. As to the independence of the judicial power after March 10, I shall not say even a word, as I am in no mood for jokes. No matter how you stretch, shrink, or mend it, there is not a single comma of Article 148 applicable to the events of July 26. Let us put it aside until such time as it may be applied to those who do incite an uprising against the Constitutional Powers of the State. I shall return later to the Code, in order to refresh the memory of the prosecutor on certain circumstances which, unfortunately, he has forgotten.

I warn you that I have just begun. If there remains in your heart a vestige of love for your country, for humanity, and for justice, then listen to me attentively. I know that I shall be silenced for many years. I know they will try to conceal the truth by every possible means. I know that there will be a conspiracy to force me into oblivion. But my voice will never be drowned; for it gathers strength within my breast when I feel most alone, and it will give my heart all the warmth that cowardly souls deny me.

I listened to the dictator on Monday, July 26, from a shack in the mountains, when there were still eighteen of us under arms. Those who have not lived similar moments will never know the meaning of bitterness and scorn. Just as the long-cherished hopes of liberating our people came tumbling down, we saw the despot rise up over them more vicious and arrogant than ever. The flood of stupid, hateful, and repugnant lies and slanders that gushed from his mouth were only equal to the enormous flood of pure and youthful blood being spilled since the night before with his full knowledge, consent, complicity, and approval, by the most heartless gang of murderers conceivable. To have believed what he said, for even one second, would have been a mistake sufficient to make a conscientious man live repentant and ashamed for the rest of his life. With a ring of more than a thousand men closing in on us, carrying weapons of longer range and greater power than ours and with orders to return with our bodies, I did not even have the hope then of branding on his miserable forehead the truth which would stigmatize him for the rest of his days and for all time. But today, with the truth beginning to be known, with these words I am pronouncing, I conclude the mission I imposed on myself completely fulfilled. I can die a peaceful and happy death. Therefore, I shall withhold no blows against those furious murderers.

It is necessary that I pause to consider the facts. It has been said by the government that the attack was carried out with such precision and perfection that participation of military experts in the elaboration of the plan was evident. Nothing could be more absurd! The plan was drawn up by a group of young men—none with military experience. I am going to reveal their names, except for two who are neither dead nor in prison: Abel Santamaría, José Luis Tasende, Renato Guitart Rosell, Pedro Miret, Jesús Montané, and myself. Half of them are dead, and as a just tribute to their memory I can say that they were not military experts, but they did have enough patriotism to give, on equal terms, a royal beating to all the generals of March 10 put together, who are neither soldiers nor patriots.

It was most difficult to organize, train, and mobilize men and arms under the surveillance of a repressive regime which spends millions of dollars on espionage, bribery, and informers. The tasks were carried out by those young men and many others with a truly unbelievable sense of responsibility, discretion, and tenacity. What is still more praiseworthy, they were willing to give an ideal everything they had, including life itself.

The final mobilization of the men, who came to this province from the remotest towns of the island, was carried out with absolute secrecy and precision. It is equally true that the attack was carried out with magnificent coordination. It began simultaneously at 5:15 A.M. in Bayamo[10] and Santiago de Cuba. One by one, to the exact minute and second previously planned, the buildings surrounding Moncada Fortress fell into our hands. However, in honor of the truth, I am going to reveal a fact that was fatal to our venture, even though it may lessen some of our merit: Because of a lamentable error, half of our forces, the best armed at that, got lost on entering the city and were missing

[10] The cradle of Cuban independence. Eds.

at the crucial moment. Abel Santamaría had taken over the Civil Hospital with twenty-one men. A doctor and our two girls went with him to attend the wounded. Raúl Castro occupied the Palace of Justice with ten men; and it was my responsibility to attack Moncada Fortress with the rest of ninety-five men. I arrived with the first group of forty-five men, preceded by an advance guard of eight men which forced Post No. 3. It was here precisely that the battle began when my car ran into a perimeter patrol armed with machine guns. The group in reserve having almost all the heavy weapons—the advance group only carried small arms—by mistake took the wrong street and wandered about in a city which none of them knew. I must clarify that I do not harbor the least doubt with regard to the bravery of those men who, on seeing themselves lost, must have suffered great anguish and desperation. The kind of action being waged, and the identical color of the uniforms used by both sides, made contact practically impossible. Many of them met death with true heroism when arrested later.

Everyone had strict orders to be, above all, humane in battle. Never was a group of fighters more generous with the adversary. From the very first we took numerous prisoners—about twenty for sure—and there was an instance at the outbreak of fighting when three of our men, Ramiro Valdés, José Suárez, Jesús Montané, after overrunning Post No. 3, managed to enter one of the barracks and held nearly fifty soldiers prisoner for a while. Those prisoners testified before this court and with no exception acknowledged that they were treated with absolute respect and did not even suffer the sound of an insulting word. On that aspect I want to express my heartfelt thanks to the prosecutor for having admitted in the trial of my *compañeros*, the incontestable facts that attested to the high sense of humaneness we showed during the struggle.

The discipline on the part of the enemy was quite bad. In the last analysis, they won because they had a fifteen-to-one superiority in men, and they had the cover which the fortress afforded. Our men, according to the soldiers, were better marksmen, and courage ran high on both sides.

Considering the causes for our tactical failure, apart for the regrettable error already mentioned, I think we made a mistake by dividing the commando unit which we had carefully trained. Of our best-trained men and boldest chiefs, there were twenty-seven in Bayamo, twenty-one in the Civil Hospital, and ten in the Palace of Justice. Had we distributed the forces otherwise, the outcome might have been different. The clash with the patrol (purely accidental, for the patrol would not have been at that point twenty seconds earlier or twenty seconds later) gave the camp time to mobilize. Otherwise it would have fallen in our hands without firing a shot, for the guard post was already in our control. On the other hand, except for the .22-caliber rifles for which we were well stocked, our side was very short of ammunition. Had we had hand grenades, they would not have been able to resist for fifteen minutes.

Once I had convinced myself that all efforts to take the fortress would be in vain, I began to withdraw our men in groups of eight and ten. The withdrawal was protected by sharpshooters under the command of Pedro Miret and Fidel Labrador, who heroically blocked the advancing soldiers. Our losses in battle had been insignificant: 95 percent of our dead were the result of the cruelty and inhumanity which began once the last shot was fired. The group at the Civil Hospital had only one casualty, the rest being trapped when the troops blocked the only exit, and laying down their arms only after they had fired their last bullet. With them was Abel Santamaría, the most generous, loved, and intrepid of the young men. His glorious resistance will immortalize him in Cuban history. We shall soon see the fate they all met and, also, the kind of lesson Batista wanted to teach our rebellious and heroic youth.

Our plan was to continue the struggle from the mountains in case the attack on the regiment failed. I was able to gather in Siboney about a third of our forces, but many were already discouraged. Some twenty decided to turn themselves in. We shall also soon see what happened to them. The rest, eighteen men, followed me into the mountains with the weapons and ammunition we had left. The terrain was completely unknown to us. For a whole week we held the top of the Gran Piedra range and the army occupied its base. We could not go down and the soldiers decided not to come up. It was not the weapons we were facing that sapped our resistance, but hunger and thirst. I had to distribute the men in small groups. Some managed to slip through the lines of soldiers; others were taken before the authorities by Archbishop Pérez Serantes.[11] When only two *compañeros* remained with me, José Suárez and Oscar Alcalde, all three of us completely exhausted, a detachment of soldiers commanded by Lieutenant Sarría surprised us at dawn on Saturday, August 1, while we slept. The slaughter of prisoners had already ceased on account of the strong reaction of the people and this officer, a man of honor, prevented some killers from murdering us hand-tied right there in the field.

I have no need to deny here the stupid statements which Ugalde

[11] He saved the lives of many rebels. Eds.

Carrillo[12] and his like invented to stain my name, believing that in so doing they would be able to cover up their cowardice, their incapacity, and their crimes. The facts are extremely clear.

It is not my purpose to entertain the court with epic narrations. Everything I have said here is essential to a more exact understanding of what I shall say later.

I wish to bring out two important facts so that you may calmly judge our attitude. First, to facilitate capture of the regiment, we could simply have detained all higher officers at their homes. This possibility was rejected out of the very humane consideration of avoiding all scenes of tragedy in the presence of their families. Second, we decided not to take any radio station until the army camp had been secured. This attitude on our part, seldom seen in its gallantry and greatness, saved the population a river of blood. Ten men were all I needed to take any radio station and then hurl the people into the struggle. You should entertain no doubt as to the people's will to fight. I had the record of the last speech delivered by Eduardo Chibás on the CMQ radio network, and I also had patriotic poems and battle hymns which would have stirred the most indifferent into action, especially when they could hear the thunder of combat. But I did not want to make use of any of these, although our situation was desperate.

It has been repeated emphatically by the government that the people did not support the movement. Never before have I heard a statement less ingenious and at the same time so full of bad faith. They pretended to prove with that statement the cowardice and submission of the people. They almost claimed that the people support the dictatorship— and they did not know how deeply that would offend the brave people of Oriente. The population of Santiago de Cuba believed at first that soldiers were fighting one another. Who could doubt the bravery, the civic pride, the unlimited courage of the rebellious and patriotic people of Santiago? If the Moncada Barracks had fallen into our hands, even the women of Santiago would have taken up arms! Many rifles were loaded for the combatants by the nurses at the Civil Hospital! They also fought! We shall never forget it.

It was never our intention to engage in battle with the soldiers of the regiment. Rather, we wanted to seize control by surprise. With this done we would have called the people to arms, and afterward would have assembled the soldiers and invited them to leave the banner of tyranny and embrace that of *freedom* to defend the better interests of the nation and not the petty interests of a small group; to

[12] Former chief of the Military Intelligence Service and later commander of Batista's armed forces in Oriente Province. Eds.

turn their rifles and fire against the enemies of the people instead of against the people, their own parents and children; to fight next to the people, like the brothers they are, and not against the people as enemies would, which is what the government wants them to be; and to unite in the beautiful and worthy ideal of offering their lives for the greatness and happiness of the fatherland. To those who doubt that many soldiers would have joined us I ask, What Cuban does not love glory? What soul does not become inflamed by the dawn of freedom?

The navy did not fight against us and, undoubtedly, would have joined us later. It is known that this branch of the armed forces was the least friendly to the tyranny, and that there is a very high civic conscience among its members. But with regard to the rest of the national army, would it have fought against a people up in arms? I affirm that it would not! The soldier is a man of flesh and blood, a man who thinks, observes, and who has feelings. He is susceptible to the influence of opinions, beliefs, sympathies, and antipathies of the people. If you ask him for his opinion, he will answer you that he cannot express it. But that does not mean that he has no opinion. He is affected by the same problems that affect other citizens: subsistence, rent, the education of his children and their future, and so forth. Each of his relatives is a point of inevitable contact with the people and with the present and future situation of the society in which he lives. It is foolish to think that just because a soldier receives a salary from the state—a very modest one at that—he has solved the essential problems which, being a member of a family and of a community, his necessities, duties, and feelings impose on him.

I have had to make this brief explanation regarding the soldier because thereon rests a fact to which very few have given any thought up to now, and that fact is that the soldier feels a profound respect for the sentiments of the majority of the people. During Machado's regime the loyalty of the army visibly decreased in the same proportion that the antipathy of the people grew. This was proved when a group of women were at the point of producing a rebellion at Camp Columbia. But a more recent event proves my assertion more clearly. While Grau San Martín's regime maintained its maximum popularity among the people, none of an infinite number of conspiracies, led and encouraged by unscrupulous officers and ambitious civilians, found an echo in the mass of the soldiers.[13]

The coup of March 10 took place at a moment when the prestige

[13] Grau San Martín was elected to the presidency in 1944. He ruled for four years. Eds.

of the government was at its lowest ebb, Batista and his gang taking advantage of this circumstance. Why did they not strike after the first of June of the same year, which was to be the date for the presidential election? Simply because had they waited for the majority of the nation to express its sentiments at the polls, no conspiracy would have found an echo among the troops. Consequently, I can make a second affirmation that no army has ever risen against a regime based on the majority of the people. You will find these truths in history. And if Batista is determined to remain in power at all costs, against the will of the absolute majority of the people, his end will be more tragic than that which befell Gerardo Machado.

I can express my ideas with regard to the armed forces because I defended them when all others remained silent; and I did it not to conspire, or for any other personal interest of any kind, for we were enjoying full constitutional normalcy. I did it simply out of humane sentiments and as a civic duty. At that time *Alerta* was one of the most widely read newspapers due to its position in national politics, and its pages carried the memorable campaign I waged against the system of forced labor to which soldiers were subjected on the private estates of the higher-ups in the military and civil world. I brought forth data, photographs, films, and facts of every kind. I took all that evidence to court on March 3, 1952. In my writings I said, more than once, that increasing the salary of the men who served in the armed forces would be only elementary justice. I would like to know the name of anyone who raised his voice on that occasion to protest against such injustice. Certainly, it was not Batista and his gang, who lived on his well-protected estate enjoying all kinds of guarantees, while I ran a thousand risks without a bodyguard or weapon.

Just as I defended the soldier then, now when all remain silent again, I tell them that they let themselves be deceived miserably; and to the stain, the deceit, and the shame of March 10, a stain and a shame a thousand times greater has been added: the frightful and unjustifiable crimes of Santiago de Cuba. The army uniform was spotted with blood from the very moment those crimes were committed. And if on a previous occasion I said and denounced before the court that there were soldiers working like slaves on private estates, today I bitterly say that there are soldiers who are bathed in the blood of many tortured and murdered young Cubans. And I repeat also that if the soldiers serve the Republic, defend the nation, respect the people, and protect the citizens, then it is just that they be paid no less than $100 a month; but if they are to kill and murder, if they oppress the people and betray the nation to benefit the interests of a small group, then the Republic should not spend a single cent on them, and Camp Columbia should be converted into a school and, instead of soldiers, ten thousand orphans should be housed there.[14]

Because above everything I want to be just, I cannot consider all army men in solidarity with those shameful crimes, which are but the work of a few traitors and criminals. But every soldier of honor and dignity, who loves his career and his institution, has the duty to demand and fight for the removal of those stains, for the avenging of that deceit, and for the punishment of those crimes. Otherwise it would be forever considered a dishonor rather than a source of pride to wear a soldier's uniform.

Of course, the coup of March 10 had no other alternative but to release the soldiers from working on private estates; however, this was only to place them as gatekeepers, drivers, servants, and bodyguards for all the political fauna which make up the dictatorship's party. Any fourth- or fifth-rate official thinks he has the right to have a soldier drive his car and be his bodyguard, as though he were in constant fear of a well-deserved kicking.

If they really had the purpose of establishing a good government, why did they not confiscate all money and property from those who, like Genovevo Pérez Dámera, made their fortunes fleecing the soldiers, making them work like slaves, and stealing the funds of the armed forces?[15] But no. Genovevo and the others have soldiers guarding their farms, and because all the generals who participated in the coup of March 10 are planning to do the same, they cannot set such a precedent.

The tenth of March was a miserable hoax indeed: His political downfall being imminent at the pools, Batista and a gang of rotten and disreputable politicians took advantage of the army's discontent and used it as an instrument to climb to a position of power on the backs of the soldiers. I know there are many disgruntled men because they have been disappointed—salaries were increased and then decreased through discounts and cuts; a large number of old elements no longer in the armed forces were returned to the ranks, holding down the advancement of able, young, valuable men; deserving soldiers were condemned to oblivion because there prevails nothing but the most scandalous favoritism and nepotism. Many soldiers are asking themselves now, what necessity was there for the armed forces to assume

[14] Camp Columbia was turned over to the Ministry of Education on September 14, 1959. Eds.

[15] Genovevo Pérez Dámera was a former chief of the army under presidents Grau San Martín and Carlos Prío. Eds.

the tremendous historic responsibility of destroying our constitution in order to place in power a group of men void of either morality or prestige, who had no chance whatsoever to occupy public office again unless they were backed by a bayonet—a bayonet they would never grasp themselves.

On the other hand, the soldiers are suffering today a tyranny worse than that to which civilians are subjected. They are being watched constantly, and not one of them can feel secure in his position. Any unjustified suspicion, any bit of gossip, any intrigue, any secret information is enough cause for transfer, dishonorable discharge, or imprisonment. Did Tabernilla not issue an order forbidding soldiers to talk to civilians opposing the regime, that is, to 99 percent of the people?[16] What distrust! Such a rule was not even imposed on the vestal virgins of Rome! The often boasted number of small houses built for soldiers does not exceed three hundred over the whole island. Yet, with the money spent on tanks, guns, trucks, and other weapons, a house could have been built for every enlisted man. For all appearances, Batista is not looking after the army but rather he wants the army to look after him. His power to oppress and kill has been increased, but that has not improved the welfare of the men. Triple guard duty, constant call to quarters, perennial unrest, the enmity of the citizenry, insecurity for the future—that is what Batista has given the soldier. To put it more plainly,

> Soldiers, you should die for the regime; give it your sweat and blood. We shall dedicate a speech to you and promote you in rank posthumously—when it no longer matters—and afterward . . . we shall continue living comfortably and getting richer. Kill, trample them under your foot, oppress them, and when the people get tired of such maltreatment and the situation comes to an end, you will pay for our crimes and we shall go to live abroad like princes. And if we return someday, don't you or your children dare knock on the door of any of our mansions, for we shall be millionaires and millionaires do not know the poor. "Kill, oppress the people, die for the regime, give it your sweat and blood. . . ."

But if a small fraction of the armed forces, blind to that sad reality, had decided to fight against the people who were to free them also from tyranny, victory would have been on the side of the people.

The prosecutor seemed very interested in knowing what our possibilities of success were. Our possibilities were based on technical, military, and social reasons. Some have tried to establish the myth that modern arms make impossible an open and frontal fight of the people against tyranny. Military parades and pompous exhibitions have, as a

[16] Tabernilla was chief of staff under Batista. Eds.

primary objective, the fomenting of this myth, thus creating among the citizens a complex of absolute impotence. But no weapon, no force, is capable of defeating a people who have decided to fight for their rights. Past and present historical instances to that effect are numberless. There is the recent case of Bolivia, where the miners smashed and defeated entire regiments of the regular army with sticks of dynamite. Fortunately, we Cubans have no need to look for examples in other countries, for we would not find any as beautiful and eloquent as those we find in our own country. During the war of 1895, there were stationed about half a million Spanish soldiers in Cuba, a number infinitely superior to that which the dictatorship has in order to oppose a population now five times greater. The weapons of the Spanish army were incomparably more modern and powerful than those of the Mambises.[17] Often the Spanish army was equipped with artillery, and its infantry used a rifle with a loading action similar to that of modern rifles. In general, the Cubans had no weapons other than their machetes, their cartridge belts being almost always empty. There is an unforgettable passage of that war recorded by General Miró Argenter, Antonio Maceo's chief of staff, which I was able to bring copied on this note in order not to abuse my memory.[18]

> The young recruits commanded by Pedro Delgado, armed for the most part with machetes, were so decimated when they hurled themselves against the Spaniards that it is not exaggerated to say that out of every fifty men at least half of them fell. They attacked the Spaniards with their fists, without pistols or machetes or knives! Searching among the bushes along the Hondo River, we found fifteen more dead belonging to the Cuban forces. At that moment we had no way of knowing to which group they belonged: There was nothing to indicate that they carried arms, their clothes appeared complete, and only tin cups hung from their waists. Two feet away, there was a dead horse with equipment intact. The culminating passage of the tragedy was then reconstructed. Those men, led by the brave Colonel Pedro Delgado, won laurels for true heroism. They had thrown themselves against the Spanish bayonets barehanded; the noise of metal heard was that of tin cups hitting against the saddle horns. Accustomed as no other man to seeing death in all its forms, Maceo was stirred and murmured this panegyric: "I had never seen recruits with only a tin cup as a weapon attack the Spaniards. And I dare call them an impediment!"[19]

[17] The Cuban patriots were called Mambises. Eds.

[18] Maceo, Cuba's greatest warrior, was nicknamed "the Titan." Eds.

[19] Term applied to the unarmed men who often "impeded" the free movement of troops. Eds.

That is the way the people fight when they want to regain freedom! They throw rocks at the planes and turn the tanks upside down!

Once we had the city of Santiago de Cuba in our hands, we would have immediately put the people on a war footing. Bayamo was attacked in order to place our advance forces next to the Cauto River. Do not forget that this province, which today has a million and a half inhabitants, is without doubt the most warlike and patriotic of all the provinces; that this province maintained for thirty years the flame of independence and paid the greatest tribute in blood, sacrifice, and heroism. In Oriente one can still breathe the air of that glorious epic. At dawn when the cock crows, like a bugle blowing reveille for the soldiers, and the sun rises brightly over the mountain crest, each day seems to be once again that of Yara or that of Baire.[20]

I said that the second consideration on which our possibilities of success were based was of a social nature because we were sure we could count on the people.

When we speak of the people, we do not mean the comfortable and conservative sectors of the nation which welcome any regime of oppression, any dictatorship, and any despotism, prostrating themselves before the master of the moment until they break their foreheads against the ground. When we mention the people in connection with the struggle, we mean the unredeemed masses to whom everything is offered but nothing is given except deceit and betrayal; those who yearn for a more dignified and just fatherland; those with ancestral longings for justice, having suffered injustice and mockery generation after generation; those who desire great and wise transformations in all the order of things, being ready to give the last drop of blood in order to attain them once they believe in something or in someone and, especially, when they believe sufficiently in themselves.

The first condition of sincerity and good faith in an undertaking is to do precisely that which no one else does, that is, to speak clearly and without fear. Demagogues and professional politicians work the miracle of being right in everything and with everyone and, of necessity, deceive everyone in everything. But the revolutionaries must proclaim their ideas valiantly, define their principles, and express their intentions clearly in order that no one, friend or foe, be deceived.

When we speak of the people and we refer to the struggle, we mean the *six hundred thousand* Cubans who are out of work and who want to earn their daily bread honestly, living here instead of having to emigrate in search of a livelihood; we mean the *five hundred thousand*

[20] Names of the towns where Cubans rebelled against Spain in 1868 and 1895. Eds.

farm workers who live in miserable huts, who work four months and go hungry the rest of the year, sharing with their children the misery of not having an inch of land to farm, and whose existence would move anyone without a heart of stone to compassion; we mean the *four hundred thousand* industrial workers and laborers whose retirement funds have been stolen, and from whom all benefits are being taken away, whose homes are wretched rooms in tenement houses,[21] whose salaries go from the hands of the employer to those of the moneylender,[22] whose future is a cut in wages and dismissal, whose life is one of never-ending work, and whose only hope for rest lies in the grave; we mean the *one hundred thousand* small farmers who live and die working land that is not theirs, contemplating it as Moses did the promised land, only to die before owning it and, like feudal slaves, having to pay for the use of that parcel of land with a large part of the crop, who cannot love that land or improve it or beautify it by planting a cedar tree or an orange tree because they do not know when the bailiff will come around with the rural guard to tell them they must leave; we mean the *thirty thousand* self-sacrificing and devoted teachers and professors, so necessary for the better destiny of future generations, who are so badly treated and poorly paid; we mean the *twenty thousand* debt-ridden small merchants, ruined by economic crises and plagued by grafting and venal public officials who deal the finishing blows; we mean the *ten thousand* young professionals—doctors, engineers, lawyers, veterinarians, dentists, teachers, pharmacists, journalists, painters, sculptors, and so forth—who leave the schools with their degrees, willing to fight for a living and full of hope, only to find themselves in a dead-end alley, with all doors closed to their clamor and pleas. These are the people, the ones who suffer all the misfortune and because of it are capable of fighting courageously! To these people, whose road of anguish is paved with deceit and false promises, we were not going to say, "We are going to give," but rather, "Here you are, now fight with all your might so that you may be free and happy!"

In the summary of the proceedings there must be the five revolutionary laws that were to have been proclaimed and broadcast by radio to the nation immediately after the fall of the Moncada Barracks. It is possible that Colonel Chaviano deliberately destroyed those documents; if he has, it does not matter, I still remember them.

The first revolutionary law would return sovereignty to the people, proclaiming the Constitution of 1940 as the true supreme law of the

---

[21] These were known as *cuarterias* and consisted of single rooms. Eds.
[22] *Garrotero:* moneylender who charged exorbitant interest. Eds.

state until such time as the people would decide to modify or change it. And in order to reestablish the Constitution, mete out exemplary punishment to all those who have betrayed it, there being no organization for holding elections to carry this out, the revolutionary movement, as the momentary incarnation of that sovereignty which is the only source of legitimate power, would assume all the faculties inherent in sovereignty (such as the powers to legislate, to enforce the laws, and to judge), except that of modifying the Constitution itself.

This measure and its purposes could not be more clearly stated or freer of sterile charlatanism. A government acclaimed by the mass of combatants would receive and be vested with the necessary power to proceed to establish effectively the will of the people and true justice. From that moment, the judicial power which since March 10 has placed itself against the Constitution and outside the Constitution would recess as such, and we would proceed to an immediate and total purification of it before it would again assume the faculties which the Supreme Law of the Republic concedes to it. For if we place the custody of the Constitution in the hands of those who dishonorably gave in without taking these prior measures, the return to legality would be a deceit, a hoax, and a new betrayal.

The second revolutionary law would have granted property, nonmortgageable and nontransferable, to all planters, tenant farmers, renters, sharecroppers, and squatters holding parcels of five *caballerías*, the state to compensate landowners on the basis of the average income they would have received from said land over a ten-year period.

The third revolutionary law granted the workers and employees of all the large industrial, mercantile, or mining concerns, including sugar mills, the right to 30 percent of the profits. Companies classified as agricultural were excepted because they would come under other agrarian laws to be implemented.

The fourth revolutionary law would have granted all planters the right to share 55 percent of the sugar production and also allotted a minimum grinding quota of 900,000 pounds of cane to all small planters who had been growing sugar cane during the last three years or more.

The fifth revolutionary law ordered the confiscation of all the wealth of those who had misappropriated public funds in previous regimes, as well as those of their heirs and legatees.[23] This law was to be enforced by a special court with full legal access to all sources susceptible to investigation, said court being endowed with the right to intervene for

[23] Law No. 78, February 13, 1959, established the Ministry of Recuperation of Stolen Public Funds and Properties. Law No. 112, February 1959, ordered confiscation of all such funds or properties. Eds.

the above purposes in all corporations registered or operating in Cuba, wherein or under the cloak of which ill-gotten gains might be concealed, and to request from foreign governments the extradition of persons and the embargo of property. Half the value of property thus recovered was to go to the retirement fund of workers and the other half to hospitals, asylums, and orphanages.

We stated also that the Cuban foreign policy in America would be one of close solidarity with the democratic peoples of the continent and that those persecuted because of their political beliefs by the bloody tyrannies which oppress brother nations would find generous asylum and brotherly love and food in the country of Martí, in direct contrast to the persecution, hunger, and betrayal which is found here today.

These laws would have been proclaimed immediately and were to be followed, once the battle had ended and after a minute study of their contents and scope, by another series of laws and measures, all fundamental, such as the agrarian reform,[24] the integral reform of the educational system, the nationalization of the electric trust and telephone trust, calling for the restitution to consumers of the illegal excess which these companies have been charging and for the payment to the Public Treasury of all monies which these companies have failed to pay.[25]

All these and other laws would be inspired by the strictest fulfillment of two of the most essential articles of our constitution, the first of which directs that latifundia be proscribed, and to that end the law should define the maximum amount of land that any person or entity may own for each kind of undertaking, adopting the necessary measures to revert all lands to the Cubans. The other article categorically orders the state to employ all the means within its reach to provide work for all those who might need it, and to assure dignified living to every manual and intellectual worker.

Neither of the two laws, therefore, can be labeled unconstitutional. The first government to come out of the first free election held would have to abide by these laws, not only because it would have a moral obligation toward the nation, but also because when people achieve what they have eagerly sought through various generations there is no force in the world strong enough to take it away from them.

The problem of land, the problem of industrialization, the problem of housing, the problem of unemployment, the problems of education and the health of the people—there we have, concretely, the six points

[24] Enacted on May 17, 1959. Eds.
[25] Telephone rates were reduced March 3, 1959. Electricity rates were cut 30 percent in August 1959. Eds.

toward which, together with the return of public liberty and political democracy, we would have resolutely directed all our efforts.

This exposition might appear cold and theoretical if, perhaps, one did not know the frightful tragedy the country is suffering in those six fields and to which the most humiliating political oppression must be added.

Eighty-five percent of the small Cuban farmers are paying rent and live under the ever-present threat of eviction. More than half of the best cr., lands are in foreign hands. In Oriente, which is the widest province, the lands owned by the United Fruit Company and West Indian Company run from the northern coast to the southern coast. *Two hundred thousand* farmers and their families do not have a single foot of land on which to raise vegetables for their hungry children whereas nearly 9,900,000 acres of fertile land remain uncultivated in the hands of powerful interests. If Cuba is an eminently agricultural country; if farmers make up a large proportion of the population; if the cities depend on the rural sector; if that rural sector waged our war of independence; if the greatness and the prosperity of our nation depends on a healthy and vigorous farmer who loves his land and knows how to cultivate it and on a state that would protect and guide him, how can this state of affairs go on forever?

With the exception of some food, timber, and textile industries, Cuba continues to be a producer of raw materials. We export sugar in order to import candy; we export hides in order to import shoes; we export iron ore in order to import plows. Everyone agrees that Cuba must be industrialized; that we need heavy industry; that we must improve cultivation and cattle breeding as well as the production of our food industries in order to meet the ruinous competition waged by European cheese, canned milk, liquors, and olive oil, as well as by the North American canned food industry; that we need merchant ships; and that the tourist industry could be an enormous source of wealth. On all of that we all agree. But the people with capital sit by and demand that workers be sacrificed, that the state keep its arms folded, and that industrialization wait for the Greek calends.

The tragedy of housing is just as bad or worse. There are in Cuba *two hundred thousand* shacks and huts. *Four hundred thousand* families in the rural area and in the cities live slavelike in cramped quarters, one-room flats, and in tenement houses lacking all hygienic and health requirements.[26] *Two million two hundred thousand* people of our urban population pay between one fifth and one third of their monthly income for rent. And *two million eight hundred thousand* of our rural

[26] In the original, *barrancones, cuarterias,* and *solares.* Eds.

and suburban population have no electricity. Here the same problem comes up. If the state plans to reduce the rent on houses, the landlord right away threatens to paralyze construction; if the state abstains from reducing it, they keep on constructing as long as they can collect a high rent—otherwise they will not lay another brick even though the rest of the population lives exposed to the elements. The same goes for the electric power monopoly. They extend power lines up to the point where they can make a satisfactory profit; from there on, it makes no difference if the people live in darkness for the rest of their lives. And the state sits there doing nothing while the people continue without shelter or electricity.

Our educational system is a perfect complement to the other problems: In a country where the farmer is not the owner of the land, why should any man want agricultural schools? In a city where there is no industry, what need is there for technical or industrial schools? Everything falls within the same logic: There is neither one thing nor the other. In any small European country, there are more than two hundred technical schools and schools for industrial arts. In Cuba, there are only six, and the boys who come out of them with degrees cannot find a place to work. Less than half of the children of school age attend rural public schools, and those who do are barefoot, half-naked, and undernourished. Many times it is the teacher who buys the necessary school materials with his own salary. Is this the way to make a nation great?

The only way to be delivered from such misery is to die, and here the state is most helpful. *Ninety percent* of the children in the countryside are ridden with parasites which enter their bodies through their bare feet. Society shudders at the news of a small child being kidnapped or murdered, but remains criminally indifferent to the mass murder of so many thousands of children who die every year in agonizing pain because of lack of resources, and whose innocent eyes reflect the shadow of death and appear to look into infinity as if they were asking that so much human selfishness be pardoned and that God's wrath not befall man. How can a man buy clothes and medicine for his children when he only works four months out of the year? His children must grow dwarflike; at thirty they will not have a tooth left but will have heard ten million political speeches; and at the end, they will die of misery and disappointment. A bed in one of the public hospitals, always filled to capacity, is only possible through the recommendation of a powerful politician who, in turn, demands from the unfortunate one his vote and that of his family so that Cuba may continue the same or worse.

With such a background it is easy to understand why from May to

HISTORY WILL ABSOLVE ME   189

December there are a million people without work to do, and that
Cuba, with five and a half million inhabitants, has at the present time
more unemployed than France and Italy put together, each of these
having a population of more than forty million.

When you judge a defendant who has been accused of robbery,
Your Honor, you do not ask him how long he has been out of work,
how many children he has, on how many days of the week he eats,
and on how many he does not. You do not worry in the least about his
social environment. You send him to jail without hesitation. But the
rich who set fire to warehouses and stores to collect the insurance do
not go to jail—even though human beings may be cremated—because
they have more than enough money to hire lawyers and bribe judges.
You send to jail the poor unfortunate who steals because of hunger;
but none of the hundreds of thieves who have stolen millions from the
state has ever spent a night behind bars. You dine on New Year's Eve
with them in some aristocratic place, and they have your respect. In
Cuba, when a public official becomes a millionaire overnight and enters
the fraternity of the rich, he can be received and drunk to with the
toast made by Balzac's famous character, Taillefer, when he drank to
the young men who had just inherited a great fortune:

> Gentlemen, let us drink to the power of gold! Mr. Valentin, now
> a six-time millionaire, has just ascended the throne. As king, he
> can do anything, for he is above all, as all the rich are. From now
> on equality before the law as prescribed by the constitution will
> be a myth to him, for he shall not be subject to the law, but
> rather the law shall be subject to him. There are no courts or
> sanctions for millionaires.

The future of the nation and the solution of its problems can no
longer depend on the selfish interests of a dozen financiers, nor on
the cold computation of profits by ten or twelve magnates in their
air-conditioned offices. The country cannot continue on its knees,
begging for a miracle from some golden calf like that of the Old
Testament which the wrath of the prophet cast down. The golden
calf cannot perform miracles of any kind. The problems of the
Republic can be solved only if we devote ourselves to fighting for it
with the same energy, honesty, and patriotism as did our liberators in
creating the Republic. It is not with statesmen like Carlos Saladrigas,
whose statesmanship consists of leaving everything as it is, mouthing
nonsense about the "absolute freedom of enterprise," "guarantees for
the investment of capital," and "the law of supply and demand," that
we are going to solve our problems.[27] The bones of those who today

---

[27] Carlos Saladrigas was a member of Batista's cabinet (1940–1944) and was
defeated as a presidential candidate in the 1944 election. Eds.

demand urgent solutions will turn to dust while those ministers happily chat in some Fifth Avenue mansion in Havana. In the real world, no social problem is solved by spontaneous generation.

A revolutionary government with the support of the people and the respect of the nation, once it cleans out all venal and corrupt officeholders, would proceed immediately to industrialize the country, mobilizing all inactive capital (currently over 1,500 million dollars) through the National Bank and the Bank for Industrial and Agricultural Development, submitting that giant task to the study, organization, planning, and final realization by technicians and men of absolute capability, free from political meddling.

A revolutionary government, after making the 100,000 small farmers owners of the land for which they now pay rent, would proceed to end the land problem once and for all. This would be done first by establishing, as the Constitution orders, a limit to the amount of land a person may own for each type of agricultural undertaking, acquiring any excess by expropriation; by recovering the lands usurped from the state; by improving swamplands; by setting aside zones for tree nurseries and reforestation. Second, it would be done by distributing the rest of the land available among rural families, preferably to those large in number; by promoting cooperatives of farmers for the common use of costly farm equipment, cold storage, and technical-professional guidance in the cultivation of crops and the breeding of livestock. Finally, it would be done by making available all resources, equipment, protection, and know-how to the farmers.

A revolutionary government would solve the problem of housing by lowering rent 50 percent, by giving tax exemption to houses inhabited by their owners; by tripling the taxes on houses built to rent; by substituting the ghastly one-room flats with modern multistory buildings; and by financing housing projects all over the island on a scale never before seen, which would be based on the criterion that if in the rural area the ideal is for each family to own its parcel of land, then in the city the ideal is for each family to own its house or apartment. There are enough bricks and more than enough manpower to build a decent house for each Cuban family. But if we continue waiting for the miracle of the golden calf, a thousand years will pass and the problem will still be the same. On the other hand, the possibility of extending electrical power to the farthest corner of the Republic is today better than ever before because today nuclear energy applied to that branch of industry, lowering production costs, is already a reality.

With these three initiatives and reforms, the problem of unemployment would disappear dramatically, and sanitation service and the struggle against disease and sickness would be a much easier task.

Finally, a revolutionary government would proceed to undertake the complete reform of the educational system, placing it at the same level as the foregoing projects, in order to prepare adequately the future generations who will live in a happier fatherland. Do not forget the words of the apostle Martí:

> A grave error is being committed in Latin America. In nations which live almost completely off the products of their land, the people are educated exclusively for urban life and are not prepared for life on a farm.
> The happiest people are those who educate their children in how to think for themselves and on how to guide their sentiments.
> An educated people will always be strong and free.

The soul of education is the teacher, and teachers are now poorly paid in Cuba. Yet there is no one more in love with his vocation than the Cuban teacher. Who of us did not learn his alphabet in a public school? It is high time to stop paying with alms those men and women to whom is entrusted the most sacred mission in the world today and tomorrow—the mission to teach. No elementary teacher should earn less than $200, and no secondary school teacher should receive less than $350 if we want them to devote themselves entirely to their high mission free of want and privation. Moreover, the teacher who works in the rural districts should be given free transportation, and every five years, at least, all teachers should be given a six-month leave with pay in order that they may attend special courses here or abroad to keep up to date on the latest pedagogical trends, thus improving constantly their programs and systems. Where can we get the necessary money? When there is an end to robbery, when there are no corrupt public officials who let themselves be bribed by big companies to the detriment of the public treasury; when the great resources of the nation are mobilized and the state ceases to buy tanks, bombers, and cannons to oppress the people in a country which has no frontiers; and when the state decides it wishes to educate instead of killing—then there will be money enough.

Cuba can support splendidly a population three times larger than it now has; there is no reason then for the misery among its inhabitants. The markets should be flooded with produce, pantries should be full, all hands should be industriously producing. All this is not inconceivable. It is inconceivable that there are men who go to bed hungry while there remains one inch of uncultivated land. It is inconceivable that there are children dying without medical assistance. It is inconceivable that 30 percent of our farmers do not know how to write their names, and that 99 percent of them do not even know Cuba's history. It is inconceivable that the majority of the families on our farms are living under worse conditions than the Indians Columbus found when he discovered the most beautiful land that human eyes have ever seen. For those who call me a dreamer because I say these things, I tell them as Martí did,

> A real man does not look around to see on which side he can live better, but rather on which side duty lies. That man is the only practical one; his dream today will be law tomorrow, for he who has set his eyes on the universal and has seen peoples boil up inflamed and blood drenched from the cauldrons of centuries knows that the future, without exception, is on the side of duty.

Only by realizing that such high aims inspired those who fell in Santiago de Cuba can we understand their heroism. Our scarce material means prevented sure success. The soldiers were told that Prío had given us a million dollars. They did not want the most important fact to be known—that our movement had no connection whatever with the past, that it was a new Cuban generation with its own ideas rising up against tyranny; that our movement was made up of young men who were barely seven years old when Batista began to commit his first crimes back in 1934. The lie about the million dollars could not be more absurd. If with less than $20,000 we armed 165 men and attacked both a regiment and a squadron, with a million dollars we could have armed 8,000 men and would have attacked fifty regiments and fifty squadrons. And Ugalde Carrillo would not have learned about it until Sunday, July 26, at 5:15 A.M. Let it be known that for every man who came to fight there were twenty more perfectly trained ones who could not come because we had no arms to give them. Those men paraded with the students' demonstration through the streets of Havana when Martí's centennial was commemorated, packing six city blocks completely. Two hundred more who could have come to fight, or twenty hand grenades, could have possibly saved this honorable court a lot of trouble.

While politicians spend millions in their campaigns bribing consciences, a handful of Cubans who wanted to save the honor of their country had to face death empty-handed because of lack of resources. That explains how the country has been governed until now, not by generous and self-sacrificing men, but by those who constitute the underworld of our public, the scum of the nation.

With greater pride than ever, in accordance with our principles I can say that no politician of yesterday ever saw us knocking on his door asking for a single cent. Whatever weapons we had we gathered with unparalleled examples of sacrifice such as that of Elpidio Sosa, who sold his job and came to me one day with $300 "for the cause";

of Fernando Chenard, who sold the photographic equipment with which he earned his living; of Pedro Marrero, who contributed his salary for many months (and it was necessary to forbid him to sell his furniture); of Oscar Alcalde, who sold his pharmaceutical laboratory; and of Jesús Montané, who gave the money he had saved for five years. And in the same way many more gave us what little they had.

One must have great faith to act in such a way, and these remembrances of idealism lead me directly to the most bitter part of this defense: the price that tyranny made them pay for wanting to free Cuba from oppression and injustice.

> Beloved corpses that once
> Were the dreams of my fatherland,
> Cast upon my forehead
> The dust of your worm-eaten bones!
> Touch my heart with your hands,
> Groan in my ears!
> Each of my moans will be
> Tears of one more tyrant!
> Gather round me; stay so that
> My being may receive your spirit
> And give me the fright of the tombs
> For tears are not enough
> When one lives in infamous slavery!

Multiply the crime of November 27, 1871, by ten and you will have the monstrous and disgusting crimes committed on July 26, 27, 28, and 29, 1953, in Oriente Province.[28] The events are still fresh, but when the years pass and the sky over the nation clears, when troubled spirits become calm and fear does not darken the mind, then the magnitude of the massacre will begin to be seen in all its frightful reality and the coming generations will look with terror on this unprecedented act of barbarism. But I do not want anger to blind me, because my mind needs to be clear and my broken heart serene so that I can relate the events as they occurred, with simple words, void of dramatic exaggeration because, as a Cuban, I feel ashamed that soulless men could have perpetuated crimes which defy description, disgracing our country before the world.

Tyrant Batista was never a scrupulous man who would hesitate to tell the people the most fantastic lies. When he tried to justify the coup of March 10, he did so by inventing a tale about a military coup which was to take place in April, adding that he "wanted to avoid the

---

[28] On November 27, 1871, eight medical students were executed after being falsely accused of desecrating the tombstone of Spanish newspaperman Gonzalo Castañón. The execution brought about a popular outcry. Eds.

submersion of the Republic in blood," a ridiculous fable that no one believed. And when he wants to submerge the Republic in a bloodbath by suppressing with terror, torture, and crime the rebellion of young men who refuse to be his slaves, he invents still more fantastic lies. How very little respect one must have for the people when one so miserably tries to deceive them! The very day I was arrested, I assumed publicly full responsibility for the armed movement of July 26, and if any of the things the dictator said against our combatants in his speech of July 27 had been true, I would have had no moral ground on which to stand during these proceedings. Yet why was I not brought to trial? Why the faked medical certificate? Why were all laws of procedure violated, and why were all the court's orders dismissed so contemptuously? Why were things done, heretofore never seen in any public trial, to prevent at all costs my appearance in court? I did my utmost to be present. I demanded from the court that I be brought to trial in strict compliance with the law, denouncing the maneuvers being made to prevent it. I wanted to argue with them, face to face. They did not.

Who, then, had the truth and who did not?

The statements made by the dictator from Camp Columbia would be something to laugh at if they were not so soaked in blood. He said the attackers were a group of mercenaries among whom there were many foreigners; he said that the main purpose of the plan was an attempt on his life—him, always him, as if the men who attacked Moncada Barracks would not have been able to kill him and twenty others like him, if such an attempt had been in accordance with our methods. He said that the attack had been conceived by former president Prío, who also provided the money, and yet we have proved beyond any doubt that there is no connection whatsoever between our movement and the past regime. He said that we were armed with machine guns and hand grenades, and yet army technicians have testified here that we had only one machine gun and no hand grenades. He said that we slit the throat of the guard at the gate, and yet here, in the evidence presented, both the death and usual medical certificates showed that none of the soldiers killed or wounded suffered a knife wound. But, above all, he said that we had knifed the sick in the Military Hospital and yet the doctors of that same hospital—army doctors, no less!—have testified at this trial that the Military Hospital was never occupied by us, that no patient was killed or wounded there, and that the only casualty suffered was that of a sanitation employee who imprudently looked out from one of the windows.

When a chief of state (or whoever pretends to be one) makes a statement to the country, he does so not just for the sake of speaking. He always harbors a purpose, seeks an effect, is propelled by an intention. If we had already been vanquished militarily and we no longer were a real danger to the dictatorship, why were we slandered in such a manner? If it is still not clear to you that his was a bloody speech, if it is not evident that he wanted to justify the crimes which had been committed since the night before as well as those that were to be committed afterward, then let statistics speak for me: On July 27, in his speech from Camp Columbia, Batista said that we had suffered thirty-three dead; by the end of the week, the number of our dead had risen to more than eighty. Where, and in what battles, did those young men die? More than twenty-five prisoners had been murdered before Batista spoke; after he spoke fifty more were murdered.

A high sense of honor was shown by those modest army technicians and army professionals who, on appearing before the court, did not disfigure the facts but gave their reports adhering to the strictest truth! They honor the uniform, they are men indeed! Neither a true soldier nor a true man is capable of tarnishing his life with lies and crime. I know they feel terribly indignant about the barbarous murders committed. I know they feel revulsion and shame for the stench of homicidal blood that permeates every stone of the Moncada Barracks.

I defy the dictator to repeat now his base slanders, if he can, in the face of the testimony given by those honorable soldiers. I defy him to justify before the Cuban people his speech of July 27. Let him not be silent, let him speak! Let him tell who the inhuman, pitiless assassins are. Let him tell if the Cross of Honor which he came here to pin on the chests of the heroes of that massacre was to reward the repugnant crimes they committed. Let him, as of now, assume that responsibility before history, so that he may not try to say later that it was done by the soldiers without his orders. Let him explain to the nation the seventy murders. There was much bloodshed! The nation needs an explanation, the nation demands it, the nation requires it!

It is known that in 1933, when the battle at the Hotel Nacional had ended, some officers were killed after surrendering, which prompted *Bohemia* magazine to protest energetically.[29] It is also known that after the surrender of Atarés Fortress, the besiegers machine-gunned a row of prisoners and that a soldier, asking who was

[29] Some 400 deposed officers had gathered at the hotel after the revolt of the sergeants led by Batista on September 4, 1933. Eds.

Blas Hernández, felled him with a shot right in the face—the soldier being rewarded for this cowardly action with a promotion to officer.[30] It was known that the murder of prisoners was fatally linked in Cuban history to Batista's name. What foolish ingenuousness of us not to see clearly and understand it to be so. Yet on those occasions the events occurred in a matter of minutes, no more that the burst of a machine gun, while nerves were still on edge, although such a procedure will never be justified.

But here in Santiago de Cuba it was not like that. Here all forms of cruelty and barbarism were surpassed. It was not a minute, an hour, a day, the time they took to kill. Throughout the week beatings, torture, men thrown from rooftops to the street, shooting, were expertly and ceaselessly carried out by perfect artisans of crime. Moncada Barracks was converted into a shop for torture and death. Dishonorable men exchanged their military uniforms for butchers' aprons. The walls were splashed with blood, and bullets were left in them, encrusted with fragments of human skin, brains, and hair blackened by point-blank shots. The grass was covered with dark, sticky blood. The criminal hands that rule the destiny of Cuba had written at the entrance of that realm of death, for all the prisoners to see, the infernal inscription: "Abandon here all hope."

They did not even bother to cover up; they did not worry about disguising what they were doing. They thought they had fooled the people with their lies and ended by fooling themselves instead. They felt and acted like lords and masters of the universe—absolute owners of human life and death. The scare they had at dawn in the attack was dissipated in a festival of corpses, in a true drunken spree of blood.

Chronicles, who have recorded four and a half centuries of our history, tell us of many cruel deeds from the slaughter of defenseless Indians, the atrocities of the pirates who preyed on coastal towns, the cruelties to the guerrillas during our struggle for independence, the shooting of Cuban prisoners by Weyler's army, the horrors of Machado's regime, to the killings of March 1935. But there is still to be written as sad, somber, and bloody a page, given the number of victims and the cruelty of the oppressors, as that of Santiago de Cuba. During those centuries only one man, Batista, has spilled the blood and sunk his claws into the flesh of two generations of Cubans. And he waited for the celebration of Martí's centenial to release a river of blood such as has never been seen before. Our republic, which cost so many lives for the liberty, respect, and happiness of all Cubans, had

[30] Blas Hernández was the revolutionary leader who had taken the fortress. Eds.

just completed fifty years of existence. Still worse is the crime, and more to be condemned, because it was perpetrated by a man who for eleven years had governed a people who by tradition and sentiment love liberty and repudiate crime with all their soul; a man, moreover, who has never been loyal, sincere, honorable, or a gentleman for one minute of his entire public life.

It was not enough. The treason of December 1933,[31] the crimes of March 1935, and the forty-million-dollar fortune which crowned his first eleven-year period were not enough for him. The treason of March 10, 1952, the crimes of July 1953, and other millions of dollars that only time will reveal were necessary. Dante divided his hell into nine circles. He put the criminals in the seventh, thieves in the eighth, and traitors in the ninth. What a dilemma Satan will face when he tries to find a place for this man—if this man has a soul! He who encouraged the atrocious crimes of Santiago de Cuba does not even have a soul.

I know many details—soldiers truly ashamed told me of the scenes they had witnessed—of how the crimes were committed.

After the battle, they threw themselves like wild beasts on the city of Santiago de Cuba and on its defenseless population. In the middle of a street, and far from where the battle had taken place, a child who was playing in front of his home was shot through the chest; when the father approached to recover the body, they shot him through the forehead. Another small boy, Cala, was shot without so much as a word when he was on his way home carrying a loaf of bread. It would be impossible to tell about all the crimes perpetrated on the civilian population. If they dealt in such fashion with those who took no part in the action, you can imagine the horrible fate suffered by those who did participate or who were thought to have participated. Because, just as they have involved many innocent people in this case, so they killed many of those first arrested who had nothing to do with the attack. These victims are not included in the number of dead, which refers exclusively to our men. Some day the total number of those sacrificed will be known.

The first prisoner assassinated was our doctor, Mario Muñoz, who had neither weapon nor uniform but wore his physician's white coat uniform; he was a generous and competent man who took care of all the wounded, friend or foe, with the same devotion. He was shot in the back while being taken from the Civil Hospital to Moncada, his body left face down in a pool of blood. But the mass slaughter of prisoners

---

[31] Batista forced provisional president Grau out of office in early 1934. Eds.

did not begin until 3:00 P.M. Until that time they waited for orders. General Martín Díaz Tamayo had just arrived from Havana with precise orders after meeting with Batista, the chief of staff, the chief of the Military Intelligence Service, and others. He said that "it was a shame and a dishonor for the army to have had three times as many losses in combat as had the attackers and that ten prisoners had to be killed for every dead soldier." That was the order!

In every human group there are men of low instincts, born criminals, beasts who carry all the ancestral atavisms dressed in human form, monsters loosely tied by discipline and social conventions who, if given a river of blood to drink, will not stop until it runs dry. And what these men needed was precisely that order! As a consequence, the best, the bravest, the most honorable, the most idealistic men of Cuba perished at their hands. The tyrant called them mercenaries, while they were dying like heroes at the hands of men who were collecting a salary from the Republic and were given weapons to defend it but were serving the interests of a gang and assassinating the finest citizens.

In the midst of torture, life was offered to our men provided they betray their ideals by declaring falsely that Prío had given them money. When this proposal was indignantly rejected, the torture continued. They crushed their testicles and pulled out their eyes but no one yielded, neither a plea nor a lament was heard. Even when they had been deprived of their sexual organs, they were a thousand times more manly than all of their torturers put together. Photographs do not lie, and their corpses appear mutilated. They tried other means as well: They could not overcome the courage of the men, so they tested the courage of the women. Carrying a bleeding eye in his hands, a sergeant accompanied by other men went to the cell where *compañeras* Melba Hernández and Haydée Santamaría were being held. Addressing the latter and showing her the eye, the sergeant said, "This belonged to your brother. If you don't tell us what he would not, we will tear out his other eye." Miss Santamaría, who loved her courageous brother above everything else, replied with dignity, "If you took one of his eyes out and he didn't tell you anything, much less will I."[32] Later they returned to apply lighted cigarettes butts to her arms until finally, full of malice, they addressed her again: "You no longer have a fiancé because we have killed him also." Once again, imperturbable, she answered, "He is not dead because to die for one's country is to live." Never before has Cuban womanhood reached a higher point of heroism and dignity.

[32] Castro made up this story, because it never occurred. Eds.

They had no mercy even for those wounded in battle who had been taken to different hospitals throughout the city. They searched for them like vultures after prey. They entered the surgery room of Centro Gallego Hospital at the moment that two badly wounded men were being given a blood transfusion. They dragged them off the tables, and as they could not walk, they dragged them to the ground floor, where they arrived dead.

They could not do the same at the Colonia Española Hospital where Gustavo Arcos and José Ponce were, because Dr. Posada valiantly prevented it by telling them that they would have to do it over his dead body.

At the Military Hospital Pedro Miret, Abelardo Crespo, and Fidel Labrador were injected with air and camphor in the veins to kill them. They owe their lives to Captain Tamayo, an Army doctor and true soldier of honor, who, at gun point, snatched them from their executioners and transferred them to the Civil Hospital.

These five young men were the only wounded who managed to survive.

In the early dawn, groups of our men were removed from Moncada and transferred to the towns of Siboney, La Maya, Songo, and other places, where already deformed by torture, they were bound and gagged in order to kill them in isolation. They wanted to make it appear later as if they had died in combat with the army. This was carried on for several days, and few of the captured prisoners survived. Many were even forced to dig their own graves. One of them, while he was digging, turned and stuck the pick into the face of one of the murderers. Others were buried alive, with their hands tied to their backs. Many solitary places served as a cemetery for those brave men. On the army shooting range alone, there are five men buried. Someday their bones will be dug up and carried on the shoulders of the people to the mausoleum which a free nation will erect beside Martí's tomb to the "Martyrs of the Centennial."

The last young man assassinated in the zone of Santiago de Cuba was Marcos Martí. He and *compañero* Ciro Redondo were captured in a cave at Siboney on the morning of July 30. As they were being taken along a road, hands over head, the former was shot in the back, a volley of bullets finishing the job while he was lying on the ground. The latter was taken to the army camp. When Major Pérez Chaumont saw him, he exclaimed, "Why have you brought me this one?" The court could hear this youth himself tell the facts, as he survived, thanks to what Major Pérez Chaumont called "the stupidity of the soldiers."

The order to kill was given throughout the province. Ten days after the attack a newspaper published that on the highway from Manzanillo to Bayamo two young men had been found hanged. Later on, the bodies were identified as those of Hugo Camejo and Pedro Vélez. Something extraordinary also occurred there: The victims were to have been three. They had been removed from the army barracks at Manzanillo at 2:00 A.M. and at a certain spot along the highway were beaten senseless and then strangled with a rope. But when all of them had been left for dead, one, Andrés García, recovered consciousness and sought refuge in the house of a farmer. Thanks to him, the court learned all the details of the crime. This young man was the only survivor of all the prisoners taken in the zone of Bayamo.

Near the Cauto River, in a place known as Barrancas, there were found at the bottom of a well the bodies of Raúl de Aguiar, Armando del Valle, and Andrés Valdés, assassinated at midnight on the road from Alto Cedro to Palma Soriano by the chief of Miranda Barracks, Sergeant Montes de Oca, Corporal Maceo, and the lieutenant in charge of Alto Cedro, where they had been arrested.

In the annals of the Moncada Barracks crime, Sergeant Eulalio González, nicknamed "the tiger," deserves honorable mention. This man did not show any shame at all when bragging about his monstrous deeds. It was he, with his own hands, who murdered our *compañero* Abel Santamaría. Yet he was not satisfied. One day, on his way to Boniato Prison backyards, where he raised fighting cocks, he boarded the same bus in which Abel's mother was riding. When the monster found out who she was, he began to talk in a loud voice about his deeds. Raising his voice still more so that the lady, dressed in mourning, could not help but hear, he said, "Well, I have pulled out many eyes, and I intend to continue pulling them out." The sobbing of the mother on hearing the cowardly insult proffered by the murderer of her son expresses better than words the unprecedented moral opprobrium our country is suffering. When those same mothers went to Moncada Barracks to inquire about their sons, with unheard-of cynicism the answer was, "Of course, Madam! Go to Hotel Santa Ifigenia—you'll find them registered there."[33] Either Cuba is not Cuba or those responsible for these deeds must suffer a terrible punishment. These soulless men even insulted the people who took off their hats as the dead bodies of the revolutionaries passed through the streets on the way to the cemetery.

There were so many victims that the government still has not

[33] Santa Ifigenia is a cemetery near Santiago de Cuba. Eds.

dared to publish a complete list, they know the number of our losses is too great if compared with their losses. They have the names of all the dead because before murdering the prisoners they took down all the data. All that routine of identification which the National Bureau of Identification went through was pure pantomime. There are families who still do not know the fate of their sons. If three months have gone by already, why, then, do they not say the last word?

I want to confirm that they searched the pockets of the corpses looking for their last cent, and they also took personal belongings such as rings and watches, all of which the murderers are brazenly wearing today.

Honorable Magistrates, a great deal of what I have just said you already known from my *compañeros*. But you see that they do not allow many key witnesses to attend this trial, although they were permitted to attend the other sessions of the trial. For example, the nurses of the Civil Hospital are absent, in spite of the fact that they are working right here beside us, in the same building in which this trial is being held. They were not permitted to be present so they could not testify before the court and answer my questions on whether or not, aside from Dr. Mario Muñoz, twenty other men were alive when arrested. They were afraid that through my questioning the witnesses, I might secure very dangerous testimony for the official records.

But Major Pérez Chaumont did come before this court and could not evade my questioning. From what I did to that hero of battles against unarmed, handcuffed men you can get an idea of what would have happened in the Palace of Justice had they not kidnapped me from the trial. I asked him how many of our men had been killed in his famous Siboney combat. He hesitated. I insisted and, finally, he said twenty-one. As I knew that such a battle never occurred, I asked him how many wounded we had. "None," he answered. "They were all dead." Astonished, I replied by asking if the army had used atomic weapons. Of course, when you murder by shooting point-blank, you have no wounded. And I asked him how many losses the army had suffered. He told me that two soldiers were wounded. Finally, I asked if any of the wounded had died, and he said none. I waited. Days later all the wounded soldiers paraded before this court, and none of them had been at Siboney. That very same Pérez Chaumont, who would hardly quiver at having killed twenty-one defenseless young men, has built himself a palace for over a hundred thousand dollars at Ciudamar Beach with the savings he has made in the few

months since March 10, 1952. Now if a major has been able to save
that much so far, how much have the generals?

Honorable Magistrates: Where are over sixty of our companions
who were arrested on July 26, 27, 28, and 29 in the zone of Santiago
de Cuba? Only three men and the two girls have appeared; the rest of
the accused were all arrested later. Where are our wounded *compañeros?* Only five have appeared; the rest were murdered also.
The figures are irrefutable. On the other hand, twenty soldiers we
had taken prisoner testified before you in this court, and they all
admitted that we had not offended them in any way. Thirty wounded
soldiers, many of them wounded in street fighting, also testified before
you, which proves that they were not finished off. If the army suffered
nineteen dead and thirty wounded, how is it possible for us to have
had eighty dead and five wounded? Who has ever seen a battle with
twenty-one dead and no wounded, like the famous battle mentioned by
Major Pérez Chaumont?

Here you have the figures for the losses suffered in the fierce combats, including victories and defeats, waged by the Invading Column
in the war of 1895. Battle of Los Indios: twelve wounded, no dead;
Battle of Mal Tiempo: four dead, twenty-three wounded; Battle of
Calimete: sixteen dead, sixty-four wounded; Battle of La Palma: thirty-
nine dead, eighty-eight wounded; Battle of Cacarajícara: five dead,
thirteen wounded; Battle of Descanso: four dead, forty-five wounded;
Battle of San Gabriel del Lombillo: two dead, eighteen wounded. In
all these battles the wounded outnumber the dead two, three, and
sometimes ten to one. Even though at that time no advanced techniques in medicine existed to treat the wounded, how can the fantastic
ratio of sixteen dead for each wounded be explained, unless it is by
finishing off the wounded in the hospitals and murdering defenseless
prisoners? These numbers speak for themselves.

"It is a shame and dishonor for the army to have three times as
many losses as the attackers. Ten prisoners must be killed for every
dead soldier." That is the concept of honor held by the petty corporals
promoted to generals on the tenth of March, and that is the kind of
honor they want to impose on the National Army. False, faked, out-
wardly apparent honor based on lies, hypocrisy, and crime: Murderers
who wear a mask of honor made with blood. Who told them that to
die fighting is a dishonor? Who told them that the honor of an army
rests on the killing of the wounded and prisoners of war?

In war, the armies that murder prisoners have always earned the
scorn and contempt of the world. There is no justification for such
cowardice even if the enemy were an army invading the national

territory. This was very well expressed by a South American liberator when he wrote, "Not even the strictest military obedience can turn the sword of a soldier into an executioner's knife." A soldier of honor does not murder a defenseless prisoner, but treats him with respect; he does not finish off the wounded, but helps him; he sees that no crime is committed, and if he is unable to prevent it, he does as the Spanish captain, who, on hearing shots from the firing squad which executed some students, indignantly broke his sword and refused to serve any longer in that army.

Those who killed the prisoners were not worthy companions of their own dead. I saw many soldiers fight with uncommon courage, as did those of the patrol who fired their machine guns at us in an almost hand-to-hand fight; or, the sergeant who, defying death, managed to sound the alarm to mobilize the camp. Some are alive, for which I am happy; others died, believing they were doing their duty, and for me that makes them worthy of admiration and respect. I only regret that brave men should fall defending a bad cause. When freedom reigns again in Cuba, the widows and orphans of those brave men who fell fighting us will be respected, protected, and aided by the nation. They are innocent victims of Cuba's misfortunes. They are just so many more victims of this nefarious situation.

But the honor the soldiers won by dying in battle was stained by the generals who ordered the killing of prisoners after the combat. Men who became generals overnight without even firing a shot, men who bought their stars with high treason to the Republic, men who ordered the murder of prisoners taken in a battle in which they took no part—those are the generals of March 10. They are generals who would not have been fit to drive the mules which carried the equipment for the army of Antonio Maceo.

If the army had three times as many losses as we had, it was due to the magnificent training of our men and to the tactics employed, as the soldiers have acknowledged. If the army did not play a more brilliant role, if it was taken completely by surprise in spite of the millions that the Military Intelligence Service spends on espionage, if their hand grenades did not explode because they were too old, it is all due to generals like Martín Díaz Tamayo and colonels like Ugalde Carillo and Alberto del Río Chaviano. We were not 17 traitors infiltrating the ranks of the army as on March 10, but 165 men from one end of the island to the other who dared to face death boldly. If the army chiefs had any military honor at all, they would have resigned their posts instead of washing away their shame and personal incompetence in prisoners' blood.

To kill defenseless prisoners and then say they died in combat, that is the military capacity of the generals of March 10. In the cruelest years of our war of independence, Valeriano Weyler's worst butchers behaved that way. The *Chronicles of the War*[34] narrate the following passage:

> On February 23, Officer Baldomero Acosta entered the town of Punta Brava at the head of some cavalry at the same time that a platoon of Spanish troopers under the command of a sergeant nicknamed Barriguilla[35] was advancing from the opposite direction. Acosta's men exchanged shots with the Spaniards and then retreated along the trail that goes from Punta Brava to a small town, Guatao. Reinforced by a company of Spanish volunteers from Marianao under the command of Captain Calvo, Barriguilla kept after Acosta's men. As his vanguard entered Guatao, he initiated a slaughter of civilians, twelve being murdered and the rest taken prisoner. Not satisfied with their outrages, they killed one of the prisoners and horribly wounded the rest on the outskirts of the town. Roguish court soldier the marquis of Cervera reported the costly victory to Weyler. But a soldier of honor, Major Zugati, denounced the incident to the Spanish government and told how it really had happened, calling the deaths caused by Captain Calvo and Sergeant Barriguilla plain murder of peaceful townspeople.

Weyler's tacit consent to this horrible massacre and his joy on learning its details is shown in the official dispatch he sent to the Minister of War immediately afterward:

> A small detachment organized by Marianao's military commander with garrison troops battled and destroyed groups commanded by Villanueva and Baldomero Acosta near Punta Brava, killing twenty who were turned over to the Mayor of Guatao for burial and taking fifteen prisoners, one of them wounded, believing more wounded carried away by the enemy. On our side one badly wounded and several slightly wounded—Weyler.

In what way does Weyler's war communiqué differ from that of Colonel Chaviano reporting Major Pérez Chaumont's victories? Only in that Weyler reported twenty dead to Chaviano's twenty-one; Weyler reported one wounded in his ranks, Chaviano reported two; Weyler reported one wounded and fifteen prisoners, and Chaviano recorded neither prisoners nor wounded.

Just as I admire the bravery of the soldiers who died fighting, I also admire the many soldiers who conducted themselves worthily and did not stain their hands in that orgy of blood. Many of the pris-

---

[34] Compilation of General Antonio Maceo's campaign records made by General José Miró Argenter. Eds.

[35] Means "potbelly." Eds.

oners now alive owe their lives to the honorable conduct of men like Lieutenant Sarría, Lieutenant Campa, Captain Tamayo, and others who treated them as gentlemen. If men such as these had not saved in part the honor of the armed forces, today it would be more honorable for a man to wear an apron than an army uniform.

I do not demand vengeance for my dead *compañeros*. Priceless as their lives were, those of all the criminals together could not ever be payment enough. It is not with blood that they can pay for the lives of the young men who died for the good of the country. The happiness of that country is the only worthwhile price that can be paid for them.

My *compañeros*, besides, are neither forgotten nor dead. They are alive today as never before. Their terror-stricken murderers shall see how from those heroic corpses there will rise the victorious specter of their ideals. Let Martí speak for me:

> There is a limit to grief at the graves of the dead, and it is the infinite love for country and glory which their bodies reflect, ever fearless, ever tireless, ever unabated—for the bodies of the martyrs are the most beautiful altar to honor.
>
> . . . When one dies
> In the arms of the grateful fatherland,
> Death ends, prison is broken,
> At last, with death, life begins!

Up till now I have dwelt almost exclusively upon events. As I do not forget that I am before a court of justice judging me, I shall now prove that right rests on our side and that the sanctions imposed on my *compañeros* and that which it is pretended should be imposed on me have no justification whatsoever before reason, before society, and before true justice.

I personally wish to be respectful to the honorable magistrates, and I shall be thankful if you do not take the rudeness of my truths as animosity toward you. My reasoning will be aimed only at demonstrating the false and erroneous position assumed in the present situation by the judicial power, of which each court is but one of the wheels forced to a certain extent to keep turning along the path previously traced, which does not justify, of course, a man going against his principles. I know perfectly well that the greater responsibility falls on the high oligarchy, which without the slightest gesture of protest servilely pledged itself to the dictates of the usurper, betraying the nation and thus renouncing the independence of the judicial power. Men who are honorable exceptions have tried to cover up the dishonor with dissenting opinions, but these efforts by a small minority have hardly transcended the pliable and sheepish attitude of the majority. However, this fatalism will not deter me from stating here the truths which back me up. If bringing me before this court is nothing more than pure comedy, to give arbitrariness an appearance of legality and justice, then I am ready to rip off with a firm hand the infamous veil which covers so great a shame. It seems odd that those that bring me before you to be judged and condemned are the same ones who not even once have obeyed the orders of this court.

If this trial, as you have said, is the most important ever held since the establishment of the Republic, what I may say here perhaps will get lost in the dictatorship's plot to silence me. But all that you hear posterity will review again and again. Think not that you are judging a man now, but that you shall be judged over and over again when the present shall be submitted to the crushing criticism of the future. Then, what I may have said here will be often repeated, not because I was the one who said it, but because the problem of justice is eternal, and the people have a profound sense of it over and above the opinions of jurists and theoreticians. The people have a simple but implacable logic, at odds with all that is absurd and contradictory; and if any people heartily hate privilege and inequality, it is the Cuban people. They know that justice is represented by a blindfolded woman holding a scale and a sword. If they see her kneeling before some and furiously brandishing the sword against others, they will imagine her a prostitute holding a dagger in her hand. My logic is the simple logic of the people.

I am going to tell you a story. Once upon a time there was a republic. It had its constitution, its laws, its liberties; a president, congress, and courts. Everyone could meet, associate, speak, and write freely. The men in government did not satisfy the people, but the people could change them, and it was only a few days before they would have done so. There existed a public opinion which was respected and obeyed, all problems of collective interest being freely discussed. There were political parties, educational radio programs, polemic programs on television, public meetings, and there was enthusiasm among the people. The people had suffered long; and if they were not yet totally happy, they wanted to be and had the right to be. They had been deceived many times and looked back with terror on the past, blindly believing that it could never return. They were proud of their love for liberty and believed that it would be respected as a sacred right. They had placed a noble trust in the certainty that no one would dare commit the crime of attacking their democratic institutions. They wanted a change, an improvement; they wanted to take a step forward, and they saw it near. All of their hopes rested on the future.

Poor people! One morning they awoke with a shock. In the shadows of the night, while they were asleep, the ghosts of the past had plotted and now had them by the feet and throat with both hands. Those claws, those fangs, those jaws of death, those boots they well knew. No, it was not a nightmare. It was stark and terrible reality! A man named Fulgencio Batista had just committed the crime no one expected.

It then happened that a humble citizen of that republic who wanted to believe in its laws and in the integrity of its judges—although he had often seen them oppress the underprivileged—sought the Code of Social Defense to find out what punishment had been prescribed for the author of such deeds and found the following:

> Anyone who performs an act directly aimed at changing in whole or in part, by means of violence, the Constitution of the State or the form of government established will incur a sentence of from six to ten years in prison.
>
> The author of an act aimed at fomenting an uprising of armed men against the Constitutional Powers of the State, shall be sanctioned for a period of from three to ten years in prison. In case the insurrection is carried out, the penalty shall be from five to twenty years.
>
> He who performs an act with the determined purpose of impeding, in whole or in part, even though temporarily, the Senate, the House of Representatives, the President of the Republic, and the Supreme Court of Justice from exercising their Constitutional functions shall incur a sentence of from six to ten years in prison.
>
> He who tries to impede or block the holding of general elections shall incur a sentence of from four to eight years in prison.
>
> He who introduces, publishes, propagates, or tries to enforce in Cuba a dispatch, order, or decree . . . which would tend to provoke a nonobservance of the laws in force shall incur a sentence of from two to six years in prison.
>
> He who without any legal faculty or order from the government shall take the command of troops, military sites, fortresses, military posts, cities, warships or war planes shall incur a sentence of from five to ten years in prison.
>
> The same penalty shall be imposed on whoever usurps the exercise of a function attributed by the Constitution as proper of any of the Powers of the State.

Without saying a word to anyone, with the Code in one hand and papers in the other, the aforesaid citizen presented himself at the old building in the capital where the competent court functioned, a court which was under obligation to pass judgment and punish those responsible for that deed. He presented a complaint listing the wrongs committed, asking that Fulgencio Batista and his seventeen accomplices be sentenced to from one to eight years in prison, as ordered by the Code of Social Defense, with all the aggravating circumstances of recurrence, malice, and stealth.

The days and the months went by. What a disappointment! The accused was not even bothered. He walked about the republic as if he were its lord. He was called "Honorable Sir" and "General." He appointed and dismissed judges, and on no less than the day of the opening of court he was seen seated in the place of honor among the august and venerable patriarchs of our justice.

Many more months and days went by. The people got tired of the farce and abuses. People do get tired! It came to the struggle, and then that man who was an outlaw, who had seized power by violence against the will of the people and, transgressing all legal order, tortured, killed, jailed, and accused before the courts all those who had decided to fight for the law and for the return of freedom to the people.

Honorable Magistrates: I am that humble citizen who one day, to no avail, presented himself before the courts to ask that the ambitious men who had violated the laws and destroyed our institutions be punished. And now, when it is I who am being accused of wanting to overthrow this illegal regime and reestablish the legitimate Constitution of the Republic, I am held incommunicado for seventy-six days, not being allowed to speak to anyone, nor even to see my own son. I am taken across the city between high-caliber machine guns, and they finally bring me to this hospital to be judged secretly with all the severity of the law and to face a prosecutor who solemnly asks, with the Code in his hand, that I be sentenced to twenty-six years in prison.

You will reply that on the previous occasion the judges did not impart justice because they were prevented by force from doing so. Then, confess it: This time force again will oblige you to condemn me. The first time you could not punish the guilty; now you will have to punish the innocent—the maiden of justice twice raped by force.

How much charlatanry to justify the unjustifiable, to explain the unexplicable, and to reconcile the irreconcilable! And from there they have gone as far as to hold, as supreme reason, that might makes right. That is to say that, by hurling tanks and soldiers into the streets and taking the Presidential Palace, the Treasury Department, and other public buildings, and by aiming their weapons at the hearts of the people, they vested themselves with a lawful right to govern the people. The same argument was used by the Nazis when they occupied European nations and installed puppet governments.

I admit, because I so believe, that revolutions constitute a source of law. But the nocturnal, armed assault of March 10 can never be called a revolution. Commonly, as José Ingenieros[36] has said, the name *revolution* is usually given to those small disorders which dissatisfied groups provoke to take away political plums or economic advantages from the well fed, such revolutions always ending in a mere change of some men for others, in a new distribution of jobs and benefits. But that is not the criterion of the philosopher of history, nor can it be that of a cultured man.

Neither in the sense of making profound changes in the social body nor even in the surface of this public swamp of ours has there been seen a way of a reform that will agitate the reigning rottenness. If the previous regime was full of political quackery, thievery, pillage, lack of all respect for human life, the present regime has multiplied political quackery by five, pillage by ten, and the lack of respect for human life by one hundred.

It was known that Barriguilla[37] had robbed and murdered; that he was a millionaire; that he owned many apartment buildings in Havana, thousands of shares of stock in foreign companies, and fabulous bank accounts in North American banks; that he distributed capital gains to the tune of eighteen million dollars; that he stayed in the most luxurious Yankee millionaires' hotel. But no one will ever believe that Barriguilla was a revolutionary. Barriguilla is Weyler's sergeant, who murdered twelve Cubans in Guatao. In Santiago de Cuba there were seventy—*de te fabula narratur*.

Four political parties governed the country before the tenth of March: Auténtico, Liberal, Democratic, and Republican. Two days after the coup, the Republicans joined; a year had not passed and the Liberal and Democratic parties again held positions of power. Batista did not restore the Constitution, he did not restore public liberty, he did not restore Congress, he did not restore the direct vote, he did not restore any of the democratic institutions torn from the people. But he did restore Verdeja, Guas Inclán, Salvito García Ramos, Anaya Murillo, and with them the high chiefs of the traditional parties in the government, the most rapacious, corrupt, conservative, and antediluvian groups of Cuban politics. This is Barriguilla's revolution!

[36] Well-known Argentine writer and political philosopher. Eds.
[37] Refers to Fulgencio Batista. The term, however, implies laziness while acquiring a fortune. Eds.

Void of the most elemental revolutionary content, Batista's regime has set Cuba back twenty years. Everyone has had to pay dearly for Batista's return, but especially the humble classes who suffer hunger and misery while the dictatorship, which has ruined the country with commotion, ineptness, and anguish, practices the lowest kind of politics inventing one formula after another to perpetuate itself in power, even if it has to be on top of a mountain of corpses in a sea of blood.

Not one courageous measure has been dictated. Batista is bound hand and foot to big business. It could not be otherwise because of his mentality, devoid as he is of ideals or principles, lacking the faith, confidence, and support of the masses. It was but a simple change in redistribution of loot among cronies, relatives, accomplices, and a group of voracious parasites who make up his political retinue. How much opprobrium have they made the people suffer in order that a small, selfish group of egoists without consideration for the country may find in public life an easy and comfortable way of living!

How right Eduardo Chibás was when he said in his last speech that Batista was planning the return of the colonels, the castor oil, and the fugitive law.[38] Immediately after the coup of March 10 there flourished again the same acts of vandalism that the people thought had been forever banished from Cuba: the assault on the studios of the "University of the Air;"[39] an unprecedented attack on a cultural institution by members of the Military Intelligence Service (SIM) intermingled with young hoodlums from PAU;[40] the kidnapping of reporter Mario Kuchilán, dragged from his home during the night and afterward savagely tortured almost beyond the point of recognition; the killing of the student Rubén Batista and the criminal volley of shots at a peaceful demonstration of students parading before the wall against which the Spaniards executed eight students in 1871; and the cases of men like Dr. García Bárcena, who vomited blood in front of the judges as a consequence of the barbarous tortures applied to him by members of repression groups. I do not have to tell here of the hundreds of citizens who have been unmercifully beaten without distinction as to sex or age. All of that happened before the twenty-sixth of July. Afterward, as you know, not even a prince of the Catholic Church, Cardinal Arteaga, was safe from such beatings. Everyone knows that he was a victim of repressive agents. The government officially announced that it was the work of a gang of thieves. For once they told the truth—for what else is this government?

[38] The "law" of shooting a suspect on the pretext of escape. Eds.
[39] "Universidad del Aire," a radio program on station CMQ. Eds.
[40] PAU: Batista's political party, Partido Acción Unitaria. Eds.

The citizenry, horrified, have just seen the case of a newspaperman who was kidnapped and tortured by fire for twenty days. From every act of violence there arises unheard-of cynicism and infinite hypocrisy, the cowardice of evading responsibility and always charging crimes to opponents of the regime. The procedures of this government have nothing to learn from the worst gangsters. Not even the Nazis were so cowardly, for Hitler himself assumed all responsibility for the slaughter of June 30, 1934, saying that he had been the Supreme Court of Germany for twenty-four hours. The henchmen of this dictatorship cannot be compared with any others for baseness, vileness, and cowardice. They kidnap, they torture, they murder and then afterward loathsomely charge the crime to adversaries of the regime. These are the typical methods of Sergeant Barriguilla.

In all these cases I have mentioned, Honorable Magistrates, not once have the guilty ones been presented before the courts to be judged. How is this! Was this not to be a regime of order, of public peace and respect for human life?

I have said all this mainly to have someone tell me whether such a political situation as the one we are facing can be termed a law-engendering revolution; whether it is legitimate or not to fight against it; and whether the courts of the Republic must be prostituted if citizens are sentenced to jail for fighting to free their country from infamy.

Cuba is suffering a cruel and ignominious despotism, and you well know that resistance to despotism is legitimate. This is a universally recognized principle, and our Constitution of 1940 consecrates it in paragraph 2 of Article 40: "Adequate resistance for the protection of previously guaranteed human rights is legitimate." But even if this right were not so consecrated in our Fundamental Law, it is presupposed that without this right the existence of a democratic collectivity cannot be conceived. The difference between a political and juridical constitution is established by Professor Infiesta in his book on constitutional law:

> At times constitutional principles are included in juridical constitutions, and even though they might not be so classified they would carry just the same force because of the people's consent. Such principles, for example, are those of majority rule and representation in our democracy.

The right to rebel against tyranny is one of those principles which, whether included or not in juridical constitutions, is always enforced in a democratic society. Bringing up this question before a court of justice is one of the most interesting problems of public law. Duguit[41] has said in his *Treatise on Constitutional Law* that "if the insurrection fails, there would be no tribunal which would dare to declare that there was no conspiracy or attempt against the security of the State on the grounds that the government was tyrannical and the intention to overthrow it was legitimate." But, notice that he did not say, "the tribunal should not," but that "there would be no tribunal which would dare. . . ." Speaking more clearly, we may say that there is no tribunal that would dare because there is not one with sufficient courage to do so under a tyrannical government. There is no alternative to the question; if this tribunal is a courageous one and complies with its duty, it will not dare to condemn me.

Recently there has been a noisy discussion as to the validity of the Constitution of 1940. The Court of Constitutional and Social Guarantees ruled against it and in favor of the Statutes. Nevertheless, Honorable Magistrates, I maintain that the Constitution of 1940 is still in force. This assertion may seem absurd and extemporaneous, but do not be astonished. It is I who am astonished that a court of law should have attempted to inflict a vile blow on the legitimate Constitution of the Republic. Adhering rigorously to the facts, to truth, and to reason, as I have done up to now, I shall prove what I have just affirmed.

The Court of Constitutional and Social Guarantees was instituted by Article 172 of the Constitution of 1940, subsequently complemented by Organic Law No. 7 of May 31, 1949. This Court was granted by these laws specific powers to rule on all matters pertaining to the constitutionality of law, decrees, laws, resolutions, or acts which would deny, diminish, restrict, or adulterate the normal functioning of the organs of the state. Article 194 establishes very clearly that "judges and Courts are obliged to solve the conflicts arising between the laws imposed and the Constitution, and are to adhere to the principle that the latter prevails over the former." So in accordance with the laws that created it, the Court of Constitutional and Social Guarantees should always rule in favor of the Constitution. If that court permitted the Statutes to prevail over the Constitution of the Republic, it went beyond its competence and powers and such an act is juridically null and void. Moreover, the decision is in itself absurd; and that which is absurd has no force in either fact or law, for metaphysically absurdity does not even exist. Regardless of how venerable a court may be, it

---

[41] Leon Duguit, a French revolutionary thinker and jurist, known as an authority on constitutional law. He argued that the state had no sovereign power and governments were bound by the rules of law derived from social necessity. Eds.

can never rule that a circle is a square or, what is the same, that the grotesque Statutes of April 4 can be considered to be the Constitution of the State.

A constitution, as we understand it, is the fundamental and supreme law of a nation; it defines the political structure and regulates the functioning of the organs of the state, placing a limit to its powers. It must be stable, enduring, and to a certain extent rigid. The Statutes do not fill any of these requisites. They do confirm, when referring to the integration of the Republic and the principles of sovereignty, the following most shameless, cynical, and monstrous contradiction. Article 1 states, "Cuba is an independent and sovereign State, organized as a democratic Republic." Then Article 2 states, "The sovereignty resides in the people, from whom all powers are derived." But then comes Article 118, which says, "The President of the Republic shall be designated by the Council of Ministers." It is no longer the people who choose the president, but the cabinet. And who chooses the cabinet? Paragraph 13 of Article 120 reads, "The President should have the power to name and remove freely the Ministers and to substitute them as the occasion demands." Who then elects whom? Is it not the classical problem of the chicken and the egg, which no one has solved yet?

One day eighteen adventurers met. The plan was to attack the Republic and get hold of its 350-million-dollar budget. Cloaked by treachery and in the shadows of the night, they achieved their purpose. "And now, what shall we do?" one of them said to the others, "You appoint me prime minister and then I will appoint you generals." When this was done, he looked around for twenty spineless flatterers and said to them, "I will appoint you all ministers and then you appoint me president." Thus, they appointed each other generals, ministers, president, and kept the Republic's Treasury for themselves.

It is not a question of someone usurping sovereignty once in order to appoint ministers, generals, and a new president; but rather that in some statutes one man should proclaim himself to have absolute sovereignty and also control of the life and death of every citizen as well as the very existence of the nation. Therefore, I hold it to be evident that the attitude of the Court of Constitutional and Social Guarantees is not only traitorous, vile, cowardly, and repugnant but also absurd!

In the Statutes there is an article which has hardly been noticed but which gives the key to this situation, and from it we are going to draw decisive conclusions. I refer to the clause contained in Article 257, which says, "This Constitutional Law may be reformed by the Council of Ministers if there is a quorum of two-thirds of its members." Here mockery reached its maximum. It is not only the fact that they have taken advantage of sovereignty to impose, without the people's consent, a new constitution and elect a government which concentrates all powers in its hands; but, rather, that by Article 257 they vested themselves with the most essential attributes of sovereignty, that is, the right to reform or amend the supreme and fundamental Law of the nation. They have done that several times since March 10 in spite of the fact that with all cynicism it is stated in Article 2 that the sovereignty resides in the people and from them are derived all powers.

If, to carry out any reform or amendment, only a quorum of two-thirds of the Council of Ministers is needed, and the president is the one who appoints the members of the Council of Ministers, then the right to make and unmake the Republic rests on the will of one man, a man who is the most unworthy of all Cubans ever born in this land.

And if all this was accepted by the Court of Constitutional and Social Guarantees, does it mean that all derived from such acceptance is legal, and valid, and binding? Very well, you will see what the Court accepted: "This Constitutional Law can be reformed by the Council of Ministers with a quorum of two-thirds of its members." Such a power recognizes no limits—any article, any paragraph, any chapter, the entire law can be modified. For example, Article 1, which I have mentioned, says that "Cuba is an independent and sovereign State organized as a democratic Republic," even though it is a bloody satrapy today. Article 3 says that "the territory of the Republic is made of the Island of Cuba, the Isle of Pines, and the other adjacent islands and keys. . . ." Yet Batista and his Council of Ministers can modify these articles under the provision of Article 257. He can modify them to say that Cuba is no longer a republic but a hereditary monarchy and appoint himself, Fulgencio Batista, its king. He can dismember the national territory and sell a province to a foreign country, as Napoleon did with Louisiana. He can suppress the right to live and, like Herod order new-born babies killed: All these measures would be legal and you would have to send to prison all those who may oppose them, just as you intend to do with me at this time. I have stretched the examples so that you may better understand how sad and humiliating our situation is. To think that such omnipotence is enjoyed by men who are capable of selling the Republic with all its inhabitants!

If the Court of Constitutional Guarantees accepted such a situation, why are they waiting to hang up their togas? It is an elemental principle of public law that there does not exist any unconstitutionality where both the executive and the legislative powers are one and the same. If the Council of Ministers makes the laws, the decrees, the regulations, and at the same time has the power to modify the Constitution in ten minutes, cursed be the need for a Court of Constitutional Guarantees! The decision it rendered is irrational, inconceivable, and contrary to logic and to all the laws of the Republic, which you, Honorable Magistrates, swore to defend. When the Court voted in favor of the Statutes, our Supreme Law was not abolished, but rather the Court of Constitutional and Social Guarantees placed itself outside that Supreme Law, renounced its powers, and juridically committed suicide. May it rest in peace!

The right to revolt established by Article 40 of the Constitution is fully in force. Was it approved so that it might function with the Republic under normal conditions? No, because that article was to the Constitution what a life boat is to a ship on the high seas. It is not used unless the ship has been torpedoed by enemies in its course. Because the Constitution of the Republic was betrayed and all powers were wrested from the people, there only remains this right to resist oppression and injustice, and no one can take that right away from the people. If there is still any doubt of that, there is an article in the Code of Social Defense, which the Prosecutor should not forget, that says "the authorities named by the government or by popular election who do not resist the insurrection with every means at their disposal shall incur a penalty of interdiction of their civil rights of from six to ten years." It was the duty of the judges to have resisted the treacherous coup of March 10. It is then perfectly understandable why when no one has complied with the law and when no one has complied with his duty, those men who have complied with the law and their duty are sent to jail.

You cannot deny that this system of government which has been imposed on the nation goes against its tradition and its history. In his book *The Spirit of the Law*, which served as the basis for the modern division of powers, Montesquieu distinguished, according to its nature, three types of government:

> The Republican, in which all the people or a part of the people have the sovereign power; the Monarchical, in which only one person rules in accordance with certain fixed laws; and the Despotic, in which only one person rules, without laws and without regulation, acting only according to his own will and caprice.

Then he adds,

> A man whose five senses tell him constantly that he is everything and the rest are nothing is, naturally, ignorant, loathful, and licentious. And as virtue is necessary in a democracy and honor in

a monarchy, so there must be fear in a despotic government, for virtue would not be necessary and honor would be dangerous.

The right to rebel against despotism, Honorable magistrates, has been recognized since the most ancient times by men of all doctrines, ideas, and beliefs.

In the theocratic monarchies of remote antiquity, in China for instance, it was practically a constitutional principle that when an emperor governed blunderingly and despotically he was to be deposed and replaced with a virtuous prince.

The thinkers of ancient India encouraged active resistance to arbitrary authority. They justified revolution and often carried their theories into practice. One of India's spiritual guides said that "An opinion held by the majority is stronger than the king himself. A rope of many strands is strong enough to drag a lion."

The city-states of Greece and the Roman Republic not only accepted but praised the violent deaths of tyrants.

In the Middle Ages, John of Salisbury, in his work *The Book of a Statesman*, says that when a prince does not govern according to law and becomes a tyrant, his violent overthrow is legitimate and justified. He recommended that a dagger, not poison, be used against a tyrant.

St. Thomas Aquinas, in the *Summa Theologica*, rejected the doctrine of tyrannicide but nevertheless maintained the thesis that the tyrant should be deposed by the people.

Martin Luther proclaimed that when a ruler degenerates into a tyrant, violating the law, the subjects become free of all duty of obedience. His disciple, Philipp Melanchthon, maintains the right of resistance when the rulers become tyrants. Calvin, the most famous thinker of the Reformation from the point of view of political ideas, postulates that the people have the right to take up arms against any usurpation.

None other than Spanish Jesuit Juan Mariana during the period of Philip II in his book *De Rege et Regis Institution* affirms that when the ruler usurps power or when, once elected, he rules tyrannically, his assassination by a private citizen, by his own hand or availing himself of trickery, with the least disturbance possible, is legitimate.

The French writer François Hotman maintained that between the people and the government there exists a contract and that the people can rise in rebellion against the tyranny of the government when the latter violates that pact.

At the same time there appeared a widely read pamphlet entitled *Vindiciae Contra Tyrannos*, signed with the pseudonym of Stephanus Junius Brutus, which openly proclaimed that resistance to the government when it oppresses the people is legitimate and that it was the duty of honorable judges to lead the battle.

The Scotch reformers John Knox and John Poynet maintained the same point of view. The most important book of that movement, written by George Buchanan, says that if a ruler obtains power without the consent of the people or rules their destinies in an unjust and arbitrary manner, he has become a tyrant and can be overthrown, or killed as a last recourse.

John Althusius, a German jurist of the early seventeenth century, writes in his *Treatise on Politics* that sovereignty as the supreme authority of the state is born from the voluntary concourse of all its members that governmental authority emanates from the people, and that its unjust, illegal, or tyrannical exercise exempts the people from the duty of obedience and justifies resistance and rebellion.

Up to now, Honorable Magistrates, I have mentioned examples from antiquity, from the Middle Ages, and from the beginning of the Modern Age. I have selected these examples from writers of all ideas and creeds. Moreover, as you see, the right to rebellion is at the very root of our political existence. And thanks to it you are today able to wear those togas of Cuban magistrates that I wish served the cause of justice.

It is well known that in England during the seventeenth century two kings, Charles I and James II, were dethroned for acts of despotism. These events coincided with the birth of liberal political philosophy, which was the ideological foundation for a new social class then struggling to break the bonds of feudalism. Against the tyrannies based on divine right, the new philosophy upheld the principle of the social contract and of the consent of the governed, and constituted the foundation of the English Revolution of 1688 and the American and French revolutions of 1775 and 1789. These great events opened up the liberation process of the Spanish colonies in America—the last link being Cuba. On this philosophy our political and constitutional thought was nourished and from it evolved the first Constitution of Guáimaro to that of 1940, the latter showing the influence of present-day socialistic trends when it consecrated the principle of the social function of property and the inalienable right of man to a decent living, the efficacy of these principles having been blocked by great vested interests.

The right to rebel against tyranny was consecrated definitively at that time, and was converted into an essential postulate of political freedom.

Already in 1649, John Milton was writing that political power resides in the people, who can name and dethrone kings and who have the duty to remove tyrants from the government.

John Locke, in his *Treatise on Government*, maintains that when the natural rights of man are violated, the people have the right and the duty to suppress or change the government. "The only remedy against force without authority is to oppose it with force."

Jean Jacques Rousseau eloquently states in his *Social Contract*,

> When a people sees itself forced to obey, and obeys, it does well; as soon as it can shake off the yoke, and shakes it off, it does better, for it recovers freedom by the same right with which it was taken away. The strongest is never sufficiently strong to be the master forever if he does not transform force into right and obedience into duty. . . . Force is a physical power; I do not see how morality can be derived from its effects. To cede to force is an act of necessity, not of will; everything else is an act of prudence. In what sense can this be considered a duty?
>
> To renounce freedom is to renounce the quality of being a man, the rights of humanity, including its duties. There is no possible reward for he who renounces all. Such renunciation is incompatible with man's nature, and to take away all freedom of self-determination is to take away all morality of the action. Finally, it is a vain and contradictory conviction to stipulate absolute authority for one side and unlimited obedience for the other.

Thomas Paine said that "A just man is more worthy of respect than a crowned ruffian."

Only reactionary writers, like that clergyman from Virginia, Jonathan Boucher, were opposed to this right of the people: "The right to revolt was a condemnable doctrine derived from Lucifer, the father of rebellion."

The Declaration of Independence of the Congress of Philadelphia, July 4, 1775, consecrated this right in a beautiful paragraph:

> We hold these truths to be self-evident; that all men are created equal; that they are endowed by their Creator with certain inalienable rights; that among these are Life, Liberty, and the Pursuit of Happiness. That to secure these rights, Governments are instituted among men, deriving their just powers from the consent of the governed, that whenever any form of government becomes destructive of these ends, it is the right of the people to alter or abolish it, and to institute new Government, laying its foundation on such principles and organizing its power in such form, as to them shall seem most likely to effect their safety and happiness.

The famous French Declaration of the Rights of Man bequeathed to coming generations the following principle:

> When the government violates the rights of the people, insurrection is for them the most sacred of rights and the most imperative

of duties. . . . When one person seizes sovereignty, he should be condemned to death by free men.

I believe that I have sufficiently justified my point of view. They are stronger reasons than those which the Prosecutor brandished when requesting that I be sentenced to twenty-six years in jail. All of them favor men who fight for the freedom and happiness of the people; none of them favors those who oppress, debase, and pitilessly rob the people. That is why I have had to expound many reasons while the Prosecutor did not expound even one.

How was the Prosecutor to justify Batista's right to power, when he obtained it against the will of the people, violating by treason and by force the laws of the Republic? How was he to qualify as legitimate a regime of blood, oppression, and ignominy? How was he to call a government revolutionary, when it was composed of the most reactionary men, ideas, and methods of our public life? How was he to consider juridically valid the high treason of the court whose mission was to defend our constitution? By what right can he send to jail citizens who came to give their blood and their lives for the honor of their country? That would be a monstrous thing in the eyes of the nation and in the face of principles of true justice!

But we have one more reason on our side, a reason stronger than all the others: We are Cubans and to be a Cuban implies a duty; not to fulfill this duty is to commit a crime, to commit treason. We are proud of the history of our country. We learned it in school; as we grew up, we heard people speak of liberty, justice, rights. Early in life we were taught to look up to the deeds of our heroes and martyrs. The names Céspedes, Agramonte, Maceo, Gómez, and Martí were the first ones to be engraved in our minds. We were told that the titan Maceo had said that you do not beg for freedom, but that you win it with the edge of the sword. We were taught that for the education of the citizens in a free country, Martí had written in his *Edad de Oro,*

> The man who conforms to obeying unjust laws and permits the man who mistreats him to trample the country in which he was born is not an honest man. . . . In the world there must be a certain amount of honor, as there must be a certain amount of light. When there are many men without honor, there are always others who have in themselves the honor of many men. These are the ones who rebel with terrible force against those who rob the people of their right to be free, which is the same as robbing men of their honor. In those men there are thousands of men, a whole nation, human dignity itself.

We were taught that October 10 and February 24 are glorious dates of patriotic rejoicing because they were the dates on which the Cubans rebelled against the yoke of infamous tyrannies. We were taught to love and defend the beautiful flag of the lone star, and to sing every afternoon a hymn whose verses say that to live in chains is to live in disgrace and abject submission, and that to die for the fatherland is to live. We learned all that and we shall not ever forget it, even though today in our fatherland men are being killed and jailed for putting into practice the ideas they were taught from the cradle. We were born in a free country which was left to us by our fathers, and we would rather the island sink into the sea than consent to be anyone's slave.

It looked as if the apostle Martí was going to die in the year of the centennial of his birth. It looked as if his memory would be extinguished forever, so great was the affront! But he lives. He has not died. His people are rebellious, his people are worthy, his people are faithful to his memory. Cubans have fallen defending his doctrines. Young men, in a magnificent gesture of reparation, have come to give their blood and to die at the side of his tomb so that he might continue to live in the hearts of his countrymen. Oh, Cuba, what would have become of you if you had let the memory of your apostle die!

I conclude my defense, but I shall not end it as all lawyers for the defense do, asking for acquittal of the defendant. I cannot ask for acquittal when my companions are already suffering in the ignominious prison on the Isle of Pines. Send me there that I may share their fate. It is conceivable that honest men should be dead or in prison when the president is a criminal and a thief!

To you, Your Honors, my sincere gratitude for having allowed me to express myself freely, without base coercion. I feel no rancor toward you. I recognize that in some aspects you have been humane, and I know that the presiding judge of this court, the man of unimpeachable background that he is, cannot disguise his repugnance for the reigning state of things which forces him to dictate an unjust verdict.

There still remains for the court a graver problem to solve. I am referring to the seventy cases of murder which should be more aptly called the greatest massacre we have ever known. The guilty ones are still at large carrying their weapons, and that is a perennial threat to the lives of citizens. If the full weight of the law does not fall on them because of cowardice or because the court cannot do anything about it, and as a consequence thereof all the judges do not resign to a man, I bemoan the honor of your names and I weep for the unprecedented stain that will besmirch judicial power.

As for me, I know that jail will be as hard as it has ever been for anyone, filled with threats, with vileness, and cowardly brutality;

but I do not fear this, as I do not fear the fury of the miserable tyrant who snuffed out the life of seventy brothers of mine.

Condemn me, it does not matter. *History will absolve me!*

A Letter from Prison
(December 12, 1953)

Dear Brother Luis Conte:

With the blood of my dead brothers I am writing you this letter; they are the ones who inspire it. More than liberty or even life for ourselves, we ask justice for them. Justice is not at this moment a monument to the heroes and martyrs who have fallen in combat or were murdered afterward. Justice is not even a grave in which to rest in peace for those whose remains lie all over the fields of Oriente, in places known only to their murderers. We cannot even speak of peace for the dead in this oppressed land. Posterity, which is always more generous with the good, will build those monuments in their memory, and in due time future generations will revive the tribute owed to those who saved the fatherland's honor in this time of infinite shame.

Luis, why have the barbaric and insane mass tortures and murders which have cut down the lives of seventy young prisoners on July 26, 27, 28, and 29 not been courageously denounced? That is the inescapable duty of the living and to fail to do so is a stain that will never be erased. The history of Cuba knows of no similar massacre either as a colony or as a republic. I understand that terror paralyzed men's hearts for a long time, but now it is no longer possible to endure the mantle of total silence that cowardice has thrown on those horrendous crimes, the reaction of despicable and brutal hatred by a tyranny that defies description. It exacted its vengeance on the justified and rebellious action of the enslaved children of our heroic people—the most pure, generous, and idealistic flesh of Cuba. Silence is shameful complicity, as repugnant as the crime itself; the tyrant must be licking

Written from the Isle of Pines Prison on December 12, 1953. This letter was later edited and released as "Manifesto to the Nation," by Luis Conte Agüero. Agüero was at the time a radio commentator and leader of the Ortodoxos. He has been in exile since 1960. Luis Conte Agüero, *Cartas del presidio, anticipo de una biografía* (Havana: Editorial Lex, 1959), pp. 13–24, and Marta Rojas, ed., *Mártires del Moncada* (Havana: Ediciones R, 1965), pp. 7–16.

his lips with satisfaction over the ferocity of the executioners who defend him and the terror he exerts on the enemies who combat him.

It seems as if the reestablishment of constitutional guarantees and the lifting of censorship has been granted in exchange for silencing those facts. There is a pact between the oppressor and the spokesmen of public opinion, a tacit or explicit pact, and this is infamous, detestable, maddening, repugnant.[1]

Truth cannot be ignored. All of Oriente knows it; the entire country whispers it. They also know that the shabby accusations they made against us to the effect that we were inhumane to the soldiers are false. During the interrogation, the government was unable to maintain its accusations. The twenty soldiers whom we imprisoned at the outset and the thirty who had been wounded and did not even suffer a verbal offense came to testify. The forensic doctors, experts, and even the state's witnesses destroyed the government's version. Some testified with admirable honesty. It was proved that the weapons had been acquired in Cuba, that there was no connection with politicians of the past, that no one had been knifed, and that at the Military Hospital there was only one victim, a patient who was wounded looking out of his window. Even the prosecutor himself had to recognize in his conclusion to this very unusual case "the honorable and human conduct of the attackers."

On the other hand, where were our wounded? There were only five in total. Ninety dead and five wounded: Can we conceive of such proportions in any war? What happened to the others? Where were the fighters who had been arrested from the twenty-sixth through the twenty-ninth? Santiago de Cuba knows the answer well. The wounded were dragged from private hospitals, even from operating rooms, and murdered immediately thereafter—sometimes even before they left the hospital (two prisoners with their guards entered an elevator alive and came out dead). Those who were admitted to the Military Hospital received air and camphor injections in their veins. One of them, the engineering student Pedro Miret, survived this mortal procedure and narrated everything. I repeat, only five remained alive; two were courageously defended by Dr. Posada, who did not allow them to be taken away from the Colonia Española.[2] These combatants were José Ponce and Gustavo Arcos. There are three others who owe their lives to Captain Tamayo, an army doctor, who with the courageous act of an honorable professional, gun in hand, transferred the wounded, Pedro Miret, Abelardo Crespo, and Fidel Labrador, from the Military

[1] This paragraph does not appear in the revised version mentioned above. Eds.
[2] Hospital in Santiago de Cuba. Eds.

Hospital to the Civil Hospital. They did not want even those five to be left alive. These numbers are of indisputable eloquence.

As far as the prisoners are concerned, the Moncada Barracks could very well have hung in its main entrance the poster which appeared at the door of Dante's Inferno: "Abandon all hope." Thirty were murdered the first night. The order was received through General Martín Díaz Tamayo, who said "it was shameful for the army to have had three times more casualties than the attackers during the battle and that now it was necessary to have ten deaths for each soldier." That order was the product of a meeting held by Batista, Tabernilla, Ugalde Carrillo, and other chiefs. To solve legal difficulties, the Council of Ministers on that same Sunday night suspended Article 26 of the Statutes, which established the responsibility of the custodian for the life of the arrested individual. The watchword was fulfilled with horrible cruelty. When the dead were buried, they had no eyes, teeth, or testicles;[3] and they were even stripped of their personal belongings by their killers, who shamelessly exhibited them later.

Scenes of indescribable courage took place among the tortured. Two girls, our heroic *compañeras* Melba Hernández and Haydée Santamaría,[4] were arrested at the Civil Hospital where they worked as first-aid nurses. Once in the barracks that evening, the latter was shown her brother's eyes by Sergeant Eulalio González (nicknamed "Tiger"), holding them in his bloody hands right after they had been pulled out.[5] Later she was informed that her fiancé, also a prisoner, had been murdered. Filled with boundless anger, she faced the murderers and told them, "He is not dead because to die for the fatherland is to live."[6] The women were not murdered; the savages halted before a woman. Those women are exceptional witnesses to what occurred in that hell.

Around Santiago de Cuba, forces under Major Pérez Chaumont murdered twenty-one unarmed and dispersed combatants. Many were forced to dig their own graves. A courageous man turned his pick and wounded one of the killers in the face. In Siboney, there were no such battles;[7] those who still had weapons retreated with me to the mountains and the army did not engage us until six days later when, due to carelessness, they surprised us, completely exhausted and asleep

---

[3] This is highly questionable. Eds.

[4] Both women participated in the planning of the Moncada Barracks attack. Eds.

[5] This event never occurred. Eds.

[6] "To die for the fatherland is to live" is a line from Cuba's national anthem. Eds.

[7] A few miles from Santiago de Cuba. Eds.

due to fatigue and hunger. Already the massacre had ceased due to the enormous popular outcry. Even then, only the miracle of a scrupulous official and the fact that we were not recognized until after reaching the hospital prevented our assassination.

On the twenty-seventh at midnight on kilometer 39 of the Manzanillo-Bayamo Highway, the captain of the area strangled the youths Pedro Félix, Hugo Camejo, and Andrés García and later dragged them from a jeep with a rope around their necks, leaving them for dead. One of them, the last one, recovered a few hours later and, presented by Monsignor Pérez Serantes,[8] has told the story.

In the early hours of the twenty-eighth by the Cauto River on the way to Palmas, the youths Raúl de Aguilar, Andrés Valdés, and another were murdered by the lieutenant in charge of the Alto Cedro Post, Sergeant Montes de Oca, and Corporal Maceo, who buried their victims in a dwelling by the river's shore near a place known as Bananea. These young men had succeeded in getting in touch with friends of mine who helped them; later we learned of the fate which awaited them.

It is completely false that the identification of bodies up to today—less than half the total—has been the work of the Department of Fingerprints. In all cases they proceeded to take the name and other details of the victims before killing them, and have been revealing the names little by little. The complete list has never been released. Through fingerprints they identified only some of the combatants who died in battle. The suffering and uncertainty caused to their families by these procedures is beyond description.

These and similar facts were denounced by us during the trial in the presence of soldiers who, armed with machine guns and rifles, invaded the courtroom in an evident coercive attitude. Even they were impressed by the account of the atrocities that had been committed.

I was dragged from court during the third session, thus violating all procedural law, in order to prevent me, as a lawyer, from clarifying facts. The trial was a true scandal, for other lawyers took charge of clarifying them.

From the accusations made by us during our testimony, three lawsuits were specified for murder and torture: 938, 1073, and 1083 of 1953 in the Emergency Court of Northern Santiago del Cuba; in addition, there were others dealing with continuous violation of individual human rights. All have been ratified by us before the Emergency

[8] Archbishop of Santiago de Cuba. Eds.

Court of Nueva Gerona. We have accused Batista, Tabernilla, Ugalde Carrillo, and Díaz Tamayo as the men who ordered the killing of prisoners, something we know for sure, and as the executors Colonel Alberto del Río Chaviano and all the officers and soldiers who were the best known in the bloody orgy.

Except in Batista's case, according to current law, it falls within the jurisdiction of civilian courts to judge those responsible for these facts. The Court of Appeals of Santiago de Cuba has taken a fairly strong stand up to now. Undoubtedly, silence about these events is the greatest favor one can grant these criminals, as well as the most efficient incentive for them to continue killing without restraint of any sort. I do not dream, of course, even remotely, about a legal sentence; no, that is absurd in a regime where murderers and torturers can live freely, wear a uniform, and represent authority while honest men suffer imprisonment for committing the crime of defending liberty, human rights, and the Constitution which the people chose. For them there are no jails, no sentences, not even courts. In addition, they will enjoy absolute moral impunity without a forceful voice rising to accuse them, when so many have generously died fighting them, when so many suffer the disgrace of prison.

Having heard the denunciations made on the death of Mario Fortuny,[9] in spite of all inconveniences—the Law of Public Order, etc.—I believe the moment has come to clarify matters. Tell me, Luis Conte, do those who kept silent in the face of the horrendous crimes committed in Santiago have no responsibility for this horrible crime? Is it just to accuse only the regime, when the opposition has stimulated it with its shameful cowardice? Does the opposition not comprehend that such behavior produces bitter results? When denunciation is the only restraint, the crime that is silenced opens a new grave. Why, then, does everyone hurry to protest Fortuny's death? Perhaps because this barbaric act was much smaller than the other and the government is ready to tolerate denunciations which are minor in scope—as long as the "taboo" issue is not touched? Or could it be, Luis Conte, still sadder, that Fortuny had loyal friends among his politically militant comrades who know how to accuse and stimulate denunciations, whereas my party brothers lie in their graves forgotten by their *compañeros* inside the party, who thus prize the generous sacrifice of lives of men who fought for the ideals they so often preach?

Those courageous men who marched to death with the supreme

[9] Member of AAA, an insurrectionary group led by Aureliano Sánchez Arango, murdered by Batista's police. Eds.

smile of happiness on their lips, consumed by the flame of duty, had to die because they were not born to be resigned to the miserable and hypocritical life of these times. They died, after all, because they could not accept that repugnant and dishonorable reality.

These considerations bring to my mind the forceful thoughts that agitated their anxious minds, the indignant revolt against selfish and repugnant mediocrity, the desire to give an example and do something great for the fatherland. Every day that goes by justifies their sacrifice more.

A few days ago November 27 was commemorated.[10] All those who wrote or spoke about the matter used ferocious and irate language, with high-sounding epithets and fake indignation, to denounce the men who shot those eight students; however, not a single syllable was used to condemn the assassination of 70 youths, as clean, honest, and idealistic as those of time past. Innocents, with their warm blood still on the heart of Cuba! The curse of history shall fall on the hypocrites! The students killed in 1871 were not tortured; they were submitted to an apparent trial, buried in known places, and the ones who committed the horror believed themselves to be in possession of a right four centuries old, granted by a divine hand and consecrated by time, legitimate and eternal—beliefs now abolished by man. Nine times eight were the number of youths who fell in Santiago de Cuba under torture and bullets, without any kind of trial, in the name of an illegitimate and detested usurpation of power sixteen months old. It has no God or law, it violates the most noble Cuban traditions and the most sacred human principles, as later it spreads the remains of its victims throughout unknown places in a republic established by our liberators to respect the dignity and honor of man, in the year of the centenary of Apostle Martí. What was the crime? To follow his teachings:

> When there are many men without honor, there are always some who have within themselves the dignity of many men. Those are the ones who revolt with terrible force against those who steal the people's freedom, which is to steal men's honor.

Whose interest has been hurt? The unlimited ambition of a group of Cains that exploit and enslave our people for the sole benefit of their personal selfishness.

If the hatred that inspired the massacre of November 27 "was born from the womb of man," according to Martí, what bowels engendered

---

[10] On November 27, 1871, several university students were killed by the Spanish colonial regime in Cuba because they supposedly made fun of a deceased Spanish authority. Eds.

the massacre of July 26, 27, 28, and 29? Moreover, I do not know of
any officer of the Cuban army who has broken his sword, resigning
from his post.[11] The only honor of that army consisted in "killing ten
youths for every soldier killed in battle"—that was the honor decreed
by the military staff.

Luis, I have as much faith in the Cuban people as I have scorn and
distrust for the rottenness choking the surface of our society. You
are a part of the people who stand above that rotten environment.

Someone called on a friend once.[12] It was three o'clock in the morning of a memorable day. He was going to invite him to liberate his
fatherland. But the friend was not there; he was very far away at the
moment. Great disappointment! Why does destiny weave such strange
circumstances? Destiny itself answers. That is why many believe in
destiny. What would have been known of the eight students put to the
wall if Fermín Valdés Domínguez[13] had been with them?

Luis, take on yourself this honorable cause, for you have more than
enough intelligence, courage, and greatness. I believe it pertinent to tell
you that if our revolutionary effort had triumphed it was our objective
to place power in the hands of the most devoted Ortodoxos.

The reestablishment of the 1940 Constitution, conditioned of course
to the abnormal situation, was our first proclamation to the people.
Once in control of Oriente's capital, we would have decreed immediately six basic laws of profound revolutionary content. One was
aimed at giving the tenant farmer, renter, sharecropper, and squatter
ownership of the land with due indemnification by the state to those
damaged. One would have given the workers the right to share in
the final profits of the enterprise, and the tenant farmers the right
to participate in 55 percent of the sugar-cane production. (These
measures, naturally, would have to be matched with a dynamic and
energetic policy by the state directly intervening in the creation of
new industries, mobilizing the great reserves of the national capital,
and destroying the organized resistance of powerful interests.) Another decree would have dismissed all judicial and administrative
functionaries at the municipal, provincial, or national level who had
betrayed the Constitution by swearing the Statutes.[14] Finally, we

---

[11] A Spanish officer did so in 1871. Eds.

[12] On July 26, Fidel Castro went to Luis Conte Agüero's house in Santiago to
invite him to participate in the attack on the Moncada Barracks, but Luis Conte
was not there. Eds.

[13] In 1871, he was unable to participate with the eight, just as Agüero had
missed the Moncada attack. Eds.

[14] Statutes decreed by Fulgencio Batista after his coup, which had to be
sworn by those officials who wanted to remain in office. Eds.

would have passed a law to confiscate misappropriated wealth under all governments, after a process of intensive investigation.

I have expounded all this for you to know that we bore a courageous and advanced program, which in itself was an essential part of the revolutionary strategy. The government has made sure that none of these documents is available.

The people were unable to learn anything because we chose not to take over the radio stations before securing the barracks in order to prevent a massacre of the people if we failed. The recording of Chibás's last speech would have been broadcast constantly and would have spontaneously made clear that the revolutionary explosion was independent of men of the past.

Our triumph would have meant the immediate ascent to power of the Ortodoxos, first provisionally and later through general elections. This has been so true with regard to our goals that, even failing, our sacrifice has meant a strengthening of the true ideals of Chibás, as shown by the current of events.

The pusillanimous would say that we were mistaken, considering *juris de jure* the foolish argument of success or failure. Failure occurred due to cruel details at the last minute, so simple that it drives one crazy to think about them. The possibilities for success were determined by our means; if we could have relied on them I have no doubt that we would have fought with a 90 percent possibility of success.

Speak with Dr. Agramonte,[15] and show him this letter. Tell him that we feel completely loyal to the purest ideals of Eduardo Chibás, that those who fell in Santiago de Cuba were militants of the party he founded and with him learned to die when the fatherland needed heroic sacrifice to raise the faith of the people and bring about the inevitable realization of its historic destiny.

There should have been no room within the Directing Council[16] for sterile and inappropriate theories about putsch or revolution, when the time called for the denunciation of monstrous crimes committed by the government in murdering more Cubans in four days than in the prior eleven years. Besides, who in Cuba have given more proof of greater faith in the masses, in their love of liberty, in their repudiation of dictatorship, in their desperate misery, and their mature consciousness? Do you think, Luis, that your actions to try to raise the Maceo Regiment on the morning of March 10, when all other commands

[15] Dr. Roberto Agramonte, at the time a leader of the Partido del Pueblo Cubano. He is today in exile. Eds.
[16] The *Consejo Director* of the party. Eds.

had been surrounded, would have been called a putsch? Is there less desire for freedom today than on the morning of October 10, 1868?[17]

What should be considered before starting a battle for freedom is not how many weapons the enemy has, but how many virtues are found in the people. If in Santiago de Cuba one hundred courageous youths fell, it means only that in our fatherland there are 100,000 youths ready to die. Look for them and you will find them. Guide them and they will march forward regardless of how difficult the road may be. The masses are ready, they only need to be shown the true road.

To denounce the crimes is a duty! That is a terrible weapon! That will be a formidable and revolutionary step forward! All the accusations have been verified; demand the punishment of the murderers! Demand their imprisonment! Appoint, if necessary, a private accuser! Do not allow, by any means, the murderers to be placed arbitrarily under military jurisdiction! Recent events are favorable toward that campaign. The simple publication of what has been denounced will have tremendous repercussions on the government. I repeat that if this is not done, it will be an indelible stain.

I beg you to visit Quevedo[18] and exhort him to do the same. Remind him about the Nacional event,[19] his protest against the murdered officers, even when the victims on that occasion did not represent a good cause and were killed in battle, not systematically and coldly for four days as was the case of the Moncada Barracks. It is not enough to publish indirect allusions, like pictures of Korea; it is necessary to deal directly with the matter. If De la Oza makes up his mind, he will help greatly. Mañach[20] mentioned this aspect of the problem; why don't you talk with him?

I am going to ask you a favor: Make up a manifesto to the people following the content of this letter,[21] sign it with my name, and give it to Mirta.[22] She will try to get it published in *Alma Mater*.[23]

Express our gratitude to Ricardo Miranda for his constant campaign on behalf of the political prisoners.

[17] On that date the war of independence began in Cuba. Eds.

[18] Miguel Angel Quevedo, director of the magazine *Bohemia*. He died in exile in 1969. Eds.

[19] On September 15, 1933, a number of officers from the army and navy entrenched themselves in the Nacional Hotel to oppose Batista's takeover of power. The American ambassador lived there. Eds.

[20] Enrique De la Oza and Jorge Mañach were political commentators for the magazine *Bohemia*. Eds.

[21] Called "Manifiesto a la nación," it almost entirely follows this letter. Eds.

[22] Castro's wife at the time. Eds.

[23] University publication. Eds.

One last request: With the exception of the money already spent, use the rest of the money collected to help the widows and relatives of the dead men. We need nothing, we want nothing. Needless to say, we shall not celebrate Christmas, we shall not even drink water, to show our mourning. Make this known as such, because I believe in that way the objective will be more noble and humane. It makes no sense for prisoners like us to hope to share the joys of Christmas; we prefer to see those who lost their loved ones and breadwinners have money to pay rent or to eat.

Luis, I congratulate you for everything you are doing as well as the brilliant, intelligent, and appropriate manner in which you are approaching the problems. I am sure that the people's sympathy for you must be great. Use this sympathy ever more in the service of truth and justice, disregarding the consequences of the sacrifice that is solidly based.

I long for the day when, in a free fatherland, we shall travel together in the fields of indomitable Oriente, picking up the bones of our heroic *compañeros* and gathering them all by the grave of Martí as martyrs of the centennial. Their epitaph should have a thought of Martí:

> A martyr never dies in vain, and an idea is never lost in the movement of the winds. It might move closer or farther away, but there always remains the memory of having seen it pass by.

Luis, we still have strength for dying and fists for fighting. A strong embrace from all of us.

Fidel

Letter to Melba Hernández
(April 17, 1954)

Dear Melba:

Mirta will tell you how to communicate with me every day if you want.[1] Keep that information absolutely secret and only tell Yeyé about it when she returns.[2] Mirta has told me about the great enthu-

---

Letter written on April 17, 1954, from the prison in the Isle of Pines in Cuba. The letter was addressed to one of the women who participated in the attack on the Moncada Barracks on July 26, 1953. Luis Conte Agüero, *Cartas del presidio, anticipo de una biografía de Fidel Castro* (Havana: Editorial Lex, 1959), pp. 37–38.

[1] Mirta Díaz Balart was at the time Fidel Castro's wife. Eds.
[2] Yeyé is the nickname of Haydeé Santamaría. Eds.

siasm with which you are fighting; my regret is only due to the immense nostalgia of being absent. I want you to consider things which I believe to be important.

1. Propaganda cannot be abandoned for a single minute, because it is the soul of every struggle. Ours should have its own style and adjust itself to the circumstances. The murders must be denounced unceasingly. *Mirta will talk to you of a pamphlet of decisive importance for its ideological content and its tremendous accusations. I would like you to give it your closest attention.*[3] Also it is necessary for the twenty-sixth of July to be commemorated with dignity. We must have a meeting on the front steps of the university (that will be a terrible blow to the government), which is necessary to prepare from now on with great care, as well as high school meetings in Santiago de Cuba and abroad. The latter will be the case of the Comité Ortodoxo of New York, Mexico, and Costa Rica. Gustavo Arcos should speak with the leaders of the FEU.[4]

2. The work of our people here and abroad must be coordinated. To that end you should plan a trip to Mexico as soon as possible so that you meet with Raúl Martínez and Lester Rodríguez,[5] and after studying the situation with care you should decide the line to be followed. Extreme precaution must be considered for any design of coordination with other groups, because they might simply want to use our name as was done with Pardo Llada[6] and others. They have used the tactic of discredit to get rid of groups [that challenge their leadership]. The slightest degree of underestimation cannot be allowed; all agreements must be based on firm and clear foundations, those that will probably succeed and bring about a positive benefit to Cuba. If not, it is preferable to march alone while you maintain our standard high until the formidable young men in prison, who prepare themselves with great care for the struggle, are freed. "To know how to wait," said Martí, " is the great secret of success."

3. Deal with the people artfully and with a smile. Follow the same tactic used in the trial: Defend our viewpoints without making unnecessary enemies.[7] There will be enough time later to crush all the cockroaches together. Do not be discouraged because of anything or anyone, as we were in the most difficult moments. A last piece of advice: Beware of envy. When you have glory and prestige, mediocre people always easily find motives and pretexts for susceptibilities.

[3] Refers to the pamphlet "History Will Absolve Me" in this volume.
[4] Federación Estudiantil Universitaria. Eds.
[5] Coordinators of the anti-Batista opposition abroad. Eds.
[6] Radio commentator and leader of the Ortodoxo Party. Eds.
[7] The original is *sin levantar ronchas.* Eds.

Welcome everyone who wishes to help, but remember: Do not trust anyone. Mirta has instructions to aid you with all her soul. I have placed all my faith in you. I will speak with Vega, if I see him today, about those things that I might think convenient.

A strong embrace for you and my dearest Yeyé. More firm than ever,

Fidel

Letter to René Guitart
(December 16, 1954)

Mr. Guitart:

It is difficult for me to start this letter, to address you in some way, to find the words that will express at the same time my gratitude, my emotion, and deep recognition for that very moving letter of yours, so kind and so full of paternal love and affection. You call me "dearest Fidel." What should I call you? Very few times in my life have I felt so honored as when I received your letter, and so stimulated to be good, honorable, and loyal to the last moment of my existence.

That long embrace to which you refer and that I shall give you someday with all my heart, how much I would have wanted to do so under other circumstances: without the cruel physical absence of Renato,[1] without the bitter bite of adversity where everything turns against one and only conviction and faith sustain one. Because in such circumstances you come to me to offer your deep and generous affection, I recognize in all your goodness and nobility the father worthy of the son who was worthy of you.

But I shall not talk to you of him as if he were absent—he is not and never will be. These are not mere words of consolation. Only those of us who feel him real and perpetually in our souls can understand this. Physical life is ephemeral, it passes inexorably, as the lives of so many generations have passed, as our own will pass soon enough. This truth should teach all human beings that above life we find the immortal values of the spirit. What meaning does life have without

Letter written on December 16, 1954, from the Isle of Pines prison. Luis Conte Agüero, *Cartas del presidio, anticipo de una biografía* (Havana: Editorial Lex, 1959), pp. 69–70.
[1] Renato Guitart was the son of René Guitart. He died in the Moncada attack. Eds.

spirit? What is it to live, then? How could men die who, understanding it, generously sacrifice themselves to goodness and justice! God is the supreme idea of goodness and justice. To God go all those who die for one or another cause in our fatherland.

I admire the courage, endurance, and greatness with which you have faced the enormous sacrifice of your son's ideals. Those ideals he found himself, but you also gave them to him. Your courage when faced with sorrow is as heroic and generous as his when faced with self-sacrifice. He would be proud of you, as you have more than enough reasons to be proud of him. I have a wish that comes from the depths of my soul—that Cuba will always have men like you and like him.

I shall never give you reason to repent of the beautiful words you sent me. I am infinitely grateful, and I shall keep them always. I hope that in our affection and above all in our behavior you will find a relief to your sadness. I hope the same for your wife. I know that she is a spartan mother, filled with resignation, goodness, and faith. "The son who dies remains in the soul of his mother." To her I send our devout and fervent love, as well as to your daughter, who has in all of us many brothers.

Words are useless when sentiments wish to speak. It is necessary to guess what one feels, because it cannot be expressed. You will understand my feelings, as I guess yours and understand them. Renato is and will continue to be among us; and he will be every day more in the hearts of all Cubans. He was all idealism, courage, dignity, and character, an unforgettable example. He knew that those who die as he did never die.

Yours,
Fidel

Letter to Luis Conte Agüero
(March 1955)

My very dear friend:

To be imprisoned is to be condemned to forced silence, to listen and read what is said and written without being able to respond, to suffer

Letter written in March 1955 from the prison on the Isle of Pines. Luis Conte Agüero, *Cartas del Presidio, anticipo de una biografía de Fidel Castro* (Havana: Editorial Lex, 1959), pp. 81–86.

the attacks of cowards who take advantage of the circumstances to oppose those who cannot defend themselves. They make proposals which, were we able to answer, would receive our immediate reply.

All of this must be suffered with stoicism, calmness, and courage, as part of the bitterness and sacrifice that all idealism demands. But there are times when all obstacles must be overcome, because it is impossible to keep silent when our dignity is wounded. I am not writing these lines to seek applause, which so often is excessively granted to apparent merit or to a theatrical gesture, while it is denied to those who know how to carry out their duty simply and naturally. I write to clear my conscience and because of the consideration, loyalty, and respect I owe to the people. And I address the Cuban people to express my opinion (which I should not silence for any reason of convenience) on a problem that affects us directly and that occupies a great deal of public attention, namely, political amnesty. I want to state my position through you, as a brother more than a friend, and through your civic "Tribuna Libre,"[1] requesting you at the same time to make my words available to equally honorable radio stations and newspapers.

The interest that an immense portion of the citizenry has shown in favor of our freedom originates in the innate sense of justice in the masses and in a deep human feeling of a people who cannot be indifferent. An orgy of demagoguery, hypocrisy, opportunism, and bad faith has arisen around this incontestable feeling. To know what we political prisoners think of all this is probably the question that thousands of citizens and perhaps not a few members of the regime are asking. The interest in this question increases when, as in this case, prisoners from Moncada are involved. They are excluded from the benefit of amnesty, they are the object of all kinds of persecution, and are the key to the whole problem. I wonder if we are the most hated or the most feared. . . .[2]

Some government spokesmen already have said that "even the Moncada prisoners will be included." We cannot be mentioned without the qualification of "even," "included," or "excluded." They doubt, hesitate, knowing for sure that if a survey were made, 99 percent of the people would request amnesty for us, because it is not easy to deceive or to hide the truth from the people. But the government is not sure of what the 1 percent wearing a uniform think. They fear displeasing them and rightly so. In their own self-interest they have poisoned the hearts of the military against us, falsifying facts, impos-

---

[1] Radio program.
[2] Ellipses in original. Eds.

ing censorship for ninety days and the Law of Public Order[3] to conceal the truth of whose conduct was humane in the battle and who carried out acts that will be related someday by a horror-stricken historian.

How strangely the regime has dealt with us! They call us assassins in public and gentlemen in private. They fight us rancorously in public and come to make our acquaintance in private. One day it is an army colonel who gives me a cigar, offers me a book, and everybody is very courteous. Another day three cabinet ministers, smiling, affable, respectful, appear. One of them says, "Don't worry, this will pass; I planted many bombs and I used to organize ambushes on the Country Club against Machado. I, too, was once a political prisoner."

The usurper holds a press conference in Santiago de Cuba and declares that public opinion is not in our favor. A few days later an incredible event takes place: The entire people of Oriente, at the meeting of a party to which we do not belong[4]—which, according to reporters, was the biggest mobilization of the campaign—incessantly shout our name and demand our freedom. A formidable answer from a unique and loyal people, who are well aware of the history of Moncada![5]

Now it is proper for us to answer the moral demand made on us by the regime in declaring that there will be an amnesty if the prisoners and the exiled will behave and make a tacit or express agreement to respect the government.

Once upon a time the Pharisees asked Christ whether or not they should pay tribute to Caesar. Their idea was that his answer should be displeasing either to Caesar or to the people. The Pharisees of every era know that trick. And so today an attempt is made to discredit us before the people or to find a pretext for leaving us in prison.

I am not in the least interested in making the regime think that they should grant us this amnesty—I am not worrying about it. I am interested only in showing up the falsity of their demands, the insincerity of their words, the despicable and cowardly maneuver being carried out against the men who are in prison because they fought the regime.

They have said they are generous because they feel strong, but I say they are vengeful because they feel weak. They have said they do not

---

[3] Decree announced on August 3, 1953, providing severe prison sentences and fines for attacks against the "national dignity, peace, public confidence, stability of the government, the economy, and national credit." Eds.

[4] Refers to a mass meeting held by the Partido Revolucionario Cubano. Eds.

[5] The shouting was done mainly by Castro followers who attended the meeting. Eds.

harbor hate, and yet they have displayed more hate against us than ever has been shown against any group of Cubans.

"There will be amnesty when there is peace." With what moral backing can men make such a statement, when during the last three years they have been proclaiming that they made a military coup in order to bring peace to the Republic? Then there is no peace; *ergo,* the coup did not bring peace; therefore, the government does not acknowledge its lie after three years of dictatorship. They must confess that Cuba has had no peace from the very day they seized power.

"The best proof that there is no dictatorship is that there are no political prisoners," they said for many months. Today, when prisons are full and exile is a common word, they cannot say that we are living under a democratic and constitutional regime. Their own words condemn them.

"If amnesty is to be granted, the adversaries of the regime must change their attitude." In other words, for having committed a crime against the rights of the people we are made hostages and treated as was the populace of the occupied countries by the Nazis. That is why we are hostages of the dictatorship rather than simply political prisoners.

"In order to have an amnesty, a prior agreement to respect the regime is necessary." The wretches who suggest such a thing assume that those of us who have gone through twenty months of imprisonment and exile on this island have lost our integrity under the hardships they imposed on us. From their comfortable and well-paid official positions, where they would like to live forever, they have the baseness to talk in these terms to those who, a thousand times more honorable than they, are buried in the cells of the penitentiary. I have been isolated in a cell for sixteen months, but I have sufficient energy to respond with dignity. Our imprisonment is unjust. I do not see why those who assault army headquarters to overthrow the legal Constitution chosen by the people can be considered in the right, whereas those who would like to defend it are not. I do not see how reason can be with those who deprived the people of their sovereignty and freedom, but not with those who have struggled to return it to the people; nor why the regime should have the right to govern the Republic against the will of the people while we, through loyalty to its principles, languish in prison. Let the lives of those in power be examined, and it will be found that they are filled with shady activities, frauds, and ill-gotten fortunes. Let their lives be compared with those who died in Santiago de Cuba or those who are here in prison, unstained by fraud or dishonor. Our personal freedom is an inalienable right as citizens born in a country which does not acknowledge lords of any kind. We can be deprived of those rights and of everything else by force, but no one will ever succeed in getting us to accept enjoyment of those rights through an unworthy agreement. Thus, we shall not yield one atom of our honor in exchange for our freedom.

They are the ones who should promise to respect the laws of the Republic, for they shamelessly violated them on March 10. They are the ones who should respect the sovereignty and the will of the people, for they scandalously mocked them on November 1. They are the ones who should favor an atmosphere of calm and peaceful coexistence in the country, for they have maintained unrest and anxiety for three years. The responsibility falls on them. Without the March 10 coup, the 26th of July revolt would not have been necessary, and there would be no Cuban suffering political imprisonment.

We are not professional agitators or blind supporters of violence if the better land for which we hope can be attained with the weapons of reason and intelligence. No people would follow a group of adventurers trying to sink the country in a civil war if justice predominated there or if peaceful and legal means were open to the citizens to settle a civic conflict of ideas. We believe, like Martí, that "one who starts a war that can be avoided is a criminal, as is one who fails to start a war that is inevitable." The Cuban nation will never see us starting a civil war that can be avoided, but I repeat that whenever shameful circumstances like those following the cowardly coup of March 10 arise in Cuba, it would be a crime to fail to start an unavoidable rebellion.

If we thought that a change of circumstance and positive constitutional guarantees demanded a change of tactics in the struggle, we would do so out of respect for the nation, but never as a cowardly and shameful agreement with the government. And if that agreement is demanded of us in order to gain our freedom, we emphatically say no.

No, we are not tired. After twenty months we are as firm and unmoved as on the first day. We do not want amnesty at the price of dishonor. We shall not undergo the Caudius gallows[6] of ignoble oppressors. We shall suffer a thousand years of imprisonment rather than humiliation! A thousand years of imprisonment rather than sacrifice our dignity! We proclaim it with calmness, without fear or hate.

If what Cuba needs at this time are Cubans willing to sacrifice themselves to save the country from shame, we offer ourselves with

[6] Refers to the method by which prisoners were forced to follow a line of conduct totally opposed to the beliefs of the prisoners. Eds.

pleasure. We are young, and we have no selfish ambitions. The politicians should not fear us then, because in different ways, more or less disguised, they climb on the bandwagon of personal ambitions, forgetful of the great injustices which harm the nation.

Amnesty does not concern us; we shall not even demand that the prison system, through which the regime has shown us all its hate and fury, be improved. As Antonio Maceo once said, "The only thing we would accept willingly from our enemies is the bloody scaffold that our other comrades in arms, more fortunate than we, have faced with their heads high and the peace of mind of those who died on the altar of the just and holy cause of freedom."

In the face of today's shameful compromises, seventy-seven years after his heroic protest, the Bronze Titan will see in us his spiritual children.[7]

[7] In 1878, Antonio Maceo, a black leader of the independence struggle against Spain, waged his "Protesta de Baraguá," a protest by which he denounced a compromise reached between the Cuban rebels and the Spanish authorities. Maceo has often been called the "Bronze Titan." Eds.

Interview with Agustín Alles Soberón (May 22, 1955)

REPORTER: Imprisonment has strengthened Fidel Castro spiritually. The political fighter in him comes out with the first words by the Ortodoxo leader with this reporter.

CASTRO: We Cubans want peace, but we can attain it only through the road of freedom. Peace cannot be a way for despotism to consolidate privilege and oppression and use appeasement to comfortably enjoy usurped power. In order to have true peace, it is essential that the trampling of the citizenry cease, as well as the violation of democratic rights. Only then will the Republic be saved.

REPORTER: The former student leader, embracing a little girl whose father fell in the Moncada attack, declares to Bohemia:

CASTRO: The amnesty is the result of the extraordinary popular mobilization, masterly support by the Cuban press, which has won the

Interview given after being released from prison. Agustín Alles Soberón, "Del Moncada al presidio y a la libertad," Bohemia (Havana), May 22, 1955, pp. 22, 73.

most impressive battle. Our message of gratitude, therefore, is for the people and journalists, to whom we shall always be deeply grateful. How can the government claim any generosity with regard to the amnesty if they were intransigently against it until the moment when public opinion forced them to give in?

REPORTER: Fidel Castro listens attentively to radio and news broadcasts related to the liberty of political prisoners. He is concerned that his ideas be quoted truthfully. Beside him is Ortodoxo leader Max Lesnick.

CASTRO: The elections for a constitutional assembly will only serve to prolong the present government through the reelection of General Batista. Partial elections solve nothing; the nation is not interested in them, but a little group of opportunists is, those who want to install themselves as mayors and congressmen. There is no formula or national solution other than general elections at the earliest time, with guarantees for all. Under those conditions, the end of the dictatorship would be inevitable.

I am exhausted. We have borne many days of impatience. If you will excuse me, I will take my shoes off, since I haven't been this comfortable for many months. Now that we are free we assert without any reservations that, since we are not professional agitators, if the present circumstances were to change and if the regime were to respect the rights of all, we would change the tactics of our struggle. We would do so because of our respect for the supreme interests of the nation. But we shall never change our tactics because of a compromise with those who are in power, disregarding the sovereign will of the people. Now it is up to the men of the regime to demonstrate that those guarantees are real and not, as up to now, false promises.

REPORTER: Summarizing his political projections, Dr. Fidel Castro declared the following:

CASTRO: I have studied the program of my party—which could be no other than that of Chibás—and those of the recently formed movements Liberación Radical de la Nación and Humanista, as well as MNR and the Partido Nuevo.[1] They all agree on what is fundamental: the need for thorough political, social, and economic reforms to establish a regime of justice and freedom. Ideological differences do not exist that will justify at this difficult hour the weakening of these forces. In the ranks of the party of Cuban independence everyone did not have the same degree of revolutionary consciousness, but we were

[1] Left-of-center political groups. Eds.

freed from prison because of the unity attained by all. The present moment is also one that calls for unity, but beneath a single banner.

REPORTER: The main participant in the attack on·the military barracks at Santiago de Cuba on July 26, 1953, reflects deeply. Twenty-two months of political imprisonment have matured him. He does not even mention the past.

CASTRO: Someday that story will be told, at its proper time. Meanwhile we must look to the future. An army must not turn its rifles to shoot at the past. We shall not do what is convenient for the government, that is, engage in conspiratorial activities, but we shall do what is beneficial for the fatherland, that is, to work tirelessly for the union of all the moral forces of the country under the flag of Chibás's thought. For that endeavor I am thinking of staying in Cuba, struggling openly, for we are not men of hate or resentment, as some suppose. Perhaps many exiles will not return until they see what happens to us, until they see whether or not guarantees exist.

REPORTER: Raúl Chibás and Roberto Agramonte[2] are the first ones to arrive at the small apartment where Fidel Castro has been living since leaving the Isle of Pines Prison. He explains to the Ortodoxo leaders the declarations which he made on recovering his liberty and ratifies his plan to struggle in the ranks of the PPC (Ortodoxo). To Raúl Chibás he says:

CASTRO: The Ortodoxo Party has taken a good step in designating you president. I understand that without being a politician you are giving lessons on politics and decency. This is what Cuba needs! Decent politicians!

REPORTER: The brother[3] of the Ortodoxo Party founder replies:

"The party is happy that you are all free. We hope that the courageous youths of the Moncada will work with us, in the same civic spirit that they have worked up to today, to return democratic normalcy and the full enjoyment of its trampled freedom to Cuba."

[2] Ortodoxo leaders. Eds.
[3] Raúl Chibás. Eds.

Part 4
Organizing in Cuba

Declaration on the Arrest of Pedro Miret
(May 25, 1955)

When we left prison, we stated that the men who attacked the Moncada Barracks would become guinea pigs to find out if there were political guarantees or not. After a series of attacks and persecutions, yesterday the police entered in the late hours of night for the second time, without judicial authorization, the home of *compañero* Pedro Miret Prieto, who recently had been released from prison with us.[1] He was arrested, as were his wife's uncle and the owner of the house.

In such circumstances we truly feel that there are no guarantees of any kind and believe that the exiles should not return to Cuba if things continue this way.[2]

Amnesty is becoming a bloody hoax played on the people and the press, who fought so much for it, as well as on those who were given amnesty, who are trying to encourage a peaceful climate through a calm and respectful attitude. But even when we feel there are no guarantees for us, we plan to remain in the country in an effort to find a decent solution without bloodshed to the tragic situation of Cuba.

At this moment our lives and personal security are exposed to attack, but we remain here gladly because our departure from Cuba would definitely end any possibility of a peaceful solution.

I have just explained this situation to the magistrates of the Court of Appeals.

Fidel Castro

Press release issued by Fidel Castro on May 25, 1955. "Detenido un amnistiado del Cuartel Moncada," *El Mundo* (Havana), May 25, 1955, p. 1.

[1] Pedro Miret was a participant in the attack on the Moncada Barracks; he was, with Fidel Castro, one of the early founders of the 26th of July Movement. He is presently a major in Cuba. Eds.

[2] At the time the issue of the return of the exiles was of great importance. The Batista regime, as well as some opposition groups, favored the return. Castro used every opportunity he had to oppose it, arguing that nothing had really changed. Eds.

Chaviano, You Lie!
(May 29, 1955)

In reply to an editorial in *Bohemia* which courageously denounced the fascist nature of the castor oil treatment suffered by two CMKC broadcasters from agents of Colonel Alberto del Río Chaviano, the latter has written an unfortunate letter which has filled the citizenry with surprise, bewilderment, and outrage. As yet I do not believe that such a great absurdity has come under the inside censure of official government spokesmen who, as the directors of *Pueblo* and *Gente*, saluted our amnesty from imprisonment. Anyone who has the most basic understanding of public opinion would realize the great damage that could result for the government out of such a clumsy and offensive public pronouncement.

What is Mr. Chaviano's objective in that letter? Is it part of a criminal plan to provoke those who have just left the prisons? Had he thought perhaps that, because of his colonel's brass and being used to absolute power when he gave orders in the brave land of Oriente, we who return to the struggle after twenty-two months of unjust imprisonment—with only the weapons of reason and honor—would not know how to reply to him vigorously and thoroughly? *Bohemia* challenged him to explain the brutal abuse of the freedom of expression and individual rights, but far from answering with convincing arguments he writes a long provocative paragraph—offensive, libelous, and poisonous —against us. Is his subconscious betraying him? Is his conscience so atrociously disturbed that he pretends to excuse himself from other acts a thousand times worse than to choke two defenseless broadcasters with castor oil for having denounced illegal gambling? Just as for Lady Macbeth, the waters of the ocean will not suffice to wash the blood from his hands.

As we left prison, we said that we had not learned to hate either those who insulted us or those who conspired against us. Our first embrace was with an honorable armed forces officer. The people admired our gesture. The citizenry welcomes with approval and admiration the words of a group of combatants who proved their courage through danger and sacrifice and yet knew how to express themselves without resentment or haughtiness, placing their enthusiasm and dignity at Cuba's service. We said of the prison that although we were

"Mientes, Chaviano!" *Bohemia* (Havana), May 29, 1955, pp. 57, 95–96.

mistreated without end, we were leaving it without prejudice in the mind or poison in the soul—which could becloud our thoughts on the path to follow—and that the people of Cuba could always expect a calm and dignified attitude worthy of the circumstances from us. Those who spoke in that manner remained in the national territory with honor and a clean conscience, as can only be done by those who know how not to fear, have no blemish on their souls, and know how to fulfill their duty simply and naturally.

While I was still in prison some spoke about amnesty with conditions. We rejected them energetically even if it meant indefinite imprisonment. When the amnesty was finally decreed without conditions, our statements had no hatred, baseness, or vengeance. If we reply to humiliation with dignity, to a decent act we reply with decency.

How little nobility! How little responsibility! How small is the sense of honor in the mind of the miserable provocateur who answers our attitude with insults, lies, and dishonor!

Mr. Chaviano called us criminals filled with hatred, while he describes himself as a prestigious and honorable military man who is consecrated for life to the military profession, and says that he has never used force abusively and is proud to have respected the lives of prisoners and wounded on July 26.

To the description he makes of us as criminals full of hatred, I reply with the words of the prosecution at the Urgency Court of Santiago de Cuba, published in the section "En Cuba" in the same issue of *Bohemia* where the unfortunate letter appeared (page 63, column 2, paragraph 4). It reads: "On the part of the revolutionaries, it is not difficult to say that they acted with honesty. They were sincere, courageous, and patriotic in their confessions. They also behaved with generosity and honor. One example is right here in the Palace of Justice where they respected the lives of a group of armed forces members whom they could have killed. . . ."

Never before in a trial of this nature have similar words been heard by a prosecutor. It was the result of the irrefutable proof presented during the trial to the effect that no soldier was wounded by knives, no patient at the Military Hospital was murdered, no prisoner mistreated, and that all soldiers who fell did so in fair combat. The death certificates signed by military doctors, the statements of many honest military men who never failed to fulfill their oath to tell the truth, and endless other proofs left the events clarified beyond a doubt.

The people of Oriente know the whole story; the people of Oriente, in the greatest demonstration the region has ever seen, clamored excitedly for hours for the Moncada fighters. And the people, Mr.

Chaviano, neither clamor nor rave for criminals. On the contrary, those who applauded, those who had gone out to give everything for Cuba's dignity, cried incessantly, "Down Chaviano!"

But because Mr. Chaviano wants it, because he insists in repeating the charges brought against the Moncada attackers, I am going to state why those fantastic lies were forged against us. It is very clear: to degrade heroism; to justify the barbaric massacre that followed; to drown the youth, who did not want then or now to be slaves to anyone, in terror and mud. Nero acted no differently when he tried to justify the assassination of Christians, accusing them of having set homes afire—something he had ordered himself. The Cuban people, intelligent as they are, soon understood the whole affair.

From prison and in spite of the isolation and rigors, we won the battle for the truth. Why then the 90 days of censorship, why then the Law on Public Order, if not so that the true story of July 26 would never be known? It is really extraordinary that with half a dozen clandestine publications the truth overcame the whole apparatus of official propaganda with its Goebbelslike methods of repeating the same slander. Today only a fool with vested interests (more vested interests than foolishness) and only a wicked person with no conscience could repeat those lies. This time nothing remains of the slander.

Let us see if Mr. Chaviano is capable of answering the following facts and data:

When Batista spoke from the military polygon of Columbia the day following the events, he said the attackers had thirty-three deaths; toward the end of the week our deaths rose to over eighty. In which battles, which places, in which combat did those young men die? Before Batista spoke, twenty-five prisoners had been killed; and after the speech, fifty more were killed. Is this the manner in which Chaviano respected the prisoners' lives?

Our total wounded, those who survived, were five. If our adversaries had nineteen dead and thirty wounded, how is it possible that we could have had eighty dead and five wounded? Who ever saw battles with twenty-one dead and no wounded, as the famous ones of Pérez Chaumont in Siboney?

Here are the statistics on the casualties of the harsh combat of the invading column in the 1895 war, casualties of battles both lost and won. Combat of Los Indios in Las Villas: twelve wounded, no dead; combat of Mal Tiempo: four dead, twenty-three wounded; combat of Calimete: sixteen dead, sixty-four wounded; combat of La Palma: thirty-nine dead, eighty-eight wounded; combat of Cacarajicara: five dead, thirteen wounded; combat of Descanso: four dead, forty-five wounded; combat of San Gabriel del Lombillo: two dead, eighteen wounded. In absolutely all of them the number of wounded is twice, three times, and even ten times greater than the dead. There were no modern achievements in medical science, then, which diminish the proportion of dead. How could this fabulous proportion of sixteen dead for each wounded be explained if not by finishing them off in the hospitals and killing the defenseless prisoners afterward? These numbers speak irrefutably. Is that how Mr. Chaviano took care of the wounded? Furthermore, if these facts and numbers are not enough I produce, for the public, testimony of Mr. Waldo Pérez Almaguer, who during this time was none other than the governor of Oriente, and who, according to his own words, was removed from his job due to his unwillingness to acquiesce in the horrendous massacre of prisoners. Oh! If only Waldo Pérez Almaguer were willing to courageously tell everything he knows! He has parliamentary immunity, and we hope he will also have the necessary civic spirit.

Mr. Chaviano mentions that the life of the revolutionaries' leader was respected on his surrender to the armed forces. That is not an argument. Let it be said once and for all—because much trouble has been made due to my arrest—that I never surrendered to the army. After resisting an encirclement of fifteen hundred men during one week with seventeen *compañeros*, on the morning of Saturday, August 1, in the company of José Suarez and Oscar Alcalde and completely exhausted by hunger and thirst, a patrol commanded by Lieutenant Sarría woke us up with their rifles on our chests. Sarría was accompanied by Cabo Suárez and soldiers Rodríguez, Batista, and several others. None recognized me at first glance. When some members of the patrol were preparing to kill us right in the field and with our hands tied behind our backs, the officer to whom I have referred cried out energetically to them, "Don't do it, for ideas cannot be killed." When I saw that singular gesture, I stood up before him and gave him my name, informing him that I was the main leader of the combatants. As an answer, that military gentleman begged me to keep my identity secret, became my own guardian, and took me to the headquarters of the political police of Santiago de Cuba where it became impossible to assassinate me once the people and the press knew my whereabouts. Six days had gone by since the events, and an immense clamor arose from the people against the unprecedented massacre of the prisoners.

Although on that occasion I kept silent about Lieutenant Sarría's beautiful words, I expressed, through Cadena Oriental de Radio, before Chaviano himself and other military personnel, the way in which I was arrested.[1] All of Cuba heard it. No one could or will be able to deny it. The interview published by *El Crisol* prompted the collection of the Monday edition of August 3, 1953.

In no way was the attitude of Mr. Chaviano an honorable one. A few days after I entered the Boniato Prison, he ordered the suspension and expulsion from the armed forces of the honorable officer and supervisor who refused to poison me. The poison had already been prepared, as well as a statement to be made public giving the version that it had been suicide. Do I need to tell the name of the officer and publicly quote from his testimony? To him, as well as Sarría, I owe my life. On the other hand, Chaviano expelled an honorable military man who refused to accept crime; he cannot find those who abused the CMKC broadcasters as yet.

What then does Mr. Chaviano want? Does he want me to narrate the "hair-raising" crimes committed against the prisoners? To speak of the torn-out eyes and of men buried alive? To point out each of the murderers by name and each of those responsible, whether big or little? If he wants it that way, I am willing to discuss with him through the press, radio, or television whenever he wants the facts in full detail. Let the responsibility for the passions which could be unleashed fall on him, for he has tried to provoke us in a cowardly manner, although from the very beginning I have had only generous words for the soldiers who fell courageously before us and for their families as well as for my comrades' families. This is so because I am a Cuban who wishes the good of all and not one group, because we want a fatherland with all and for the good of all. I educated my mind in Martí's thought, which preaches love, not hatred. The Apostle Martí is the guide of my life and, just as he did, I have seen in myself the need to grasp arms to struggle against an oppression which closes all avenues for peace; just as he, before saluting the adversary in death, we would have liked to have embraced him in liberty; and as he, we shall know how to fall facing the sun, struggling for the good of those who combat us.

The soldiers who fell in combat will always have our respect as adversaries without hate or fear, and the families will receive generous help when the magnanimous and concerned revolution attains power, just as those who today do not have aid will have it as the relatives of our *compañeros* who fell victims of crime, repression, and hate.

We have fought with the soldiers, facing each other; we have never used them as a pedestal to climb to offices. I defended them more than

[1] Cadena Oriental de Radio was a radio station in Oriente Province. Eds.

anyone before March 10, and there are my articles in the newspaper *Alerta* as irrefutable proof. I never asked anything in exchange.

My sincere sympathies go to the military man who, without hate or anger, knows how to fulfill what he thinks and believes is his duty, who knows how to die fighting but who will never murder a defenseless prisoner.

I have respect for the Sarrías, Camps, Tamayos, Roger Pérez Diazes, and all honorable military men even though they might not think as I do. My admiration goes to that gentleman, Major Izquierdo, police chief of Santiago de Cuba, who having lost a brother in combat spoke to me amiably and without a trace of resentment because we had gone to fight a system of government and not against any particular military man.

Do you now see, Mr. Chaviano, that I, an adversary, can speak in this manner; you cannot, because with the blood of your fallen *compañeros* you knead a fortune of millions which all of Cuba knows about. Smuggling, vice, and any murky business venture finds a magnificent entrepreneur in you. Even political nominations are controlled completely by you, as denounced by the governmental legislator Morcate. Do you want me to list your businesses one by one?

Finally, I would like to know whether the High Command consented to the publication of that letter. If so, the regime would be lying when they speak of cordiality and peaceful coexistence. Does Mr. Chaviano desire to raise a hate-flag within the armed forces? What macabre design is hidden behind his attitude?

No honorable military man would be in accord with this manner of acting. My aim is just to refute him because in this article I am not attacking the armed forces, but rather one who dishonors them with his acts and with an unjustifiable and cowardly provocation at a time when the country requires the good sense of all more than ever. The uniform is to be honored; one should know how to wear it, and not launch cowardly and cunning attacks while hidden in the armed forces.

It does not matter that our hands are without weapons. Today we are moral columns of the fatherland, and as columns we shall collapse rather than fall individually. We remain in Cuba, despite the risks; we do not fear the hired bullet.

Murderers' Hands
(June 7, 1955)

After March 10, 1952, the Yateras bullies disappeared,[1] but it seems that all of them have come to Havana. Cuba does not want bullies. And in the name of Cuba the government will put an end to all bragging. The government wants to be calm and patient. Some people believe that to be a weakness; but listen well. We do not want bullies or braggarts around. Let not the attacks made against us be repeated by some who have received amnesty, because I do not want them to provoke our men anymore. And let it not be said afterward that force was out of our hands, for the men and women of the ruling parties have brains, hearts, and also hands. And with regard to courage, let us not talk about it, because the only one who has courage here is the one who rules close to the people with dignity and affection.[2]

Should a chief of state express himself in such terms? Are those the proper words for one who has in his hands all the instruments of power, knowing that any statement of his could have far-reaching national repercussions? Is this the tone which Mr. Batista desires to set in the public debate? Is this the example the master wishes to set for servants in greater need of restraint than ever? Has not the new Torquemada[3] we have in charge of censorship closed opposition papers for much less?

It was depressing enough to see the spectacle offered by Mr. Batista when he inaugurated a boulevard with his name before a dangerous mob of bootlickers who screamed "Let us have twenty years of Batista." In such an atmosphere of vanity and ridiculous puppetry it is not surprising that a so-called President should have descended to ugly, threatening, and vulgar language.

Less than a week ago, after our article "Chaviano, You Lie!"[4] which was a reply to a letter published the previous week, Batista publicly demanded an end to provocations "from both sides," which was clearly an order to his followers, for I was the one provoked. Despite his declarations, Batista's spokesmen unleashed an unprecedented barrage of insults and epithets against me. They called me "beast, damn

"Manos asesinas," *La Calle* (Havana), June 7, 1955, p. 3.
[1] Yateras is a region east of the city of Guantánamo. In Cuban slang it meant a place where most thugs and tough people hang around. Eds.
[2] Statement made by Fulgencio Batista at a rally on June 5, 1955. Eds.
[3] Refers to Ramón Vasconcelos, minister of communications in the Batista administration. Eds.
[4] In this volume. Eds.

beast, gangster, murderer, nut, crazy." Either the servants revolted
against their master, or the master ordered one thing in public and
another in private. What would happen if the opposition used the
same epithets against Batista? Is it logical then that after a week filled
with insults, Batista himself, who was apparently disobeyed by his
well-paid spokesmen, should come out stating that the bullies have
moved to Havana, that the government will not permit any bragging,
and that those who have been released should end their provocations?

When have we insulted anyone, in any public statement, since we
were released? Does Mr. Batista call bullying and bragging my calm
reply to an insolent and inappropriate letter in which we were called
criminals filled with hatred, without even excluding those who died?
Is bragging telling the truth using facts and undeniable evidence? What
do you want me to do? To seek refuge in a foreign embassy? Do you
want me to kneel down while you threaten and insult me?

At the moment when, without any pretense, the regime's spokesmen
have publicly demanded my head, the following dangerous words
have been uttered by Batista:

> And let it not be said afterward that force was out of our
> hands, for men and women of the ruling parties have brains,
> hearts, and also hands.

If a political crime were committed after those words, could it be
said that Batista was exempt from guilt? Could it be denied that
murder is insinuated in those words? Could not a henchman be
inspired by those words?

Why speak about hands when we are debating the truth? Who has
used force in the polemic centering on what happened in the Moncada? The polemic was provoked by Mr. Chaviano, who forced some
radio announcers to drink castor oil, and placed himself in a hardly
defensible position. One should not speak about hands, hands that
could murder, when we speak about facts. If the government lacks
rationality, then it is logical to speak about hands, murderers' hands.

But one should not overlook the immense cowardice hiding behind
their arguments about hands and force. Their hands have weapons,
ours do not. I am aware that the men in the government have hands
which they could use. As Batista declared before a mob that cried
"Let us have Batista for twenty years," they have hands—a fact which
many courageous Cubans have discovered. They have hands, but I do
not believe they have brains or hearts.

To reply to the portion of Batista's speech where he states that he
is the only man around with courage, I am going to be a little respectful, for it is not nice to degrade another person, regardless of what

position he holds. A great psychologist once said, "Everyone boasts about what he lacks." Batista, I suppose, is not a coward, but I am sure he is conceited, vain, dishonest, and wrong.

He thinks he is the only one capable of ruling the Republic and of making revolutions, when he has been the mere instigator of plots without doctrine or ideology. He said once that he taught the Cubans how to make constitutions, provoking the indignant protest of the illustrious Don Cosme de la Torriente,[5] who reminded him of our glorious history, when a republican constitution was made during the war of independence.

As if that were not enough, his clique, insulting our courageous people, affirms that Batista is the only real man around. Such words are a slap in the face of the entire nation. That is a grave mistake: A worthy and honest nation is humiliated and vilified by a handful of men who have no conscience. That is what provokes rebelliousness and endangers the peace the nation needs so much.

It is not courage to oppose the people by force; courage is to give the people the rights that were destroyed one sad day. The wild beast that attacks defenseless nations in the dark of night is not courageous. A courageous wild beast, when overburdened by "the Indian," lies down and dies, as José Martí said.[6]

Batista, be courageous! Have the courage to overcome the sinister interests that surround you, and return to the nation its rights. Do not insult and humiliate the people any longer with your speeches and actions. They hurt Cuba's sensibility. Remember that "tyranny sooner or later creates the virtues that will destroy it." This is the reply of a loyal adversary who does not need to offend anyone to fight you.

[5] Veteran of the war of independence. Eds.

[6] Martí's remark, concerning the wild llama of the Andes, is also used here as a punning reference to Batista, who was called "the Indian" by his followers. Eds.

Against Terror and Crime
(June 11, 1955)

Last night was a tragic night: There were seven bombings and one assassination. To guess who set off the bombs would take a magician. These were the strangest, most stupid, and most ridiculous of all the

"Frente al terror y frente al crimen," *La Calle* (Havana), June 11, 1955, p. 3.

bombs that have recently exploded in the streets of Havana and other places in Cuba.

I stated my suspicions on the matter when I left prison, because, as I said then to the reporters; a man in his right mind cannot conceive of hurting the regime by blowing up a Chinese store outside Havana with a few little bombs. The greatest service that can be performed for a dictatorship that stresses order is to use the barbaric and inhumane method of dynamite, because the oppressors are then given the justification for terrorism.

In the last few weeks I have spoken with hundreds and hundreds of persons, young and old, politicians, revolutionaries, some more radical than others. I have heard all types of ideas and opinions while gathering the views of those who came to greet me. Of all those, not one has uttered a word in favor of terrorism. To tell the truth, I believe I know the thoughts of all the men in the opposition, and all of them, like all the people, absolutely reject terrorism.

To set off bombs, then, can only be the work of scoundrels without conscience who want to serve the government instead of fighting it. I am so convinced of the immense harm that they are doing to the struggle against the dictatorship that I would not hesitate to publicly denounce the bunch of savages who render such a formidable service to Batista while pretending to be revolutionaries.

The bombs last night coincided with a brutal political assassination. Jorge Agostini was assassinated, there is no doubt about it.[1] Even if the police version is to be believed, it is clear that a crime was committed. The police release read: "Agostini had a physician's satchel, and inside it were found a pistol and ammunition."

If that is the case, then Agostini did not shoot, did not use a weapon; he did not even try to use it. Unless they could divine it, the assassins could not have had any way of knowing that a pistol and bullets were inside the physician's bag.

Supposedly he was killed so he could not escape. But could one have the slightest possibility of escape from a block completely surrounded by the police?

Agostini's body was riddled with bullet holes. That many holes are not given to a man to prevent his escape. There are only such signs in the body of a victim when there is cruelty; he was shot even after he fell.

---

[1] Former minister of the navy under the Grau administration (1944–1948). Agostini fought in the Spanish Civil War, participated in the Cayo Confites expedition (1947), and was underground coordinator for Aureliano Sánchez Arango's AAA. Eds.

Why that manhunt against a person who was not sought by any court? Agostini was one of the persons who benefited from the recent amnesty law. According to the government, he was meeting with subversives at his Vedado home. Should people be shot because of simple rumors?

Agostini was not a gangster. I never had the honor of meeting him, and never had any type of relationship or acquaintance with the movement of which he was a member, but everyone agrees that he was an honest man, loved by his followers. He never abused or killed anyone; he never stole. His hands were free of blood or filth. In exile he lived a humble life, leaving no capital of any sort to his children. It is almost impossible to believe that an honest former officer of the navy could be killed like a dog.

His death, aside from politics or tactics, hurts us all. It has no justification, and can have none. These are the first consequences of the speech made by Mr. Batista, when he said at "Batista Boulevard" that "his men had hands."

In our article "Murderers' Hands," answering Batista's threats, we said,

> If a political crime were committed after those words, could it be said that Batista was exempt from guilt? Could it be denied that assassination is insinuated in those words? Could not a henchman be inspired by those words?[2]

Unfortunately, our worries were well grounded.

What is going to be the reaction of the opposition parties, of the neutral press and the public-opinion makers, in the face of this monstrous political murder, which has placed the entire nation in a state of uncertainty? To keep silent is to be a shameful accomplice. The citizenry will carefully observe all the stands to see who remains calm and public spirited in the face of the terror unleashed by the regime.

Will this savage act remain unpunished? Do a handful of men have the right to take away the lives of others with greater impunity than the worst gangsters of the past? Today it is Jorge Agostini, a new martyr of our struggle for national liberation. Who will be the next to fall, riddled with bullets? No one should take personal vengeance for his death! National mobilization should be the answer to political assassination! It is the only correct revolutionary tactic.

Let us stop crime with vigorous and courageous denunciations. Let us test the honesty of our judges and courts. No more crimes without punishment! Justice, justice, justice!

[2] In this volume. Eds.

Part 5
Exile

Letter to Prominent Political Leaders
(July 7, 1955)

I am leaving Cuba because all doors of peaceful struggle have been closed to me.

Six weeks after being released from prison I am convinced more than ever of the dictatorship's intention to remain in power for twenty years masked in different ways, ruling as now by the use of terror and crime and ignoring the patience of the Cuban people, which has its limits.

As a follower of Martí, I believe the hour has come to take rights and not to beg for them, to fight instead of pleading for them.

I will reside somewhere in the Caribbean.

From trips such as this, one does not return, or else one returns with the tyranny beheaded at one's feet.

Fidel Castro Ruz

Letter written before leaving Cuba for Mexico, July 7, 1955. Edmundo Desnoes, ed., *La sierra y el llano* (Havana: Casa de las Américas, 1961), p. 7.

Against the Return of Carlos Prío from Exile
(July 10, 1955)

Carlos Prío cannot return to Cuba without being sent to the Castillo del Príncipe,[1] where several Cubans are falsely accused of terrorism in a trial in which he is included as the one mainly responsible for the dreadful plan. Therefore, it is impossible to believe what Batista and his minister, Santiago Rey, have declared publicly—that Prío will not be bothered—when there are three orders for his arrest decreed by the Court of Appeals. For Prío to return to Cuba without difficulties, a new political amnesty would have to be approved or, on the other hand, it would be necessary to admit that the courts do exactly what the minister of government and Dictator Batista order.

If Carlos Prío can return to Cuba and peacefully live in his residence

"Opiniones sobre el regreso de Prío." *Bohemia,* July 10, 1955, p. 64.
[1] Prison located in Havana. Eds.

at "La Chata," then why, at the moment I make these statements, are Juan Pedro Carbó, Manuel Carbonell Duque, José Machado, and others imprisoned, accused in the same cause as Prío? Why have Pascasio Lineras, Manuel Alfonso, and Evelio Duque been in jail for over two weeks?

My own brother had to take the road of exile, accused in the same trial of having placed a bomb in a movie theater in Havana when he was a thousand kilometers away with my sick father in Oriente Province. Consequently, I do not know if Prío's words announcing his return to Cuba in peace are sincere.

Would he be allowed to speak? Would they let him appear on television? Would they allow him to write? Would they give him the opportunity to undertake public acts? If so, we would have to acknowledge that Prío is very fortunate in this situation because I, a citizen just as any other and with the same rights according to the supposedly enforced Constitution, am absolutely forbidden any of those legal activities. Through an unusual personal expedient open for an indefinite time in the Ministry of Communications, as evident in telegram 142, R-OV-OF Urgent, dated June 13, 1955, sent to Unión Radio and Channel 11,[2] I am not allowed to speak. All this happened even before the drastic measure of closing the newspaper *La Calle*.

Prío could come under such conditions, and perhaps Batista would be grateful for it; but I am not willing to do any favors for this ignominious regime. I am already packing my suitcase to leave Cuba, although I have even had to borrow money for the passport because I am not a millionaire but a Cuban who has given everything and will continue to do so for Cuba. We shall return when we can bring our people freedom and the right to live decently, without despotism and without hunger.

After six weeks in the streets[3] and after seeing the intention of the ruling cliques ready to remain in power twenty years, as the flatterers and the opportunists are asking, I do not believe even in general elections. All the doors being closed to the people for peaceful struggle, there is no solution except that of '68 and '95.[4] The outrage which this regime represents for all who have fallen for the dignity of Cuba, from Joaquín de Agüero to Jorge Agostini, must be remedied.[5]

[2] Radio and television stations in Havana. Eds.
[3] Castro had been released from Isle of Pines Prison, where he was sent after the Moncada Barracks assault. Eds.
[4] The references is to the 1868 and 1895 wars for Cuban independence from Spain. Eds.
[5] Joaquín de Agüero, an anti-Batista politician, was murdered by the police. On the latter, see "Against Terror and Crime" in this volume. Eds.

As I said before the Court of Appeals in Santiago de Cuba, when I was on trial for the events of July 26, we are Cubans and to be a Cuban implies a duty: not to fulfill it is a crime and treason. We are proud of the history of our fatherland; we learned it in school and we have grown up hearing of freedom, of justice, and of rights. We were taught at an early age the glorious examples of our heroes and martyrs. Céspedes, Agramonte, Maceo, Gómez, and Martí were the first names engraved in our minds. We were taught that the titan Maceo had said, "Freedom is not to be begged for but conquered with the edge of the machete." We were taught what the apostle Martí had written in his *Edad de Oro* in order to have a free fatherland: "When there are many without honor, there are always some who have within themselves the dignity of many men. Those are the ones who revolt with terrible force against those who steal the people's freedom." We were taught that October 10 and February 24 are glorious dates on which the Cubans rebelled against the yoke of infamous tyranny.[6] We were taught to love and defend the beautiful flag of the solitary star[7] and to sing an anthem every afternoon, the verses which say that "to live in chains is to live sunk in shame and dishonor" and that "to die for the fatherland is to live."[8]

[6] October 10, 1868, was the date on which the independence struggle against Spain began in Cuba. The struggle continued after an unstable peace on February 24, 1895. Eds.

[7] Cuba's flag. Eds.

[8] Last lines of Cuba's national anthem. Eds.

Manifesto No. 1 to the People of Cuba (*August 8, 1955*)

I live for my fatherland and for its true freedom, although I know that my life may not last long enough to enjoy the fruit of my labors and that this service must be given with the certainty and thought of receiving no reward for it.

JOSÉ MARTÍ

My duties to the fatherland and to my convictions stand above all personal concerns; that is why I shall be free or shall perish for the redemption of my people.

ANTONIO MACEO

Manifesto issued on August 8, 1955, from Mexico. "Manifiesto No. 1 del 26 de Julio al pueblo de Cuba," *Pensamiento Crítico* (Havana), no. 21 (1968), pp. 207–220.

Under this battle cry, which recalls past national rebellion, the Cuban revolutionary movement is today organized and prepared for its great task of redemption and justice.

By the express agreement of its leaders, I have been entrusted with the drafting of this first manifesto to the country and those which in the future will be published clandestinely.

In carrying out this mission which duty imposes on me, I do not hesitate to assume the responsibility involved in signing these proclamations that will be a constant reminder to the people, an open call for revolution, and a frontal attack against the clique of criminals who trample the honor of the nation and rule its destiny counter to its history and the sovereign will of the people. And although at the present time I am absent from the soil of our nation and therefore outside the jurisdiction of the courts that issue the sentences ordered by the master, I did not hesitate to unmask the executioner when that court was judging me there, or from prison to accuse by name the dictator and his bloodthirsty generals of the Moncada Barracks' crimes in a manifesto dated January 6, 1954, or to reject amnesty with conditions attached, or again, when freed, to show the people evidence of the cruel and inhuman character of the Batista regime. What a cruel and inhuman apparatus Batista's regime has! I do not care what accusations they may make against me in the special courts! Cuba is my fatherland, and I shall never return to it or I shall return with the dignity I have pledged myself to. The bridges have been burned: Either we conquer the fatherland at any price so that we can live with dignity and honor, or we shall remain without one.

> The fatherland means something more than oppression, something more than a piece of land without freedom and without life.[1]

It is hardly necessary to justify the use of this means to set forth our ideas. The closing down of the newspaper *La Calle*, whose courageous stand won it the sympathy of the people, increasing its circulation to more than 20,000 copies in only a few weeks, made clear the more or less concealed muzzle which the dictatorship has maintained over the legal press in Cuba for more than three years.

The censorship and the Law on Public Order, by which the regime sought to conceal from the people the barbarous Moncada massacre, are a threat to the mass media. The closing down of the civic-spirited newspaper of Luis Orlando[2] was yet another warning to the press that their opinions cannot exceed certain limits, in reality so as not to

[1] The editors have not been able to ascertain the origin of this quote. Eds.
[2] Luis Orlando Rodríguez was the editor of *La Calle*. Eds.

threaten those in power. The same warnings were given on other occasions with the torture of Mario Kuchilán and Armando Hernández, the assault on the "University of the Air"[3] and the newspaper *Pueblo*, the castor oil torture of the CMKC announcers, the attacks on numerous photographers, the sentencing of Luis Conte Agüero and Pincho Gutiérrez, the confinement of Pardo Llada, Guido García Inclán, Max Lesnick, Rivadulla, García Sifredo, and other arbitrary actions which make the list of attacks on the free expression of thought since March 10 interminable.

The governmental "inquisition" was especially cruel with regard to this writer. After our article in *Bohemia* answering the cowardly provocation of a miserable henchman who went out for blood but ended up bleeding, our appearance on any radio or television program was drastically and categorically prohibited.

On two consecutive occasions the Partido del Pueblo Cubano broadcasts were prevented. The broadcasts could continue only on the condition that I would not be heard by the people. In an urgent telegram dated June 13, 1955, the network was informed that proceedings had been initiated to deprive me of this right. This was an unprecedented case: It was not a radio station or a program that was censured, but a citizen. That great hustler of governmental favors, Ramón Vasconcelos, who bought a newspaper when he was a minister under Carlos Prío and who launched the most terrible attacks against him when Prío took off with everything, was not closed down—and he was not even a Batista supporter just prior to March 10, because he was trying to obtain a senatorial post through the Ortodoxo Party. He has found his own method of concealing the truth.[4]

Every instrument of power was used successfully to impose silence on me everywhere, which demonstrates to what extent any new moral protest is doomed today in Cuba because of the shameful coalition of oppression, vested interests, and general hypocrisy.

Thus, Santiago Rey, another cynic who was a Prío follower until March 10, 1952, a Batista follower until October 10, 1944,[5] and a Machado follower until August 12, 1933,[6] ordered the closing of the newspaper *La Calle* the day our article entitled "One Can No Longer Live Here" appeared. We answered one of the stupid accusations of Colonel Carratalá and challenged him to go to the courts and denounce the names of the police chiefs who have gotten rich from the proceeds

---

[3] A radio program transmitted from Havana. Eds.
[4] Ramón Vasconcelos was communications minister at the time. Eds.
[5] Date when Ramón Grau San Martín became president of Cuba. Eds.
[6] Date when dictator Gerardo Machado was overthrown. Eds.

of illegal gambling. We were left without a platform from which to express our views.

The same happened with every public gathering at which it was known we would be present, beginning with the meeting to welcome the political prisoners on the university steps. They went to the extreme of prohibiting the showing of a film of our visit to the National News Agency with Guido García Inclán, for they were irritated by the demonstrations of sympathy expressed by the public. We were left without the right to speak or write or hold public gatherings or to exercise civic rights of any kind—as if we were not Cubans, as if we had no rights in our fatherland, as if we had been born pariahs and slaves in the glorious land of our immortal liberators. Can this be called constitutionality, equality before the law, guarantees for peaceful struggle?[7]

In Cuba one only has the right to write what pleases the six libelous papers the dictatorship maintains with the money stolen from teachers and public employees. In Cuba only the unconditional supporters of the regime or those who play the game of a docile and inoffensive opposition have the right to meet freely. In Cuba only those who get down on their knees have the right to live.

The bad faith of the regime, the mean spirit in which the amnesty the people demanded was granted, has been obvious from the very first moments. Three days after we had been freed the first false accusation of subversive activity was hurled at us, when our families had not even had time to welcome us and express their joy in the naïve belief that a different stage of calm and respect for the citizen was beginning, and that their children would not find themselves again involved in the maelstrom of revolutionary struggle, agony, and martyrdom which has already lasted three and a half years. In this struggle the greatest pain is not that of the fighter who struggles resolutely, without worrying about the risk, but that of the mothers who, as Martí said, weep with inconsolable sorrow "out of love and not reason."

We had changed prisons. The spectacle of hunger and injustice was everywhere. And the harsh struggle that idealism required, dignity demanded, and duty ordered, began again, to end only when no oppressors remain in Cuba or when the last revolutionary falls on this sad and martyred land.

Those who doubt the determination with which we shall carry forward our promise, those who believe that we are reduced to impotence because we have no private fortune to put at the disposal of

---

[7] In the original the term used is *lucha cívica*. Eds.

our cause nor millions stolen from the people, should remember the twenty-sixth of July. They should remember that a handful of men who had been ignored, without economic resources of any kind, and without any weapons except their dignity and their ideals, stood up to the second largest military installation in Cuba and did what others with vast resources have not yet done. They should remember that there is a people with faith in its honored defenders, ready to gather the necessary funds penny by penny so that those who will achieve freedom with honest blood and honest money will not be without weapons again. Finally, let them remember that for each one of the young men who fell at Santiago de Cuba there are thousands more awaiting the signal to go into battle, that the revolutionary reserves of the people now include a hundred thousand idealists. And for each of those writers who preach cowardice, vilification, defeatism, and compromise with the oppressors, advising our people to submit peacefully to the tyranny, renouncing their tradition as a rebellious and honorable people as if nothing had happened in Cuba on March 10, there are a million voices cursing them.

The voices are those who suffer hunger in the countryside and the cities, the desperate voices of those who have no work or hope of finding any, the indignant voices of our workers for whom it was a cursed hour when Batista snatched power, the voices of an entire people trampled on and deceived, who have seen their children murdered in the shadows and who are not resigned to living without rights and freedom.

Stubborn fools are those who believe that a revolutionary movement can be measured by the millions available to it and not by the reason, idealism, determination, and honor of its fighters! "What matters," Martí said, "is not the number of weapons in one's hand, but the number of stars on one's forehead!"[8] To those who ask us to abandon the revolutionary struggle and accept the crumbs of legality the regime offers, we answer, Why do you not ask Batista to abandon office first?

He is the only obstacle. It was he who used violence when all legal paths were open. He protects and ,safeguards the henchmen who murder and kill. He, only he, is the man who has provoked this situation of uncertainty, unrest, and ruin.

Why ask a people to renounce their rights instead of asking a lucky adventurer to abandon a power that does not belong to him? To those who impudently advise participation in partial elections as a national

---

[8] This is a literal translation of a quotation often used by Castro. It is meant to contrast the physical with the mental or spiritual, emphasizing the importance of the latter. Eds.

solution, we answer: Who is concerned with those elections? The discontent is found, not on the part of the politicians who seek posts, but in the people who seek justice. Those who believe that serious political, social, and economic problems can be solved by simply satisfying the appetites of a hundred or so miserable candidates for a few posts as mayors and representatives think very badly of Cuban citizens. What have petty politics given the country in the last 50 years? Speeches, sinecures, congas,[9] lies, compromises, deceit, betrayals, improper enrichment of a clique of rogues, empty talk, corruption, infamy. We do not view politics as the traditional politicians do. We are concerned not with personal benefit but with the benefit of the people whom we serve as missionaries of an ideal of redemption. Glory is worth more than triumph, and "there is only one glory for certain—that of a soul at peace with itself."[10] Those electoral crumbs with which Batista buys his unimportant enemies should not be offered to us. The pride with which we put them aside is worth more than all of the electoral posts put together.

To those who speak of general elections, we ask: Elections with or without Batista? The general elections of November 1 with Batista were the most scandalous and fraudulent in our republican history, a permanent stain on our democratic tradition that set us back to a stage which it seemed we had transcended. What answer have the defenders of an election presided over by Batista? What arguments do they have left after this unprecedented scandal? Did they not employ precisely the same reasons, the same words, the same lies before? Can anyone forget the mobilization of tanks along the highways and the dramatic farewells by Tabernilla[11] at the terminal station, as if the soldiers were leaving for the battlefield? After that November experience, after the March 10 coup within 80 days of elections, for the simple reason that they did not have the slightest chance of winning, can anyone make our skeptical people believe in honest elections with Batista in power? Those who want to create the illusion that the events of 1944[12] could be repeated deliberately and criminally betray the people. They pretend to make us believe that the circumstances are the same. They forget the signs of the times. They do not distinguish between the present moment in which America has been invaded by reactionary dictatorships and 1944, when the world was shaken by a wave of popular enthusiasm and democratic optimism, a

[9] Cuban dance. It has the connotation of irresponsibility. Eds.
[10] The editors have not been able to ascertain the origin of the quote. Eds.
[11] General Francisco Tabernilla. Eds.
[12] When Batista allowed free elections and transferred power to the opposition. Eds.

world which with the last shots in Europe conceived hopes for a happier and more humane future for its peoples. Batista then yielded to world public opinion, as the cowardly ruling cliques of Peru, Venezuela, Guatemala, and other countries of the American continent yielded.

Therefore, the only civic solution we would accept, the only honest, logical, and just solution, is immediate general elections without Batista. Meanwhile, we shall continue tirelessly our revolutionary line. And we have a question for those who demand general elections as the only solution: What will you do if Batista flatly refuses to allow elections? Will you cross your arms and weep like Mary Magdalene for what you lacked the courage to demand with honor? "Rights are taken, not begged; they are seized, not pleaded for."[13] The people await the answer too.

To those who affirm that the 1940 Constitution has been reestablished, we state that they are brazenly lying. A fundamental principle of our constitution categorically prohibits presidential reelection, and Batista reelected himself to that post on November 1. He did not even resign his post: He asked for a leave of absence and left a lackey in the presidential palace. If the Constitution states that anyone who has occupied that post cannot do so again until eight years have gone by, Batista's continuation in the presidency is unconstitutional.

Another precept establishes that sovereignty resides in the people and that from them all powers are derived. If this is true, and the Constitution is in effect, none of those who elected themselves in the unilateral and fraudulent November first elections has the right to occupy the posts he holds. All of them should resign immediately. Sovereignty resides in the people and not in the barracks. Batista is the main enemy of our constitution, which he ignominiously destroyed on March 10. There is no room for both in the same republic.

To those who accuse the Revolution of upsetting the economy of the country, we answer: There is no economy for the rural workers who have no land; there is no economy for the millions of Cubans who are unemployed; there is no economy for the railroad, port, sugar, hemp, textile, and bus workers and those in the many sectors whose wages Batista has mercilessly reduced. And there will be an economy for them only through a just revolution that will redistribute the land, mobilize the vast resources of the country, and equalize social conditions, putting an end to privilege and exploitation. Is it possible to expect that miracle from the candidates running in the forthcoming partial elections?

[13] Quote from Antonio Maceo. Eds.

Or are they talking perhaps of the economy of the senators who earn 5,000 pesos a month, of the millionaire generals, of the foreign trusts that exploit the public services, of the great landowners, of the tribe of parasites who thrive and get rich at the expense of the state and the people? Then we welcome the Revolution that upsets the economy of a few who so greedily profit from it! After all, man does not live by bread alone.

Another question for those who speak of the economy: Has not Batista jeopardized the credit of the country for 30 years? Has not the public debt increased to more than 800 million pesos? Is there not a deficit of more than 100 million? Are not the monetary reserves of the nation pledged to foreign banks in a desperate search for money? Were not 350 million pesos of the most recent loan wasted on the purchase of jet planes and things of that nature, without plan or program, for no other reason than personal whim? Can one play in this manner with the destiny of a nation? Did anyone authorize him to undertake those insane credit ventures? Did he consult the people in any way? Finally, how many millions have individuals very close to Batista transferred periodically to North American banks? It is for us more than anyone else to be concerned because we and future generations will have to pay the terrible consequences of that corrupt and unchecked policy. The country's economy requires an immediate and radical change of government.

To those who assert that the Revolution brings sorrow to Cuban families, we answer: Sorrow is caused by the hunger decimating families in the Cuban countryside; sorrow is caused by the corrupt politicians who steal hospital funds; sorrow is caused by the henchmen who murdered Rubén Batista, the Santiago couple Oscar Medina Salomón and María Rodríguez, the Camagüey labor leader Mario Aróstegui, the Auténtico leader Mario Fortuny, the revolutionary soldier Gonzalo Miranda Oliva, the naval commander Jorge Agostini, and the seventy young prisoners in the Moncada Barracks. This is the blood of students, workers, professionals, honest military men, men and women of all parties and all social classes—honest blood, Cuban blood, the blood of fighters who could not defend themselves at the moment they were sacrificed.

Today more than ever the spokesmen of the dictatorship emphasize public discussion and legal methods as the path their opponents should follow. They did not think that way when on March 10 they perpetrated the most unjustifiable crime conceivable against the nation, and at that time all legal paths were really open for political struggle! Now that they have blocked all paths toward peace, they speak of peace. Now that everything has been arranged through force to suit them, they defend legality. Now after four years of being in power, a power to which they have no right, getting rich and profiting under the eyes of the entire nation, distributing privileges and sinecures among friends, unconditional supporters, and relatives of the whole clique, having constantly used abuse and force to maintain their privileges, now they shout that the only just and decent way of fighting them is through politics. Politics, as conceived by Martí and as we understand it, is the art of keeping the peace and greatness of the country, but not the vile art of creating a fortune at its expense.

> The fatherland is not a tool we can use or discard as we choose; nor is the Republic a means of maintaining the lazy and the haughty, well fed and housed, who in the baseness of their egotism believe themselves to be the natural responsibility of the country and the inevitable masters of their inferior people.[14]

Those who chant their devout songs in favor of peace as if there could be peace without freedom, peace without law, peace without justice, have still not found the words to condemn *the one hundred crimes* which have been committed since March 10, nor the daily outrages, the raids on homes in the middle of the night, the arbitrary arrests, the false accusations, the unjust convictions. What have they said about the young man from Guantánamo, a humble employee of the newspaper *La Calle*, who was atrociously tortured and on whose strangled testicles corrosive acid was thrown by his executioners? Nothing! Absolutely nothing!

Beware, Cubans, of those who advise cowardly submission to the tyranny, whatever the source of this advice, because these people are paid a price for their hypocritical sermons by Batista.

The peace Batista wants is the peace Spain wanted. The peace we want is the peace Martí wanted.

To speak of peace under tyranny is to offend the memory of all those who died for the freedom and happiness of Cuba. Then as well there were reformists and autonomists who fought with cowardly fury the honorable attitude of our liberators and accepted as a solution the electoral crumbs offered by the masters of that era.[15]

The streets and the parks of our cities and towns bear the names and proudly display the statues of Maceo, Martí, Máximo Gómez, Calixto García, Céspedes, Agramonte, Flor Crombet, Bartolomé Masó,

14 José Martí. Eds.
15 Refers to the *reformistas* and *autonomistas* of the nineteenth century in Cuba who opposed independence from Spain and favored a compromise with the Spanish authorities. Eds.

and other illustrious heroes who had the courage to rebel. The schools teach our glorious history, and October 10 and February 24 are celebrated with devotion.[16] These were not dates of submission or of resigned and cowardly acceptance of the existing despotism, nor were those individuals the ones who extended a begging hand to receive from Spain a post as a deputy to the royal court or in the senate of the colonial master.

All the regime's efforts will be futile. The 26th of July Movement will send its revolutionary message to all corners of Cuba. Tens of thousands of our revolutionary manifestos will circulate clandestinely throughout the country, invading factories, farms, and villages. Men and women who want to aid our cause will reproduce them by hand or machine everywhere, knowing that thereby they are doing their little bit in this heroic struggle of the nation against its oppressors. They will even penetrate the barracks, the warships, the police stations, and the military camps.

We do not fear talking to the military, we have no hatred in our hearts for honest Cubans—the military man who has been vilely used as a tool so that cliques of politicians gain power and wealth, the military man who is forced to constant and cruel guard duty to safeguard the interests of a handful of scoundrels who take no risks; the military man who is forced to die without glory for a regime hated by the people; the military man whom Batista miserably deceives. Batista has not yet found a way of justifying the unlimited enrichment of the high commanders, nor the violations of military seniority in favor of the families and friends of the generals, setting aside merit and ability, nor the presence of gangsters in the government, nor the frequent decreases in wages while every senator whom no one elected and who represents no one collects 5,000 pesos. Batista himself has increased his income to the fabulous sum of 70,000 per month, seventy times what the prime minister of England earns. We defended the military when no one defended them, and fought them when they supported the tyranny, but we shall welcome them with open arms when they join the cause of liberty. We shall tell the military the truth, as one Cuban to another, as one man to another, without fear or flattery, and the hands and the hearts of many honest soldiers will be reached by our revolutionary proclamations. The military must be freed from the tyranny too.

The 26th of July Movement is formed without hatred for anyone.

[16] On October 10, 1868, the war of independence began in Cuba. After ten years of fighting a truce was signed between the Cubans and the Spaniards, but on February 24, 1895, the war started again. Eds.

It is not a political party but a revolutionary movement. Its ranks are open to all Cubans who sincerely desire to see political democracy reestablished and social justice introduced in Cuba. Its leadership is collective and secret, formed by new men of strong will who are not accomplices of the past. Its structure is functional. Young and old, men and women, workers and peasants, students and professionals, can join its fighting groups, its youth cadres, its secret workers' cells, its women's organizations, its economic sections, and its underground distribution apparatus throughout the country, for not all can take up arms. There will never be sufficient weapons to equip each of those who wishes to give his life in the struggle, but each can participate to the extent that he can, contributing money, distributing proclamations, or leaving work in a gesture of solidarity and proletarian support when the revolutionary call to struggle comes. Above all, this must be a revolution of the people, with the blood of the people and the sweat of the people. Its broad and courageous program can be synthesized in the following essential points:

1. Outlawing of the latifundia, distribution of the land among peasant families; permanent and untransferable granting of property to all existing small tenant farmers, sharecroppers, small holders, and farm laborers; state economic and technical aid; reduction of taxes.

2. Reestablishment of all the workers' gains taken away by the dictatorship; the right of the worker to broad participation in the profits of all the large industrial, commercial, and mining enterprises, which should be paid out in addition to salaries or wages at given intervals during the year.

3. Immediate industrialization of the country by means of a vast plan made and promoted by the state, which will have to decisively mobilize all of the human and economic resources of the nation in the supreme effort to free the country from the moral and material prostration in which it finds itself. It is inconceivable that there should be hunger in a country so endowed by nature; every shelf should be stocked with goods and all hands employed productively.

4. Drastic decrease in all rents, effectively benefiting the 2,200,000 persons who are today spending a third of their income on rent; construction by the state of decent housing to shelter the 400,000 families crowded into filthy single rooms, huts, shacks, and tenements; extension of electricity to the 2,800,000 persons in our rural and suburban sectors who have none; initiation of a policy designed to transform each renter into an owner of the apartment in which he lives on the basis of long-term amortization.

5. Nationalization of public services: telephone, electricity, and gas.

6. Construction of ten children's cities to fully shelter and edu-

cate 200,000 children of workers and peasants who cannot currently feed and clothe them.

7. Extension of education, following a previous reform of all teaching methods, to the farthest corner of the country, so that every Cuban will be able to develop his mental and physical aptitudes in a decent living environment.

8. General reform of the tax system and establishment of modern methods for the collection of taxes to avoid tax evasion and mishandling of funds, so that the state can meet its needs and the people will know that what they pay from their income goes back to society to benefit all classes.

9. Reorganization of public administration and establishment of administrative training.

10. Establishment of an inviolable military roster safeguarding the members of the armed forces so that they can be removed from their posts only for good reasons proved in administrative litigation courts. Elimination of the death penalty in the Military Penal Code for crimes committed during peacetime. Rendering of socially beneficial services by the armed services throughout the country, making economic surveys, land surveys and demarcation, and building by their corps of engineers, with special remuneration, hygienic schools and decent housing for peasants, workers, and members of the armed forces themselves, who will retain ownership when they retire from service.

11. Generous and decent pay to all public employees: teachers, office workers, and members of the armed forces, retired civilian and military personnel.

12. Establishment of adequate measures in education and legislation to put an end to every vestige of discrimination for reasons of race or sex which regrettably still exists in our social and economic life.

13. Social security and state unemployment compensation.

14. Reorganization of the judicial branch and abolition of the treasury courts.[17]

15. Confiscation of all the assets of embezzlers acquired under all past governments, without exceptions of any kind, so that the Republic can recover the hundreds of millions which have been taken from it with impunity. These will be invested in the implementation of some of the undertakings described above. Does anyone doubt that they could have been possible if the nation had had honest governments?

These points will be fully explained in a pamphlet that will be distributed throughout the country.

The Cuban Revolution will carry out all of the reforms following the spirit and the letter of our 1940 Constitution, without taking from anyone what is legitimately his and compensating everyone for the

[17] The Spanish term used is *tribunales de hacienda*. Eds.

losses he has suffered, fully aware that in the long run all of society will be benefited.

The Cuban Revolution will firmly punish all the acts of violence against the individual committed under the tyranny, but it will reject and repress any evidence of ignoble vengeance inspired by hatred or base passions.

The Cuban Revolution does not compromise with groups or persons of any sort, nor does it offer anyone governmental employment or posts within the armed forces. It will respect competence and merit wherever it may be found, and it will never regard the state as the booty of a triumphant group. A revolutionary movement which has already given the fatherland a legion of heroic martyrs who neither prospered from the nation nor had any ambition but to serve their country tirelessly and without self-interest can speak thus to the nation.

In adopting again the line of sacrifice, we assume before history responsibility for our actions. And in making our declaration of faith in a happier world for the Cuban people, we think like Martí that a sincere man does not seek where his advantage lies but where his duty is, and that the only practical man is the one whose present dream will be the law of tomorrow.

On behalf of the 26th of July Revolutionary Movement,

Fidel Castro

Message to the Congress of Ortodoxo Militants (August 15, 1955)

Comrades in ideals:

It is hard writing these words from a distance when our thoughts never for a moment leave our martyred and enslaved fatherland, for whose redemption we work unceasingly.

It is not even possible to be assured now as I write this letter that the Congress will be allowed, because in Cuba there is no security for anything. The only rights that survive are not given as inherent prerogatives of all citizens and political parties, but are offered as charity as long as one sinks down on one's knees. For three and a half years we

Letter written on August 15, 1955, from Mexico. Luis Conte Agüero, *Fidel Castro, vida y obra* (Havana: Editorial Lex, 1959), pp. 300–307.

have pleaded on our knees for freedom, and this has only served to facilitate placing the yoke on our bended necks.

Looking at Cuba and all that happens in it, closely following, despite the distance, all the stands and intentions, I believe that the Congress of Militants can have a decisive importance for the life of the party and the struggle for national liberation. It could become a historic event of great consequence if, moving away from useless lengthy statements, vacillation, and the paralysis that has reduced Cuba's greatest political party to impotence, it has the courage and boldness to adopt decisions appropriate to the crucial moment that the Republic faces.

The time is ripe for false historical analogies that the worst advisers of the people want to skillfully exploit.

Those who believe that the history of 1944 will be repeated deceive themselves or deceive others.[1] They disregard the signs of the times, forgetting that that event occurred in a world agitated by popular enthusiasm and the democratic optimism awakened by the end of the war. Batista, like many other dictators of Latin America, yielded to world public opinion then. The times are different: Just look at Latin America and you will see the panorama of our continent, invaded by reactionary dictatorships, in full democratic retrogression.

We are in the 1950s and not in the 1940s, and these years are very different in the historical perspective of the continent. In 1958, the history of 1954 will be repeated, but never that of 1944. Batista will not refrain from leaving a puppet of his in the presidential palace in order to continue ruling from his estate, like Trujillo, Somoza, Carías, and others cut from the same cloth.

Have we not listened to all his speeches from Camp Columbia since March 10? Even the story of the crane, has it not awakened the naïve to reality?[2]

Can anything else be expected from a man who never vacillated in destroying the Constitution eighty days before general elections because he knew he could not win; who, against the opinion of the immense majority of the country, never vacillated in reelecting himself without even resigning formally from his post? Can anything else be expected from a man who permitted the murder of seventy young prisoners in the Moncada Barracks, who keeps in their respective commands those responsible for that unprecedented massacre, who arms

[1] In 1944 Batista ceded power to a political opponent when Grau won the presidential elections. Eds.

[2] The crane was the symbol of Batista's political party, which was said to have acquired health after very severe threats to its existence. Eds.

himself more and more and establishes new intelligence and repressive agencies? Can we not see everywhere the symptoms that denote the intention of remaining permanently in power? Or is this the reverse of the famous story? Are we going to believe that under the disguise of the wolf we shall find a harmless grandma?

The calling of general elections, considered by all sectors of public opinion as the only formula for a peaceful solution of the tragedy Cuba is living, will never be granted by the regime, especially when faced by an unarmed opposition that has not demonstrated its intention to demand in stronger form the rights snatched from the people. It is enough to observe how many insults have been hurled at the venerable person of Don Cosme de la Torriente and the Sociedad de Amigos de la República as a reply to their negotiations.

It is really difficult to believe that the smallest concession from the dictatorship can be attained when the prologue of all the demands begins with a beatific confession of pacifism. In other words, it means: "Batista please grant us such and such demands, but be completely assured that if you deny them absolutely nothing will happen, because we shall not resort to means other than that of energetic declarations in the newspapers."

Batista in a ringing voice says: peace, peace, peace. And many of his stupid adversaries only want to declaim also: peace, peace, peace.

It does not occur to anyone to cry aloud, with all the force of reason: In order to have peace it is necessary to have justice; in order to have peace it is necessary to have rights; in order to have peace it is necessary to have freedom, and the president of the republic must resign. Batista's ambition, his unlimited eagerness to rule and to enrich himself, these are the only reasons why there is no peace, and why so much Cuban blood has been spilled and so much grief can be found in every home. It is because of these that the economy is bankrupt, and the Republic has been in continual distress for more than three years. Batista, you should resign, because the whims of an adventurer cannot be put ahead of the interests of six million Cubans; if you do not resign, and if you keep trying to impose yourself through force, the six million also will use force, and we shall sweep you and your clique of infamous murderers from the face of the earth.

The opposition asks for immediate general elections. A question can be asked in this respect: elections with or without Batista? General elections with Batista took place on November 1, and they were the most scandalous elections recorded in our history, an unforgettable stain on our democratic tradition that took us back to the early years of the Republic. General elections were to be held on June 1, 1952, and Batista, foreseeing his defeat, eighty days prior to the elections, stabbed the nation in the back on March 10. After these experiences, who can make our skeptical people believe that honest elections could be held with Batista in power? Does he want them? If he wants them, what about the generals? If he wants those elections, if the generals want them, if elections were to be held, if they were honest, how many months would we have to wait to see repeated the unpunished treason of March 10?

But an even more important question could be asked. The opposition asks for general elections *as the only formula for a peaceful solution.* What will be done if Batista, as is possible, refuses to grant that formula considered to be the only solution? Will they cross their arms and cry like Mary Magdalene because they lack the courage to demand anything with honor? We know already that many will cry, "Every man for himself!" And they will dash headlong to place their names on the electoral ticket to participate in the partial elections offered—elections that will not be held because sooner than that we shall be fighting on Cuban soil.

Cuba finds itself at a crossroads, moving toward the most shameful political and moral prostration. It could last twenty years, as it has lasted in Santo Domingo and other countries of Latin America, or Cuba can free itself once and for all from oppression.

One road is called partial elections: compromise with the tyranny, recognition of the legitimacy of the regime, unlimited ambitions for municipal posts and congressional seats, hunger, misery, injustice, dishonor, betrayal of the people, and criminal neglect of our dead.

The other road is called *revolution:* the exercise of the right of all people to revolt against oppression, historic continuation of the struggle of 1868, 1895, and 1933, adamant intransigence toward the treacherous coup of March 10 and the shameful masquerade of November, justice for the oppressed and hungry people, dignity, selflessness, sacrifice, and loyalty to the dead.

There is no other alternative. The Ortodoxos know that the hour has come to choose one or the other.

What awaits those who choose the former is the contempt of the people and infamy. The ephemeral personal advantages they might obtain will be the twelve coins with which Batista buys his spineless enemies. I doubt that anyone will follow them; a people is not moved to satisfy the appetites of a dozen timid candidates with the pretext that positions should be obtained (for them!!!). The Ortodoxo Party was not founded by obtaining positions. Eduardo Chibás became great by renouncing such positions, and those who followed him abandoned power and went to struggle in the open, sacrificing ministries, senatorial posts, and mayoralties. There are the examples of Luis Orlando Rodríguez, who was sports director; Rubén Acosta, who was an election supervisor; Orlando Castro, Hugo Mir, Erasmo Gómez, and hundreds of other *compañeros* who resigned from duties which they honestly had carried out. The Ortodoxo Party will be condemned to disappear and will soon find itself at the end of the ballot if it participates in partial elections. What a sad fate for a party whose emblem was carried by one of the greatest men of the Republic! The name of Chibás made into a standard for thieves and ambitious men!

The other alternative is the one we have already adopted irrevocably. It is one of sacrifice, but also of honor; it is honest, useful, worthy, heroic, and is a part of our glorious tradition. Who can forget those words of Martí to Gómez when, as today, there were Cubans who begged for posts in the Spanish court in return for putting up a harmless opposition!

> Great moments require great sacrifices; and I come to you to plead that you leave in the hands of your children and your wife the wealth you have made through hard labor, and come to help conquer Cuba's freedom, with risk of death. I come here to ask you to change your comfort and your glorious peace for the hazards of revolution and the grief of a life consecrated to the service of men.

It is not honest in good times to ask the people to vote for us because we are the best, the ones who sacrificed the most, the ones ready to give all for Cuba; and then, when times change and the rights of the people are destroyed, and they are mistreated, dispossessed, humiliated, to go quietly to our homes, unable to face the sacrifices that the moment demands from us.

There are some among us who—let us say so now—at election time use all their savings and even mortgage their homes in order to assure their own victory. It is hard to say this! Then, when the time came to do the same for Cuba, there were men who had to die practically empty-handed because we lacked resources. Abel Santamaría, Fernando Chenard, Pedro Marrero, Elpidio Sosa, Boris Luis Santa Coloma,[3] to mention only a few—unknown young men who did not aspire to official posts. They gave all, even their lives, while others wasted thousands of dollars in politicking and refused to give a miserable dollar for the fatherland.

The Ortodoxos must analyze their behavior from March 10 on,

---

[3] Young men who died in the attack of the Moncada Barracks on July 26, 1953. Eds.

when victory was snatched from our hands. From being the most radical party in the opposition, we allowed those without morality, prestige or the backing of the people to capture the vanguard position of the struggle against the dictatorship. It has been sad to see the spectacle of thousands of our best men serving in the subversive organizations of those who just yesterday were our greatest adversaries. They cut our cadres by a tenth and this reduced the mass of Ortodoxo fighters. All of this was due to the fact that we did not know how to face the situation with dignity, investing our best energies in futile and endless squabbles that have left us with a fear of action.

I know that I am touching the sore points in the progress followed by the Ortodoxos since March 10. But the truth should be told once and for all if we want to get rid of the cursed helplessness that has burdened us since then.

The Congress of Militants has met. It is a great step; we congratulate sincerely its organizers and Raúl Chibás, who gave it all of his support. There is a program: Immediate general elections, the repeal of repressive laws, and other points are demanded. Good, but not enough! The masses will be mobilized behind these watchwords! But it is not enough! A further step forward must be made. What the Ortodoxos will do if the regime refuses to grant these demands must be stated. The answer must be ready for the time when the people, tired of abstract phrases, will ask, "And then, what do we do?" This question cannot be postponed. Our great sin has been to postpone things. We have done so for three years. We have to work with foresight. Now or never! Tomorrow, as Ingenieros says, is the pious lie with which feeble wills deceive themselves.

The fighters of the 26th of July await the determined support of the best Ortodoxos of the whole island. We do not constitute a tendency within the party; we are the revolutionary apparatus of Chibasismo[4] which is rooted in its cadres and from which it emerged to struggle against the dictatorship when the Ortodoxo Party lay impotent and divided in a thousand pieces. We have never abandoned its ranks, and we have remained loyal to the purest principles of the great fighter whose death will be commemorated tomorrow. The man[5] who occupies his place today has all our sympathies because of his selflessness, his unifying prestige, and his zeal to move the party forward. We hope to receive from him and all good Ortodoxos the maximum of encouragement in our unbreakable decision to fight, a decision which is sealed with the blood of 80 of our comrades.

4 Eduardo Chibás's followers. Eds.
5 Refers to Raúl Chibás. Ed.

In conclusion, before ending, I wish to clarify a personal matter. I read in several newspapers that in the Camagüey meeting of activists it was agreed, among other things, to solicit my return to Cuba. Perhaps the information is mistaken. If it is true, I do not doubt the love and good intentions that are behind such an invitation. It is not right, however, to ask for the return of a fighter to whom all civic means of struggle were closed without clarifying the terms of the return. I plan to return, as our independence fighters returned whenever tyranny threw them out of Cuban territory; I shall never return any other way. This is not the hour to ask a revolutionary to submit, a comrade that for four years has fulfilled his duty without rest, who has not gone abroad to relax, who lives honestly and poorly because he did not take with him a fortune stolen from the people. This is the hour to help with all resources available, not him, but the honorable idea of freedom that he represents and that he has promised to fulfill.

I wish the last words of this letter to be a fervent remembrance of the great leader whose heroic death will be commemorated tomorrow.

I think of him, whose history was formed fighting Machado's dictatorship and not aspiring to posts in the elections convoked by the tyrant. I think of the man who rejected power, with all its advantages, to pick up the banner of the betrayed revolution; the man who, when they tried to gag him with a decree, did not hesitate to mobilize the people and move forward under attack toward the CMQ.[6] I think what he would have done now. I think of the man who when he believed sacrifice necessary did not hesitate to kill himself, a last knock on the door that resounded in the hearts of thousands and thousands of Cubans. A last knock on the door that fell on a vacuum! He is the example, he who taught us that an example is worth more than a man. He tells us today that this struggle should only end when no oppressors are left in his fatherland or the last revolutionary has died on this enslaved and sorrowful soil.

With a fraternal embrace to all the *compañeros*, I request the chairman to read this message.

Fidel Castro

---

[6] Radio and television station in Havana where Chibás died. Eds.

Letter to Melba Hernández
(October 4, 1955)

My dear doctor:[1]

Yesterday, Monday, at 9:00 P.M., Alex arrived from the interior greatly satisfied with the tour he made.[2] He is not writing you today because he is very tired from the trip, but he has expressed to me some of his viewpoints, which I shall transmit to you.

As soon as he arrived, I gave him Ñ's report, which he read right away showing his satisfaction.[3] All here have found it very good. Alex will answer him, as well as the labor leader, point by point.

Alex wants you all to be very clear on the matter of the election of a secretary general for the Juventud.[4] He cannot be a candidate for that position, nor can he present himself as such at any time. This is the criterion of all of us and the only point where we disagree with Ñ's magnificent report. It will be convenient for our people within the Juventud to make a declaration to the effect that Alex has never aspired to any position within the party, that he rejected the post offered him as a member of the party's executive council, as well as the post of president of Havana's Municipal Assembly, and that you are certain he would not accept under any circumstances the post of secretary general of the Juventud. Also, it should state that the militants of the 26th of July, within the working masses and Cuban youth, only aspire to be in the vanguard of the inevitable Revolution—to which Alex is committed today body and soul—gathering for it in a solid movement the firmest and most militant elements of our generation. The struggle within the Juventud Ortodoxa is only a part of the larger plan we are developing within the revolutionary sectors of our country.

You should draw up the declaration following essentially the ideas stated above so that the present conflict will not confuse public opinion as to Alex's role in this whole process. It would be a good idea if the "lawyer" skillfully wrote the declaration in such a manner that

Letter written on October 4, 1955, from Mexico City. Luis Conte Agüero, *Fidel Castro, vida y obra* (Havana: Editorial Lex, 1959), pp. 314–318.

[1] *Doctor* was Melba Hernández's underground name. Eds.

[2] Alex was a pseudonym used by Fidel Castro. Eds.

[3] Ñ was the underground name used by Antonio López, coordinator of Havana's clandestine 26th of July Movement. He died on April 9, 1958. Eds.

[4] Refers to Juventud Ortodoxa, youth section of the Ortodoxo Party. Eds.

instead of weakening, it will strengthen the work of the 26th of July militants inside the Juventud.

If the break is inevitable, we ask ourselves why not have as secretary general of the Juventud Ortodoxa a veteran of the Moncada? Although Anillo[5] is an intelligent and capable person, we all believe that Ñ should be the person for the post. His concept of the role of the Juventud in this whole process has been marvelously stated in his report. We believe that he is capable, due to his inexhaustible energy, of carrying the plan forward. If you agree with us, and he does not, you should convince him. He will be obliged to accept the post as an order of the Movement's leadership. We are concerned about his family and economic situation, but we are ready to sacrifice in order to provide him with the necessary resources.

It is very important that amid the maneuvers of the struggle within the Juventud we begin to demand, from now on, the payment of the membership dues. We should emphasize incessantly that the fulfillment of this duty will be the index by which the loyalty of our militants to principles and to revolutionary discipline will be judged. The more rigorous this demand, the more we insist on it, the greater the fighting spirit of the organization will be. This is an axiom of every politico-revolutionary movement: If we tolerate the nonfulfillment of duties, our fighting spirit and faith are weakened. Also, the collection of funds is the stepping-stone of our struggle. Alex is completely sure that if this point is satisfactorily fulfilled everything else will be possible and easy. He has studied the circumstances in which our plan will develop, and as you know it covers many practical details.

We think that the idea of developing the Movement within the Juventud around a program is very good. It demonstrates how every day our men assimilate the techniques of revolutionary struggle and improve the methods of action and organization. To carry out this norm to its maximum should be our principal point. It is encouraging to see how in the middle of so many difficulties, surrenders, and betrayals, our legion of revolutionary youth resolutely advances toward its objectives and creates an unbreakable fighting spirit. That spirit can be found in our youth, the proletariat, and the fighting groups, and it will spread to the people, preparing them for the final battle. It will do away with the passing skepticism planted by Prío's insurrectional frustration. Just look how our movement has never given up action, activity, and its fighting spirit. The faith with which we

[5] Refers to René Anillo, then studying law at the University of Havana and closely associated with the Directorio Revolucionario.

work will end by breaking the curtain of silence that the government and politicians of the pseudo-opposition have tried to encourage.

The people will end by firmly supporting those who do not vacillate today. It does not matter what comments the press makes about our daily struggle, as it has done with regard to the Juventud. In fact it helps us because it agitates those young people who are inactive and awakens passion toward the task we are carrying out. It also shows that the revolutionary current grows daily and that the insurrectional resolution adopted at the Congress of Ortodoxo Militants will not become another hollow promise in the country's political comedy. One by one all the redoubts of the party will fall. In our general plan of action we will take the workers', women's, and youth sections of the party. When we control them we will see what the executive council will do. To all these must be added all the revolutionary fighters that do not belong to any political party, the young students, the worker's cells in all the labor unions—all of which will not see in our movement a Fico, a Gerardo Vázquez and his clique,[6] but rather, new, humble, fighting, and poor people who never had a government post or participated in dirty business or in politicking. Our movement presents itself with an ambitious social program which is mainly concerned with the exploited and humble classes.

We are interested in knowing what has been the reaction of the Civic Front of Women for Martí[7] to our call for joining our movement. Do not abandon for a single moment that aim and exhaust all your efforts to fulfill it, so that we can complete our cadres.

To the action groups we will dedicate our complete attention later. With regard to finances, Alex says that he is ready to write one thousand letters if you send him the names of persons who might contribute one hundred dollars. We have to collect money in the Juventud, the labor unions, among the women and the people in general. To that effect economic sections should be formed in all the towns using the services of those people who have prestige and from whom we cannot demand any other type of work. Until the hour comes to take a rifle, even if we are all near-sighted and hunchbacked from writing so much, we will continue writing, asking for help. This effort cannot stop due to lack of money.

Alex will write to the labor leaders, the youth leaders and to Fouche soon.[8]

There is a minor point that has made us unhappy: the issue of the

6 Rich Ortodoxo leaders. Eds.
7 Anti-Batista women's organization. Eds.
8 Fouche was the underground name of Pedro Miret. Eds.

manifesto. It does not escape our attention, even though we are far away, that work has been deficient in this respect. The organization of the printing press has to be improved. Next time we will send the plates in order to make things easier. The delay of two months in publishing Manifesto No. 1 gives a very bad impression.[9] Speaking of this, as soon as the *compañero* of the J. M. group from Marianao returns, he will put you in touch with a printing press that will print all we need.[10] The only way we can assure the efficiency of the printing is to have three or four different places where we can print, so that we will not have any problem in coming out with a manifesto. Two or three persons should be put exclusively in charge of developing those contacts.

We realize that you all are working hard, but we have to insist on every single thing to be done there, just as we here impose on ourselves the maximum of security in the functions we must carry out.

Alex had to go to the countryside all by himself due to lack of funds. Soon we will have to augment our security measures in general.

We send a big embrace from the *compañeros* living here and the warmest congratulations for the effort and enthusiasm that you all show.

[9] See "Manifesto No. 1 to the People of Cuba" in this volume. Eds.
[10] J. M. refers to Juan Manuel Márquez. Marianao is a Havana suburb. Eds.

Speech in New York
(November 1, 1955)

I do not live in a particular place. I reside somewhere in the Caribbean and can feel as much at home in a city like this one as on a barren and deserted little island. I live committed to the struggle, and the contingencies and sacrifices of this difficult life do not concern me; The two years I spent in solitary confinement have prepared me very well.

We all live very modestly. There are no millionaires here. Each of our men in exile sustains himself with far less than the cost of a horse to the army. None of us will ever be seen in a nightclub or bar. The first revolutionary manifesto was printed with the money from

Speech given on November 1, 1955, at the Palm Garden on 52nd Street in New York City. Vicente Cubillas, "Mitin oposicionista en Nueva York," *Bohemia* (Havana), November 6, 1955, pp. 82–83.

a pawned overcoat; but that did not undermine our morale, because we believed in the justice and reasonableness of our ideas. And today in New York alone there are thousands of Cubans ready to give a part of their salaries every month. To this must be added the Cubans who are organizing with great enthusiasm in Bridgeport, Union City, Elizabeth, Long Island, and other cities. We are doing with the émigrés the things our Apostle Martí taught us in a similar situation. Those thousands of families thrown into exile by misery and oppression, who arrive by the hundreds every month, filled with sadness and sorrow, people exiled from a land where no one speaks out, who have never been the concern of politicians because they cannot vote but are desperate to return to their fatherland if they could live an honorable life. They love Cuba greatly and today are formidable bulwarks of national liberation. The Cuban people there and here will support us. Just look at what is happening here in the Palm Garden; thousands of dollars are collected in a second. This struggle will be carried forward only with the resources of the people.

> We will find magnanimous aid in all honest hearts. And we will knock on all doors. And we will ask for contributions from town to town. And they will give because we will ask with honor.[1]

I can inform you with complete reliability that in 1956 we will be free or we will be martyrs. This struggle began for us on March 10; it has lasted almost four years, and will end with the last day of the dictatorship or our death. One of our most famous liberators stated once that whoever tried to conquer Cuba would get its soil drenched in blood.[2]

The regime is totally disoriented with regard to our revolutionary activities. Often, however, they will publish imaginary information in order to give the impression of being well-informed and to sow confusion. We have developed invincible methods of organization and work. Our apparatus of counterespionage functions much better than their espionage. Whenever their agents abroad inform the government, we immediately get the information here. All information offices and Batista's spies abroad are carefully watched by us. They want to ignore us, and they want to ignore the tens of thousands of men around the 26th of July, because we do not seek electoral posts. Moral hypocrisy has reached such a level in terms of what is said or written in Cuba that it seems that to seek a post, whatever the price of one's submission, is a virtue. To be a revolutionary ready to sacrifice for

---

[1] José Martí. Eds.
[2] Refers to Antonio Maceo. Eds.

an ideal, without asking for anything, is a crime. This is the politics of the ostrich which refuses to see reality. The surprise is going to be great for everyone!

The militants of the 26th of July will attend all the meetings to be organized in Cuba, regardless what opposition party organizes them, to shout a speech for the masses: Revolution! Revolution! Anyone who gets permission for a public meeting can count on an assured public—we also know how to use political tactics.

We are against violent methods aimed at persons from any opposition organization that disagrees with us. We are also radically opposed to terrorism and personal assault. We do not practice tyrannicide. When someone proposed to Maceo the assassination of an enemy leader, he answered,

> The man who exposes himself to death and can kill his opponent on the battlefield does not use the treacherous and disgraceful means of assassination.

Look, the Cuban people want something more than a simple change of command. Cuba longs for a radical change in every aspect of its political and social life. The people must be given something more than liberty and democracy in abstract; decent living must be given to every Cuban. The state cannot ignore the fate of any of its citizens who were born and grew up in this country. There is no greater tragedy than that of the man capable of and willing to work who suffers hunger with his family because he lacks a job. The state is unavoidably obliged to provide him with a job or to support him until he finds a job. None of the armchair formulas discussed nowadays includes a consideration of this situation, as if the grave problem of Cuba comprised only how to satisfy the ambitions of a few politicians who have been ousted from power or who want to get it. But if there is any possibility of finding a peaceful solution to this situation, we have a formula: immediate general elections without Batista. Let him resign and give power to Don Cosme de la Torriente! Every Cuban would agree with that solution!

Don Cosme de la Torriente has all of our consideration. The government's spokesmen, without respecting his venerable gray hair, have insulted him deplorably. Although there are natural differences due to time between his ideas and ours, we are aware of his patriotic intentions. His behavior will produce a positive result in this struggle to recover the democratic institutions. But what is most critical in this situation is the fact that the regime has clearly refused to listen to the proposals of all the opposition presented through the Sociedad de Amigos de la República (SAR). Now SAR will have to call forth

civic resistance; however, its activity will lack any meaning and will
be discredited in the most lamentable way. The opposition parties that
have backed SAR have reached their most critical point. What will
they do after the clear-cut negative reply of the regime? It is necessary
to repeat the words of Martí:

> No longer do the cheeks of beggars have room for slaps.
>
> When has a nation ever been built by people who have to beg
> for their rights?
>
> Fear does not resolve a situation that can only be resolved with
> courage.

We are the only ones today in Cuba who know where we are going
and do not depend on the dictator's last word.

Greetings to the Cuban people, and the most firm promise that we
shall return!

Speech at Flagler Theater
(November 20, 1955)

The regime fears this Flagler meeting much more than the meeting of
the Sociedad de Amigos de la República. Here we have those who do
not fear the bayonets. I swear it here: In Cuba, they are finished or
we are finished. Now we are planning to sow the seed. These are our
first meetings. When we return to Miami we will hold a meeting at
the Auditorium, because if twelve activists got together one thousand
persons, then one thousand activists can mobilize five thousand persons. There can be no ambivalence toward the fatherland. A Cuban is
not one who calls himself that; a Cuban is one who is ready to serve
Cuba. You are more than exiles, you are émigrés of hunger. The
politicians do not talk about the émigrés because you do not vote. The
Revolution is interested in the émigrés because we are concerned not
with votes but with conscience. We come to seek the moral strength
of the émigrés. In three years of tyranny, 26,000 Cubans were pushed
here by oppression. The Cubans have to leave a rich land, whereas
in Holland the people have to snatch every inch of land from the sea.
"The return of the exiles" was a demagogic slogan, because the

Speech delivered on November 20, 1955, in Miami, Florida. Luis Conte
Agüero, "Del Muelle de Luz al Teatro Flagler," *Bohemia* (Havana), December
4, 1955, pp. 78, 79, 80.

exiles were few and some of them were millionaire thieves. What matters is the return of the émigrés. My son is right there; if he were old enough I would take him to battle.

The flag the Cuban students of Miami gave me I will put beside that given to me by the mothers of those who died when I was released from prison. The Moncada, a solitary event, will not occur again, but to those who call it suicide, I would recall the 300 Spartans who fought against 2 million Persians at the Thermopylae. Three thousand years have passed, and Greece is still proud of them. Suicidal was the act of sacrifice committed by the seven heroic children who jumped from the Chapultepec tower, and today they constitute the richest spiritual source of Mexico.

We do not care if we have to beg for the fatherland, we do so with honor. No one will repent of having contributed, but even if the help is insufficient, we will go to Cuba. We will go with 10,000 rifles or with only one. Only in this way can responsibility be assumed in a struggle like this. What an extraordinary spectacle is this generous contribution of the humble émigrés! The money stolen from the Republic cannot be used to make revolutions. With the money stolen from the Republic not a single shot has yet been fired. Revolutions are based on morals. A movement that has to rob banks or accept money from thieves cannot be considered revolutionary. We cannot recognize as our allies the thieves who attempt to ingratiate themselves with the people by giving 10 percent of what they have stolen. We do not want the people to owe their freedom to thieves. We will knock at their doors when the Revolution attains power.

We are against the false and conventional justice that has dominated Cuba for fifty years, a justice imprisoning the poor who steal because of hunger while tolerating with total impunity the big-time thieves the Republic has suffered. We shall unite our compatriots behind the ideal of full dignity for the Cuban people, justice for the hungry and forgotten, and punishment for the truly guilty. Ideas make the people. Here is Tampa, a town as Cuban as any in Cuba, whose inextinguishable patriotism was founded on the fervor of Martí's ideas.[1]

We want to reestablish the honorable fatherland, assaulted by the "insolent sergeant" and the politicians who want to substitute for the dictatorship that replaced them. They are as much embezzlers as the ones now ruling. With embezzlers the Republic cannot be redeemed. Don Cosme de la Torriente has very good intentions, but is running around with bad company. But let me make clear that Raúl Chibás, the

---

[1] Tampa is a town in Florida traditionally populated by Cuban exiles. Eds.

FEU, Liberación Radical, and other groups are not bad company. But it was a depressing thing at the SAR meeting to listen to the voices of men who have enriched themselves in power, who represent no moral ideals, and who are as guilty of Cuba's ills as Batista himself. Raimundo Abreu, for example, who owns in Pinar del Río half a dozen farms that I have seen in the property registers, acquired them with the money of sick people. He spoke in the name of the Partido Demócrata Abstencionista, a party that does not exist, even metaphysically. That was a farce! The guilt of great embezzlers who now want to bathe themselves in the Jordan of the anti-Batista cause cannot be exonerated with the pretext of mobilizing public opinion. Embezzlers have no public opinion. The embezzlers cannot be enemies of the dictatorship because the dictatorship is protecting their ill-gotten gains. Embezzlers prefer tyranny to revolution, as they demonstrated last Saturday by attacking the men of the 26th of July—men who have given to the revolutionary cause eighty martyrs—while they played the government's game in a rigged electoral process. That is why the embezzlers want the Sociedad de Amigos de la República to make an agreement with the regime in order to ensure their political survival. And I ask SAR if there can be any honorable compromise with those who murdered our comrades of the Moncada and many other courageous Cubans, without even demanding their resignations? It is immoral to speak of the dead in order to plead for an arrangement with the executioners. What is the use of a bad agreement if in three years there would be another March 10? I am one of the Cubans who is worried very seriously about the country's future if such deeds remain unpunished.

That is why we maintain that the solution must begin with Batista's resignation and the transference of power to Don Cosme de la Torriente, who will preside over the general elections even if Don Cosme does not wish to run for office, because what matters is not what Don Cosme wants but what the Republic wants. If Batista does not resign, the SAR should decree mass resistance and the regime will crumble. If the electoral formula does not include Batista's resignation, without which no one will believe in the honesty of the elections, then the Revolution will occur before the elections are held. The petty politicians will be punished and disqualified for a number of years from active or passive participation in politics. New men will occupy the three powers of the state, posts which up to now have been occupied by bad politicians.

Some are surprised that we have stated the year in which the Revolution will take place. We talk about the year, but we do not say the month, day, hour, or place it will happen. We know what can be said and what cannot be said. No one can teach us that art. It is not the same thing to conspire with a few unhappy individuals and to conspire with the masses who most know their role in the struggle. Martí never denied his revolutionary aims when he spoke to the émigrés. This technique cannot be understood by those with a putschist mentality on the same style of March 10. Besides these words there is the work organized by committed men. Help the fatherland! Help the martyr! It is not enough to love the fatherland with words, it must be aided with deeds. The fatherland must be helped, as I said in New York, with what is spent in going to the movies or in drinking whiskey every week. Those who do not help do not have the right to criticize, and those who help will not be disappointed, because the men who lead this task know how to carry it out or die. Let us stand up and sing the immortal hymn whose verses say that to live in chains is to live under shame and insult, and to die for the fatherland is to live!

Manifesto No. 2 to the People of Cuba *(December 10, 1955)*

> We will find generous help in all honest hearts. And we will knock on all doors. And we will ask for contributions from town to town. And they will give, because we will ask with honor.
>
> JOSÉ MARTÍ

I am addressing these lines essentially to the generous men and women of my fatherland. I still remember the unforgettable scenes I witnessed among the Cuban émigrés to the United States. Everywhere I saw Cubans standing, their hands raised high, swearing not to rest until they saw their land redeemed, and then en masse they deposited in the *mambí*[1] hat the product of their sweat which they earned through hard work. But that was not their only contribution. One does not need to look for the exiled Cubans to obtain their aid; after every public gathering they can be seen in the streets asking for the address of the Patriotic Club where they join and offer their weekly contributions.[2] Every Sunday Cuban parties are organized, and what is collected is

Manifesto issued on December 10, 1955 from Nassau. "Manifiesto no. 2 del 26 de Julio al pueblo de Cuba," *Pensamiento Crítico* (Havana), no. 21 (1968), pp. 221–227.

[1] *Mambí* is the term used to refer to those who fought in Cuba's war of independence in the nineteenth century. Eds.

[2] Patriotic clubs formed abroad to aid financially those who were fighting the Batista dictatorship. Eds.

given entirely to the Revolution. The first of these, held just a few days ago in New York, produced hundreds of pesos. All the beauty of our historical tradition is evidenced by the Cuban exiles with astonishing fervor. Already there are Patriotic Clubs functioning in Bridgeport, Union City, New York, Miami, Tampa, and Key West. New groups will be organized in Chicago, Philadelphia, Washington, and other places where the Cubans who have had to leave their native land have settled. Seven weeks of tireless effort dedicated to organizing the Cubans from the Canadian border to the glorious Key have produced the best of results.

The 26th of July Movement, which unites and organizes all of the country's revolutionary forces in a close and disciplined organization, breaking away from the traditional framework in which petty Cuban politics have existed up to the present, has called on our émigré brothers—who are also Cubans suffering from the misfortunes of Cuba—to struggle. The émigrés have responded unanimously to the appeal of the 26th of July. They have provided hundreds of young fighters, many of them veterans of the European and Pacific theaters in World War II, who now want to fight for the cause of liberty in their own land. Moreover, they are providing abundant economic resources so that the noble and virile individuals who will challenge the tyranny once again with the cry "liberty or death" on their lips will not go unarmed.

There are some who have not yet understood the meaning of the public preaching of a revolutionary idea, and they wonder if this does not put the oppressors on guard. They forget many things, but mainly that we are not millionaires with huge sums deposited in banks. They forget that we are not rich, nor do we have private means to make available to our cause. We would offer them without hesitation if we had them, just as we are offering all that we do have—our energy and our lives. They forget that a revolution, unlike a military putsch, is the work of the people, and it is necessary that the people know beforehand what they must do in the struggle. In revolution, as Martí stated, "the methods are secret and the goals are public."

Does anyone believe that when our liberators publicly solicited aid from the cigarmakers of Tampa and Key West they wanted to conceal from the Spanish authorities that a revolution was developing in Cuba? If we are not embezzlers or rich men, how can we obtain the resources essential for the struggle if we do not ask the people for them? And how can we ask the people for resources if we do not tell them what we will do with the money? If the Revolution robs a bank to get funds, the enemy will call us gangsters. If the Revolution accepts aid from embezzlers who have plundered the Republic, the Revolution will be betraying its principles. If the Revolution solicits aid from vested interests, it will be compromised before it attains power.

We have already gone to battle once with the limited resources we could obtain, each of us giving what little he had and quietly soliciting the aid of some generous individuals, and the result was defeat and the horrible crimes which followed. It would have been useless then to ask for help publicly, because no one would have paid attention to us. Faith lay with other men who were expected to do everything against oppression. Today, after paying such a high price in sacrifice and lives for the confidence of our compatriots, we shall do what we could not do then. We shall publicly appeal to the people to help us, to prepare the country for revolution on a major scale, without possibility of failure. We shall set forth the actions the masses must carry out everywhere when national rebellion breaks out like a storm, so that the fighting detachments, well armed and led, and the active youth cadres will be supported by the workers throughout the country, organized from below in revolutionary cells, capable of unleashing a general strike. What the enemy will never know is where the weapons are hidden and at what moment and how the insurrection will erupt. If the corrupt politicians publicly preach their electoral thesis, the Revolution must publicly preach its thesis of rebellion.

To preach revolution aloud will undoubtedly produce better results than to speak of peace in public and conspire in secret, which was the method used for three and a half years by the group removed from power on March 10. Their secret conspiracy was never a secret to anyone. Thanks to our campaign it is clear that, despite the return of the Auténticos from exile, many of whom erroneously thought that the insurrectional stage had ended, revolutionary feeling and agitation are stronger than ever throughout the nation. Our cry "Revolution! Revolution!" is the slogan of the masses wherever people gather. All of the electoral plans of the regime to maintain itself in power with the complicity of the political cliques of the pseudo-opposition have been destroyed by our strategy. Only the blind, the greedy, the envious, or the impotent could deny this.

The national panorama is clearing. Events are finally proving us right. The massacres of workers, the street battles between students and police, the increasing economic crisis with its hunger and misery, the unchecked rise of the public debt which has compromised the credit of the nation for thirty years, the men who have disappeared without a trace, the crimes committed with impunity, the daily embezzlements, and the haughty and categorical refusal by the dictator to one hundred thousand citizens who gathered at the Muelle de Luz[3] indicate that no alternative remains for the country but revolution. Those who to date have maintained other theses now have only two choices: They must either surrender to the regime or join the Revolution, whose standard we alone held high when everyone was running around in search of an electoral compromise with the dictatorship. Even the most humble citizen correctly interprets the situation in Cuba when he says that Batista and his clique of millionaire generals have been deceiving the public for four years and that they will not give up their power unless they are thrown out by force. To the cowards who say that he has the tanks, the guns, and the planes, the answer of a nation with dignity must be, "Well then, we too have to get together the necessary weapons. We have to give the fighters the economic resources they need. If the tyranny forces us by taxes to purchase its weapons and pay its police, we should contribute our resources voluntarily to those who for four years have been fighting and dying for our freedom. We have to aid them because the duty to sacrifice oneself for the fatherland is the duty of all and not just a few. We have to aid them because the frivolous life, the life of indifference when the country is in agony, is a crime when others are suffering in prison or in exile or are already buried in debased soil."

Each citizen should give a dollar, each worker should contribute the earnings of one day's work, as the Cuban émigrés are going to do on January 28, and you will see how the tyranny resoundingly collapses in less time than many imagine.

Those of us who lead an austere and poor life, devoted without rest or respite to the struggle, giving the country our youth and our life, working for six million Cubans without asking anything of anyone, we feel that we have the moral authority and courage to speak to the nation in these terms. To beg is bitter, even if it is done for the fatherland, but it is more bitter still to live oppressed as we are living. It is more bitter to see a husband tolerate insults to his wife in the street from a uniformed officer; a mother see her son or husband taken away from home in the middle of the night; a father, despite his age and position, find himself beaten and harassed without any respect at a police station; a businessman see the very policeman who should protect him from thieves taking a handful of cigars or a pound of meat or a cup of coffee from him, and, if he is refused, imposing a fine or making an unjust accusation of some violation; barefoot children walking the streets begging alms; men standing idle on street corners;

---

[3] At the Muelle de Luz, Fidelistas disrupted a meeting held by the proponents of the civic dialogue. Eds.

lines formed outside foreign consulates for visas to leave the country; infinite injustices occurring daily before our very eyes.

Let the people who see us suffer, who see us fight, who see us asking for help for the fatherland, heed us.

Others ask for themselves, and they offer as security a house, a farm, or some asset. We ask for Cuba and offer as security our lives. Each dollar deposited in our hands is a check drawn against the existence of men who have pledged to die before abandoning the undertaking in which we are engaged. And those who out of egotism or pettiness refuse to help them, knowing that they are right and fighting for a just cause, for a noble ideal, for a worthy principle, for the common good, will see them die, their consciences full of remorse.

We know that this appeal will not be wasted. Already on one occasion, when it appeared necessary to close down the newspaper *La Calle* because of lack of funds, we made a similar appeal and the people immediately began to provide splendid help. The regime had to close it down. This time we are not asking for a newspaper but for the entire nation. We are asking for money to free six million slaves, to save the nation. The contribution, therefore, should be a thousand times more generous and more spontaneous.

The collection of funds by a movement functioning underground is a difficult task, but perfectly feasible in this case, given the organization and discipline of our cadres throughout the island.

Nonetheless, it is essential that the following rules be followed:

No citizen should give anything to anyone if he does not have absolute confidence in the honesty, seriousness, and moral reputation of that individual. One must be certain that what has been donated will reach the treasury of the Movement.

No one will have any identification or document from this Movement for the specific purpose of collecting funds. The only valid credential of an activist of ours for these purposes will be the reputation he enjoys in the place where he lives or works.

No one should give a cent to any person coming from another place of employment or a place where he says he works, so that no person who is not known in any given place can claim to be a member of the 26th of July Movement in order to collect funds.

No one will be given a receipt or bond as proof of his contribution, for any paper of this sort would be dangerous to the person giving it or receiving it. When the time comes, when the present circumstances of repression have been eliminated, honor rolls listing the names of the persons who have contributed will be drafted based on the reports of the members of our economic section.

The dictatorship cannot take effective measures against this economic campaign because it is confronted with a mass conspiracy.

Any impostor pretending to be a member of our movement who tries to collect funds on its behalf will be discovered promptly by our militants and will be given the punishment deserved, as happened in the province of Matanzas to a rogue named Ramón Estévez who undertook that despicable deception using a photograph of us pasted on false credentials. No vigilance is more effective than *collective vigilance*.

Any form of collection by means of coercion or violence is entirely alien to our methods.

The preceding rules for collecting funds apply only in Cuba, in which our underground organization functions. This will not be the case abroad, where Patriotic Clubs will carry out their tasks legally.

The treasury of the Movement maintains detailed accounts of income and expenditures, of which a full report will be rendered to the nation when its work is concluded.

On behalf of the national leadership of the 26th of July Revolutionary Movement, signed on the island of Nassau,

Fidel Castro

Against Everyone!
(December 25, 1955)

Four years ago, no one was interested in me. I passed unnoticed by the powerful men who discussed the fate of the country. Today, strangely, all plot against me. Why? the people might ask. What offense has he committed? Did he give up? Did he abandon his ideals? Did he change his line? Did he sell out for a position or money? Did he betray his principles? No, far from it!

The amazing thing is that the selfish, cowardly plot of the embezzlers and the spokesmen of the regime against me, a fighter who has stood up for four years without rest against the tyranny (sixteen months of silent and hard work prior to the twenty-sixth of July, two years in prison, and six months in exile), is due precisely to the contrary: It is due to my keeping a firm line of conduct since March

Article written on December 25, 1955. "Frente a todos!" *Bohemia* (Havana), January 8, 1956.

10, when so many have changed their attitude, just as one changes shirts. They attack me because everyone knows that my revolutionary integrity cannot be bought for money or position, and my loyalty to an ideal is free from duplicity and vacillation. I am loyal to a truth which I preach and practice and to a task which, although harsh and difficult, I am carrying out successfully regardless of a multitude of obstacles and powerful interests.

The spokesmen of the dictatorship, who insult me with so much hate and so much rage, would not even mention my name if I remained indifferent to the crimes that are committed against Cuba. If I were a mercenary, a sellout, a bootlicker, the libelous press would dedicate great headlines to praise me.

If on leaving prison I had chosen to run for any electoral position, using my imprisonment and sacrifice as a political platform, the submissive politicians and the users of politics would have said that I was an excellent citizen, a great patriot, a public-spirited and sensible man. It is fashionable to be shameless nowadays.

If on undertaking once more the road of sacrifice and risk by leaving the country when the dictatorship clumsily closed all doors to civic protest, if then I had knocked at the doors of the embezzlers to plead for a part of the gold that they stole from the Republic to make the Revolution, I would have at this moment hundreds of thousands of dollars at my disposal, and no embezzler would have made common cause with the spokesmen of the tyranny against me.

But I did the opposite.

I gave up any electoral ambition from the outset. I renounced the presidency of the Municipal Assembly of Havana, which the Ortodoxo Party offered me, a post coveted by all as the second most important position in the Republic. I gave up an appointment in the executive council of the party. At the same time I gave up a salary of $500 per month that an insurance company offered me, because I do not profit from my prestige—a prestige that does not belong to me but to a cause. I gave up the salary that an important Havana newspaper offered me, and instead I wrote for Luis Orlando's newspaper, which could not pay me a single cent. I gave up everything that meant personal tranquility and safety. I gave up silence—a comfortable refuge of those who fear defamation and danger. I denounced crimes and unmasked murderers and have made very clear what happened in the Moncada Barracks.

I left Cuba without a single cent, determined to carry out what others had failed to do with millions of dollars. Instead of knocking on the doors of those who had enriched themselves, I went to the

people, visited the emigrants, issued a manifesto to the country soliciting help. I begged for the fatherland, to gather penny by penny the
necessary funds with which to achieve our freedom. How comfortable and simple, how free from sacrifice and sweat, from hard work
and fatigue would have been the easy way. The way that others, less
convinced of the purity of their cause and the greatness of their people, would have adopted by soliciting aid from those who have a lot
of money because they have stolen it, to ask for a small portion of their
fortune in exchange for a promise of security and respect! It would
have been easy to get into the good graces of the powerful men of
money; political finagling could have been used! But no. I did the
opposite! Strange mania, that of doing the opposite of what everyone
has done up to now.

I publicly stated at Palm Garden, New York,

> . . . the Cuban people want something more than a simple change
> of command. Cuba longs for a radical change in every aspect of
> its political and social life. The people must be given something
> more than liberty and democracy in abstract; decent living must
> be given to every Cuban. The state cannot ignore the fate of any
> of its citizens who were born and grew up in this country. There
> is no greater tragedy than that of the man capable of and willing
> to work who suffers hunger with his family because he lacks a
> job. The state is unavoidably obliged to provide him with a job or
> to support him until he finds a job. None of the armchair formu-
> las discussed nowadays includes a consideration of this situation,
> as if the grave problem of Cuba comprised only how to satisfy
> the ambitions of a few politicians who have been ousted from
> power or who want to get it.[1]

On Flagler Street I said publicly,

> We shall unite our compatriots behind the ideal of full dignity
> for the Cuban people, justice for the hungry and forgotten, and
> punishment for the truly guilty. . . . The money stolen from the
> Republic cannot be used to make revolutions. Revolutions are
> based on morals. . . . A movement that has to rob banks or accept
> money from thieves cannot be considered revolutionary. We can-
> not recognize as our allies the thieves who attempt to ingratiate
> themselves with the people by giving 10 percent of what they
> have stolen. . . . We will knock at their doors when the Revolu-
> tion attains power. . . . Embezzlers have no public opinion. The
> embezzlers cannot be enemies of the dictatorship because the dic-
> tatorship is protecting their ill-gotten gains. Embezzlers prefer
> tyranny to revolution. . . . That is why the embezzlers want the
> Sociedad de Amigos de la República to make an agreement with
> the regime in order to ensure their political survival.[2]

[1] See "Speech in New York" in this volume. Eds.
[2] See "Speech at Flagler Theater" in this volume. Eds.

These words are truer than ever because right now the embezzlers and the tyrants are almost at the point of making, not a gentlemen's agreement as they would like to call it, but a bandits' agreement whose first clause will be to forget all the crimes and thefts committed in the past and to respect all privileges and consecrate all injustices.

I was impugned in a recent article in *Bohemia* entitled "The Nation Is Not Fidel's,"[3] in which it was stated,

> No one can really say that Fidel has benefited from public funds. It is also fair to state that there has been no opportunity to test his honesty, because he never was a minister and never had a chance to snatch an appetizing and enticing chunk of taxes with the impunity of doing so without leaving any fingerprints. Possibly the only abundant money Fidel has ever had the chance to handle in his life is the money that the Cuban emigrants are now placing in his hands.

I can reply simply that I have handled money on previous occasions. It was not as considerable, perhaps, as what Justo Luis del Pazo handed over to the organizing committee of the Auténtico Party to carry out the reorganization that would precipitate the electoral farce of November 1, thanks to which Batista now says his government is constitutional and legitimate. But I have handled nearly twenty thousand pesos which modest young men like Fernando Chenard saved through many sacrifices, including selling all of the photographic equipment with which he earned his living; like Pedro Marrero, who mortgaged his salary for many months and whom we had to prohibit from selling the furniture of his home; like Elpidio Sosa, who sold his job for three hundred dollars. How different from those men mentioned by the author of the article cited, who on November 1, as a token of civic example "gambled their economic future in order to go to the polls, mortgaging even their bones"! The men I mentioned are dead; those who "mortgaged even their bones" are now collecting from the Republic five thousand pesos monthly in the Senate.

I have handled almost twenty thousand pesos, and how many times my son could not drink milk! How many times the Cuban Electric Company cut off my electricity! I still keep the ominous court papers by which landlords dispossess tenants from their houses. I did not have a personal income; I practically lived on the charity of my friends. I know what it is to see a hungry son while having the money of the fatherland in my pockets.

I have never believed that the fatherland belongs to me. Martí once said, "The country belongs to no one; and if it did, it would belong

---

[3] Refers to an article by Miguel Hernández, "La patria no es de Fidel," *Bohemia* (Havana), December 18, 1955, pp. 107, 154. Eds.

to those who serve it unselfishly, and then only in spirit." Those who evidently thought that the country was theirs are the embezzlers who exploited it when they were in power as if it were a private piece of real estate.

It is as unfair to affirm that one can be honest only when one does not handle public funds (as though our unfortunate people could not produce a single honest man) as it is to make the absurd and inconceivable statement that those who surround me "were not humble emigrants, but rather happy owners of real estate in Miami." I would like to know which of those suffering and humble Cubans who attended our meetings and set up the revolutionary clubs of Bridgeport, Union City, New York, Miami, Tampa, and Key West, who are earning a living by hard work away from their country, is a happy owner of real estate. If any owned a private home, it would be an exception, and without a doubt the product of many years of honest work and not of stealing from the Republic. I saw how they lived in small apartments where no children are allowed, where women have to wash and cook after returning tired from working ten hours in a factory; where life is hard, tiring, and unhappy; and where only one exclamation is heard—"I would prefer to live in Cuba on only half of what I make here!"

Previously much was said about the exiles. There were little more than one hundred. Many were well off; their children's pictures appeared in the papers often; they longed for their little friends and homes in their native land. But no one remembered the poor children of the emigrants who in the Northern states had to live in a very cold climate, who had no school where they could learn their own language, no doctors who could understand the language of their parents. To state that they are happy real estate owners demonstrates the resentment of the politicians toward the Cuban emigrants, because those tens of thousands of families who live abroad constitute a sad and living accusation of the bad governments that have plagued the Republic. The politicians said, "The Cuban problem will be solved when the exiles can return." We revolutionaries say, "The problem of Cuba will be solved when the emigrants can return."

In the same article, it is capriciously affirmed that in the magazine *Bohemia* I "recommended that my friends vote for Grau because I was thinking of attaining freedom promptly by means of his justice. . . ." An evident lack of seriousness and capacity is shown here which disqualifies anyone as a polemicist and a public man. I never made such a recommendation because I do not involve myself in such contradictions of principle. I shall give up my public life if someone shows me the issue of *Bohemia* in which that recommendation appears.

I could not have wanted my freedom in that dishonorable way when, at the time discussions over amnesty centered around whether the men who attacked the Moncada should be included and there was talk of conditions for our release, I wrote a public letter to *Bohemia* that stated,

> If a compromise is demanded of us in order to gain our freedom, we emphatically say no. No, we are not tired. After twenty months we are as firm and unmoved as on the first day. We do not want amnesty at the price of dishonor. We shall not undergo the Caudius gallows of ignoble oppressors. We shall suffer a thousand years of imprisonment rather than humiliation! A thousand years of imprisonment rather than sacrifice our dignity![4]

Only a scoundrel without arguments or a coward convinced that because I am engaged in a cause, above personal grievances, I cannot call him to account, only such a person would dare to say so irresponsibly that I attacked "colleagues and men who were also pure idealists in their own way." I do not have to resort to lies to combat an adversary, because I have sufficient bases from which to draw facts and reasons.

Perhaps if the writer of the article believes what he says, he lacked the courage to say it when gangsterism was in full swing; at that time, I never saw him writing any articles against gangsterism. My enemies so lack any basis that in order to attack me they resort to digging up the old slanders from the government's sewers; they are indeed good allies of the tyranny against the Revolution. Every time my adversaries tried the vile and selfish procedure of involving me with gangsterism, I stood resolutely against their slander, I appealed to the courts, and honest judges (there are only a few) like Hevia or Riera Medina can certify my innocence.

Thousands of students, who are professionals today, saw my actions in the university for five years. I always had their support (because I have always fought with the weapon of public denunciation, going to the masses). It was with their cooperation that I organized large meetings and protests against the existing corruption. They can testify to my conduct. There they saw me—newly arrived and inexperienced but full of youthful rebellion—challenge the empire of Mario Salabarría. (I refrain from personal attacks because he is in prison and one should not attack those who cannot defend themselves. One might ask why he is imprisoned and not those who were murderers of eighty prisoners in Moncada.)[5] I shall only say, for the sake of information,

---

[4] See "Letter to Luis Conte Agüero" in this volume. Eds.

[5] Mario Salabarría was taken to the firing squad several years after Castro took over. Eds.

that at the time, in the first years of Grau's government, Salabarría controlled all the forces of repression, no less repressive than those of today, and he was the owner of the capital.

At a time when corruption was unprecedented, when many youth leaders could get dozens of government positions and so many were corrupted, it is worthy of some merit to have led student protests against that regime for a number of years without ever having appeared on any government payroll.

It is extraordinary, cynical, and shameful that the sponsors, protectors, and subsidizers of gangsterism should use this argument to attack me. They could not be more barefaced! To mention gangsterism in the home of the great imposter [Batista] is like mentioning the rope in the home of the hanged. The members of the regime find themselves in a similar situation. They shipped Policarpo Soler[6] to Spain loaded with money, and at the same time murdered "El Colorado"[7] on Durege Street. It should be mentioned with respect to the latter that by dying in active opposition to the tyranny he vindicated his errors. Strange things occurred before March 10! Very strange things! For example, those who bombed the Ingelmo shoe store or those who murdered Cosío del Pino[8] have never been found.

Because he is forcing me to do so, will it be necessary to publish again the statement I filed with the Court of Accounts on March 4, 1952, which was published in the newspaper *Alerta* on March 5, naming one by one the 2,120 persons that the groups had in the ministries? Who ever dared to file such a statement? It certainly was not Batista, who lived in his Kuquine farm thoroughly protected by Carlos Prío and who had permission to go armed and with a personal guard. I walked the streets of Havana alone and unarmed.

From that work of mine, suffice it now to quote the paragraph with which I opened the statement (which was a premonition): "To the Court of Accounts I appeal to patriotically ask . . . for the miracle that may save the nation from the constitutional disaster that threatens it."

The miracle did not occur, and a week later the disaster of March 10 materialized. Gangsterism was the pretext, but the man who invoked it had been one of its founders when he encouraged university gangs through Jaime Mariné.[9] That evil germinated in the Auténtico

[6] A thug of the Machado dictatorship and later of Batista's. Eds.

[7] Orlando León Lemus, also a famous political gangster in Havana, was murdered by Batista. Eds.

[8] Alejo Cosío del Pino was killed in early 1952. Eds.

[9] Jaime Mariné was a Spaniard who became a major in the army during the Machado dictatorship. Eds.

Party and had its roots in the resentment and hate that Batista sowed during his eleven years of abuse and injustice. Those who saw the murder of their comrades wanted to avenge them, and a regime that was unable to establish justice allowed such vengeance. The blame cannot be placed on the young men who, moved by natural yearning and the legend of a heroic era, longed for a revolution that had not taken place and at the time could not be started. Many of those victims of deceit who died as gangsters could very well be heroes today.

In order that the mistake not be repeated, the Revolution that has not occurred will be fought at a time when it can be fought. To avoid vengeance, we shall have justice. When we have justice, no one will consider himself a wandering avenger, and the full weight of the law will fall upon him. Only the people, who constitute sovereign power, have the right to punish or pardon.

There has never been justice in Cuba. To send a poor man to prison because he steals a chicken, while the big embezzlers enjoy immunity, is simply an unjustifiable crime. When has a judge sentenced a powerful man? When has a sugar-mill owner gone to jail? When has a rural guard been arrested? Are they pure? Are they saints? Or is it that in our social order justice is a vile lie applied only when it is convenient to the vested interests?

The fear of justice has united the embezzlers and the tyranny. The embezzlers, perplexed by the shouts of "Revolution!" that recur with increasing force at every large meeting like bells calling the wicked to final judgment, have listened to the prudent words of Ichaso in his column "Cabalgata Política" of *Bohemia*, dated December 4, 1955:

> Fidel Castro is too dangerous a competitor for certain leaders of the opposition, who during three and a half years have failed to take a correct stand toward the Cuban situation. Those leaders know it too well. They now feel displaced by the size the 26th of July Movement is acquiring in the battle against March 10. The logical reaction of the politicians in the light of this evident fact should be to face the revolutionary action of Fidelismo with a resolute political stand.

The embezzlers have listened to the cordial appeal made by Batista's Havana alderman, Pedro Alomá Kessel, in a government publication dated December 14:

> All of us politicians, without exception, are deeply interested in stopping Fidel Castro's insurrectionist plans. If we disregard this threat and continue stubbornly to close all political solutions, we shall be opening the revolutionary road to Fidel Castro. I would like to see who, either in the opposition or in the government, is going to save us if Fidelismo triumphs in Cuba.

They know that I left Cuba without a single cent; they know that
I have not knocked at the doors of the embezzlers. Nevertheless, they
fear that we may start a revolution. In other words, they recognize
that we can count on the support of the people.

The nation is at the point of witnessing the great betrayal of the
politicians. We know that for us, for those who maintain a dignified
stand, the struggle will be hard. But we are not frightened by the
number of enemies we shall have to face. We shall defend our ideals
against all. "To be young is to feel within oneself the strength of one's
own destiny, it is to believe in it while facing resistance and to sustain
that belief against all vested interests."

The politicking opposition is fully eclipsed and discredited. First
they demanded a neutral government and general elections in 1956.
They no longer talk about a particular year; they will end up by
taking off their last little fig leaf and accepting any arrangement with
the dictatorship. They did not discuss principles, but only details of
time in order to join in robbing the budget of our unfortunate republic.

But this business will not be as easy as they think! The people are
alert!

The peasants, tired of speeches and promises of agrarian reform and
distribution of land, know they can expect nothing from the politicians. A million and a half Cubans who are unemployed due to the
incapacity, avarice, and lack of foresight by all the bad governments
know they can expect nothing from the politicians.

Thousands of sick people, with neither beds nor medicine, know
that those politicians who seek their votes in exchange for a little favor
and whose business consists of always having a large number of needy
people whose consciences can be bought at a very low price, know
they can expect nothing.

The hundreds of thousands of families living in huts, open sheds,
empty lots, and tenements, or paying exorbitant rents; workers who
earn salaries of hunger, whose children have no clothes or shoes to
wear to school; citizens who pay for the highest priced electricity in
the world, or who requested telephone service ten years ago and have
not been served yet; in other words, all who have had to suffer or
still suffer the horrors of misery know they can expect nothing from
the politicians.

The people know that with the hundreds of millions removed by
foreign trusts from our country, plus the hundreds of millions that
the embezzlers have stolen, plus the graft that thousands of parasites
have enjoyed without rendering service or producing anything for the

community, plus the losses of all types due to gambling, vice, the black market, and so forth, Cuba would be one of the most prosperous and rich countries of America, without emigrants, without unemployed, without the hungry, without sick people with no beds, without the illiterate, and without beggars.

From political parties, organizations of godparents for the purpose of appointing congressmen, senators, and majors, the people expect nothing. From the Revolution, an organization of fighters united by a great patriotic ideal, the people expect everything, and they will get it!

Letter to Celestino Rodríguez
(February 12, 1956)

Dear Celestino:

Before anything else I beg you to forgive my delay in answering your beautiful letter of January 22. We all enjoyed your letter, which we are keeping in our files among documents of true interest, for the day the modest history of this struggle is written.

The system you have adopted could be used as a model for other clubs.[1] I would like your authorization to send copies of your letter to other places, even if at this time it would only be as proof of the way the work of the clubs could have been accomplished. In a letter to Luis García I expressed my bitter complaint because of the very poor work done by the *compañeros* remaining as heads of the other organizations, not because of lack of enthusiasm among the émigrés or the leaders, but rather because of the predominance of petty rivalries over the larger interest of our cause. At times I have the feeling that in the comfortable refuge of a country where work is abundant and high salaries are earned, where the people are not forced from their homes in the middle of the night, or tortured or persecuted, the émigrés forget the desperate situation of our brothers in Cuba, in that distressed island suffering the hell of tyranny and misery. And least important, but nevertheless not least painful, they forget the agony of

Letter written on February 12, 1956, from Mexico. Celestino Rodríguez at the time was the head of a group of Cubans in Bridgeport, Connecticut. "Una carta de Fidel," *Revolución* (Havana), February 2, 1959, p. 12.
[1] Patriotic clubs of the 26th of July Movement. Eds.

us who await, with the impatience of death itself, the aid offered in order to fulfill our duty to the fatherland.

In a letter to the different clubs I am demanding greater sacrifice. In due time I shall send you a copy of the letter I sent to Miami and the one I shall write to New York. I suggest to those organizations that instead of the extensive work of collective fund raising, always humiliating, full of transactions and paperwork, also demanding great use of time and energy, they should concentrate on a reduced number of selected and generous persons who will be capable of larger donations at one time. In this manner I have set quotas for each club to be fulfilled in no more than two and a half months, because the extremely difficult situation of the country demands that we act rapidly.

If the Cuban émigrés do not respond appropriately to the call I make, perhaps we shall find ourselves forced, before giving up the noble ideals for which so many *compañeros* died, to sacrifice more, and that sacrifice will always be more rewarding than the shameful prostration of an inert people. These reproaches are not addressed to you, because you embody the most encouraging virtues of our people. It is just that I cannot write without expressing my deepest feelings, whether of joy or sadness. It hurts to think how others who did not have an honest public life could count on millions of dollars to stage a revolutionary comedy whereas we, with an unalterable decision to struggle to the end, tied to a pure cause, find ourselves impotent due to the poverty produced by honesty and loyalty. Not impotent! One is not impotent when there is the last recourse of giving one's life and the conviction that each penny begged for will be used to fight as long as there is a man capable of holding a weapon.

As much as the limitations of our resources prevent us from giving all the momentum to our activities which Cuba's grave situation demands, it deeply hurts to think of the possibility that a group of ambitious military men, aware that the building is collapsing, would run to give the final blow to the regime. Using the pretext of improvised liberators—which is easily done when people are desperate—they would lay the foundations with the complicity of a clique of politicians of a new and ignominious military regime. Do not all of these reasons justify desperation and even the sacrifice of those who have thrown their fate with the honor of the fatherland and the people?

Forgive this bitter reply to your beautiful and encouraging words. It is not the voice of hopelessness, because there is spirit and strength to continue; it is the voice of dignity that rebels against petty material needs and expresses its determination to overcome them.

I can speak like this to you, and other good *compañeros* like you, because you understand me.

A fraternal embrace for all from one who will never give you reason to regret the friendship with which you honor me.[2]

Fidel Castro

[2] Celestino lives in exile now. Eds.

The Condemnation They Demand of Us (March 5, 1956)

In the section "On Cuba" of the last issue of *Bohemia*, the incident that occurred during the meeting of the national leadership of the Ortodoxos on February 2 is narrated.[1] There is a paragraph in which it is affirmed that the explanation given by *compañero* Antonio López to the effect that the 26th of July Movement had nothing to do with what happened there did not satisfy those present and that is why "the leaders of the Partido del Pueblo consider themselves as having the right to expect from Fidel Castro himself the explicit condemnation of the assault."

Article written on March 5, 1956, in Mexico. "La condenación que se nos pide," *Bohemia* (Havana), March 11, 1956, pp. 59, 69.

[1] This refers to a meeting sponsored by Cosme de la Torriente and the Sociedad de Amigos de la República, which attempted to establish a civic dialogue with the Batista regime. Dr. Manuel Dorta Duque invited the leaders of the Partido del Pueblo, of which Castro was a member, to discuss in his home whether the party should engage in those activities. As the leaders entered several persons gathered in the vicinity of Duque's residence and began to shout "Down with the traitors." In spite of the harassment the deliberations began. The following persons participated: Raúl Chibás, Luis Conte Agüero, José Iglesias, Armando Muza, Ernesto Stock, Raúl Primelles, Mario Rivadulla, Marta Freyre, Pastora Núñez, Nazario Sargen, Rubén Acosta, Omar Borges, Erasmo Gómez, Max Lesnick, Enrique Barroso, José Manuel Gutiérrez, Roberto Agramonte, Pelayo Cuervo, and Manuel Bisbé. In the middle of the discussion, the group which had assembled outside the house entered it. Enrique Barroso, who was guarding the entrance to the house, was knocked down to the floor, kicked, and finally beaten with a stick. The intruders left when the police reached the house. There was indignation and outrage at what had happened among the persons gathered there. As the vote was being taken by the Ortodoxos Antonio López, who belonged to the wing following the ideas of Fidel Castro, stated that their movement had absolutely nothing to do with what had happened. It seems, nonetheless, that Fidelistas were the ones who had intruded and assaulted those participating in the deliberations. For more on this, see "Sección en Cuba," *Bohemia* (Havana), March 4, 1956, pp. 69–72. Eds.

Because of the veracity and attention which the opinions in the section "On Cuba" of *Bohemia* merit, I am breaking the discreet silence which I have maintained for more than two months to fulfill the painful duty of clarifying my relations with men to whom I am united by years of comradeship and with the party to which I have dedicated my greatest efforts since its inception. I am doing this in order to put things in their place and to inform the public. I do not believe, however, that I owe any explanation to the members of the central committee of the Ortodoxos because no one should be obliged to give explanations of events for which he is not responsible. After all, due to the conduct I have always maintained within the party, my open and sincere behavior, the respect, consideration, and even personal friendship I have with all of its members *without exception*, what right have those leaders to suppose that what happened was the consequence of an order given by our movement? Why was not the least consideration given to the statement of a self-denying and valiant *compañero* who fought in Bayamo on the twenty-sixth of July, who spent two years in exile in Mexico and slept in parks in the winter and fainted from hunger because he refused to beg for charity from the rich exiles, a man who in Cuba has been at the vanguard of street demonstrations, suffering blows and daily persecution, and who spends the dawn in the market of Havana working hard to support his family and his father lying paralyzed in a hospital due to a grave illness, and who during the day works without rest for his fatherland, who is a living example for all of idealism and sacrifice? He has, in a party where true merit is recognized, more right to speak, to be heard, and to be believed than many who believe they fulfill their duties toward Cuba by merely meeting once a month to enunciate some declarations without importance while spending the rest of their time at their businesses, professions, and particular interests.

That, in the final analysis, is to echo the most spurious accusations of the regime! For a long time, our enemies, the enemies of the Revolution, the disguised or declared friends of the tyranny, have tried to throw over us the stigma of a violent and unbridled people. That tactic began on July 26, 1953, when we were accused cynically of having committed brutal deeds against our adversaries, when in fact they were the ones who at that very moment were murdering prisoners by the dozens after having tortured them.

While we were imprisoned and with no communication to the outside world for more than two years, logically we could not be accused of the underhanded activities which were occurring within the Ortodoxo leadership. For example, there was the occasion when Márquez

Sterling and his followers met in the Artística Gallega Hall to solicit aid for the party, which had been registered in the elections for November 1, and were attacked with eggs and tomatoes by a group of dissenters. Ah! But then it was a matter of being Márquez Sterling, who was maintaining different criteria from those of the abstentionist group—some of whom already have taken an amazing turn of 180 degrees toward the partial elections. But the group which has been attacked now, perhaps by the same dissenters who then attacked Márquez Sterling, did not raise its voice of indignant protest nor did it shroud anyone with stupid suspicions. Today those same party members are being called alcoholics and men without scruples.

The campaign of defamation against us on the part of the regime, whose game some are now foolishly playing though they consider themselves adversaries, continued with renewed intensity as soon as we left prison.

Pardo Llada[2] came on a vacation to Mexico; he had the kindness to get in touch with me, exchanging impressions over a long period of time in the presence of his wife and other friends. He even expressed his skepticism concerning the civic dialogue and recognized the foundations of our revolutionary position as well. The spokesman of the regime were fearful that perhaps there would be a revolutionary rapprochement between the most important radio commentator with the largest audience in Cuba and the 26th of July Movement. Thus, they publicized the infamous version that his trip had served the purpose of offering me a dishonorable return to Cuba, and that consequently I had attacked him with my fists. So absurd, unfounded, and ridiculous was all of this that it did not merit, I thought, a public statement.

When the efforts toward mediation were making some headway and a meeting for all the parties concerned was imminent, the delegates of the opposition parties began to receive threatening letters signed supposedly by the executives of the 26th of July Movement. One of these is today in my hands due to the courtesy of René Fiallo, who received it and who is one of the few who did not enrich themselves while in power during the preceding regime. In spite of the fact that we think differently politically, he has had, for those who have fallen and for us, words of recognition for which we must be grateful. One of these letters accused him of misappropriation. It had been drawn up with phrases gathered from our manifestos, trying to imitate our style and, naturally, had been typed and had no written signature. Imme-

2 José Pardo Llada, the radio commentator, was an Ortodoxo leader aided by the *Fidelista* cause, but in 1960 he sought refuge from the Castro government in Colombia. Eds.

diately the spokesmen of the regime spent their time raising the specter
of the twenty-sixth of July for all the political parties, recommending an
immediate electoral compromise. Some fearful delegates took this
seriously—they must have had a bad conscience!—and the famous
apocryphal letters received the honor of a discussion in the SAR.[3]
What need had we to threaten anyone with private letters if our viewpoint on mediation and the concept we have of compromise and com-
promisers have been expressed over and over again in these same pages
of *Bohemia* for hundreds of thousands of readers to see and signed with
our own hand?

A young female student is kidnapped, beaten, tortured, and abandoned on the highway; a young man from Camagüey is kidnapped,
burned on the feet, and likewise abandoned in the city of Florida. So
now, the spokesmen of the regime do not hesitate to suggest that this
is the work of those who dissent from the mediation efforts, as if the
dictatorship had not set sufficient precedents by their attacks on the
"Universidad del Aire"; blows inflicted on the journalist Mario
Kuchilán; burns of another journalist, Armando Hernández; the bomb
which exploded on the stomach of the worker Mario Arostegui; the
castor oil which Chaviano forced the radio commentators of CMKC
to drink; the horrendous tortures they inflicted on the distributor of
the paper *La Calle* in Guantánamo; the disappearance of Narciso
Hernández Báez, whose remains still have not been found (incidentally, it never occurred to the mediators to claim the cadaver), and
an infinity of other abuses.

Yet I shall never support the immorality of affirming or suggesting
that the incidents which occurred at the residence of Dr. Dorta Duque
were the work or inspiration of elements of the government. And if we
had promoted that unfortunate incident, we would not hesitate to say
so publicly. Open and sincere conduct which takes the responsibility
for its good judgment as well as for its mistakes, rather than the infamy
and the cowardliness that are enveloped in the subterfuge and the lie,
is always healthier and more useful. When I was arrested in the
Moncada, in spite of the fact that at that time we were classified as
war criminals and an immense portion of the country was confused, I
did not hesitate to declare resolutely that I assumed all responsibility
for that action. If there is something that we have always fought
against, it is hypocrisy and Pharisaism; if something has always characterized our style, it is the frankness with which we have expressed
ourselves and an unconditional devotion to truth.

I cannot justify by any means those who damaged the residence of

[3] Sociedad de Amigos de la República. Eds.

Dr. Dorta Duque and interrupted the meeting, but I can understand it perfectly: It was a spontaneous and lawless action by unorganized elements of the masses. We already know what the reactions of individuals are when they meet in a multitude of this type, regardless of the part of the world. They understand only what is simple and clear. They do not understand complex analysis of the strategic convenience or inconvenience of a dialogue with Anselmo Alliegro, Santiago Rey, or Justo Luis del Pozo; they see it as treason and they act accordingly. The fact that the masses are destructive but highly moral, as Gustave LeBon says, is demonstrated in what occurred at the home of Dr. Duque, where pictures were thrown on those who met there but not a single object was stolen.

If that mass reached a peak of excitement that produced such an uncivilized act, I, who have not produced one single declaration in the last two months, cannot be blamed. Blame the Ortodoxo policies, blame the national leadership which two weeks before the incident adopted a radical pronouncement opposing any conversation with the regime while a state of oppression and a lack of guarantees continued to prevail. It demanded seven points, none of which was conceded. The state of repression did not cease. Far from it; it was increased for days. The students of the School of Commerce of Camagüey were abused; then, of course, the cases of Enelida González and José Carballo occurred. The act of commemorating the infamous assassination of the revolutionary Matico Fernández was prohibited; citizens of all parties were the victims of attacks everywhere. When the indignation of the people was at its peak because of these incidents, the national leadership of the Partido del Pueblo, which had set public sensibility on fire, made a complete turnabout and retracted their proclamations.

I am not questioning whether this was the last resort given the theatrical appeal of Don Cosme, or an isolated situation in which this clique was going to abandon the one who accompanied it on this adventure. But I do question the right of party leaders to adopt radical agreements and to act like a sailboat whose course is decided by the wind—in this case the worst kind of political opportunism. If they adopt and later retract them, playing with the feelings of their own masses, they should blame no one for the consequences of their acts. I have never attempted to pressure any leaders of the party, either publicly or privately, individually or collectively, nor have I believed that they would allow themselves to be intimidated. I shall dishonor no one nor shall I dishonor myself with such procedures as are resorted to by cowards or by those who accuse others of being cowards.

Numerous facts have demonstrated this thought of ours. When

conflicts within the Ortodoxos' youth section began, a directive was issued to our militants demanding that they prevent personal incidents at any cost. Later, with a sincere effort on both parts, all of the difficulties were definitely overcome.

Right after the last incident that happened to Márquez Sterling as he was leaving a television program on CMQ, which the government press tried to attribute to us, I immediately stated through *Bohemia* (version of the Palm Garden meeting): "We are radically opposed to the methods of violence directed toward persons of any opposing organization that disagrees with us, just as we are equally opposed to terrorism and personal assassination." He who knows the idiosyncrasies of the Cuban people knows that if they are willing to sympathize with all noble rebelliousness, they deplore with all their soul coercion and aggression. And after so much struggle to define our position on this matter clearly, we cannot allow some leaders of the party in order to mask their mistakes to make unjust attacks against the Movement which today they are serving. Let it be said once and for all: The true followers of the preachings and example of Eduardo Chibás are those who have fought alone against the regime, those who alone have been maintaining a struggle for the last four years against the dictatorship and the political cliques, those of us who have not sat at the same table with those who were anathema yesterday, those of us who have not considered sitting and conversing with the delegates of the tyranny, those of us who will continue to maintain our stand while there is a single worthy man in the nation—and no one will be able to throw this or anything else in our faces because we have been able to follow a correct line without contradiction.

In the end, the Ortodoxo movement will depend on the thousands of its best members following those who remain loyal to the principles of its great founder. The true historical Ortodoxos are men like Luis Orlando Rodríquez, Juan Manuel Márquez, Rubén Acosta, Pastorita Núñez, Erasmo Gómez, Orlando Castro, Pepín Sánchez, and others of that handful of founders who together with Chibás saved the party when the provincial chieftains wanted to carry it into coalition with Miguel Suárez and the Democratic Party. These founders, who opposed the action then, would be in accord with our revolutionary line today. On that occasion, those affiliated with the party together with Eduardo Chibás made their protest heard in the meetings.

What did some of those men do who today promote mediation? They abandoned the organization leaving Chibás alone in the most decisive moment of his public life, while they became candidates for governor and senator for the Liberal Party. Who can assure us that the obsession for a senatorial position is not evident once again?

What can come out of the Casa de la Cultura[4] in the best of cases? Elections presided over by Batista and his gang of murdering generals; the forgetting of all the assassinations; the legalization of all the fortunes which had been acquired through robbery; the right of Batista to make as many coup d'états and fraudulent elections as he would like, faced only by a bunch of impotent politicians and the kiss of Judas on a mountain of blood and muck. If the Ortodoxo leadership does not have faith in the dialogue, the result of which can be none other than that mentioned previously, why did it not courageously declare the fact from the very first instant? Why did it attend the farce, led around by the nose as a toy of the most spurious political interests, completely remote from the great historical mission that we must fulfill? Why did it allow itself to get tangled in the net that was sewn by its adversaries? Why did it not audaciously adopt its own policies? Why did it leave us alone before July 26? Why does it leave us alone today? Why did it spend $100,000 in political reorganization and campaigning for the House of Representatives and town mayors when the hour had arrived to demonstrate that in truth it was as humble and committed as it had been proclaiming from the podium, when the moment had arrived to prove that it was capable of sacrificing for Cuba in the same manner as it had solicited the votes of citizens and demanded the greatest sacrifices of them? It has not been willing to give a miserable cent to free the fatherland from misery, hunger, tyranny, and dishonesty. How different from the affiliated members, those who never aspired to the House of Representatives or to senatorial posts! There lies the undebatable proof of their generosity and adherence to our cause, in the thousands of dollars that are being gathered cent by cent, given by humble hands to prepare the great and final redemption, consecrating as a beautiful reality the faith that we place in the virtues of our people.

It would be profoundly painful for a break to occur between the leadership of the party and its revolutionary wing, the 26th of July Movement. Among other reasons, I harbor great sympathies for Raúl Chibás, I love Conte, I feel sincere affection that I will preserve in any circumstances for José Manuel Gutiérrez, Pelayo Cuervo, Agramonte, Carone, Bisbé, and many others. What I wish the most is for us to unite in that line which has been demonstrated to be the right and just one; for us together to make the effort, together to free the

[4] Where oppositionists met with the government. Eds.

country from this shameful situation; for us together to govern the Republic tomorrow, the technicians in their places, the men of struggle and action in theirs.

Today I defend myself from an unjust accusation, from a suspicion I do not merit, from the attitude of some leaders of the party who have questioned our conduct before the public. Let it suffice in the way of an epilogue to end these painful clarifications that the young man Jorge Barroso, who suffered injuries on the twenty-third at the residence of Dr. Dorta Duque, is an old friend of mine from university studies and struggle, and he is also a very dear member of our movement. On December 7, he was at the meeting of the Key West émigrés with us. Raúl Cervantes, responsible for the finances of the Movement in the city of Ciego de Ávila, granted me, before he died, the very high honor of sending me his pen through the family, and a message in which he said that he was content to be reunited with his fallen friends because he had absolute faith in the victory of our ideals.

To the people of Cuba, we express our satisfaction in knowing that the day in which we shall fulfill our work is not far away.

And if any *compañero* of the party still doubts the sincerity with which I write these declarations, he will have time to verify the fact that the 26th of July Movement was organized to combat face to face the regime that possesses tanks, cannons, jet planes, napalm bombs, and all kinds of modern weapons and not to attack a tranquil dwelling where a group of defenseless citizens have gathered.

The 26th of July Movement
(March 19, 1956)

The names of those who obstruct the task of liberating their country should be recorded in the same place of dishonor and shame as the names of those who oppress it. In Cuba there are, unfortunately, many who have up to now done nothing to redeem the nation from tyranny and, at the same time, have stood in the way as much as possible. Those of us who for years have not rested a single minute in fulfilling our rough and difficult duty know this very well.

Ten months ago, when we left prison, we clearly understood that the rights of the people would never be restored unless the people con-

"El Movimiento 26 de Julio," *Bohemia* (Havana), April 1, 1956, pp. 54, 70–71. This article was written on March 19, 1956.

quered them. From then on we engaged in the creation of a strong revolutionary organization and provided it with the necessary elements to wage the final battle against the regime. For those of us who have made it our life's work, this was not the hardest part. Much more arduous and fatiguing has been the struggle against the bad faith of the politicians, the intrigues of the incompetent, the envy of the mediocre, the cowardice of vested interests, and the selfish and cowardly plots which always oppose any group of men who attempt a great and worthy accomplishment in their surroundings.

The military coup that plunged the country into chaos and despair was an easy task. The people and the government were taken by surprise. The coup was conceived secretly by a handful of disloyal persons who moved freely and perpetrated their criminal plans while the unsuspecting and innocent nation slept. In a few hours Cuba, a democratic country, became, as the world watched, one more link in the group of Latin American nations chained by tyranny. The task of returning the international prestige of the country, recovering the freedom which was snatched from the people, and establishing a new era of true justice and redemption for those who suffer most from exploitation and hunger is, in contrast and by a bitter paradox, incomparably more difficult.

For four years we have been fighting to rebuild what was destroyed in one night. We are fighting a regime that is alert and fearful of the inevitable attack. We are fighting political cliques that apparently are opposed to the situation but in fact are not interested in a radical change in the life of the country. Instead they want to push it further backward to the deadly and sterile politics of fabulously profitable legislative posts and high bureaucratic posts with fortunes attached that can be assured for a lifetime and, if possible, transferred from father to son. We are fighting the intrigues and maneuvers of men who speak in the name of the people but who lack their support. We are fighting the wicked preachings of false prophets who speak against revolution in the name of peace and forget that in hungry, fearful, mournful homes there has been no peace in the last four years. We are fighting those who attempt to denounce our uncompromising stand, offering as the saving panacea the poison of an electoral compromise and, at the same time, taking precautions to hide the fact that during the fifty-four years of our republican life maneuver and mediation have not only failed to cure the evils at their root but have produced the horrible misery of our countryside and the industrial poverty of our cities. The result is clear: Hundreds of thousands of families, descendants of our liberators, have no land; more than a million persons are unemployed; the embarrassing figure of 40 percent of our population is illiterate. Compare all these with the fortunes, the land, the palaces, and the personal advancement of hundreds of politicians throughout our republican existence. Stolen money is invested in Cuba, in the United States, and all over the world. And all this has become natural, while the most elemental justice clearly has been forgotten, and moral concepts have become so contradictory and paradoxical that the Sociedad de Amigos de la República, for example, recently made dramatic statements against general amnesty because of the threat it would represent to society if crimes were allowed with impunity. At the same time, they established a solemn dialogue with Anselmo Alliegro, Santiago Rey, Justo Luis del Pozo,[1] and other government figures on whose shoulders, as representatives of past and present situations where blood has been spilled and theft committed, rests more blame than all that could be found in all the occupants in the Isle of Pines prison put together.

I am not resigned to the political fatalism under which we have lived up to now; I want a better destiny for my country, a more dignified public life, a higher collective moral level. I believe that the nation does not exist for the exclusive benefit and privilege of a few, but belongs to all. Each and every one of its six million inhabitants, and the millions to be born in the future, is entitled to a decent life and to justice, work, and well-being. It is because we fight for that ideal without hesitating at any risk or sacrifice, without qualms in giving up the best years of our youth and life, as is being done by hundreds of men of our generation with incomparable selflessness, that our opponents try to present us to the public as outcasts of society or capricious advocates of a position that at the moment is the most honorable, loyal, and patriotic.

This article, therefore, is not only a reply to the last one published against us in the magazine *Bohemia* by one who, forgetting the many links of comradeship and of struggle—as though it were convenient to reject them in difficult times—expressed the thought of the group that officially leads the Ortodoxo Party (mediationist faction).[2] It is also a reply to all those who fight us in good or bad faith; it is a reply to the politicians who repudiate us because of either self-interest or cowardice; it is a reply on behalf of our entire movement to all those who are blind and lack faith in our people.

It is necessary to clear up concepts and put things in their place, so

[1] Officials of the Batista government. Eds.
[2] Refers to an article by Enrique Barroso, "Palos si bogas, y palos si no bogas," *Bohemia* (Havana), March 18, 1956, pp. 53, 81. Eds.

we begin by repeating here what we stated in the message to the Congress of Ortodoxo Militants on August 16, 1955:

> [The 26th of July Movement does] not constitute a tendency within the party; we are the revolutionary apparatus of Chibasismo which is rooted in its cadres, and from which it emerged to struggle against the dictatorship when the Ortodoxo Party lay impotent and divided in a thousand pieces. We have never abandoned its ranks, and we have remained loyal to the purest principles of the great fighter whose death will be commemorated tomorrow.[3]

That message proclaiming a revolutionary line was unanimously approved by the 500 representatives of the Ortodoxo Party from all parts of the island, who stood to applaud it for a full minute. Many of the official leaders were present and none of them spoke against it. From that moment our revolutionary thesis was the thesis of the masses of our party, who had expressed their sentiments unequivocally; from that moment the masses and the leaders began to march down different paths. When did the party militants repeal that agreement? Was it at the provincial mass meetings where the unanimous cry was "Revolution! Revolution!"? And who but we maintained the revolutionary thesis? And what organization could carry it into practice but the revolutionary apparatus of Chibás's followers, the 26th of July Movement?

Seven months have gone by since then. What did the official leaders do from that day on? Defend the thesis of dialogue and mediation. What did we do? Defend the revolutionary thesis and put ourselves to the task of carrying it out. What was the result of the former? Seven months lamentably lost. What was the result of the latter? Seven months of fruitful effort and a powerful revolutionary organization that soon will be ready to go into combat.

I speak about facts and not fantasies; they are based on truths and not sophisms. We could prove that the immense majority of the members of the party—the best of them!—follow our line, yet we do not proclaim it daily. We do not go around speaking in the name of the Ortodoxo Party as do others whose hypothetical backing is very questionable at this point. A lot of water has gone under the bridge since the last reorganization *five years ago!* Who has said that leaders are eternal, that situations do not change, and even more in a process of convulsion where everything is altered with dazzling speed? Things change so much that someone, a product of that reorganization like Guillermo Zéndegui, is today comfortably installed in the government!

---

[3] See "Message to the Congress of Ortodoxo Militants" in this volume. It should be noted that the dates given in these two documents are different. Eds.

At the same time, it is still unknown in what part of Oriente Raúl de Aguiar and Víctor Escalona, delegates from the glorious municipal assembly of Havana, are buried. It would have been a good thing to have questioned the government commissioners who attended the affable meetings concerning the civic dialogue, but they only remember electoral offices and not the dead.

It should be pointed out that an examination of my record in the party, where everyone saw me fighting incessantly, does not show that I occupied any post. I have never been a protagonist, either before or after March 10, of those disgraceful polemics that caused so much harm to the faith of the masses. The newspapers are full of those quarrels, and my name appears in none of them. I have dedicated my time and energies entirely to organizing the struggle against the dictatorship, without any backing from the exalted leaders. The unforgivable thing is that history repeats itself and that at the moment the civic dialogue breaks down and events demonstrate how right our thesis is, when it would be expected for the political apparatus of the party to support our movement, we have received from it the most unjustifiable aggression, using as a petty pretext an incident for which we are not in the least responsible. They have presented that ridiculous episode as a heroic triumph, not against Batista, but rather against the movement that is in the vanguard of the struggle against the regime. Besides being false and a lie, the supposed victory will be a pyrrhic one! Now even more infamous still is the fact that they are trying to absolve me from all blame and to put the full weight of the intrigue on my self-denying comrades in the national directorate of our movement. They do this to men who wage the hardest and most dangerous struggle in Cuba, who never appear in any newspaper because they know silent sacrifice and have no desire for publicity. They do not practice the shameful exhibitionism of those who, under the banner of patriotism, are already campaigning for alderman, congressman, and senator. Their names do not appear publicly today, because they will appear tomorrow in our history. The envious detract from them now, and if any of them falls in battle, those same ones who belittle them would not hesitate to invoke their names when giving speeches. They would be called martyrs, and then the audience would be asked to vote for the speaker.

I do not want to allow my calm indictment to be called a merciless attack, as my previous article was described. But I shall not neglect to clarify points of principle in order to demonstrate who has interpreted best the thought of the founder of the Ortodoxo Party. Let us make a brief summary of the party's history after March 10. As a result of the Montreal meeting, the party was divided into three factions. The interminable conflict between Agramonte and Ochoa[4] became a schism when Pardo Llada[5] made a motion at the Artística Gallega meeting in favor of reaching an understanding with the other parties to wage an insurrectional struggle against the regime. The group in favor of maintaining a line of political independence stated, through a dramatic speech by Professor Bisbé[6] that there was no room for discussion because it was a matter of principle and, consequently, he left the meeting with integrity. From there on three tendencies arose: the Montrealists, the independentists, and the inscriptionists.[7] The independentists excommunicated Pardo Llada, arguing that he had violated the line of independence because he sat down in Montreal with Tony Varona, Hevia, and other Auténticos.[8] The Montrealist group, in turn, defined the position of the independent group as static and inoperative. Both of them excommunicated the inscriptionist group, alleging that it had chosen to follow the electoral legislation of the dictatorship. The party members entered a state of despair and disorder. Many sincere Ortodoxos joined the Triple A of Aureliano Sánchez Arango,[9] feeling that any road was good for overthrowing the regime; others could not transcend the scruples of their conscience, which had been awakened by Chibás's preachings for an independent line; and others, although very few, joined the cadres of the inscriptionists.

The Ortodoxos who sympathized with the Montrealist faction felt dissatisfied with their ideological position; those who followed the independent group found themselves unhappy by the lack of action. It was then, in the midst of that chaos, that within the ranks of the party arose a movement that, because of its stand, was capable of satisfying the true aspirations of the people. It was a movement which, without violating the line of independence set by Chibás, resolutely accepted revolutionary action against the regime. It was a movement which could not provoke qualms of conscience in anyone fulfilling his pure and honest duty. This was the 26th of July Movement.

The question to be asked is not whether we were successful that first time; Chibás did not attain success in 1948, but it was, nonetheless,

[4] Roberto Agramonte and Emilio Ochoa were leaders of the Ortodoxo Party. Eds.

[5] José Pardo Llada was a radio commentator who led the opposition against the Batista government. Eds.

[6] Manuel Bisbé, language professor, leader of the Ortodoxo Party, and after 1959 in the diplomatic corps of the Cuban Revolution. Eds.

[7] The inscriptionists favored elections. Eds.

[8] Tony Varona and Carlos Hevia were leaders of the Auténticos. Eds.

[9] Auténtico insurrectional group. Eds.

a moral victory.[10] What has to be asked is what could have been done by an anonymous group from the people, without resources of any kind, that demonstrated all that can be expected of decent and honorable men. The question to be asked is whether success would have been possible if we could have counted on the support of the party. I am one of those who firmly believe that when the military coup took place if the Ortodoxo Party—with its firm moral principles, the immense influence that Chibás left on the people, and the good reputation that he enjoyed even among the armed forces (for the propaganda made against the party displaced from power could not be directed against the army)—had stood resolutely against the regime, raising the revolutionary banner, today Batista would not be in power. To calculate the possibilities of collecting funds for the struggle, one only has to remember the public collection of one cent per person to free Millo Ochoa, which in twenty-four hours reached seven thousand pesos. Men and women on the street said, "If it is for the revolution, I am ready to give ten pesos instead of one cent."

Three years have passed since then, and only the Movement has maintained its position and principles. The independent group that excommunicated the Montrealists because on that occasion they sat down with the representatives of other parties now sit beside the leaders of the parties they had previously rejected. It is curious that those who rejected an understanding for revolutionary action with the other parties now join those parties to plead for general elections. It is more curious that all those who excommunicated the inscriptionist group for accepting the regime's legislation now meet with the dictatorship's delegates to seek an electoral agreement.

And what infamy! There, in that same meeting, in the presence of the hired sycophants of the dictator, the delegate of the mediationist Ortodoxo faction declared that "the line of Fidel Castro does not have the support of the executive committee." Our line was, however, the line approved unanimously at the Congress of Ortodoxo Militants on August 16, 1955. Today they renounce my name. But they did not disavow my name when, on my leaving the prison where I suffered two honorable years, they needed my declarations of support to strengthen the battered prestige of the official leadership—then my modest apartment was constantly honored with the visits of those same leaders. Today, when to support the worthy line of one who has honestly fulfilled his duty can be dangerous, it is logical to intone a *mea culpa* before the exacting delegates of the tyranny.

[10] In 1948, Chibás was defeated for the presidency by Auténtico candidate Carlo Prío Socarrás. Eds.

It is true that the same delegate defended us later; he defended us in his own way. He said that our attitude was justified because the regime had closed every other opportunity for us to act in Cuba. And I ask the group in whose name the delegate spoke, if our line is justified because the regime closed all other avenues of action in Cuba, is not the adoption of that line more than justified for a party from which victory was snatched eighty days before elections and which for four years has not been allowed to act in Cuba?

The mediation has ended in complete failure. We were resolutely opposed to it because we discovered from the outset the regime's maneuver, whose only purpose since March 10 has been to perpetuate itself indefinitely in power. Behind the formula of the Constitutional Assembly is the intention of reelecting Batista once his term has ended. The dictatorship wanted to gain time—and it has fully achieved that aim thanks to the prodigious unaffected simplicity of Don Cosme, whom they insulted first, then praised, and now insult again.[11] Batista received him in the Presidential Palace in the most critical days of his government, when the country was convulsed by the heroic student rebellion and the formidable sugar workers' movement, which demanded the sugar differential that had not been given to the workers.[12] Batista needed a break: He summoned Don Cosme once again for fifteen days hence. In the first meeting he implied that he would grant everything; in the second Batista was more reserved and in this way gained almost three months, until March 10, when from Camp Columbia, in the middle of the civic dialogue, he carried out another coup against the naïve opposition leaders.

If they did not believe in the results of the dialogue, what did they expect by participating in it? Was their goal to unmask the regime before the people? Do the people need to be shown that this regime is an atrocity and a shame for Cuba? Was it necessary to waste so many months when the time could have been dedicated to another type of struggle? Or did someone sincerely believe in finding a solution through this path? Can anyone be so naïve? Is it not enough to observe how the leaders and representatives of the regime openly enrich themselves and buy country homes, residential districts, and businesses of all types throughout the country, in view of the nation, making evident the intention to remain in power for many years? Do not the smelting of Batista's statue at Camp Columbia and the modern

[11] Cosme de la Torriente, former colonel of the Liberation Army, which was in itself an institution in Cuba politics. He died on December 8, 1956. Eds.

[12] The sugar differential refers to the proportional increment in salaries when the price of sugar is increased on the world market. Eds.

weapons of all types that are constantly being acquired say anything?

It is really deceitful to sit down there with the government's delegates when it is not yet known where many men murdered by the regime have been buried, when not a single one of those who have killed more than a hundred compatriots has been punished. Are the dead to be forgotten? And the ill-gotten fortunes, will they be retrieved? And the March 10 treason, will it go unpunished so that it can be repeated? And the ruin of the Republic, the horrible hunger of hundred of thousands of families, will that remain without hope of a real and effective solution? It is not our fault if the country has been led toward an abyss from which there is no solution other than revolution. We do not love force; we detest force, and that is why we refuse to be governed by force. We do not love violence; we detest violence, and that is why we are not disposed to go on supporting the violence that for four years has been exercised on the nation.

Now it is a people's struggle. The 26th of July Movement has been organized and strengthened to aid the people in their heroic struggle to recover the freedoms and rights that were snatched from them.

The twenty-sixth of July against the tenth of March!

The 26th of July Movement is not different from the Ortodoxo Party for the followers of Chibás. It is the Ortodoxo movement without a leadership of landlords like Fico Fernández Casas, without sugar plantation owners like Gerardo Vázquez, without stock-market speculators, without commercial and industrial magnates, without lawyers for the big interests or provincial chieftains, without incompetent politicians of any kind. The best of the Ortodoxos are beside us waging this beautiful struggle. To Eduardo Chibás we offer the only homage worthy of his life and death: the freedom of his people. This can never be offered by those who have done nothing other than shed crocodile tears on his grave.

The 26th of July Movement is the revolutionary organization of the humble, for the humble, and by the humble.

The 26th of July Movement is the hope of redemption for the Cuban working class, who cannot be offered anything by the political cliques; it is the hope of land for the peasants who live like pariahs in the country that their grandparents liberated. The 26th of July Movement is the hope of return for the emigrants who had to leave their country because they could not live or work in it; it is the hope of food for the hungry and justice for the forgotten.

The 26th of July Movement makes its own the cause of all those who have fallen in the hard struggle since March 10, 1952, and serenely proclaims before the nation, before their wives, their children, their parents and brothers, that the Revolution will never compromise with their executioners.

The 26th of July Movement is the warm invitation to close ranks, extended with open arms to all revolutionaries of Cuba, without miserable sectarian differences and regardless of any previous differences.

The 26th of July Movement is the healthy and just future of the fatherland. Our honor is pledged before the people; the promise will be fulfilled.

On the Arrest of Cuban Revolutionaries in Mexico (June 22, 1956)

I trust that Mexico will continue to be loyal to its noble tradition toward the politically persecuted. For myself, nothing will make me desist from my efforts to retrieve freedom for my fatherland. No one in Cuba is unaware of my position toward communism, for I was a founder of the Partido del Pueblo Cubano along with Eduardo Chibás, who never made a pact nor accepted any type of collaboration with the Communists. Furthermore, our movement has nothing to do with other political groups on the island, nor does it maintain contact with former president Carlos Prío Socarrás.

On June 22, 1956, Fidel Castro and six of his followers were arrested in Mexico for planning a revolt against Batista. That same day, Castro released this statement from prison. "Exilados, cambio de política?" *Bohemia* (Havana), July 1, 1956, pp. 61–62.

Enough Lies! (July 15, 1956)

I had thought of waiting until the termination of the proceedings to give the people of Cuba an explanation of what has occurred in Mexico. However, the report by Mr. Luis Dam, published in the last

"Basta ya de mentiras!" *Bohemia* (Havana), July 15, 1956, pp. 63, 84–85.

issue of *Bohemia* under the pompous title "The Group of the 26th of July in Jail,"[1] forces me to write these lines from prison itself.

The truth is that the newsman was not even allowed to enter the jail, and the picture published of us was taken from the files of the Federal Bureau of Security. He does not deny it and begins affirming that, in spite of the efforts he made, he was not allowed to communicate with us. Afterward, he wrote a news report based only and exclusively on the information of the police, who have acted in self-evident partnership with Batista. The people were unable to read one word by the Cubans who have been victims of persecution and whose opinion, one can suppose, is also of interest to the country for whose destiny they suffer.

When a news report must be written under those conditions, it is best to abstain because of the risk that the truth will not be made known. The reporter can do nothing but echo some criminal lies, and his conduct can appear suspicious if, not knowing the public background of those mentioned, he emphasizes those libelous points which constitute the cowardly theme of the defamation campaign unleashed against us. That the declared enemies of our cause attempt to do us as much harm as possible and behave with opportunism and covetousness can be understood perfectly; but it is bitter and painful that, under the title of impartial reporter, a one-sided version is chosen in an attempt to confuse the Cuban nation at the moment when a group of its most sacrificing sons are mistreated, slandered, persecuted, and even tortured outside their fatherland.

In matters like this, to write superficially is to write criminally.

When at this instant there are *compañeros* who were kidnapped by the police and have vanished without their possibly terrible fate being known, when a cry of alarm given on time could save their lives, what has the reporter done with his lack of impartiality to better the fate of our *compañeros*?

It seems a common thing in my public life to have to wage the most difficult battle in favor of truth from a cell. It is not the first time, and perhaps will not be the last. The dishonorable adversaries use every kind of weapon and take advantage above all of adverse moments (when one is imprisoned or incommunicado and they believe one to be defenseless) to try to win before the public, through lies, the battle they have been waging vainly for the last four years.

At this instant we are prisoners in a foreign country; we have been sequestered in its prisons for over twenty days, without their fulfilling

[1] Refers to an article by Luis Dam, "El grupo 26 de Julio en la cárcel," *Bohemia* (Havana), July 8, 1956. Eds.

the most elemental requirement of placing at our disposition a competent authority. No one will protest officially this violation of rights; no ambassador will speak in the name of the faraway fatherland. We do not have consuls or diplomats to represent us; any common delinquent of any country in that sense is more fortunate. Those who in the name of Cuba figure here—anointed representatives of the country by pure fiction—are those who furiously instigate persecution and scatter slander with hands full of mercenary gold. Then, more than ever, one experiences the bitter sensation that Cubans have no fatherland.

But this is not the time for sentimentalism because here, in spite of all mishaps and dirty plots, our morale is as high as ever.

The history of what has occurred in Mexico is very different from that expressed in the official report, and I am going to refer to it with the moral authority of having always written with absolute honesty.

I had received repeated warnings from Cuba, and on occasion the plea of our *compañeros* and sympathizers, to adopt greater precautionary measures, for an attempt against my life was being plotted. I had received the news through several channels worthy of complete trust.

The idea of eliminating me physically already had hovered in the minds of some elements of the regime for several months, but it was only recently, as the dictatorship grew more desperate and the strength of our movement was growing visibly, that the plan took official character and the first steps were taken to that effect. They were faced with the problem of preventing a scandal as much as possible and not leaving a trail. I must say they elaborated the plan minutely and in almost perfect form, which partly because we were informed of it and above all due to pure luck was not carried out. I shall leave the exact facts and details for another occasion.

The agent in charge of this mission made two trips to Mexico in the last few months. On both occasions he stayed in the Prado Hotel, the most luxurious in Mexico. The first time he was discovered by some of our *compañeros* while he hovered about the house at Emparan. Apparently discouraged, he returned to Cuba, reporting that it was not easy to carry out his mission. Weeks later he returned with two other agents. It was then they were assured that the only person capable of successfully realizing the undertaking in Mexico was a Cuban subject, a fugitive from justice, who resides in Mexico with forged papers, known here as Arturo, "El Jarocho," who is also an agent of the Secret Service and a confidant of General Molinari, the chief of police. I understand, however, that Molinari had nothing to do with this matter, for the Cuban agents dealt directly with "El Jarocho" and stipulated a price of $10,000 that he would have to share with another individual who was to arrive from Venezuela (for "they did not want Mexicans in on this matter").

They know that someone always accompanied me, and they intended to eliminate him also. The plan was to present themselves in uniform in a police patrol car, arrest us, place handcuffs on us, kidnap us, and make us disappear afterward without any trail. I have been assured that they had a paper with my signature perfectly forged with which they thought of sending a letter from another country to Emparan 49 stating that I urgently had to take leave of Mexico. Although the plot was childish, they intended to sow confusion with it initially, while several other versions were made up. Having drawn up all the details, the agents returned to Cuba around June 10.

We had to await the events calmly, knowing that a vulgar assassin was plotting our death for the price of $10,000. What we did was to take basic precautionary measures, going out seldom and not frequenting the same places.

I must confess that we did not foresee all the dangers of our situation. When they realized that we were on alert and ready to defend ourselves, that it was very risky to realize their original plan, they circulated our automobile license plates and threw the Federal Security Agency on us.

I was not arrested in the ranch, as the news report affirms, but in the middle of the street, by agents of that corps. Had these men not acted with extreme caution, proceeding to identify themselves previously, a grave incident could have taken place. Perhaps this also entered into the calculations of the plan's authors.

Behind the whole plot was a river of gold. In contrast, when we were arrested, we only had $20 in the Movement treasury.

The Cuban Embassy knew everything. They knew about the arrest before anyone else and immediately began a propaganda campaign through their agents. Everything was perfectly planned with repugnant cynicism. They immediately announced that "seven Cuban Communists were imprisoned for conspiring against Batista." They inserted a number of facts pertaining to the Moncada, the imposed sentence, and so forth, which only the embassy could have known. They added the stupid statement that I had entered Mexico "with a passport obtained thanks to the recommendations of Lázaro Peña and Lombardo Toledano"[2]—as if no one knew how a passport is processed in Cuba, without anyone's recommendations, and the visa in the Mexican con-

---

[2] A Cuban and Mexican Communist respectively. Eds.

sulate, for which a mere bank letter is the requirement, though it was not even demanded from me when the consul granted me the visa with sympathetic and hospitable words.

Naturally the accusation of my being a Communist was absurd in the eyes of all who knew my public path in Cuba, without any kind of ties with the Communist Party. But that propaganda is elaborated for the consumption of Mexican public opinion and international news agencies and for the purpose of adding the pressure of the American embassy to that which they have been applying to the Mexican authorities.

The Batista regime must be feeling very weak when in the face of the growing strength of our movement it must resort to that miserable lie of calling for the interference of powerful international interests.

I totally denounce Mr. Luis Dam's report where he says, "Incidentally the Federal Security Police affirms that it has verified that Fidel is a member of the Communist Party." Captain Gutiérrez Barros himself read me the report forwarded to the President of Mexico after a week of minute investigation; among its observations it was categorically affirmed that we had no ties whatsoever with Communist organizations. An extract of that report was published in all the newspapers. I have before me *Excelsior* of June 26, page 8, column 6, paragraph 5, where it reads as follows: "The Federal Bureau of Security emphasized that the 26th of July group has no Communist ties nor receives help from the Communists."

If this was what was confidentially affirmed to the President of Mexico and also appeared in the newspapers, why would they have told something else to Mr. Dam?

The intrigue is ridiculous besides and without the least foundation because I have been a militant in only one Cuban political party, and that is the one founded by Eduardo Chibás. What moral authority, on the other hand, does Mr. Batista have to speak of communism when he was the Communist Party presidential candidate in the elections of 1940, if his electoral posters took shelter under the hammer and sickle, if his pictures beside Blas Roca and Lázaro Peña are still around, if half a dozen of his present ministers and trusted collaborators were well-known members of the Communist Party?

There is talk about an arsenal of weapons, and all that the Mexican police encountered were five old rifles and four pistols. In any peaceful ranch there are more weapons than that.

But there are other points to clarify. Why is it assiduously affirmed that "the Mexican press energetically condemns the attitude of Fidel Castro and his *compañeros*"? The press published at the very outset what the police reported and the versions sent out by the embassy. But as soon as the truth opened its way, the honest press, the honest journalists who are also plentiful here, reacted unanimously in our favor.

The newspaper *Excelsior*—one of the most prestigious and with the greatest circulation in Mexico, a million readers—in its editorial of July 4, under the title "Significant Habeas Corpus," among other things wrote the following:

> The federal judge Miguel Lavalle Fuentes has granted habeas corpus to the 25 Cuban citizens whom the Federal Bureau of Security has kept imprisoned for several days. The reason for the imprisonment, or the pretext, is that the above mentioned police have accused them of preparing a revolt against President Batista. . . . To confirm it, the accusers presented several objects, among them pistols and old rifles, which are considered inoffensive weapons. . . . Because of that accusation they have been kept incommunicado. Three Cubans have been tortured in the infamous jail of Pocito. . . . Federal justice must be warmly praised for undoing, though tardily, one of the maneuvers of the misnamed Mexican Security Police. This is not the only case, and all Mexico knows it. The reputation that the Mexican police agency has built for itself is truly shameful. A corps of that nature must be abolished for the honor of Mexican justice.

In the same newspaper, *Excelsior*, there is an in-depth attack in the editorial of July 5 against Batista, under the title "Consequences of Political Persecution." It reads as follows: "The arrogance of dictators usually implicitly carries its own perdition. . . . In his furious madness, the despot does not care that harassed people make, out of the innocent victims of dictatorial insanity, heroes whom they elevate to myth." After mentioning the cases of Sandino and Galíndez, it concludes,

> It is not hazardous to affirm that Dr. Fidel Castro never thought to become paladin of Cuba's freedom and he has come to be considered a version of Martí. Notwithstanding what General Batista has wanted, by unleashing such unjust persecution against him, Castro Ruz overnight has become a man whom his people trust to free them from tyranny, and a political exile on whom converge the sympathies of the Mexican people—who do not quite understand how it has been possible for the reprisals of a dictator to exercise themselves in Mexican territory, which has been a safe place for the politically persecuted and wide refuge for the trampled liberties of the continent.

"Equislogismos," another one of the most widely read sections in the Mexican press, says with irony,

At least habeas corpus still exists in Mexico. It is very bad that there exist policemen who play at intelligence without demonstrating it and who, together with the Cuban exiles who possessed two harquebuses, one musket, and perhaps a bow and arrow, "mistakenly" arrested two Peruvians who neither had those deadly weapons in their possession nor much less were interested in overthrowing any Creole dictator.

A headline in the newspaper *Ultimas Noticias* says, "Mexico Will Judge the Cubans, It Will Not Deliver Them to the Executioner."

Carlos Denegri, widely read columnist of an afternoon newspaper, adds his pen to our cause, remembering the asylum which Cuba gave Mexicans during the period of the Revolution.

Journalist Roberto Roldán of *La Prensa* writes,

Sifting the first impressions of the Cuban case, it becomes clear that it is nothing but a powerful maneuver on the part of dictators to extend their underhanded persecution of their adversaries. Fidel Castro and his friends are not Communists; the "abundant arsenal of weapons" which preoccupied the Mexican Security Police never existed. This is why we have asked from the very beginning the greatest caution in these things in which the subtleness and power of the dictators becomes evident through their remote control.

It would be endless to enumerate similar reports which we have filed, as well as the numerous letters addressed to newspapers by Cuban and Mexican citizens. Dr. Carlos Vega, an Auténtico youth leader, goes directly to the point when he says in a letter to the editor of *Excelsior*,

Today, Mr. Editor, I was overwhelmed by surprise as I read in the press a cable from Havana which stated that a high-ranking functionary of the Presidential Palace in Cuba gave reports emanating from the investigations undertaken by the Mexican Security Policy—details which are still not known in Mexico. That boastful declaration only showed that Batista's money and fist are behind the persecution of Cuban refugees in this country.

The police procedures and the tortures used in Mexico on Cubans have nothing to learn from those used in Cuba. The Federal Security was more prudent before the firmness of the arrested, understanding that it was useless to use torture. But the same day, the twenty-first, *compañeros* Cándido González, Julio Díaz, and Alfonso Zelaya were arrested by the Secret Service, *a true nest of gangsters*. For six days they were not given food or water. In the early dawn hours, with temperatures of almost zero, they were put in tanks of freezing water with hands and feet tied and completely naked; they were dunked and when they were about to suffocate they were pulled out by the hair for a few seconds before being submerged once again. This procedure was repeated many times; then they were taken from the water and beaten unconscious. A hooded man, who spoke with a Cuban accent, gave the interrogation, without obtaining results. They were Batista's agents. They were the only ones who have been violating Mexican hospitality, Mexican laws, and even Mexican sovereignty, because as fugitives of justice they falsified Mexican papers, they bribed and corrupted functionaries, tortured and prepared the treacherous murder of political adversaries. The stay of those henchmen here is corroborated by the newspaper *Ultimas Noticias* of June 25, column 4, page 1, which reads as follows: "A real cloud of special agents of Cuba's SIM,[3] a greatly feared organization in the island, remains in our country and travels daily to airports, harbors, and other places where Cuban political exiles arrive in Mexico."

On Tuesday, July 3, during the evening, *compañero* Jesús Reyes was kidnapped by several men in a car. It is not known whether they were federal agents or of the Secret Service. More than six days have gone by, and there is no news about him. We do not know what fate he has met.

Batista has invested hundreds of thousands of dollars to unleash this persecution. The Mexican citizenry and exiles of all countries residing in this capital are indignant about this unusual event.

The behavior of the police corps and the Secretary of Government violates the Mexican Constitution, as they have refused to comply with the order of the federal judge to either free us or bring us before the courts. We have been imprisoned for twenty days already. An extraordinary current of sympathy is awakening in this noble people for the Cubans who, in spite of torture and threats of deportation, have behaved with exemplary dignity. The incident has served, besides, to closely unite all Cubans in exile. It will also serve to show that the enemies of the liberation of our people are many and in order to carry it out it is necessary to unite, without exception or exclusion of any sort, all Cubans who want to fight.

The 26th of July Movement, which preserves intact all its forces, its spirit of struggle, proclaims the necessity to unite all men, all weapons, and all resources against the tyranny which divides us, persecutes us, and assassinates us if we are separate. The dispersion of forces is the death of the Revolution; the union of all revolutionaries is the death of the dictatorship.

Fidel Castro
Miguel Schultz Prison
Mexico, July 9, 1956

[3] Military Intelligence Service. Eds.

Interview in Mexico
(August 7, 1956)

Q: How were you treated during your recent arrest in Mexico?
A: The incident should be forgotten; I do not want it to leave any resentment in Cubans against Mexico. Prison and maltreatment are prices we have to pay in our profession as fighters. If instead of revolutionaries we had been Batistianos, the embassy would have protected us. But we are adversaries of the tyranny, and its mission consisted of seeking the worst for us. Persecution and defamation emanated from the embassy. Those who suffered the tortures of the Secret Service in the Pocitos Prison were not considered Cubans by the embassy; we were considered something even worse than enemies of the fatherland.

They repeat the sad role of the Spanish consuls against the Cubans who fought for independence. I have proof of what I say. They are criminals with fancy suits who invest the Republic's money in persecuting our compatriots in exile, making the embassies into centers of espionage instead of publicizing our sugar and seeking markets for our products and supporting the commercial and spiritual trade of our countries. This is the inevitable policy of any dictatorship.

Q: What is your opinion on the partial elections? Do you think that the opposition should participate?
A: After four years of ruling the country with blood and fire, imposing invariably the interests and whims of a clique, appointing its few supporters to all state posts in the provinces, municipalities, and autonomous organizations, it is a bloody mockery to the nation that the dictatorship now offers the formula of partial elections to solve the crisis it provoked by its ambition and treachery. This plan does not solve, it only divides. Don Cosme de la Torriente already has expressed his disagreement; almost all the parties have rejected this formula. The fact that a few ambitious and opportunistic politicians have accepted the formula proves nothing. Cuba does not want to be ruled through force any longer. The nation demands a government elected by the people.

No one can deny the people that inalienable right; it cannot be restricted or questioned. The people will not renounce that right regardless of its price or how long the struggle goes on. This is a principle that cannot be renounced. If that right were taken away from the people by force, it would be recovered by force. Our rights, as

Francis L. McCarthy, "Admite Fidel Castro cambio en su táctica," *El Mundo* (Havana), August 7, 1956, pp. 1, A10.

José Martí taught us, are not to be begged but demanded; they are to be taken by the people.

Q: What would be your position? Are you going to continue your efforts?

A: Some politicians change positions as one changes shirts. Men of firm convictions are loyal to their ideas regardless of sacrifices. Our liberators, who fought for thirty years to achieve independence, were never dismayed. Our line remains the same as the one we adopted on March 10, 1952, a line for which hundreds of courageous Cubans have died. Not a single young man who respects himself and is honest will dare talk to the people while having personal aspirations; the people will not allow it. Even at the time when Grau agreed to participate in the elections of November 1, one could speak, at least theoretically, of a total change in power. Now not even that is possible. I do not see how the politicians are going to tell the people to vote for them under such conditions. The people will go to those meetings of the pseudo-opposition to mock the politicians. Those meetings will have no participation and will be surrounded by soldiers. Wherever a voice is raised to propose this poor formula, the people will raise their voice to oppose it. The cry of revolution continues to be the speech of the masses.

There can be no capitulation when the nation needs to be intransigent with its rights.

Q: Do you think then that the revolution has not failed?

A: Some of us have seen the extraordinary examples of courage and idealism, have felt the energy of a new generation ready to sacrifice itself; this is a generation eager to fight and full of faith in the future of Cuba, aided by reason and history. We know that the Revolution cannot fail.

For every politician willing to sacrifice the fatherland to benefit himself, there are 1,000 young men ready to sacrifice themselves to benefit the nation. As long as three rebels remain in Cuba, the Revolution will not be defeated. War, as Martí said, begins when there are reasons for it; it grows from the impatience of courageous men.

Those who proclaim the failure of the Revolution are the turncoat politicians who have no scruples and who justify their cynicism. They keep smiling while the master mistreats them. The most famous enemies of the Revolution today carried a "bazooka" on their shoulders two years ago. But they lacked the courage to carry out their ideas to their ultimate consequences. Essentially they were mere simulators.

Q: Do you think that there is a youth capable of governing the country?

A: Politics has been prostituted to such an extent in Cuba that thousands of honorable and capable persons have separated themselves from it. Our people, luckily, are very rich in human resources. This is so not only with our youth but among all age groups. There are very valuable and capable men who will be disposed to serve the fatherland when public administration is cleansed of the stigma it suffers today. Mainly youth respond to this first phase, because they are much more combative.

We know very well that we have to distinguish between the men of action and the administration men. Each one has a function to fulfill. When the first phase of the struggle concludes, the constructive phase will begin. At that time we intend to invite the best human resources of our country to aid us in building a new fatherland that will be democratic in the political sphere and socially just. The Revolution will reach power free from compromises, personal interests, and ambitions.

Q: What plan do you have with respect to Cuba? Are you going to return or stay in Mexico?

A: We have stated that in 1956 we shall be free or become martyrs, and we shall be true to our word.

Q: What do you have to say about the last military conspiracy? What about Goicuría?[1]

A: I believe that Colonel Barquín, Major Borbonet,[2] and his comrades are the most genuine representatives of the military honor that our army used to have. They did not conspire against the Constitution or against a government chosen by the people, nor did they try to make a coup eighty days prior to general elections; on the contrary, they wanted respect for our Magna Carta, the reestablishment of popular sovereignty, and immediate general elections, without Batista, as our people want. That was recognized by Blanco Rico, chief of the Military Intelligence Service himself, before the military tribunal. What right do those who achieved power through a military coup have to call these officers detestable traitors? Are the soldiers of the Republic good soldiers when they overthrow the Constitution to benefit a clique that has no votes or prestige, and bad ones when they want to overthrow that small clique to restore the Constitution?

[1] Military conspiracy uncovered on April 3, 1956, led by a number of military men and professionals, also known as the Montecristi group. The attack on the Goicuría Barracks occurred on April 29, 1956; led by Reynold García, it was aimed at sabotaging the Civic Dialogue that was taking place at the time. Eds.

[2] Military men who opposed the Batista dictatorship. Eds.

If the officers of April 3 are traitors, what should we consider the officers of March 10? Or perhaps do military men have to be loyal only to a man who has oppressed the nation for fifteen years while enriching himself? Are military men supposed to be loyal to despotism and not loyal to the Republic, to the people, to the fatherland, to the men who sustain them with their sweat? What crimes have these officers committed? By what right can Batista condemn a military coup when he achieved power by a military coup? How can the men who carried out a military coup on March 10 judge the military men who revolted on April 3? I honestly believe that they should be freed immediately. I do not see how some politicians can talk about elections while those men are imprisoned.

One of the first measures of the victorious revolution will be the reinstatement of those honest military men to their posts.

With regard to the Goicuría incident, it is clear that the government was well informed about the planned attack on the barracks. The government could have prevented it; nevertheless, it preferred the massacre. Then the history of the Moncada was repeated: the prisoners were murdered. Nonetheless, this event demonstrated once again the indomitable courage of our people.

Q: What is your opinion of the Sociedad de Amigos de la República and Don Cosme de la Torriente?

A: The SAR has been very skillful in making its plan—unite the political parties, mobilize public opinion—but very weak in carrying out its thesis to its logical consequence. If SAR had called for civic resistance when Batista broke the negotiations by rejecting the unanimous demand for general elections, there would be no dictatorship today. SAR should coordinate its action with the revolutionary forces so that at a given moment, if necessary, those forces could second the SAR's demands with weapons at hand. If this is not done, the dictatorship will laugh at SAR's impotence and the demands will be similar to those made by José Antonio Saco to Spain, when he confessed beforehand that Cuba was unable to win them. Needless to say, the reforms were never granted.

We consider Don Cosme a virtuous and patriotic man, even though, logically, there is a difference of half a century between our way of thinking. If Don Cosme were 29 years old today, he would support the revolutionary thesis. Did he not demonstrate that in 1895?

Q: What do you think of Pardo Llada and his present position?

A: When the news from Mexico reached Cuba announcing the raid against us, Pardo Llada believed that the revolutionary thesis was definitively defeated. It was a mistaken estimate. Our arrest did not imply greater consequences because all of our fighting resources are in Cuba awaiting the precise moment. Besides, soon the unity of all fighting forces existing in Cuba, with all their weapons, transcending all personal or political differences, will be achieved so that the isolated sacrifices of a Moncada or a Goicuría will not be repeated.

I know Pardo's feelings and I do not now think that he will adopt a line that would remove him irremediably from the historic line of our generation. Pardo had very sincere friends among us. I hope we can exchange viewpoints with him.

Q: What do you think of Prío? Should he return to Cuba?

A: Batista has been merciless with Prío beyond all limits, by insults, taunts, and humiliation. Now Batista wants him to return after he rooted up Prío and his family with machine guns from their home one morning. Batista violently expelled Prío from the country with his clothes in a handbag as if he were a beggar and not a former president. A person cannot be offended so much and remain unpunished. I am sure Prío will act consistently. When we were arrested in Mexico, and people spoke insistently about our deportation, Prío—a man I have fought several times—was very much a gentleman. He wrote in his capacity as former president of Cuba an open letter to the president of Mexico asking him not to deport us.

Our reply to the Batista regime is directed at uniting in a single front all the revolutionary forces. The fierce repression of a handful of young men in the attack on the Goicuría Barracks, Prío's expulsion from Cuba, the persecution unleashed against us in Mexico, the reprisals against our courageous young students, against the labor sectors who demand their rights, the imprisonment and retirement of many military men known for their competence and honesty, in other words, the persecution of everyone who has opposed the regime, demonstrates without doubt that the dictatorship's tactics have been to divide and conquer its adversaries. That is why it is useful for the Revolution to unite these people. Martí taught us never to do what our adversary wants us to do. All the political parties, without exception, united to demand uselessly an electoral solution; it is more dignified to unite in order to demand our freedom. No one has a right to criticize that.

Some might think that this declaration implies a change of tactics on our part. I accept it. A tactical change is necessary within the revolutionary line. It is foolish to disregard the lessons of reality. Later we can argue; now the only honest thing to do is to fight.

Cuba and the Dominican Republic
(August 26, 1956)

Dear friend:

It is urgently necessary for me to write you this letter. My heart is paralyzed with bitterness, and my hands are weary from so much struggle, from writing so much against infamy and evil; sometimes it is even repugnant to me to take up my pen to fight against the lowest and most vulgar tricks. But none of these will stop me from doing my duty. I do so with the same faith I had four and a half years ago, and it will only end with the fulfillment of my promise or death.

The barrage of slanders hurled at us by the dictatorship is beyond all limits. Only five weeks ago I had to send you an article to reply to a report made by Luis Dam in which I was accused of being a member of the Mexican-Soviet Institute and an active member of the Communist Party.[1] Weeks later, in spite of the responsible conduct of all my comrades in Mexico, who have never been seen in a bar or a cabaret and whose high standard of morality and discipline is recognized by all (including the Mexican police itself), a writer subsidized by the [Cuban] embassy was vile enough to affirm that on several occasions he had to defend Cubans who "had created public scandals by excessive drinking" and things of that sort.

Now I open the August 19 issue of *Bohemia* in its section "On Cuba" and read a summary of the denunciation made by Salas Cañizares[2] where he is sufficiently barefaced to cynically and shamelessly link my name—the name of a tireless fighter against the tyranny that oppresses our people—to that of the despicable tyrant who has oppressed the Dominican people for 25 years.[3]

As the chief of police has attributed to himself the right to pass political judgment and to write whatever he wants about the reputation of the dictatorship's adversaries in reports to the courts which are published everywhere in the national and foreign press, and as these wicked, criminal, and cowardly denunciations are taken as a basis by the spokesmen of the regime for repeating with Goebbelslike emphasis the evil slogans of the government, I consider it my duty to defend

---

Letter written on August 26, 1956, to the editor of the weekly *Bohemia*. *Bohemia* (Havana), September 2, 1956, pp. 35, 82, 83.

[1] See "Enough Lies!" in this volume. Eds.

[2] Cañizares was chief of police under Batista until he was killed on October 24, 1956, while trying to enter the embassy of Haiti to arrest some political refugees. Eds.

[3] Rafael Leónidas Trujillo. Eds.

my prestige and my right to pass judgment on my opponents. I do this even though I do not have at my disposal all the mass media of the Republic which they have and which they use to fight without respite an exiled opponent who is even persecuted with unequaled cruelty beyond the borders of his own country.

I have the right to defend myself because a life is not devoted to a cause, sacrificing for it everything that others cherish and care for—tranquility, career, home, family, youth, and even existence—just so a handful of evildoers who enjoy power through fire and blood against the people, for the exclusive benefit of their personal fortunes, can throw mud, lies, and shame with impunity at those whose sacrifices, self-denial, and disinterest have a thousand times served a pure ideal.

It is sickening to have to answer such an accusation, but if I do not overcome my disgust the dictatorship's spokesmen will be able to keep on slandering people without anyone taking a stand and telling them a few facts.

There can be no understanding between Trujillo and ourselves, just as there can be no understanding between Batista and us. The same ideological and moral abyss separating us from Batista separates us from Trujillo. Is there any difference between the two dictatorships? Trujillo has oppressed the Dominican people for twenty-five years; Batista, in his two ruling periods, has done the same for fifteen years and is on the way to emulating his Dominican colleague.

In Cuba, as in Santo Domingo, there is a dictator. In Cuba, as in Santo Domingo, a regime is maintained by raw force. In Cuba, as in Santo Domingo, elections are a farce without guarantees for the adversaries of the regime. In Cuba, as in Santo Domingo, a fawning, rapacious, and ambitious clique enjoys all the offices of the state, provinces, and municipalities while enriching only itself. In Cuba, as in Santo Domingo, the master hires and fires officers, rules from his private estate, and seats a servant in the presidential chair. In Cuba, as in Santo Domingo, terror and repression prevail, homes are broken into at midnight, men are arrested, tortured, and disappear without leaving a trace. In Cuba, as in Santo Domingo, massacres are practiced as was the case of the Moncada and the Goicuría. In Cuba, as in Santo Domingo, civic meetings are prohibited, the press is censored, newspapermen are beaten, and newspapers closed. In Cuba, as in Santo Domingo, defenseless peasants are beaten with machetes, workers are repressed with rifle butts, and the most elemental rights are denied to the humble. Trujillo's goons kidnap and murder opponents in exile—Jesús de Galíndez, Mauricio Báez, Andrés Requena;[4] Batista's goons persecute

---

[4] Dominican exile leaders murdered by Trujillo's secret police abroad. Eds.

and plan the assassination of opponents in exile. Today the newspaper *Ultimas Noticias* publishes on page 5, column 1, the following:

> The chief of the Cuban Bureau of Investigation, Colonel Orlando Piedra, and the chief of the Subversive Activities Bureau, Captain Juan Castellanos, have just arrived in Mexico to investigate privately the Cuban refugees who have been involved in plots against General Batista. The presence of these Antillian policemen has sown alarm among the Cuban residents in our country, who fear being the object of reprisals on the part of the agents of General Batista's government. Colonel Piedra and Captain Castellanos came to our country accompanied by various agents who, as simple "tourists," will investigate the activities of Cubans who are in disagreement with the present policy of the Cuban government in power.

What difference is there between these two tyrannies?

The desire of the Cuban people, as well as that of the Dominican people, is to rid themselves of Batista and Trujillo respectively. Cuba and Santo Domingo will be happy the day both men are overthrown. Trujillo's was the first government to recognize with delight the March 10 coup. From the opposition Batista repeatedly criticized the Auténtico governments for the generous help offered to Dominican revolutionaries.

Neither Batista nor Trujillo wants to see a democratic regime in either country. The most that Trujillo can hope for is the establishment of a *tanquista*[5] military dictatorship of a gangster mafia. The Revolution led by the 26th of July Movement would give all its support to a democratic Dominican movement. Now that our movement is the vanguard of the revolutionary struggle, the only thing convenient for Trujillo is that Batista remain in power. No dictator will act against his own interests regardless how great may be his personal grudge. Are not Batista's relations with Pérez Jiménez[6]—a dictator just like Trujillo—magnificent? Was it not there that Santiago Rey[7] proclaimed Batista's reelection? Why did Batista not denounce Trujillo in Panama?[8] Is it not true that Batista cordially embraced the brother of the Dominican jackal? Why, on the other hand, did the democratic president José Figueres[9] refuse even to salute the Cuban dictator? What explanation can the regime give for these contradictions?

If Batista's dictatorship felt strong against us, if it were not sure that

---

[5] Refers to the group of military officers led by the Tabernilla family, who controlled the tank units of the armed forces. Eds.

[6] Venezuelan dictator at the time. Eds.

[7] Official of the Batista government. Eds.

[8] In 1956, the presidents of the hemisphere met in Panama. Eds.

[9] President of Costa Rica (1953–1958). Eds.

the explosion was inevitable and definitive, it would not have used the vile hoax of suggesting an agreement between Trujillo and us. To use such a trick implies an irresponsibility without limits.

They intend to create a state of confusion so that when the fighting starts the revolutionary struggle will be called a Trujillo-sponsored plot in order to put a brake on the people and throw the soldiers against us under the pretext of defending the sovereignty of the nation rather than fighting a revolution that even has the sympathy of many military men. This maneuver must be exposed.

If it were true that an insurrectional pact existed between Trujillo, Prío, and us, it would imply an open and brazen intervention by a foreign tyrant in the internal affairs of our country. Then what is Cuba waiting for to reply with dignity to such an aggression? The government cannot make an official denunciation like that and then remain indifferent. The time has come to unmask this infamous maneuver. Either the government denies that an insurrectionl pact exists between the 26th of July Movement and Trujillo, or the government declares war on Trujillo in order to defend the honor and sovereignty of the nation. The regime is obliged to be consistent in its charge or to deny it.

If at any time the sovereignty and dignity of our fatherland were attacked, the men of the 26th of July Movement would fight side by side with the soldiers of our army. But this kind of game that plays with the prestige and revolutionary honor of the country by calling anyone opposing a regime very similar to that of Trujillo a Trujillista cannot be allowed. If certain gangsters such as Policarpo Soler,[10] who left Cuba through the national airport in Havana with Batista's help, are now in evil alliance with the Dominican despot, it is unfair to involve those men who have given more than enough proof of their idealism, honesty, and love for Cuba.

It is a fact that *tanquista* officers of March 10 were in contact with Trujillo. Pelayo Cuervo[11] valiantly denounced this and ended up in a downtown Havana prison. The regime has not said a word about this; instead it accuses all of its adversaries of being Trujillistas when in fact Trujillismo was born within the ranks of the regime. I am sure that the charge is equally false with regard to Prío.

If I have defended the thesis of uniting all revolutionary forces, and gangsters are excluded, it is precisely because I believe that we Cubans by ourselves can achieve our liberation without receiving any aid that would stain the cause for which we fight. This attitude has been mortal

---

[10] Well-known thug in the 1930s and 1940s in Cuba. Eds.
[11] Opposition leader murdered by Batista on March 13, 1957. Eds.

for the tyranny and has angered the representatives of the regime. I declared that position publicly, in the face of the criticisms of our detractors, because I am a revolutionary who thinks only of what can benefit his country; I am not an electoral candidate demagogically calculating the number of votes that I could get in an election.

Four and a half years I have been engaged in this struggle, for which I have sacrificed all, while being persecuted and slandered constantly, half of the time imprisoned at home or abroad, incommunicado for long months in solitary confinement, constantly threatened by the murderous bullets of my enemies, without a minute of rest, without a moment of hesitation, having only the clothes I wear—these are proofs enough of my disinterest and loyalty to Cuba. I have had the honor of being the target of the roughest, most constant, and most infamous attacks of the tyranny. I have withstood them and shall continue to do so to the end.

My firm democratic convictions and my loyalty to the cause of the Dominican people cannot be questioned by Mr. Salas Cañizares. Juan Rodríguez,[12] Juan Bosch,[13] and all the Dominican leaders in exile can testify to my struggle in the university in favor of Dominican democracy, to the three months I lived outdoors on a sandy islet waiting for the signal to leave,[14] and to the many times I declared myself ready to go to fight Trujillo. They can speak for me, they know their real friends, and they have reasons to be better informed than most regarding the maneuvers of the dictator who oppresses their fatherland. The stand I took when I was a student is my present stand, and it will always be my stand regarding Trujillo.

I believe that in a revolution principles are more important than guns. We went to fight at Moncada with .22 caliber rifles. We have never counted the number of weapons the enemy has; what counts, as Martí said, is the stars on one's forehead.

We would not exchange a single one of our principles for the weapons of all the dictators in the world. This stand, of men who are ready to fight and die against forces that have uncomparably superior resources, without accepting aid from outside, is the most dignified reply we can give the spokesmen of the tyranny.

In contrast, Batista will not give up the tanks, cannons, and planes that the United States sends him, all of which will not serve to defend democracy but to massacre our helpless people. In Cuba we are losing

[12] General Juan Rodríguez, a Dominican, organized from Cuba an expedition against Trujillo in 1947. Castro participated in the training but the invasion never materialized. Eds.

[13] Anti-Trujillo leader who spent most of his exile in Cuba. In 1963, he was elected president of the Dominican Republic and overthrown later that year. Eds.

[14] This was Rodríguez's abortive invasion. Eds.

the habit of telling the truth. The campaign of infamy and slander will have its true reply one day in the fulfillment of our promise that in 1956 we shall be free or shall be martyrs.

Today I calmly ratify this statement with full understanding of its implications four and a half months from December 31. Nothing will stop us from fulfilling our promise. To a people who have become skeptical from so much deceit and betrayal, one cannot speak in any other terms. When that hour comes, Cuba will know that those of us who are giving our blood and our lives are her most loyal children and that the weapons with which we shall achieve its freedom were not paid for by Trujillo but by the people, cent by cent and dollar by dollar. If we die, as Martí told that great Dominican Federico Hernández y Carbajal,[15] we shall die also for the freedom of the Dominican people.

I request you to publish these lines in your impartial and fair magazine.

Sincerely,
Fidel Castro

[15] A good friend of José Martí who aided the Cubans in their independence struggle in the 1890s. Eds.

Mexico Pact
(September 1956)

The Federación Estudiantil Universitaria (FEU) and the 26th of July Movement, the two organizations formed by a new generation that has earned through sacrifice and struggle the sympathies of the Cuban people, have agreed to address the following declaration to the country. That

1. Both organizations have decided to unite solidly their efforts in order to overthrow the tyranny and carry out the Cuban Revolution.

2. To collaborate with partial elections after having demanded general and free elections for four years constitutes a submissive and treacherous attitude which will not attain its ambitious goals because the Revolution will not permit it.

This document, known as the "Mexican pact," was signed in September 1956 by José Antonio Echevarría, leader of the University Federation of Students (FEU), and Fidel Castro, leader of the 26th of July Movement in Mexico. The pact was made to coordinate the activities of both organizations for the *Granma* landing that was to take place in November 1956. "Pacto de México" in *13 documentos de la insurrección* (Havana: Organización Nacional de Bibliotecas Ambulantes y Populares, 1959), pp. 37–39.

3. If the Cuban Revolution, which already has the sympathy of America's democratic public opinion, is defeated in the inevitable struggle, the dictatorship will not offer even that niggardly concession which it offers today because it fears revolution. On the heads of the ambitious electoral candidates will fall the blood of those who sacrifice themselves.

4. We consider the social and political conditions of the country ripe for revolution and the preparations sufficiently advanced to offer the people their liberation in 1956. The insurrection supported by a general strike throughout the country will be undefeatable.

5. A foreign tyrant, Rafael Leónidas Trujillo, has intervened openly in the internal affairs of our country and forged a conspiracy against Cuba with the complicity of a group of officers who participated in the March 10 coup: Alberto del Rio Chaviano, Martín Diaz Tamayo, Leopoldo Pérez Coujil, Manuel Ugalde Carrillo, Manuel Larrubia, Juan Rojas, Rego Rubido, and a gang of henchman led by Policarpo Soler, who left Cuba right after the coup d'état with Batista's protection, in spite of being wanted by the courts of justice.

6. Weapons from Trujillo were introduced in Cuba with the clear complicity of those military men.

7. Dictator Batista did not have the courage at the Panama Conference to denounce this aggression on Cuba's honor and integrity; instead he embraced the brother of the Dominican murderer.

8. On returning to Cuba, hiding the truth from the people, Batista gave himself to the ignoble task of accusing the Cuban revolutionaries of being followers of Trujillo, a relationship that is impossible because of our democratic convictions.

9. In reply to the cowardly maneuver, we challenge Batista to give the FEU and the fighters of the 26th of July Movement the weapons of the Republic, which he has not known how to use with dignity, so that we may show our willingness to settle the matter with the Dominican dictator and save our nation's honor.

10. Cuba must answer the offense it has suffered with dignity; consequently, we support armed action against the tyrant Trujillo, which will free the Dominicans from an oppression that has already lasted over twenty-five years. We challenge Batista to say the last word or to unmask himself before the Cuban people.

11. The weak, opportunistic, and cowardly attitude of the regime toward Trujillo is treason to the fatherland.

12. Trujillo and Batista are dictators who endanger democratic sentiment in America and disturb the peace, friendship, and happiness of Cubans and Dominicans.

13. While the pro-Trujillo military remain in their posts, the best

men of the armed forces, the officers most capable of defending the fatherland, are imprisoned and treated inhumanely on the Isle of Pines.

14. The FEU and the 26th of July Movement consider Colonel Barquín, Major Borbonet, and other imprisoned officers as the most honorable representatives of the army. They are the men who have the sympathy of the armed forces today.

15. The army, led by those honorable and prestigious officers, serving the Constitution and the people, will have the respect and sympathy of the Cuban Revolution.

16. The FEU and the 26th of July Movement adopt as their watchword the unity of all the revolutionary, moral, and civic forces of the nation—students, workers, youth organizations, and all men of dignity —so that they will support us in this struggle which will end in our victory or our death.

17. The time has come for political parties and the Sociedad de Amigos de la República to cease their useless pleading for friendly solutions—an attitude which might have been patriotic at other times but which after four years of rejection, contempt, and refusal is infamous.

18. As the Revolution faces a struggle to death against the tyranny, victory will belong to those of us who fight on the side of history.

19. The Revolution will take power free of compromises or vested interests to serve Cuba with a program of social justice, freedom, and democracy. There will be respect for just laws and the full recognition of the dignity of all Cubans without petty hatreds against anyone. Those of us who lead the Revolution are ready to sacrifice our lives in order to achieve our pure intentions.

José Antonio Echevarría Bianchi   Fidel Castro Ruz

Letter to the Gutiérrez Family
(November 24, 1956)

Inside the car that is taking me to my departure in order to fulfill a sacred duty to my fatherland and my people, I wish to leave this will in case I die in the struggle—for this is a task from which one does not return.

I leave my son in the custody of Engineer Alfonso Gutiérrez and

Letter written on November 24, 1956, a few hours before leaving in the yacht *Granma* for Cuba. Luis Conte Agüero, *Fidel Castro, vida y obra* (Havana: Editorial Lex, 1959), pp. 428–429.

his wife Orquidea Pino. I am making this decision because I do not want, in my absence, to see my son Fidelito in the hands of those who have been my most ferocious enemies and detractors, those who, in a base act without limits, and using my family ties, attacked my home and sacrificed it to the interest of a bloody tyranny that they continue to serve. Because my wife has demonstrated herself to be incapable of breaking away from the influence of her family, my son could be educated with the detestable ideas that I now fight.

I am adopting this measure not out of resentment, but solely thinking of my son's future. I leave him to those who can educate him best, a good and generous family, my best friends in exile, in whose house the Cuban revolutionaries found a true home. I leave my son to them and to Mexico, so that he can grow and learn in this friendly and free country where children have turned into heroes. He should not return to Cuba until it is free or he can fight for its freedom.

I hope that this just and natural desire on my part with regard to my son, the only one I have, will be fulfilled.

Part 6
Guerrilla War

An Expression of Gratitude
(December 25, 1956)

On setting out again on the march toward the Sierra Maestra, where we shall continue fighting until we meet victory or death, we wish to thank *compañero* Ramón Pérez Montano and his family, who helped us to regroup the first contingent of our force, fed us for eight days, and put us in touch with the Movement in the rest of the island. The help that we have received from him and many others like him in the most critical days of the Revolution encourages us to continue to struggle with more faith than ever, convinced that a people such as ours deserves every sacrifice. We do not know how many of us will fall during the struggle, but here are the signatures of all of us, as a testimony of our infinite gratitude.

December 25, 1956

Letter written 23 days after Castro and his men had landed in Cuba. The signatures that appear in the document are those of Fidel Castro, Raúl Castro, Juan Almeida, Camilo Cienfuegos, Ernesto Guevara, Ciro Redondo, Ramiro Valdés, Efigenio Ameijeiras, Universo Sánchez, and René Rodríguez. *Gramma Weekly Review* (Havana), January 5, 1969, p. 9.

Sierra Maestra Manifesto
(July 12, 1957)

From the Sierra Maestra, where a sense of duty has united us, we issue this call to our compatriots.

The time has come when the nation can save itself from tyranny through the intelligence, courage, and civic spirit of its children, through the efforts of all those who feel deeply the destiny of this land where we have the right to live in peace and freedom.

Is the nation incapable of fulfilling its high destiny or does the blame for its impotence fall on the lack of vision of its public leaders? Can we not offer the fatherland in its most difficult hour the sacrifice of all personal aspirations, as just as they may seem, of all petty passions,

This manifesto was issued on July 12, 1957, after Castro had a conference with Raúl Chibás and Felipe Pazos, leaders of the Ortodoxo Party. "Al pueblo de Cuba," *Bohemia* (Havana), July 28, 1957, pp. 69, 96–97.

personal or group rivalries, or in short, of whatever selfish or small sentiment has prevented placing on the alert, as one man, this formidable Cuban nation, awakened and heroic? Or is the self-centered desire of an aspirant to public office worth more than all the blood that has been spilled for this republic?

Our greatest weakness has been disunity. The tyranny, conscious of it, has promoted it by all means in all its forms, offering half solutions, tempting ambitions, and using the good faith or naïveté of its adversaries. They have divided the parties into antagonistic factions, divided the political opposition into different groups and, when the revolutionary current gained strength and became more threatening, they attempted to set the politicians against the revolutionaries, with the only goal of beating the Revolution now and deceiving the parties later.

It is no secret that if the dictatorship managed to defeat the rebel bulwark of the Sierra Maestra and crush the underground movement, once free from the revolutionary danger there would be left not even the remotest possibility of honest elections in the midst of general grief and skepticism.

Their intentions were made evident when they approved the senatorial minority, perhaps too soon, disregarding the Constitution and poking fun at the obligations contracted with the very delegates from the opposition. Once again they tried to divide and prepared the way for the electoral farce.

That the Interparliamentary Commission failed is recognized by the party that proposed it in Congress.[1] The seven opposition organizations that participated in it say so categorically today and denounce the whole thing as a bloody joke. All the civic institutions affirm it; above all, the facts affirm it. It was bound to fail because it wanted to ignore two forces that have made their appearance in Cuban public life: the new revolutionary generation and the civic institutions, much more powerful than any little clique. Thus, the interparliamentary maneuvers could only prosper on the basis of the extermination of the rebels. The fighters of the Sierra were not offered anything in that wretched solution but prison, exile, or death. One should never accept discussions on those terms.

Unity is now the only patriotic way. Unity is what all political, revolutionary, and social sectors that combat the dictatorship have in common. And what do all the opposition political parties, the revolu-

[1] The Interparliamentary Commission was established to achieve a peaceful transition of power in Congress. Eds.

tionary sectors, and the civic institutions have in common? The desire to put an end to a regime based on force, the violation of individual rights, the infamous crimes, the desire to seek the peace that we all long for by the only road possible, the democratic and constitutional path of our country.

Do the Sierra Maestra rebels not want free elections, a democratic regime, a constitutional government? It is because they deprived us of those rights that we have fought since March 10. We are here because we want them more than anyone else. To demonstrate it, there are our fighters dead in the mountains and our comrades murdered in the streets or secluded in prison dungeons. We are fighting for the beautiful ideal of a free, democratic, and just Cuba. What we do not do is to agree with the lies, farces, and compromises of the dictatorship.

We want elections, but with one condition: truly free, democratic, and impartial elections.

Is it not nonsensical, a deception of the people, what is happening here daily? Can there be free, democratic, and impartial elections under a tyranny which represents antidemocracy and partiality?

Of what value is the direct and free vote, the immediate counts, and other fictitious concessions if on the day of the elections no one is allowed to vote and the ballot boxes are filled at bayonet point? Of what use was the Committee on Suffrage and Public Liberties in halting the closing of radio stations and the mysterious deaths that continued to occur?

Has it done any good for public opinion to make demands? Have the exhortations for peace, the tears of mothers done any good?

With more blood, they want to put an end to the rebellion; with more terror, they want to end terrorism; with more oppression, they want to put an end to the desire for freedom.

Elections should be presided over by a provisional, neutral government, with the support of all, that will replace the dictatorship in order to induce peace and move the country toward democratic and constitutional normalcy.

This should be the slogan of a great civic-revolutionary front that comprises all political parties of the opposition, all civic institutions, and all revolutionary forces.

Consequently, we propose to all opposition political parties, all civic institutions, and all revolutionary sectors the following:

1. To create a civic-revolutionary front with a common strategy of struggle.

2. To designate as of now a person to preside over the provisional government, whose election will be left to the civic institutions to show the disinterest and impartiality of opposition leaders.

3. To declare to the country that due to the gravity of events there is no possible solution other than the resignation of the dictator and the transference of power to the person who has the confidence and the support of the majority of the nation, expressed through its representative organizations.

4. To declare that the civic-revolutionary front does not invoke or accept mediation or intervention of any kind from another nation in the internal affairs of Cuba. In contrast, it supports the denunciations of the violation of human rights made by Cuban emigrants before international organizations and asks the government of the United States that as long as the present regime of terror and dictatorship persists to suspend all arms shipments to Cuba.

5. To declare that the civic-revolutionary front, by republican and independent tradition, will not allow any type of provisional military junta to rule the Republic.

6. To declare that the civic-revolutionary front plans to separate the army from politics and to guarantee the apolitical nature of the armed forces. Military men have nothing to fear from the Cuban people, but it is the corrupt clique that sends them to their death in a fratricidal struggle.

7. To declare under formal promise that the provisional government will hold general elections for all offices of the state, the provinces, and the municipalities at the end of a year following the norms of the 1940 Constitution and the Electoral Code of 1943, and that power will be given immediately to the elected candidates.

8. To declare that the provisional government must adjust its mission to the following program:

   a. Immediate freedom for all political, civil, and military prisoners.

   b. Absolute guarantee of freedom of information, of the spoken and written press, and of all the individual and political rights guaranteed by the Constitution.

   c. Designation of provisional mayors in all the municipalities after consultation with the civic institutions of the locality.

   d. Suppression of embezzlement in all its forms and adoption of measures that tend to increase the efficiency of all state agencies.

   e. Establishment of the civil service on a career basis.

   f. Democratization of labor politics, promoting free elections in all unions and industrial federations.

   g. Immediate initiation of an intensive campaign against illiteracy, and civic education emphasizing the duties and rights
of each citizen to his society and fatherland.

   h. Establishment of the basis for an agrarian reform to distribute
barren lands and convert into owners all the tenant farmers,
sharecroppers, squatters, and lessee planters who have small
parcels of land, be it property of the state or of private persons, with prior indemnification to the owners of the land.

   i. Adoption of a healthy financial policy that safeguards the
stability of our currency and tends to use the credit of the
nation in productive works.

   j. Acceleration of the process of industrialization and the creation of new jobs.

Special emphasis must be put on two points of this document.

First: The need to name now the person called to preside over the
provisional government of the Republic, to demonstrate before the
world that the Cuban nation is capable of uniting behind the ideal of
freedom and supporting the person who, meeting the conditions of
impartiality, integrity, capability, and decency, can represent that
ideal. There are more than enough men in Cuba capable of presiding
over the Republic!

Second: That this person must be designated by all civic institutions
because those organizations are apolitical and their backing would free
the provisional president of partisan compromises and lead to absolutely
clean and impartial elections.

To form this front it is not necessary that the political parties and
the civic institutions declare themselves in favor of the insurrectional
thesis and come to the Sierra Maestra. It is enough that they deny all
support to the regime's electoral compromise and declare heroically
before the nation, before the armed forces, and before world opinion
that after five years of useless effort, of continuous deceit and rivers of
blood, in Cuba there is no other solution than the resignation of
Batista, who already has ruled the destiny of the country in two stages
for sixteen years, and that Cuba is not disposed to fall into the situation
of Nicaragua or Santo Domingo.

It is not necessary to come to the mountains to discuss this. We can
be represented in Havana, in Mexico, or wherever may be necessary.

It is not necessary to decree the Revolution: Organize the front that
we propose and the downfall of the regime will follow, perhaps without spilling another drop of blood. One has to be blind not to see that
the dictatorship is in its last days, and that this is the moment when all
Cubans must put forth the best of their intelligence and effort.

Can there be another solution in the midst of civil war with a government incapable of guaranteeing human life, which no longer even controls the action of its own repressive forces and whose continued tricks and games have made completely impossible the slightest public confidence?

No one should be deceived by the government propaganda concerning the situation in the mountains. The Sierra Maestra is already an indestructible bulwark of freedom that has taken root in the hearts of our compatriots, and here we shall know how to honor the faith and confidence of our people.

Our call may not be heard, but the fight will not stop because of it, and the victory of the people, although it will be much more costly and bloody, will not be prevented by anyone. We hope, however, that our appeal will be heard and that a real solution will halt the spilling of Cuban blood and will bring an era of peace and freedom.

Letter to Frank País
(July 21, 1957)

Sierra Maestra
July 21, 1957

Dear David:

Little by little, as we go along, I am going to try to write you these lines.

The present revolutionary upsurge is taking place at a moment when the morale of our men is very high. Moreover, we are strong and well fed. We shall be ready for whatever comes.

I am enclosing a sincere testimony of solidarity signed by our officers on behalf of all our combatants. We were deeply shocked by the cruel blow.[1] It served to arouse our spirit, and it has had an enormous influence in raising our combat spirit these past few days.

I must confess that I am overcome by a feeling of suspense every time I listen to the radio and hear that some young man was found murdered in the streets of Santiago. Just today they announced they had found the unidentified body of a young man, about 24 years old,

Granma (Havana), July 7, 1968, p. 9. David was the underground name of Frank País, leader of the urban resistance in Santiago de Cuba, Oriente Province, for the 26th of July Movement. Fidel Castro's *nom de guerre* was Alejandro.
[1] Refers to the murder of Josué País, Frank's brother, on June 30, 1957. Eds.

with a mustache, etc., etc. This worry will remain with me for hours until I know the identity of the man. One cannot help but worry even if it is perhaps absurd. Really, we are going through very difficult hours.

There may be a couple of things I have forgotten but, on the whole, I think I have covered the questions that interest you the most. Write as soon as you can. A big hug from

Alejandro

Letter from the Rebel Army to Frank País (July 21, 1957)

Dear Brother:

Under circumstances such as this it is difficult to find the words, if they exist, to express how deeply we feel. Perhaps a strong and silent embrace would replace words and express our feelings much better. We cannot embrace, just as you could not be with your brother in his last moments because you were at your combat post.

If fate permits us, we will go together to his tomb one day to tell him and all the young heroes that we have done our part in this struggle and that with the same determination and spirit of sacrifice we are ready to finish the work of our generation, with them as the supreme judges of our future actions.

They have cleansed with their blood the past of the generations that have preceded us, and the essential duty of those who follow them in this struggle will be to see to it that the blood shed and the tears shed by many mothers shall not be in vain; that our magnificent people not be deceived again; that the memory of the dead not be betrayed and desecrated again; that none abandons the trail blazed by those who fell, or turns his back on the route that leads to the happiness this suffering people so justly deserves and that constitutes the goal for which we are fighting.

We shall soon reap the fruits of our struggle in a land so often bathed in innocent blood.

We all admire your serene courage in the face of last week's bitter blow. We revolutionaries find relief in struggle.

This letter was handwritten by Raúl Castro and dictated by Fidel Castro. The letter was written on July 21, 1957 from the Sierra Maestra. *Granma* (Havana), July 7, 1968, p. 9.

Please convey the condolence of all the fighters and officers of the Sierra Maestra to your mother and other relatives. As for you, dear brother, there is nothing else to be said, because we also share the pain for the loss of the young fighter.

We are all very proud and happy about the way you are carrying on your work of leadership. As far as the Sierra is concerned, when the history of this stage of the Revolution is written, two names should appear on the cover: David and Norma.[1]

[1] Underground names used by Frank and Josué País. Eds.

On the Death of Frank País
(August 1, 1957)

I cannot express the bitterness, anger, and infinite pain that overwhelms us.

Barbarians! Like cowards they hunted him in the street, using all the advantages they enjoy to persecute an underground fighter. Monsters! They did not know the intelligence, character, and integrity of the man they assassinated.

The people of Cuba do not even suspect who Frank País was, what greatness and promise there was in him. It hurts to see him thus, killed in full maturity, despite the fact that he was twenty-three years old when he gave the best of himself to the Revolution.

How much sacrifice this filthy tyranny is costing!

How long are the Salas Cañizares, Cruz Vidals, Venturas, Fagets, Masferrers, Santiagos Rey,[1] amassers of fortunes, people without scruples, without hearts, without souls, going to keep sowing death and grief at will without falling themselves, riddled with bullets from the just hand of the people?

After seeing the assassination of Frank País, the most courageous, useful, and extraordinary of all our fighters, what is holding back the thousands of Cubans anxious to do something? Are we not really seeing a heroic stage in which the sacrifice of lives to save the fatherland concerns no one? Have we not seen our men advance under a hail

Radio broadcast made on August 1, 1957, from the Sierra Maestra after Frank País was murdered. "Palabras ante la muerte de Frank País," in *13 documentos de la insurrección* (Havana: Organización Nacional de Bibliotecas Ambulantes y Populares, 1959), p. 51.
[1] Members of the Batista regime. Eds.

of fire to take a position? Are we not seeing our imprisoned men advance resolutely toward the most horrible of deaths, the hunger strike? Are we not seeing our women move forward in street demonstrations, defying bullets and beatings? Did we see Frank País abandon his post in spite of the imminent danger that threatened him? No!

The hour has come to demand of all those who call themselves revolutionaries, all those who call themselves oppositionists, all who claim to be honorable and decent persons, regardless of the institution, party, or organization to which they may belong—to put an end to childish dreams.

Letter to the Cuban Liberation Junta (December 14, 1957)

Gentlemen, leaders of Partido Revolucionario Cubano, Partido del Pueblo Cubano, Organización Auténtica, Federación Estudiatil Universitaria, Directorio Revolucionario, and Directorio Obrero Revolucionario:

A moral, patriotic, and even historical duty forces me to address this letter to you, based on facts and circumstances that have worried us deeply during these last weeks (which, by the way, have been the most arduous and busy ones since we arrived in Cuba). It was precisely on Wednesday, November 20, that our forces sustained three battles in only six hours (and this gives an idea of the sacrifice and effort made by our men here without the slightest aid from other organizations). On that same day, the surprising news was received in our zone of operations of the document containing the public and secret bases of the unity pact which purports to have been supported in Miami by the 26th of July Movement and those organizations to which I now address myself.

The arrival of those papers, as another irony of fate at a time when what we needed were arms, coincided with the most intense offensive launched by the tyranny against us.

Under the conditions of our struggle, communications are difficult. In spite of everything, it has been necessary to call together the leaders of our organization in the midst of a campaign in order to attend

Letter written on December 14, 1957. "Carta de Fidel Castro," *Bohemia* (Havana), February 2, 1958, supplement, pp. 48, 83–85.

to this matter, in which not only the prestige but also the historical rationale of the 26th of July Movement is at stake.

For those who are fighting an enemy incomparably superior in numbers and in arms, with no support for a whole year other than the dignity with which one should fight for a cause that one loves with sincerity and conviction, a cause worth dying for; for those who are bitterly forgotten by other compatriots who, having had all the ways and means, have systematically (not to say criminally) refused their help; for those who have seen so closely daily sacrifice in its purest and most selfless form and have felt so often the grief of seeing the best comrades fall in battle, and when one does not know which of those on our side are going to fall in new and inevitable holocausts without even seeing the day of victory for which they fight so earnestly, with no aspiration or consolation other than the hope that their sacrifice will not be in vain, it must be understood that the news of a broad and intentionally publicized agreement, which binds the future conduct of the Movement without even the consideration—not to mention the elemental obligation—of having consulted its leaders and fighters, has to be highly offensive and irritating for all of us.

Improper procedure always brings the worst consequences. This is something that should be kept in mind by those who consider themselves capable of such an arduous undertaking as overthrowing a tyranny and, what is even more difficult, gaining the recognition of the country after a revolutionary period.

The 26th of July Movement did not designate or authorize any delegation to discuss such negotiations. However, there would have been no objection to designating a delegate if it had been consulted, and very concrete instructions would have been given to its representatives in view of the fact that something so serious for the present and future activities of our organization was to be considered.

On the contrary, the information we had regarding the relations with some of those sectors was limited to a report by Lester Rodríguez, delegate for military affairs abroad, with powers limited exclusively to these matters. It reads as follows:

> With respect to Prío and the Directorio,[1] I held a series of conversations with them to coordinate plans of a military character, *solely and exclusively*, until a provisional government could be formed that would be guaranteed and respected by the three sectors. Logically, my proposal was the acceptance of the Sierra Maestra Manifesto in which it was stated that the government

[1] Directorio Revolucionario, a student movement based mainly in the universities. Ed.

should be formed in agreement with the civic forces of the country. This brought the first difficulty. When the commotion of the general strike occurred, we held an emergency meeting. I proposed the immediate use of all the resources at hand in an attempt to solve the problem of Cuba once and for all. Prío replied that he did not have the sufficient resources to do something that would bring about victory and that it would be madness to accept my proposal. I answered that when he considered that he had everything ready, he should let me know, so that we then could talk about possible agreements, but that in the meantime he should do me the favor of letting me and what I represent within the 26th of July Movement work with complete independence. In conclusion, there exists no compromise with those people, and I do not believe that in the future it is desirable to have one, for at the moment when Cuba most needed it, they denied having the material which a few days ago was captured from them and which amounts to so much that it moves one to indignation. . . .

This report, which speaks for itself, confirmed our suspicions. That is, the rebels could not expect any help from outside.

If the organizations you represent had considered it proper to discuss the bases of unity with some members of our movement, such bases (so much more so because they altered fundamentally the demands made by the Sierra Maestra Manifesto) could not be published under any conceivable circumstance as a settled agreement, without the knowledge and the approval of the national directorate of the Movement.[2] To act in any other way is to make agreements for the sake of publicity and to fraudulently invoke the name of our organization.

We have the astounding fact that when the national directorate, operating clandestinely somewhere in Cuba, received the news and was ready to reject the public and private points that were put forth as a basis for the pact, it learned through clandestine newsletters and from the foreign press that the points had been published as a settled agreement. We were confronted with an accomplished fact, in the opinion of the nation and the world, and with the alternative of having to deny it—with the consequences of harmful confusion that such a denial would imply—or accepting it without even supporting its stand. And, as is logical to suppose, when the document reached us in the mountains, it had already been published for several days.

In this predicament, the national directorate (before proceeding with a public denial of the said agreements) informed you of the necessity of having the junta develop a series of points which would

---

[2] The national directorate was composed of Fidel Castro, Frank País (before he died), René Ramos Latour, Armando Hart, Faustino Pérez, David Salvador, Carlos Franqui, Manuel Ray, Francisco González, Enrique Oltuski, Vilma Espín, and others. Eds.

cover the demands of the Sierra Maestra Manifesto, while at the same time a meeting was called in rebel territory in which the thoughts of all the members were taken into consideration and a unanimous agreement was adopted thereon, as set forth in this document.

Naturally, any unity agreement would have to be well received by national and world opinion, because among other reasons the real situation of the political and revolutionary forces opposing Batista is not known abroad. And in Cuba the word *unity* had much prestige when the arrangement of forces was quite different from what it is today. Finally, it is always positive to join all efforts, from the most enthusiastic to the most timid.

But most important for the Revolution is not unity itself but rather the bases of such unity, the form in which it is made viable, and the patriotic intentions that inspire it.

To arrange such unity without even having discussed the bases, to have it signed by unauthorized persons, and to make it public without further procedure from a comfortable city abroad thereby placing the Movement in the situation of having to confront a public deceived through a fraudulent pact, is a trap of the worst sort into which a truly revolutionary movement cannot let itself fall. To do so is to deceive the nation and the world.

This type of thing is only possible because of the simple fact that while the leaders of the organizations signing that agreement are abroad carrying out an imaginary revolution, the leaders of the 26th of July Movement are in Cuba making a real revolution.

These lines, however, would be unnecessary, they would not have been written no matter how bitter and humiliating the effort to bind the Movement to such an agreement, if the discrepancies in the form did not detract from the essentials. We would have accepted, in spite of everything, due to the positive value of unity, the usefulness of certain plans put forth by the junta, and the aid offered to us (and which we really need) if we were not simply in disagreement with certain essential points of the bases.

No matter how desperate our situation may be, no matter how many thousands of soldiers the dictatorship (in its efforts to annihilate us) may mobilize against us—and perhaps we shall fight even more zealously, for a burdensome condition never humiliates more than when the circumstances are pressing—we shall never accept the sacrifice of certain principles fundamental to our conception of the Cuban Revolution. These principles are included in the Sierra Maestra Manifesto.

To suppress from the unity document the express declaration of refusing any kind of foreign intervention in the internal affairs of

Cuba is evidence of lukewarm patriotism and a self-evident act of cowardice.

To declare that we are against intervention is not only to ask that the Revolution be allowed no favors because it would be detrimental to our sovereignty and detrimental to a principle that affects all the peoples of America. It is also to ask that no intervention be made in favor of the dictatorship by sending planes, bombs, tanks, and the modern weapons that keep it in power and that no one has suffered physically as have we and especially the rural population of the Sierra. In short, to succeed in stopping intervention is in itself to overthrow the tyranny. Are we going to be so cowardly as not even to demand that no intervention be made in favor of Batista? Or so insincere as to demand in an underhanded way that others pull the chestnuts out of our fire? Or so mediocre as not to dare to utter a word about all these? How, then, can we call ourselves revolutionaries and support a unity document with presumptions of historic importance?

In the unity document, our express declaration of refusing any kind of provisional military junta rule of the Republic has been eliminated.

The most tragic thing that could happen to the nation at this time is to replace Batista by a military junta, creating the deceptive illusion that Cuba's problems have been solved by the mere absence of the dictator. And some civilians of the worst breed, including accomplices of the March 10 coup who are today estranged from power, perhaps because of their great ambitions, are thinking of those solutions which could only be looked on favorably by the enemies of progress in our country.

Experience has demonstrated in America that all military juntas drift toward autocracy; the worst evils that have afflicted this continent are the spreading roots of the military castes in countries that have fought fewer wars than Switzerland and have more generals than Prussia. One of the most legitimate aspirations of our people in this crucial hour, which decides whether their democratic and republican destiny is saved or lost for many years, is to guard—as the most precious legacy of their liberators—the civil tradition which was initiated with the wars of independence, and which was broken the day that a military junta presided over the Republic (something that never was attempted by the most glorious generals of our independence either in war or in peace). At what point are we going to renounce everything by suppressing such an important declaration of principle for fear of wounding susceptibilities (more imaginary than real among the honest military men who can support us)?

Do the people not understand that an opportune definition could prevent the danger of a military junta taking power, which could serve no purpose other than to perpetuate the civil war? Very well! We do not hesitate to declare that if a military junta substitutes for Batista, the 26th of July Movement resolutely will continue its campaign of liberation. It is preferable to struggle more today than to fall tomorrow into new and insurmountable abysses. No military junta, nor a puppet government serving the military! Civilians must govern decently and honestly, the soldiers must stay in their barracks, and each must fulfill his duty!

Or are we waiting for the generals of the March 10 coup, to whom Batista would gladly cede his power, when he considers it untenable, as the most viable way of guaranteeing the transition without the least damage to his interests and those of his clique? How long will the lack of foresight, the absence of worthy aims, or the lack of a true will to fight continue to blind Cuban politicians?

If there is no faith in the people, if there is no confidence in their great energy and will to fight, then there is no right to lay hands on their destiny, to twist or misdirect it in the most heroic and promising moments of their republican existence. Neither the methods of bad politics, nor puerile ambitions, nor the desire for personal aggrandizement, nor prior plans for dividing the spoils can be allowed to interfere in the revolutionary process. In Cuba, men are dying for something better. Let the politicians become revolutionaries if they wish, but let them not convert the Revolution into bastard politics; there is too much blood shed and the sacrifices are too great on the part of the people in this hour for them to deserve such thankless future frustration!

Aside from these two fundamental principles omitted in the unity document, we are in total disagreement with other aspects of the same.

Even if we are to accept clause *b* of the secret agreement number 2 relative to the power of the Liberation Junta (which reads, "to appoint the President of the Republic who shall exercise this office in the provisional government"), we cannot accept clause *c* of said point, which includes among other powers, "to approve or disapprove, as a whole, the cabinet appointed by the President of the Republic, as well as the changes therein in case of total or partial crisis."

How can the power of the President to appoint or substitute his collaborators be subject to the approval of a body outside of the powers of the state? Is it not clear that said junta is formed by representatives of different parties and sectors and therefore, having different interests, the appointing of the cabinet members could be converted into a distribution of positions as the sole means of arriving at an agreement in each case? Is it possible to accept an agreement that implies the establishment of two executive powers within the state? The only guarantee that all sectors of the country should demand from the provisional government is the adjustment of its mission to a given minimum program and absolute impartiality as a moderating power in the transitional period toward complete constitutional normalcy.

To try to interfere in the appointment of each member implies the desire to control the public administration so as to put it at the service of political interests, explicable only in parties or organizations lacking the support of the masses. Such organizations can survive only within the canons of traditional politics, but this is at variance with the high revolutionary and political goals which the 26th of July Movement pursues for the Republic.

The mere presence of secret agreements which do not refer to questions of organization for the struggle or plans of action, but rather to questions of interest to the nation such as the structuring of the future government—and which, therefore, should be publicly proclaimed—is in itself unacceptable. Martí said that in a revolution, the methods are secret but the aims should always be public.

Another point which is inadmissible to the 26th of July Movement is the secret agreement number 8 which says, "The revolutionary forces will be incorporated into the regular armed forces of the Republic with their weapons."

First of all, what is understood by "revolutionary forces"? Is a police, navy, or army badge to be given to anyone coming in at the last moment with a weapon in his hands? Are uniforms and authority to be granted to persons who today have their weapons hidden, only to bring them out on the day of victory, and who remain with their arms crossed while a small group of compatriots fight all the forces of the tyranny? Are we going to allow the very germs of gangsterism and anarchy which were the shame of the Republic not so long ago to enter a revolutionary document?

Experience acquired in the territory dominated by our forces has taught us that the maintenance of public order is a vital question to the country. The facts have shown us that as soon as the existing order is abolished, a number of bonds are unloosed and delinquency springs up everywhere if not checked in time. The timely application of severe measures, with the full approval of the public, can put an end to banditry. The citizens, previously accustomed to seeing the authorities as enemies of the people, extended their hospitality to the persecuted or those running from justice. Now that they see in our soldiers the defenders of their interests, complete order prevails and their best guardians are the citizens themselves.

Anarchy is the worst enemy of a revolutionary process. To combat it from the outset is a fundamental necessity. If someone does not want to understand, it is because he is not concerned about the destiny of the Revolution; and it is logical that those who have not sacrificed themselves for it should not be concerned. The country should know that justice will be done, but within the strictest order, and crime will be punished regardless of who commits it.

The 26th of July Movement claims for itself the function of maintaining public order and reorganizing the armed forces of the Republic for the following reasons:

1. Because it is the only organization with organized and disciplined militias throughout the nation and an army in active service with twenty victories over the enemy.

2. Because our fighters have shown a chivalrous spirit free from any hate of the military, invariably respecting the life of the prisoners, healing their wounds, never torturing an adversary even when knowing that he is in possession of important information. They have maintained this conduct in war with unprecedented equanimity.

3. Because the armed forces must be inculcated with the spirit of justice and chivalry which the 26th of July Movement has sown in its own soldiers.

4. Because the calmness with which we have acted in this struggle is the best guarantee that the honorable military have nothing to fear from the Revolution, nor do they have to pay for the faults of those who, by their deeds and crimes, have covered the military uniform with disgrace.

There are still some aspects which are difficult to understand in the unity document. How is it possible to reach an agreement without having a definite strategy of struggle? Do the Auténticos continue to think about a putsch in the capital? Will they continue to accumulate more and more weapons, which sooner or later will fall into the hands of the police before they are handed over to those who are fighting? Have they accepted finally the thesis of a general strike maintained by the 26th of July Movement?

Moreover, there has been, as we understand it, a lamentable underestimation of the importance of the struggle in Oriente from a military standpoint. At this moment the war in the Sierra Maestra is not a guerrilla war but rather a war of battle lines.[3] Our forces, inferior in numbers and equipment, take advantage of the terrain, constantly keep an eye on the enemy, and have great speed in their movements. It is hardly necessary to mention that morale is of great importance in

[3] The term used is *una guerra de columnas,* which could be translated as a war fought by columns.

this struggle. The results have been astounding, and someday they will be known in full detail.

The whole population is in revolt. If they had arms, our detachments would not have to patrol any zone. The peasants would not permit a single enemy to pass through. The defeats of the tyranny, which insists on sending numerous forces, would be disastrous. Not enough can be said about how courage has been awakened in these people. The dictatorship carries out barbarous reprisals. The mass murder of peasants is no different from the massacres perpetrated by the Nazis in any European country. Each defeat the enemy suffers is avenged on the defenseless population. The bulletins of the General Staff announcing casualties among the rebels are always preceded by some massacre. This has pushed the people to a state of absolute rebellion. What hurts, what makes one's heart bleed, is to think that no one has sent a single rifle and that the peasantry here see their houses burned and their families murdered, imploring desperately for rifles. There are weapons hidden in Cuba which are not being used even to annihilate a miserable criminal, and they wait for the police to pick them up or for the tyranny to fall or for the rebels to be exterminated.

The conduct of many compatriots could not have been more ignoble, but there is still time to rectify and aid those who are fighting. From our own personal viewpoint, it is not important. No one should bother to think that these words are prompted by self-interest or pride. Our fate is sealed, and no uncertainty troubles us. Either we shall die here down to the last rebel and an entire young generation will perish in the cities, or we shall triumph against most incredible odds. For us, defeat is no longer possible. The year of sacrifice and heroism which our men have lived through cannot be erased. Our victories stand and cannot be easily erased either. Our men, firmer than ever, will know how to fight to the last drop of blood.

The defeat will be for those who have refused us their help; for those who, having obligated themselves to us at first, abandoned us; for those who, lacking faith in dignity and idealism, wasted their time and prestige in shameful dealings with Trujillo's despotism;[4] for those who, having arms, like cowards hid them at the time of the struggle. They are the deceived, not we.

There is one thing we can state with certainty: If we had seen other Cubans fighting for liberty, persecuted almost to the point of

---

[4] At the time there were rumors that a number of anti-Batista groups were receiving aid from dictator Leónidas Trujillo of the Dominican Republic. Up to the present this issue has not been cleared up, even though there seems to be some evidence that points toward such occurrences. Eds.

extermination, if we had seen them resist day after day without giving up or hesitating in their determination, we would have joined them and, if necessary, died with them. This is because we are Cubans, and Cubans do not stand by idly even when the struggle for liberty is in another country of America. Have the Dominicans joined together on a small barren island to liberate their people? For every Dominican, ten Cubans arrive. Do Somoza's henchmen invade Costa Rica? The Cubans rush there to combat them. How is it that when the most violent battle for freedom takes place in their own country, there are Cubans in exile, expelled by the tyranny, who refuse to aid the Cubans who are fighting?

Or is it that to help us they demand the lion's share? Must we offer the Republic as a booty to gain their aid? Must we abjure our ideals and convert this war into a new art of killing fellow men to gain their aid? Must we shed blood uselessly without promising the country the benefits that await from so much sacrifice?

The leadership of the struggle against the tyranny is and will continue to be in the hands of the revolutionary fighters in Cuba. Those who now or in the future might wish to be considered revolutionary leaders should be inside the country directly facing the responsibilities, risks, and sacrifices that Cuba now demands.

Exiles should cooperate in this struggle, but it is absurd for anyone to try to tell us from abroad what peak we should take, what sugarcane fields we should burn, what sabotage we should carry out, or at what moment, in what circumstances, and in what form we should call a general strike. Besides being absurd, it is ridiculous. Let aid come from abroad by collecting funds among the Cuban exiles and emigrants, by campaigning for the Cuban cause in the press and among the public. Denounce the crimes that we are suffering but do not attempt to direct from Miami a revolution that is being waged in all the cities and fields of the island through combat, agitation, sabotage, strikes, and a thousand other forms of revolutionary action which have been the strategy of struggle of the 26th of July Movement.

The national directorate is ready, and has made this clear several times, to talk in Cuba with the leaders of any opposition organization in order to coordinate specific plans and produce concrete acts which may be considered useful in the overthrow of the tyranny.

The general strike will be carried out through the effective coordination of the efforts of the Civic Resistance Movement,[5] the National Labor Front,[6] and any other sector outside partisan politics and in

[5] Movimiento de Resistencia Cívica. Eds.
[6] Frente Obrero Nacional. Eds.

close contact with the 26th of July Movement, which up to now is the only opposition organization fighting throughout the country.

The labor section of the 26th of July Movement is organizing strike committees in every work center and industrial sector with the opposition elements of all militant groups who are willing to strike and offer moral guarantees that they will do so. The organization of these strike committees will include the National Labor Front, which will be the only representative of the proletariat that the 26th of July Movement will recognize as legitimate.

The overthrow of the dictator involves the displacement of the spurious Congress, of the leadership of the Cuban Confederation of Labor, and of all the mayors, governors, and other functionaries who directly or indirectly have supported the so-called elections of November 1, 1954, or the military coup of March 10, 1952, in order to attain public office. It also implies the immediate release of political, civil, and military prisoners as well as the indictment of all those who have had complicity in crime, arbitrary acts, and the tyranny itself.

The new government will be guided by the Constitution of 1940, will assure all rights recognized therein, and will be outside of any political partisanship.

The executive will assume the legislative functions that the Constitution attributes to the Congress of the Republic, and its main duty will be to lead the country to general elections following the Electoral Code of 1943 and the Constitution of 1940 and to develop the minimum ten-point program set forth in the Sierra Maestra Manifesto.

The present Supreme Court will be dissolved because it has been powerless in solving the lawless situation created by the coup d'état, but later some of its present members shall be eligible for appointment, provided that they have defended the principles of the Constitution or maintained a firm attitude against crime, arbitrary acts, and the abuses of these years of tyranny.

The President of the Republic will decide how the Supreme Court will be constituted, and the latter in turn will proceed to reorganize all the courts and autonomous institutions, relieving of their functions all those whom it may consider to have acted in evident complicity with the tyranny and bringing them to justice when necessary. The appointment of the new officers will be made in accordance with the provisions of the law in each case.

Political parties will have only one right under the provisional government: freedom to defend their program before the people, to mobilize and organize the citizens within the broad framework of our constitution, and to participate in the general elections to be held.

In the Sierra Maestra Manifesto, the necessity of appointing the person to preside over the Republic was stated, and our movement made clear its criterion that such a person should be selected by all civic institutions. In view of the fact that five months have passed without this step having been taken, because it is more urgent than ever to let the country know the answer to the question of who will succeed the dictator, and because it is not possible to wait one more day without answering this national question, the 26th of July Movement now answers it. We present to the people the only formula possible that will guarantee the legality and the development of the aforementioned bases of unity and of the provisional government itself. That person should be the distinguished magistrate of the Court of Appeals of Oriente Province, Dr. Manuel Urrutia Lleó.[7] It is not we but his own conduct which designates him, and we hope that he will not refuse this service to the Republic.

The self-evident reasons which point to him are the following:

1. He was the member of the judiciary who raised the name of the Constitution highest when he declared, on the bench of the tribunal that tried the *Granma* expeditionaries, that it was not a crime to organize armed forces against the regime but perfectly legal according to the spirit and the letter of the Constitution and the laws. This is unprecedented, coming from a magistrate, in the history of our struggles for freedom.

2. His life, dedicated to the strict administration of justice, is the guarantee that he has sufficient preparation and character to serve fairly all legitimate interests at the moment when the tyranny shall be overthrown by the action of the people.

3. No one could be more impartial to partisan politics than Dr. Manuel Urrutia Lleó, for he does not belong to any political group precisely because of his judicial functions. And there is no other citizen of his prestige who, free from any group, has identified himself so much with the revolutionary cause.

Moreover, by virtue of his being a magistrate, it is the closest formula to the Constitution.

If our conditions are rejected, the disinterested conditions of an organization which no other exceeds in sacrifice, an organization which was not even consulted when its name was included in a unity

---

[7] Urrutia Lleó was sworn in as provisional president of the Republic on January 1, 1959, and resigned on July 17, 1959, after Castro made a speech attacking him. He remained under house arrest until April 1961, when he succeeded in obtaining political asylum in the Venezuelan embassy. In 1963, he left Cuba for the United States. Eds.

manifesto it did not sign, we shall continue the struggle alone as we have done up to now, without weapons other than those we seize from the enemy in each battle, without help other than that of the suffering people, and without support other than that of our ideals.

Because, after all, the 26th of July Movement has been and still is carrying out actions throughout the country; only the militants of the 26th of July Movement have carried out sabotage, executed criminals, burned sugarcane fields, and other revolutionary actions. Only the 26th of July Movement has been able to organize in a revolutionary fashion the workers of the entire nation; only the 26th of July Movement can undertake today the strategy of strike committees, and only the 26th of July Movement has cooperated in the organization of the Civic Resistance Movement now holding together the civic sectors of almost all of Cuba.

To state all this might be considered arrogant by some; but the fact is that only the 26th of July Movement has declared that it does not want to participate in the provisional government, and that it places all its moral and material support at the disposal of the citizen most competent to preside over the necessary provisional arrangement.

Let it be well understood that we have renounced bureaucratic positions or participation in the government; but let it also be known once and for all that the militants of the 26th of July Movement will never renounce guiding and directing the people from the underground, from the Sierra Maestra, or from the graves of our dead. And we shall not renounce that duty because it is not we but a whole generation that is morally committed to the Cuban people to provide substantial solutions for its great problems.

And we shall know only how to conquer or to die. The struggle will never be harder than when we were only twelve men, when we did not have an organized group with experience in war in the Sierra Maestra, when we did not have (as we have today) a powerful and disciplined organization all over the country, when we did not count on the formidable support of the masses, as evidenced in the burial of our unforgettable Frank País.

To die with dignity does not require company.

For the national directorate of the 26th of July Movement,

Fidel Castro

Why We Fight
(February 1958)

As this is written, our armed campaign on Cuban soil against Cuba's dictatorial regime is entering its second year. Though it has been given many meanings and many interpretations, it is essentially a political struggle. In this struggle, we have sustained few reverses and a good many victories, while dictator Batista can point to a single successful achievement: he has effectively muzzled all public communications in our country, silenced TV, radio, and the press, and so intimidated our news publishers that not a single Cuban reporter has ever been assigned to *our* side of what is, in effect, a spreading civil war.

One of the unexpected results of this iron censorship, augmented by a military blockade around the combat zone, has been that our program—the aims, plans and aspirations of the 26th of July Movement—has never been published or explained adequately. In obtaining and publishing this exclusive article—the only first-person story written by me since we landed in Cuba on December 2, 1956—*Coronet Magazine* has given us the opportunity to state our aims and to correct the many errors and distortions circulating about our revolutionary struggle.

Though dictatorship, ignorance, military rule, and police oppression have spawned a great many evils among our people, all these evils have a common root: the lack of liberty. The single word most expressive of our aim and spirit is simply—freedom. First of all and most of all, we are fighting to do away with dictatorship in Cuba and to establish the foundations of genuine representative government.

To attain this, we intend to eject from office Fulgencio Batista and all his cabinet officers; to place them under arrest and impeach them before special revolutionary tribunals. To replace the unconstitutional Batista regime, we will aid in setting up a provisional government to be nominated by a special convention made up of the delegates of our various civic organizations: Lions, Rotarians, professional bodies such as the physicians' or engineers' guilds, religious associations, and so forth. This will be a break with established procedure, but we feel certain that it will prove workable. Once appointed, the provisional government's chief task will be to prepare and conduct truly honest general elections within twelve months.

The question has presented itself whether I aspire to the presidential office of this provisional government or the elected government which will succeed it. The truth is that, quite apart from my personal reluctance to enter the presidential competition so soon, our Constitution, as it now stands, would prohibit it. Under its age requirement clause, I am, at 31, far too young to be eligible for the presidency, and will remain so for another ten years.

We do have, however, a number of program points which might serve as a basis for action by the provisional government. They are the following:

1. Immediate freedom for all political prisoners, civil as well as military. Although the outside world knows little about it, Batista has imprisoned dozens of officers and hundreds of enlisted men from his own armed forces who have shown revulsion or resistance to his bloody suppression of political discontent.

2. Full and untrammeled freedom of public information for all communication media—broadcasting, TV, the daily and periodical press. Arbitrary censorship and systematic corruption of journalists has long been one of the festering sores of our nation.

3. We want to reestablish for all citizens the personal and political rights set forth in our much-ignored Constitution.

4. We want to wipe out corruption in Cuban public life. Those who have grown accustomed over the years to dealing with venal policemen, thieving tax collectors, rapacious army bosses here in Cuba may think this an optimistic resolution. But we intend to attack this problem at its very roots, by creating a career civil service beyond the reach of politics and nepotism and by making sure that our career functionaries get paid enough to be able to live without having to accept bribes.

5. We want to sponsor an intensive campaign against illiteracy. Though no one knows the exact number of our illiterates, they run into the hundreds of thousands, perhaps even up to a million. Our farm children get little schooling at best; many of them get none at all. Hundreds of thousands of small farmers feed their families on roots and rice, simply because no one has ever taught them how to grow tomatoes, lettuce, or corn. No one has ever shown them how to utilize water. No one has ever told them how to choose a wholesome diet or how to protect their health.

6. We are in favor of land reform bills adjusting the uncertain owner-tenant relations that are a peculiar blight of rural Cuba. Hundreds of thousands of small farmers occupy parcels which they do not own under the law. Thousands of absentee owners claim title to

properties they have hardly ever seen. The titles, in fact, have been seen by no one and it is often impossible to establish who actually owns a particular property. We feel that in settling the question of legal ownership, preferential treatment should be given to those who actually occupy and cultivate the land. We will support no land reform bill, however, which does not provide for the just compensation of expropriated owners.

7. Finally, we support speedy industrialization of our national economy and the raising of employment levels.

Apart from political misconceptions about my ambitions and those of our movement—we have been often accused of plotting to replace military dictatorship with revolutionary dictatorship—nothing has been so frequently misunderstood as our economic program. Various influential U.S. publications have identified me as a tool of big business, as a dangerous radical, and as a narrow reactionary manipulated by the clergy. U.S. companies with business interests in Cuba have been repeatedly warned that I have secret plans in my pocket for seizing all foreign holdings.

Let me say for the record that we have no plans for the expropriation or nationalization of foreign investments here. True, the extension of government ownership to certain public utilities—some of them, such as the power companies, U.S.-owned—was a point of our earliest programs; but we have currently suspended all planning on this matter. I personally have come to feel that nationalization is, at best, a cumbersome instrument. It does not seem to make the state any stronger, yet it enfeebles private enterprise. Even more importantly, any attempt at wholesale nationalization would obviously hamper the principal point of our economic platform—industrialization at the fastest possible rate. For this purpose, foreign investments will always be welcome and secure here.

Industrialization is at the heart of our economic progress. Something must be done about the staggering mass of over one million unemployed who cannot find jobs during eight months out of twelve. They can hope to work only during the four months of the cane harvest. A million unemployed in a nation of six million bespeaks a terrible economic sickness which must be cured without delay, lest it fester and become a breeding ground for communism.

Fortunately, improvement is by no means as difficult as Cuba's present rulers would lead us to believe. Our country is rich in natural resources. What we need is an adequate canning industry to utilize our superb fruit crops; expanded industrial facilities for the processing of sugar and its important by-products; expanded consumer industries for the production of light metal, leather, paper, and textile goods which would go far toward improving our trade balance; and the beginnings of a long-range cargo fleet.

The state would not need to resort to expropriation to take a guiding part in such economic developments. By reforming its tax collection system, which now consists of paying off the revenue collector instead of paying the state, it could increase its budget many times and turn its attention to the sorely needed extension of our road network.

And with rising living standards and growing confidence in government will come rapid progress toward political stability under a representative, truly democratic government. That, ultimately, is what we are fighting for.

As long as we are forced to fight, however, our constructive projects must wait. Our immediate task is something entirely different: it is the burning of Cuba's entire sugar cane crop. It was a terrible decision, and now that we are about to carry it out, it is a terrible job. Sugar cane is Cuba's principal source of revenue; it contributes about one third of the total national income and employs two fifths of the labor force. Half of our farm income is dependent on sugar. Yet it is the very importance of the cane crop that compels us to destroy it.

If the cane goes up in flames, the army will grind to a standstill; the police will have to disband, for none of them will get paid; and the Batista regime will have to capitulate. What is more, we will gain this decisive victory with comparatively little bloodshed by expending this year's crop.

I well know the heavy personal losses involved. My family has sizable holdings here in Oriente, and my instructions to our clandestine action groups state clearly that our crop must be the first one to burn, as an example to the rest of the nation. Only one thing can save the cane, and that is Batista's surrender.

But even if the crop will have to burn down to the last single cane, the flames will set fire to the dictatorship which weighs heavily on us now. Once the tyranny has gone up in smoke, we will see the way to a decent, democratic future.

To the Rebels of Las Villas
(February 2, 1958)

We have received with profound happiness the news that a group of Cubans is fighting in Las Villas Province.

Regardless of the revolutionary militancy of the group, we have given instructions to the Movement[1] to give you all possible help.

We wish to know your situation. There is very little we can do directly for you because of the distance, but we want to express our great and sincere solidarity.

We consider it useful for the struggle against the tyranny that your front maintain itself at any price. We can imagine initial difficulties that you might be facing. If the topography of the zone makes it impossible for you to resist or ammunitions run out, I advise you to move closer to us, walking at night and hiding in the daytime in places where the air force cannot see you, following a zig-zag route. When the enemy is ambushed several times, it will cease to follow you. You can advance about twenty to thirty kilometers every night. We have a patrol between Bayamo and Victoria de las Tunas that can serve you as a bridge. We shall try to intensify the campaign here to alleviate the pressure there. The messenger[2] can inform you about details and experiences that might be of interest. I await news. We pray that the front will succeed, and we send your courageous fighters a fraternal embrace.

Fidel Castro

In November 1957, guerrilla groups began to operate in the mountains of Las Villas. The guerrillas were independent of the 26th of July Movement. On February 2, 1958, Fidel Castro sent this message to the guerrillas. Max Lesnik Menéndez, "Por que se disuelve el II Frente Nacional del Escambray," *Bohemia* (Havana), March 6, 1960, p. 56.

[1] The 26th of July Movement. Eds.

[2] A girl called "Edelmira," who died in battle later in the Sierra Maestra, was the courier between Fidel Castro and the forces of Eloy Gutiérrez Menoyo. Eds.

Interview with Andrew St. George
(February 4, 1958)

ST. GEORGE: Dr. Castro, your death has been officially reported many times, but you look hearty. For fourteen months, you've waged a jungle-mountain war against the Cuban Army of some thirty thousand men with all its modern weapons. What have you accomplished?

CASTRO: In December, 1956, we were a dozen men in the bush. Now, one thousand strong, we rule a liberated zone of fifty thousand people. Our army is kept small, mobile, combative; we turn down fifty volunteers for every one we take. Our doctors, who serve without pay, as do our soldiers, give these people medical care they've never had before. We also set up classes in captured areas whenever possible to teach children their first letters.

Most important, this year our movement has won the respect and affection of the Cuban people, long sunk in political apathy. They are revolted by the regime's increasing terrorism and corruption, the outright assassinations and atrocities. Recently, forty-seven simple farmers near here were rounded up and shot, and their deaths were announced as those of "rebels" killed in combat. These are only *officially* reported deaths.

The dictator has used every strategy against us—air strafing and bombing, infantry assaults, bombardment from the sea. Teams of assassins continually infiltrate our lines to murder me. But all these tactics have failed.

Now Batista says he'll starve us out, by ringing the Sierra Maestra with troops and stopping all incoming shipments of food and medical supplies. Rumors persist that he will also bomb us with mustard gas. This is risky business, since the U.S. naval base at Guantánamo is nearby.

ST. GEORGE: You say you will burn Cuba's entire sugar crop. The island's economic life depends on it. What can you gain by this?

CASTRO: Our intent is to burn the harvest to the last stalk, including my own family's large sugar-cane farm here in Oriente Province. It is a *hard* step. But it is a legitimate act of war. From sugar taxes, Batista buys bombs and arms, pays his newly doubled army. Only their bayonets now keep him in power. Once before, Cubans burned their cane, razed their very towns, to wrest freedom from Spain. During

Andrew St. George, "Cuban Rebels," *Look*, February 4, 1958, p. 30.

your revolution, didn't the American colonists throw tea into Boston Harbor as a legitimate defense measure?

ST. GEORGE: What do you rebels want, besides toppling Batista? And what of reports you will nationalize all foreign investments in Cuba?

CASTRO: First, we must overthrow the dictatorship, forced on us by the military coup d'état in 1952 when Batista saw he would lose any free election. Next, we'll set up a provisional government, whose heads are to be elected by some 60 Cuban civic bodies, like the Lions, Rotarians, groups of lawyers and doctors, religious organizations. Within a year, this caretaker regime would hold a truly honest election. In a manifesto issued last July, we called for the temporary government to free immediately all political prisoners, restore freedom of the press, reestablish constitutional rights.

We must eventually root out the fearful corruption that has plagued Cuba so long; set up an adequately paid civil service beyond the reach of politics and nepotism; wage a war against illiteracy, which runs as high as 49 per cent in rural areas; speed industrialization, and thus create new jobs. For in this little nation of six million, a million work only four months a year, under an antiquated, one-crop economy.

Our 26th of July Movement has never called for nationalizing foreign investments, though in my twenties I *personally* advocated public ownership of Cuba's public utilities. Nationalization can never be as rewarding as the right kind of private investment, domestic and foreign, aimed at diversifying our economy. I know revolution sounds like bitter medicine to many businessmen. But after the first shock, they will find it a boon—no more thieving tax collectors, no plundering army chieftains or bribe-hungry officials to bleed them white. Our revolution is as much a moral as a political one.

ST. GEORGE: Will you run for President? And have you thought of negotiating a compromise with Batista, who has promised he will not run in the next Presidential elections?

CASTRO: Under our constitution, I am far too young to be a candidate. As for Batista, did President Roosevelt think of compromising with Hitler just before D-day?

ST. GEORGE: Charges have been made that your movement is Communist-inspired. What about this?

CASTRO: This is absolutely false. Every American newsman who has come here at great personal peril—Herbert Matthews of the New York *Times*, two CBS reporters and yourself—has said this is false. Our Cuban support comes from all classes of society. The middle class is strongly united in its support of our movement. We even have many wealthy sympathizers. Merchants, industrial executives, young people, workers are sick of the gangsterism that rules Cuba. Actually, the Cuban Communists, as your journalist John Gunther once reported, have never opposed Batista, for whom they have seemed to feel a closer kinship.

ST. GEORGE: What do you expect of Americans?

CASTRO: Your public opinion should know more about Latin American movements that are democratic and nationalist. Why be afraid of freeing the people, whether Hungarians or Cubans?

Why is it assumed that outmoded dictators are the best guardians of our rights, and make your best allies? And what is the difference between dictatorship by a military caste, like Batista's, and the Communist or Fascist dictatorships you say you abhor? To any North American, it would be absurd, outrageous, if an army officer or police chief deposed or disposed of the governor of a state and then declared *himself* governor. Who would recognize him as such? Yet this happens all too frequently in Latin America. By furnishing arms to these usurpers of power—the men of the infamous "international of sabers" —tyrants like Pérez Jiménez of Venezuela, exiled Rojas Pinilla of Colombia, Trujillo of the Dominican Republic—you kill the democratic spirit of Latin America. Do you think your tanks, your planes, the guns you Americans ship Batista in good faith are used in hemispheric defense? He uses them to cow his own defenseless people. How can he contribute to "hemispheric defense"? He hasn't even been able to subdue us, even when we were only a dozen strong!

I firmly believe that the nations of Latin America can achieve political stability under representative forms of government, just as other nations have. We need material progress, first, to raise low living standards; we need a climate of freedom, in which we can develop democratic habits. This is never possible under tyranny.

Efforts at self-government in many Latin nations are far from perfect, I realize. But we can cure ourselves of these ills—unless dictators step in and strangle this natural political evolution, and are given aid and recognition by other countries. I repeat, by arming Batista you are really making war against the Cuban people.

Message to Che
(February 16, 1958)

Che:

If everything depends on the attack from this flank without the support of Camilo and Guillermo, I do not believe anything suicidal should be done as we shall be risking too many casualties and fail to reach the objective.

I strongly recommend that you be careful. As a final order, you should not fight. Take charge of leading the men well. That is what is indispensable at the present time.

Fidel

Letter written on February 16, 1958. Ernesto Guevara, "Pino del Agua, II" *Verde Olivo* (Havana), January 12, 1964, pp. 7–8.

On the Political Solution Offered
by the Episcopate (March 9, 1958)

Free Territory of Cuba
Sierra Maestra, March 9, 1958
10:45 A.M.

News Editor of CMKC
Santiago de Cuba
Distinguished journalist:

By means of this worthy and patriotic eastern broadcasting station, we wish to declare to the people of Cuba:

1. That the Cuban Episcopate should define what it means by "Government of National Unity."

2. That the top ecclesiastical hierarchy should clarify to the country whether it considers it possible for any dignified and self-respecting Cuban to sit down in a council of ministers presided over by Fulgencio Batista.

3. That this lack of definition on the part of the Episcopate is enabling the dictatorship to channel its efforts toward a compromising and counterrevolutionary arrangement.

"Fidel rechaza la componenda del Episcopado con Batista," *Revolución* (Havana), July 26, 1962, p. 9.

4. That consequently the 26th of July Movement flatly rejects any contact with the Conciliation Commission.

5. That the 26th of July Movement is only interested in expounding its thoughts to the people of Cuba and therefore reiterates its desire to do so before a commission of representatives of the national press.

6. That a week having elapsed since our public challenge to the dictatorship without its giving a reply, thus trampling once more the rights of the Cuban press, we set Tuesday the eleventh of the present month as a deadline for the tyrant to say, without further delay or playing games, whether he will or will not permit the transit of journalists through the territory dominated by his troops.

7. That on expiration of that deadline, the 26th of July Movement will make a definitive pronouncement to the country, launching the final watchwords of the struggle.

8. That from this instant the entire people should be on the alert and put all their forces in readiness.

9. That after six years of shameful, repugnant, and criminal oppression, with private rejoicing of the fighters who have fulfilled their duty without resting for a minute in such a long task, we can announce to the country that because of the victories of our unbending and invincible people, who have left on the path hundreds of their best sons, the chains are about to be broken and the anxiously awaited dawn, which in these hours nothing and no one can prevent, already is visible on the horizon.

I beg of you very fraternally to furnish this declaration to all mass media.

Fidel Castro Ruz

Total War against Tyranny (March 12, 1958)

In refusing authorization to the Cuban press to visit the field of operations and know the stand of the 26th of July Movement, dictator Batista has shown not only moral cowardice and military impotence but has said the last word on the final outcome of this struggle.

Manifesto issued from the Sierra Maestra on March 12, 1958, and signed by Fidel Castro, commander in chief of the Rebel Forces, and Dr. Faustino Pérez, delegate of the national directorate of the 26th of July Movement. Gregorio Selser (ed.), *La revolución cubana* (Buenos Aires: Editorial Palestra, 1960), pp. 141–146.

He could have rendered an invaluable service to the country in this final moment, in the midst of all the harm he had done, namely, by resigning in order to save the coming bloodshed, for he has irremediably lost this contest.

If it is unjustifiable to rule the country by brute force and sacrifice human lives in the selfish desire to remain in power, as he been doing for the last six years, it is a thousand times more unjustifiable to sacrifice those lives when the unbreakable will of the nation, expressed in all social, political, cultural, and religious sectors, against which it is impossible to govern, has decreed the immediate and inexorable end of this regime.

Those of us who know intimately the values the fatherland is sacrificing in its fight for freedom; those of us who know the lives it costs to take every position and to carry out every action; those of us who always hold before us the memory of Frank País and José Antonio Echevarría as symbols of hundreds of other equally courageous young men who have died to fulfill their duty, and who know how much the fatherland will need them in the creative moment which is close at hand, with deep sorrow, with uncontainable indignation, we understand and suffer as no one else the monstrous and futile crime being committed against Cuba.

If the right to know the truth is denied the people, how can one expect the slightest respect for physical integrity, personal freedom, and the right of meeting, organizing, and electing rulers?

The tyranny could not grant anything without the danger of disintegrating; the tyranny has no other possible alternative than its immediate disappearance.

If the rebels are vanquished, if the troops of the regime dominate the mountains and the valleys, if our forces do not fight and are impossible to locate, if what exists are small groups engaged in misdeeds, and if against us there stands a strong, invincible, disciplined, and combative army, as the General Staff in its cynical reports states, why were newspapermen not permitted to come to the Sierra Maestra? Why, if they once ostentatiously sent them in a plane to see that no one was here, why do they not allow newspapermen now to even come close to the southern zone of Oriente? Why do they not remedy this insult among the many they have conferred on the Cuban press?

The explanation to the denial of authorization to the newspapermen lies in the shameful defeats that the dictatorship has suffered in the military offensives that, over and over again, we have destroyed; in the unprecedented acts of barbarism that their henchmen have committed against the defenseless civilian population; in the real and true fact that their troops have been expelled from the Sierra Maestra and the 26th of July army is now on the offensive in the north of the province; in the demoralization and cowardice that have reached such a degree in their ranks that women and children are used as shields to prevent the action of our detachments; and in the ever more numerous cases of soldiers and officers coming to our side with their weapons, sickened by the corrupt and criminal regime they have been defending.

The dictatorship did not want the newspapermen to know on the spot, directly and irrefutably, that more than 400 peasants were murdered during the six months of suspended guarantees and press censorship; that in Oro de Guisa in Oriente Province alone fifty-three peasants were killed in one day; that a mother lost her nine children and husband in a single blow. It did not want the newspapermen to see the hundreds of humble homes, built through sacrifice, reduced to ashes in brutal reprisal, children mutilated by the bombing and machine-gunning of defenseless hamlets. It did not want them to know the lies that the General Staff reported after each combat, trying to deceive not only the people but the army itself. We were going to take the newspapermen to the scenes of the defeats and the crimes of the tyranny; we were going to show them the prisoners we have taken and the soldiers that have joined our side. If all the truth of the Sierra Maestra were to reach the Cuban newspapermen, the regime would fall by the frightening discredit it would have suffered in the eyes of the members of the armed forces.

No other reason could exist for refusing to grant them permission. In our territory, the newspapermen can move around and report freely what they see. There is no censorship here, which demonstrates that freedom of information is not incompatible with military security and that restrictions on the freedom of the press are not justified in the midst of war.

We were sure of the negative reply because we knew the deep reasons for it, but we wanted to unmask the dictatorship, unmask its moral bankruptcy and military weakness, show the Cuban people that they must have faith in our victory, that faith our men have acquired fighting under the most adverse circumstances, that invincible faith always held by representatives of just causes, because what matters, as Martí said, is not the number of weapons at hand but the number of stars on one's forehead. Now we can fight with the power of our reason and the power of our numbers, with the power of justice as well as the power of arms. The promise that we made one day to the nation will soon be a beautiful reality.

The dictatorship has just suspended guarantees and reestablished the hated censorship. This demonstrates its tremendous weakness. It was enough to announce that the chains were about to be broken and the rapid advance of Column 6 toward the heart of Oriente Province would soon precipitate the measure in the midst of an atmosphere of general strike. The ministers are resigning, the ship is sinking, and the people are rising.

Meeting at the camp of Column 1, general headquarters of the rebel forces, the national directorate of the 26th of July Movement unanimously agreed on the following:

1. To consider that due to the visible disintegration of the dictatorship, the growth of the national consciousness, and the belligerent participation of all social, political, cultural, and religious sectors of the country, the struggle against Batista has entered its final stage.

2. That the strategy of the final blow is based on the general revolutionary strike, to be seconded by military action.

3. That revolutionary actions should be progressively intensified from this moment on, until they end in the strike which will be ordered at the proper time.

4. The citizenry should be alerted and warned against any false order. Therefore, contacts and communications should be defined and ensured.

5. The general strike and the armed struggle will continue resolutely if a military junta should try to take over the government. The position of the 26th of July Movement on this point is unchangeable.

6. To ratify the appointment of Dr. Urrutia to preside over the provisional government, to invite him to select freely and in the shortest possible time his aides, and to determine the governmental measures to be taken when the tyranny falls in accordance with the minimum program set forth in the Sierra Maestra Manifesto and in the Letter to the Cuban Liberation Junta.[1]

7. The organization and direction of the strike in the labor sector will be charged to the National Labor Front, which will assume in turn the representation of the proletariat before the provisional revolutionary government.

8. The organization and direction of the strike in the professional, commercial, and industrial sectors will be charged to the Civic Resistance Movement.

9. The organization and direction of the student strike will be charged to the National Student Front.

10. Armed action will be charged to the rebel forces, the militias of

[1] Both in this volume. Eds.

the 26th of July Movement, and all the revolutionary organizations that support the Movement.

11. The underground papers, *Revolución, Vanguardia Obrera, Sierra Maestra, El Cubano Libre,* and *Resistencia,* will orient and inform the people, and they will be distributed through underground channels in order to prevent faked issues.

12. To exhort all newspapermen, radio announcers, graphic arts workers, and all newspaper, radio, and television enterprises to rapidly organize in order to strongly answer the new censorship, so that they become, as in Venezuela, the leaders of the people in the final struggle for liberation.

13. To exhort the students of the country to maintain now more than ever the indefinite strike already started, so that the valiant student youth, who have fought heroically for freedom, will be the vanguard of the general revolutionary strike. No student should return to class until the dictatorship falls.

14. From April 1, for military reasons, all highway or railway traffic is prohibited throughout Oriente Province. Any vehicle passing through those routes by day or by night may be fired on without warning.

15. From April 1, the payment of any type of tax to the state, province, or municipality in the entire national territory is prohibited. All payments made after that date to the state treasurer of the dictatorship will be declared null and will have to be paid again to the new provisional government, aside from the fact that noncompliance with this measure will be considered an unpatriotic and counterrevolutionary act.

16. The continuance of any person in an office of trust in the executive branch from the presidency of government councils to paragovernmental agencies subsequent to April 5 will be considered treason to the fatherland.

17. Due to the state of war existing between the people of Cuba and the Batista tyranny, any officer, noncommissioned officer, or enlisted man in the army, navy or police who continues to render service against the oppressed people after April 5 will lose his right to continue service in the armed forces. There is no valid pretext to use weapons against the people under circumstances such as those of today. Every enlisted man has the duty to abandon the army, rebel, or join the revolutionary forces. All those who come with their weapons will be received in our ranks, their rights respected, and they will be promoted to the rank immediately above and will be exempt from the obligation to fight against their fomer comrades.

18. The 26th of July Movement will reject only the collaboration

of those military men who have been directly responsible for inhuman acts or theft. Having fought against us does not prohibit any military man from serving his fatherland in this decisive hour.

19. In view of the news that seven thousand more men will be drafted into the army to fight the Revolution, the 26th of July Movement declares that any citizen enlisting in the armed forces subsequent to the date hereof will be subject to court martial and judged as a criminal.

20. Likewise, after April 5, any judicial functionary, magistrate, or district attorney who wishes to preserve his right to continue in office must resign from his post, because the absolute lack of guarantees and of respect for legal procedure has converted the judiciary into a useless body.

21. To communicate to the country that Column 6 of the rebel forces, under the command of Major Raúl Castro Ruz, having left the Sierra Maestra has invaded the northern part of Oriente Province; that Column 3 of the rebel forces, under the command of Juan Almeida, has invaded the eastern part of the same province; that rebel patrols are moving in all directions through the entire province and that the action of armed patrols will intensify throughout the nation.

22. From this moment, the country should consider itself in total war against the tyranny. The weapons of the army, navy, and police belong to the people. They should serve the people. No one has the right to use them against the people, and anyone doing so should not expect the least consideration. In order to give the leaders of the revolutionary movement time to act, the campaign of extermination against all those who serve the tyranny with weapons will not begin until April 5. From that date, the war on the military will be relentless in order to recover those weapons which belong to the nation and not to the dictator. The people will find it necessary to annihilate them wherever they may be, as the worst enemies of their freedom and happiness.

The entire nation is determined to be free or to perish.

A Call to Strike
(April 9, 1958)

Attention Cubans! Attention Cubans! The 26th of July Movement is calling for a general revolutionary strike. Today is the day of libera-

This call was made at 11:00 A.M. on April 9, 1958, over three Cuban radio stations. "Llamamiento a la huelga," in *13 documentos de la insurrección* (Havana: Organización Nacional de Bibliotecas Ambulantes y Populares, 1959), p. 59.

tion, the day of the general revolutionary strike. All throughout Cuba at this very moment the final struggle which shall end in the overthrow of Batista has begun.

Major Camilo Cienfuegos Appointed Military Chief (April 16, 1958)

For tactical convenience and considering the need to coordinate our forces, Major Camilo Cienfuegos is named military chief of the triangle formed by the cities of Bayamo, Manzanillo, and Victoria de las Tunas.

The obligations of Major Camilo Cienfuegos are those of his rank and the coordination of efforts of the different guerrillas operating in the zone. This appointment must be communicated to the different captains, lieutenants, and those in charge of small groups.

Also under his command is the urban area of the cities of Bayamo, Victoria de las Tunas, and Holguín, and the coordination of supplies and sabotage in the towns. Moreover, under his responsibility is the organization of agrarian reform and the modification of the system of justice.

Fidel Castro

This appointment was made on April 16, 1958, from the Sierra Maestra. "El guerrillero," *Verde Olivo* (Havana), October 29, 1960, p. 22.

Letter to Celia Sánchez (June 5, 1958)

Dear Celia:[1]

When I saw rockets firing at Mario's house, I swore to myself that the North Americans were going to pay dearly for what they are doing. When this war is over, a much wider and bigger war will commence for me: the war that I am going to wage against them. I am aware that this is my true destiny.

Fidel

Letter written on June 5, 1958, from the Sierra Maestra. It should be noted that this letter was not made available to the public until the fall of 1967. *Gramma Weekly Review* (Havana), August 27, 1967, p. 8.

[1] One of the founders of the 26th of July Movement and Castro's aide. Eds.

Letter to Major José Quevedo
(June 9, 1958)

Dear friend:

It was difficult to imagine that you and I, seeing each other at the University, would someday be fighting each other, in spite of the fact that perhaps we do not harbor different feelings with respect to the fatherland, which I am sure you venerate as much as I do.

Many times I have remembered that group of young soldiers which attracted my attention and awakened my sympathies because of their great desire for culture and their efforts to continue their studies. I knew how to appreciate it when in my mind the things that are occurring now were far away.

I did not have then, as I do not have today—in spite of the sad circumstances which have placed the armed forces beside the most nefarious politics in our history—any hatred of the military. I have judged with harsh words the behavior of many in general and the army in particular, but never have my hands or those of any of my *compañeros* been tarnished with the blood or degraded by the mistreatment of an imprisoned soldier. In one of our battles at Uvero, there were thirty-five prisoners; none was mistreated, and today all of them are free and in the service. However, on that same occasion, one of our wounded men was left with the military doctor due to his critical state, but once cured he was not freed as an elemental gesture of reciprocity toward those who had freed thirty-five adversaries. That *compañero*, invalid as a result of the wound inflicted, is today in the Isle of Pines. How different everything has been, my friend! How many horrible acts have dehumanized the uniform you wear! Yet my testimony is not needed. Any educated, conscious, and sensitive man would investigate and analyze events by himself.

Not even the esprit de corps, a unifying factor, a sentiment that has been exploited by those who have carried the army into an absurd and foolish war, exists today. That is the case because even the most worthy, the most honorable of soldiers can be arrested, humiliated, beaten, and thrown into the dungeons of a prison as a common delinquent on mere suspicion, which will never be tolerated by any army with a true esprit de corps among its officers.

Letter written on June 9, 1958, to an officer in Batista's armed forces. "Por qué se rindió el Comandante José Quevedo," *Bohemia* (Havana), January 18–25, 1959, p. 53.

Many times I have asked myself about you and the other *compañeros* who were studying with you. I have asked myself, I wonder where they are? Have they been arrested and dismissed in one of the many conspiracies? What a surprise to know you are around here! And even though the circumstances are difficult, I am even happy to know about one of you, and I write you these lines without thinking of them, without telling you or asking you anything, only to salute you and wish you, very sincerely, good luck. Your friend,

Fidel Castro

Letter to Camilo Cienfuegos (June 12, 1958)

Sierra Maestra
June 12, 1958, 2 P.M.

Major Cienfuegos:

Yesterday I sent you through another channel an order that in essence is as follows:

To assemble all the well-armed men in your column and march until you make contact with me in the Santo Domingo region.

Leave there a patrol of riflemen whose only objective should be to stall off the army's forces in that zone.

Carry out this action in complete secrecy, so that no one knows your destination.

Take all precautions in crossing enemy lines.

Proceed to carry out this order as soon as you receive either of my two messages.

Fidel

Major Cienfuegos was in Monte de Guinea when Castro called him due to the offensive launched by Batista's forces. "Camilo Cienfuegos," *Verde Olivo* (Havana), October 25, 1964, pp. 9–12.

Letter to Camilo Cienfuegos
(June 27, 1958)

Camilo:

Things here are a little difficult, but the chance to capture an enemy column is getting nearer. You should come here at the pace the physical state of your men allows.

                                                                        Fidel

Letter written on June 27, 1958, from the Sierra Maestra. "El guerrillero," *Verde Olivo* (Havana), October 29, 1960, p. 24.

The First Battle of Santo Domingo
(June 29, 1958)

On Saturday, June 28, the 22nd Battalion, made up of three companies, left its headquarters in Santo Domingo and headed toward the Yara River area, south of the Estrada Palma sugar mill, where Lieutenant Colonel Sánchez Mosquera had already been encamped for several days with another battalion under his command.

This battalion had tried to scale the foothills of the Sierra Maestra and had been driven back by rebel forces always on the alert for the troops of the tyranny.

When the 22nd Battalion, under the command of Major Villavicencio, arrived on the banks of the Yara River, Sánchez Mosquera, according to reports received from captured soldiers, ordered them to go upriver in order to scale the Sierra Maestra. He did this without reporting that guerrillas from the 26th of July Movement were in the area. The 22nd Battalion, comprising three companies, advanced toward the Sierra Maestra, but a powerful mine of more than 60 pounds of TNT almost completely destroyed the 1st Company's formation. At the same time, they were subjected to rifle and 30- and 50-caliber machine-gun fire by rebel soldiers. The 1st Company was completely decimated by the rebel forces. Major Villavicencio ordered the 2nd Company to go to the rescue of the 1st, but a new rebel column at-

Communiqué issued on June 29, 1958, from the Sierra Maestra. *Granma* (Havana), July 7, 1968, p. 9.

tack on the right flank of the 2nd Company blocked this attempt and the 2nd Company was subjected to merciless attack by machine-gun and 60-caliber mortar fire by the revolutionaries. Meanwhile, several new rebel columns were put on the alert in order to cut off the retreat of the 3rd Company of the 22nd Battalion, which was also under heavy attack.

Major Villavicencio ordered a retreat, and the Batista soldiers fled in complete disorder, abandoning a large number of dead and wounded and a large amount of equipment on the battlefield. The rebels captured 28 soldiers, who surrendered unconditionally, and proceeded to gather up the dead and the equipment abandoned by the Batista troops. Meanwhile, Lieutenant Colonel Sánchez Mosquera, who had always been well known for his cruelty to the rebels, did not move his battalion to protect the soldiers he had sent in to attack. Comfortably ensconced in his camp, Sánchez Mosquera sent in another company to try to protect those who had been abandoned and were besieged by the rebels, this new force under the command of a first lieutenant. But the rebels, who had become stronger with the weapons and ammunition abandoned by the Batista soldiers, prepared a new ambush with another TNT mine, which was exploded in the midst of the new company's front ranks, decimating them, many soldiers being either killed or surrendering without offering any resistance. A large part of that company abandoned their equipment and fled in disorder through the mountains with the rebel soldiers following closely. Sánchez Mosquera did not move from his post, abandoning the soldiers he had sent out to a sure death. The rebel soldiers stopped attacking when night fell, but their last shot could be heard on Monday, the thirtieth, at 8:30 A.M. Cuban time.

On the Arrest of U.S. Citizens
(July 3, 1958)

Today I have informed the international press and the United States government that in the general headquarters of the Rebel Army in the Sierra Maestra no report has been received on the case of North American citizens allegedly arrested. That zone of operations, which

Rebel Radio broadcast on July 3, 1958, the following message by Fidel Castro to Raúl Castro, chief of Column 6, operating in the northern sector of Oriente Province. Editors' tape.

is situated one hundred miles away, has no radio transmitters, and if it is true that the United States citizens are being held by rebel forces their release will be ordered.

I have informed them that it is possible that such a thing might have occurred as a reaction to the recent delivery of 300 rockets from the North American naval base at Caimanera to Batista's planes, with which civilian populations are being bombed in the territory occupied by the rebels. I have been able to gather fragments of these rockets, some of which have complete serial numbers. Despite all this, today I am publicly ordering their release. The order should be received and carried out, if it is true that North Americans are being held by some revolutionary troops, because I believe that these North American citizens cannot be blamed for the shipment of bombs to Batista by the government of their country.

I am certain that no rebel forces would make hostages of United States citizens so they could observe the results of the inhuman bombings of Cuban civilians with weapons sent by the United States. However, in view of the difficulty of communications, we cannot be certain that they are not in the hands of our troops.

I have stated also that the 26th of July Movement is fighting for the respect of human rights. We believe that individual freedom is one of the inviolable rights of every human being and therefore no one should be arrested without a just cause. We hope that the United States government will, in like manner, respect the lives and liberty of Cubans and will not interfere in any manner whatsoever in the internal affairs of Cuba by sending weapons to Batista, which he uses to kill our fellow citizens. This is the necessary condition for the continuation of the present friendly relations between the two countries.

In accordance with my statement, should any of the rebel troops operating in this sector be holding all or any United States citizens as claimed, I order that command to contact the United States military authorities at the Caimanera Naval Base or the United States diplomatic representatives in order to turn these persons over to them, at the same time taking the necessary measures for their personal safety.

If none of the mentioned United States citizens is in the hands of the rebel troops, the foreign press and the United States government must be given available information in order to prevent the police and gangsters in the pay of the dictator from attacking the citizens of the United States and so casting doubt on the responsible conduct of the rebel forces.

Fidel Castro

Letter to Major José Quevedo
(July 15, 1958)

Sierra Maestra
July 15, 1958

Major José Quevedo:

With great sorrow I have learned, through the first prisoners, that you are in command of the surrounded troops. We know that you are a learned and honorable military officer of the Academy, with a law degree. You know that the cause for which your soldiers, as well as yourself, sacrifice and die is an unjust cause.

You are an honorable military man who knows our laws. You know that the dictatorship is a violation of all the human and constitutional rights of your people. You know that the dictatorship has no right to sacrifice the soldiers of the Republic in order to maintain a regime that oppresses the nation, snatches away all freedoms, and stays in power through terror and crime; it has no right to send the soldiers of the Republic to fight against their own brothers, who only demand to live with freedom and dignity. We are not at war against the army, we are at war against the tyranny. We do not wish to kill soldiers; we deeply lament the death of every soldier defending an ignoble and shameful cause.

We believe the army should defend the fatherland and not the tyranny.

The political thieves, the ministers, the senators, and the generals are in Havana, without taking risks or enduring hardships while their soldiers are surrounded by a circle of steel, suffering hunger and on the edge of destruction.

You and your soldiers have been sent here to die, led into a trap by putting you in a place from which there is no escape, without moving a single soldier to try to save you.

Your troop is surrounded; it does not have the slightest hope of salvation. All roads, paths and rivers are taken, defended by trenches and mined with 100-pound bombs. The entire air force and army could not save you.

You will die from hunger or from bullets if the battle is prolonged.

To sacrifice those men in a lost battle, for the sake of an ignoble cause, is a crime that a sensitive man cannot commit.

Letter written to the officer in command of the soldiers surrounded by the Rebel Army in the Sierra Maestra. José Pardo Llada, *Memorias de la Sierra Maestra* (Havana: Editorial Tierra Nueva, 1960), pp. 60–62.

In this situation I offer you a dignified and honorable surrender. All
your men would be treated with the greatest respect and consideration. The officers could keep their weapons.

Accept this offer; you will not surrender to an enemy of the fatherland but to a sincere revolutionary, a man who fights for the welfare
of all Cubans, including that of the soldiers who fight us. You will
surrender to a university classmate who wants the same things that
you want for Cuba.

Sincerely,
Fidel Castro[1]

[1] Major Quevedo surrendered at the end. See also "The Battle of Jigüe" in
this volume. Eds.

Unity Manifesto of the Sierra Maestra
(July 20, 1958)

After the treacherous coup of March 10, which interrupted the normal
democratic process of the nation, the Cuban people have opposed the
tyranny with heroism and determination. Each and every form of
defiance has been used in these six bloody years, and all sectors of
Cuba have patriotically opposed Fulgencio Batista's dictatorship. The
Cuban people, in their struggle to be free, have shed much blood,
demonstrating that they have a never-ending love for freedom.

Ever since the long-gone days of student parades and demonstrations, when the first martyrs fell, up to the recent battles, such as the
one at Santo Domingo in Oriente Province, in which the dictatorship
suffered a crushing defeat, leaving on the battlefield its dead, wounded,
and a large amount of equipment, much blood has been shed and
numerous efforts made to free the enslaved fatherland. Labor strikes,
three military conspiracies, and courageous protests by all the civic

Manifesto broadcast by Rebel Radio on July 20, 1958 (also known as the
Caracas Pact). It was issued by Fidel Castro (26th of July Movement); Carlos
Prío Socarrás (Organización Auténtica); Enrique Rodríguez Loeches (Directorio
Revolucionario); Justo Carrillo (Agrupación Montecristi); Manuel A. de Varona
(Partido Revolucionario Cubano Insurreccional); Angel Santos (Resistencia
Cívica); Lincoln Rodón (Partido Demócrata Independiente); David Salvador,
Angel Cofiño, Pascasio Linares, Lauro Blanco, José M. Aguilera (Unidad
Obrera); José Puente, Omar Fernández (FEU); Dr. José Miró Cardona (Co-
ordinador General).

institutions have aided the heroic armed struggle in Santiago, Matanzas, Havana, Cienfuegos, and Sagua la Grande. In the cities sabotage and other revolutionary tactics have tested the indomitable spirit of a generation loyal to the immortal words of our national anthem: "To die for the fatherland is to live!"

Rebellion has spread over the whole nation. In the mountains new battlefronts have been created; in the plains guerrilla columns constantly harass the enemy. Today thousands of soldiers, in Batista's largest offensive to date, are being faced by courageous rebels who are defending, inch by inch, the free territory at the Sierra Maestra. One third of Oriente Province is under the control of guerrilla column number 6. In the plains, guerrilla column number 2 is fighting throughout the area between Manzanillo and Nuevitas. In the central region of Santa Clara, the Directorio Revolucionario has been fighting bravely. There have been battles in the Escambray Mountains and the surrounding area. Members of the Partido Revolucionario Cubano and the 26th of July Movement have also been fighting in this region. At Cienfuegos and Yaguajay, revolutionary guerrillas are fighting hard. Small guerrilla forces are operating in Matanzas and Pinar del Río. In each corner of Cuba, a struggle to the death is taking place between freedom and dictatorship. Abroad many exiles are aiding in the effort to free the fatherland.

Aware that the coordination of human efforts, resources, civic forces, of political and revolutionary sectors of the opposition, including civilians, military men, workers, students, professionals, businessmen, and citizens in general is necessary to overthrow the dictatorship through a supreme effort, we pledge our united efforts. Hereby we agree to create a large revolutionary, civic coalition, made up of all of Cuba's sectors. We pledge our best and patriotic efforts to that goal because united we shall oust the criminal dictatorship of Fulgencio Batista and give Cuba peace, returning democracy to the people—the two blessings which can lead our people toward greater progress, development, and freedom. We are aware of the need to act in a united manner. Our fellow citizens demand it.

This unity of the Cuban opposition forces is based on three main points:

1. Adoption of a common strategy to defeat the dictatorship by means of armed insurrection, reinforcing—as soon as possible—all the fronts and arming the thousands of Cubans willing to fight for freedom. The popular mobilization of all labor, civic, professional and economic forces, culminating in a great general strike on the civilian

front; while, on the military front, action will be coordinated throughout the country. From this common determination, Cuba will emerge
free, and the painful spilling of blood will come to an end. Victory
will be ours in any case, but it will be delayed if our activities are not
coordinated.

2. Guiding our nation, after the tyrant's fall, to a normal state of
affairs, a brief provisional government will be formed to establish full
constitutional and democratic rights.

3. A minimum governmental program will be formed to guarantee
the punishment of those who are guilty of crimes, workers' rights,
fulfillment of international agreements, public order, peace, freedom,
as well as the economic, social, and political progress of the Cuban
people.

We ask the government of the United States of America to cease
all military and other types of aid to the dictator, and also reaffirm our
defense of our national sovereignty and the nonmilitary, republican
tradition of Cuba.

To our soldiers, we say that the moment has arrived to deny their
support to the tyranny. We trust them because we know that there
are decent men in the armed forces. In the past hundreds of officers
and enlisted men have paid with their lives, imprisonment, exile, or
retirement from active duty because of their love of freedom, and
there must be many others who feel the same way. This is not a war
against the armed forces of the Republic but against Batista, the only
obstacle to the peace desired and needed by all Cubans, both civilian
and military. We urge workers, students, professionals, businessmen,
sugar plantation owners, farmers, and Cubans of all religions, ideol-
ogies, and races to join this liberation movement which will overthrow
the infamous tyranny that has soaked our soil with blood, decimated
our best human resources, ruined our economy, destroyed our republican institutions, and interrupted the constitutional and democratic
evolution of our country, thus bringing about a bloody civil war
which will come to a triumphant end only with a revolution backed
by all the people.

The hour has come when the intelligence, patriotism, courage, and
civic virtues of our men and women—especially those who feel deeply
the historic destiny of our nation, its right to be free and to adopt the
democratic way of life—will save the oppressed fatherland. Our great
future is assured by our history and our natural resources and the
people's capacity to sacrifice. We call on all the revolutionary organizations and the civic and political forces of our nation to support this

declaration of unity. Later, as soon as possible, we shall hold a meeting with every representative delegate to discuss and approve all the points of our pledge.

They Are Losing the War
(July 21, 1958)

A company of Column 8, commanded by Captain Jaime Vega, suffered a serious setback in the zone of operations in the province of Camagüey. We have not published any information about what happened more than two weeks ago because we were awaiting results of the investigation ordered.

Any war unit can suffer a tactical misfortune, because the course does not necessarily have to be an uninterrupted chain of victories against an enemy that has always had superior weapons and resources and which, nevertheless, has always borne the worst part of this conflict.

We consider it our duty in the command of our army to announce any setback that any of our forces in action suffers, because according to our moral and military standards we consider it wrong to conceal from the people or the combatants any reverses we may suffer.

The misfortunes should be published because valuable lessons can be learned from them and we can thus prevent the errors committed by one unit from being repeated by others, and carelessness on the part of one revolutionary officer being repeated by other officers.

In war, human shortcomings will not be overcome by concealing them or by deceiving soldiers, but by making them known, always alerting commanders and demanding new and redoubled efforts in the planning and execution of movements and actions.

But in this case the action was characterized by subsequent facts that the people should know, mainly because they affect very seriously the fate of the armed forces of the nation and if they continue happening could have very grave consequences for their future.

We have repeatedly proclaimed that we are not at war against the armed forces, only against the tyranny. But the unheard-of barbarities

Communiqué released on July 21, 1958. Jules Dubois, *Fidel Castro—Liberator or Dictator?* (Indianapolis: Bobbs Merrill, 1959), pp. 306–311.

of certain officers and members of the army responsible could reach
a degree in which a military man in active service today could find
it hard to justify his freedom from guilt for what has been happening
and prove that only the unlimited ambitions of an unscrupulous dictator, plus the treason of a few officers of the tenth of March movement, led the army to assume the unconstitutional, undemocratic, and
undignified role it is now playing. The facts to which we refer are as
follows:

Not observing the tactical measures of security contained in his
instructions, which should always be followed in enemy-controlled
territory, Captain Jaime Vega was advancing in trucks on the night of
the twenty-seventh of September on a railroad embankment leading
from Central Francisco to Central Macareno, in the south of Camagüey
Province.

Company 97 of the enemy forces, lying in ambush along the embankment, opened fire on the column by surprise at two o'clock
the morning of the twenty-eighth, with heavy machine-gun support.
The heavy enemy fire against the vehicles caused eighteen dead, and
eleven wounded prisoners could not be recovered because of the darkness and the superior position of the machine-gun emplacements.

The wounded rebel prisoners were taken to the hospital at Macareno,
where they were attended by the resident doctor and two other
doctors from Santa Cruz del Sur, sent for by Lieutenant Suárez, in
charge of Company 97.

On the following day Colonel Leopoldo Pérez Coujil arrived by
plane, and shortly after Lieutenant Suárez Suquet, Major Domingo
Piñeyro and his bodyguard, Sergeant Lorenzo Otano, arrived by car.

Colonel Pérez Coujil distributed a gift of $1,000 in cash among the
soldiers. Thereupon, the first thing he did was to strike one of the
wounded prisoners in the face, and after questioning them instructed
Lieutenant Colonel Suárez Suquet to kill all of the wounded. Suárez
Suquet appointed Major Piñeyro to feign a rebel attack in the course
of transferring the wounded to Santa Cruz del Sur.

They prepared trucks with mattresses, on which the wounded were
placed, and after going a few miles the soldiers started to shoot, while
Major Piñeyro shouted, "The rebels are attacking us." Whereupon
Sergeant Otano threw two hand grenades at the trucks carrying the
wounded who, thinking they were really being attacked by their
rebel colleagues, shouted, "Don't shoot, companions; we are wounded."

Sergeant Otano leaped forward, climbed on the trucks and, machine
gun in hand, finished off the wounded, who were already half dead.
Some lost arms and legs, others were badly mutilated, some decap-

itated; inside the trucks there was nothing but a mass of human blood and flesh.

From then on, Sergeant Otano was known by his fellow soldiers as the Butcher.

Then they placed the corpses in a truck, carried them to Santa Cruz del Sur, opened a huge ditch and buried them.

The narration of these deeds is enough to outrage even the most indifferent person. But no Cuban can feel the facts so much as the rebel doctors who cared for more than 100 wounded enemy prisoners when the offensive against the Sierra Maestra commenced, or our combatants who carried those wounded on their shoulders and on stretchers from the battlefields to the hospitals many miles away. It is possible that among those murdered rebel wounded, there could be found some who in the battle of Jigüe had carried enemy wounded from the points of action to the place where they received first aid, after having climbed almost inaccessible terrain.

Those wounded who had been murdered in Camagüey had witnessed with their own eyes how 422 soldiers of the tyranny had marched in the Sierra Maestra and were delivered to the International and Cuban Red Cross, and shared with them their medicines, their tobacco, and their food.

The lack of reciprocity could not be more repugnant or more cowardly. And this is not an isolated case on the part of an officer or a given group of troops, but a general custom of the entire army, to a nauseating degree.

They murdered prisoners when we attacked Moncada; they murdered prisoners when we landed from the *Granma;* they murdered prisoners when the presidential palace was attacked; they murdered prisoners when Calixto Sánchez landed; they murdered prisoners at the Cienfuegos revolt. But on all of those occasions, the army could still have hopes of remaining in power: it was strong, it had not suffered substantial defeats, and it could still believe that its crimes could go unpunished by virtue of the helplessness of an unarmed people. What happened in Camagüey is doubly absurd and double cause for outrage. First, because the return of hundreds of soldiers safe and sound by the rebels to the Red Cross is still fresh in the memory of the citizens; and second, because the soldiers of the tyranny are losing the war and have been beaten in several battles, giving up more and more territory every day and are retreating everywhere.

They are losing the war and yet murder the few prisoners they take, in spite of being an army now vanquished.

Through that same territory in Camagüey, Columns 2 and 8, under the command of majors Camilo Cienfuegos and Ernesto Guevara, marched victoriously without being stopped by the heavy forces that the dictatorship threw against them. The vanguard has now invaded more than thirty-five miles of territory in Las Villas Province.

What military or political sense can there be in that treacherous attack against the rebel wounded, except inflicting another stain of blood on the armed forces, which will be remembered frequently in history as an unwashable stain on the uniform of an infamous and dishonored army, that can nevermore be called the army of the Republic?

This deed will be denounced before the International Red Cross and we will demand that their delegates be sent to investigate what has happened; an open letter will be addressed to the armed forces notifying them of the responsibility they are putting upon themselves.

Besides holding several soldiers as prisoners, we also have a lieutenant colonel who, paradoxically, is wounded and is being attended in one of our hospitals, and a major and two captains.

The conduct of Colonel Leopoldo Pérez Coujil, Lieutenant Colonel Suárez Suquet, Major Triana, and the other miserable murderers constitutes an act of infinite cowardice and a total lack of consideration for their colleagues in arms who are being held prisoner by us, without any other guarantee for their lives than our attitude of calm steadfastness in the face of this kind of vandalism, the sense of humanity and justice which accompanies us in this war we are waging, the ideals which inspire us and our true concept of what honor is.

Let not those responsible for these acts think that they can escape even if at the last minute the army should rebel against them, because one of our most inflexible conditions is that even if any military coup be carried out, the war criminals and all military men and politicians who have enriched themselves with the blood and sweat of the people must surrender, beginning with Batista and ending with the last torturer. Otherwise, they will have to continue fighting the war until their total destruction, because they cannot stop this revolution at all either by the shameful farce that is being prepared for November 3 or any military coup which may be carried out without fulfilling the conditions of the 26th of July Movement or by means of any prior agreement.

Those who have sown winds will reap whirlwinds.

There is no longer any doubt that the decadent and demoralized forces of the tyranny cannot stop the victorious advance of the people. To do that they would first have to vanquish each one of the columns that are already operating successfully in four provinces, and then take the Sierra Maestra up to the very last trench at the top of Turquino Peak,[1] which will be defended by the very last rebel soldier.

Batista's army has demonstrated to the full extent that this it cannot do.

An extensive report has been received at general headquarters to the effect that invading Column 2, "Antonio Maceo," after having crossed Camagüey Province successfully, has entered Las Villas territory.[2] That report contains a detailed account of an extraordinary military achievement and will soon be read by Rebel Radio so as to give the people an opportunity of knowing about one of the most thrilling episodes of the contemporary history of our country.

[1] Highest mountain in Cuba. Eds.
[2] This did not happen until a month later. Eds.

The Battle of Jigüe
(July 24, 1958)

On Saturday the eleventh, at 5:45 in the morning, a rebel patrol fired the first shots against Battalion 18 of the enemy infantry camped at a point known as Jigüe, where the river of that name and La Plata River meet, about 7 kilometers from the south coast and 10 kilometers west of Turquino Peak. The initial fire was brief. It looked like a simple harassing skirmish; fifteen minutes later the patrol ceased firing and fell back. Its objective was to inflict casualties and provoke movement. At that time other rebel units had taken all strategic points around the battalion but were under orders not to fire on the enemy unless their presence was discovered.

At nine in the morning, two enemy platoons departed toward the beach carrying the wounded and an array of mules in search of food. Half an hour later they clashed with our forces posted along the road, forcing them to retreat leaving behind five dead, one prisoner, two Cristóbal machine guns, one Thompson machine gun, three Springfields, about one thousand bullets, and twelve rifle grenades. The rest of the rebel units remained without firing. The silence was prolonged for seventy-two hours.

Under those circumstances it was very difficult for the enemy

Communiqué issued on July 24, 1958, from the Sierra Maestra. Edmundo Desnoes (ed.), *La sierra y el llano* (Havana: Casa de las Américas, 1961), pp. 189–194.

battalion to realize its true situation. The food supply was exhausted, and three days passed before they made a second attempt. This occurred on the fourteenth. At two in the afternoon a complete company resolutely advanced down the same road. Combat began anew, and this time it lasted until nine in the evening. A platoon was cut off and tried to escape by dispersing; the other two platoons retreated. The following day the balance was five dead, 21 prisoners, 10 Springfields, 8 Garands, 2 Cristóbal machine guns, 1 Browning rifle machine gun, 39 mules with knapsacks, and 2,800 bullets. Simultaneously our forces advanced from all directions and took positions at rifle-shot distance from the enemy encampment. The encirclement was established, and from then on the harassment was unceasing.

The battalion had been immobilized and without food for the last four days, and the success of the operation from then on would depend on the fight against enemy reinforcements. On the morning of the fifteenth, the air force appeared. The aerial attack against our positions, with machine-gun strafing and 500-pound explosive bombs as well as napalm, lasted uninterrupted from six in the morning until one in the afternoon. The pasture and forest around Jigüe were left scorched, but not one of the rebel combatants moved from his position. On the sixteenth, this attack was repeated while enemy transports moved reinforcement to the mouth of the La Plata River.

On that same day at twelve noon, as we knew that the besieged troops had been without food for eleven days, we ceased fire for three hours, inviting them to surrender. The soldiers left their trenches and enjoyed the truce, but at three in the afternoon they returned to their positions without accepting surrender. On the seventeenth at six in the morning, Infantry Company G-4 left the beach. It marched slowly, exploring the road. At 2:30 P.M., 50 automatic rifles and 2 tripod machine guns (30-caliber) opened fire on it. In fifteen minutes the first two platoons were destroyed; the rest retreated. In our possession remained the 24 prisoners, 12 dead, 14 Springfields, 9 Cristóbal machine guns, 8 Garands, 1 Browning rifle machine gun, and 1 tripod machine gun (30-caliber), 18,000 bullets, and 48 rifle grenades.

The first reinforcements had been repelled. But the air force continued attacking uninterruptedly, and the transports continued landing troops at the mouth of the La Plata. On the nineteenth, an entire battalion supported by artillery fire from land, sea, and air advanced from the beach. Then the hardest battle of the whole episode, which lasted uninterrupted for almost twenty-four hours, began. The rebel forces counterattacked and forced the enemy to retreat right to the beach. One rebel captain, the courageous *compañero* Andrés Cuevas, and three other *compañeros* had fallen, another four were critically wounded, but in our possession were twenty-one prisoners, seventeen dead soldiers, fourteen Cristóbal machine guns, ten Garand rifles, two boxes of 81-caliber howitzer mortars, and one train of mules with food. Above all, the enemy reinforcements had been repelled completely.

The besieged battalion had not had any food for nine days. Our forces advanced toward the encampment; they situated themselves 50 meters from the enemy trenches, also cutting off water from them. On the same day, the nineteenth, at eleven in the evening, while the battle against the second reinforcement was being fought, a prisoner was sent to offer them surrender. On the morning of the twentieth, we ordered a cease fire from six in the morning until ten. The enemy soldiers, who were weary in the trenches, accepted the cease-fire. Little by little several of those who still could walk laboriously came close to our trenches and asked for water, food, and cigarettes. On seeing that our men did not shoot and shared the food they had in their hands, they embraced our soldiers and cried with emotion. How different was the treatment from that which they expected perhaps, fooled by the dictatorship's false propaganda! The sight was an emotional one for all. But the battalion had not surrendered yet. No one was firing, but Commandant José Quevedo, a young officer, still maintained control over the decimated, hungry, and undernourished troops. They were no longer fighting nor could they fight, but the officer still refused to surrender and the soldiers respected his decision. It was unfortunate, however, that the embraces between rebels and soldiers should turn into a struggle to death again. The commander made an effort to win time and communicated to us that until 6:00 P.M. he would not make a decision and that although his soldiers had reached the limit of physical endurance, he had given his word to the General Staff to resist until that hour, awaiting reinforcements.

Convinced of the solidity of our line, we decided to wait and not launch an unnecessary attack, which would have cost many more lives, against those who minutes before asked us for water and food. At dusk the news arrived that the reinforcements had been totally repelled. On the twenty-first at 1:00 A.M., the remainder of Battalion 18 surrendered to our forces. The conditions were honorable and humane. The officers were allowed to keep their personal weapons, food was made available to all, and they were told that all would be freed with the greatest speed. Only the commander would remain as a war prisoner. One hundred seventy officers, noncommissioned officers, and soldiers were in our power, 91 Springfield rifles, 46 Cristóbal machine guns, fifteen Garands, 4 rifle machine guns, 2 tripod machine guns, 1 bazooka with 60 projectiles, 1 mortar (81-caliber) with 60 howitzer shells, approximately 35,000 bullets, and 126 grenades.

It is just to recognize that the adversary fought with courage, resisting admirably a ten-day encirclement without consuming food, awaiting reinforcements which the dictatorship was unable to deliver. One of the best enemy units, with a capable and courageous chief, was out of combat. Even as a prisoner of war, he will be treated with the consideration he deserves because according to information in our possession, he was humane and respectful to the civilian population in the months he operated in the Sierra Maestra. We regret that in this case the defeat occurred to an honest and dignified officer. The criminals never risk themselves amidst the peaks of the Sierra Maestra. The battle of Jigüe has resulted in a balance of 249 weapons taken, 41 soldiers and officers dead, and 241 prisoners, of whom 30 were wounded.

With the objective of informing the people and their own families, we can say for the benefit of the wives, mothers, and other relatives of these soldiers that since yesterday the delegate of the International Red Cross from Geneva, to whom the wounded enemy soldiers of the last several battles in the Sierra Maestra and 240 prisoners of the battle of Jigüe were delivered, is in Vegas de Jibacoa.

Letter to Camilo Cienfuegos (August 5, 1958)

Camilo:

Send me information on the situation there. In Sao Grande it seems the guards have gained some territory. Only an attack tonight against the reinforcements can define the situation.

Inform me on what measures you have taken there.

Fidel

Letter written on August 5, 1958, from the Sierra Maestra. "El guerrillero," Verde Olivo (Havana), October 29, 1960, pp. 24–25.

Letter to Camilo Cienfuegos
(August 6, 1958, 7:45 A.M.)

Camilo:

At this very moment, in which I have received your message, the guards at Macitas are showing their intention of leaving, burning all their trenches.

If this occurs, from here on intense persecution will be initiated that will allow no truce.

The mission of your forces: to watch over the agreed place for the ambush in order to occupy it if at any moment the enemy abandons it and to give the first strong blow to the withdrawing guards. If that position is not taken, the bulk of your forces, the bazooka, and the mortar should be on the alert to attack the retreating enemy forces with the greatest intensity possible from the barren hill and along the entire flank, as soon as they show up there.

In our message I noticed your preoccupation with a plan in case they attack the hill. If nothing happens, inflict some casualties on them from there and then retreat half a mile. Try to stop or make as difficult as possible the enemy's retreat, which will be pursued from here by other forces.

Fidel

Letter written on August 6, 1958, at 7:45 A.M., from the Sierra Maestra. "El guerrillero," *Verde Olivo* (Havana), October 29, 1960, p. 25.

Letter to Camilo Cienfuegos
(August 6, 1958, 6:15 P.M.)

Camilo:

We heard on the radio that the guards are stuck out there, asking for tractors, and that they have been fired on heavily from the rear. Try to keep them there. One hundred men of ours are going to the rearguard and then one hundred more, to try to take over their tanks.

Letter written on August 6, 1958, at 6:15 P.M., from the Sierra Maestra. "El guerrillero," *Verde Olivo* (Havana), October 29, 1960, p. 25.

Pedrito should wait there. The important thing now is not to allow them to move, so that we can attack them when the moon comes out.

Fidel

Orders to Camilo Cienfuegos (August 18, 1958)

By Order of the Commander in Chief:

Major Camilo Cienfuegos is assigned the mission of leading a column from the Sierra Maestra to Pinar del Río Province to carry out the strategic plan of the Rebel Army.

Column 2, "Antonio Maceo," as the invading force will be known in honor of the glorious warrior of Independence, will leave from El Salto next Wednesday, August 20, 1958.

The major of the invading column is granted power to organize rebel units throughout the national territory until the majors of each province arrive with their columns in their respective jurisdictions; to apply the penal code and the agrarian laws of the Rebel Army in the invaded territory; to collect the contributions established by military decree; to combine operations with any other revolutionary forces which might be found in a given region; to establish a permanent guerrilla front in Pinar del Río Province, which will be the base of operations of the invading column; and to designate officers of the Rebel Army up to the rank of column major in order to carry out that plan.

The invading column, although its main objective is to wage the liberation war in the western part of the island and to that end any other tactical matter is secondary, will engage the enemy on every occasion which presents itself.

The weapons taken from the enemy will be destined preferably for the organization of local units.

In order to reward, distinguish, and stimulate heroism among officers and soldiers of the invading Column 2, "Antonio Maceo," the medal of courage "Osvaldo Herrera," a former captain of said column who took his life in the prisons of Bayamo after a gallant and heroic attitude of resistance before the tortures of the tyranny's henchmen, is created.

Message written on August 18, 1958, at 9:00 A.M., from the Sierra Maestra. "Las órdenes de Fidel," *El Mundo* (Havana), October 28, 1965, p. 8.

Report on the Offensive: Part 1
(August 18, 1958)

Exactly four months ago I used the microphones of Rebel Radio to speak to the people at a difficult time; it was after the strike of April 9. In the cities spirits had fallen, for many the days of our revolutionary forces were numbered, and there was fear that the country would remain submerged for many years in a night without hope. With the strike's failure, the tyranny's high command issued a series of false dispatches announcing that on the battlefield also the rebel forces had been defeated. Once the strike was crushed, the tyranny believed that the opportune moment had arrived to launch all its military forces against the rebel nucleus which had maintained the banner of rebellion upright for over a year.

Replying then to the enemy campaign and expressing our unbreakable will to resist, I said,

> The people of Cuba know that the struggle is being waged victoriously; the people of Cuba know that throughout seventeen months, since our landing with a handful of men who knew how to face all dangers with none giving up his obligation, the Revolution has been fighting incessantly; they know that what was born barely a year ago is today called invincible; they know that now the struggle goes on not only in the Sierra Maestra, from Cabo Cruz to Santiago de Cuba, but also in Sierra Cristál from Mayarí to Baracoa, in the Cauto Plain from Bayamo to Victoria de las Tunas, and in other provinces of Cuba. But above all the people of Cuba know that the will and boldness with which we initiated this struggle remains unbreakable; they know we are an army sprouted from the people, to whom adversity represents nothing; that after each reverse the Revolution has come back with greater strength. They know that the destruction of the *Granma* expeditionary detachment was not the end of the struggle but the beginning; they know that the spontaneous strike which followed the murder of our *compañero* Frank País did not defeat the tyranny but pointed the way for an organized strike; that no government can keep itself in power atop the pile of cadavers with which the dictatorship drowned the last strike in blood, because the hundreds of young men and workers murdered and the unprecedented

The government of Fulgencio Batista launched a military offensive against the Rebel Army on May 24, 1958. After having repelled the offensive on August 18, 1958, Castro spoke to the people of Cuba and Latin America from his clandestine radio station, Radio Rebelde, in the Sierra Maestra. Antonio Nuñez Jiménez, *Geografía de Cuba*, 2nd edition (Havana: Editorial Lex, 1959), pp. 578–588.

repression unleashed against the people does not weaken the Revolution but rather makes it stronger, more necessary, more invincible. The spilled blood increases the courage and indignation: Each fallen *compañero* in the city streets and on the battlefields awakens in his spiritual brothers an irresistible wish to give his life also; it awakens among the indifferent the wish to struggle; it awakens among the lukewarm the feelings of the fatherland bleeding to death for its dignity; it awakens sympathy and support among all the peoples of America.

And I concluded that speech with the following words: "To the people of Cuba we give assurance that this fortress will never be subdued and our oath that either the fatherland will be free or the very last combatant will die."

Today I speak again to the people from this radio station—which did not cease to broadcast even during the days when mortars and bombs exploded around it—not with a promise to be fulfilled but with an entire stage of that promise already fulfilled. The Rebel Army, after seventy-six days of incessant battle in Front No. 1 of the Sierra Maestra, repelled and virtually destroyed the cream of the tyranny's forces, inflicting on them one of the greatest disasters a modern army, trained and equipped with all the military resources, could suffer before nonprofessional forces enclosed in a territory surrounded by enemy troops, without aviation, without artillery, and without supply routes for ammunition and food.

Over thirty skirmishes and six major battles were waged. The enemy offensive began on May 24. Weeks before, along the Sierra Maestra the tyranny had been concentrating troops which slowly drew near the foot of the range. For this offensive the enemy command had been able to gather fourteen infantry battalions and seven other companies consisting of the following units: Battalion 10, Major Nelson Carrasco Artiles; Battalion 11, Lieutenant Colonel Angel Sánchez Mosquera; Battalion 12, Captain Pedraja Padrón; Battalion 13, Major J. Triana Tarrao; Battalion 14, Major Bernardo Guerrero Padrón; Battalion 15, Major Martínez Morejón; Battalion 16, Captain Figueroa Lara; Battalion 17, Major Corzo Izaguirre; Battalion 18, Major José Quevedo Pérez; Battalion 19, Major Suárez Zoulet; Battalion 20, Major Caridad Fernández; Battalion 21, Major Franco Lliteras; Battalion 22, Major Eugenio Menéndez Martínez; Battalion 23, Major Armando González Finalés; Company 1, Captain Modesto Díaz Fernández; Company K, Major Roberto Triana Tarrao; Company L, Captain Noelio Montero Díaz; Second Company, Fifth Regiment, First Lieutenant Miguel Pérez de La Llama; First Company, Third Regiment, Captain Luis Vega Hernández; Second Company, Third Regiment, First Lieutenant

Adriano Pérez Cabrera; Tank Company C, 10th of March Regiment, Captain Victorino Gómez Oquendo; an air force under the command of Lieutenant Colonel Armando Coto Rodríguez; a naval force under the command of Captain J. López Campos, and Rural Guard forces under the command of Lieutenant Colonel Arcadio Casillas Lumpuy. The enemy high command consisted of Major General Eulogio Cantillo Porras, Brigadier General Alberto del Río Chaviano, Brigadier Dámaso Sogo Hernández, Colonel José Manuel Ugalde Carrillo, Lieutenant Colonel Merob Sosa, Commanders Raúl de Talahorra, Juan Arias Cruz, Bernardo Perdomo Granela, J. Ferrer Casilda, Timoteo Morales Villazón, Raúl Martínez Trujillo; Captains Hermes Llinás Valdés, F. Bal-Lloveras, Ricardo Montero Duque, Lorenzo Fundidor, Rodolfo Ugalde Carrillo, Julio Roldán Puig, Miguel J. López Naranjo; and Second Lieutenants Heriberto M. Ruiz and Agustín G. Padrón Rivero. The dictatorship's strategy was to concentrate the core of their troops against Front No. 1 in the Sierra Maestra, headquarters of the General Command and of Rebel Radio.

After the enemy had deployed their forces and imagined ours dispersed, the Rebel Command secretly moved all columns in the south and center of the province to Front No. 1: Column 3 commanded by Major Juan Almeida, who operated in the Cobre zone; Column 2 commanded by Major Camilo Cienfuegos, who operated in the center of the province; Column 4 commanded by Major Ramiro Valdés, who operated east of Turquino Peak; Column 7 commanded by Major Crescencio Pérez, who operated in the western extreme of the Sierra Maestra, all were mobilized toward the immediate west of Turquino Peak. These columns, Column 8 commanded by Major Ernesto Guevara, and Column 1 commanded by the General Command formed a defensive compact front of around 30 kilometers in length whose principal axis was the high ground of the Sierra Maestra.

The rebel strategy was synthesized in the following instructions addressed by the General Command to the column's majors during the first few days of the month of July, which said among other things:

> We must be conscious of the minimum amount of time that we must maintain organized resistance and of each of the successive stages that are going to present themselves; that is, in this moment we are thinking of the future weeks and months. This offensive will be the longest of all, and after its failure Batista would be irremissibly lost; he knows it and therefore will make the maximum effort. This is a decisive battle which is being waged precisely in the territory best known by us. We are directing all our efforts toward turning this offensive into a disaster for the dic-

tatorship. We are adopting a series of measures destined to guarantee (1) organized resistance; (2) the draining and exhaustion of the adversary army; (3) the conjunction of elements and sufficient weapons to throw ourselves on the offensive as soon as they begin to weaken. The successive stages for defense are prepared one by one. We harbor the certainty that we shall make the enemy pay a very high price. At this moment it is evident that they are behind in their plans and even though we presume there will be much fighting to be done given the efforts they must make to gain territory, we do not know how long their enthusiasm will last. The thing is to know how to make the resistance stronger each time, and this will be accomplished to the degree that they lengthen their lines and we fall back toward strategic positions. As we consider it possible that at some points they will be able to flank the Maestra, in the enclosed document we communicate the precise instructions for each case. The fundamental objectives of this plan are (1) to ready a basic territory where the organization, hospitals, shops, and so forth will function; (2) to maintain Rebel Radio on the air, a factor of utmost importance; (3) to offer the enemy greater resistance each time as we concentrate troops and occupy the most strategic points from which to launch the counterattack.

The plan contained in these instructions was rigorously fulfilled. The guerrilla war had been abandoned to become instead a war of positions and movements. Our platoons were placed at all the natural entries of the Sierra to the north and south. It was necessary to cover 30 kilometers to the north and 30 kilometers to the south of the Maestra with our limited forces. On May 24 and 25, the enemy attacked simultaneously by the mines of Bueycito and by Las Mercedes. From the very first instant, they met tenacious resistance. To take Las Mercedes, defended by only fourteen rebels, the enemy—supported by tanks and planes—was forced to fight for thirty hours, while in Minas de Bueycito the forces of Sánchez Mosquera had to pay dearly for each meter of ground they advanced, gaining only 10 kilometers in fifteen days of combat. On June 15, the enemy attack also began in the south, from the coast, once Infantry Battalion 17 had disembarked at Las Cuevas.

The course of events which followed has been related day by day through the war dispatches on the military situation broadcast by Rebel Radio, and it would be too extensive to reproduce them textually. For thirty-five days the enemy continued to gain ground slowly. In the middle of June, Battalions 11 and 22, which had been applying pressure from the mines in Bueycito, cut diagonally through the foot of the range and advanced to Santo Domingo. Thus, all the enemy forces were west of Turquino Peak. The day which signaled the most critical moment was the nineteenth of June. In the course of those twenty-four hours, the enemy forces simultaneously penetrated Las Vegas de Jibacoa, Santo Domingo, and continued to advance toward Naranjal in La Plata from Palma Mocha, threatening with annihilation the most advanced platoons of our forces. Days later they advanced through Gaviro and flanked the Maestra through the high ground of San Lorenzo. It was the rapidity with which our untiring fighters moved from one position to another in response to the enemy movements which allowed them to face the difficult situation in each case. The most advanced points which enemy forces succeeded in establishing were Naranjal, reached by Battalion 18 of Major Quevedo advancing from the mouth of the La Plata, and Meriño, penetrated by Major Suárez Zoulet's Battalion 19.

The enemy had penetrated deeply north and south. Between the troops that were attacking from both directions barely a distance of 7 kilometers in a straight line remained, but the spirit of our troops was intact and the ammunition reserve as well as stock of highly destructive mines had been kept almost complete. The enemy had to invest much energy and time to gain ground in the mountain interior. On July 29 in Santo Domingo, the tyranny's forces, under the command of Lieutenant Colonel Sánchez Mosquera, received the first obliterating blow against one of their most aggressive troops. With the weapons and ammunitions taken in that action, which lasted three days, was initiated the thundering counterattack which expelled all the tyranny's forces from the Sierra Maestra in thirty-five days after inflicting on them almost a thousand casualties and taking over four hundred prisoners.

The battles of Santo Domingo, Meriño, Jigüe, the second battle of Santo Domingo, Las Vegas de Jibacoa, and Las Mercedes succeeded uninterrupted. The final stage of the struggle was the tyranny's desperate attempt to remove what was left of the forces utilized in the offensive from the Sierra Maestra to prevent absolutely all of them from being cut off and annihilated by our army. Even the Pino de Agua encampment was evacuated without waiting for the attack! It was a shameful flight from the battlefield which would have been sufficient anywhere in the world for an army with a sense of honor and prestige to demand the resignation of the entire high command due to the number of victims sacrificed and the military equipment stupidly and criminally lost. The soldiers who were victims of the mistakes made by the military command are not responsible for the disaster.

It can be said that panic spread first in the command post rather than among the troops, and the retreat consequently became precipitate flight.

Infantry Battalion 22 was annihilated; Battalion 11 was decimated; Battalion 19 lost all its wagons with knapsacks, food, and ammunition in Meriño. Battalion 18 was forced to surrender due to harassment, encirclement, hunger, and thirst. Company G4 was destroyed in Purialón. Company L of the infantry division was annihilated near the mouth of the La Plata River. Company 92 was encircled and forced to surrender in Las Vegas, together with the chief of Tank Company C. Company C was destroyed in El Salto. Battalion 23 was decimated in Arroyón. Battalion 17 and three other infantry battalions with tank forces which went to its rescue suffered severe punishment, abandoning the battlefield after seven days of struggle, virtually in the middle of the plain.

A total of 507 weapons remained in the possession of the rebel forces including: 2 14-ton tanks with 37-millimeter cannons; 2 81-caliber mortars; 2 3½-inch bazookas; 8 60-caliber mortars; 12 tripod machine guns; 21 rifle machine guns; 142 Garand rifles; approximately 200 Cristóbal machine guns and the remainder of M-1 carbines and Springfield rifles, over 100,000 bullets and hundreds of Howitzer mortars, bazookas, and 37-millimeter shells; 3 Minipacks and 14 CR C 10 radio transmitters. The rebel forces suffered a total of 27 dead and 50 wounded, some of whom died and were included in the number of dead. Among the dead were a rebel major, René Campos (Daniel), four captains—Ramón Paz, Andrés Cuevas, Angelito Verdecia, and Leonel Rodríguez—each of whom wrote pages of heroism which history will not forget. The high number of officers who fell reveals the profound sense of duty of the rebel officers fighting in the front line, in the post of greatest danger. If the dictatorship's army was not also under the terror of the tyranny, which does not allow the slightest judgment of its acts or the slightest manifestation of nonconformity, there would be more than enough motive to court martial those who, from their comfortable offices many leagues away from the heat of battle in a terrain which perhaps they have not even seen from an airplane, gambled with the lives of majors, captains, lieutenants, enlisted men, and draftees who, we must recognize as honest adversaries, fought tenaciously though uselessly.

What explanation can the Joint High Command, Chief of Operations General Cantillo, Executive Officer Colonel Ugalde Carrillo, and the entire staff give for the hundreds of soldiers who have died due to the lack of foresight, insensibility, and lack of capacity of the shining strategists of the tyranny? Going further, what justification can there now be for the thousands of napalm bombs, high-power explosives, and rockets, not to mention the incessant machine-gun strafings to which all the villages in the Sierra Maestra were submitted? From a human viewpoint they will never have justification; from a military viewpoint the defeat suffered justifies it less and makes their shameless, cowardly, and frustrated war techniques more criminal and cowardly. Have they sacrificed their own soldiers for that? Have they sacrificed the people for that? As a demonstration of the contempt which the tyranny feels for its own soldiers, there is the case of Las Vegas de Jibacoa where in spite of the Red Cross flag they strafed the field hospital in which wounded prisoners were kept. This can be verified by the 100 prisoners of Company 92 who were present. What we ourselves do not do with enemy soldiers was done by them to their own comrades in arms who lay in rebel hospitals for defending the tyranny, strafing them without mercy. On another occasion, during the battle of Las Mercedes instead of sending Sherman tanks ahead of the infantry to protect the soldiers, the enemy command sent the soldiers in the vanguard to protect the tanks from the rebels' electric mines, thus allowing them to be wiped out by our rifle squads.

In their attempt to deceive the troops as to reality, the military command has been involved in criminal acts to which we are eye-witnesses. Company G4 of the Eighteenth Infantry was ordered to advance from the beach at La Plata toward Jigüe, without even warning them that the position was surrounded, thus falling into a mortal and annihilating ambush. Something similar occurred with Infantry Company L, which was destroyed in the same place where Company G4 fell because they were not warned of the defeat suffered by the former two days earlier.

In El Salto during the second battle of Santo Domingo, we intercepted a communication of the executive officer who from a plane ordered Company C to advance to Santo Domingo without worry, for he had inspected the road and it was clear. Half an hour later the company was destroyed. Battalion 22 was ordered to move from Santo Domingo to Pueblo Nuevo without warning them that a day earlier a battle had taken place there with rebel forces placed along that road, where it met its destruction.

Company 92 located in Las Vegas was ordered by the executive officer from an airplane to leave, being informed that they would have no difficulties as the heights which controlled the routes had been taken over by a thousand of their soldiers—though it was true that those positions were controlled by the rebel forces.

As a loyal adversary with a human sense of war, on many occasions

I have felt true sorrow for the criminal and stupid manner by which those soldiers, who in the final analysis are Cubans, were fooled and sacrificed by the military command. From the very first skirmish in Santo Domingo, the radio equipment of Company L and Infantry Battalion 22, composed of one Minipack and one CR C 10 with its war codes, fell into the hands of our forces. The enemy command was not even aware of that detail and from then on all the tactical disposition and orders of the enemy were carried out with our complete knowledge. The June 15 secret code of the High Command, which fell into our hands the twenty-ninth of the same month, was not replaced until July 25, when a new one was given, which fell into our hands that same day with other new radio equipment when Company C was destroyed in El Salto. This code was not changed until the final days of the rebel counteroffensive. On one occasion when an enemy unit lost communication because their Minipack was broken, the rebels gave orders themselves to the enemy planes to bombard the army's position.

The technique of deceiving the soldiers by hiding from them the difficulties and defeats which other units were facing brought about the natural outcome that lies sooner or later bring about. Any troops would easily fall into the same errors which had seriously cost other troops. They would fall into the same traps and even the same ambushes that others had fallen into days earlier. No unit officer would receive the slightest news as to the experience of other groups and units. Therefore, the soldiers as well as the officers were ignorant of what was occurring around them. Right now, as the offensive is ending, the dictatorship's High Command has just issued the most fabulous of all the war dispatches which have been heard in Cuba about hundreds of rebel deaths. The truth is that the high number of rebel casualties given—which, of course, are the army's own casualties—indicates acknowledgment of the magnitude of the battles waged. The cynicism of the High Command has been so great that the same day it issued a dispatch stating that rebels were turning themselves in at Manzanillo, Bayamo, and other points we delivered 163 army prisoners and wounded to the Red Cross in Sao Grande where an act signed by the Cuban Red Cross colonels was issued which made a grand total of 422 including previous prisoners. In the 76 days which the offensive lasted, the dictatorship's forces have not captured one prisoner nor has there been one rebel deserter. What will the High Command tell the soldiers when they witness the surge of rebel troops throughout the length and breadth of the island?

Does the High Command not believe that in this moment their

soldiers will experience the most terrible surprise and the bitterest deception about their military command, which having led them to defeat lies shamelessly to the rest of the armed forces saying that the enemy has been destroyed—an enemy which at any moment can appear at the improvident gates of their barracks.

What we said four months ago should be repeated here:

> When the real history of this struggle is written and each factual happening is compared with the regime's military dispatches, it will be understood to what degree the tyranny is capable of corrupting and vilifying the institutions of the Republic, to what degree force in the service of evil is capable of reaching extremes of criminality and barbarity, to what degree the soldiers of a dictatorship can be deceived by their own leaders.

After all, what do the despots and executioners of the people care about the contradictions of history! They are concerned only to get ahead and delay their inevitable fall. I do not believe the High Command lies because of shame. The Cuban army's High Command has demonstrated that it has no modesty whatsoever. The High Command lies from self-interest, lies to prevent the demoralization of its ranks, lies because it refuses to recognize its military incapacity before the world, its condition as mercenary chiefs sold out to the most dishonorable cause one could defend; it lies because it has not been able, in spite of its thousands of soldiers and immense material resources, to defeat a handful of men who rose to defend the rights of their people. The tyranny's mercenary rifles crashed against idealistic rifles which do not collect a salary. The Military Institute or the Academy or the most modern weapons serve for nothing. When the military do not defend their fatherland but attack it, when they do not defend their people but enslave them, they cease to be an institution and become an armed gang, they cease to be military men and become malefactors, and they cease to deserve either the salary that they wrest from the people's sweat or the sun that shelters them and the soil that they are staining with blood, dishonor, and cowardice. Those of us who thought Major General Eulogio Cantillo an officer of a different breed from Ugalde Carrillo, Salas Cañizares, Chaviano, Tabernilla, Cruz Vidal, Pilar García, and so forth, have been changing our opinion because although at the beginning of the campaign he kept silent about operations with adverse consequences and dictated humane orders to the battalion chiefs about the treatment of the civilian population (even though late), to compensate for the horrible crimes previously committed, the last dispatches of the army, more cynical and false than ever, constitute a true prostitution of character and a dis-

honor to any just man. The bombardments which he ordered against
the defenseless residents of the Sierra Maestra as cruel revenge or un-
controlled panic, the eviction of peasants ordered by thousands and
thousands of leaflets thrown from the air, the crimes perpetrated by
the bloodthirsty Morejón in the outskirts of Bayamo, and other events
are more than enough to include Major General Eulogio Cantillo not
only among the cowards who have indifferently contemplated the
rosary of cadavers which their colleagues—Chaviano, Ventura, Pilar
García, and others—have spread through the cities and towns of Cuba,
but also among the men who have prostituted their honor and military
career for the tyranny.

Because of the length of this report and my desire not to abuse the
attention of the listeners, I shall continue tomorrow at the same time
to explain the present military situation, our attitude concerning the
army and the armed forces of the Republic, our position on a possible
coup d'état, the next forward advance of the Rebel Army in the remaining national territory, and the people's role in this new stage of
the struggle.

Report on the Offensive: Part 2
(August 19, 1958)

The enemy wounded attended by our doctors reached 117. Of that
total only two died. The rest are either well or on the way to full
recovery. This fact reveals two things with singular eloquence: first,
the care which the enemy wounded were given; second, the capacity
and extraordinary merit of our doctors, who, lacking all technical
resources in improvised hospitals, were able to accomplish their humane task so brilliantly. Moreover, we did not want to expose the
wounded to the inconveniences and sacrifices which are necessarily
entailed in being secluded in hospitals built in the jungle; thus, from
the very first moment we appealed to the Red Cross in order to have
them transferred to armed forces hospitals. In some cases this was
absolutely necessary to save a critically wounded limb or even life
itself; and in general all would have a better diet, more comforts, and
above all the visits and attention of their own relatives. We delivered

On August 19, 1958, Fidel Castro continued his report on the offensive. Antonio Nuñez Jiménez, *Geografía de Cuba*, 2nd edition (Havana: Editorial Lex,
1959), pp. 588–594.

422 wounded and nonwounded prisoners to the International and Cuban Red Cross besides the 21 wounded prisoners from the battle of Arroyón, who were taken to a nearby site to be picked up by the army itself, which raised the total number of enemy soldiers to 443 enlisted men and officers freed during the rebel counteroffensive. All of the wounded and other prisoners were returned without any delay whatsoever.

Does it seem illogical in the midst of the war to free enemy prisoners? This depends on the war itself and on the concept one has of war. In war one must have a policy for the enemy, just as one must have a policy for the civilian population. War is not merely a matter of rifles, bullets, cannons, and planes. Perhaps that belief has been one of the causes of the failure of the tyranny's forces. That phrase of our apostle José Martí, which could have seemed merely poetic, when he said that what is important is not the number of weapons in one's hand but the number of stars on one's forehead, has become a profound truth for us. Since we landed in the *Granma*, we have adopted an unchanging policy toward the enemy. That policy has been fulfilled rigorously, indeed as probably very few times in history. From the first battle, that of La Plata on January 17, 1957, to the last battle in Las Mercedes during the first days of August, there were over six hundred members of the armed forces in our hands in this front of the Sierra Maestra alone. *With the legitimate pride of those who have known how to follow an ethical norm, we can say that without one exception the fighters of the Rebel Army have honored their law with the prisoners. Never did a prisoner forfeit his life, and never was a wounded man left unattended. But we can say more: Never was a prisoner beaten. And further: Never was a prisoner insulted or offended. All officers who were our prisoners can verify that no one was submitted to interrogation due to our respect of their condition as men and soldiers. The victories achieved by our troops without murdering, torturing, and even without interrogating the enemy demonstrate that abuse to human dignity can never be justified.*

This attitude, maintained during twenty months of struggle, with over one hundred encounters and battles, speaks itself for the conduct of the Rebel Army. Today, in the midst of human passions, it does not have as much value as it will when the history of the Revolution is written. To have followed that policy now when we are strong is not as meritorious as when we were a handful of men persecuted like beasts in the rugged mountains. It was then, during the days of the battles of La Plata and El Uvero, that to have respected the lives of prisoners had profound moral significance. And even this would have been nothing more than an elemental duty of reciprocity if only the dictatorship's forces had respected the lives of the enemy who fell into their hands. Torture and death were the certain fate that awaited any rebel, sympathizer of our cause, or even a mere suspect who fell into enemy hands. There were many cases of luckless peasants who were murdered just to assemble corpses with which to justify the false dispatches of the tyranny's High Command. If we can affirm that six hundred members of the armed forces who fell into our hands are alive and in their homes, the dictatorship, in contrast, can affirm that over six hundred defenseless compatriots, often innocent of any revolutionary activity, have been murdered by their forces during those twenty months of struggle.

To kill makes no one stronger. Killing has made them weak; not to have killed has made us strong. Why do we not murder prisoners? (1) Only cowards and henchmen murder the enemy once he has surrendered. (2) The Rebel Army cannot use the same tactics as the tyranny we fight. (3) The politics and propaganda of the dictatorship have essentially consisted of presenting the revolutionary as the sworn and implacable enemy of any man who wears the uniform of the armed forces. The dictatorship, through deceit and lies, has tried to the utmost to bind the soldier to the regime, making him believe that to fight against the Revolution is to fight for his career and for his own life. What would be convenient for the dictatorship is not for us to cure wounded soldiers and respect the lives of the prisoners, but rather to murder them all without exception so that each member of the armed forces could then see the need to struggle to the very last drop of blood. (4) If in any war cruelty is stupid, in no war is it more so than in a civil war, where those who fight one another will have to live together some day and the executioners will meet the sons, wives, and mothers of their victims. (5) Before the shameless and depressing examples given by the dictator's murderers and torturers, we must place the example that our fighters have given before the coming generations as edifying encouragement. (6) Right now we must sow the seed of fraternity which must rule the future fatherland that we are forging for all and for the good of all. If those who fight honestly know how to respect the life of an enemy who surrenders, tomorrow in peace no one can feel he has the right to practice revenge and political crime. If there is justice in the Republic, there should be no revenge.

Why do we give prisoners their liberty? (1) To keep hundreds of prisoners in the Sierra Maestra would mean to share food, clothes, shoes, cigarettes, and so forth—which are acquired with great effort—

or on the contrary keep them so inadequately that it would be inhumane and unnecessary. (2) Due to the economic conditions and
enormous unemployment in the country, the dictatorship would never
lack men who would offer themselves for a salary. Thus, there is no
logic in thinking that we weaken them by retaining prisoners. But
from our military viewpoint, we are concerned not with the number
of men and weapons the dictatorship possesses (because we have always supposed they would have the military resources they wished,
having the Republic's treasury at their disposal) but with the number
of men and weapons that the rebels possess to fulfill our strategic and
tactical plans. Victory in war depends on a minimum of weapons and
a maximum of morale. Once the soldier's weapons are in our hands,
we are no longer concerned with him. That man would be hard put
to have any desire to fight those who have treated him so nobly. To
kill the soldier or submit him to the hardship of prison would serve
only for troops which are under siege and defeated, for example, to
resist even though militarily there may be no justification for it. (3)
A freed prisoner is the most effective proof of the tyranny's false
propaganda.

Thus, on July 24, 253 prisoners were returned at Las Vegas. The
liberation documents were signed by John P. Jequier and J. Schoen-
hozer, delegates of the International Red Cross Committee who came
from Geneva, Switzerland. On the tenth and thirteenth of August,
169 prisoners were returned at Sao Grande. The liberation document
was signed by Dr. Alberto C. Llanet, lieutenant colonel of the Cuban
Red Cross. There could be no exchange of prisoners because throughout the offensive the dictatorship did not take one rebel prisoner. We
did not demand any conditions whatsoever, as otherwise our liberation of the prisoners would cease to have the moral and political
meaning which that act entails. We only accepted the medicine which
the International Red Cross sent when we returned the second group
of prisoners because we interpreted it as a generous and spontaneous
gesture of that institution, partly compensating for the medicine we
invested in curing enemy wounded. The medicine of the International
Red Cross arrived in an army helicopter. They could have done
nothing less after we had saved the lives of so many soldiers! It is
truly a shame that the High Command and the spokesmen of the
dictatorship began politicking from such a simple and unimportant
detail, thus politicizing the meaning of that act.

Our feelings with respect to the members of the armed forces have
been demonstrated through deeds, and deeds have greater value than
words. In our dealings with the prisoners, we have observed in them

a permanent and characteristic trait: deceit. Within the army a whole machinery of lies functions constantly, directed by the High Command. We have captured numerous documents, circulars, and very revealing secret orders. The troops on campaign are deceived; they are assured that the rebels are dispersed groups, that their morale is low, that they are armed with shotguns, and so forth. Logically when the soldier clashes with the reality, he suffers.

No officer or soldier generally knows about the things which have occurred in the Sierra Maestra. If we, for example, took thirty-five prisoners in El Uvero over a year ago, curing nineteen wounded and freeing them all, the High Command contrives it so those men remain as isolated as possible. They make the soldiers believe that if they fall prisoner we torture them, castrate them, or kill them. . . .[1] At any rate, all those are things which they have done to the revolutionaries in barracks and police stations. With the press censorship, the soldier is ignorant of what occurs in the country; he reads nothing other than what appears in governmental circulars or in dispatches which the High Command uses for internal consumption. At the end of September 1957, for example, in Oro de Guisa fifty-three peasants were murdered in one day. Days later the High Command issued a circular stating that two battalions had obtained a splendid victory there, killing fifty-three rebels without suffering any casualties. The circular ended, *viva el viejo Pancho*, give them hell! etc.[2] The soldiers hear no speeches other than those forced on them in Columbia on March 10 and September 4 by Batista, Tabernilla, and company. No one ever tells them that behind that barrage of words, lies, and deceit, of which they are victims, is hidden the interest of the regime's politicians to steal, as well as the proposition that the soldiers should die defending the infamous and corrupt regime.

I am completely sure that if only for a day the soldiers and the revolutionaries could be gathered to talk instead of fight, the tyranny would disappear instantaneously, and a long and sincere peace would begin for many years. I have observed the human quality of many soldiers and sincerely have wished that instead of my enemy they were my comrades in arms. I have asked myself often how many valuable men have died deceived that they were sent to fight for something worthwhile.

The best of the army is among the front officers and soldiers, if we except the recruits who have joined during the last several months

---

[1] Edited as it appears in the original. Eds.

[2] "Pancho" was the nickname of Francisco Tabernilla, head of the Joint Chiefs of Staff of the armed forces. Eds.

without any selection whatsoever. The lieutenants, above all, have demonstrated ability and courage in combat. The Cuban army has a young officer corps which has awakened our sincere recognition during these months of struggle. They are not corrupt, they love their career and their institution. For many of them, this war in which they have been involved is absurd and illogical, but they comply with orders and individually they know of little else they can do. Among other barbarities the dictatorship has taken students of the School of Cadets from the classrooms without letting them finish their courses and has sent them to the battlefront. It looks as if they want to make the future officers responsible for the war which is waged against the people and for the crimes already committed. The young officers who have died in battle in the Sierra Maestra are too many. The worst in the army begins with the colonels and is aggravated as it gets to the generals. In large measure these are corrupt men without scruples. Those who have not become millionaires through the exploitation of gambling, vice, extortion, and shady business could be counted on the fingers of one hand, and with most of the fingers left over.

It is evident that, due to the state of affairs at which the country has arrived, with no exit for the regime and the unleashing of the latest events, a coup d'état is very possible. Before that eventuality the 26th of July Movement wants to state its position very clearly. If the coup d'état is the work of opportunistic military men whose objective is to salvage their interests and look for a way out, the best possible one for the tyranny's coterie, we are resolutely opposed to such a coup d'état even though it masks itself in the best intentions. In the final analysis, the sacrifices that have been made and the blood spilled should not serve only so things remain more or less as they are now and, thus, the history that follows the fall of Machado is repeated. If the military coup is the work of honest people and has a sincere revolutionary end, a solution of peace on a just and beneficial basis for the fatherland would be possible.

Between the armed forces and the Revolution, whose interests are not and do not need to be antagonistic, the problem of Cuba can be solved. We are at war with the tyranny, not with the armed forces. But it is up to the armed forces to free itself from the shackles which have tied it to the most infamous and hated regime our fatherland has suffered. The dilemma faced by the army in these moments is very clear: Either it takes a step forward, separating itself from that cadaver which is Batista's government, and vindicates itself before the nation, or it commits suicide as an institution. What the army can save today, it will not be able to save in a few months. If the war lasts half a year more, the army will completely disintegrate. The situation ahead could be controlled only with the backing of the whole population but, on the contrary, the whole population is identified and collaborating with the rebellion. The army itself must know better than anyone what has just occurred in the Sierra Maestra. Over two hundred officers participated in the last offensive, and they cannot ignore the disaster or stop thinking about the events. If the army cannot control one rebel nucleus by concentrating all its forces on it, it will be less able to control the rebels when they have to fight on twenty fronts. The massive desertion of soldiers is something which hardly can be dissimulated. In El Cerro on the night of July 24, by dawn thirty-one out of eighty soldiers who were stationed there had deserted. That is one example—not to cite more—of what has been occurring in the other battalions and we are very well informed about those details.

When an armed corps reaches that situation, it has the duty to analyze the mistakes that have led it to that abyss when there is still time to react and before it is too late. The objectivity with which I am speaking cannot leave any doubt as to the sincerity of these words. An agreement between the military and revolutionaries will never be desired by those who seek the continuation of the present state of affairs in the country.

That is the only salvation left for the military who are truly concerned with the future of their army and their fatherland. The young officers' corps must be alert so that the coup will not become a maneuver perhaps precipitated by the tyranny itself to save the necks of their worst coryphaei. We cannot yield one iota of the interests of the people.

These are the bases which can create a peaceful solution between the Revolution and the army. (1) The arrest and delivery of the dictator to a court of justice. (2) The arrest and delivery to courts of justice of all political leaders who share responsibility with the tyranny, as they are the cause of the civil war and have enriched themselves with the Republic's money. (3) The arrest and delivery to courts of justice of all military men who are known to have employed torture and crime in the cities as well as in the countryside and of those who have grown rich with contraband, shady businesses, and extortion, regardless of their rank. (4) Delivery of the Republic's provisional presidency to the person designated by all the sectors who fight the dictatorship, to convoke general elections in the shortest time span possible. (5) The restructuring and removal of the armed forces from political and partisan struggles so that the armed forces will never again become the instrument of any caudillo or political party, and will limit themselves to their mission of defending the country's sovereignty, the constitution, laws, rights of the citizen, so that brotherhood and mutual respect will reign between civilians and the military without fear of one or the other, in accordance with the true social ideal of peace and justice.

The Republic will demand better politicians tomorrow but also a better and more honest military. Without the just fulfillment of these conditions, no one should have illusions, because we shall all die before abandoning the goal for which our people have been struggling for the last six years and for which they have been longing for half a century. No one has, as we do, the right to demand something for the good of the fatherland because it is only we who know how to renounce all personal ambition beforehand. We await the reply on the march. The rebel columns will advance in all directions toward the rest of the national territory, with nothing and no one being able to stop us. If a leader dies, another will replace him. If a soldier dies, another will take his post. The people of Cuba must ready themselves to help our fighters. Any town or zone of Cuba can become a battlefield in the next weeks and months. The civilian population must be ready to courageously bear the privations of war. The fortitude shown by the population in the Sierra Maestra, where even children assist our troops, bearing twenty months of campaign with incomparable heroism, must be an example emulated by the rest of the Cubans so that the fatherland may be really free, cost what it may, and the promise of the Titán Maceo may be fulfilled: *"The revolution will be marching as long as there remains one injustice uncorrected."*

There is revolution because there is tyranny, there is revolution because there is injustice. There is and there will be revolution as long as a single shadow threatens our rights and our freedom.

Che Guevara Ordered to Invade Las Villas (*August 21, 1958*)

Major Ernesto Guevara is assigned the mission of leading a rebel column from the Sierra Maestra to Las Villas Province and of operating in that territory following the strategic plan of the Rebel Army.

Order issued from the Sierra Maestra on August 21, 1958. "Orden militar disponiendo que el Che Guevara inicie la invasión de las Villas," in *13 documentos de la insurrección* (Havana: Organización Nacional de Bibliotecas Populares y Ambulantes, 1959), p. 62.

Column 8, "Ciro Redondo," as the invading force will be known, will leave from Las Mercedes between the twenty-fourth and the thirtieth of August.

Major Ernesto Guevara is appointed chief of all rebel forces of the 26th of July Movement operating in Las Villas Province, whether in rural or urban areas. Powers are granted to raise and dispose of contributions for war expenses in accordance with our military rules; to apply the penal code and the agrarian reform laws of the Rebel Army in the territory where the forces would operate; to coordinate operations and plans and the administration of the territory. Militarily, organizations with military forces operating in the province shall be invited to integrate one army corps in order to structure and unify the military effort of the Revolution, to organize local fighting units and to designate officers of the Rebel Army up to the rank of Column Major in order to carry out the plan.

The strategic objective of Column 8 will be to fight unceasingly in the central section of Cuba and to intercept the enemy until it totally paralyzes the movements of those troops throughout the land, from west to east.

Fidel Castro

Interview with Enrique Meneses
(September 1, 1958)

CASTRO: To whom must I surrender the weapons we have taken from the army? To the same army, which has been fighting us for a year? The opposition would have done better to give us the weapons that we needed so much during the first months in the Sierra.[1] The weapons we have captured from the army will be returned when all possibility of a dictatorship is destroyed. We do not aspire to any political post, so we do not represent any dictatorial danger. When the armed forces are reorganized and put under the control of honorable officers, when all fears that a new military junta will replace Batista have been removed, then the 26th of July Movement will surrender its weapons to those armed forces.

Interview held in the Sierra Maestra on September 1, 1958. Unpublished manuscript supplied through the courtesy of Jay Mallin.

[1] Castro refers to statements made by a follower of Carlos Prío Socarrás on January 8, 1958. According to several sources, the followers of Prío had weapons but refused to give them to those fighting against Batista. Eds.

MENESES: What do you think about the acceptance of Manuel Urrutia as provisional president?

CASTRO: We are very happy that we all agree that Urrutia is the ideal person to preside over the Republic. We shall back him all the way whether or not Carlos Prío accepts the final conditions set by the 26th of July Movement. Carlos Prío no longer counts for anything in Cuba. The Revolution is in the hands of a new generation and not in the hands of those who would like to chain its destiny to a dishonorable past.

MENESES: Do you believe that without the help of the rest of the opposition you can defeat Batista?

CASTRO: It will take us longer, but we will do it. The days when the troops came looking for us in the mountains are gone. Today we have to go and look for them in the plains. Now one is safer here than in the rest of the Republic. This is Free Cuba.

Proclamation to Batista's Soldiers (September 15, 1958)

The General Staff has just sent to all its field commands General Order 196, by which the immediate execution of any soldier or officer who deserts from the ranks of the armed forces is ordered.

According to the order, the deserter will be judged by any member of the armed forces who has the rank immediately higher than that of the deserter. This order holds for anyone who is a soldier, a noncommissioned officer, or officer up to the rank of brigadier general. This means that now, according to the general order, any member of the armed forces can use the pretext that another member was planning to desert to murder that soldier without fear of punishment.

The 26th of July Movement and the Rebel Army express their solidarity with the members of the armed forces, who are also victims of the terror and despotism existing in our country. We offer our support through the proclamation of September 15, as a reply to the order of the dictatorship's General Staff. The proclamation reads as follows:

a. Any soldier, noncommissioned officer, or officer of the armed forces who does not wish to continue defending the ignoble and

Proclamation made on September 15, 1958. Miguel Deulofeu Ramos, "Papel de la propaganda clandestina en Oriente durante la insurrección," *Verde Olivo* (Havana), April 12, 1964, p. 77.

shameful cause of the tyranny can come to reside in free territory where his bloodthirsty persecutors will be unable to penetrate.

b. The soldier, noncommissioned officer, or officer of the armed forces who desires to live in free territory will not have the obligation of fighting against his own comrades-in-arms, nor will he have to carry out any type of warlike activity.

c. Any soldier, noncommissioned officer, or officer who accepts these conditions will continue receiving in free territory the same salary paid him by the state, so that he will be able to maintain his family. The only requisite is that he bring his weapon to us.

d. Any soldier, noncommissioned officer, or officer who, although wanting to abandon the ranks of the tyranny, fears the reprisals that might be taken against his loved ones, should know that he can come with them to free territory, where they will be offered housing and food until the end of the war.

e. To enter free territory, any soldier, noncommissioned officer, or officer of the armed forces does not require credentials, previous contacts, or any other kind of prerequisite. It is enough to come with your weapon and make contact with our posts or with the peasants, mentioning that you accept the hospitality of the Rebel Army proclaimed in the declaration of September 15.

The Rebel Army has always kept its word. Hundreds of wounded and captured soldiers given to the Red Cross are proof of the courteous treatment they received from us.

The free territory offers its generous hospitality to all military men who do not wish to continue defending the tyranny, so that they will not be murdered in the barracks due to simple suspicion.

This is our answer to the criminal General Order 196 of the dictatorship's General Staff. Not a single soldier should fear those threats when the free territory of Cuba is just a step away, a piece of the fatherland where liberty and justice reign.

Fidel Castro Ruz
Commander in Chief of the Rebel Army

To the 26th of July Movement Committees in Exile and Cuban Émigrés (September 16, 1958)

The 26th of July Movement's National Executive Council wishes to communicate that the Committee in Exile has been restructured in the following manner:

Coordinator and head of public relations: Luis Buch

Organization: José Llanusa

Propaganda: Antonio Buch

Treasurer: Haydée Santamaría

Dr. Raúl Chibás, due to his prestige, merits, and brilliant work as treasurer of the Committee in Exile, has been invited to take charge of the Department of Finance in the territory liberated by the rebel forces, which today encompasses great capital resources. He has accepted the responsibility and is moving again to the Sierra Maestra.

The 26th of July National Executive Council does not recognize organizations of the Movement other than the Committee in Exile and the sections and associations of *compañeros* and sympathizers that work under its orientation and instructions.

To the *compañeros* and sympathizers of the 26th of July Movement who have become separated from its discipline to establish other organizations under names such as "Fidel Castro Revolutionary Movement," "Acción Fidelista," or "Ortodoxo Committee Supporting the 26th of July," and who collect funds, publish propaganda, and carry out other activities, we exhort that they dissolve such organizations and incorporate themselves into the official organization. For reasons of discipline, moral principle, and revolutionary stance, the 26th of July Movement cannot accept the proliferation of collateral organizations which carry a *caudillista* connotation, divide the effort, and create confusion among the émigrés and the people.

Discipline is essential. Without discipline, there can be no revolutionary organization.

It is necessary that the promotion of our ideas and objectives be defined by only one authority. Without a single direction, the propaganda would be chaotic, divergent, and at times contradictory.

It is necessary that funds be disposed of by only one administrator. Without a single direction, there can be neither administration nor

Written in the Sierra Maestra on September 16, 1958. Rafael Humberto Gaviria, *Fidel Castro: La revolución de los barbudos* (Lima: Ediciones "Tierra Nueva," 1959), pp. 83-91.

control of the funds, and we have no right to call for the sacrifices of our fellow men only to spend them without plan or order.

The duty of all Cubans is to fight the tendency characteristic of our temperament that leads us so many times to dilute our efforts in useless and sterile conflicts, which as long ago as the wars of liberation frustrated the best energies of the émigrés. The ill effects are suffered by those who are fighting and who need to receive from their fellow men aid which must not be obstructed by passions or personalities.

The reasons are clear enough to be understood by any *compañero* or honest sympathizer with sincere patriotism. Within the Movement there is room for all efforts and all enthusiasms. There also will be room, with time and good will as we struggle for an ideal, without ambition, to overcome the deficiencies or natural imperfections of any human organization that could be cause for nonconformity but should never be a pretext to disperse energies in these decisive moments for the fatherland.

Émigré aid has been large, but it could be even larger if it unites and is more disciplined.

Let the efforts of our émigrés march parallel to the advance of our invading columns, which in these moments march to liberate the rest of the fatherland.

In the name of the Executive Council of the National Directorate of the 26th of July Movement,

Fidel Castro

The Battle of El Cerro
(September 27, 1958)

Two battles of importance and other minor actions have taken place in Fronts 1 and 3 of the Sierra Maestra. While Major Juan Almeida was informing us that rebel troops of Front 3 had defeated a battalion of the dictatorship, capturing Lieutenant Colonel Nelson Carrasco Artiles and five other soldiers, inflicting on them twenty-five casualties and capturing ten weapons, another victorious battle many miles away was being waged by Front 1 against the tyranny's troops.

A strongly entrenched enemy battalion had camped in El Cerro,

Communiqué issued on September 27, 1958, from the Sierra Maestra. René Ray Rivero (ed.), *Libertad y Revolución* (Havana: n.p., 1959), pp. 81–84.

4 kilometers from Estrada Palma. After a thorough study of the terrain and the careful observation of enemy positions, forces from Columns 1 and 12 supported by mortars and machine guns surrounded the place during the early morning hours of Friday, September 27. At 11:45 P.M., a 60-caliber mortar and two 50-caliber machine guns, under the command of Captain Braulio Coronou, opened fire on the enemy camp; five minutes later, at 11:50, under the command of Captain Pedro Miret, only 240 meters away from the enemy positions, a battery of mortars opened fire, initiating a barrage of mortar fire over an area 150 meters long and 100 meters wide where the enemy battalion was located. The mortars fired for one whole hour. Fifty-four howitzer shells fell on the camp. The camping tents, command post, and other enemy installations were blasted. At 12:50 A.M., two rebel infantry platoons commanded by Major Eduardo Sardiñas, throwing flares to warn the mortars of their movements, advanced to a ditch a few meters away from the enemy trenches. The rebels and the dictatorship's soldiers were so close that they could see each other by the light from the detonations. Their automatic weapons were discharged there against the enemy garrison, which almost collapsed. The dictatorship's troops fought desperately, attempting to prevent the whole camp from falling into rebel hands. They had 50-caliber machine guns, mortars, and cannons for their defense. The moon was full, and the air force came to their aid. From Estrada Palma the dictatorship's Sherman tanks, camping in the sugar mill, fired heavy 75-millimeter cannons at El Cerro. But not one reinforcement troop was moved to assist the encircled battalion. As the enemy remained paralyzed throughout the night without making any troop movements, at dawn our forces returned to the mountains. Five of our fighters died heroically when Major Eduardo Sardiñas advanced to the enemy trenches. On Saturday a large helicopter of the dictatorship descended six times to pick up the wounded.

According to reports which arrived through different channels, the enemy suffered sixty-seven casualties among the dead and wounded. In these cases the facts are difficult to tell with exactitude. The rebel deaths were Lieutenant Raúl Verdecia, Lieutenant Arturo Vázquez, enlisted men Juan Sardiñas, René Ibarra, and Miguel López. They died in front of the enemy trenches. Their weapons and the bodies of three of them were recovered under predawn enemy machine-gun fire.

Major Eduardo Sardiñas, the men under his command, and the two platoons which realized the assault on the trenches deserve special mention because of their courage.

Major Eduardo Sardiñas and the troops under his command—which today form Column 12, "Simón Bolívar"—were the officer and soldiers who fought the most in the Sierra Maestra during the last offensive of the dictatorship. They were a mere platoon when the victorious battle of Santo Domingo was initiated.

With less than twenty men he destroyed the enemy vanguard, taking their automatic weapons, with which the battle was continued. After that action, they participated in all the battles fought thereafter: in Meriño, Jigüe, in the second battle from Santo Domingo to Providencia, in Cuatro Caminos and Las Mercedes. In Santo Domingo they captured over 50 weapons; in Meriño they captured all the enemy supplies. In Purialón during the Jigüe battle, with Majors Cuevas and Paz, who died gloriously, they destroyed Company G-4 Battalion 18 and Company L, which was one of the tyranny's best units. In Santo Domingo during the second battle on that site, together with the forces of Major Guillermo García of Column 3, they defeated Lieutenant Colonel Sánchez Mosquera, who received a critical wound in the skull.

In El Cerro, the last battle, they demonstrated their worth and courage as one of the most experienced and efficient units of our army. In the combat of El Cerro, Major Pedro Miret, chief of the mortar battery, also distinguished himself for his courage and efficiency, as he inflicted a great number of casualties on the enemy. The platoon of rebel women, "Mariana Grajales," engaged in combat for the first time in this action, withstanding the cannon fire of the Sherman tanks firmly, without moving from their positions. This was one of the combats where great precision and coordination was achieved among the different units.

Each day the tactical and strategic superiority of the rebels over the decadent and demoralized forces of the tyranny is more clear, in spite of their planes, heavy tanks, and all the modern resources of war, employing everything including deadly gases. They continue to lose more territory, more men, and more weapons.

Only the blind could fail to see that the Revolution grows and becomes stronger in a geometrical progression. Deluded are those who imagine there is a possible salvation for the tyranny, even if it surrendered power to the opposition, a false opposition that today carries on its opportunistic campaign with the money the dictator gives it. The shameful and disgusting farce which is being prepared for November 3 will serve only to aggravate their desperate and terrible situation.

Little time will remain to their poor soldiers to gather identification cards and rig the ballot boxes for they can barely breathe.

A terrible war awaits them everywhere and at all hours. The defeat of two battalions and the imprisonment of a lieutenant colonel within the last 48 hours should have said something to those who have failed to see reality with the defeat of 14 battalions, 400 prisoners, 800 casualties, and 500 captured weapons in only 36 days in the Sierra Maestra.

Dr. Fidel Castro
Commander in Chief

Letter to Major Juan Almeida
(October 8, 1958)

Major Almeida, Sierra Maestra, October 8, 1958, 8 A.M.

Dear Almeida:

I have fought to advance the preparations for Operation Santiago as much as possible, so that it will coincide with the electoral farce. Our objective is to force the enemy into a battle of giant proportions then, which together with other measures we are going to take will prevent it from taking place.

I was also thinking of moving to that territory with the greatest possible amount of materiel this very month; but after analyzing everything, I realized it was impossible for several reasons: (a) the supply of arms and ammunitions has not yet reached its maximum; (b) the numerous matters and tasks of all kinds which must be faced this month would remain unsolved or solved halfway if I were to leave here to undertake that long march. As persistent as you know I am in my objectives, I have paid dearly to renounce my ideal of leaving. At the same time, in order to quickly utilize all forces in view of the elections, I have initiated a series of movements toward several territories of the province, but establishing for those movements specific objectives in relation to November 3, which also would serve as basis for the strategy to be developed weeks after that date. That is, the troops which I am now sending to Victoria de las Tunas, Puerto

Fidel Castro, . . . Y la luz se hizo (Havana: Cooperativa Obrera de Publicidad, n.d.), pp. 24–26.

Padre, Holguín, and Jibara will fulfill important objectives in the last months of the year.

I am substituting the plan of taking over Santiago de Cuba first for the plan of taking over the province. The takeover of Santiago and other cities would thus be a lot easier, and, above all, they can be held. First, we will take over the countryside; within approximately twelve days all municipalities will be invaded; then we will take over and, if possible, destroy all communications routes by land, highways and the railroad. If, parallel to this, the operations of Las Villas and Camagüey progress, the tyranny may suffer a complete disaster like the one it suffered in the Sierra Maestra.

This strategy is a lot safer for us than any other, and meanwhile, far from concentrating the bulk of our forces in one direction, which takes time and requires great accumulation of food and implies risks worth considering, we would distribute them in such a manner as to maintain the enemy under constant harassment everywhere. Your front, which is the Front of Santiago de Cuba, is assigned columns 3, 9, and 10. You must make those troops a potent and disciplined force which will progressively dominate and above all study minutely the zone for when the hour arrives. There are many arms which recently arrived without bullets. The prolonged sojourn of Pedro Luis has delayed the supply of provisions, and this problem of the bullets must be solved.

You must organize people who will try to buy them from the soldiers; if necessary you can pay up to one dollar for each 30.06 or M-1 caliber bullet. It is a tempting price, and we can afford it; we should not care if we spend half a million dollars on half a million bullets. What we cannot do for any reason is be left out without bullets. I would urge delivery from outside the country, but every time there are more rifles and we must find other means to solve the problem. If I receive some bullets this week, I shall send them to you without fail. Now I am sending you two 50-caliber guns with all the bullets available, nearly 800; 2 antitank guns with 5 clips and 120 bullets for each; and 2 rifles that have a similar sight to the antitank one, so I placed them together.

Fidel Vargas is going with all this and the rank of lieutenant. I will send you four mines right away, if Crespo has them ready. I hope these weapons will make the fellows happy. I have 60 Springfields and 30 M-1's here without one bullet, but I prefer to send you these 2,000 because if I receive some in the next few days, you will be receiving these in advance.

After November 3, all your thoughts must be directed to preparations for the moment when we decide to isolate and besiege all cities simultaneously. Your forces will have to isolate the cities of Palma Soriano and Santiago de Cuba. You must start thinking about highway destruction, which means destruction of bridges, digging antitank ditches, and studying heights and strategic points nearby. You must start gathering the greatest quantity of picks and shovels, as well as cables and batteries to make detonators; the installation of mines in the asphalt highways is a technical problem that must be solved. We must make the greatest possible number of holes and bumps in the highway so that a mine can be placed in any of them. If the highway is completely smooth, the first time the enemy can be surprised by a mine in the asphalt, but thereafter any other bump will become suspicious. In the same degree that our control over the highways increases, we must produce bumps with picks, at least while we cannot make antitank ditches.

You can be sure that once one or two mines have exploded in the highway, a patrol at night could dig up the asphalt at several points and the tanks would have to stop and search them one by one. Also the mines can be placed in mounds of dirt, one at each side and facing the other, to explode simultaneously. The explosion would come from the mound against the tank's side, which if compressed between two explosions, I think, will have no resistance, but this is a matter of distance and other details. The important thing is that we must solve the problem of using mines on asphalt highways because they are our most powerful weapon against armored vehicles, and this I leave to your imagination and the always prodigious intelligence of the rebels.

Meanwhile, we must maintain at all times, before and after the third, a systematic war against transport, as you all are doing now. We must ruin the transportation companies if they do not cancel traffic on the highways and railroads. I am sure they will not be able to withstand the losses and they will have to halt, thus creating one of the most serious problems for the dictatorship. Communications must be improved day by day, establishing the largest possible number of plants. I spoke about this to José Antonio when he was here.

Another thing is that the men must try not only to inflict casualties on the enemy but also to be concerned about their weapons. I was thinking that the three columns by this date could have captured more weapons. It seems that the *micro-ondas*[1] have been frightened, and it is going to be difficult to hunt them after the shows of force that have been displayed. They will be quartered too soon, and it would have

---

[1] Refers to vehicles with radio equipment used by Batista's authorities. Eds.

been convenient if we had staged a fishing expedition along the high-ways before this. At any rate, when they are quartered and leave less frequently, we must initiate the systematic destruction of high-ways and roads; then we will place a Maginot line from town to town; then we will not allow the entry of food or water, and you will see how humble we will make them all. But it is of utmost importance that these plans be absolutely secret; therefore, take good care of them. Experience teaches me that even majors lack discretion. I am not re-ferring to you, because I know you are an old fox in these matters, but I remind you because of those under your command.

Above all, we must keep secret the strategy to follow November 3, so that the unsuspecting enemy will not be able to make preparations to resist. I will be moving and placing forces and at the opportune moment will give the order. I consider it to be still a matter of months. To very few will I reveal my intentions; each will receive his instructions by parts.

Send me the greatest number of reports about the communications and terrain of your zone. You must assign that task to some person capable of taking care of it. Find maps and elaborate as many charts as you consider necessary for good information and send me a copy.

For the moment I do not have any other important matter to discuss with you. Impatiently I am awaiting news from Che and Camilo. I am under the impression that the advance has been hard for them, but they have done well. I congratulate you for the formidable blow you delivered to the lieutenant colonel. I received the little stars and the identification card. When he is well, send him out here. Write me then with news about everything: economic, military, public order, and so forth. A strong embrace to you.

Fidel Castro

No-Election Decree
(October 10, 1958)

WHEREAS the tyranny prepares a new and raw electoral farce for the third of November, totally behind the back of the interests of the people in the midst of the pool of blood into which the Republic has

Issued on October 10, 1958. Jules Dubois, *Fidel Castro: Liberator or Dictator?* (Indianapolis: Bobbs-Merrill, 1959), pp. 316–317.

been converted in full civil war—in which the military forces retreat before the victorious push of the rebel troops—without finding formulas capable of masking the elections such as even the technical re-establishment of individual guarantees and of freedom of the press; against a citizenry, in sum, that is persecuted, in mourning and determined to recapture their liberties and rights through the definite end of the usurper regime of thieves, traitors, and murderers who have converted the fatherland into the feudal estate of their infinite ambitions.

WHEREAS the participation in the election farce constitutes an act of betrayal of the interests of the fatherland and the revolution, and is classified as opportunism on the part of those who think only of their debased personal conveniences and work in the shadows at the expense of the Republic when they serve the plans of the tyranny while the best of our people offer their lives on the battlefield.

WHEREAS it is necessary for the last time to alert the Cubans who have not yet understood the profound question that is being debated in Cuba and who, insensible to the tragedy that surrounds them, have enlisted in the company of actors of the comedy which the tyranny prepares November 3 by stubbornly lending their names as candidates for posts they never will hold.

THEREFORE, in use of the powers that are found invested in this command, the following Law No. 2 is dictated about the electoral farce:

I. Everyone who takes part in the electoral farce the third day of November of 1958, as a candidate to any elective post, without prejudice to the criminal responsibility which he may incur, will be barred for a period of thirty years from the date of this law from holding a public or elective post or one by appointment by the state, the province or the municipality.

II. The period having expired in which a candidate cannot resign so that his name does not appear on the ballot, he will show his non-participation in the electoral farce by absenting himself from the country and previously presenting himself in the free territory of Cuba, or, in any case by reporting his resignation to the foreign press or through the broadcast means of the Rebel Army by the thirtieth of October.

III. Any political agent who dedicates himself to the corrupt system of collecting voting cards[1] will be tried by a summary court-martial and executed on the spot.

IV. The candidate to any elective post who may be captured in the zone of operations of the free territory will be tried and condemned

[1] For voting purposes. Eds.

to a penalty that may fluctuate, in accordance with the greater or lesser degree of responsibility, from ten years to the death sentence.

V. In the urban zones the death sentence may be executed against the guilty either by the rebel troops or by the militia operating in the towns and cities.

Fidel Castro

Letter to Camilo Cienfuegos
(October 14, 1958)

Dear Camilo:

The emotion with which I have just read your report of October 9 is indescribable. There are no words to express the happiness, the pride, and the admiration I have felt for you all. What you have done is enough to earn you a place in the history of Cuba and of great military feats.

I hurry to write you through the same channel to give you the following instructions:

Do not continue the advance march until further orders. Wait and meet Che in Las Villas. The politicorevolutionary situation there is complex, and your presence in the province is indispensable to help establish it solidly.

Before continuing the advance march, it is necessary that

1. Your men recover physically.

2. The struggle intensify in the provinces of Oriente, Camagüey, Las Villas, and Pinar del Rio, forcing the enemy to use all its forces on all fronts, preventing it from concentrating the bulk of its forces against you as happened in Camagüey.

3. Rebel units be created all along your path.

4. Careful preparation and study of your advance plans be made, gathering guides, making advance contacts, and carefully foreseeing the difficulties you might encounter. Also, you must use several fast patrols that will disorient the enemy and make your march easier.

5. Above all: Your line of march be kept completely secret. The

Letter written on October 14, 1958, from the Sierra Maestra, after receiving a report from Cienfuegos that described his march toward the province of Las Villas. Castro wrote the orders at a moment when a clash developed between the guerrilla forces of the 26th of July Movement and those of the Segundo Frente del Escambray in Las Villas Province. Comandante William Gálvez, "Camilo en Las Villas," *Verde Olivo* (Havana), January 17, 1965, pp. 4–7.

enemy must be led to believe that you have given up your plans so that it can be taken completely by surprise.

If you wish to make any objections or suggestions to these instructions, I am willing to consider them, but I hope you agree with me.

An embrace of infinite admiration and love for the heroic soldiers of your column.

Fidel

A Reply to the State Department
(October 26, 1958)

A communiqué received from the Second Front, "Frank País," announces the possibility that the Nicaro zone, where a United States nickel plant is located, will become a battlefield.

Three days ago the dictatorship, surprisingly, without any military reason, withdrew the troops that had been stationed at that point. Following the usual tactics, the rebel forces immediately took the territory abandoned by the enemy, offering the employees and functionaries of the installation full guarantees to continue operating. Then today, the Rebel Command intercepted an order from Colonel Ugalde Carrillo ordering his forces to land again at Nicaro, which inevitably will produce an armed clash.

All this forms part of a Batista maneuver, in complicity with Ambassador Earl E. T. Smith and high officials of the United States Department of State, to precipitate the intervention of the United States in the civil war in Cuba.

The dictatorship, in its despair, is trying to produce a grave incident between the rebels and the United States.

The first attempt took place in July, when the General Staff of the dictatorship, in agreement with Mr. Smith, withdrew its troops from the Yateritas aqueduct, which supplies water to the United States Naval Base at Caimanera (Guantánamo), and solicited from the authorities there soldiers to be sent to that point of our national territory to protect the aqueduct.

Batista and Mr. Smith sought to cause a clash between the North

Declaration made on October 26, 1958, in reply to statements issued by Lincoln White of the State Department on the kidnapping of North American citizens by the rebel forces. Gregorio Selser (ed.), *La revolución cubana* (Buenos Aires: Editorial Palestra, 1960), pp. 171–174.

American Marines and the rebels. A great campaign of public opinion in all of America, the responsible attitude of the rebel forces in the face of that evident provocation, and the negotiations of the Civic Revolutionary Front permitted a diplomatic solution to the matter. The North American Marines were withdrawn without incident.

An unimportant event that occurred a few days ago accidentally encouraged the intrigue of the North American embassy and the Batista dictatorship against the sovereignty of our country.

Two North Americans and seven Cubans working at the Texaco plant fell into an ambush of Cuban patriots who awaited the advance of enemy forces. Due to strict security, for the employees as well as for our own forces, the men traveling in the vehicle were detained and moved to a safe place. This was done not because they were North Americans or Cubans, but simply because when an ambush is discovered by civilians and they do not immediately announce it to the forces of the tyranny to prevent their falling into the ambush, the dictatorship takes reprisals against them. If, on the contrary, the civilians announce our position, it could be surrounded by superior forces and attacked. That is why in these cases civilians are detained in a safe place for reasons of security, theirs as well as that of our troops, and for as long as the operation may last.

This act cannot be called kidnapping. No one wanted to detain them from their jobs, absolutely nothing was demanded in exchange for their freedom, and they were treated with all consideration. This was simply what happened, and they were freed as soon as the commander of the column withdrew our forces from the road.

Then, immediately taking advantage of this incident, seeking the smallest pretext to interfere in the internal affairs of Cuba, Lincoln White, spokesman of the North American State Department, made insulting declarations about the Cuban patriots, which contained a clear threat to the integrity of our territory and the sovereignty of our people.

The Batista dictatorship has murdered more than one North American citizen, on a number of occasions has attacked and even murdered newspapermen from other countries, but the State Department has remained silent with regard to those events, not informing North American public opinion about them.

What then is the reason for Lincoln White to hurl a series of threats and accusations against the 26th of July Movement because of a simple incident?

Simultaneously the town of Nicaro was abandoned by the forces of the dictatorship and, three days later, when the patriots had occupied the territory, the dictatorship ordered its troops to land again.

Now it is planning to make that place, where the nickel plants of the United States government are to be found, the scene of a battle so material damages to the plants can be caused and then a pretext found for sending North American troops to our national territory. It is a plan similar to the one hatched for the Yateritas aqueduct. It is the worst betrayal that a government could make of its own fatherland.

We want to denounce these acts to the public of the United States and Latin America.

Why did the forces of the dictatorship abandon the nickel plants if they were not attacked by the rebels? Why was a new landing of troops ordered there? What is the relationship between these events and the aggressive declaration of Lincoln White?

The Rebel Command never has been moved by unfriendly or hostile sentiments toward the United States. When a group of North American citizens was held in the north of Oriente Province so that they could witness and contemplate the effects of the bombardment of the peasant population with bombs and planes of U.S. origin, this command, as soon as it heard of the matter, ordered the immediate return of those citizens to the authorities of their country because we considered that they should not be molested because of the mistakes of their government.

When I gave that order, a North American newspaperman was in the Sierra Maestra and he immediately transmitted it to the wire services.

The latest incident with those two North Americans was purely a matter of chance and a consequence of the reasons we have mentioned already. The presence of the seven Cubans held with them is proof that a question of nationality was not involved.

If Lincoln White classifies as an assault on civilized standards the detention of two of his compatriots who were treated with decency and freed as soon as the danger for them and for our soldiers had passed, how do we classify the death of so many helpless Cuban civilians, killed by the bombs and planes that the North American government has sold to dictator Batista?

Mr. White, Cuban citizens are human beings like North American citizens; however, not a single North American has ever died by Cuban bombs and planes. You cannot accuse Cuban patriots of those deeds, but we can accuse you and your government.

The war that our fatherland is now suffering causes losses and inconveniences, not only to the citizens of your country, but to all the residents of Cuba as well. This war is not the fault of Cubans who want to recover our democratic system and our freedom, but the fault of the tyranny that has been oppressing our fatherland for six years and that has counted on the support of North American ambassadors.

Our conduct is open to public scrutiny. In the territory liberated by our forces, there is no censorship of the press. North American newspapermen have visited us on a number of occasions, and they can do so as many times as they want to freely inform the public opinion of their country of our activities. The only accounting that we value of our acts, of our free determination, is that of public opinion, of the opinion of our people and the world.

It is proper to observe that Cuba is a free and sovereign nation; we want to maintain the best friendly relations with the United States. We do not wish any conflict to arise between Cuba and the United States that could not be solved through reason and the right of the peoples. But if the North American State Department continues to allow itself to be dragged into the intrigues of Mr. Smith and Batista, and incurs the unjustifiable mistake of forcing that country to commit an act of aggression against our sovereignty, then be sure that we shall know how to defend ourselves with honor.

There are duties toward our fatherland that cannot be left unfulfilled, cost what they may. A large and powerful country like the United States cannot be honored by the words and threats made in your recent statements. Threats are useful against cowardly and submissive people but are useless against men who are willing to die in defense of their people.

Fidel Castro

Santiago de Cuba Is Surrounded (November 2, 1958)

Powerful columns of the Rebel Army are surrounding Santiago de Cuba. The enemy troops are besieged by land, and their withdrawal is cut off.

On October 30, around noon, an enemy force tried to get out via the Santiago-El Cristo highway. It was intercepted and completely

Statement made on November 2, 1958, over Rebel Radio with headquarters in the Sierra Maestra. Editors' tape.

defeated by the troops of Column 9, which captured Major Hubert Matos. The fighting began at 1:30 P.M. and lasted almost two hours. Only one enemy tank was able to escape. Three mobile microwave transmitters and an armored car fell to our troops. Twelve enemy soldiers were left on the battlefield. Six others were captured. Twenty-four rifles, three automatic guns, and twenty-one Garand M-1 and Springfield rifles were also taken. Three courageous rebel army soldiers fell during the violent action, but they won the laurels of victory for the army of the Revolution.

In an effort to hide its desperate situation from its own troops, the enemy General Staff issued a completely false report, announcing twenty-nine rebel losses for four enemy losses and three wounded.

It is inconceivable that the dictatorship should have tried to deny its losses to such an extent at the very doors of Santiago de Cuba, where the people would have found out the truth anyway because a battle in the vicinity of a large city and fighting in the hidden recesses of the Sierra Maestra are not the same. However, this is explained by the fact that for a besieged army like the dictator's army in Santiago de Cuba, the defeat of El Cristo is a tremendous moral defeat. The experience we acquired in the big battles in the Sierra Maestra allows us to recognize that a large number of the dictator's troops are on the verge of collapse.

Fidel Castro Ruz

On the Death of Angel Ameijeiras (November 8, 1958)

Angel Ameijeiras is the third brother who has fallen fighting for the freedom of his people.

The first gave his life on the twenty-sixth of July, 1953, in the Moncada Barracks action. The second, Gustavo, was arrested, without leaving a trace, by the hordes of Colonel Ventura; the third, Angel, fell yesterday in the streets of Havana; a fourth brother is imprisoned in the Isle of Pines, also for struggling against oppression; and the fifth, Efigenio Ameijeiras, landed with the *Granma* expeditionaries in

Speech of Fidel Castro on November 8, 1958, about the death of Angel "Machaco" Ameijeiras, broadcast by the clandestine radio station 7-R-R. "Palabras de Fidel Castro sobre Angel 'Machaco' Ameijeiras," *Revolución* (Havana), November 9, 1959, pp. 1, 4.

Playa Coloradas on December 2, 1956. He is one of the twelve who kept the flag of the Revolution uplifted during the most difficult days in the Sierra Maestra. Today, because of his merit in innumerable battles, he is major of the rebel forces and second chief of the Second Front "Frank País." Five brothers! Three dead, one in the Isle of Pines, and the other fighting on the battlefields. The stock of the Ameijeirases is a moving example of heroism which reminds us of the Maceo family.

Those who have not yet comprehended the profound meaning of this struggle and the sacrifices that our people are making to obtain their liberty should meditate on the example of this family which has already lost three sons in this epic contest.

For those who have crossed their arms before the unhappiness of the fatherland, what shame! What shame for those who, with the blood of so many generous fellow men, maintain the hateful tyranny and harvest millions in the furrows of pain watered with the tears of so many grieving mothers!

What shame for those who, in the midst of so much selflessness and sacrifice, lent themselves to an infamous election which offered nothing to the people but rather promised them the fine fruits of a poor fatherland turned into booty for opportunists and traitors.

That Angel Ameijeiras fell in combat in the streets of Havana with two heroic *compañeros*, Pedro Gutiérrez and Rogelio Perea, a few days after the elections they sought to present as the remedy of our misfortunes, is one more condemnation to those who lend themselves to that disgusting farce.

Persecuted youths, as if they were cornered beasts forced to sell their lives dearly before criminal hordes that forgive no one, who have the misfortune to fall into their hands are destroyed in the police stations. This is the only thing that the bloody despotism, which since 1952 forcefully has imposed itself on the fatherland, can promise the country for four more years.

It is a sad victory for the tyranny to announce with malicious enthusiasm the death of three courageous men and the wounding of two women. With hundreds of policemen against three cornered men, killing them is not a triumph; killing them in those circumstances is a disgrace and one more infamy.

Here in Oriente, where the struggle is face to face, where they are the ones cornered and encircled in spite of their number, their airplanes, and their tanks, they are not so courageous, they are not so aggressive, they do not sing of those victories.

The death of three heroic young men, who struggled five and a half hours against the attack of the whole police corps, is the only thing the wavering tyranny can offer as a sad trophy.

Havana is still a fief of henchmen. In Havana they still frisk about, but their hour will come. There too, as in Santiago de Cuba, they will hear at very close range the echo of the advancing liberation rifles.

Santiago de Cuba was a fief of Chaviano and Salas Cañizares; until not long ago the miserable henchmen triumphantly exhibited their shameless cruelty there. Santiago de Cuba now sees the hours of justice draw near, after having barely cleaned Frank País's blood from the pavement, and the flock of criminals who assassinated him and many others are trembling like caged rats.

Similarly, the Revolution will draw near to Havana; and on a day not far off, perhaps long before the blood of Angel Ameijeiras and his *compañeros* is washed away, the assassins will tremble and will hear the echo of our rifles.

Angel Ameijeiras continues to be a combatant for the Revolution. The courageous never die in the memory of their people. The courageous who fall continue fighting in every battle, because they are carried in the thoughts of our glorious soldiers.

Each hero who falls joins ranks in the front line, and thus there are two who command our men. Not without a purpose the columns carry the name of the fallen heroes.

Major Angel Ameijeiras, all the fighters of the Rebel Army stand at attention before you and await your orders when they draw near the streets of Havana.

Fidel Castro

Communiqué to Paralyze Transportation (November 9, 1958)

Announcement to all rebel commanders in Oriente Province!

Rail as well as bus transportation should be completely paralyzed. Food supplies to cities and towns transported in small vehicles will be permitted on Mondays, Tuesdays, and Wednesdays. All types of fuel supplies should be completely prevented from moving. Any truck that attempts to transport fuel should be driven back or destroyed.

Communiqué issued on November 9, 1958, from the Sierra Maestra. Roger González Guerrrero, "Oriente 1958," *Verde Olivo* (Havana), January 5, 1969, pp. 6–11.

All citizens are warned of the danger of riding in vehicles driven by members of the tyranny, for our forces cannot allow them to move with impunity. Henceforth, any soldier carrying a rifle while traveling in a vehicle will be shot on sight.

Fidel Castro Ruz
Commander in Chief

Posthumous Promotion
(November 9, 1958)

Militia Captain Angel Ameijeiras, who was killed while fighting against the repressive agents of the tyranny, is hereby promoted to the rank of major.

In tribute to his exemplary revolutionary conduct, his tireless spirit of struggle, his unlimited valor, and the heroism with which he fought for hours against the mercenary forces of the tyrant without regard for the numerical strength of the enemy, choosing to die rather than surrender, the Rebel Army awards him the rank of major, the highest rank in our military chain of command.

Fidel Castro
Commander in Chief

Radio broadcast from the Sierra Maestra on November 9, 1958. "Posthumous Promotion," *Granma* (Havana), November 16, 1969, p. 7.

The Enemy's Resistance Is Crumbling
(November 10, 1958)

This is Rebel Radio, organ of the 26th of July Movement, transmitting in connection with the Second Front "Frank País," Blue Station, and Apache Indian:[1]

The military barracks of the tyranny continue to surrender one after the other. For several days now they have not offered resistance.

Communiqué issued on November 10, 1958. Roger González Guerrero, "Oriente 1958," *Verde Olivo* (Havana), January 5, 1959, pp. 6–11.

[1] Underground radio stations. Eds.

The rebel forces have destroyed or paralyzed the enemy, whose lines of communications we have broken.

The enemy's resistance is crumbling in the face of the powerful offensive unleashed by the Second Front, while the main body of the Rebel Army, that is, the First, Third, and Fourth Fronts, await their respective orders to make the last move against the enemy.

Fidel Castro Ruz
Commander in Chief

Orders to the Rebel Army
(November 13, 1958)

To all the commanders and leaders of the rebel columns in the provinces of Oriente, Camagüey, and Las Villas, and to the civilian population, particularly in Oriente Province:

Two worthy officers of the army together with their troops have just rebelled against the dictator and have joined the revolutionary troops on Front No. 1 of the Sierra Maestra. They have brought all their weapons and a large quantity of bullets. Two complete platoons with officers, noncommissioned officers, and soldiers are already on their way to the general headquarters. This report has caused great jubilation in the rebel ranks.

Other units have rebelled and are on their way to the Sierra Maestra. This is evidence of the complete revolutionary support found in the ranks of the armed forces. This is an extraordinary moment which could determine the early end of the tyranny. Although it is still necessary to fight very hard, everything seems to indicate that the defeat of the government is imminent, desperate though its final resistance may be.

Traffic in the province of Oriente must, therefore, remain completely paralyzed. All rebel men and units must remain at their posts. All roads leading to and from the cities as well as to and from the province of Oriente must be cut off. The Frank País Column on the Second Front must continue their advance, surrounding and conquering as many garrisons as possible in the Mayarí-San Luis-Guantánamo triangle, while the columns surrounding Santiago de Cuba must tighten the circle, preventing the slightest movement of enemy troops.

Broadcast made on November 13, 1958, over Rebel Radio. Editor's tape.

The rebel troops operating in the center and west, guarding the entrance to the province of Oriente, must fight tenaciously against all troops the government sends to the province. The cities which fall into the hands of our troops will be declared open cities and, therefore, no rebel troops shall camp there to prevent the bombing of defenseless towns. We shall request the intervention of the Red Cross to this effect. Absolute order is necessary in all circumstances. The soldiers who surrender or join the Revolution will have to receive the most fraternal treatment. Any official of the armed forces wishing to join the Revolution with his troops will have to do so under the commanders and the rebel leaders of each region.

Each rebel commander must take special care that the weapons held in the large garrisons are unloaded and placed in a secure place while awaiting orders for their distribution to the pupils of the various revolutionary soldiers' schools where they are being trained at present. The rebel troops of the province of Camagüey must support the battle of Oriente, intensify the attacks against enemy transportation in Camagüey, and attack the rearguard of the troops which are to be sent to that province.

The invasion columns 2 and 8 of the Rebel Army situated in Las Villas, with the support of all the other revolutionary forces fighting there, must also block the railheads and railways to prevent passage of the enemy forces to Oriente Province and to prevent those remaining with the tyranny and fighting in this extreme end of the island, where they are already almost completely surrounded by our troops, from withdrawing.

The people must cooperate with the Rebel Army to the best of their ability. They must be the chief preservers of order in each liberated city and must prevent pillaging, destruction of property, and bloodshed. No one must take revenge on anyone. Those who have committed inhuman acts against the people will be detained and imprisoned and later tried by revolutionary courts. In the decisive moments which are approaching, the people must give the highest proof of civic sense, patriotism, and a sense of order so that later no dishonorable accusation can be made against our revolution which, because it is the highest goal of the Cuban nation and the most extraordinary proof of the people's desire for peace and of their dignity, must suffer no blemish.

Fidel Castro

The Battle of Guisa
(December 7, 1958)

Yesterday at 10:00 P.M., after ten days of struggle, our forces entered Guisa. The battle took place across from Bayamo, where the rebel post is located. We fought nine enemy reinforcements that arrived successively, supported by heavy tanks, artillery, and air force. The battle of Guisa began on November 20 at exactly 8:30 A.M., when our forces intercepted an enemy patrol which was making its daily trek from Guisa to Bayamo, opening fire a few minutes later. At 10:30 A.M. of the same day, the first enemy reinforcements, against whom we fought until 6:00 P.M. when they were repulsed, arrived. At 4:00 P.M., a T-17 30-ton tank was destroyed by a powerful land mine. The impact of the explosion was such that the tank was raised several meters in the air, falling forward with its wheels upside down and the tower stuck in the highway pavement. Hours before, a truck full of soldiers also had been destroyed by another powerful land mine. At 6:00 P.M., the reinforcements retreated. The following day the enemy advanced, supported by Sherman tanks, and was able to reach Guisa, where it left a number of soldiers in the garrison.

On the twenty-second our forces, recovered from the weariness of two days of continuous struggle, again took position on the highway from Bayamo to Guisa.

On the twenty-third, enemy troops attempted to advance through the Corojo road but were driven back. On the twenty-fifth, an infantry battalion, preceded by two T-17 tanks, again advanced on the Bayamo-Guisa highway in a convoy formed by fourteen trucks.

Two kilometers from this point, rebel troops fired on the convoy from both sides of the highway, curbing their retreat, while a mine paralyzed the vanguard tank; then one of the most violent combats ever fought in the Sierra Maestra was initiated. The Guisa garrison, as well as the complete battalion which had come as reinforcement, was under siege. The latter had two T-17's. At six in the evening, the enemy had to abandon all the trucks grouped around the two tanks. At 10:00 P.M., while a rebel battery of 81-millimeter mortars punished the enemy force, revolutionary recruits armed with picks and shovels opened a trench in the highway by the tank destroyed on

Communiqué issued on December 7, 1958, from the Sierra Maestra. "La batalla de Guisa," *Verde Olivo* (Havana), January 22, 1967, pp. 8–11.

the twentieth, so that between its remains and the trench the exit of the two T-17 tanks inside the circle would be blocked.

At two in the morning a rebel company advanced toward the enemy, firing against the tanks whose men remained without food and water. At dawn on the twenty-seventh, two battalions of reinforcements from Bayamo, preceded by Sherman tanks, arrived at the site of the battle. We fought them throughout the twenty-seventh. At six in the evening, the Sherman tanks were able to leave, thanks to their four-wheel drive. One of the T-17's was dragged away, but the other one could not be withdrawn. On the enemy field numerous weapons remained—35,000 bullets, 14 trucks, 200 knapsacks, and a T-17 tank in perfect condition with abundant 37-millimeter cannon ammunition—yet the battle had not been concluded.

A rapidly advancing rebel column intercepted the retreating enemy near the central highway intersection, inflicting numerous casualties and taking over more weapons and ammunition.

The tank was attended to quickly and put in condition to engage in action. On the evening of the twenty-ninth, two rebel platoons advanced resolutely toward Guisa preceded by the tank. At 2:20 A.M. on the twenty-ninth, the rebel forces manning the T-17 placed it at the very gates of the Guisa Barracks, in the midst of numerous buildings where the enemy was entrenched, and began to fire. They had fired fifty cannon shots when two direct hits from a bazooka fired by the enemy paralyzed the tank. The crew of the rebel tank continued to fire the cannon against the barracks until no munitions were left. They then got off the tank and started to retreat.

An act of unparalleled heroism occurred. Lieutenant Hipólito Prieto, the tank machine-gunner, took the machine gun, and under crossfire and in spite of his wounds, crawled under the rain of bullets carrying the heavy weapon, without abandoning it for a single moment.

That same day, at dawn, four enemy battalions advanced from three different points (the road from Bayamo to Corojo, the Bayamo to Guisa highway, and the road from Santa Rita to Guisa). All the enemy forces from Bayamo, Manzanillo, Yara, Estrada Palma, Baire, and other points were mobilized. The column that advanced by the Corojo road was repelled after two hours of battle. The battalions advancing by the Bayamo-Guisa highway were held for the whole day, and they camped 2 kilometers away from Guisa. The ones who were coming by the Corralillo road also were driven back; they then took a detour through the town's northeastern section. On the thirtieth, the last battles were fought with the battalions that had taken positions 2 kilometers away without being able to advance. At 4:00

P.M., while units fought against the reinforcements, the Guisa garrison abandoned the town in a hurried retreat, leaving behind all ammunition and many weapons. At 9:00 P.M., our vanguard entered the town (on this same date, 61 years earlier, the forces of the Liberation Army under the command of Calixto García Iñíquez took the town of Guisa).

As this war communiqué is being written, the following equipment has been taken from the enemy:

    1 T-17 tank
    94 Springfield rifles and San Cristóbal machine guns
    3 mortars (2 60-millimeter, 1 81-millimeter)
    1 bazooka
    7 30-caliber machine guns
    55,000 bullets
    130 Garand grenades
    70 60-millimeter mortar rockets
    25 81-millimeter mortar rockets
    20 bazooka rockets
    200 knapsacks
    160 uniforms
    14 transport trucks
    food, medicine, etc.

The battlefield is still being searched, with the certainty that more weapons will be found. The enemy suffered over 200 casualties in dead and wounded during the ten days of battle. Today the Red Cross took responsibility for the numerous corpses of the dictatorship's soldiers that were abandoned on the battlefield and could not be buried while the battle lasted.

Eight wounded *compañeros* died in battle, and seven more were wounded.

The battle was waged mainly against the troops camped in Bayamo. It was a struggle of men against planes, tanks, and artillery.

The most outstanding officer of the Rebel Army was Captain Braulio Coroneaux, a veteran of numerous actions who died gloriously defending his position on the Guisa highway, through which the enemy tanks failed to pass. Under the command of captains and other officers, the rebel units fought with extraordinary spirit. The following men distinguished themselves in action: Captains Reynaldo Mora, Rafael Verdecia, Ignacio Pérez, and Calixto García; Lieutenants Orlando Rodríguez Puerta, Alcibíades Bermúdez, and Gonzalo Paneque, who led the tank crew and the battery of 81-millimeter mortars; Dionisio Montero, who handled the 60-millimeter battery; Lieutenant Raymundo Montes de Oca, instructor of the machine-gun company; Engineer Miguel Angel Calvo, chief of the mines and explosives section; and Lieutenants Armelio Manejas and Lilito Ramos. A squadron of the Mariana Grajales women's platoon fought courageously during the ten days the battle lasted, enduring with unparalleled fortitude the bombings and enemy artillery attacks.

Guisa, 12 kilometers from the command post at Bayamo, is already free territory.

Fidel Castro
Commander in Chief

The Take-over of Baire
(December 10, 1958)

This is Rebel Radio:

Rebel troops of Column 1 "José Martí" took the town of Baire yesterday at 8:30 P.M. The enemy has retreated.

An important military action is developing along a 35-kilometer stretch of the Central Highway. Numerous enemy garrisons are left with two alternatives: surrender or annihilation.

For military reasons we abstain from offering more details at the present on the results of these operations.

The victorious and unchecked advance of our forces continues.

Fidel Castro
Commander in Chief

Communiqué read on December 10, 1958. Roger González Guerrero, "Oriente 1958," *Verde Olivo* (Havana), January 5, 1969, pp. 6–11.

Instructions of the General Headquarters to
All Commanders of the Rebel Army and
the People (December 31, 1958)

Whatever the news from the capital may be, our troops should not stop firing at any time.

Communiqué released from the Sierra Maestra on December 31, 1958. Edmundo Desnoes (ed.), *La sierra y el llano* (Havana: Casa de las Américas, 1961), pp. 303–304.

Our forces should continue their operations against the enemy on all battlefronts.

Parleys should be granted only to those garrisons that want to surrender.

It seems that there has been a coup d'état in the capital. The conditions under which that coup took place are not known to the Rebel Army.

The people should be on the alert and should follow only the instructions of our general headquarters.

The dictatorship has collapsed as a consequence of the crushing defeats suffered in the last weeks, but that does not mean the Revolution already has triumphed.

Military operations will continue until an express order is sent from this headquarters, which will be issued only when the military forces that have arisen in the capital place themselves unconditionally under the orders of the Revolutionary Command.

Revolution, *yes*! Military coup, *no*!

Military coup behind the backs of the people and the Revolution, no, because it would only serve to prolong the war!

Coup d'état in agreement with Batista, no, because it would only serve to prolong the war!

Snatching victory from the people, no, because it would only serve to prolong the war until the people obtain total victory!

After seven years of struggle the democratic victory of the people has to be absolute, so that never again will there be in our fatherland another March 10.

No one should be confused or deceived!

To be on the alert is the order!

The people and very especially the workers of the entire Republic should listen attentively to Rebel Radio and rapidly prepare all centers of work for the general strike. And as soon as the order is given they should begin it, if it should be necessary to stop any attempt at a counterrevolutionary coup.

The people and the Rebel Army must be more united and more firm than ever in order not to let the victory that has cost so much blood be snatched from them!

Fidel Castro
Commander in Chief

Letter to Colonel Rego Rubido
(December 31, 1958)

Colonel:

A regrettable error has been made during the delivery of my message to you. Perhaps it was due to the rush in which I answered your note and the rapidity of the conversation I held with the messenger. I did not tell him that one of our conditions in the agreements reached here was the surrender of the garrison at Santiago de Cuba to our forces. To have done so would have been a discourtesy, as well as an undignified offense to the military men who have frequently come close to us. The problem is something else. An agreement has been reached between the leader of the military[1] and ourselves, and a plan was adopted which should have begun on December 31, at three o'clock in the afternoon. Even the minor details were considered after we carefully analyzed the problems we would have to face. The plan was to begin with the uprising of the Santiago de Cuba garrison. I persuaded General Cantillo of the advantages of beginning in Oriente and not at Columbia, as the people would distrust any coup coming from the capital's barracks, thus making it difficult to incorporate the people into the movement. He fully agreed with my views and was concerned only with preserving order in Havana. Thereafter we agreed on measures to stop any dangers. One of the measures was precisely the advance of our column on Santiago de Cuba. It was to be a joint action taken by the military, the people, and our forces. Such a revolutionary movement from the outset could count on the support of the entire nation. Immediately after, following our agreement, we suspended operations and began to move our forces toward other points such as Holguín, where it was certain that well-known henchmen would resist the revolutionary-military movement. When all the preparations were ready on our part, I received yesterday's message notifying me that the coordinated action would not take place.

Apparently there were other plans, but I was not informed or told of the reasons behind them. It was none of our doing; everything had been changed and our forces placed in danger, as they had been sent to undertake difficult operations following agreed upon plans.

Letter written on December 31, 1958, to the military commander of Santiago de Cuba garrison. *Revolución* (Havana), January 5, 1959, pp. 1, 4.

[1] General Eulogio Cantillo, who days earlier had been in command of all the armed forces in Oriente. Eds.

We were then dependent on General Cantillo, and his frequent trips to Havana could become militarily disastrous for us. You must recognize that everything is quite confusing at this moment, and that Batista is a clever individual who knows how to maneuver well. The change could be for the worse.

We cannot be asked to renounce all the advantages that we have gained in the last weeks and patiently wait for events to unfold. I said quite clearly that there could be no unilateral action by the military. We did not fight for two horrible years to get just that. We cannot be asked to fold our arms in this decisive moment. It is not power in itself which concerns us, but rather the fulfillment of the Revolution. I am even worried that the military, due to an unjustified excess of scruples, will allow the guilty to escape and go overseas with their great fortunes in order to further harm the fatherland.

I personally can add that power does not interest me nor do I plan to take any post. I will only be on guard so that the sacrifices of so many compatriots will not be in vain, regardless of what my destiny might be.

I have always acted with loyalty and frankness. One cannot call a victory that which has been achieved through deceit. The language of honor, which you all understand, is the only one I know. In our meeting with General Cantillo the word *surrender* was never mentioned, and what I said yesterday I repeat today: after 3:00 P.M., December 31, the agreed date, we will end the truce with Santiago de Cuba, even though it might injure the people.

Last night the rumor reached us that General Cantillo had been arrested in Havana, that several youths had been murdered in the cemetery of Santiago de Cuba, and I had the feeling that we had wasted precious time. Today it seems that General Cantillo still remains at his post. What need is there for running these risks? What I told the messenger about surrender was not transmitted literally—which is clear from your message. I said the following: If hostilities break out because what we had agreed on is not fulfilled, we would be forced to attack the garrison of Santiago de Cuba. This is inevitable because we have directed our efforts toward this objective for the last several months. If that happens, we will demand the surrender of the troops defending Santiago. This does not mean that we think they will surrender without fighting, because I know that even without out reason to fight Cuban military men would defend their positions, and they have cost me many lives.

I only meant that once the blood of our men is shed in the conquest of an objective no other solution could be accepted even if it costs us many lives, for due to the present conditions of the regime's forces they could not lend support to Santiago, and it would inexorably fall into our hands.

This has been the basic objective of our campaign during the last months, and a plan of such importance cannot be suspended for a week without grave consequences. If the military revolt does not take place, this is the opportune time for us to move—when the dictatorship is suffering great defeats in Oriente and Las Villas. We have been faced with the dilemma of renouncing the advantages of our victory or recognizing a sure triumph in exchange for what in the end will be a limited victory. Do you believe that with yesterday's ambiguous message, containing a unilateral decision, I should suspend the rebel's plans?

As a military man you must agree that we are being asked the impossible. You have not stopped making trenches for a minute, and those trenches can be used against us by a Pedraza, Pilar García, or a Cañizares. If General Cantillo is dismissed from his command and with him the men he trusts, we cannot remain inactive. You must see that we are being promised absurdities. Even though you courageously defend your positions, there is no other thing to do but to attack, because we also have sacred obligations to fulfill. More than allies I wish that honorable military men would be our *compañeros* in only one cause: the cause of Cuba. I wish above all that you, *compañero*, would not have a mistaken impression of my attitude, and would not believe I have been strict in regard to the cease-fire in Santiago de Cuba. In order to dispel any doubts, I certify that operations could begin any time and that from today on it should be known that an attack could take place at any moment. For no reason whatsoever shall we alter our plans again.

Fidel Castro

Proclamation to the People of Santiago (January 1, 1959)

People of Santiago:

The Santiago de Cuba Barracks is surrounded by our forces. By 6:00 P.M. today the barracks should lay down its arms. If not, our

With the departure of Fulgencio Batista in the early hours of January 1, 1959, a military coup occurred in Havana in order to take power away from the revolutionary forces that overthrew the dictatorship. Consequently Fidel Castro made this proclamation on January 1, 1959. *Bohemia* (Havana), January 2, 1969, p. 74.

troops will advance toward the city and will take by assault the enemy positions. After 6:00 P.M. today all air and maritime traffic in the city is prohibited.

Santiago de Cuba, the murderers who have assassinated so many of your children will not escape as Batista escaped, or those greatly responsible, who along with a number of officers carried out the sly coup last night.

Santiago de Cuba, you are not free yet, in your streets are those who have oppressed you for seven years; the war has not ended because the murderers remain armed. The military men who carried out the coup argue that the rebels cannot enter Santiago de Cuba; we have been prohibited from entering a city that we could take with courage and efficiency as our fighters have done before. They want to prohibit the entrance into the city of Santiago de Cuba to those who have liberated the fatherland. The history of 1895 will not be repeated, today the *mambises* will enter Santiago de Cuba.[1]

Santiago de Cuba, you will be free because you deserve it more than any other and because it is indecent to see defenders of the tyranny in your streets.

Santiago de Cuba, we count on your support.

Fidel Castro

[1] In 1898, American troops did not allow Cuban freedom fighters—*mambises*—to enter the city of Santiago de Cuba. Eds.

Orders to Camagüey and Las Villas Commands (January 1, 1959)

Major Victor Mora, chief of Camagüey Province, is ordered to advance on all cities, subduing them by force of arms with the cooperation of the people and honest leaders of the enemy's army with troops under their command.

Major Mora must close all access routes to towns, especially the Central Highway, and the Santa Cruz del Sur and Nuevitas to Camagüey highways. Major Camilo Cienfuegos, with his glorious invasion column no. 2, should advance toward the city of Havana, to subdue and take over the military camp of Columbia.

Major Ernesto Guevara has been invested with the rank of chief of

Orders issued from Rebel Radio on January 1, 1959, by Fidel Castro. "Se cursan órdenes militares a los mandos de Camagüey y de las gloriosas columnas 2 y 8 de Las Villas," *Revolución* (Havana), July 26, 1962, p. 2.

La Cabaña Military Camp and consequently will advance with his
forces on the city of Havana, while subduing the fortresses of Matanzas.

Also, orders have been imparted to Major Belarmino Castilla to
threaten the Mayarí forces into surrender; to Major Raúl Castro for
the surrender of Guantánamo; and to Majors Sardiñas and Gómez
Ochoa the surrender of Holguín and Victoria de las Tunas.

Also these commands are ordered to maintain the greatest order in
the cities which surrender and to make immediate arrests so that all
guilty in the present situations will be submitted to summary trials.

Major Escalona, military chief of Pinar del Río, must act in accord
with the preceding instructions.

Meanwhile columns 1, "José Martí," 3, 9, and 10 under the direct
command of the Commander in Chief Fidel Castro and Major Juan
Almeida are advancing toward Santiago de Cuba.

Fidel Castro

General Strike Proclamation
(January 1, 1959)

To the Cuban people and especially to the workers:

A military junta in complicity with the tyrant has taken power in
order to assure the escape of Batista and the principal murderers and to
try to block the revolutionary movement from taking power.

The Rebel Army will continue its resolute campaign, accepting
only the unconditional surrender of the military garrisons.

The Cuban people and the workers should immediately prepare to
initiate a general strike throughout the country on January 2 to support the revolutionary forces and guarantee the total victory of the
Revolution.

Seven years of heroic struggle, thousands of martyrs whose blood
has been spilled in every corner of Cuba, cannot serve those who were
accomplices of the past regime by allowing them to continue holding
power in Cuba.

The Cuban workers led by the worker's section of the 26th of July
Movement today should take over all the labor unions controlled by

Message read over Rebel Radio on January 1, 1959. "Fidel ordena la huelga
general," *Revolución* (Havana), July 26, 1962, p. 8.

the former government, and the workers should organize in all factories and working centers in order to start the total paralyzation of
the country tomorrow morning.

Batista and Mujal[1] have fled. But their accomplices have stayed;
they control the army and the labor unions. A coup d'état to betray
the people cannot be permitted. To do so will only prolong the war.
Camp Columbia must surrender in order to end the war. This time
nothing and no one can impede the triumph of the Revolution.

Workers: This is the moment for you to assure the victory of the
Revolution.

Cubans: For freedom, democracy, and the triumph of the Revolution, *support the general revolutionary strike in all the territories that
have not been liberated.*

Fidel Castro

[1] Eusebio Mujal, pro-Batista labor leader. Eds.

Annotated Bibliography of Fidel Castro's Works (1948–1958)

"Conferencia de prensa," *Diario de la Marina*, February 26, 1948, p. 25.
Denial of participation in the assassination of student leader Manolo Castro.

"Primeros pasos del movimiento latinoamericano contra el coloniaje europeo en este continente," *Bohemia*, March 17, 1957, pp. 62–63.
Position paper presented to the Federation of University Students (FEU) at the University of Havana in 1948 on European colonialism in Latin America.

"Ciudadano, esconde tu kilo!" *Bohemia*, January 30, 1949, pp. 51, 54–55.
Speech at a rally calling for a militant opposition to any increase in bus fares.

"Carta a Amador García," *Bohemia*, April 26, 1959.
Letter written in December 1951 to an Ortodoxo senator.

"El derrumbe constitucional," *Alerta*, March 4, 1952.
Describes Prío administration financing of gangster groups.

"Yo acuso," *Alerta*, January 28, 1952.
Deals with Prío's illegal businesses.

"Revolución no, zarpazo!" *El Acusador* (mimeographed leaflet), March 13, 1952, p. 1.
Denunciation of Batista's coup.

"Al Tribunal de Urgencia," *Granma*, July 26, 1966, p. 5.
Brief presented on March 24, 1952, to the Court of Appeals calling for the punishment, through the legal system, of those who participated in the military coup.

"Recuento crítico del PPC," *El Acusador* (mimeographed leaflet), August 16, 1952, p. 1.
Summary of the history of the Partido del Pueblo Cubano and its weak stand toward Batista.

"Asaltado y destruído el estudio del escultor Fidalgo," *Bohemia*, February 8, 1953, pp. 66, 81.
First article written by Castro in the national magazine *Bohemia* exposing the destruction of the studio of an Ortodoxo militant by the police.

"Manifiesto del Moncada" in *13 documentos de la insurrección* (Havana: ONBAP, 1959), pp. 19–21.
Manifesto written by Fidel Castro and Raúl Gómez García calling for a

The bibliography has been arranged chronologically. All the magazines and newspapers used were published in Cuba, with the following exceptions: *Coronet* (New York), *Look* (New York), *O Cruzeiro* (Rio de Janeiro), *Revista Elite* (Caracas), and *Ultimas Noticias* (Mexico).

popular revolution in order to implement the ideals of past generations. The document was issued on July 23, 1953.

"Este movimiento triunfará," *Verde Olivo*, July 26, 1964, p. 5.
Speech delivered to the men who were to attack the Moncada Barracks on July 26, 1953.

"Carta al Tribunal de Urgencia," *Bohemia*, July 27, 1962, p. 67.
Letter to the Court of Appeals written on September 26, 1953, from prison, stating the maneuvers used in order to allow Castro to defend himself.

History Will Absolve Me (New York: Lyle Stuart, 1961), 79 pages.
Well-known pamphlet which allegedly reproduces the defense plea made by Fidel Castro on October 16, 1953. There are no transcripts of the trial in existence.

"Carta a Luis Conte Agüero" in Luis Conte Agüero (ed.), *Cartas del presidio, anticipo de una biografía* (Havana: Editorial Lex, 1959), pp. 13–25. (Henceforth *Cartas*.)
Letter written on December 12, 1953, describing the massacre of young men after the Moncada attack.

"Carta a Melba Hernández" in *Cartas*, pp. 37–40.
Letter written on April 17, 1954, showing Castro's organizational skills.

"Carta a Luis Conte Agüero" in *Cartas*, pp. 25–30.
Letter written on June 12, 1954, reflecting on prison life as well as a vehement exposition of his will to fight.

"Carta a Luis Conte" in *Cartas*, pp. 31–36.
Letter written on June 19, 1954, calling for an organized campaign to demand the amnesty of political prisoners.

"Carta a Luis Conte" in *Cartas*, pp. 41–42.
Letter written on July 6, 1954, expressing the strong friendship between both men.

"Carta a Mirta" in *Cartas*, pp. 43–44.
Letter to his wife written on July 17, 1954, making clear his disbelief that she is receiving a government sinecure.

"Carta a Luis Conte" in *Cartas*, pp. 45–46.
Letter written on July 17, 1954, arguing that the sinecure issue was made up by the government to hurt him politically.

"Carta a su hermana" in *Cartas*, pp. 47–48.
Letter written to his sister on July 22, 1954, affirming that the sinecure issue, while true, will not hurt him.

"Carta a Luis Conte" in *Cartas*, pp. 49–54.
Letter written on July 31, 1954, expressing deep sorrow at finding out that it was true his wife was receiving a monthly check from the government.

"Carta a Luis Conte," in *Cartas*, pp. 59–62.
Written on August 14, 1954, this letter states Castro's plans for divorce.

"Carta a su hermana" in *Cartas*, pp. 63–64.
Letter written on October 25, 1954, to his sister in which the emotion felt at listening to a political rally on the radio is described.

"Carta a su hermana" in *Cartas*, pp. 65–66.
Letter written on November 29, 1954, giving instructions to his sister on the steps to be taken toward bringing about his divorce.

"Carta a su hermana" in *Cartas*, pp. 67–68.
Letter written on December 8, 1954, discussing what should be done with his son.

"Carta a René Guitart" in *Cartas*, pp. 69–70.
Letter written on December 16, 1954, to the father of one of the men who died in the Moncada attack. The letter is extremely spiritual.

"Carta al Dr. Jorge Mañach" in *Cartas*, pp. 71–74.
Letter written on March 13, 1955, discussing the amnesty campaign.

"Carta a su hermana" in *Cartas*, pp. 75–78.
Written on March 13, 1955, this letter reiterates his views on a political amnesty.

"Carta a René Guitart" in *Cartas*, pp. 79–80.
Written on March 18, 1955, this letter categorically states Castro's commitment to a revolutionary stand.

"Carta sobre la amnistía," *Bohemia*, March 27, 1955, pp. 63, 94.
Document stating that he will not abandon his political beliefs in order to be freed.

"Carta a Maria Lobarde" in *Cartas*, pp. 87–88.
Polite letter written in March 1955 to a young girl who had sent him comforting notes.

"Carta a su hermana" in *Cartas*, pp. 89–93.
Letter written on May 2, 1955, from prison, announcing the ascetic life he will live in the future while fighting for Cuba's freedom.

"Declaraciones al salir de prisión," *El Mundo*, May 17, 1955, p. A8.
Statement made after leaving prison on May 15, 1955.

"Que se prueben en mi persona las garantías que ha prometido el gobierno," *Diario de la Marina*, May 17, 1955, p. 1.
Skeptical viewpoint on the existence of political rights made in an interview with Cuba's conservative daily.

"Yo soy un combatiente sin odios ni resentimientos," *Bohemia*, May 22, 1955, pp. 22, 73.
Press conference announcing his future political plans.

"Declaraciones sobre el arresto de Pedro Miret," *El Mundo*, May 25, 1955, p. 1.
Press release denouncing the lack of freedom for the opposition.

"Mientes Chaviano!" *Bohemia*, May 29, 1955, pp. 57, 95–96.
Virulent attack on the statements made by the officer who was in charge of the Moncada Barracks when the attack occurred in 1953.

"Manos asesinas," *La Calle*, June 7, 1955, p. 3.
Comments on a speech made by Fulgencio Batista days earlier.

"Lo que iba a decir y me prohibieron," *La Calle*, June 8, 1955, p. 3.
Article asking the people to materially support the newspaper in which he writes.

"Frente al terror, frente al crimen," *La Calle*, June 11, 1955, p. 3.
Article denouncing terrorist tactics.

"Carta denuncia de la oposición pacífica a Batista," *Diario de la Marina*, January 5, 1959, p. 1.
Letter addressed to opposition leaders on July 5, 1955, in which he states it is impossible to continue waging a peaceful struggle against the Batista dictatorship and announces his departure from the island.

"Manifesto No. 1 del 26 de Julio al pueblo de Cuba," *Pensamiento Crítico*, no. 21, 1968, pp. 207–220.
Manifesto issued on August 8, 1955, from Mexico outlining his revolutionary goals.

"Mensaje al Congreso de Militantes Ortodoxos" in Luis Conte Agüero, *Fidel Castro, Vida y Obra* (Havana: Editorial Lex, 1959), pp. 300–307.
Message to the Partido del Pueblo Cubano in which the 26th of July group is defined as the militant arm of the party.

"Carta a Melba Hernández" in Luis Conte Agüero, *Fidel Castro, Psiquiatría y Política* (Mexico: Editorial Jus, 1968), p. 223.
Letter written on October 4, 1955, giving directions to a young woman on steps to be taken with regard to the Partido del Pueblo Cubano.

"Discurso en New York," *Bohemia*, November 6, 1955, pp. 82–83.
Speech to Cuban émigrés reasserting the need for radical change in the island.

"Sirvo a Cuba," *Bohemia*, November 20, 1955, pp. 59, 81–83.
Reply to an article published in *Bohemia* which accused him of aiding the Batista dictatorship by espousing an insurrectional thesis to solve Cuba's problems.

"Discurso en el Teatro Flagler," *Bohemia*, December 4, 1955, pp. 78–80.
Speech analyzing the moves by the opposition to find a peaceful solution.

"Manifesto No. 2 del 26 de Julio al pueblo de Cuba," *Pensamiento Crítico*, no. 21, 1968, pp. 221–227.
Manifesto of December 10, 1955, describing his activities among exile circles in the United States and defining the 26th of July Movement.

"Frente a todos!" *Bohemia*, January 8, 1956, pp. 81–82, 89.
Article written on December 25, 1955, discussing the plots made against him in order to undermine his rebelliousness.

"Carta a Celestino Rodríguez," *Revolución*, February 2, 1959, p. 1.
Letter of February 12, 1956, summarizing the procedures to be used to organize patriotic clubs in exile.

"La condenación que se nos pide," *Bohemia*, March 11, 1956, pp. 59–69.
Article commenting on political developments in Cuba.

"El movimiento 26 de Julio," *Bohemia*, April 1, 1956, pp. 54, 70–71.
Article denouncing the creation of the 26th of July Movement in
Mexico.

"Declaración desde México," *Bohemia*, July 1, 1956, p. 62.
Statement on the arrest of Cuban revolutionaries by Mexican authorities.

"Basta ya de mentiras!" *Bohemia*, July 15, 1956, p. 84.
Article denying links with Communists.

"Declaraciones al periódico," *Ultimas Noticias*, July 26, 1956, p. 1.
Interview in which Castro expresses the hope that Mexico will not oppose Cuba's revolutionary struggle.

"Pacto de México," *El País*, September 3, 1956, p. 1.
Political pact signed by Castro and the leader of the Directorio Revolucionario in August 1956.

"Entrevista en México," *El Mundo*, August 7, 1956, pp. 1, A10.
Interview outlining a change in tactics.

"Carta sobre Trujillo," *Bohemia*, September 2, 1956, pp. 35, 82–83.
Letter of August 26, 1956, denying any connections with the dictator of
the Dominican Republic.

"Entrevista con Benjamín de la Vega," *Alerta*, November 19, 1956.
Interview given a few hours before leaving for Cuba.

"An Expression of Gratitude," *Granma Weekly Review*, January 5, 1969,
p. 9.
Letter of December 25, 1956, giving thanks to a peasant who helped
Castro and his followers after they landed on the island.

"Al pueblo de Cuba," *Bohemia*, July 28, 1957, pp. 69, 96–97.
Manifesto by Fidel Castro, Raúl Chibás, and Felipe Pazos released on
July 12, 1957, calling on the people to fight against tyranny. A proposal is
made on steps to be taken by the opposition.

"Carta a Frank País," *Granma*, July 7, 1968, p. 9.
Letter of July 21, 1957, stating the high morale of the guerrillas and
commenting on the struggle waged in Santiago de Cuba.

"Palabras sobre Frank País," *Revolución*, July 30, 1962, p. 13.
Radio broadcast of August 1, 1957, made after the assassination of Frank
País, leader of the urban underground.

"Carta a la Junta Cubana de Liberación," *Verde Olivo*, January 5, 1964,
pp. 33–39.
December 14, 1957, document opposing the agreements reached by the
opposition groups in exile.

"Carta a los rebeldes de Las Villas," *Bohemia*, March 6, 1960, p. 56.
Letter of February 2, 1958, affirming the sincere solidarity of the Sierra
Maestra guerrillas toward those who opened a new front in the center of
the island.

"Why We Fight," *Coronet*, February 1958, pp. 80–86.
Article for North American consumption playing down the radicalism
of the 26th of July Movement.

"Interview with Andrew St. George," *Look*, February 4, 1958.
Interview with North American reporter in which Castro answers numerous questions related to U.S.-Cuban relations.

"Carta al Che," *Verde Olivo*, January 12, 1964, pp. 7–8.
February 16, 1958, message advising Che to be careful in his military campaign.

"Orden militar ascendiendo a comandante a Juan Almeida," *Verde Olivo*, March 17, 1968, p. 7.
Document of February 27, 1958, making Juan Almeida a major in the Rebel Army.

"Dr. Manuel Urrutia Lleó Appointed Provisional President" in Manuel Urrutia Lleó *Fidel Castro & Company, Inc.* (New York: Praeger, 1964), p. 16.
Unilateral move by Castro on March 9, 1958, appointing a judge who had stated it was a right to revolt against the Batista dictatorship. The appointment was made to undermine other opposition groups.

"Fidel rechaza la componenda del Episcopado con Batista," *Revolución*, July 26, 1962, p. 9.
March 9, 1958, statement dismissing the proposals for a peaceful solution to Cuba's problems made by the Cuban Church.

"Guerra total contra la tiranía" in Gregorio Selser (ed.), *La revolución cubana* (Buenos Aires: Editorial Palestra, 1960), pp. 141–146. (Henceforth *La revolución cubana.*)
Manifesto issued on March 12, 1958, from the Sierra Maestra calling for a total war against the Batista regime and a general strike.

"Manifesto to the Workers" in Jules Dubois, *Fidel Castro, Rebel, Liberator or Dictator?* (Indianapolis: Bobbs-Merrill, 1959), pp. 248–249. (Henceforth Jules Dubois, *Fidel Castro.*)
April 1958 manifesto calling for a general strike.

"Llamado a una huelga general" in *13 documentos de la insurrección* (Havana: ONBAP, 1959), p. 59.
Message read on April 9, 1958, over Rebel Radio and other underground radio stations.

"Entrevista con Jorge Massetti," *Revista Elite*, April 12, 1958.
Interview with an Argentine journalist in which the general goals of the revolutionary movement are outlined.

"Mensaje a Camilo Cienfuegos," *Verde Olivo*, October 29, 1960.
Letter of April 16, 1958, appointing Camilo Cienfuegos a major of the Rebel Army and outlining the military strategy to be followed.

"Con Fidel Castro na 'zona da morte,'" *O Cruzeiro*, May 3, 1958, pp. 40–45.
Interview with Carlos María Gutiérrez in which the political and social goals of the 26th of July Movement are stated.

"Ataque y toma del Cuartel de Uvero," *Revolución*, August 1, 1962, p. 10.
Radio broadcast of May 28, 1958, describing the battle of Uvero and the revolutionary strategy of the Rebel Army.

"Letter to Celia Sánchez," *Granma Weekly Review*, August 27, 1967, p. 8.

Letter written on June 5, 1958, in which Castro attests the necessity of fighting against the United States after Batista is overthrown.

"Carta a Camilo Cienfuegos," *Verde Olivo*, October 25, 1964, pp. 9–12.

Letter written on June 12, 1958, giving military orders to one of Castro's rebel majors.

"Carta al Comandante Camilo Cienfuegos," *Verde Olivo*, October 29, 1960, p. 24.

Written on June 27, 1958, this letter describes the difficulties faced by the guerrillas during the military offensive of the Batista troops.

"The First Battle of Santo Domingo," *Granma*, July 7, 1968, p. 9.

Communiqué of June 29, 1958, reporting the defeat suffered by government troops.

"Carta al Comandante José Quevedo" in José Pardo Llada, *Memorias de la Sierra Maestra* (Havana: Editorial Tierra Nueva, 1960), pp. 60–62.

Written on July 15, 1958, this is a letter to a Batista officer.

"La batalla de Jigüe" in Edmundo Desnoes (ed.), *La sierra y el llano* (Havana: Casa de las Américas, 1961), pp. 189–194.

Communiqué released on July 24, 1958, describing a major battle in which the government forces suffered a great defeat.

"Unity Manifesto of the Sierra Maestra" in Jules Dubois, *Fidel Castro*, pp. 280–283.

Manifesto of July 20, 1958, broadcast from Rebel Radio announcing the unification of all opposition groups under the leadership of Fidel Castro.

"Carta al Comandante Camilo Cienfuegos," *Verde Olivo*, October 29, 1960, pp. 24–25.

Letter written on August 5, 1958, asking for more military information in order to plan further actions.

"Carta al Comandante Camilo Cienfuegos," *Verde Olivo*, October 29, 1960, p. 25.

Letter written on August 6, 1958, ordering an ambush.

"Las órdenes de Fidel Castro," *El Mundo*, October 28, 1965, p. 8.

Message written on August 18, 1958, ordering Major Camilo Cienfuegos to invade Pinar del Rio Province.

"Orden militar disponiendo que el Che Guevara inicie la invasión de las Villas" in *13 documentos de la insurrección* (Havana: ONBAP, 1959), p. 62.

Military order issued on August 21, 1958, ordering Major Ernesto Guevara to invade Las Villas Province.

"La ofensiva" in Antonio Núñez Jiménez, *Geografía de Cuba* (Havana: Editorial Lex, 1959), pp. 578–588. (Henceforth *Geografía*.)

Radio broadcast of August 18, 1958, giving a detailed account of the military offensive unleashed by the Batista regime.

"La ofensiva II" in *Geografía*, pp. 588–594.

Radio broadcast of August 19, 1958, giving further details of the Batista military offensive.

"Interview with Enrique Meneses," unpublished. Research Institute for Cuba and the Caribbean, University of Miami, 2 pages.
Interview made on September 1, 1958, by a Spanish journalist.

"Proclama a los soldados de Batista," *Verde Olivo*, April 12, 1964, p. 77.
Proclamation issued on September 15, 1958, to Batista's soldiers.

"A los comités del Movimiento 26 de Julio" in Rafael Humberto Gaveira, *Fidel Castro (La revolución de los barbudos)* (Lima: Ediciones Tierra Nueva, 1959), pp. 83–91.
Circular released on September 16, 1958, setting the directions for a more coherent and efficient revolutionary movement.

"La batalla de El Cerro" in René Ray Rivero (ed.), *Libertad y Revolución* (Havana: n.p., 1959), pp. 81–84.
Communiqué written on September 27, 1958, analyzing the military defeat of enemy forces in Oriente Province.

"Carta al Comandante Juan Almeida" in Fidel Castro, *Declaraciones en el juicio contra el ex-Comandante Hubert Matos* (Havana: CTC–R, 1959), pp. 24–26.
Letter written on October 8, 1958, reviewing the strategy and tactics of the guerrilla movement.

"No-Election Decree" in Jules Dubois, *Fidel Castro*, pp. 316–317.
Radio broadcast of October 10, 1958, telling the Cuban people not to participate in the forthcoming national elections.

"Carta al Comandante Camilo Cienfuegos," *Verde Olivo*, January 17, 1965, pp. 4–7.
Message written on October 14, 1958, to the invading force marching toward Pinar del Rio Province.

"Acusación a los Estados Unidos" in *La revolución cubana*, pp. 171–174.
Radio broadcast of October 26, 1958, commenting on the kidnapping of U.S. citizens by guerrillas under the command of Raúl Castro and the statement made by the State Department.

"Palabras sobre Angel Ameijeiras," *Revolución*, November 9, 1959, pp. 1, 4.
Radio broadcast of November 8, 1958, announcing the death of a Cuban revolutionary.

"Communicado de Noviembre 9, 1958," *Verde Olivo*, January 9, 1969, pp. 6–11.
Communiqué issued on November 9, 1958, describing the political and military situation in the island.

"El enemigo pierde terreno," *Verde Olivo*, January 5, 1969, p. 8.
Radio broadcast of November 10, 1958, detailing the various victories of the Rebel Army.

"Este es un minuto extraordinario," *Verde Olivo*, January 5, 1969, p. 8.
Radio broadcast of November 11, 1958, ordering the last rebel offensive on the Batista regime.

"El ataque al Cuartel de Imias," *Verde Olivo*, January 5, 1969, p. 8.
Communiqué of November 14, 1958, outlining the battle of Imias.

"La batalla de Guisa," *Verde Olivo*, January 22, 1967, pp. 8–11.
    Thorough account broadcast on December 7, 1958, of one of the most important battles fought against Batista's forces.

"La toma de Baire," *Verde Olivo*, January 5, 1969, p. 11.
    Communiqué of December 10, 1958, announcing the fall of a very important town in Oriente Province.

"La toma de Palma Soriano," *Verde Olivo*, January 5, 1969, p. 11.
    Communiqué of December 10, 1958, announcing the fall of a town in the center of Oriente's sugar-producing area.

"Proclama al pueblo de Santiago," *Bohemia*, January 2, 1969, p. 47.
    Proclamation issued on December 31, 1958, announcing the surrounding of Santiago de Cuba, Cuba's second most important city.

"Se cursan órdenes militares a los mandos de Camagüey y de las gloriosas columnas 2 y 8 de Las Villas," *Revolución*, July 26, 1962, p. 8.
    Orders issued on the night of December 31 telling rebel commanders to continue their struggle until the armed forces surrender.

"Fidel ordena el avance rebelde sobre Santiago y La Habana y proclama la huelga general," *Revolución*, July 26, 1962, p. 8.
    Document issued on January 1, 1959, ordering the military take-over of Santiago de Cuba and a general strike in order to stop any counterrevolutionary plan.

Index